# Corporate Taxation

Aspen Casebook Series

# Corporate Taxation

**George K. Yin**
Edwin S. Cohen Distinguished Professor
of Law and Taxation
University of Virginia School of Law

**Karen C. Burke**
Warren Distinguished Professor of Law
University of San Diego School of Law

Wolters Kluwer
Law & Business

Published by Wolters Kluwer Law & Business in New York.

Wolters Kluwer Law & Business serves customers worldwide with CCH, Aspen Publishers, and Kluwer Law International products. (www.wolterskluwerlb.com)



To contact Customer Service, e-mail customer.service@wolterskluwer.com, call 1-800-234-1660, fax 1-800-901-9075, or mail correspondence to:

Wolters Kluwer Law & Business
Attn: Order Department
PO Box 990
Frederick, MD 21705

Printed in the United States of America.

1 2 3 4 5 6 7 8 9 0

ISBN 978-0-7355-2630-3

**Library of Congress Cataloging-in-Publication Data**

Yin, George K.
Corporate taxation / George K. Yin, Karen C. Burke.
p. cm.
Includes index.
ISBN 978-0-7355-2630-3
1. Corporations — Taxation — Law and legislation — United States. I. Burke, Karen C., 1951- II. Title.

KF6450.Y56 2011
343.7305′267 — dc23

2011035813

# About Wolters Kluwer Law & Business

Wolters Kluwer Law & Business is a leading global provider of intelligent information and digital solutions for legal and business professionals in key specialty areas, and respected educational resources for professors and law students. Wolters Kluwer Law & Business connects legal and business professionals as well as those in the education market with timely, specialized authoritative content and information-enabled solutions to support success through productivity, accuracy and mobility.

Serving customers worldwide, Wolters Kluwer Law & Business products include those under the Aspen Publishers, CCH, Kluwer Law International, Loislaw, Best Case, ftwilliam.com and MediRegs family of products.

**CCH** products have been a trusted resource since 1913, and are highly regarded resources for legal, securities, antitrust and trade regulation, government contracting, banking, pension, payroll, employment and labor, and healthcare reimbursement and compliance professionals.

**Aspen Publishers** products provide essential information to attorneys, business professionals and law students. Written by preeminent authorities, the product line offers analytical and practical information in a range of specialty practice areas from securities law and intellectual property to mergers and acquisitions and pension/benefits. Aspen's trusted legal education resources provide professors and students with high-quality, up-to-date and effective resources for successful instruction and study in all areas of the law.

**Kluwer Law International** products provide the global business community with reliable international legal information in English. Legal practitioners, corporate counsel and business executives around the world rely on Kluwer Law journals, looseleafs, books, and electronic products for comprehensive information in many areas of international legal practice.

**Loislaw** is a comprehensive online legal research product providing legal content to law firm practitioners of various specializations. Loislaw provides attorneys with the ability to quickly and efficiently find the necessary legal information they need, when and where they need it, by facilitating access to primary law as well as state-specific law, records, forms and treatises.

**Best Case Solutions** is the leading bankruptcy software product to the bankruptcy industry. It provides software and workflow tools to flawlessly streamline petition preparation and the electronic filing process, while timely incorporating ever-changing court requirements.

**ftwilliam.com** offers employee benefits professionals the highest quality plan documents (retirement, welfare and non-qualified) and government forms (5500/PBGC, 1099 and IRS) software at highly competitive prices.

**MediRegs** products provide integrated health care compliance content and software solutions for professionals in healthcare, higher education and life sciences, including professionals in accounting, law and consulting.

Wolters Kluwer Law & Business, a division of Wolters Kluwer, is headquartered in New York. Wolters Kluwer is a market-leading global information services company focused on professionals.

To Mary,
Elizabeth, and Laura

G.K.Y.

# Summary of Contents

# Table of Contents

# Preface

This book concerns the federal income taxation of corporations. Corporate tax is a core part of the business law curriculum of most law schools, and often the first tax course taken by students after the introductory income tax course. Although the course has always been very challenging, its difficulty has been compounded in recent years by uncertainty regarding key aspects of the law as well as complicated developments in response to corporate tax shelter activity.

To help students overcome these challenges, this book emphasizes the policy choices that lend structure and coherence to the law, and distinguish it from a mere collection of rules. While acknowledging the law's flaws, we have tried to prevent these flaws from obscuring the policies and principles that constitute the underlying fabric of corporate tax. We believe this emphasis facilitates an understanding of the specific details of corporate tax as well as other tax law areas (since the policies and patterns followed in corporate tax are repeated elsewhere). More generally, it helps prepare students for the practice of law, when they will have to make informed judgments even though the applicable law is unclear or incomplete.

In general, corporations are taxed in two different ways. Nearly three-fourths of corporations (termed "S corporations") are generally disregarded for tax purposes, with the corporation's income taxed as if it were earned directly by the shareholders. The taxation of S corporations is a natural extension of principles learned in the introductory income tax course, and we build upon that common foundation by introducing the subject in chapter two. The general manner in which S corporations are taxed — commonly referred to as "passthrough taxation" because the tax items of the corporation are "passed through" and taxed to its owners — is replicated elsewhere in corporate tax (such as the taxation of intercorporate investment, including corporations filing a consolidated tax return (chapter fourteen)), partnership tax, and other areas.

Most other corporations — including virtually all publicly traded ventures — are treated for tax purposes as taxpayers separate and distinct from their shareholders. We explain in chapter three the essential features of separate entity taxation. In addition, we discuss both the policy and practical implications of the foundational choice to tax business income under either a passthrough or separate entity approach.

Beginning with chapter four and continuing through the balance of the book, we consider the tax treatment of transactions involving corporations and their shareholders, a key part of most corporate tax practice. We present this material using a building-block approach, progressing from an analysis of basic to more complex transactions. This approach enables students to see that transactions may be structured in different ways to achieve similar economic (but potentially different tax) results, and that the taxation of complex transactions to some extent flows naturally from how simpler ones are taxed. The book prepares students to think rigorously and creatively about the kinds of problems they will encounter as practitioners of tax and business law.

One transaction carried out in many different ways is a distribution of cash or property by a corporation to its shareholders. Although we examine piecemeal the tax treatment of ordinary distributions (chapter five), redemptions (chapter six), section 304 transactions (chapter eight), stock distributions (chapter nine), and, finally, liquidations and reorganizations (chapters ten through twelve), we emphasize throughout the common features of these transactions and the policy considerations dictating their tax results.

Corporate tax is marked by a number of transactions — sometimes referred to as "nonrecognition events" — in which taxpayers are generally allowed to defer paying tax on gains and losses realized. Most students will have had some exposure to the taxation of nonrecognition events in the introductory income tax course, but corporate tax provides ample opportunity to learn additional nuances. As with the material on distributions, we consider piecemeal the tax consequences of transfers to controlled corporations (chapter seven), parent-subsidiary liquidations (chapter ten), and reorganizations (chapters eleven and twelve), while highlighting their common patterns and principles. This background is helpful in understanding the tax treatment of other nonrecognition transactions, including those encountered in partnership tax.

Finally, overlaid on top of corporate tax (and, indeed, tax law generally) is the question of whether the tax consequences of a transaction follow from its "form" or its "substance." This has always been a crucial question in corporate tax, but its significance may be more important than ever due to the recent codification of a judicially-developed doctrine focusing on the "economic substance" of transactions. We examine this issue very early in the materials (chapter four), and repeatedly return to it throughout the rest of the course.

Throughout the book, we emphasize the core source material of the law — the statute and regulations — as amplified in interpretive administrative materials and judicial decisions. We have deliberately tried to make background explanations and illustrative examples concise without being cryptic, based on our firm belief that actively engaging students with the actual source material enhances the learning process. We have interspersed many explanations, problems, and questions to help lead the students through the material. Although corporate tax certainly deserves its challenging reputation, we are confident that students will emerge from the course equipped to analyze and evaluate the critical issues they will encounter in practice.

In preparing this first edition, we have enjoyed the luxury of starting from a clean slate, without being constrained by past editorial, organizational or pedagogical choices. During the long genesis of these materials, corporate tax has seen dramatic change in its rules and underlying premises. Using our combined experience in teaching, private practice, and government, we have taken a fresh look at the subject matter and tried to identify the most important issues and themes that will confront future lawyers in this area.

We gratefully acknowledge the valuable contribution of Michael Lang in helping to develop portions of early drafts, as well as insightful comments from Rosanne Altshuler, Larry Axelrod, David Lenter, and Ethan Yale. We also acknowledge with appreciation meticulous research assistance from Tim Knox, Kristyn Medina, Meghann Morrill, and Becca Reeb, and useful feedback from many classes of students who were taught from earlier versions of the materials.

As a matter of editorial prerogative, we have freely edited judicial decisions and other materials to focus attention on essential analysis and holdings. Footnotes are numbered consecutively within each chapter, and many footnotes in the original sources have been deleted or renumbered. Internal citations and cross-references in cases and other authorities have been omitted without so indicating, while substantive omissions are indicated by an ellipsis (" . . . ").

George K. Yin
Charlottesville, VA

Karen C. Burke
San Diego, CA

September 2011

# Acknowledgments

We gratefully acknowledge the permission extended by Elsevier Limited to reprint an excerpt from the material listed below:

"US Income Taxation of New Financial Products," by Alvin C. Warren, Jr., reprinted from Journal of Public Economics, Volume 88, pages 899-923, copyright © 2004, with permission from Elsevier.

# Corporate Taxation

# Chapter 1

# Introduction to Corporate Tax

From prior study, you are already familiar with the basic concepts of income taxation, including what income is, when it arises, and what its character is. No doubt, you have also been exposed to the fictional legal entity known as a "corporation" and some of the rules and policies pertaining to it. This course explores what happens when income is earned by a business that is organized in corporate form or treated as one for tax purposes.

Let us begin with an example. Assume that your daughter, Laura, decides to invest $10 of her savings to operate a lemonade stand. She uses the $10 to purchase the items necessary to get the business started — the stand, cups, lemons, and so forth. She then proceeds to hawk her drinks out by the curb in front of your house. The day is hot, the drinks are cool, your daughter is cute and efficient, and your neighbors are kind, and she therefore successfully sells a number of drinks by day's end.

If necessary, we might calculate her income for the day using familiar principles. First, she should have income from services, that is, her compensation for sitting out all day in the hot sun peddling her drinks. Further, as the owner of the enterprise, she may have business income equal to her total receipts less properly allowable expenses (including the compensation her business pays to her). The business income might be thought of as the return she obtains from investing her $10 for one day in the manner described. Our principal concern in this course will be with the taxation of the business income, the income from her $10 capital investment.

Should the tax treatment of the business income vary, depending upon the *form of organization* of the business? For example, the foregoing describes how the business profits might be taxed if the lemonade stand is operated as a *sole proprietorship*. But suppose your daughter has only $5 in her piggy bank and therefore seeks out her older sister, Elizabeth, for the remaining capital needed to start up the business. Elizabeth provides the additional $5 but only on condition that the two sisters form a partnership and share equally in any profits from the business. How should the profits of the *L&E partnership* be taxed?

At least in theory, it is difficult to see why the profits of the partnership should be taxed any differently from those of the sole proprietorship. There is simply more than one owner now. But the economic activity undertaken in the two situations is exactly the same. Moreover, taxing the two situations differently would have the effect of either encouraging or discouraging the pooling of capital.

In fact, partnerships *are* taxed essentially along the lines of the sole proprietorship model. This method of taxation is variously referred to as "passthrough," "flowthrough," "conduit," or "aggregate" taxation. The legal entity (the partnership in this case) is generally ignored for purposes of paying tax. Instead, it is treated as a "conduit" and the income tax items relating to the business are passed through to the owners of the enterprise—the partners—who are the real (and only) taxpayers in interest. Under this approach, the partnership is conceived of as an "aggregate" of owners, each of whom is taxed as if she owned an individual interest in the partnership's assets and conducted the partnership's business directly.

Suppose the two sisters decide to incorporate their business, perhaps out of concern about the potential liabilities arising from it or for other good business reasons. The sisters agree to take back equal shares in the corporation. How should the profits of *L&E, Inc.* be taxed?

Again, at least in theory, perhaps the same partnership/sole proprietorship model should be followed. The underlying economic activity of the business seems to be the same, no matter what the form of organization. Therefore, why not tax the results of the underlying economic activity in the same way, regardless of the form of organization? Why not simply treat the legal entity (the corporation, here) as a mere conduit for tax purposes and have it pass through all tax items to the shareholders, the real taxpayers in interest?

Under current law, about 70 percent of all corporations (referred to as "S corporations" because they are governed by subchapter S of the Code (I.R.C. §§ 1361-1379)) *are* treated as conduits for tax purposes. Their taxable income and other tax items are passed through to their shareholders who must report and pay tax on such amounts. Chapter two focuses on the taxation of S corporations and their shareholders. Not all corporations, however, qualify for S corporation treatment or choose to be taxed in that manner. The law does not provide passthrough treatment for most other corporations (including essentially all public corporations), sometimes termed "C corporations" because they are principally governed by the rules of subchapter C of the Code (I.R.C. §§ 301-385). Indeed, unlike S corporations, C corporations are respected as taxable entities separate and distinct from their shareholders. Business profits earned by a C corporation, therefore, may be taxed twice: the entity may pay tax on them and the shareholders may pay another tax when they receive the earnings. As we shall see, however, many businesses organized as C corporations are able to avoid that result to a large extent and to achieve the equivalent of a passthrough result.

Chapter three explains what types of business entities are treated as corporations for tax purposes and therefore are taxed as C corporations if they have not elected or are ineligible for S status. The chapter also describes how the business profits of C corporations are taxed and the various ways in which the "double tax" may be reduced or avoided altogether. The chapter concludes with several proposals to reform the taxation of C corporations. The most important are proposals to "integrate" the corporation and shareholder income taxes so that corporate-source income is not taxed more than once. We consider why all corporations are not treated as conduits for tax purposes and whether there are other ways to achieve roughly the same outcome.

Beginning with chapter four and continuing through to the end of the book, we turn to the taxation of *transactions* between corporations and their shareholders and between one corporation and another. Consideration of these issues requires us to delve into some of the wonderful mysteries of subchapter C of the Internal Revenue Code. We examine these transactions carefully, moving from the simple to the complex, and identify the continuing themes in the taxation of corporate transactions that provide some coherence to this body of law. For example, the final chapter of the book, dealing with the taxation of tiers of C corporations that have been organized into "affiliated groups" filing a single, "consolidated return," requires us to revisit the passthrough tax principles first encountered in chapter two in order to ensure that the income of such groups is not excessively taxed.

As we shall see, the complexity of corporate transactions, their potential importance to the economy and the fisc, and the inventiveness of taxpayers and their advisors, have all contributed to the creation of a detailed and complicated set of laws specifying the tax consequences of the transactions. However sensible each of these laws may be if considered in isolation, their interaction with one another in the context of a particular transaction has almost inevitably led to some nonsensical results surely not contemplated by the drafters of the laws. Thus, an important issue frequently arising in tax law in general, and in corporate tax in particular, is how literally the law should be interpreted and applied. We focus on that topic specifically in chapter four but consider it throughout the book.

Let us not get too far ahead of ourselves, however. For now, let's return to our incorporated lemonade stand. What types of conceptual problems are raised if the legal entity is ignored for tax purposes? How might those problems be addressed?

# Chapter 2

# Taxation of S Corporations

This chapter describes the consequences of taxing a corporation known as an "S corporation" as a conduit or passthrough entity. What does it mean to disregard the corporate entity for tax purposes? Part A presents the principal features of the passthrough system under subchapter S. Part B then examines which corporations qualify as S corporations and part C concludes with some data relating to S corporations and other business entities.

## A. Passthrough System under Subchapter S

### 1. *Tax Responsibilities of the S Corporation*

Read I.R.C. § 1363(a)-(c). Like sole proprietorships and partnerships, an S corporation is generally not subject to income tax. Nevertheless, an S corporation must perform virtually all of the tasks of a taxpayer, including calculating its income, gain, loss, deductions, and credits (collectively referred to as the corporation's "tax items") and making many tax elections (such as choosing an accounting method and taxable year). The corporation thus serves as the "central headquarters" that takes essentially all of the steps necessary to determine the tax liability of the enterprise. The final step — the payment of tax — is the responsibility of the shareholders. The corporation must allocate its tax items among the shareholders and inform them of their respective shares (on a tax schedule labeled "K-1") so that they can include the items on their own tax returns. See I.R.C. § 1366(a)-(c). Importantly, the allocation is made (and shareholders must report their shares of tax items) without regard to whether the corporation makes any distribution to its shareholders.

The division of responsibility may give rise to ambiguity in some situations. Various tax provisions are applicable only to "corporations" or "individuals." An S corporation is a "corporation" yet, as described in part B, most of its shareholders are "individuals." Therefore, when an S corporation calculates its tax items, which tax law provisions apply? Section 1363(b) provides that an S corporation must generally compute its taxable income in the same manner as an *individual.* Thus, an S corporation is not entitled to claim the dividends-received deduction under section 243(a) (discussed in chapter five), which is only available to corporations. An S corporation, however, also may not claim the deduction for personal exemptions available to individuals. I.R.C. §§ 1363(b)(2), 703(a)(2)(A). Why not?

Finally, consistent with the "central headquarters" role of the S corporation, the character of tax items is determined at the corporate level with the S corporation then passing through items of the appropriate character to its shareholders. Read I.R.C. § 1366(b).

### *NOTES*

1. *Applicability of subchapter C (and payment of corporate tax).* Section 1371(a) makes subchapter C of the Code, which deals with the tax treatment of transactions involving *corporations*, generally applicable to an S corporation. Section 1363(b) is therefore limited to the manner in which an S corporation calculates its taxable income. When an S corporation participates in a transaction, it is recognized as a corporation, and the material beginning with chapter four of this book generally applies equally to C and S corporations. In addition, certain S corporations that were previously C corporations (or have succeeded to C corporation tax attributes) may be subject to a corporate-level tax. See I.R.C. §§ 1374, 1375. These provisions, and the policies behind them, are considered in chapter ten.

2. *Income character change?* Suppose an individual would realize ordinary income upon sale of a parcel of real estate because the individual is considered a dealer in real estate. Assuming that the individual could transfer the parcel in a tax-free manner to her wholly-owned S corporation, could the S corporation sell the parcel, realize a long-term capital gain (assuming that the S corporation is not treated as a dealer), and pass through income of that character to the individual? The partnership tax law contains a specific rule prohibiting a change in the character of income in that situation. See I.R.C. § 724(b). Although there is no comparable statutory provision applicable to S corporations, the regulations supply a similar rule. See Reg. § 1.1366-1(b)(2) (denying capital gain treatment if S corporation is "formed or availed of" for the principal purpose of changing the character of the income). This example illustrates a potential problem with having the S corporation determine certain issues (such as dealer status) that affect tax liability, since the corporation's determination may be different from that of each shareholder (whose determination may also differ from one another).

## 2. *Shareholder Inclusion of Tax Items*

Read I.R.C. §§ 1366(a) and (c) and 1377(a). Each shareholder of an S corporation must take into account her "pro rata share" of the corporation's tax items. This share is determined by assigning an equal portion of each item to each day in the corporation's taxable year and then to each share of stock outstanding on such day. The pro rata allocation is a simple rule that could be easily abused if shareholders were allowed to share the corporation's *economic* items in a different way. As described in part B of this chapter, however, S corporations are barred from having more than one class of stock. I.R.C. § 1361(b)(1)(D). This prohibition is intended to ensure that the amount of tax items allocated to a shareholder will eventually be matched by a distribution of the corporation's economic items.

Because an S corporation selects its own taxable year in computing its tax items, a rule of reconciliation is needed for allocation purposes when the corporation's taxable year differs from a shareholder's taxable year. That rule is contained in section 1366(a)(1), which requires a shareholder to report her share of each item in the "shareholder's taxable year in which the taxable year of the S corporation ends." Because this rule may allow a shareholder to defer reporting a tax item beyond the point she would have had to report it as a sole proprietor, the law restricts the taxable years that an S corporation may elect. Read I.R.C. §§ 1378 and 444 and skim I.R.C. § 7519.

**Problem 2-1:**

(a) What tax items of an S corporation must be passed through? May the items be lumped together or must they be separately stated? Why? Are there any tax items that need not be passed through?
(b) Ms. A owns 90 percent of X corporation, a calendar year S corporation. On July 1 of Year 1, she sells all of her X shares to Mr. B who retains the shares for the remainder of the year. Throughout the year, Ms. Q owns the other 10 percent interest in the corporation. Assume that X has $100,000 of taxable income during the first six months of Year 1 and only $30,000 during the last six months. Describe two permissible methods of allocating X's Year 1 income among its shareholders. Under what conditions may those methods be used?
(c) D, a calendar year taxpayer, is the sole shareholder of corporation Z, an S corporation. May Z select a taxable year ending either March 31 or September 30? If either taxable year is permissible, would it be advantageous to D for the corporation to do so? Why or why not?
(d) Suppose in question (c), Z uses a September 30 taxable year and on October 31 of Year 1, D sells all of his Z stock to Ms. E. D, E, and Z all consent to the section 1377(a)(2) election. In which return must D report his share of corporate income or loss from October 1 to October 31 of Year 1? See Reg. § 1.1377-1(b)(3)(i) and (iii), and -1(c) (ex. 2(iii) and (iv)).

*NOTE*

*Elective termination of taxable year.* As illustrated by questions (b) and (d) of **problem 2-1**, if a shareholder's interest in an S corporation is terminated during a taxable year, the corporation and all affected shareholders may elect to treat the event as if it terminated the corporation's taxable year. I.R.C. § 1377(a)(2). This election allows a corporation's tax items to be allocated more precisely to those shareholders owning shares when the tax item arose. When the election is made, the corporation's taxable year is deemed to terminate only for purposes of determining each shareholder's share of the corporation's tax items, the amount of adjustments to certain of the corporation's tax attributes, and the tax effect of distributions. The regulations extend this election (for the same limited purposes) whenever there is a "qualifying disposition" of the corporation's stock. In general, a qualifying disposition includes, during any 30-day period, either a 20 percent or greater disposition of stock by an existing shareholder or the issuance of stock to a new shareholder equal to 25 percent or more of the amount previously outstanding. Reg. § 1.1368-1(g). In effect, the regulations allow taxpayers to bypass the arbitrary general rule whenever there is some significant shift in the shareholders' percentage interests.

### 3. *Shareholder Basis Adjustments*

Although subchapter S generally disregards the existence of the corporate entity for the important purpose of paying tax on the corporation's income, the entity is nevertheless respected for other legal purposes. For example, shareholders own shares in the corporation's stock and *not* direct interests in the corporation's assets. Rather, it is the corporation that owns the assets and earns the business income.

This inconsistency between the tax and corporate law treatment of S corporations creates the need for certain additional rules. Consider the following example:

> **Example 2-1:** Assume that your daughter, Laura, operates a lemonade stand as a sole proprietorship and in Year 1, the business has net profits of $20. Laura's basis in the business is automatically increased by $20, either in the form of money retained or business assets acquired with the money, because there is no legal separation between a proprietor and her proprietorship. The basis increase ensures that upon a subsequent sale of the business, Laura will not have to pay tax again on the same $20.
>
> Now assume the same facts except that Laura incorporates her business and it qualifies for "S" status. Under the passthrough system, the $20 in Year 1 business profits is not taxed to the corporation but instead is passed through to Laura and taxable to her in that year. While the corporation increases *its* basis in its assets by $20 if it retains the profits, some mechanism is also necessary to adjust Laura's basis in her stock. Otherwise, on a subsequent sale of that stock, she might be taxed again on the same profits.

Current law addresses this problem by prescribing a series of increases and decreases to shareholder stock basis, sometimes referred to as "outside basis," depending upon certain events affecting the S corporation. (The corporation's basis in its assets is sometimes referred to as "inside basis.") Read I.R.C. § 1367(a) and (b)(1). In general, these adjustments take into account the S corporation's income, loss, deductions, and distributions. The adjustments are effective as of the close of the corporation's taxable year in which the event occurs. However, if a shareholder disposes of her stock in the corporation, the adjustments allocable to such shareholder are effective immediately prior to the disposition. See Reg. § 1.1367-1(d).

**Example 2-1** illustrates an important objective of any passthrough tax system. Because transactions of legal significance may occur at either the "corporate level" or the "shareholder level," the law must anticipate the possibility of separate tax consequences arising at each level. Yet if the goal of taxing an S corporation's income like that of a sole proprietor is to be achieved, there must be coordination between the tax consequences to make sure a stream of income is not taxed more than once. In general, events producing tax consequences "inside" the corporation (such as income earned by the corporation and an increase in aggregate inside basis) should be accounted for "outside" the corporation (through increases to the stock basis of the shareholders). Similarly, events having tax consequences "outside" the corporation (such as a sale of corporate stock by a shareholder at a gain and an increase in aggregate outside basis) should be accounted for "inside" the corporation (through increases to the basis of the corporation's assets). A key principle of passthrough taxation is to maintain equivalence between the entity's aggregate inside basis in its assets and the owners' aggregate outside bases in their interests in the entity. As we will see, subchapter S achieves this objective only imperfectly.

**Problem 2-2:**

(a) In **example 2-1**, what happens to Laura's basis in her stock assuming that she is the sole shareholder of the corporation? Does your answer change if the corporation's profits consist entirely of capital gains?
(b) Same as (a), except that Laura, for whatever reason, fails to include in her taxable income the $20 in business profits allocated to her. Will there be any change to her stock basis now?
(c) Same as (b), except that the reason Laura fails to include the $20 in her taxable income is that it is tax-exempt interest income. Answer the same question as in (b). Does your answer reach a sound policy outcome?
(d) Suppose that after earning the $20 in profits, the corporation distributes that amount as a dividend to Laura. What effect should these events have on Laura?
(e) Explain the rationale behind section 1367(a)(2)(D).

### 4. *Limitation on the Passthrough of Losses*

One area where subchapter S fails to coordinate the tax consequences arising "inside" and "outside" an S corporation is when the corporation borrows money.

Although the amount borrowed is not income, it nevertheless increases the corporation's basis in its assets. Thus, a proper coordination rule would require outside basis to be increased by the amount borrowed, which is the rule for partnerships under subchapter K. See I.R.C. § 752(a) and (b). There is, however, no comparable rule in subchapter S. A practical effect of this omission is to prevent taxpayers who are not well-advised from claiming certain losses incurred by their S corporations. Many taxpayers fall into this trap. Read I.R.C. §§ 1366(d)(1) and (2) and 1367(b)(2) and the following case.

## Uri v. Commissioner

949 F.2d 371 (10th Cir. 1991)

HOLLOWAY, Cir. J.

The issue . . . is whether a shareholder in a subchapter S corporation who personally guarantees a bank loan to the corporation may increase his or her adjusted basis in the corporation's stock by the prorated amount of the guarantee in order to increase the available loss deduction under . . . I.R.C. § [1366(d)]. In the cases before us, the Tax Court approved the Commissioner's disallowance of petitioners' enhanced loss deductions. Guided by a recent Tenth Circuit opinion concerning this controlling issue, we affirm.

. . . During the tax years in question, petitioners Cathaleen Uri and Stevens J. Townsdin were stockholders in The Old Opera House Mall Company (referred to as "the corporation" in this opinion), formed by Mrs. Uri and Mr. Townsdin as the business vehicle for renovation of a building in downtown Concordia, Kansas. After renovation, the corporation planned to operate a small retail mall and a dinner theater in the building. Mrs. Uri and Mr. Townsdin, also partners in an accounting firm, each contributed $10,000 cash to capitalize the corporation and received 50% of the corporation's stock. The corporation elected to be taxed as a small business corporation under subchapter S of the Internal Revenue Code. The corporation borrowed money from a local bank to repay interim loans for construction and equipment. This loan was secured by the real estate and assets of the corporation and by the personal guarantees of Mrs. Uri and Mr. Townsdin. Ninety percent of the loan was also guaranteed by the Small Business Administration (SBA).

Unfortunately, after the building was renovated, business was not sufficiently profitable to cover the loan payments, and the corporation suffered severe financial losses. After the SBA sent petitioners a demand for satisfaction under their guarantees on the accelerated note, petitioners filed individually for bankruptcy under Chapter 7 and their personal guarantees of the loan were discharged in the bankruptcy proceedings. Eventually, after strenuous efforts to financially revive the corporation failed, the corporation filed for bankruptcy. Under Chapter 7 liquidation, its real property and other assets were sold at a marshal's sale.

I.R.C. § [1366(d)] allowed a pro-rata pass-through of net corporate losses to subchapter S corporate shareholders up to the amount of the taxpayer's adjusted basis in corporate stock plus the adjusted basis of the corporation's debt to the same taxpayer. In this case, [the shareholders' bases] in the corporate stock that resulted from their initial respective investments of $10,000 were extinguished by the losses they claimed on their 1981 returns. However, . . . petitioners claimed that their adjusted basis included a pro-rata share of the amount of the corporate loan each had personally guaranteed, resulting in their claims of a net business loss deduction for [1982 and 1983].

The Commissioner disallowed these pass-through losses. In denying the amount personally guaranteed as part of petitioners' § [1366(d)] allowance for subchapter S loss pass-through, the Commissioner noted that petitioners were never called upon to make an actual economic transfer for the benefit of the corporation under the guarantee.

In their petitions to the Tax Court, petitioners noted that they had suffered considerable economic impact because the guarantees had forced each of them into personal bankruptcy at significant personal financial loss. They noted that the interrelationship of their personal finances, the finances of their joint accounting firm, and the prospective finances of the corporation were all taken into account when the bank extended the loan to the corporation. Petitioners argued that because the loan was made primarily on the strength of their personal financial worth and the income from their accounting business, it was in substance a loan to them and a subsequent contribution by them of the funds to the corporation's capital. In the alternative, they characterized the loan as corporate debt to them because the bank would not have made the loan without their personal guarantees. Under either argument, they claimed that the amount of the guarantee should be part of their pass-through loss limitation under [§ 1366(d)].

The Tax Court denied the taxpayers' petitions, citing its opinion in Estate of Leavitt v. Comm'r, 90 T.C. 206 (1988), aff'd, 875 F.2d 420 (4th Cir.), cert. denied, 493 U.S. 958 (1989). Under the Tax Court ruling, petitioners' basis in the corporation's stock was limited to contributions of cash or other property, in accord with the definition of "basis" from I.R.C. § 1012 and the definition of "cost" from Treas. Reg. § 1.1012-1(a). The Tax Court held that because petitioners' personal guarantees were neither cash nor other property, the guarantees could not be considered as part of petitioners' adjusted basis in the corporation's stock. In addition, in rejecting application of debt-equity principles to this transaction, the court cited its ruling in *Estate of Leavitt*, requiring actual economic outlay by petitioners rather than characterizing a mere demand for payment under the guarantee as corporate debt to petitioners. Petitioners appealed to this court.

Petitioners correctly note a split among the circuits which have considered this issue. *Compare* Selfe v. U.S., 778 F.2d 769 (11th Cir. 1985) (approving theory of pro-rata inclusion of personal loan guarantees in shareholders' adjusted basis in subchapter S corporate stock for the purpose of the pass-through loss deduction, emphasizing analysis of whether the lender looked primarily to the shareholder or to the corporate entity for repayment . . . ) *with Estate of Leavitt* (disapproving such inclusion and . . . emphasizing that subchapter S shareholders must abide by the form of the transaction of which they are a part, rather than using hindsight to construct an explanation of the transaction which gives them the best tax result) and Brown v. Comm'r, 706 F.2d 755, 756 (6th Cir. 1983) (subchapter S shareholder/guarantor must make economic outlay to convert loan guarantee into investment). After this appeal was filed two more circuits, including this one, have considered the issue and joined the Fourth and Sixth Circuits in their analysis, leaving the Eleventh Circuit alone in the minority position. See Goatcher v. U.S., 944 F.2d 747 (10th Cir. 1991). . . .

We are bound by our decision in *Goatcher*. There, this court refused to recharacterize a transaction as a different relationship between the parties than that reflected on the face of the financial documents used to structure the transaction. Under *Goatcher*, taxpayers must choose a form for transactions which accurately reflects the substance of the transactions. The same requirement can be applied to petitioners' "debt-equity" argument here. They contend that the loan from the bank to the "thinly capitalized" corporation, personally guaranteed by the shareholders, was in substance a loan to the shareholders themselves, who then contributed the loan proceeds to the corporation as a capital infusion. However, *Goatcher's* analysis that the form of a taxpayer's transactions govern the tax ramifications of those transactions applies to this argument as well. Recharacterization of the transaction in pursuit of tax advantages was properly disallowed. . . .

### *NOTES AND QUESTIONS*

1. *Debt basis.* Losses may be passed through to a shareholder up to the amount of the shareholder's stock basis *plus* her basis in any of the corporation's debt to her. I.R.C. § 1366(d)(1)(B). This rule mitigates slightly the potential harshness of the result illustrated in *Uri* when an S corporation borrows money but outside basis is not adjusted. Any losses passed through first reduce stock basis to zero before reducing debt basis. If debt basis is reduced, a subsequent positive basis adjustment first restores debt basis to its original amount before increasing stock basis. See I.R.C. § 1367(b)(2). This ordering rule increases the likelihood that a subsequent repayment of the debt is simply a nontaxable return of basis, the "normal" result expected by most taxpayers (and perhaps reported by them even when repayment exceeds the amount of their basis). Positive basis adjustments at most restore debt basis to its original amount; any further adjustments increase stock basis, not debt basis.

2. *Suspended losses.* Losses not allowed by reason of section 1366(d)(1) are suspended. Suspended losses are treated as arising again and pass through in each succeeding taxable year (subject to the section 1366(d)(1) limitation applicable at that time) to the same shareholder entitled to the original loss. I.R.C. § 1366(d)(2). If a shareholder transfers all of his stock in the corporation prior to being able to deduct the suspended loss, may the shareholder or anyone else claim the loss? Why or why not? Does it matter whether the transferee is the spouse of the transferor? See I.R.C. § 1366(d)(2)(B); Reg. § 1.1366-2(a)(5)(i) and (ii).

3. *Use of collateral.* May a shareholder increase outside basis for a corporate loan if the shareholder guarantees the loan and provides personally owned assets as collateral for the guarantee? See Harris v. U.S., 902 F.2d 439 (5th Cir. 1990) (collateral did not constitute economic outlay and therefore did not affect outside basis).

4. *Substance vs. form. Uri* illustrates a very common issue in corporate tax — to what extent should the tax consequences of a transaction follow from its "form" as opposed to its "substance"? In the case, the taxpayer argued that the tax consequences should be determined by the substance of the transaction (a shareholder borrowing followed by a contribution of the proceeds to the corporation either in the form of a loan or additional equity) rather than by its form (a corporate borrowing). A court may resist such an invitation if it disagrees with the taxpayer's characterization of the facts or simply because it believes that taxpayers must live with the consequences of their transactions. Since the form of a transaction chosen by taxpayers is generally determinative of its tax consequences, taxpayers should not be entitled to back away from their own form in the selected situations where it is advantageous to do so. See Maloof v. Comm'r, 456 F.3d 645, 651 (6th Cir. 2006) (quoting from Williams v. Comm'r, 429 U.S. 569 (1977), that "while a taxpayer is free to organize his affairs as he chooses, nevertheless, once having done so, he must accept the tax consequences of his choice, whether contemplated or not . . . and may not enjoy the benefit of some other route he might have chosen to follow but did not"). In the *Selfe* case mentioned in *Uri*, however, the Eleventh Circuit accepted the taxpayer's invitation to ignore form in favor of substance. In a subsequent case, the Eleventh Circuit described *Selfe* as presenting an "unusual set[] of facts"; because the S corporation was a thinly capitalized, fledgling enterprise run by a novice in a highly competitive field, the court was persuaded that, in reality, the loan had been made directly to the shareholder. Sleiman v. Comm'r, 187 F.3d 1352, 1359 (11th Cir. 1999).

The reluctance of courts to disregard the form of a transaction does not, of course, apply when it is the *government* making the plea because the government plays no role in selecting the form. For example, in Oren v. Comm'r, 357 F.3d 854 (8th Cir. 2004), the taxpayer controlled three different S corporations, two of which had incurred losses. In order to increase his basis in the two loss corporations, the taxpayer borrowed funds from his remaining, profitable S corporation and then loaned those amounts to the two loss corporations. They, in turn, loaned the same funds back to the third, profitable corporation. Thus, in the end, there was simply a circular flow of money among the taxpayer and his three controlled corporations. Even though all formalities were observed, the court refused to accept the form of the transaction, which would have increased the taxpayer's basis in his two loss corporations and enabled his greater use of their losses. The court indicated that the possibility of personal economic loss to be suffered by the taxpayer as a result of the transactions would require the occurrence of "a great number of unlikely facts." Id. at 859. Accordingly, because the taxpayer had not made any "economic outlay" to the loss corporations, his basis in the corporations did not increase and he was not entitled to claim the losses passed through to him. The proper role of substance and form in determining tax consequences is discussed more generally in chapter four.

5. *Other gatekeepers.* Even if a shareholder has enough stock or debt basis to satisfy section 1366(d)(1), the shareholder's use of any losses passed through may still be prevented by the "at risk" (I.R.C. § 465) or "passive loss" (I.R.C. § 469) rules.

6. *Policy.* Because the partnership tax rules provide for an adjustment to outside basis when the partnership borrows money, it generally does not make a difference for tax purposes whether a borrowing is made directly by a partnership or by a partner who then contributes or loans the proceeds to the partnership. Is there any policy justification for not allowing the same adjustment in subchapter S? One possible rationale is that under state corporate law, shareholders are generally insulated from liability for their corporation's debts. The same liability shield, however, is generally available to the members of an LLC, and if the LLC is taxed like a partnership, the members are permitted to adjust their outside basis by the amount of any LLC debt.

7. *Charitable contributions by S corporations.* In computing its taxable income, an S corporation may not claim a deduction for charitable contributions. Rather, the amount of such contributions made by the corporation is passed through to the shareholders and any deduction is potentially claimed by them. I.R.C. §§ 1363(b)(2), 703(a)(2)(C), 1366(a)(1) (last sentence), 702(a)(4). The general reason for this procedure is to protect charitable contribution limitations and elections that are personal to the taxpayer making the contribution. See I.R.C. § 170(b)(1). If property other than cash is contributed by an S corporation to a charity, the passthrough of the contribution reduces the shareholder's outside basis by the *basis*, and not the value, of the property contributed. I.R.C. § 1367(a)(2) (flush language). Consistently, the section 1366(d)(1) limitation applies only if the basis of the contributed property exceeds the shareholder's stock and debt basis. I.R.C. § 1366(d)(4); Rev. Rul. 2008-16, 2008-1 C.B. 585. These rules enable the shareholder to avoid recognizing any gain on a charitable contribution of appreciated property, and are consistent with the goal of maintaining parity between aggregate inside and outside basis. The rules currently expire at the end of 2011 but will likely be extended.

**Problem 2-3:** Jan organizes Q corporation and exchanges $20,000 for all of Q's stock. Q has an operating loss of $24,000 in Year 1. During Year 2, Jan lends Q another $20,000; Q loses another $24,000 in Year 2. In Year 3, Q is expected to show a profit of $15,000. For all three years, Q has a valid S election in effect.

(a) How much of Q's loss can Jan deduct in Years 1 and 2?
(b) How much will she be able to deduct in Year 3 if the profit expectations materialize? In that event, what will be her basis in the stock and indebtedness of Q after the end of Year 3?

(c) If Q is expected to show a profit of only $3,000 in Year 3, what can Jan do before the end of Year 3 to increase her allowable loss deduction for that year?

---

The holding of the following case was reversed by Congress in 2002. See I.R.C. § 108(d)(7)(A) (addition of the words beginning with "including"). Nevertheless, *Gitlitz* remains a useful (and challenging) case in terms of understanding the structure of subchapter S and interpreting statutes like the tax code. It also illustrates the type of problems that arise because outside basis is not adjusted by the amount of an S corporation's debt.

By way of background, income generally includes the amount of a discharge of indebtedness. I.R.C. § 61(a)(12). If, however, the taxpayer is insolvent at the time of the discharge, the discharged amount is excluded from gross income. I.R.C. § 108(a)(1)(B). As a condition for this exclusion, the taxpayer must reduce certain tax attributes, including any net operating losses (NOLs), by the amount excluded. I.R.C. § 108(b)(1) and (2)(A). If there is a dollar-for-dollar reduction in the taxpayer's NOLs, then section 108 operates as a deferral provision rather than an exemption. *Gitlitz* resolves what happens when an S corporation incurs the debt and the debt is discharged when the corporation is insolvent. Which opinion — the majority or the dissent — seems to have the better view?

## Gitlitz v. Commissioner

531 U.S. 206 (2001)

Justice THOMAS delivered the opinion of the Court.

... In this case we must answer two questions. First, we must decide whether the Internal Revenue Code (Code) permits taxpayers to increase bases in their S corporation stock by the amount of an S corporation's discharge of indebtedness excluded from gross income. And, second, if the Code permits such an increase, we must decide whether the increase occurs before or after taxpayers are required to reduce the S corporation's tax attributes.

... David Gitlitz and Philip Winn were shareholders of P.D.W.&A., Inc., a corporation that had elected to be taxed under subchapter S of the Code. ... In 1991, P.D.W.&A. realized $2,021,296 of discharged indebtedness. At the time, the corporation was insolvent in the amount of $2,181,748. Because it was insolvent even after the discharge of indebtedness was added to its balance sheet, P.D.W.&A. excluded the entire discharge of indebtedness amount from gross income under § 108(a) and (d)(7)(A). On their tax returns, Gitlitz and Winn increased their bases in P.D.W.&A. stock by their pro rata share (50 percent each) of the amount of the corporation's discharge of indebtedness. Petitioners' theory was that the discharge of indebtedness was an "item of income" subject to pass-through under

§ 1366(a)(1)(A). They used their increased bases to deduct on their personal tax returns corporate losses and deductions, including losses and deductions from previous years that had been suspended under § 1366(d). Gitlitz and Winn each had losses (including suspended losses and operating losses) that totaled $1,010,648. With the upward basis adjustments of $1,010,648 each, Gitlitz and Winn were each able to deduct the full amount of their pro rata share of P.D.W.&A.'s losses.

The Commissioner determined that petitioners could not use P.D.W.&A.'s discharge of indebtedness to increase their bases in the stock and denied petitioners' loss deductions. . . . [T]he Tax Court [agreed]. . . . The Court of Appeals affirmed. It assumed that excluded discharge of indebtedness is an item of income subject to passthrough to shareholders pursuant to § 1366(a)(1)(A), . . . but held that the discharge of indebtedness amount first had to be used to reduce certain tax attributes of the S corporation under § 108(b), and that only the leftover amount could be used to increase basis. The Court of Appeals explained that, because the tax attribute to be reduced (in this case the corporation's net operating loss) was equal to the amount of discharged debt, the entire amount of discharged debt was absorbed by the reduction at the corporate level, and nothing remained of the discharge of indebtedness to be passed through to the shareholders under § 1366(a)(1)(A). . . . Because Courts of Appeals have disagreed on how to treat discharge of indebtedness of an insolvent S corporation, . . . we granted certiorari. . . .

Before we can reach the issue addressed by the Court of Appeals — whether the increase in the taxpayers' corporate bases occurs before or after the taxpayers are required to reduce the S corporation's tax attributes — we must address the argument raised by the Commissioner. The Commissioner argues that the discharge of indebtedness of an insolvent S corporation is not an "item of income" and thus never passes through to shareholders. Under a plain reading of the statute, we reject this argument and conclude that excluded discharged debt is indeed an "item of income," which passes through to the shareholders and increases their bases in the stock of the S corporation.

Section 61(a)(12) states that discharge of indebtedness generally is included in gross income. Section 108(a)(1) provides an express exception to this general rule:

> "Gross income does not include any amount which (but for this subsection) would be includible in gross income by reason of the discharge . . . of indebtedness of the taxpayer if— . . . (B) the discharge occurs when the taxpayer is insolvent."

The Commissioner contends that this exclusion from gross income alters the character of the discharge of indebtedness so that it is no longer an "item of income." However, the text and structure of the statute do not support the Commissioner's theory. Section 108(a) simply does not say that discharge of indebtedness ceases to be an *item of income* when the S corporation is insolvent. Instead it provides only that discharge of indebtedness ceases to be *included in gross income.* Not all items of income are included in gross income, see § 1366(a)(1) (providing that "items of income," including "tax-exempt" income, are passed through to shareholders), so mere exclusion of an amount from gross income does not imply that the amount ceases to be an item of income. Moreover, §§ 101 through 136 employ the same construction to exclude various items from gross income: "Gross income does not include. . . ." The consequence of reading this language in the manner suggested by the Commissioner would be to exempt all items in these sections from pass-through under § 1366. However, not even the Commissioner encourages us to reach this sweeping conclusion. Instead the Commissioner asserts that discharge of indebtedness is unique among the types of items excluded from gross income because no economic outlay is required of the taxpayer receiving discharge of indebtedness. But the Commissioner is unable to identify language in the statute that makes this distinction relevant, and we certainly find none.

. . . [The statute] presumes that discharge of indebtedness is always "income," and that the only question for purposes of § 108 is whether it is includible in gross income. If discharge of indebtedness of insolvent entities were not actually "income," there would be no need to provide an exception to its inclusion in gross income; quite simply, if discharge of indebtedness of an insolvent entity were not "income," it would necessarily not be included in gross income.

Notwithstanding the plain language of the statute, the Commissioner argues, generally, that excluded discharge of indebtedness is not income and, specifically, that it is not "tax-exempt income" under § 1366(a)(1)(A). [1] . . .

[T]he Commissioner argues that excluded discharge of indebtedness is not "tax-exempt" income under § 1366(a)(1)(A), but rather "tax-deferred" income. According to the Commissioner, because the taxpayer is required to reduce tax attributes that could have provided future tax benefits, the taxpayer will pay taxes on future income that otherwise would have been absorbed by the forfeited tax attributes. Implicit in the Commissioner's labeling of such income as "tax-deferred," however, is the erroneous assumption that § 1366(a)(1)(A) does not include "tax-deferred" income. Section 1366 applies to "items of income." This section expressly includes "tax-exempt" income, but this inclusion does not mean that the statute must therefore exclude "tax-deferred" income. The section is worded broadly enough to include

1. The Commissioner also contends, as does the dissent, that because § 108(d)(7)(A) mandates that the discharged debt amount be determined and applied to reduce tax attributes "at the corporate level," rather than at the shareholder level, the discharged debt, even if it is some type of income, simply cannot pass through to shareholders. In other words, the Commissioner contends that § 108(d)(7)(A) excepts excluded discharged debt from the general pass-through provisions for S corporations. However, § 108(d)(7)(A) merely directs that the exclusion from gross income and the tax attribute reduction be made at the corporate level. Section 108(d)(7)(A) does not state or imply that the debt discharge provisions shall apply *only* "at the corporate level." The very purpose of Subchapter S is to tax at the shareholder level, not the corporate level. Income is determined at the S corporation level, see § 1363(b), not in order to tax the corporation, see § 1363(a) (exempting an S corporation from income tax), but solely to pass through to the S corporation's shareholders the corporation's income. Thus, the controlling provision states that, in determining a shareholder's liability, "there shall be taken into account the shareholder's pro rata share of the corporation's . . . items of income (including tax-exempt income). . . ." § 1366(a)(1). Nothing in § 108(d)(7)(A) suspends the operation of these ordinary pass-through rules.

any item of income, even tax-deferred income, that "could affect the liability for tax of any shareholder." § 1366(a)(1)(A). Thus, none of the Commissioner's contentions alters our conclusion that discharge of indebtedness of an insolvent S corporation is an item of income for purposes of § 1366(a)(1)(A).

... Having concluded that excluded discharge of indebtedness is an "item of income" and is therefore subject to pass-through to shareholders under § 1366, we must resolve the sequencing question addressed by the Court of Appeals — whether pass-through is performed before or after the reduction of the S corporation's tax attributes under § 108(b). Section 108(b)(1) provides that "[t]he amount excluded from gross income under [§ 108(a)] shall be applied to reduce the tax attributes of the taxpayer as provided [in this section]." Section 108(b)(2) then lists the various tax attributes to be reduced in the order of reduction. The first tax attribute to be reduced, and the one at issue in this case, is the net operating loss. See § 108(b)(2)(A). Section 108(d)(7)(B) specifies that, for purposes of attribute reduction, the shareholders' suspended losses for the taxable year of discharge are to be treated as the S corporation's net operating loss. If tax attribute reduction is performed *before* the discharge of indebtedness is passed through to the shareholders (as the Court of Appeals held), the shareholders' losses that exceed basis are treated as the corporation's net operating loss and are then reduced by the amount of the discharged debt. In this case, no suspended losses would remain that would permit petitioners to take deductions. If, however, attribute reduction is performed *after* the discharged debt income is passed through (as petitioners argue), then the shareholders would be able to deduct their losses (up to the amount of the increase in basis caused by the discharged debt). Any suspended losses remaining then will be treated as the S corporation's net operating loss and will be reduced by the amount of the discharged debt. Therefore, the sequence of the steps of pass-through and attribute reduction determines whether petitioners here were deficient when they increased their bases by the discharged debt amount and deducted their losses.

The sequencing question is expressly addressed in the statute. Section 108(b)(4)(A) directs that the attribute reductions "shall be made *after* the determination of the *tax imposed* by this chapter for the taxable year of the discharge." (Emphases added.) ... In order to determine the "tax imposed," an S corporation shareholder must adjust his basis in his corporate stock and pass through all items of income and loss. See §§ 1366, 1367. Consequently, the attribute reduction must be made *after* the basis adjustment and pass-through. In the case of petitioners, they must pass through the discharged debt, increase corporate bases, and then deduct their losses, all before any attribute reduction could occur. Because their basis increase is equal to their losses, petitioners have no suspended losses remaining. They, therefore, have no net operating losses to reduce. ...

[C]ourts have discussed the policy concern that, if shareholders were permitted to pass through the discharge of indebtedness before reducing any tax attributes, the shareholders would wrongly experience a "double windfall": They would be exempted from paying taxes on the full amount of the discharge of indebtedness, *and* they would be able to increase basis and deduct their previously suspended losses. . . . Because the Code's plain text permits the taxpayers here to receive these benefits, we need not address this policy concern.[2] . . .

Justice BREYER, dissenting.

I agree with the majority's reasoning with the exception of footnotes 1 and 2. . . . As the majority acknowledges, . . . § 108 contains a subsection that sets forth a special exception. The exception [§ 108(d)(7)(A)], entitled "Special rules for S corporation," says:

> "(A) Certain provisions to be applied at corporate level.
> "In the case of an S corporation, subsections (a), (b), (c), and (g) shall be applied at the corporate level." . . .

If one reads this language literally as exclusive, both the COD exclusion (§ 108(a)) and the tax attribute reduction (§ 108(b)) would apply only "at the corporate level." Hence the COD income would not flow through to S corporation shareholders. Consequently, the insolvent S corporation's COD income would not increase the shareholder's basis and would not help the shareholder take otherwise unavailable deductions for suspended losses.

The Commissioner argues that we should read the language in this way as preventing the flow-through of the corporation's COD income. . . . He points to the language of a House Committee, which apparently thought, when Congress passed an amendment to § 108, that the Commissioner's reading is correct. . . . ("The exclusion and basis reduction are both made at the S corporation level (sec. 108(d)(7)). The shareholders' basis in their stock is not adjusted by the amount of debt discharge income that is excluded at the corporate level"). . . .

The Commissioner finds support for his literal, exclusive reading of § 108(d)(7)(A)'s language in the fact that his reading would close a significant tax loophole. That loophole—preserved by the majority—would grant a *solvent* shareholder of an insolvent S corporation a tax benefit in the form of permission to take an otherwise unavailable deduction, thereby sheltering other, unrelated income from tax. See Witzel v. Comm'r, 200 F.3d 496, 497 (CA7 2000) (Posner, C. J.) ("It is hard to understand the rationale for using a tax exemption to avoid taxation not only on the income covered by the exemption but also on unrelated income that is

---

2. The benefit at issue in this case arises in part because § 108(d)(7)(A) permits the exclusion of discharge of indebtedness income from gross income for an insolvent S corporation even when the S corporation shareholder is personally solvent. We are aware of no other instance in which § 108 directly benefits a solvent entity. However, the result is required by statute. Between 1982 and 1984, § 108 provided that the exclusion from gross income and the reduction in tax attributes occurred at the shareholder level. . . . This provision, which paralleled the current taxation of partnerships at the partner level, see 26 U.S.C. § 108(d)(6), prevented solvent shareholders from benefiting as a result of their S corporation's insolvency. In 1984, however, Congress amended the Code to provide that § 108 be applied "at the corporate level." . . . It is as a direct result of this amendment that the solvent petitioners in this case are able to benefit from § 108's exclusion.

not tax exempt"). Moreover, the benefit often would increase in value as the amount of COD income increases, a result inconsistent with congressional intent to impose a "price" (attribute reduction) . . . on excluded COD. . . .

The majority acknowledges some of these policy concerns and confesses ignorance of any "other instance in which § 108 directly benefits a solvent entity," but claims that its reading is mandated by the plain text of § 108(d)(7)(A) and therefore that the Court may disregard the policy consequences. . . . It is difficult, however, to see why we should interpret that language as treating different solvent shareholders differently, given that the words "at the corporate level" were added "in order to treat all shareholders in the same manner." H.R. Rep. No. 98-432, pt. 2, p. 1640 (1984). And it is more difficult to see why, given the fact that the "plain language" admits either interpretation, we should ignore the policy consequences. . . .

The arguments from plain text on both sides here produce ambiguity, not certainty. And other things being equal, we should read ambiguous statutes as closing, not maintaining, tax loopholes. Such is an appropriate understanding of Congress' likely intent. Here, other things are equal, for, as far as I am aware, the Commissioner's literal interpretation of § 108(d)(7)(A) as exclusive would neither cause any tax-related harm nor create any statutory anomaly. . . .

The majority, in footnote 1, says that the words "at the corporate level" in § 108(d)(7)(A) apply to the exclusion of COD income from corporate income and to "tax attribute reduction" but do not "suspen[d] the operation of . . . ordinary pass-through rules" because § 108(d)(7)(A) "does not state or imply that the debt discharge provisions shall apply *only* 'at the corporate level.'" It is the majority, however, that should explain why it reads the provision as nonexclusive (where, as here, its interpretation of the Code results in the "practical equivalent of [a] double deduction" . . . ). I do not contend that § 108(d)(7)(A) *must* be read as having exclusive effect, only that, given the alternative, this interpretation provides the best reading of § 108 as a whole. And I can find no "clear declaration of intent by Congress" to support the majority's contrary conclusion regarding § 108(d)(7)(A)'s effect. It is that conclusion from which, for the reasons stated, I respectfully dissent.

## *NOTES AND QUESTIONS*

1. *Tax-deferred income.* Do you agree with the Court's assertion that the term "items of income" in section 1366(a)(1)(A) is broad enough to include not only "tax-exempt income" but also "tax-deferred income"? Suppose an S corporation engages in a like-kind exchange under section 1031 with the result that gain realized of $1,000 is not recognized but deferred. Should there nevertheless be a passthrough of the $1,000 of "tax-deferred income" and an accompanying $1,000 increase to shareholder stock basis in the year of the exchange? If so, is there anything in the statute to prevent *another* passthrough and increase to stock basis when the deferred income is recognized in a later year? Furthermore, consider the goal of a passthrough system to maintain parity between aggregate inside and outside basis. Following the like-kind

exchange by an S corporation, is aggregate inside basis changed? Should there be any change to outside basis?

2. *Sequencing question.* The Court resolves the sequencing question through a plain reading of section 108(b)(4)(A). Read that provision carefully. Its meaning seems clear enough if the taxpayer is an individual (or a corporation other than an S corporation). But if the taxpayer is an S corporation, there is a potential ambiguity as to whether it should be applied to the "determination of . . . tax imposed" by the *S corporation* or by the *shareholders* of the corporation.

The Court interprets the provision as referring to the "determination of . . . tax imposed" by the shareholders. This view is arguably consistent with the approach of subchapter S, which disregards the corporate entity for purposes of paying tax. On the other hand, we have learned that the S corporation (and not the shareholders) must perform virtually every other role necessary to make the "determination of . . . tax imposed." So how should this ambiguity be resolved? Does section 108(d)(7)(A) and (B) provide any help?

3. *Capital contribution is not "item of income."* In Nathel v. Comm'r, 615 F.3d 83 (2d Cir. 2010), an S corporation passed through losses to its shareholders that reduced their stock basis to zero and their debt basis to less than the debt's principal amount. The issue was the effect on the shareholders' stock and debt basis of a subsequent capital contribution made by them to the S corporation. Normally, a capital contribution increases a shareholder's basis in stock of the corporation. Based on the reasoning in *Gitlitz*, however, the taxpayers argued that the contribution represented a tax-exempt "item of income" to the corporation (see I.R.C. § 118(a)), which, when passed through to them, restored their debt basis before having any effect on stock basis. I.R.C. § 1367(b)(2)(B). By this claim, the taxpayers hoped to avoid ordinary income when the debt was repaid (as opposed to simply reducing their capital gain when they disposed of their stock). The court concluded that a capital contribution was not an "item of income" for purposes of sections 1366 and 1367.

4. *Current law.* Current law now provides that the amount of income excluded by section 108(a) is not an item of income under section 1366(a) and therefore does not affect outside basis. I.R.C. § 108(d)(7)(A). Any losses suspended by section 1366(d)(1) are treated as net operating losses of the S corporation, which must be reduced by the amount of excluded income. I.R.C. § 108(b)(1) and (2)(A) and (d)(7)(B). If the corporation has multiple shareholders, the regulations require that the suspended losses of all shareholders be pooled for purposes of the attribute reduction. Following such reduction, any remaining suspended losses are then allocated pro rata among the shareholders based on their "excess amount." The excess amount is (1) the suspended loss of the shareholder prior to such reduction less (2) the amount of cancellation of indebtedness income that would have been allocated to the shareholder under section 1366(a) had the income not been excluded by section 108(a). Reg. § 1.108-7(d)(2)(ii). If the suspended losses are of different character, the regulations provide ordering rules that preserve proportionately the character of any remaining losses. Reg. § 1.108-7(d)(3) and (e) (ex. 5(iii)).

### 5. *Absence of Inside Basis Adjustments*

In addition to not permitting any adjustment to outside basis when an S corporation incurs a loan, subchapter S also fails to provide any adjustment to inside basis to take into account taxable events occurring outside the corporation, such as the recognition of gain or loss by a shareholder upon sale of the corporation's stock. In *Uri*, we saw how a failure to maintain parity between inside and outside basis worked to the disadvantage of a taxpayer who was not well-advised. As the following tax shelter notice illustrates, these disparities may sometimes provide "planning opportunities" for the well-advised.

## Notice 2002-65

2002-2 C.B. 690

... This transaction involves a series of preplanned steps. First, Taxpayer and one or more other shareholders form a corporation that elects to be treated as an S corporation under § 1362(a) of the Internal Revenue Code. Taxpayer initially has a minority stock interest in the S corporation.

The S corporation enters into straddles on foreign currencies and may acquire other assets. The S corporation terminates the gain leg of a foreign currency straddle, and allocates the gain to the shareholders pro rata according to their stock ownership. The gain increases each shareholder's basis in the stock of the S corporation under § 1367(a)(1). The S corporation redeems the stock of all of the shareholders other than Taxpayer, and the other shareholders claim a loss as a result of the redemption. The S corporation files an election under § 1377(a)(2) to treat the S corporation's taxable year as though it consists of two separate taxable years, with the first year ending on the date of the redemption.

After the redemption, the S corporation terminates the loss leg of the foreign currency straddle. In order to maximize the allowable loss, Taxpayer also may engage in a transaction that is intended to increase Taxpayer's basis in the S corporation. For example, Taxpayer may make a loan to the S corporation.

The entire loss from the loss leg of the straddle passes through to Taxpayer, the sole remaining shareholder in the S corporation, under § 1366. The loss reduces Taxpayer's basis in the stock (and indebtedness, if any) of the S corporation under § 1367(a)(2). Due to the reduction in Taxpayer's basis in the S corporation's stock (and indebtedness, if any), Taxpayer will recognize gain when the corporation makes additional payments to Taxpayer or Taxpayer disposes of Taxpayer's interest in the S corporation. ...

### *NOTES*

1. *The basis for the tax shelter.* The key to the transaction in Notice 2002-65 is the failure to reduce inside basis when the shareholders other than Taxpayer were

redeemed at a loss. This decrease would have eliminated the built-in loss that remained behind in the corporation after the redemption. Thus, the adjustment to inside basis would have eliminated the tax advantage of the plan. But subchapter S does not require any such adjustment. In contrast, under subchapter K, an inside basis reduction in a comparable situation is required if the built-in loss exceeds $250,000. I.R.C. § 734. In the remaining portion of the notice, the IRS describes the various ways in which the claimed outcome of the transaction may be challenged. The notice also adds the transaction and any substantially similar one to the category of "listed transactions," which imposes certain disclosure requirements on taxpayers and results in increased penalties if the taxpayer's position ultimately produces a tax deficiency. Listed transactions are discussed further in chapter four.

2. *Other differences between subchapters S and K.* A more common situation where an outside event is not taken into account inside an S corporation is when a shareholder disposes of her stock or dies while holding the stock. For example, suppose a shareholder dies when the corporation holds several appreciated assets. The transferee — the person inheriting the stock from the decedent — ordinarily obtains a "stepped-up" basis in such stock equal to its fair market value at the date of death. I.R.C. § 1014(a)(1). There is no analogous change, however, to the transferee's share of the inside basis of the corporation in its assets. Therefore, upon a subsequent sale of assets, the corporation may recognize gain that accrued prior to the decedent's death, which is then passed through and taxed to the transferee. By contrast, in the case of a partnership, subchapter K provides a procedure, which is generally elective, to adjust the transferee's share of the inside basis of the partnership's assets if there is a transfer of a partnership interest by sale or exchange or upon the death of a partner. See I.R.C. §§ 743 and 754.

Subchapters K and S treat the transferor as well as the transferee differently on a sale of ownership interests. To some extent, subchapter K fragments the sale to take into account the type of assets held by the partnership at the time of sale. For example, a taxpayer who sells a partnership interest generally has ordinary income consequences from the sale if the partnership holds assets whose sale would generate ordinary income. See I.R.C. § 751(a). In contrast, a sale of S corporation stock is generally treated as the sale of an interest separate and apart from the assets of the corporation. Thus, a taxpayer who sells such stock generally has capital gain or loss if the stock is a capital asset in the taxpayer's hands.

As a result of section 1(h)(5)(B), however, a transferor of S corporation stock must take into account the allocable portion of any unrealized appreciation in collectibles held by the S corporation at the time of sale. (For this purpose, a "collectible" is an item such as a work of art, antique, gem, stamp, or coin held for more than one year.) This rule ensures that gain from the stock sale may be taxed at rates as high as 28 percent, the rate applicable to gain from collectibles, rather than at the lower rate for long-term capital gain. Under the regulations, the taxpayer may have taxable gain from collectibles even though the balance of the transaction results in a loss. See Reg. § 1.1(h)-1(f) (ex. 4). The Treasury has regulatory authority to fragment a sale of S corporation stock even further to take into account the other categories of gain specified in section 1(h). Thus far, that authority has not been exercised. See I.R.C. § 1(h)(9) and (10)(C).

These selected differences between subchapters K and S—there are other important ones—are illustrative of a more general difference between these two areas of law. In general, subchapter K implements the theory of passthrough taxation more precisely than subchapter S, but at the cost of much greater complexity.

### 6. *Distributions by S Corporations Without E&P*

This section describes the shareholder-level tax consequences of distributions by S corporations that have no "earnings and profits" ("E&P"). As we will learn in chapter five, E&P is a concept relevant to C corporations. Thus, this part considers the tax treatment of distributions from corporations without any history as a C corporation, such as one that has always maintained "S" status. The shareholder-level treatment of distributions by S corporations with a C history, as well as the corporate-level consequences of a distribution, are taken up in chapter five.

The passthrough method of taxing S corporations requires that *all* income earned by the corporation, whether distributed to the shareholders or not, must be reported currently by them on their tax returns. A logical implication of this rule is that a subsequent distribution of profits should not be a taxable event to the shareholders. Such a distribution is like withdrawing funds from a bank account—it is a receipt of previously taxed income, and therefore should not be taxed to the recipient. On the other hand, it might be possible to distribute an amount, such as the proceeds of a borrowing against unrealized appreciation of the S corporation's property, that has not yet been taxed to the shareholders. What is needed, therefore, is some account to keep track of the amount previously taxed to shareholders.

Read I.R.C. § 1368(a) and (b). Distributions from S corporations without E&P are excluded from gross income to the extent the distribution does not exceed the distributee's stock basis. Because stock basis reflects the net amount of income passed through to a shareholder, see I.R.C. § 1367(a), it is used as the measure of "previously taxed income." Given the limited role of *debt basis*, should it ever be relevant in determining the tax consequences of a distribution to a shareholder? See I.R.C. §§ 1366(d)(1), 1367(b)(2).

When a distribution is excluded from gross income, the "previously taxed income" account, i.e., stock basis, is appropriately reduced. I.R.C. § 1367(a)(2)(A). Because, however, the passthrough of losses is also dependent upon the amount of stock basis and reduces that account, see I.R.C. §§ 1366(d)(1)(A) and 1367(a)(2)(B), an ordering rule must be provided. Read very carefully I.R.C. §§ 1366(d)(1)(A) and 1368(d)(1), and the last sentence of I.R.C. § 1368(d). These rules give priority to distributions over losses in adjusting basis. The tax treatment of a distribution is tested after the section 1367(a)(1) positive stock basis adjustments for the year (such as a passthrough of income) are taken into account, and stock basis is reduced by the amount of any excluded distribution. Only then is the passthrough of losses considered. Stock basis adjustments are generally made in the following order: (1) section 1367(a)(1) basis increases, (2) basis decreases due to section 1367(a)(2)(A) distributions, (3) basis decreases due to the passthrough of section 1367(a)(2)(D) and (E) items, and (4) basis decreases due to the passthrough of section 1367(a)(2)(B) and (C) loss or deduction items. Taxpayers may elect to reverse the order of the third and fourth categories. Reg. §§ 1.1367-1(f) and (g), 1.1366-2(a)(3)(i).

> **Example 2-2:** Ms. A, the sole shareholder of an S corporation with no E&P, has a $500 basis in her stock at the beginning of Year 1. She owns no debt of the corporation. During Year 1, she is distributed $600, and the corporation has $500 in capital gains and a $900 operating loss. The tax treatment of the distribution is tested after taking into account the positive stock basis increase for the passthrough of the capital gain. Thus, since she has a $1,000 stock basis ($500 initial basis plus $500 increase for passthrough of capital gain), the $600 distribution is excluded from income, which reduces her stock basis to $400. Therefore, only $400 of the loss may be claimed by her and the $500 remaining loss is suspended. After the loss passthrough, her stock basis is reduced to zero.

The rules of section 1368 apply to any distribution otherwise subject to section 301(c), a provision we examine in chapter five. In general, section 301(c) applies to ongoing distributions to continuing shareholders as well as certain distributions in redemption of stock.

## *NOTE*

*Compensation vs. share of S income.* As explained in chapter three, a very common question for a C corporation is whether an amount paid to a shareholder represents compensation (which is generally deductible by the corporation) or a distribution (not deductible). This issue frequently arises on audit and has resulted in many judicial decisions involving whether a payment to a shareholder exceeds a "reasonable allowance for salaries or other compensation." I.R.C. § 162(a)(1).

Since S corporations are generally not subject to tax, the issue of "excessive" compensation normally does not arise. Indeed, for at least two reasons, S corporations have reason to *understate* the amount of their compensation payments to shareholders, and the IRS and courts must once again ferret out whether the characterization comports with reality. Consider first an S corporation owned by a number of family members who are taxed in different tax brackets. In this case, the less "compensation" paid by the corporation to one of its high-bracket shareholders, the more taxable income it will have left to pass through to all of its shareholders, including the low-bracket ones. Thus, by paying less than reasonable compensation to its high-bracket shareholders, the corporation can potentially shift income from such persons to low-bracket owners, resulting in an aggregate reduction in income tax liability. Section 1366(e) of the Code authorizes the government to adjust the amount of compensation paid to shareholders in this situation although, as in the case of compensation paid by C corporations, the inquiry is highly fact-specific.

Even where there is no income-shifting advantage, employment taxes provide another reason for an S corporation to minimize the amount of compensation payments to shareholders. Suppose an S corporation earns $250,000 and pays all of it to its sole shareholder. Regardless of whether the payment is characterized as compensation or a distribution of S income, the shareholder must report $250,000 of income. The characterization, however, affects the employment tax consequences of the payment. Under current law, there are generally no such consequences if the amount represents a share of S income. (Beginning in 2013, there is a scheduled 3.8 percent employment tax on the net investment income of high-income taxpayers (individuals and joint filers with AGI over $200,000 and $250,000, respectively). This tax would apply to a share of S income if it constitutes income from a passive activity (within the meaning of section 469) with respect to the shareholder.) In contrast, if the income is compensation, a portion is subject to both the employer and employee share of the FICA tax, covering old age, survivors and disability insurance as well as hospital insurance (in 2011, both portions equaled 12.4 percent of wages up to $106,800 plus 2.9 percent of all wages), plus state and federal unemployment taxes (which are fairly modest, with the federal taxes largely offset in most states by credits for participating in the state unemployment insurance system). (Beginning in 2013, there is a scheduled additional 0.9 percent tax on all wages over $200,000 ($250,000 for joint filers).) The IRS may pursue a corporation not only for taxes it should have paid on its own account, but also for any taxes it should have withheld and paid over to the government.

In Radtke v. U.S., 712 F. Supp. 143 (E.D. Wis. 1989), aff'd per curiam, 895 F.2d 1196 (7th Cir. 1990), the taxpayer-lawyer spent all of his time working for his wholly-owned S corporation but did not report receiving any salary. Instead, the taxpayer received corporate distributions whenever he needed them. The court recharacterized the distributions as salary subject to employment taxes. More generally, the GAO has estimated that about 13 percent of S corporations understated their compensation amounts by over $23.6 billion in tax years 2003 and 2004. The vast majority of understatements were by S corporations with three or fewer shareholders.

In 2010, the House of Representatives approved legislation that would generally impose employment taxes on the full pro rata share of S corporation income allocated to a shareholder who provides substantial services with respect to certain professional service businesses. Income constituting the taxpayer's share of rental income, dividends, interest, and certain capital gains of the corporation would be exempt. In general, the rule would apply if the S corporation is either (1) engaged in a professional service business whose principal asset is the reputation and skill of three or fewer employees, or (2) a partner in certain partnerships engaged in a professional service business. H.R. 4213 (2010) (as passed by the House on May 28, 2010), § 413.

**Problem 2-4:** Assume that the corporations in these questions have no E&P.

(a) Alma contributes $10,000 for all of the stock of a new S corporation and holds no debt in the corporation. In its first year of operation, the corporation has a net loss of $1,000 but, nonetheless, distributes $3,000 to Alma. During the corporation's second year, it loses $8,000 and makes no distributions. In its third year, it earns and distributes $10,000 to Alma. What are the tax consequences to Alma as a result of her corporate investment during these three years? What is her basis in the corporation's stock at the end of the period?

(b) Same as (a), except that in the corporation's second year, in addition to its $8,000 loss, the corporation pays a $5,000 fine to a local government. The fine is not deductible (see I.R.C. § 162(f)) and it therefore qualifies as a section 1367(a)(2)(D) expense. Answer the same questions as in (a). See Reg. §§ 1.1366-2(a)(3)(i) and 1.1367-1(f) and (g). Should Alma make the Reg. § 1.1367-1(g) election?

(c) Bob owns a successful S corporation in which several of his friends and relatives have invested. During a particular year, the corporation earns a significant profit, which will have to be reported by the shareholders. Bob would like to keep as much of the profit as possible in the corporation to expand the business, but his friends and relatives are unhappy at the prospect of having to pay tax on income that they have not received. What should Bob have the corporation do?

## B. Eligibility and Election

In order to qualify for S status, a corporation must satisfy various conditions and elect to be taxed as an S corporation.

### 1. *Eligibility for S Status*

Read I.R.C. § 1361(a), (b)(1) and (2), and (c)(1). To qualify as a "small business corporation" (within the meaning of section 1361(b)) eligible to elect S status, a corporation must be incorporated in the U.S. and not be taxed under certain special tax regimes, such as those applicable to certain financial institutions and insurance companies. In addition, the corporation must comply with limits on the number and type of shareholders and its financial structure. Taken together, the eligibility rules generally carry out a policy of limiting S status to those corporations that can easily comply with the operative rules of subchapter S. In addition, since subchapter S generally exempts the corporation from paying tax, the eligibility rules try to ensure that some other taxpayer is responsible for paying tax on the corporation's income and that such taxpayer obtains economic benefits and burdens commensurate with the tax items reported.

### a. Limited Number of Shareholders

An S corporation may not have more than 100 shareholders and for this purpose, a husband, wife, certain members of a family, and their estates are all treated as one shareholder. The definition of a "family" for this purpose is very broad and generally includes an ancestor of a shareholder going back up to six generations, any lineal descendant of such ancestor, and any spouse or former spouse of such ancestor or lineal descendant. Thus, as a practical matter, very few nonpublic corporations are excluded from S status by reason of the limit on the number of shareholders. Moreover, in the unusual circumstance where a nonpublic venture finds itself constrained by the limit, the IRS has indicated that the venturers may form multiple S corporations, which join together as partners of a common partnership. According to the IRS, such an arrangement is unobjectionable because it does not undermine the administrative simplicity at the corporate level of any single S corporation. See Rev. Rul. 94-43, 1994-2 C.B. 198. To facilitate compliance and enforcement of the law, it might be easier to eliminate the number-of-shareholder limitation and simply exclude "publicly traded corporations" from those eligible to elect S. Cf. I.R.C. § 7704(b) (defining "publicly traded partnership"). Most S corporations have far fewer than 100 shareholders. According to data predating the current rule permitting certain members of a family to be counted as one shareholder, about 60 percent of S corporations have only one shareholder, 90 percent have one or two shareholders, and over 99 percent have ten or fewer shareholders.

### b. Only Individuals and Certain Entities May Be Shareholders

Read I.R.C. § 1361(b)(1)(B), (c)(2), (3), and (6), (d) and (e). Aside from individuals, the only permissible shareholders of an S corporation are estates (including bankruptcy estates), certain trusts, and certain exempt organizations. In general, an S corporation may not have a shareholder consisting of any other entity, such as a nonqualifying trust, partnership, limited liability company, or another corporation.

The importance for estate planning purposes of allowing a trust to hold stock in an S corporation has presented a special challenge for subchapter S because of the possibility that a trust may accumulate income on behalf of contingent and unknown beneficiaries. If a trust with such beneficiaries is allowed to be a shareholder of an S corporation, to whom and when would the S corporation's income be taxed? Would the person taxed ultimately receive the corresponding economic benefits and burdens? Moreover, how would the corporation's compliance with some of the other eligibility requirements, such as the limitation on number of shareholders, be determined? In general, for these reasons, the only trusts that were allowed to be shareholders of S corporations until 1996 were (1) voting trusts, (2) trusts (such as grantor trusts) whose assets are treated as owned by only one individual who is a U.S. citizen or resident (generally because of the individual's powers over the income or corpus of the trust), (3) certain testamentary trusts (but only for up to two years), and (4) "qualified subchapter S trusts" ("QSSTs"). This last type of trust is quite restrictive; a QSST may have only a single income beneficiary, who is treated as a shareholder of the S corporation, and all of the income of the trust must be currently distributed to that beneficiary. In 1996, Congress added an important category of eligible trust shareholder, an "electing small business trust" ("ESBT"), which may have multiple beneficiaries and also accumulate trust income. The following ruling describes the type of administrative questions that have arisen with respect to QSSTs, and the note after the ruling provides a brief description of ESBTs.

## Rev. Rul. 92-64

1992-2 C.B. 214

. . . If the income beneficiary of a qualified subchapter S trust (QSST) dies and the trust has income for the period between the last distribution date and the date of the income beneficiary's death, to whom may this income be distributed without violating the requirement under section 1361(d)(3)(B) of the Internal Revenue Code that the trust distribute all of its income currently to one individual?

. . . X is a small business corporation that made a valid election for its 1988 taxable year to be an S corporation. In 1989, A transferred shares of X to a trust, T. Under the terms of the trust instrument, B is the current income beneficiary and C is the successor income beneficiary of T. B and C are individuals who are citizens of the United States. The terms of the trust instrument satisfy the QSST requirements of section 1361(d)(3)(A) of the Code. B made a valid election under section 1361(d)(2) to treat T as a trust described in section 1361(c)(2)(A)(i) and thus as an eligible shareholder of X.

The Revised Uniform Principal and Income Act provides that, unless the governing instrument provides otherwise, on termination of an income interest in a trust, the income beneficiary whose interest is terminated, or the income beneficiary's estate, is entitled to income undistributed on the date of termination. . . . T is subject to the laws of a state that has adopted the Uniform Principal and Income Act.

The trust instrument provides that all of T's income (within the meaning of section 643(b) of the Code) is to be distributed on June 30 and December 31 of each year. B died on May 1, 1991. At that time T had undistributed income for the period between the last distribution date, December 31, 1990, and the date of B's death. T also received income after B's death and before the next distribution date, June 30, 1991.

*Situation 1.* The trust instrument makes no provision for the distribution of T's income for the period between the last distribution date and B's death.

*Situation 2.* The trust instrument provides that any income T has for the period between the last distribution date and B's death is to be distributed to the successor income beneficiary, C.

. . . [Under s]ection 1361(d)(1)(B) of the Code . . . , if the beneficiary of a QSST makes an election under section 1361(d)(2) with respect to the QSST, the beneficiary is treated as the owner of that portion of the trust which consists of stock in an S corporation with respect to which the election is made. . . .

A QSST is defined in section 1361(d)(3) of the code. Under section 1361(d)(3)(A), the terms of the trust must contain certain requirements for the trust to be a QSST. . . . In addition, section 1361(d)(3)(B) provides that a trust is a QSST only if all of the income of the trust (within the meaning of section 643(b)) is distributed (or required to be distributed) currently to one individual who is a citizen or resident of the United States.

Section 1366(a)(1) of the Code provides that in determining the taxable income of a shareholder of an S corporation, the shareholder's pro rata share of the corporation's items of income, loss, deduction, or credit is taken into account.

Section 1377(a) of the Code generally provides that each shareholder's pro rata share of any item for any taxable year is the sum of the amounts determined with respect to the shareholder by assigning an equal portion of the item to each day of the taxable year, and then by dividing that portion pro rata among the shares outstanding on that day.

. . . As the beneficiary of T, a QSST, B is treated for income tax purposes as the owner of that portion of T that consists of X stock. Accordingly, B must take into account B's pro rata share of X's items of income, loss, deduction, or credit, regardless of the timing of distributions from X to T or from T to B.

The income held by T at the time of B's death is required to be distributed according to state law and the terms of the trust instrument. Although B is taxed on B's pro rata share of X's income until B's death, T is not required to distribute any income received from X or elsewhere until June 30, 1991.

In *Situation 1*, under applicable state law the income received by T between the last distribution date, December 31, 1990, and the date of the income beneficiary's death, is required to be distributed to B's estate. The income received by T after B's death and before June 30, 1991, is required to be distributed to the successor income beneficiary, C. Hence, on June 30, 1991, T distributes income to two different income beneficiaries. Although section 1361(d)(3)(B) of the Code requires that T's income be distributed currently to one individual, the statute does not specify to whom T's income should be distributed in the year of death of the current income beneficiary. In this instance, B's estate, on behalf of B, receives the income for the period ending with B's death and C receives the income for the period after B's death. Therefore, on any particular day, there is only one income beneficiary of T. Accordingly, neither of the distributions by T on June 30, 1991, adversely affects T's QSST status.

In *Situation 2*, the trust instrument provides that any income for the period between the last distribution date and B's death is to be distributed to the successor income beneficiary, C. Under applicable state law specific provisions of the trust instrument control the rights to trust distributions. Therefore, all the income received by T after December 31, 1990, and by June 30, 1991, is required to be distributed to C on June 30, 1991. Section 1361(d) of the Code does not specify that income received by T that is undistributed upon the death of the current income beneficiary must be distributed to the deceased income beneficiary's estate. Rather, section 1361(d)(3)(B) requires that T's income be distributed currently to one individual, and, under the terms of the T trust instrument, on June 30, 1991, that individual is C. Therefore, the distribution to C does not adversely affect the qualification of T as a QSST. . . .

## *NOTES AND QUESTIONS*

1. *Current distributions to one income beneficiary.* The requirement that QSST income be distributed currently to one individual (who is generally treated as the owner of the trust's S stock) reflects the general goal under subchapter S that tax items be allocated to taxpayers commensurate with the economic benefits and burdens obtained by the taxpayer from the venture. As a result of the QSST requirement, the same person generally reports the S corporation's tax items (allocated to the owner of the stock) and receives the corresponding economic items (through the current distribution). Examine closely, however, both situations described in Rev. Rul. 92-64. Does each satisfy this larger policy objective?

2. *ESBTs.* Review I.R.C. § 1361(c)(2)(A)(v) and (B)(v) and (e) and read I.R.C. § 641(c). An electing small business trust (ESBT) is an eligible S corporation shareholder. Unlike a QSST, an ESBT may have multiple beneficiaries and accumulate income. An S corporation with an ESBT shareholder must count every "potential current beneficiary" of the ESBT as a shareholder of the corporation and if there are no such beneficiaries, the trust is treated as a shareholder. A "potential current beneficiary" is any person who for a particular period is entitled to receive, or may receive at the discretion of any person, a distribution from the income or principal of the trust. Thus, a person need not be an actual current beneficiary to be classified as a "potential current beneficiary" and counted as a shareholder of the S corporation. A corporation is not eligible for S status if it has an ESBT as a shareholder and one of the potential current beneficiaries of the ESBT is not eligible to be a shareholder of an S corporation. See Reg. § 1.1361-1(m)(5)(iii).

The accumulated portion of an ESBT's income attributable to its stock in an S corporation, except for its share of long-term capital gain or qualified dividend income passed through to it by the S corporation, is taxed at a flat rate equal to the highest income tax rate for individuals (currently 35 percent). This tax rate is Congress's way of ensuring that use of an ESBT is for estate planning or other business purposes and not for tax avoidance.

3. *Tax-exempt shareholders.* In 1996, Congress allowed pension trusts and charitable organizations to be shareholders of an S corporation on condition that the tax-exempt entity's share of S income is taxable as unrelated business income. See I.R.C. §§ 1361(b)(1)(B) and (c)(6), 512(e). According to the Senate report,

> . . . the present-law prohibition of certain tax-exempt organizations being S corporation shareholders may inhibit employee ownership of closely-held businesses, frustrate estate planning, discourage charitable giving, and restrict sources of capital for closely-held businesses. The Committee seeks to lift these barriers by allowing certain tax-exempt organizations to be shareholders in S corporations. However, the provisions of subchapter S were enacted in 1958 and substantially modified in 1982 on the premise that all income of the S corporation (including all gains on the sale of the stock) would be subject to a shareholder-level income tax. This underlying premise allows the rules governing S corporations to be relatively simple (in contrast, for example, to the partnership rules of subchapter K) because of the lack of concern about "transferring" income to non-taxpaying persons. Consistent with this underlying premise of subchapter S, the provision treats all the income flowing through to a tax-exempt shareholder, and gains and losses from the disposition of the stock, as unrelated business taxable income. [S. Rep. No. 104-281, 104th Cong., 2d Sess. 197 (1996).]

4. *Traditional and Roth IRAs as shareholders.* In general, traditional and Roth individual retirement accounts (IRAs), which are trusts or custodial accounts treated as trusts that accumulate income tax-free for the retirement benefit of individuals and their beneficiaries, are not eligible to be shareholders of an S corporation. They are neither qualifying trust shareholders nor eligible tax-exempt shareholders. Reg. § 1.1361-1(h)(1)(vii); Taproot Administrative Services, Inc. v. Comm'r, 133 T.C. 202 (2009). There is a limited exception for certain S corporations that are banks. I.R.C. § 1361(c)(2)(A)(vi).

5. *S corporations controlling other corporations and investing in other business entities.* For post-1996 taxable years, Congress eliminated the rule prohibiting an S corporation from owning 80 percent or more of the stock of another corporation. Thus, there are currently no restrictions on the type of entities in which an S corporation may invest. For example, an S corporation may be a partner in a partnership or a member of an LLC, own portfolio shares in other corporations, and have corporate subsidiaries. An S corporation, however, is not allowed to file a consolidated income tax return with its corporate subsidiaries. See I.R.C. § 1504(b)(8).

A special rule allows an S corporation to elect to treat a wholly-owned subsidiary as a "qualified subchapter S subsidiary" (QSub). Read I.R.C. § 1361(b)(3). The separate corporate existence of a QSub is generally disregarded for tax purposes and all of its assets, liabilities, and tax items are treated as belonging to the parent S corporation. One key consequence of this treatment is that an unlimited number of tiers of wholly-owned subsidiaries under the parent S corporation may all qualify as QSubs. See Reg. § 1.1361-2(d) (exs. 1-3). In addition, because QSubs are not recognized as separate from their corporate parent for tax purposes, they are in effect entitled to join the parent's tax return. This is not technically a consolidated income tax return since the assets of the subsidiary are treated as those of the parent. A QSub need not elect S status, but the parent S corporation must elect to treat the subsidiary as a QSub.

The election of a subsidiary as a QSub is generally treated for tax purposes as a liquidation of the wholly-owned subsidiary into its parent. See Reg. § 1.1361-4(a)(2)(i). As we will see in chapter ten, this transaction is almost always a nonrecognition event to both corporations, with the subsidiary's basis in its assets and its other tax attributes preserved in the hands of the parent corporation. Conversely, the termination of a QSub election is treated as a transfer by the parent S corporation of all of the subsidiary's assets and liabilities to a new corporation in exchange for all of the stock of the new corporation. See I.R.C. § 1361(b)(3)(C), Reg. § 1.1361-5(b)(1)(i). Once again, this transaction is usually a tax-free transaction to all parties, with the subsidiary taking a transferred basis in its assets equal to the parent's former basis (see chapter seven). If a QSub election is terminated, the subsidiary is generally not eligible to be a QSub again or an S corporation for five years. See I.R.C. § 1361(b)(3)(D). Relief is provided in the case of certain inadvertent terminations of an election as well as inadvertently invalid elections in the first instance. See I.R.C. § 1362(f).

### c. No More Than One Class of Stock

Finally, an S corporation may not have more than one class of stock. This constraint is the key eligibility condition of subchapter S: it provides some assurance that the pro rata allocation of tax items to the shareholders is consistent with their economic shares. When S income is distributed as a dividend or in liquidation of the corporation, the holders of the single class of shares should generally receive economic benefits consistent with their prior reporting of that income. Subchapter S is able to avoid the most complicated issue in subchapter K—the allocation of a partnership's tax items among its partners—only because there are default tax rules applicable to all corporations (C corporations) not eligible for, or electing, S status. Thus, the law allows corporations to segregate themselves based in part on their financial structures; only those corporations willing to comply with the "one class of stock" rule potentially have the option to be taxed under a straightforward form of passthrough taxation.

#### Paige v. United States

580 F.2d 960 (9th Cir. 1978)

SKOPIL, District Judge:

... Tackmer is a small California company that was first incorporated [and elected to be an S corporation] in 1965. When Tackmer first issued stock, it received two different kinds of consideration. Plaintiffs and another party assigned their rights to an exclusive license agreement in exchange for Tackmer stock ("property shareholders"). Eight other parties paid cash ("cash shareholders").

The Articles of Incorporation state that "No distinction shall exist between the shares of the corporation [or] the holders thereof." The applicable California Corporation Code, § 304 (West 1949), stated that there could be no distinction between shares unless specified in the Articles.

Before Tackmer could issue any stock, it was required to obtain a permit from the California Department of Corporations. The California Corporation Code gave the Department authority to impose conditions on corporations for the protection of the public. Pursuant to this authority the Department had a policy of imposing certain conditions on small corporations such as Tackmer which were capitalized with both cash and property that had an indeterminate value. The purpose of the conditions was to protect the shareholders who paid with cash from having their interests diluted by overissue of stock to the shareholders who paid with property.

The conditions imposed by the Department of Corporations were as follows:

> (a) The stock had to be deposited in escrow and could not be sold without the Department's consent;
>
> (b) If the company defaulted on dividend payments for two years, the cash shareholders would have irrevocable power of attorney to vote the property shareholders' shares for the board of directors;
>
> (c) On dissolution, the property shareholders had to waive their rights to the distribution of assets until the cash shareholders had received the full amount of their purchase price plus any unpaid accumulated dividends at 5% per year;
>
> (d) The property shareholders had to waive their rights to any dividends until the cash shareholders annually received cumulative dividends equal to 5% of the purchase price per share;
>
> (e) The conditions were to remain in effect until the shares were released from escrow. The conditions were in effect from 1965 to 1970.

The property shareholders signed an agreement with the company stating that they would abide by the conditions. The taxpayers admit that the conditions could have been waived by the cash shareholders. Notwithstanding the conditions, the differences between the two kinds of shareholders were never taken into account and all dividends were distributed on a pro rata basis.

... [The taxpayers reported their share of Tackmer's tax items on their individual income tax return and the Commissioner challenged this position.] The reason ... was that the conditions imposed by the California Department of Corporations created more than one class of stock, disqualifying Tackmer for subchapter S treatment. ...

The taxpayers contend that because the Articles and state law authorized only one class of stock, there can be only one class for subchapter S purposes. We hold, however, that the interpretation of subchapter S qualifications is a federal question. ...

[The regulations] provide that "If the outstanding shares of stock of the corporation are not identical with respect to the *rights* and interests which they convey in the control, profits, and assets of the corporation, then the corporation is considered to have more than one class of stock" [emphasis added]. The cash shareholders had preferred rights over property shareholders, notwithstanding that the cash shareholders chose not to exercise those rights. The possibility of the exercise of differing rights is enough to disqualify a corporation, for subchapter S tax treatment.

Taxpayers' assertion that Tackmer in fact made all distributions on a pro rata basis is irrelevant. A corporation's qualifications for subchapter S status is judged at the date of election. . . . The court may not consider Tackmer's actual distributions after its election. The language in the statute is clear. Tax planners must be able to assume that the court will give it its plain meaning. . . .

There is a strong policy behind the requirement that subchapter S corporations have only one class of stock. The corporations themselves pay no corporate income tax. The shareholders pay individual income tax on a pro rata share of all corporate income, regardless of whether any money or property has actually been distributed to the shareholder. If the statute allowed more than one class of stock, complicated allocation problems could arise.

The example given in the government's brief illustrates the potential problems. Assume that during its first taxable year Tackmer had earnings and profits of $5,500 and had declared and paid a preference dividend to the cash shareholders only. Pursuant to Condition (d) of the California Department of Corporations requirements, the minimum dividend would be $2,575. This would leave the corporation with an undistributed taxable income of $2,925. This sum would be taxed pro rata to all the shareholders:

| | |
|---|---|
| To the cash shareholders (who have 5,100 of the 14,300 shares) | $1,043 |
| To the property shareholders (who have 9,200 of the 14,300 shares) | $1,882 |
| | $2,925 |

If Tackmer had no earnings and profits its second year, it would still be obligated to pay $2,575 under Condition (d). It would pay the distribution out of funds generated during its first year. That is, it would pay to the cash shareholders money that had been taxed to, but not received by, both cash and property shareholders. In computing the proper liability of cash shareholders with respect to this distribution, it would be necessary to attribute in an equitable manner to cash shareholders taxes paid by property shareholders. This would introduce substantial complexity in the administration of subchapter S. It was this type of *potential* difficulty which Congress sought to avoid by limiting subchapter S corporations to one class of stock.

We agree with the taxpayers that the purpose of subchapter S is to benefit small corporations such as the one here. It is unfortunate that a requirement of state law has caused a result that no one intended. However, the taxpayers' subjective intent to create one class of stock cannot be allowed to override statutory requirements. . . . Congress has set forth specific objective requirements for subchapter S qualification, and we must follow the mandate of the statute. . . .

*NOTES*

1. *Subchapter K.* There is no comparable "one class of stock" rule in subchapter K. Thus, the partnership tax rules must determine how to allocate the tax items of a partnership among partners who have differing income, distribution, and liquidation rights. In general, the rules make this determination by relying upon the "capital accounts" of the partners, the accounts that set out the economic interests of the partners in the venture vis-à-vis one another. The tax law generally validates an allocation for tax purposes only if it is consistent with the allocation made in the capital accounts. To achieve conformity across partnerships, the law specifies how capital accounts must be maintained. The law further imposes requirements to make sure the capital account balances are respected by the partners in dividing up their economic shares in the enterprise. These and many other complications are avoided in subchapter S because of the one class of stock rule.

2. *What rights must be the same and what may be different?* To satisfy the one class of stock requirement, all of the outstanding shares of a corporation must confer identical rights to distribution and liquidation proceeds. The determination is made based upon the corporation's governing documents, state law, and binding agreements relating to distribution and liquidation proceeds, which are collectively referred to in the regulations as the "governing provisions." See Reg. § 1.1361-1(*l*)(1) and (2)(i). Section 1361(c)(4) explicitly allows an S corporation to have more than one class of common stock if the sole difference between the classes is in their voting rights.

3. *Debt as possible second class of stock.* An oft-litigated issue in the past has been whether debt of an S corporation contains enough equity features to be treated as a prohibited second class of stock. Section 1361(c)(5) provides a safe harbor to prevent "straight debt"—generally, debt that does not provide the holder with the possibility of a residual equity-like return, is not convertible into stock, and is issued to a holder who is generally a permissible S corporation shareholder or who is in the business of lending money—from being reclassified as a prohibited second class of stock of an S corporation. More generally, the regulations provide that an instrument will not be treated as a second class of stock unless (1) it is treated as equity under general principles of tax law, and (2) a principal purpose for its issuance is to circumvent the one class of stock rule or the limitations on the number and type of permissible S corporation shareholders. Reg. § 1.1361-1(*l*)(4)(i) and (ii)(A).

4. *Restricted stock and stock rights.* In determining whether the one class of stock limitation has been satisfied, all outstanding stock of an S corporation is considered. For this purpose, stock that is not transferable and is subject to a substantial risk of forfeiture is not considered "outstanding stock" unless the holder has made a section

83(b) election with respect to such stock (in effect treating receipt of the stock as a taxable event). See Reg. § 1.1361-1(b)(3). Conversely, a right to acquire stock, such as a call option or warrant, is generally taken into account and treated as a prohibited second class of stock if the option is substantially certain to be exercised and has a strike price substantially below the fair market value of the stock at the time the option is issued or certain other times. If the option's strike price is equal to at least 90 percent of the fair market value at those times, the option will not be treated as a second class of stock. See Reg. § 1.1361-1(*l*)(4)(iii)(A) and (C). The existence of restricted stock and stock rights creates the possibility that the shareholders' economic shares may not ultimately match the allocation of tax items.

5. *Nonresident aliens.* An S corporation may not have a shareholder who is a nonresident alien. See I.R.C. § 1361(b)(1)(C). A principal reason for this rule is to avoid potential complexity in complying with the "one class of stock" rule. In general, nonresident aliens who are not effectively connected with a U.S. trade or business are taxed by the U.S. only on certain types of U.S.-source income, such as dividends paid by U.S. corporations. Typically, this U.S. tax liability is enforced through a withholding tax imposed on the U.S. payor of the income.

Suppose the income of an S corporation were allocable to both U.S. shareholders and a nonresident alien. If the withholding tax with respect to the nonresident alien shareholder were imposed on the corporation only upon the actual distribution of funds to such shareholder, the U.S. tax due on this share of income would be inappropriately deferred. In that case, the U.S. shareholders would pay tax on their share of S corporation income as the income is earned, without regard to a distribution, whereas the nonresident alien shareholder would pay tax only upon a distribution. On the other hand, if the withholding tax were imposed at the time of the allocation to the nonresident alien shareholder, even without any distribution, then the S corporation would have an accounting burden to make sure the amount of its future distributions is correct. The corporation would need to make sure that any future distribution to the nonresident alien shareholder takes into account the amount of income previously allocated to such shareholder net of the corporation's prior withholding of tax. It should be noted, however, that a similar problem arises if U.S. shareholders of S corporations are subject to different state laws that require corporate withholding of state income taxes on behalf of such shareholders. The regulations provide that such differences do not violate the one class of stock rule so long as after taking into account the actual and constructive payments to the shareholders resulting from these state law tax obligations, the shares confer identical rights to distribution and liquidation proceeds. Differences in timing, where a corporation pays state tax on behalf of one shareholder prior to an actual distribution to some other shareholder, are disregarded. See Reg. § 1.1361-1(*l*)(2)(ii) and (v) (ex. 7).

An S corporation that desires to raise capital from a nonresident alien can circumvent the eligibility restriction by forming a partnership with the alien. As previously noted, the IRS has permitted S corporations to join partnerships in order to avoid violating an eligibility restriction, and the partnership tax regulations explicitly bless the use of a partnership for this purpose. Reg. § 1.701-2(d) (ex. 2).

6. *Affirmative use of doctrine by taxpayer*. Minton v. Comm'r, 562 F.3d 730 (5th Cir. 2009), involved an unusual case in which the taxpayer rather than the Commissioner argued that an S corporation had more than one class of stock. The taxpayer had become estranged from the other shareholders and, in the year at issue, had been passed through an abnormally large amount of corporate income without any accompanying distribution. If the corporation lost its S status, the taxpayer's tax liability for the year would thus have been reduced. The court held that the taxpayer failed to establish that a side agreement entitling certain shareholders to receive payments from the corporation constituted an impermissible second class of stock.

**Problem 2-5:** George and Hal, two brothers living in Virginia, own equal shares of an S corporation. Would any of the following provisions in their ownership agreement violate the eligibility requirements for S corporations? See Reg. § 1.1361-1(*l*)(1) and (2).

(a) If the brothers decide to split up for any reason, George would have an option to purchase Hal's stock for 75 percent of its share of the corporation's book value at the time of the split-up, and if he does not exercise the option, Hal would have a similar option to purchase George's stock.
(b) Upon the death of either of them, the corporation will redeem the decedent's interest from his estate for 60 percent of the interest's share of the corporation's book value at the time of death.
(c) If either of them should move out of Virginia, the rights of the brothers to share in corporate income would be adjusted to ensure that each receives the same dollar amount of corporate income per share after taking into account all state and local income taxes.

## 2. *Election and Termination of S Status*

Even if qualified, a corporation must make an affirmative election to be taxed under subchapter S. Read I.R.C. §§ 1361(a)(1), 1362(a)-(c). Once made, an election may be terminated either intentionally or inadvertently. If an election has been terminated, a corporation generally cannot make a new election for five years. Read I.R.C. § 1362(d)(1) and (2), (e)-(g). Why might a taxpayer intentionally terminate an S election? What might cause an inadvertent termination? Can taxpayers be rescued if there is such a termination?

**Problem 2-6:**

(a) Who files the S election? When? For what years is an election effective? Suppose that an election is filed for an eligible corporation using the calendar year on February 15 of Year 1, and the filing includes the consent of all shareholders (all of whom are eligible as of that date). However, an ineligible or nonconsenting shareholder held some shares on February 1 of Year 1 (prior to the election). Is the election effective? For what years? Is there any way for the election to be effective for all of Year 1?

(b) If a valid election for a calendar year corporation is made on March 1, and an eligible shareholder who objects to the election acquires stock on April 14, will the objection have any effect on the election? Is there anything the new shareholder can do to terminate the election? Is there any way in which the election can be terminated retroactively?

## *NOTES AND QUESTIONS*

1. *Section 1362(f) relief.* The many eligibility conditions contained in subchapter S can easily lead to an inadvertent loss of S status. For example, the shares of a deceased shareholder might be transferred to a nonqualifying trust that holds the shares longer than the permissible two-year period. I.R.C. § 1361(c)(2)(A)(iii). Section 1362(f) provides the IRS with discretion to disregard an invalid election or inadvertent termination. The following excerpt explains the circumstances in which an inadvertent termination may be disregarded:

> If the Internal Revenue Service determines that a corporation's subchapter S election is inadvertently terminated, the Service can waive the effect of the terminating event for any period if the corporation timely corrects the event and if the corporation and the shareholders agree to be treated as if the election had been in effect for such period.
>
> The Committee intends that the Internal Revenue Service be reasonable in granting waivers, so that corporations whose subchapter S eligibility requirements have been inadvertently violated do not suffer the tax consequences of a termination if no tax avoidance would result from the continued subchapter S treatment. In granting a waiver, it is hoped that taxpayers and the government will work out agreements that protect the revenues without undue hardship to taxpayers. . . . It is expected that the waiver may be made retroactive for all years, or retroactive for the period in which the corporation again became eligible for subchapter S treatment, depending on the facts. . . . [S. Rep. No. 97-640, 97th Cong., 2d Sess. 12-13 (1982).]

2. *Why elective?* There are clear costs to allowing corporations to be taxed in two different ways, with one of the ways being available only to eligible taxpayers who make an appropriate election. Taxpayers have to be aware of and understand the significance of their choice; take whatever steps are necessary, including ensuring eligibility and filing a timely election, to exercise their choice effectively; and then monitor subsequent events to make sure the choice is not unintentionally forfeited. Could some of the cost of maintaining two tax systems be reduced by eliminating the

elective feature of subchapter S? For example, would it be preferable from a policy standpoint to make subchapter S mandatory for any corporation satisfying its eligibility requirements? Or, if an election should be retained, would it be preferable to switch the default so that an eligible corporation must elect *out of* S status?

3. *What happens to suspended losses?* Suppose a corporation has its S status terminated at a time when losses are still suspended for a particular shareholder. May the shareholder ever deduct those losses? Under what circumstances? See I.R.C. §§ 1366(d)(3), 1377(b).

> **Problem 2-7:** Z corporation, a calendar year S corporation, is owned equally by individuals A, B, and C. On May 1 of Year *y*, B sells her one-third interest in Z to partnership P. During Year *y*, Z has $360,000 income, $100,000 arising prior to May 1 (based on Z's method of accounting) and the balance earned on and after that date. Describe two permissible methods of reporting the Year *y* income of corporation Z. Would your answer change if on May 1, *both* B and C sell their respective one-third interests to partnership P?

## C. Some Data on S Corporations and Other Business Entities

**Figure 2-1** shows the changing number of C and S corporations and partnerships (including LLCs) between 1980 and 2008. Tax law developments help to explain both the growing number of passthrough entities and the generally declining number of C corporations during this period. For example, enactment in 1986 of an inverted rate structure in which the top individual income tax rate was lower than the top corporate tax rate fueled an increase in the number of S corporations and a decrease in the number of C corporations. In addition, legislative changes in 1986 curtailing tax shelters reduced the attractiveness of partnerships, but liberalized classification rules adopted in the mid-1990s (and discussed in chapter three) permitting LLCs to be treated as partnerships for tax purposes led to sharp growth in the use of that type of entity. Interestingly, although the LLC may have replaced to some extent the C corporation, the popularity of S corporations continues unabated. As previously discussed, the tax rules for S corporations are less precise and flexible, but simpler and generally more familiar, than those for entities taxed as partnerships. Particularly for firms with one or very few owners, the choice of an S corporation can often satisfy most tax and nontax objectives. Thus, S corporations have thrived despite the availability of an organizational form (LLC) providing both state law limited liability protection to owners and passthrough taxation under subchapter K.

**Figure 2-2** disaggregates the number of entities taxed as partnerships into its three main categories—LLCs and general and limited partnerships—and compares them to the number of S corporations between 1986 and 2008. As can be seen,

**Figure 2-1. Number of C Corporations, S Corporations, and Partnerships (including LLCs), 1980-2008**

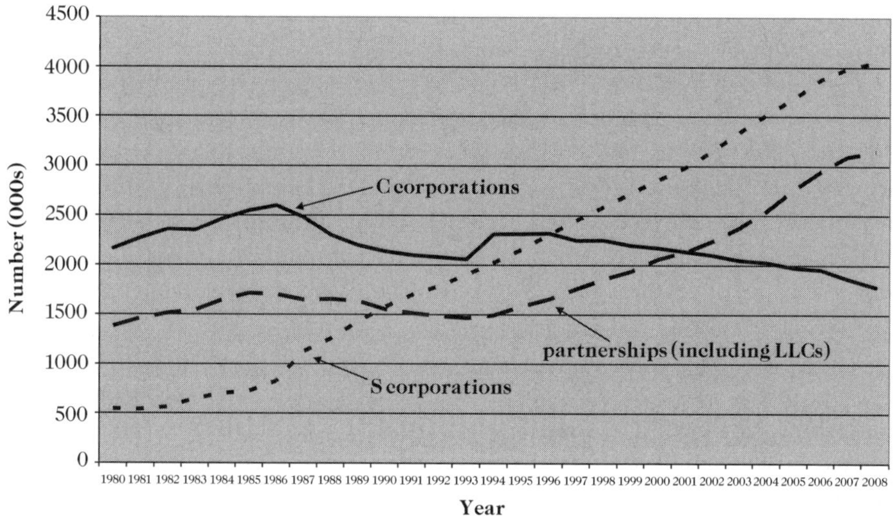


Source: IRS, Statistics of Income, http://www.irs.gov/taxstats/index.html

**Figure 2-2. Number of S Corporations, LLCs, General Partnerships, and Limited Partnerships, 1986-2008**

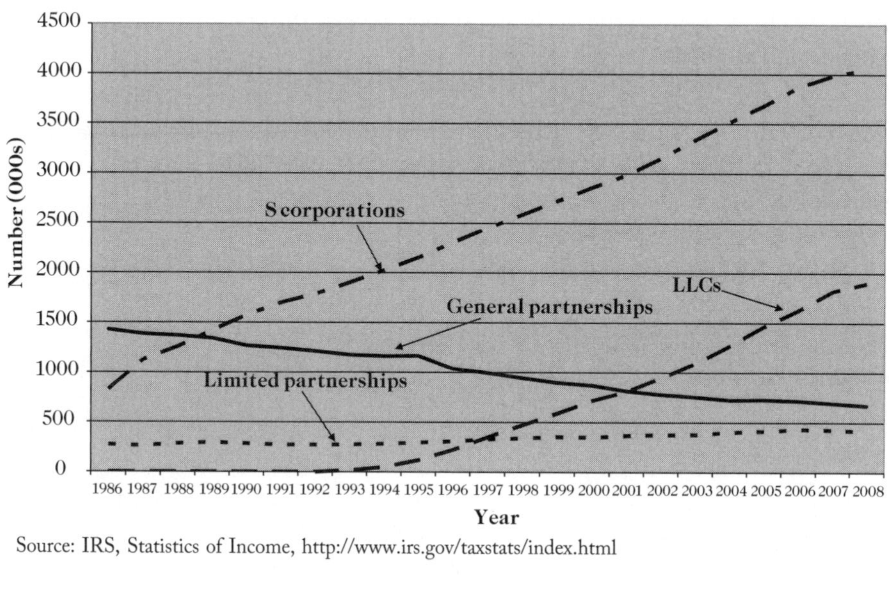


Source: IRS, Statistics of Income, http://www.irs.gov/taxstats/index.html

there has been steady growth in the number of both S corporations and LLCs and more gradual growth in the number of limited partnerships. In 2008, there were over four million S corporations, 1.9 million LLCs (or 60 percent of all firms taxed as partnerships), and about 1.8 million C corporations. Almost 70 percent of corporations were S corporations. The principal category of business entity not represented in either **Figure 2-1** or **2-2** is the nonfarm sole proprietorship; by number, such proprietorships far exceeded all of the other categories, increasing from 8.9 million in 1980 to 22.6 million in 2008.

**Figure 2-3** shows the average income (net of deficits) reported by S corporations, partnerships (including LLCs), and nonfarm sole proprietorships between 1980 and 2008. The use of partnerships as tax shelters prior to 1986 is reflected in the very small amount of net income, or net losses, reported by those entities throughout the 1980s. Since then, however, both partnerships and S corporations have reported positive and generally increasing amounts of average income. The average income of all three business forms declined in 2008 with the onset of the most recent recession.

**Figure 2-4** illustrates the changing share of total business income (that reported by C and S corporations, partnerships (including LLCs), and nonfarm sole proprietorships) attributable to passthrough entities. The share of business income reported by S corporations was less than one percent in 1980 but increased to 22 percent by 2008. If income from partnerships (including LLCs) is included, the share of business income attributable to passthrough entities grew to 54 percent in 2008 (compared to less than four percent in 1980). Finally, if income from nonfarm sole proprietorships is also included, the share of such business income grew to 73 percent in 2008 (compared to just over 20 percent in 1980 and 1981). Thus, an increasing portion of business income is taxed under the income tax for *individuals*. This fact helps to explain the declining importance of the corporate income tax as a revenue source in this country.

**Figure 2-3. Average Income (Net Deficit) of S Corporations, Partnerships (including LLCs), and Nonfarm Sole Proprietorships, 1980-2008**

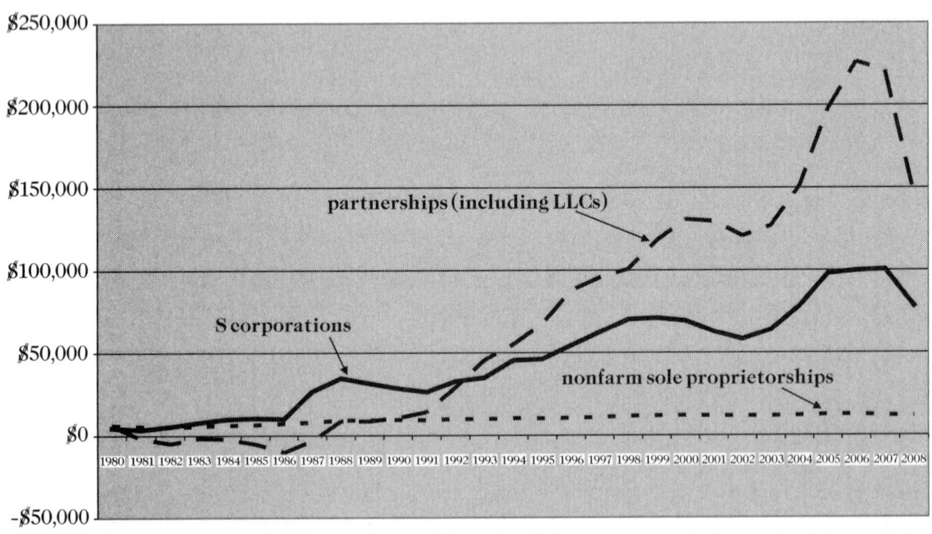


Source: IRS, Statistics of Income, http://www.irs.gov/taxstats/index.html

**Figure 2-4. Portion of Total Business Income Reported by S Corporations, Partnerships, and Nonfarm Sole Proprietorships, 1980-2008**

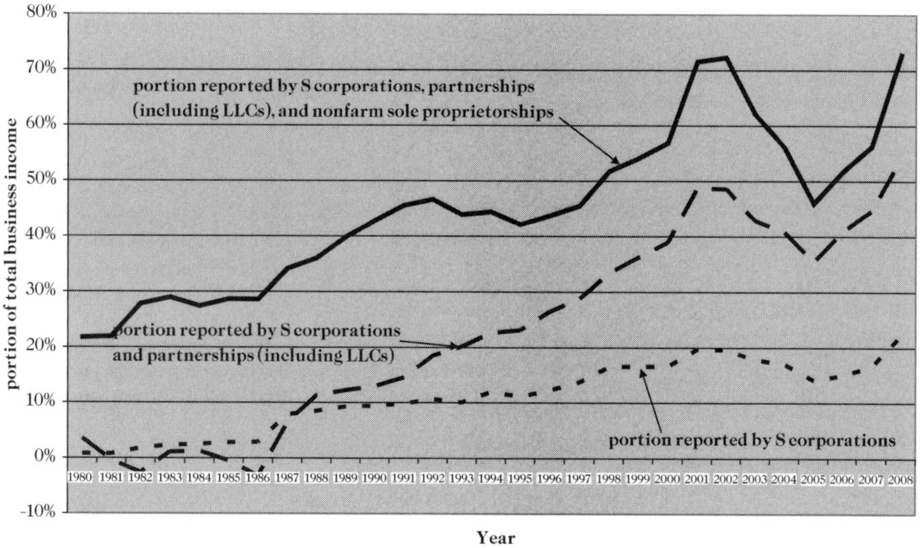


Source: IRS, Statistics of Income, http://www.irs.gov/taxstats/index.html

**Figure 2-5. Portion of All Corporations and Corporate Assets Represented by S Corporations, by Corporate Asset Class, 2005**

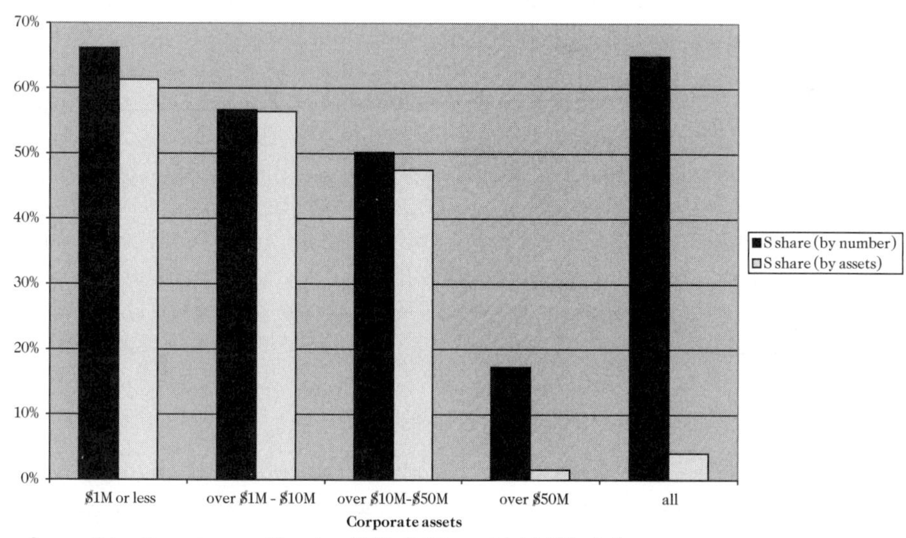


Source: Joint Committee on Taxation, JCX-48-08, pp. 14-15 (tbls. 3,4)

**Figures 2-5** and **2-6** compare S and C corporations and show the portion of corporations, corporate assets, and corporate receipts attributable to S corporations in 2005, as classified by corporate asset classes (**fig. 2-5**) and amount of corporate

**Figure 2-6. Portion of All Corporations and Corporate Receipts Represented by S Corporations, by Corporate Receipts Class, 2005**

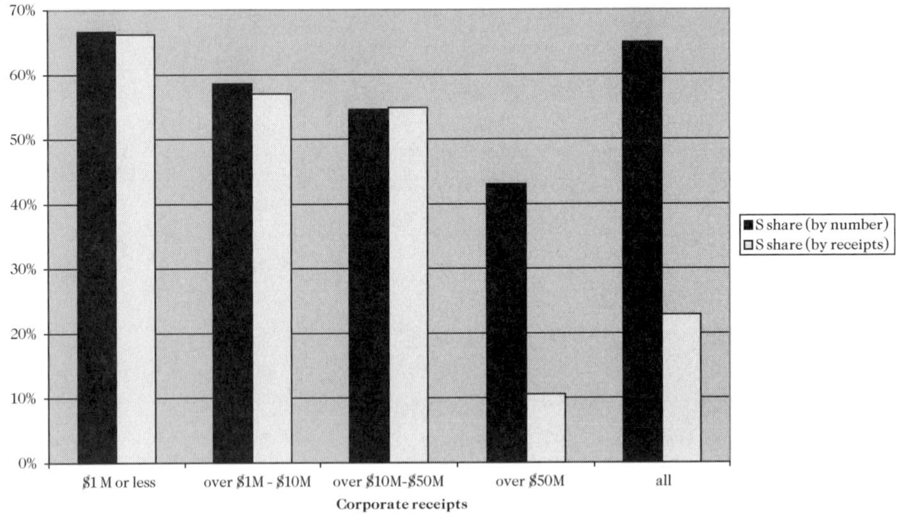


Source: Joint Committee on Taxation, JCX-48-08, pp. 14-15 (tbls. 3,4)

receipts (**fig. 2-6**). The figures reveal that S and C corporations were comparable in average size, in terms of both assets and receipts, in all of the lower asset and receipt classes. That similarity changes, however, for corporations with assets or receipts of over $50 million because of the inclusion of large, public corporations (which are all C corporations). For example, in 2005, S corporations represented over 40 percent of all corporations with receipts of over $50 million but had only about 10 percent of the receipts of those corporations (**fig. 2-6**). The impact of public corporations also explains why, in 2005, S corporations comprised over 60 percent of all corporations but held only about four percent of all corporate assets (**fig. 2-5**).

Finally, **figure 2-7** segregates S corporations in 2008 by the number of shareholders of the corporation. The figure shows that the average size of an S corporation, based on both assets and income, increased with the number of shareholders. As previously indicated, however, the vast majority of S corporations have very few shareholders.

---

Future legislation may alter some of the trends shown in the foregoing figures. For example, if (as seems likely) individual income tax rates are increased and corporate income tax rates reduced, there may be a revival of interest in using C corporations rather than S corporations, LLCs, and partnerships. The C corporation also remains, and will almost certainly continue to be, the mandatory entity form for virtually all public ventures. Thus, the balance of this course deals mainly with the rules of subchapter C.

**Figure 2-7. Percentage of S Corporations, Assets, and Income (Net Deficit), by Number of Shareholders of the S Corporation, 2008**

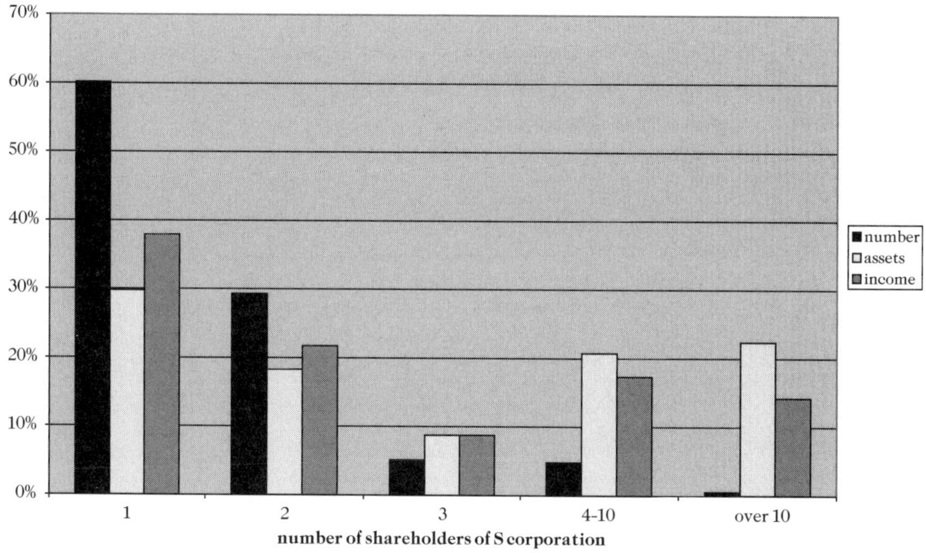


Source: IRS, Statistics of Income, http://www.irs.gov/taxstats/index.html

For at least two reasons, however, we are not yet through thinking about subchapter S issues and S corporations. First, there are some important, special provisions applicable to S corporations that were formerly C corporations or have succeeded to the tax attributes of C corporations. We will cover these special provisions once we have learned the relevant concepts in subchapter C. Second, and more importantly, the transactional rules of subchapter C, governing matters such as corporate formations, redemptions, mergers, acquisitions, divisions, and liquidations, are generally applicable to both S and C corporations. Hence, you should keep S corporations and their special form of passthrough taxation in mind as we proceed to encounter the wonderful world of subchapter C.

## Chapter 3

# Taxation of C Corporations

As explained in chapter two, a certain class of corporations, termed S corporations, are treated as passthrough entities for tax purposes. These corporations are generally not subject to a separate entity-level tax. Rather, the taxable income and other tax items of such corporations are passed through to their shareholders and taxable to them.

In contrast, corporations not qualifying or electing to be treated as S corporations, sometimes termed C corporations, *are* generally subject to a separate corporate-level income tax. In addition, any profits (net of the corporate tax) are taxed again to the shareholders when received as a distribution or through a sale of corporate stock. Hence, C corporation profits may be taxed twice.

Part A of this chapter explores the classification question of which entities are subject to the corporate-level income tax. Most incorporated entities are taxable as corporations but some *un*incorporated ones are as well. An entity treated as a corporation for tax purposes is generally taxed as a C corporation unless it is eligible for and has elected S status.

Part B reviews how the profits of a C corporation are taxed. As we shall see, the number of times income of a C corporation is taxed is less important than the timing of the tax, the measurement of the tax base, and the applicable tax rate. Hence, the actual impact of the double taxation regime depends on a variety of circumstances. In some cases, the profits of a C corporation may end up being taxed more favorably than those of an S corporation.

Finally, part C considers several possible reforms to the taxation of C corporations. One important reform, termed "corporate integration," would end the "classical system" of taxing C corporation profits twice. Other reforms would retain the classical system but revise the manner in which the corporate income tax is determined. As you review the material in this part, consider whether any of the reforms are sensible and how they might be implemented.

## A. Classification Issues

What business entities are subject to the two-tier tax? We have already reviewed the conditions for qualifying as an S corporation. Are the profits of all other corporations, by default, taxed twice? Might any *un*incorporated entities be taxed in the same manner?

### 1. *Incorporated Entities*

Most domestic *incorporated* entities are taxable as either C or S corporations. There are a few statutory exceptions involving corporations with specialized functions. See, e.g., I.R.C. §§ 851 et seq., specifying a form of passthrough taxation for "regulated investment companies," more commonly known as mutual funds. As the following case illustrates, common law principles may also be relevant.

#### Commissioner v. Jesse C. Bollinger

485 U.S. 340 (1988)

Justice SCALIA delivered the opinion of the Court.

. . . Respondent Jesse C. Bollinger, Jr., developed, either individually or in partnership with some or all of the other respondents, eight apartment complexes in Lexington, Kentucky. (For convenience we will refer to all the ventures as "partnerships.") Bollinger initiated development of the first apartment complex, Creekside North Apartments, in 1968. The Massachusetts Mutual Life Insurance Company agreed to provide permanent financing by lending $1,075,000 to "the corporate nominee of Jesse C. Bollinger, Jr." at an annual interest rate of eight percent, secured by a mortgage on the property and a personal guaranty from Bollinger. The loan commitment was structured in this fashion because Kentucky's usury law at the time limited the annual interest rate for noncorporate borrowers to seven percent. Lenders willing to provide money only at higher rates required the nominal debtor and record title holder of mortgaged property to be a corporate nominee of the true owner and borrower. On October 14, 1968, Bollinger incorporated Creekside, Inc., under the laws of Kentucky; he was the only stockholder. The next day, Bollinger and Creekside, Inc., entered into a written agreement which provided that the corporation would hold title to the apartment complex as Bollinger's agent for the sole purpose of securing financing, and would convey, assign, or encumber the property and disburse the proceeds thereof only as directed by Bollinger; that Creekside, Inc., had no obligation to maintain the property or assume any liability by reason of the execution of promissory notes or otherwise; and that Bollinger would indemnify and hold the corporation harmless from any liability it might sustain as his agent and nominee.

Having secured the commitment for permanent financing, Bollinger, acting through Creekside, Inc., borrowed the construction funds for the apartment complex from Citizens Fidelity Bank and Trust Company. Creekside, Inc., executed all necessary loan documents including the promissory note and mortgage, and transferred all loan proceeds to Bollinger's individual construction account. Bollinger acted as general contractor for the construction, hired the necessary employees, and paid the expenses out of the construction account. When construction was completed, Bollinger obtained, again through Creekside, Inc., permanent financing from Massachusetts Mutual Life in accordance with the earlier loan commitment. These loan proceeds were used to pay off the Citizens Fidelity construction loan. Bollinger hired a resident manager to rent the apartments, execute leases with tenants, collect and deposit the rents, and maintain operating records. The manager deposited all rental receipts into, and paid all operating expenses from, an operating account, which was first opened in the name of Creekside, Inc., but was later changed to "Creekside Apartments, a partnership." The operation of Creekside North Apartments generated losses for the taxable years 1969, 1971, 1972, 1973, and 1974, and ordinary income for the years 1970, 1975, 1976, and 1977. Throughout, the income and losses were reported by Bollinger on his individual income tax returns.

Following a substantially identical pattern, seven other apartment complexes were developed by respondents through seven separate partnerships. For each venture, a partnership executed a nominee agreement with Creekside, Inc., to obtain financing. . . . The corporation had no assets, liabilities, employees, or bank accounts. In every case, the lenders regarded the partnership as the owner of the apartments and were aware that the corporation was acting as agent of the partnership in holding record title. The partnerships reported the income and losses generated by the apartment complexes on their partnership tax returns, and respondents reported their distributive share of the partnership income and losses on their individual tax returns.

The Commissioner of Internal Revenue disallowed the losses reported by respondents, on the ground that the standards set out in National Carbide Corp. v. Comm'r, 336 U.S. 422 (1949), were not met. The Commissioner contended that *National Carbide* required a corporation to have an arm's-length relationship with its shareholders before it could be recognized as their agent. . . . Since, in the Commissioner's view, the corporation rather than its shareholders owned the real estate, any losses sustained by the ventures were attributable to the corporation and not respondents. . . . The Tax Court held that the corporations were the agents of the partnerships and should be disregarded for tax purposes. On appeal, the United States Court of Appeals for the Sixth Circuit affirmed. . . .

For federal income tax purposes, gain or loss from the sale or use of property is attributable to the owner of the property. . . . The problem we face here is that two different taxpayers can plausibly be regarded as the owner. Neither the Internal Revenue Code nor the regulations promulgated by the Secretary of the Treasury provide significant guidance as to which should be selected. It is common ground between the parties, however, that if a corporation holds title to property as agent for a partnership, then for tax purposes the partnership and not the corporation is the owner. Given agreement on that premise, one would suppose that there would be agreement upon the conclusion as well. For each of respondents' apartment complexes, an agency agreement expressly provided that the corporation would "hold such property as nominee and agent for" the partnership, and that the partnership would have sole control of and responsibility for the apartment complex. The partnership in each instance was identified as the principal and owner of the property during financing, construction, and operation. The lenders, contractors, managers, employees, and tenants — all who had contact with the development — knew that the corporation was merely the agent of the partnership, if they knew of the existence of the corporation at all. In each instance the relationship between the corporation and the partnership was, in both form and substance, an agency with the partnership as principal.

The Commissioner contends, however, that the normal indicia of agency cannot suffice for tax purposes when, as here, the alleged principals are the controlling shareholders of the alleged agent corporation. That, it asserts, would undermine the principle of Moline Properties v. Comm'r, 319 U.S. 436 (1943), which held that a corporation is a separate taxable entity even if it has only one shareholder who exercises total control over its affairs. Obviously, *Moline*'s separate-entity principle would be significantly compromised if shareholders of closely held corporations could, by clothing the corporation with some attributes of agency with respect to particular assets, leave themselves free at the end of the tax year to make a claim — perhaps even a good-faith claim — of either agent or owner status, depending upon which choice turns out to minimize their tax liability. The Commissioner does not have the resources to audit and litigate the many cases in which agency status could be thought debatable. Hence, the Commissioner argues, in this shareholder context he can reasonably demand that the taxpayer meet a prophylactically clear test of agency.

We agree with that principle, but the question remains whether the test the Commissioner proposes is appropriate. The parties have debated at length the significance of our opinion in *National Carbide Corp. v. Comm'r, supra.* In that case, three corporations that were wholly owned subsidiaries of another corporation agreed to operate their production plants as "agents" for the parent, transferring to it all profits except for a nominal sum. The subsidiaries reported as gross income only this sum, but the Commissioner concluded that they should be taxed on the entirety of the profits because they were not really agents. We agreed, reasoning first, that the mere fact of the parent's control over the subsidiaries did not establish the existence of an agency, since such control is typical of all shareholder-corporation relationships, and second, that the agreements to pay the parent all profits above a nominal amount were not determinative since income must be taxed to those who actually earn it without regard to anticipatory assignment. We acknowledged, however, that there was such a thing as "a true corporate agent . . . of [an] owner-principal," and proceeded to set forth four indicia and two requirements of such status, the sum of which has become known in the lore of federal income tax law as the "six *National Carbide* factors":

> "[1] Whether the corporation operates in the name and for the account of the principal, [2] binds the principal by its actions, [3] transmits money received to the principal, and [4] whether receipt of income is attributable to the services of employees of the principal and to assets belonging to the principal are some of the relevant considerations in determining whether a true agency exists. [5] If the corporation is a true agent, its relations with its principal must not be dependent upon the fact that it is owned by the principal, if such is the case. [6] Its business purpose must be the carrying on of the normal duties of an agent."

We readily discerned that these factors led to a conclusion of nonagency in *National Carbide* itself. There each subsidiary had represented to its customers that it (not the parent) was the company manufacturing and selling its products; each had sought to shield the parent from service of legal process; and the operations had used thousands of the subsidiaries' employees and nearly $20 million worth of property and equipment listed as assets on the subsidiaries' books.

The Commissioner contends that the last two *National Carbide* factors are not satisfied in the present case. To take the last first: The Commissioner argues that here the corporation's business purpose with respect to the property at issue was not "the carrying on of the normal duties of an agent," since it was acting not as the agent but rather as the owner of the property for purposes of Kentucky's usury laws. We do not agree. It assuredly was not acting as the owner in fact, since respondents represented themselves as the principals to all parties concerned with the loans. Indeed, it was the lenders themselves who required the use of a corporate nominee. Nor does it make any sense to adopt a contrary-to-fact legal presumption that the corporation was the principal, imposing a federal tax sanction for the apparent evasion of Kentucky's usury law. . . .

Of more general importance is the Commissioner's contention that the arrangements here violate the fifth *National Carbide* factor — that the corporate agent's "relations with its principal must not be dependent upon the fact that it is owned by the principal." The Commissioner asserts that this cannot be satisfied unless the corporate agent and its shareholder principal have an "arm's-length relationship" that includes the payment of a fee for agency services. The meaning of *National Carbide*'s fifth factor is, at the risk of understatement, not entirely clear. Ultimately, the relations between a corporate agent and its owner-principal are *always* dependent upon the fact of ownership, in that the owner can cause the relations to be altered or terminated at any time. Plainly that is not what was meant, since on that interpretation all subsidiary-parent agencies would be invalid for tax purposes, a position which the *National Carbide* opinion specifically disavowed. We think the fifth *National Carbide* factor — so much more abstract than the others — was no more and no less than a generalized statement of the concern, expressed earlier in our own discussion, that the separate-entity doctrine of *Moline* not be subverted.

In any case, we decline to parse the text of *National Carbide* as though that were itself the governing statute. As noted earlier, it is uncontested that the law attributes tax consequences of property held by a genuine agent to the principal; and we agree that it is reasonable for the Commissioner to demand unequivocal evidence of genuineness in the corporation-shareholder context, in order to prevent evasion of *Moline*. We see no basis, however, for holding that unequivocal evidence can only consist of the rigid requirements (arm's-length dealing plus agency fee) that the Commissioner suggests. Neither of those is demanded by the law of agency, which permits agents to be unpaid family members, friends, or associates. It seems to us that the genuineness of the agency relationship is adequately assured, and tax-avoiding manipulation adequately avoided, when the fact that the corporation is acting as agent for its shareholders with respect to a particular asset is set forth in a written agreement at the time the asset is acquired, the corporation functions as agent and not principal with respect to the asset for all purposes, and the corporation is held out as the agent and not principal in all dealings with third parties relating to the asset. Since these requirements were met here, the judgment of the Court of Appeals is affirmed.

Justice KENNEDY took no part in the consideration or decision of this case.

### *NOTES AND QUESTIONS*

1. *Is* Bollinger *a wise decision?* What would have happened in a case like *Bollinger* if the corporation had been profitable and it had been advantageous from a tax standpoint for the corporation (and not the taxpayer) to report the income?
2. *Was subchapter S an option in this case?* If so, would it have made any difference?
3. *Form matters.* The conclusion in *Bollinger* is quite unusual. As the Supreme Court articulated in *Moline Properties*, discussed with approval in *Bollinger*, the general rule is that in the absence of a statutory exception, incorporated entities are respected as separate from their owners for tax purposes. Thus, their income is subject to the corporate tax. Except in the very limited circumstances described at the end of the opinion, it is rare for a corporation to be treated as a mere agent of its owners or disregarded for tax purposes under some other theory.

## *2. Unincorporated Entities*

An *un*incorporated firm classified as an "association" for tax purposes is also taxed like a corporation. See I.R.C. § 7701(a)(3). Until 1997, the regulations under section 7701 defined "association" based on a mechanical corporate resemblance test, described by the Tax Court in Larson v. Comm'r, 66 T.C. 159, 172 (1976), as follows:

> The starting point of the regulations' definition of an "association" is the principle applied in Morrissey v. Comm'r, 296 U.S. 344 (1935), that the term includes entities

> which resemble corporations although they are not formally organized as such. *Morrissey* identified several characteristics of the corporate form which the regulations adopt as a test of corporate resemblance. For the purpose of comparing corporations with partnerships, the significant characteristics are: continuity of life; centralization of management; limited liability; and free transferability of interests. Other corporate or noncorporate characteristics may also be considered if appropriate in a particular case. An organization will be taxed as a corporation if, taking all relevant characteristics into account, it more nearly resembles a corporation than some other entity. . . . This will be true only if it possesses more corporate than noncorporate characteristics.

These classification regulations were developed in response to efforts by taxpayers to *achieve* "association" status for their unincorporated entities. Doctors and other professionals sought that status to take advantage of pension and profit-sharing rules more favorable to corporate employees than noncorporate ones. (Many state laws at the time prohibited such professionals from incorporating their practices.) Consequently, the regulations were widely perceived as biased against association status. As the *Larson* excerpt indicates, the regulations required a business organization to have at least three of the four "corporate" characteristics in order for the organization to be classified as an association for tax purposes.

By the mid-1970s, changes in state and federal law eliminated the need of professionals to obtain association status for their unincorporated businesses. At the same time, tax shelters started to flourish. These shelters were often organized as limited partnerships in order to permit the passthrough of losses to their investors, and the classification regulations made it easy for such partnerships to avoid association status.

In January 1977, the IRS issued proposed regulations that would have reversed the bias against association classification of entities organized as limited partnerships. The proposed regulations caused a major controversy and were promptly withdrawn. In 1980, the IRS tried again and put forward proposed regulations to the effect that an organization in which no member is liable for the debts of the organization, such as a limited liability company (LLC), would automatically be classified as an association and treated as a corporation for tax purposes. These regulations were also controversial and withdrawn.

By 1988, the IRS had clearly retreated from its prior positions. In Rev. Rul. 88-76, 1988-2 C.B. 360, it concluded that a Wyoming LLC could under certain circumstances be treated as a partnership for tax purposes. This ruling opened the floodgates as state after state authorized a similar form of business organization providing full limited liability protection for the owners of the enterprise while still maintaining enough "noncorporate" characteristics to qualify for partnership tax treatment under the classification regulations. An LLC statute was ultimately enacted by every state in the nation as well as the District of Columbia. The combination of a limited liability shield and partnership taxation made the LLC the entity of choice for many new business ventures despite initial concern about the legal status of an LLC outside its state of organization. The IRS soon found itself flooded with ruling requests for the classification of businesses organized under the new state LLC statutes. Although the rulings involved largely mechanical determinations, they required a case-by-case analysis and were time-consuming. See, e.g., Rev. Rul. 93-38, 1993-1 C.B. 233 (discussing classification of two Delaware limited liability companies with different provisions in their respective LLC agreements; one classified as a partnership and the other as an association).

In this environment, the Treasury decided in 1996 to change the classification regulations to allow certain domestic, unincorporated business organizations to elect their status for federal tax purposes. These regulations are commonly referred to as the "check-the-box" regulations. Read Reg. §§ 301.7701-1(a) and (b), -2(a), (b)(1)-(7), (c)(1) and (2)(i), -3(a), (b)(1) and (3)(i), (f)(1) and (2). The threshold question under the regulations is whether an organization qualifies as an entity separate from its owners for federal tax purposes. In general, an unincorporated organization (other than certain trusts) qualifying as a separate entity may elect corporate status. In the absence of an election, an organization with two or more owners is treated as a partnership and an organization with only a single owner is "disregarded" for tax purposes and treated as a sole proprietorship, branch, or division of its owner. Ordinary trusts — arrangements merely to protect or conserve property for beneficiaries — are not provided with a classification choice because they generally do not have associates or an objective to carry on business for profit. A separate set of rules in the Internal Revenue Code (subchapter J) specifies how they are taxed. Business or commercial trusts — which are devices created by beneficiaries to operate profit-making ventures — are permitted, however, to make the classification election.

## *NOTES AND QUESTIONS*

1. *Types of unincorporated business organizations.* The following describes the typical state-law characteristics of some of the most common forms of unincorporated business organizations eligible to make the check-the-box election. In general, the distinguishing feature of these organizations is the extent to which the owners of the organization may be held liable for its obligations. In a *general partnership*, the general partners are ordinarily jointly and severally liable for all of the obligations of the partnership. In contrast, in a *limited partnership*, comprised of both limited partners and at least one general partner, the liability of the limited partners may be limited to the amount of their investment in the venture. To retain their liability shield, however, limited partners generally may not be actively involved in the management of the business. In a *limited liability company* (LLC), all of the owners (termed "members") may have limited liability like limited partners but, unlike such partners, may also be involved in management without losing their liability protection. A *limited liability partnership* (LLP) is a special type of general partnership in which each partner is typically protected from liability for torts committed by those not under such partner's supervision. LLPs are popular among professional service firms because they may serve to insulate each partner from liabilities arising from

malpractice committed by other partners. Finally, a *limited liability limited partnership* (LLLP) is a special type of limited partnership in which each general partner typically has no vicarious liability for torts committed by other partners. The legal consequences of some of these organizational forms may not be well established.

2. *Subchapter S?* If an unincorporated entity, such as a partnership or LLC, elects to be taxed as a corporation, can it then elect to be taxed under subchapter S? Why might it wish to do so? How should the subchapter S eligibility rules, such as the single class of stock requirement, be interpreted in the context of such an entity?

3. *Corporations.* The classification election is available only to *unincorporated* firms. Thus, corporations may not choose to be taxed under subchapter K. See Reg. § 301.7701-2(b)(1) and -3(a). How might the states respond to that restriction? Is the restriction likely to move the law in a sensible direction?

4. *Public firms.* In general, firms with publicly traded ownership interests, even though not incorporated, are also ineligible to be taxed under subchapter K. Instead, such firms are taxed as corporations. I.R.C. § 7704(a); Reg. § 301.7701-2(b)(7) and -3(a). This rule does not apply to unincorporated firms that derive 90 percent or more of their income from certain categories such as interest, dividends, rent and gain from real property, and income or gain from exploiting natural resources. Firms with such qualifying income may continue to be taxed as partnerships even though their ownership interests are publicly traded. Interests are considered publicly traded if they are traded on an established securities market, a secondary market, or the substantial equivalent thereof. Certain preexisting firms are grandfathered from application of section 7704(a) if they pay a special 3.5 percent tax on gross income from their active conduct of a trade or business.

5. *Validity of regulations.* In Littriello v. U.S., 484 F.3d 372 (6th Cir. 2007), in a case of first impression, the Sixth Circuit upheld the validity of the check-the-box regulations. See also McNamee v. U.S., 488 F.3d 100 (2d Cir. 2007) (accord). In *Litriello*, the taxpayer was the sole owner of a limited liability company responsible for about $1 million of unpaid federal employment taxes. Because the company did not elect to be treated as a corporation, its status as a separate entity was disregarded for tax purposes and, therefore, the sole owner was liable for the taxes. Applying the "deferential" analysis of Chevron U.S.A., Inc. v. Natural Res. Def. Council, Inc., 467 U.S. 837 (1984), the court concluded that the regulations represented a reasonable administrative interpretation of section 7701. Revised regulations reverse the specific outcome in *Littriello* and treat an entity that is generally disregarded for tax purposes as, nevertheless, a corporation for employment tax purposes. Reg. § 301.7701-2(a) and (c)(2)(iv). This reversal was adopted in order to conform federal employment tax law with that of the states, which generally continue to make the entity responsible for the reporting, collection, and payment of state employment taxes despite the disregarded status of the entity for federal tax purposes.

6. *Classification changes.* Changes in the tax status of a firm may result either from a change in the firm's elected status or, in certain cases, from a change in the

number of its owners. If a firm classified as a partnership elects to be treated as a corporation, the partnership is deemed to contribute all of its assets to a corporation in exchange for stock of the corporation and the partnership is then deemed to liquidate. In the reverse situation where a firm classified as a corporation elects to be treated as a partnership, the corporation is deemed to liquidate (in a taxable transaction) and the former shareholders are treated as contributing the distributed corporate assets to a newly formed partnership. Reg. § 301.7701-3(g)(1). The corporate tax consequences of these deemed transactions are described in chapters seven and ten.

## B. Taxation of C Corporation Income and Loss

Both the corporation and its owners generally must pay tax on the income of a C corporation. Sections one and two provide brief overviews of the corporate- and investor-level taxes, respectively, and section three then describes how the effect of double taxation can be mitigated or avoided.

### 1. *Brief Overview of Taxation of C Corporations*

As a separate taxable entity, a C corporation must compute its taxable income and pay tax in much the same manner as an individual, except that the corporation is subject to a different rate schedule and certain other special rules. Read I.R.C. §§ 11, 1201(a), 1211(a), and 1212(a)(1) and the following excerpt as an introduction to the general rules.

#### Dept. of the Treasury, Business Taxation and Global Competitiveness (2007)

Corporations are generally subject to tax on their receipts less the cost of doing business. To compute taxable income, a corporation deducts expenses paid or incurred during the taxable year from gross business income. These expenses include wages, state and local taxes, depreciation, interest expense, and other expenses. Expenditures that produce benefits in future taxable years, such as expenditures on plant and equipment, are capitalized and recovered over time through depreciation, amortization, or depletion allowances. When deductions exceed income, a corporation has a net operating loss. Net operating losses can be carried back 2 years and carried forward for 20 years to offset taxable income. Deductions are also allowed for certain amounts for which the corporation did not make expenditures. For example, a deduction is allowed for a portion of income attributable to certain manufacturing activities. Certain other payments by corporations, such as dividends paid to shareholders, are not deductible.

U.S. corporations are subject to tax on foreign source as well as domestic source income. Although a U.S. corporation is required to pay U.S. tax currently on foreign income earned through a foreign branch, U.S. tax generally is not imposed on the active earnings of a foreign subsidiary until the subsidiary distributes the income to the parent corporation as a dividend (i.e., until income earned abroad is repatriated back to the United States). However, certain passive income, such as portfolio income, is taxed when earned regardless of whether it is repatriated to the United States. In computing U.S. tax liability, U.S. taxpayers (including corporations) are allowed a credit for foreign taxes paid.

In addition to these general rules, special rules apply to specific types of business that conduct activity in corporate form, such as insurance companies. Other special rules apply to specific types of activities, such as exploration and development of natural resources. Certain types of corporations are granted full or partial relief from corporate level tax.

Corporations are taxed at the rate of 15 percent on the first $50,000 of taxable income, 25 percent on taxable income from $50,001 to $75,000, 34 percent on taxable income from $75,001 to $10 million, and 35 percent on taxable income above $10 million. The first two graduated rates are phased out for corporations with taxable income between $100,000 and $335,000 and the 34-percent rate is phased out between $15,000,000 and $18,333,333 in taxable income.

Under the corporate income tax, there is no separate rate structure for capital gains. Thus, the maximum rate on net capital gains is 35 percent. Capital losses in excess of capital gains are not deductible, but may be carried back 3 years or carried forward 5 years.

Corporations are taxed at lower rates on income from certain production activities through the allowance of a special deduction. . . . [T]he deduction . . . is [9] percent of the income from manufacturing, construction, and certain other specified activities. . . . The 9-percent deduction is (approximately) equivalent to taxing income at a tax rate of 31.85 percent (i.e., 91 percent of income is taxed at a 35-percent rate, or 31.85 percent).

Corporations are also eligible to claim tax credits related to certain activities, such as the tax credit for research and experimentation, the low income housing tax credit, the enhanced oil recovery credit, and others.

A corporation is also subject to an alternative minimum tax, which is payable to the extent that it exceeds the corporation's regular tax liability. The alternative minimum tax is imposed at the rate of 20 percent on a base that is broader than the regular tax base. The exemption amount for the corporate alternative minimum tax is $40,000. If a corporation pays the alternative minimum tax, the amount of tax paid is allowed as a credit against the regular tax in future years.

*NOTES*

1. *History*. Under the first federal income taxes in the U.S., enacted during the Civil War, corporations were taxed in two different ways. Certain corporations were treated as passthrough entities like S corporations and partnerships today. Other corporations (as well as unincorporated businesses) in certain industries, such as railroads and banking, were taxed directly. Such direct taxation served primarily as a way to collect an income tax from the investors in those companies. In 1894, when the income tax was briefly revived, corporations were taxed directly on two percent of their net income but this tax again appears to have been largely a collection device for the tax owed by shareholders. Congress did not pass the first truly separate income tax on corporations until 1909, four years prior to ratification of the Sixteenth Amendment and introduction of the present individual income tax. Under the 1909 legislation, corporations were subject to an "excise tax" equal to one percent of their net income over $5,000. (Even though the tax was calculated based in part on the amount of a corporation's income from property, the tax was held to be a valid excise or indirect tax on the privilege of doing business, rather than an unconstitutional direct tax on property. Flint v. Stone Tracy Co., 220 U.S. 107 (1911).) When the individual income tax was enacted in 1913, Congress exempted dividends from the one percent "normal tax" imposed on individuals (but not from the progressive surtax) as a rough way to integrate that tax with the one percent corporate tax and thereby avoid double taxation. That structure was gradually modified to allow partial double taxation; full double taxation was not introduced until 1936.

2. *Incidence of the corporate tax*. An important policy question is the incidence of the corporate tax. The nominal burden of the tax is borne by the corporation, which must remit the tax to the government. Since a corporation is a legal fiction, however, the real burden must lie elsewhere. Uncertainty about the incidence of the tax has sometimes led cautious policy analysts to omit consideration of corporate tax changes from distributional analyses of legislative proposals. Such an omission may, however, result in conclusions potentially just as misleading as ones premised on an erroneous attribution of the corporate tax burden. For example, proposed legislation that offsets tax cuts for individuals with tax increases on corporations may appear to provide *only* an income tax cut for individuals if the distributional effect of the corporate tax increase is not taken into account.

A seminal contribution to the incidence question was made by Arnold Harberger, The Incidence of the Corporation Income Tax, 70 J. Pol. Econ. 215 (1962). Based on a number of key assumptions, including the existence of two exclusive sectors (corporate and noncorporate) and free mobility of capital and labor between the two, Harberger concluded that in the long run, the corporate tax is borne by *all* holders of capital, and not just corporate shareholders. Under his analysis, an additional tax imposed only in the corporate sector results in a movement of the factors of production from that sector to the noncorporate one until a new equilibrium is reached in the returns (net of taxes and risk premiums) from the factors employed in each sector. Using reasonable parameters for the U.S. economy, he found that the introduction of a corporate tax would make the existing holders of capital investment in each sector worse off. Capital owners in the noncorporate sector would see their after-tax returns decline due to the influx of new capital into their sector and the resulting reduction in pre-tax returns on investment. Capital owners in the corporate sector would also see a decrease in their after-tax returns, as the increase in pre-tax returns in their sector attributable to the reduction in capital investment would not be enough to offset the higher tax imposed on the returns from that investment. Other aspects of the model led Harberger to conclude that the burden of the corporate tax would not fall on workers or be shifted to consumers in the aggregate, although there might be individual winners and losers among consumers.

Obviously, this model abstracts away some key features of the law. For one thing, business income is taxed in both the C corporation and non-C corporation sectors; in the latter, the tax is simply imposed on the owners of the enterprise rather than on the business entity itself. True, the presence of an additional tax on distributions from C corporations means that investments in the two sectors are not taxed exactly the same, but the difference is more nuanced than a simple model that imagines the corporate tax as an "add-on" burden not found in the "noncorporate" sector. Another issue relates to restricted mobility between the two sectors, such as the current-law rule generally requiring public businesses to be part of the "corporate" sector. The Harberger model also assumed that the tax would not affect the total amount of capital, yet higher capital taxes might induce greater consumption and less savings.

Another important assumption in the initial Harberger analysis was the existence of a "closed economy," that is, one in which neither capital nor labor can cross international borders. Some later work, including Harberger's own subsequent work, concludes that in an "open economy," an important portion of the corporate tax may be borne by domestic labor in the form of lower wages. This work assumes that the international mobility of capital is greater than that of labor. Therefore, an increase in capital income taxes by one country may cause capital to shift from that country to others that have not similarly increased their taxes. Labor, being less mobile, is not able to flee to the same extent. The result is a potential decrease of capital investment in the country that initially increased its taxes (with no commensurate reduction in labor), leading to a slowing of advances in labor productivity and a reduction in wages in that country. Of course, if all countries tend to change the level of their corporate income taxes in a roughly coordinated fashion, a pattern that has actually occurred to some extent over the last few decades, then the "closed economy" model may not be an unreasonable assumption. Another factor affecting this analysis is the degree to which products produced in different countries are close substitutes for one another.

Empirical evidence concerning the incidence of the corporate tax is fairly thin and controversial. Thus, who bears the corporate tax burden remains an important puzzle in public finance.

3. *The corporate AMT.* As explained in the Treasury excerpt, corporations (like individuals) are subject to an alternative minimum tax (AMT). The corporate AMT

is imposed at a lower rate and on a broader base than the regular corporate income tax and a corporation must pay the greater of the two tax liabilities. I.R.C. § 55(a), (b)(1)(B), and (b)(2). The main differences in the base of the two taxes result from timing provisions such as accelerated depreciation; in general, capital investments may not be depreciated as quickly under the AMT as under the regular corporate tax. As a result, corporations in capital intensive industries are most heavily affected by the AMT. On average, only about one percent of corporations are affected by the AMT; corporations having average annual gross receipts of $7.5 million or less for the prior three taxable years are generally not subject to the tax. I.R.C. § 55(e). This exception alone exempts around 95 percent of all C corporations from the AMT.

The regular corporate tax correlates more closely than the corporate AMT with the business cycle. Since corporations must pay the greater of the two liabilities, they are thus more likely to have corporate AMT liability during economic downturns (when regular corporate tax liability is low) and less likely to have AMT liability during economic boom periods (when regular corporate tax liability is high). For example, in 2005 (a very good year for corporate profits), only about 0.2 percent of all corporations reported being affected by the AMT. This "pro-cyclical" effect of the corporate AMT—its tendency to rise when the economy is stressed and to decline when the economy may be overheating—makes it a frequent target for repeal. Other reasons supporting AMT repeal include its relatively small contribution to corporate tax revenue, uneven impact across industries, and contribution to tax complexity.

One factor thwarting repeal of the corporate AMT has been the problem of AMT credits. Since the AMT arises largely because of the denial of timing benefits allowed by the regular tax, payment of the AMT is in effect a prepayment of the regular tax. To avoid taxing a corporation twice on the same income, the law permits a corporation to credit against its regular tax liability amounts of AMT previously paid, but only to the extent the regular tax exceeds its AMT liability for the year. Any unused credits are carried forward for use in future years. I.R.C. § 53(a) - (c). If the AMT were repealed, some provision would have to be made for the utilization of any remaining AMT credits. Congress and the public have not viewed favorably the specter of these prepaid taxes being refunded to large corporations even though the effect is little different from tax refunds made to individuals who have been withheld an excessive amount of tax during the prior year.

4. *Graduated corporate income tax rates.* As explained in the Treasury excerpt, there is a graduated tax rate structure principally for the benefit of very small corporations with taxable income of less than $100,000. Corporations with greater amounts of income have the benefits of the lower rates gradually clawed back through imposition of a surtax above the top statutory rates of 34 and 35 percent. I.R.C. § 11(b)(1) (flush language). The net result is that any corporation with taxable income between $335,000 and $10 million must pay the equivalent of a 34 percent tax on every dollar of income and any corporation with taxable income of $18,333,333 or more must pay the equivalent of a 35 percent tax on every dollar of

income. The existence of graduated rates for corporations is difficult to justify since the amount of taxable income a corporation reports does not necessarily have any correlation with the ability to pay of the persons ultimately bearing the burden of the tax. The standard explanation for graduated rates generally does not move much beyond the flat assertion that they provide a benefit for "small businesses." One potential effect of graduated rates is to create a minor tax shelter opportunity for taxpayers who are in individual income tax brackets higher than the corporate rate. Indeed, it is presumably for this reason that some closely held corporations eligible for S status nevertheless prefer to be taxed as C corporations. The law has long included a rule preventing taxpayers from dividing their income among multiple C corporations established in an effort to obtain multiple low-bracket benefits. See I.R.C. §§ 1561, 1563.

5. *Corporate capital gains and losses.* Unlike individuals, corporations do not pay tax on their capital gains at a preferential rate. In addition, corporate capital losses are deductible only against their capital gains. Finally, unused corporate capital losses generally may be carried back three years and carried forward only five years, unlike the unlimited carryforward of unused capital losses of individuals. I.R.C. §§ 1211(a), 1212(a)(1) and (b)(1). As we will see, these generally less favorable rules relating to capital gains and losses (combined with taxpayers' ability to time the recognition of such gains and losses) have prompted corporate taxpayers to devise means, including tax shelters, to reduce their tax exposure to capital gains and to utilize fully their capital losses.

6. *The problem of "trapped" corporate losses.* C corporations with net operating losses are not permitted to pass through their losses to their owners. Rather, such losses may generally be carried back two years and forward 20 years to offset corporate taxable income. I.R.C. § 172(a), (b)(1)(A), (c). Since the amount of losses is not indexed, any losses that must be carried forward gradually lose their value, and some corporate tax planning aims to avoid that outcome. For example, because start-up ventures commonly incur losses in their early years, such ventures are typically organized as passthrough entities rather than C corporations to allow the owners to claim the losses as they are incurred. C corporations anticipating an excess of deductions over income may structure transactions, such as issuing preferred stock rather than debt or leasing assets rather than purchasing them with debt, to minimize a further accumulation of excess deductions. Finally, C corporations with significant losses may be viewed as attractive acquisition targets to allow the accumulated losses to offset income of the acquirer. Special rules, discussed in chapter thirteen, attempt to limit the tax advantage of many such acquisitions.

The tax treatment of C corporation losses presents important and difficult policy issues. The length of the carryback period is generally limited by administrative concerns. Requiring any remaining losses to be carried forward encourages the continued existence of corporations with losses, sometimes beyond the point where the corporation is economically viable. Indeed, taxpayers have an incentive not only to continue such corporations but also to infuse them with income-producing capital in order to ensure that the tax value of the losses is not completely lost. On the other hand, the principal alternative to a carryforward of losses is a refund to corporations of the tax value of the losses. Refundability is controversial partly because it may encourage corporations to engage in tax shelter activities that generate artificial tax losses.

The length of the carryback period is occasionally increased during economic downturns as a way to provide liquidity to economically distressed corporations. See I.R.C. § 172(b)(1)(H) (providing elective carryback period of up to five years for certain losses of small corporations). This type of change is sometimes criticized as simply providing windfall benefits to just one class of corporations — those that incur sizable losses during the economic slump.

7. *Foreign corporations.* The Treasury excerpt summarizes the tax rules applicable generally to U.S. or "domestic" corporations, that is, those organized under U.S. laws. I.R.C. § 7701(a)(4). All other corporations, termed "foreign" corporations, are generally taxed under the same rules as U.S. corporations, but only on income effectively connected with the conduct of a U.S. trade or business. I.R.C. § 882(a). Foreign corporations must also pay a 30 percent U.S. tax on U.S.-source investment-type income (computed without allowing any deductions) even if it is not effectively connected with a U.S. trade or business. However, this withholding tax, collected at the source of the payment, generally does not extend to capital gains or interest income on portfolio debt investments. I.R.C. § 881(a) and (c). Also, the tax rate is commonly reduced to 15 percent or less by treaty with the treaty partner making a similar concession in the taxation of U.S. corporations.

8. *Some data.* **Figure 3-1** shows the relationship of corporate income tax to both total federal receipts and gross domestic product (GDP) between 1934 and 2010. Corporate tax receipts are strongly affected by economic conditions influencing the level of corporate profits, and that factor helps to explain the year-to-year fluctuations. Reasons for the generally declining share of corporate tax revenue to total receipts and GDP during the period shown include the growing importance of employment taxes during the same period, changes in the corporate tax laws and attitudes of corporate advisors to such laws, and changing patterns of foreign and domestic investment. Another very important factor, as mentioned in chapter two, is the increasing use of passthrough entities, such as LLCs and S corporations, to carry out business activities (see **figures 2-1** and **2-4**, pp. 41, 43). The income taxes of such entities are generally reported by the owners of the entity, who may be individuals. Thus, the tax generated from passthrough business activity is accounted for, to a significant extent, as "individual" rather than "corporate" income tax revenue in the official statistics.

The vast majority of C corporations are quite small. In recent years, over half of all C corporations had assets of $100,000 or less, almost 90 percent had assets of $1 million or less, and over 97 percent had assets of $10 million or less. Conversely, the roughly 20,000 C corporations falling within the largest asset class (over $100 million) — presumably including all of the large public corporations — represented only about one percent of all C corporations but owned almost 97 percent of all assets held by C corporations.

**Table 3-1** presents a similar picture of C corporations based upon their income subject to tax in 2006. "Income subject to tax" is generally equal to a corporation's net income after taking into account any deduction for losses carried forward from prior years and the dividends-received deduction (discussed briefly in the next section and again in chapter five). As the table shows, almost two-thirds of all C corporations reported having no income subject to tax and another 25 percent reported $50,000 income or less, potentially placing them in the lowest (15%) marginal tax bracket. At the other end of the spectrum, about 3,800 C corporations, representing less than 0.2 percent of all such corporations, reported income over $18,333,333 and therefore had all of their income taxed at a flat 35 percent rate. This small group of corporations paid almost 90 percent of the corporate tax. The amount of income tax shown is after credits, the principal one being the foreign tax credit. Thus, the drop in the average tax rate (equal to income tax after credits divided by income subject to tax) of the corporations with the largest amount of income reflects to some extent the omission of foreign income taxes from this table. The average tax rate in this table should not be confused with another ratio, sometimes termed the "effective tax rate," that estimates the amount of tax paid in relation to a broader measure of income, such as income reported for financial accounting purposes. The broader measure would reflect income amounts before taking into account special deductions and exclusions allowed for tax purposes.

**Figure 3-1. Corporate Income Taxes as Percentage of Total Federal Receipts and GDP, 1934-2010**

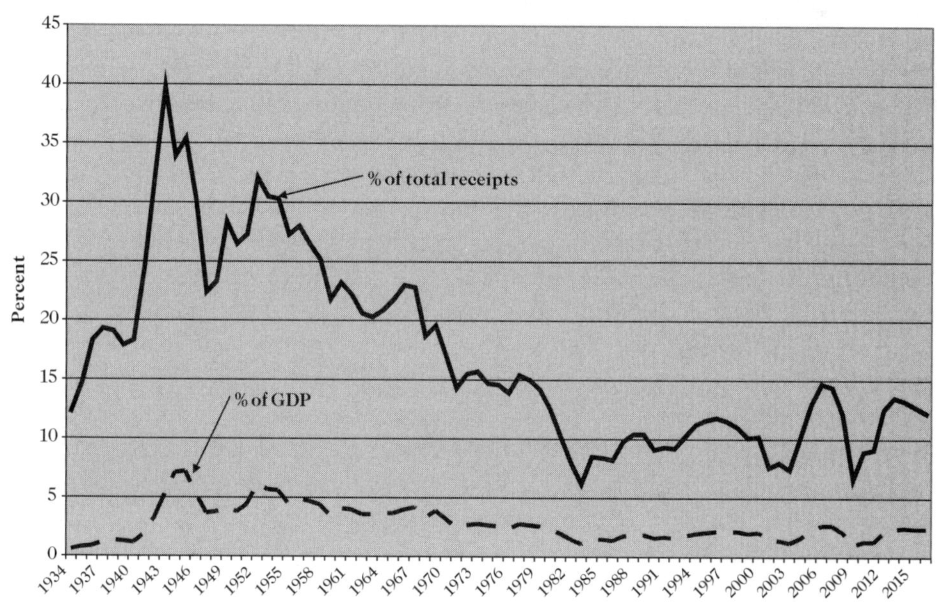


Source: Budget of U.S. Government, FY 2012, Historical Tables (tables 2.2, 2.3)

**Table 3-1**
**Distribution of C Corporations by Income Subject to Tax, 2006**

| *Income subject to tax* | *# C corps* | *% tot. C corps* | *Income subject to tax ($Ms)* | *Income tax after credits ($Ms)* | *% tot. income tax after credits* | *Marginal tax rate* | *Average tax rate* |
|---|---|---|---|---|---|---|---|
| Zero or less | 1,271,550 | 65.04% | 0 | 3,026 | 0.86% | N/A | N/A |
| $1 – $50,000 | 497,670 | 25.45% | 6,721 | 1,021 | 0.29% | 15.00% | 15.19% |
| $50,001 – $75,000 | 52,050 | 2.66% | 3,183 | 527 | 0.15% | 25.00% | 16.55% |
| $75,001 – $100,000 | 28,652 | 1.47% | 2,478 | 491 | 0.14% | 34.00% | 19.81% |
| $100,001 – $335,000 | 58,324 | 2.98% | 10,126 | 2,850 | 0.81% | 39.00% | 28.14% |
| $335,001 – $1M | 22,881 | 1.17% | 13,325 | 4,357 | 1.24% | 34.00% | 32.70% |
| over $1M – $5M | 15,503 | 0.79% | 33,968 | 11,081 | 3.15% | 34.00% | 32.62% |
| over $5M – $10M | 3,048 | 0.16% | 21,300 | 6,826 | 1.94% | 34.00% | 32.05% |
| over $10M – $15M | 1,169 | 0.06% | 14,241 | 4,541 | 1.29% | 35.00% | 31.89% |
| over $15M – $18,333,333 | 500 | 0.03% | 8,318 | 2,745 | 0.78% | 38.00% | 32.99% |
| over $18,333,333 | 3,801 | 0.19% | 1,176,101 | 314,858 | 89.37% | 35.00% | 26.77% |
| All C corporations | 1,955,147 | 100.00% | 1,289,761 | 352,322 | 100.00% | | 27.32% |

Source: IRS, Statistics of Income, http://www.irs.gov/taxstats/index.html, special tabulation

## *NOTE*

*Economic diversity of corporations.* The roughly four million S corporations, almost all of which are quite small, add to the wide economic diversity of corporations, and the heterogeneous grouping sometimes creates policy dilemmas. For example, to enhance compliance, persons in a trade or business who make certain payments of $600 or more in a taxable year are required to file an information report with the payee and the IRS. I.R.C. § 6041(a). Information reporting of payments to large corporations are generally not very useful because such corporations usually keep good account of their receipts and must, in any event, use the accrual method for tax purposes (so that reporting of cash payments provides little benefit for tax compliance purposes). I.R.C. § 448(a)(1). These considerations are not necessarily applicable, however, to payments to S corporations or small C corporations, which are generally allowed to use the cash method of accounting. I.R.C. § 448(b)(3). Because payors may not be able to distinguish "small" from "large" corporate payees, all payments to corporations have until recently been exempted from the information-reporting requirement (Reg. § 1.6041-3(p)(1)). Although this exemption was ended in 2010 (effective after 2011), the change was repealed in 2011 without ever going into effect. Despite an estimated $17 billion revenue gain (over ten years) from improved compliance, the reporting requirement was highly controversial (in part because of the perceived burdensomeness of filing unnecessary reports on payments to large corporations).

## 2. *Brief Overview of Taxation of Investors in C Corporations*

Under current law, individuals generally pay a maximum 15 percent tax on their dividends and long-term capital gain. I.R.C. § 1(h)(1) and (11). The top rate was reduced to 15 percent in 2003 in an effort to mitigate the effect of the "double tax," but the preferential rate is scheduled to expire at the end of 2012. If it expires, dividends would once again be taxed at ordinary income tax rates (currently, the maximum such rate for individuals is 35 percent), and long-term capital gain would be taxed at 20 percent.

Despite being taxed at the same rate, dividends and long-term capital gain are not treated identically. Among other differences, the capital gain tax applies only to the "gain" portion of the receipt (i.e., the excess of amount realized over the taxpayer's basis), whereas the dividend tax applies to the full amount of any dividend received. Thus, a sale of shares for $100, including a sale back to the corporation that issued the stock, may not result in the same income tax liability as the receipt of a $100 dividend from that corporation.

The rules described above do not apply to corporate shareholders. Corporations receiving dividends or capital gain from investments in C corporations must generally pay tax on such income at the regular corporate income tax rate, currently a maximum of 35 percent. However, corporate shareholders are generally entitled to deduct between 70 and 100 percent of the dividends received from a domestic corporation, depending upon how large an interest the corporate shareholder owns in the corporation paying the dividend. See I.R.C. § 243(a) and (c). The net effect, in general, is to tax corporations on their dividend income at a rate of between zero and 10.5 percent and on their capital gain at a rate of 35 percent. The corporate dividends-received deduction is often explained as a way to reduce and potentially eliminate the imposition of more than one corporate tax on a particular item of income (and more than two taxes total on the same income). The tax treatment of corporate capital gain from investments in C corporations is, however, inconsistent with that policy objective. We consider the dividends-received deduction in chapter five.

Unlike dividend and capital gain income, interest paid by a C corporation to individual or corporate debtholders is taxed as ordinary income without any preferential rate or special deduction. While interest is generally deductible by the corporate debtor, however, dividends are not.

In summary, corporate income paid out as interest is generally taxed only once, to the debtholder, at ordinary income tax rates. By contrast, corporate income paid out as dividends is generally taxed twice, once at the corporate level and then again at the shareholder level (although this second tax is currently ameliorated for both individual and corporate shareholders). Finally, corporate income realized by a shareholder as a capital gain is also generally taxed twice: once at the corporate level when earned and once again at the shareholder level on sale of the corporate stock. As noted, individuals realizing long-term capital gain pay tax at a preferential rate but corporations do not.

Because the income tax consequences to corporations and their investors are generally not tied to one another, the overall tax consequences may deviate considerably from the above summary in any particular situation. For example, corporations are generally entitled to deduct interest even if the interest is paid to an investor—such as a pension fund, qualified retirement account, charity, or foreign person (including a foreign corporation) not subject to U.S. tax on portfolio debt income—that is exempt from paying tax on the income. In 1990, the Treasury estimated that almost 60 percent of corporate debt was held by a tax-exempt holder; since then, there is some indication that foreign holdings of corporate debt have increased dramatically. Individual investors are entitled to the preferential rate for dividends and capital gain even though the income is partly or wholly exempt from tax at the corporate level due to preferences or tax shelters. Therefore, some corporate-source income may not be taxed at all, some may be subject to a full double tax or more, and some may be taxed in an intermediate way between these two extremes. In 2003, the George W. Bush Administration proposed initially to exempt individuals on their dividend income, provided that the corporation had been fully taxed on such income. In its original form, the proposal might have helped to put a brake on corporate tax shelter activity. Congress, however, decided that the proposal was too complicated; it approved instead the current preferential dividend and long-term capital gain tax rate for individuals, determined without regard to whether the income was taxed at the corporate level.

This brief overview provides some idea of the importance taxes may play on corporate and investment behavior, all with potential efficiency costs. Economists refer to the "clientele effect" as the tendency of different investments to attract different types of investors due to a variety of factors. The tax rules just described produce a number of possible clientele effects. For example, because of the dividends-received deduction, U.S. corporations generally prefer to invest in high-dividend securities, such as preferred stock, rather than low- or no-dividend securities, such as "growth" common stock. Foreign persons (including foreign corporations) generally have the opposite preference; they may be subject to a withholding tax on dividend income but are generally not taxed on their capital gain. Likewise, U.S. individuals generally prefer capital gain to dividend income, although the 2003 rate changes reduced the advantage of that choice. Tax-exempts and foreign persons have an incentive to invest in corporate debt rather than equity. For U.S. individuals and corporations, the preferred choice between debt and equity is more ambiguous; to some extent, the decision rests on whether the investor would prefer the corporate-source income to be taxed at the corporate tax rate (equity) or the investor's tax rate (debt).

The tax rules may have broader economic effects. The different tax treatment of C corporations and passthrough entities, for example, potentially alters the allocation of capital between businesses in those two sectors. The tax law affects corporate financing decisions, including whether to issue debt or equity and the terms of such securities. It also affects corporate distribution policy, such as whether to accumulate earnings or distribute them as dividends or through share repurchases. Finally, these distinctions entail administrative costs. As we will see later in this chapter and succeeding ones, the law must determine whether a particular security is debt or equity, or whether corporate-source income has been realized as a dividend rather than a long-term capital gain, because the tax consequences of those different characterizations may vary.

## NOTES

1. *The "traditional" and "new" view of dividend taxation and some implications.* Under the "traditional" view, the tax on dividends distorts corporate distribution policy because it discourages dividends and thereby locks in corporate earnings in much the same way that the capital gain tax may lock in investment and discourage sales. The traditional view predicts that dividends occur only when their nontax benefits, such as the positive signal they send regarding the health and prospects of a company, outweigh the tax costs of the transaction.

In contrast, the "new" view of dividend taxation conceives of the tax as the price that must be incurred to withdraw accumulated earnings from corporate solution. If this cost is unavoidable, then it should not distort corporate distribution policy. In other words, under the assumptions of the new view, the amount and timing of dividends would depend exclusively on nontax factors. Importantly, the new view is premised on the existence of a *uniform* corporate distributions tax, no matter when or how a distribution occurs.

To illustrate the theory of the new view, assume the existence of a uniform corporate distributions tax equal to 30 percent of any amount distributed out of corporate solution; assume further that amounts invested in or out of corporate solution earn the same after-tax annual rate of return of ten percent. If a corporation with $100 of accumulated earnings distributes that amount to a shareholder, the shareholder receives and can invest $70 after the distribution ($100 – ($100 × 30% distributions tax)) and thus would have $77 after one year ($70 + ($70 × 10%)). If the corporation instead delays the distribution for a year, then the corporation has $110 of accumulated earnings by the end of the year ($100 + ($100 × 10%)) which, if distributed to the shareholder, yields the shareholder $77 after taxes ($110 – ($110 × 30% distributions tax)). In short, the shareholder ends up in one year's time with $77 after taxes no matter what decision the corporation makes about its distribution policy. Under these assumptions, the tax system is neutral towards the amount and timing of dividends.

Of course, for a variety of reasons, current law does not impose a uniform tax regardless of when or how a corporate distribution is carried out. Thus, even under the new view's conception of the tax on dividends, the tax law is not neutral towards corporate distribution policy. But the basic insight of the new view that a corporate distribution, although triggering a tax, has an offsetting benefit of removing the amount distributed from any further exposure to "double taxation," has several useful implications.

First, the new view suggests that increased uniformity in the tax on corporate distributions, no matter how or when they are carried out, may reduce undesirable tax-induced distortions in corporate distribution policy. Thus, the theory of the new view provides a direction for possible reform.

Second, a neutral distribution tax is possible regardless of the level of tax. For example, although a "zero" tax on distributions, i.e., allowing dividends to be exempt from income altogether, would achieve the neutral objective, so would a distributions tax equal to 20 percent, 40 percent, or any other level. The key is the uniformity and inevitability of the tax, not the particular tax rate. The tax rate on distributions also need not be the same as the income tax rate of the shareholder.

Third, the new view suggests that a stock sale from one shareholder to another should be viewed as a different transaction from a stock sale back to the corporation that issued the stock. A share repurchase by a corporation, but not a sale between shareholders, removes an amount from corporate solution and hence reduces exposure to the double tax. Under the theory of the new view, therefore, a share repurchase should be taxed like any other distribution whereas a sale between shareholders might be taxed differently.

Finally, the new view has important implications for reform proposals to eliminate the double tax by, for example, repealing the tax on dividends. Under the new view, because earnings are trapped in corporate solution until payment of the inevitable distribution tax, share price should reflect this cost. If so, a repeal or reduction of the dividend tax, such as what transpired in 2003, may simply grant a windfall to existing shareholders by increasing share values, without significantly affecting the cost of capital and level of business investment. Under this view, any relief from double taxation should apply only to returns on post-relief equity contributions to a C corporation and not to earnings on preexisting accumulations.

The 2003 tax rate reduction potentially provided a natural experiment to test the validity of these two views of dividend taxation since the traditional view, but not the new view, conceives of the dividend tax as discouraging corporate distributions. Thus, a reduction in the dividend tax should increase distributions under the traditional view but have no effect on distributions under the new view (which would predict instead a one-time increase in share value). So what happened when the dividend tax rate was cut by more than one-half in 2003?

A number of studies have shown that, in general, there was an increase in the amount of corporate dividends, although there is considerable disagreement as to the reason and durability of the increase. This evidence of a spike in dividends is generally consistent with the traditional view. Unfortunately, because the 2003 tax rate reduction was only temporary (the reduced rates were originally enacted to apply only through 2008 and were later extended through 2012), this evidence does not refute the new view. The neutral impact of the dividend tax that is envisioned by the new view is premised on the existence of a uniform tax applying to both current and future distributions. Thus, the new view would predict a higher level of current distributions if, as was the case after the 2003 changes were made, a higher distribution tax applied in the future. In short, the 2003 experiment failed to provide conclusive proof in favor of either the traditional or new view of dividends.

2. *Tax benefits for small corporation investors.* Sections 1202 and 1244 provide special tax benefits for certain investors in small corporations. Section 1202(a)(1) generally permits a noncorporate shareholder to exclude 50 percent of any gain (generally up to $10 million) from the sale or exchange of "qualified small business stock" held for over five years. (A portion of the excluded gain is subject to the alternative minimum tax (I.R.C. § 57(a)(7)); for 2011, however, taxpayers may exclude 100 percent of the gain (still up to certain limits) for purposes of both the regular and minimum tax.) "Qualified small business stock" is generally stock acquired at original issue of a domestic C corporation that engages in an active business and whose gross assets do not exceed $50 million before or immediately after the issuance of the stock. I.R.C. § 1202(c)(1) and (2), (d)(1) and (2). Section 1244(a) permits an individual to claim an ordinary loss rather than a capital loss (up to $100,000 for joint filers) on the sale or exchange of "section 1244 stock." In general, "section 1244 stock" is stock of a domestic corporation whose capital contributions do not exceed $1 million and which derived over 50 percent of its gross receipts from non-passive sources during the five years ending with the date the loss is sustained. I.R.C. § 1244(c).

## 3. *Avoiding or Mitigating the Effect of the "Double Tax"*

### a. Compensation

Although C corporations are subject to a separate entity-level tax, the ultimate tax liability for such a corporation, as with all taxpayers, depends in part upon the size of the *base* for the tax. Thus, for many closely held C corporations, avoiding the double tax may be as simple as paying the right amount of deductible compensation to its shareholder-employees in order to eliminate corporate taxable income. As shown previously in **Table 3-1** (p. 64), almost two-thirds of C corporations in 2006 reported net income of zero or less, and another 25 percent reported income of $50,000 or less. The IRS frequently challenges this common strategy on the ground that a corporation may deduct only a "reasonable allowance" for salaries or other compensation. I.R.C. § 162(a)(1). As the following case illustrates, the determination of "reasonable" compensation is often difficult.

**Menard, Inc. v. Commissioner**

560 F.3d 620 (7th Cir. 2009)

POSNER, Circuit Judge.

The Internal Revenue Code allows a business to deduct from its taxable income a "reasonable allowance for salaries or other compensation for personal services actually rendered,". . . . Occasionally the Internal Revenue Service challenges the deduction of a corporate salary on the ground that it's really a dividend. A dividend, like salary, is taxable to the recipient, but unlike salary is not deductible from the corporation's taxable income. So by treating a dividend as salary, a corporation can reduce its income tax liability without increasing the income tax of the recipient. At least that was true in 1998, the tax year at issue in this case. As a result of a change in law in 2003, dividends are now taxed at a lower maximum rate than salaries—15 percent, versus 35 percent for salary. 26 U.S.C. § 1(h)(11). This makes the tradeoff more complex; although the corporation avoids tax by treating the dividend as a salary, which is deductible, the employee pays a higher tax.

But depending on its tax bracket, the corporation may still save more in tax than the employee pays, and in that event, if the employee owns stock in the corporation, he may, depending on how much of the stock he owns, prefer dividends to be treated as salary. Menards' tax bracket in 1998 was, its brief tells us without contradiction, 35 percent. Had the new law been in effect then, the corporation, if unable to deduct the $17.5 million bonus, would have paid $6.1 million in additional income tax, while Mr. Menard, had he received the bonus as a dividend and thus paid 15 percent rather than 35 percent of it in tax, would have saved only $3.5 million.

Even before the change in the Internal Revenue Code, treating a dividend as salary was less likely to be attempted in a publicly held corporation, because if the CEO or other officers or employees receive dividends called salary beyond what they are entitled to by virtue of owning stock in the corporation, the other shareholders suffer. But in a closely held corporation, the owners might decide to take their dividends in the form of salary in order to beat the corporate income tax, and there would be no one to complain—except the Internal Revenue Service.

The usual case for forbidding the reclassification (for tax purposes) of dividends as salary is thus that "of a corporation having few shareholders, practically all of whom draw salaries," Treas. Reg. § 1.162-7(b)(1), especially if the corporation does not pay dividends (as such) and some of the shareholders do no work for the corporation but merely cash a "salary" check. A difficult case—which is this case—is thus that of a corporation that pays a high salary to its CEO who works full time but is also the controlling shareholder. The Treasury regulation defines a "reasonable" salary as the amount that "would ordinarily be paid for like services by like enterprises under like circumstances," § 1.162-7(b)(3), but that is not an operational standard. No two enterprises are alike and no two chief executive officers are alike, and anyway the comparison should be between the total compensation package of the CEOs being compared, and that requires consideration of deferred compensation, including severance packages, the amount of risk in the executives' compensation, and perks.

Courts have attempted to operationalize the Treasury's standard by considering multiple factors that relate to optimal compensation. . . . We reviewed a number of these attempts in Exacto Spring Corp. v. Comm'r, 196 F.3d 833 (7th Cir. 1999), and concluded that they were too vague, and too difficult to operationalize, to be of much utility. Multifactor tests with no weight assigned to any factor are bad enough from the standpoint of providing an objective basis for a judicial decision . . . ;

multifactor tests when none of the factors is concrete are worse, and that is the character of most of the multifactor tests of excessive compensation. They include such semantic vapors as "the type and extent of the services rendered," "the scarcity of qualified employees," "the qualifications . . . of the employee," his "contributions to the business venture," and "the peculiar characteristics of the employer's business."

All businesses are different, all CEOs are different, and all compensation packages for CEOs are different. In *Exacto*, in an effort to bring a modicum of objectivity to the determination of whether a corporate owner/employee's compensation is "reasonable," we created the presumption that "when . . . the investors in his company are obtaining a far higher return than they had any reason to expect, [the owner/employee's] salary is presumptively reasonable." But we added that the presumption could be rebutted by evidence that the company's success was the result of extraneous factors, such as an unexpected discovery of oil under the company's land, or that the company intended to pay the owner/employee a disguised dividend rather than salary. The strongest ground for rebuttal, which brings us back to the basic purpose of disallowing "unreasonable" compensation, is that the employee does no work for the corporation; he is *merely* a shareholder. . . .

Comparison with the compensation of executives of other companies can be helpful if—but it is a big if—the comparison takes into account the details of the compensation package of each of the compared executives, and not just the bottom-line salary. This qualification will turn out to be critical in this case. For the Tax Court acknowledged that the presumption of reasonableness had been established but thought it rebutted by evidence that corporations in the same business as Menards paid their CEOs substantially less than Menards paid its CEO.

Menard, Inc. is a Wisconsin firm that under the name "Menards" sells hardware, building supplies, and related products through retail stores scattered throughout the Midwest. It had 138 stores in 1998 and was the third largest retail home improvement chain in the United States; only Home Depot and Lowe's were larger. It was founded by John Menard in 1962, and, at least through 1998, the tax year at issue in this case, he was the company's chief executive. . . . Uncontradicted evidence depicts him as working 12 to 16 hours a day 6 or 7 days a week, taking only 7 days of vacation a year, working even while spending "personal time" with his family, involving himself in every detail of his firm's operations, and fixing everyone's compensation. Under his management Menards' revenues grew from $788 million in 1991 to $3.4 billion in 1998 and the company's taxable income from $59 million to $315 million. The company's rate of return on shareholders' equity that year was, according to the Internal Revenue Service's expert, 18.8 percent—higher than that of either Home Depot or Lowe's.

Menard owns all the voting shares in the company and 56 percent of the non-voting shares, the rest being owned by members of his family, two of whom have senior positions in the company. Like the other executives of Menards, he is paid a modest base salary but participates along with them in a profit-sharing plan. In 1998, his salary was $157,500 and he received a profit-sharing bonus of $3,017,100, and the Tax Court did not suggest that there was anything amiss with these amounts. But the bulk of his compensation was in the form of a "5% bonus" that yielded him $17,467,800, as a result of which his total compensation for the year exceeded $20 million.

The 5% bonus program (5 percent of the company's net income before income taxes) was adopted in 1973 by the company's board of directors at the suggestion of the company's accounting firm, though there is no indication that the firm suggested a number rather than just advising the board that Mr. Menard should have his own bonus plan because of his commanding role in the management of the company. The board at the time included a shareholder who was not a member of Menard's family and he voted for the plan, which was still in force in 1998 and so far as we know had not been reexamined in the interim. That shareholder departed and the board in 1998 consisted of Menard, a younger brother of his who works for the company, and the company's treasurer.

There is no suggestion that any of the shareholders were disappointed that the company obtained a rate of return of "only" 18.8 percent or that the company's success in that year or any year has been due to windfall factors, such as the discovery of oil under the company's headquarters. But besides thinking Menard's compensation excessive, the Tax Court thought it was *intended* as a dividend. It thought this because Menard's entitlement to his 5 percent bonus was conditioned on his agreeing to reimburse the corporation should the deduction of the bonus from the corporation's taxable income be disallowed by the Internal Revenue Service or its Wisconsin counterpart and because 5 percent of corporate earnings year in and year out "looked" more like a dividend than like salary.

These are flimsy grounds. Given the fondness of the IRS and the Tax Court for a "totality of the circumstances" approach to determining excessive compensation, it was prudent (and incidentally not in Menard's personal financial interest) for the company to require him to reimburse it should the IRS successfully challenge the deduction. Nor does 5 percent of net corporate income look at all like a dividend. Dividends generally are specified dollar amounts — so many dollars per share — rather than a percentage of earnings. . . . When earnings fall, dividends may be cut, but they are cut from one fixed amount to another rather than made to vary continuously, as a percentage of earnings would do.

Paying a fixed (though occasionally altered) dividend provides the shareholder with a more predictable cash flow than if the dividend varied directly with corporate earnings, which fluctuate from year to year. It thus reduces the risk (variance) associated with ownership of common stock. Moreover, the reason for varying a manager's compensation with the company's profits is to increase his incentive to work intelligently and hard in order to increase those profits, and that reason has no application to a passive owner. Although tying compensation to the market value of the company's stock is criticized by some economists because of the many factors besides managerial effort and ability that influence the price of a publicly traded stock, stock in Menards is not publicly traded; probably it is not traded at all.

The most insignificant factor that the Tax Court thought indicative of a "concealed" dividend was that Menard's 5 percent bonus is paid at the end of each year.

Well, it would have to be paid either at the end of the year, when the earnings for the year are known, or in installments throughout the year. Bonuses are usually paid in a lump, once a year, often at Christmas, but that would not be a feasible course for Menards to follow unless it closed for the following week, because its net income for the year wouldn't be determinable until the close of the last day of the year on which the store was open. Bonuses are more likely to be paid in single payments at or near the end of the year than dividends are; dividends usually are paid quarterly. . . .

The court thought it suspicious that the board of directors that approved the 5 percent bonus in 1998 was controlled by Menard. But it could not be otherwise, since he is the only shareholder who is entitled to vote for members of the board of directors, as he owns all the voting shares in the company. The logic of the Tax Court's position is that a one-man corporation cannot pay its CEO (if he is that one man) any salary! The Tax Court has flirted with that strange logic, as we shall see.

A slightly better candidate for suspicion is that the board of directors had not sought outside advice on what appropriate compensation for Menard would be. But the only point of doing that would have been to provide some window dressing in the event of a challenge by the IRS. Menard doubtless has a strong opinion of what he is worth to his company and would not pay a compensation consultant to disagree.

It might seem that since Menards paid no formal dividend at all, some of Mr. Menard's compensation (and perhaps that of other executives as well) *must* be a dividend. But that is incorrect. . . . Many corporations do not pay dividends but instead retain all their earnings in order to have more capital. One reason that publicly held corporations — that is, corporations in which ownership is diffuse, which may enable managers to pursue personal goals at the expense of shareholder welfare — usually do pay dividends is that it helps to discipline management by making it go outside the company for money for new ventures, thus forcing it to convince the capital markets that the ventures are likely to succeed. That reason for paying dividends has no application to a corporation like Menards in which there is an almost complete fusion of management and ownership.

The main focus of the Tax Court's decision was not on the issue of "concealed dividend" (that is, whether the company was acting in good faith in paying $17.5 million as a bonus rather than as a dividend); it was on whether Menard's compensation exceeded that of comparable CEOs in 1998 — that is, whether it was objectively excessive, and hence (in part) functionally if not intentionally a dividend rather than a bonus.

The CEO of Home Depot was paid that year only $2.8 million, though it is a much larger company than Menards; and the CEO of Lowe's, also a larger company, was paid $6.1 million. But salary is just the beginning of a meaningful comparison, because it is only one element of a compensation package. Of particular importance to this case is the amount of risk in the compensation structure. Risk in corporate compensation is significant in two respects. First, most people are risk averse, and the scholarly literature on corporate compensation suggests that risk aversion is actually an obstacle to efficient corporate management because managers tend to be more risk averse than shareholders. Shareholders can diversify the risk of a particular company by owning a diversified portfolio, but a manager tends to have most of his financial, reputational, and "specific human" capital tied up in his job. . . . So the riskier the compensation structure, other things being equal, the higher the executive's salary must be to compensate him for bearing the additional risk.

That is not a critical consideration in this case because, as we said, management and ownership in Menards are not divorced. But a second significance of risk in a compensation structure is fully applicable to this case. A risky compensation structure implies that the executive's salary is likely to vary substantially from year to year—high when the company has a good year, low when it has a bad one. Mr. Menard's *average* annual income may thus have been considerably less than $20 million—a possibility the Tax Court ignored. Had the corporation lost money in 1998, Menard's total compensation would have been only $157,500—less than the salary of a federal judge—even if the loss had not been his fault. The 5 percent bonus plan was in effect for a quarter of a century before the IRS pounced; was it just waiting for Menard to have such a great year that the IRS would have a great-looking case?

Nor did the Tax Court consider the severance packages, retirement plans, or perks of the CEOs with whom it compared Menard (although it did take account of their stock options), even though such extras can make an enormous difference to an executive's compensation. . . .

We have discussed risk; with regard to responsibilities there is incomplete information about the compensation paid other senior management of Menards besides Mr. Menard himself, and no information about the compensation paid the senior managements of Home Depot or Lowe's other than those companies' CEOs. The relevance of such information is that it might show that Menard was doing work that in other companies is delegated to staff, or conversely that staff was doing all the work and Menard was, in substance though not in form, clipping coupons. The former inference is far more likely, given the undisputed evidence of Menard's workaholic, micromanaging ways and the fact that Menards' board of directors is a tiny dependency of Mr. Menard. He does the work that in publicly held companies like Home Depot or Lowe's is done by boards that have more than two directors besides the CEO. Of course they are larger companies—Home Depot's revenues were seven times as great as Menards' in 1998—so we would expect them to have more staff. But we are given no information on how much more staff they had. . . .

The Tax Court's opinion strangely remarks that because Mr. Menard owns the company he has all the incentive he needs to work hard, without the spur of a salary. In other words, reasonable compensation for Mr. Menard might be zero. How generous of the Tax Court nevertheless to allow Menards to deduct $7.1 million from its 1998 income for salary for Menard!

The Fifth Circuit has commented sensibly on the Tax Court's belief that owners don't need or deserve salaries:

> "the Tax Court questioned whether an incentive bonus tied to company performance is needed for an employee who is also a shareholder. Apparently, the argument is that

> such an employee already has sufficient incentive to make the business successful because as a shareholder he will receive the profits of the business anyway. This argument, however, misses the economic realities of the corporate form as taxed under the internal revenue code. For compensation purposes, the shareholder-employee should be treated like all other employees. If an incentive bonus would be appropriate for a nonshareholder-employee, there is no reason why a shareholder-employee should not be allowed to participate in the same manner. In essence, the shareholder-employee is treated as two distinct individuals for tax purposes: an independent investor and an employee." . . .

We conclude that in ruling that Menard's compensation was excessive in 1998, the Tax Court committed clear error, and its decision is therefore reversed.

## *NOTES*

1. *Compensation paid by public companies.* As mentioned in *Menard*, the reasonable compensation controversy arises most frequently in connection with compensation paid by closely held corporations. Nevertheless, the level of compensation paid to employees of public corporations has also come under scrutiny, principally due to corporate governance concerns, and Congress has used the tax law as one way to address these concerns. In 1993, Congress limited the amount a public corporation may deduct for compensation paid to certain key executives to $1 million per executive per year. I.R.C. § 162(m)(1). The limit does not apply to certain remuneration payable on a commission basis and other performance-based compensation. This provision appears to have had little impact on the total compensation packages paid by public companies to their executives although some believe it has influenced the composition of those packages. For example, because stock options can be structured as performance-based compensation and therefore exempt from the limitation, the 1993 change may have encouraged that form of compensation.

In 2008, as part of the legislation to provide emergency relief for certain financial institutions, Congress limited the amount that may be deducted by certain beneficiaries of that legislation for compensation paid to key executives to $500,000 per executive per year. I.R.C. § 162(m)(5). The commission basis and performance-based exceptions are unavailable, and this limit applies even if the financial institution is not a public corporation. Legislation in 2009 made these rules applicable to a broader range of firms receiving financial assistance from the government. P.L. No. 111-5, § 7001.

2. *Golden parachute payments.* The tax law also limits the amount a corporation may deduct for "golden parachute payments," which are a form of extraordinary compensation paid to an executive upon certain changes in control of the company. When the provision applies, the executive must also pay a 20 percent excise tax on the nondeductible amount. I.R.C. §§ 280G, 4999. The 2008 relief legislation for financial institutions extends the limitation and excise tax to certain severance

payments made to key executives of the benefitted companies without regard to a change of control of the company.

3. *Tax treatment of compensatory stock options.* Compensatory stock options raise tax issues regarding the amount, timing, and character of the income to the employee and the deduction to the employer. In theory, an employee might be treated as having income when the option is first granted, when the option rights vest (even though not yet exercised), when the option is exercised, or when the employee ultimately disposes of any shares acquired as a result of the option; the amount and character of income would follow from the identification of the taxable event. In addition, the amount, timing, and character of the employer's compensation deduction might match or be different from the tax treatment of the employee.

The vast majority of compensatory stock options granted today are "nonqualified" or "nonstatutory" stock options. The tax treatment of these options is generally controlled by the rules in section 83 dealing with property transfers in connection with the performance of services. In general, assuming that a nonqualified stock option received by an employee does not have a readily ascertainable value at the time the option is granted, the employee must report ordinary income equal to the bargain element of the option when the option is exercised, and the employee's basis in the shares acquired is increased by the amount of income recognized. I.R.C. § 83(a); Reg. § 1.83-7(a). An employee may elect instead to be taxed on the value of the option at the time of the grant. I.R.C. § 83(b). Although the election accelerates the taxable event, it also may limit the employee's ordinary income exposure from the transaction because any further income is potentially taxed at preferential long-term capital gain rates. A corporation granting a nonqualified stock option is generally allowed an ordinary deduction in the same amount and at the same time as the employee reports ordinary income. I.R.C. § 83(h). If the nonqualified stock option is "in-the-money" at the time of the grant (i.e., the option's exercise price is less than the fair market value of the stock) and no section 83(b) election is made, then the taxable event occurs when the option vests (even though not yet exercised) and the employee must pay an additional 20 percent penalty tax at that time. I.R.C. § 409A(a)(1); Reg. § 1.409A-1(b)(5)(i)(A) (safe harbor from section 409A only applies to options not in-the-money).

"Qualified" or "statutory" stock options, formally called "incentive stock options," are taxed under the rules of sections 421 and 422. Assuming that various corporate governance and holding period conditions are satisfied, taxation of the employee's income from an incentive stock option is deferred for regular tax purposes until the employee disposes of the shares acquired through the option, at which time all of the income potentially qualifies as long-term capital gain. The trade-off for this favorable tax treatment of the employee is to deny the employer any tax deduction for the compensatory element of an incentive stock option. The significance of the trade-off depends upon the relative tax situations of the employer and employee. In addition, the favorable treatment of the employee does not apply for AMT purposes. Upon exercise of an incentive stock option, the bargain element of the option, meaning any excess of the fair market value of the stock over the exercise price of the option, must be included in the employee's AMT base, and the employee's basis in the shares acquired by exercise of the option is, for AMT purposes, increased by the amount of such income. I.R.C. § 56(b)(3). There is an annual limit ($100,000) on the amount of stock that may be granted to a given individual pursuant to an incentive stock option. Also, qualifying incentive stock options must not be in-the-money when granted.

4. *Financial accounting treatment of stock options.* Due to a recent change in financial accounting standards, public corporations are now generally required to reduce their earnings for financial accounting purposes by the value of compensatory stock options (determined using an option-pricing model) at the time the options are granted. This treatment applies regardless of whether the option is "qualified" or "nonqualified" or whether the employee has made the section 83(b) election, all of which are significant only for tax purposes. Previously, corporations were generally not required to reduce their earnings for financial accounting purposes by the compensatory element of stock options even where the corporation claimed a tax deduction for that amount. This significant book-tax discrepancy allowed corporations to report very large amounts of financial earnings while paying little, if anything, in federal income taxes. Corporations that reported their financial earnings in this manner were, however, required to calculate and report their tax expense for financial accounting purposes as if they had not received the tax deduction.

The revised financial accounting treatment of stock options is closer to, but not the same as, their tax treatment. As previously noted, in most cases, companies obtain a tax deduction at the time an option is exercised, not when it is granted, and the amount of the deduction may be significantly different from the charge to financial earnings. If book-tax conformity were achieved by limiting the tax deduction to the accounting charge and allowing both at the time of the grant, it would be necessary to decide whether to tax the employee also on the same amount and at the same time. Alternatively, it would be possible to achieve book-tax conformity by matching the accounting charge to the tax deduction and requiring both to occur at the time of exercise. Under that approach, the financial accounting treatment of stock option compensation would not match the treatment of cash or restricted stock compensation (both of which are taken into account at grant).

5. *Some disguised dividend patterns.* Because the tax treatment of dividends is generally undesirable — the payment is not deductible by the corporation even though receipt of a dividend is includible in income (although generally taxed in a preferential way) — it is common for taxpayers to try to disguise their dividend payments as something else. One strategy is to substitute for dividends a form of payment that is deductible by the corporation, such as the compensation used in *Menard*, or rents, royalties, or interest. The possible substitution of interest for dividends is discussed further in the next section. Another strategy is to use a nondeductible form of payment that is, however, excluded from the income of the recipient, such as a purported loan or repayment of a loan by a corporation to a shareholder. Taxpayers may also attempt to transfer corporate assets to shareholders for a bargain price or transfer shareholder assets to a corporation at a

premium price. The common characteristic of a disguised dividend is a corporate transfer of money or other property to or for the benefit of a shareholder, but only if there is no genuine expectation of repayment and the transfer is made with respect to the corporation's stock.

6. *Effect of preferential dividend tax rate.* As explained at the outset in *Menard,* the current-law preferential tax rate for dividends has changed the tax advantage of a corporation paying compensation rather than dividends to its shareholder-employees. Indeed, very small C corporations whose income is taxed at less than a 35 percent rate may find it advantageous to distribute dividends rather than to pay compensation to shareholder-employees. This is particularly true if the employment tax effects of compensation are taken into account. The following table compares a compensation payment with a dividend under the assumptions that the corporate income tax rate is 15 percent, the shareholder-employee's ordinary income tax bracket is 35 percent, the dividend tax rate is 15 percent, and the corporation and shareholder both must pay a 7.65 percent FICA tax on any compensation paid to the employee. As the table indicates, a closely held C corporation in this situation would prefer to make unreasonably small (or no) compensation payments to its shareholder-employees. Chapter two described why S corporations generally have the same incentive. The different taxpayer incentives mean that "reasonable allowance" in section 162(a)(1) should be interpreted as placing both a *limit* and a *floor* on the amount of deductible compensation. In the case of S corporations, section 1366(e) provides additional authority.

**Compensation vs. Dividend**

| | *compensation* | *dividend* |
|---|---|---|
| 1. corporate pre-tax earnings | $1,000.00 | $1,000.00 |
| 2. corporate deduction | 1,000.00 | 0.00 |
| 3. corporate taxable income ((1) – (2)) | 0.00 | 1,000.00 |
| 4. corporate income tax (15% × (3)) | 0.00 | 150.00 |
| 5. corporate FICA tax (7.65% × (6)) | 71.06 | 0.00 |
| 6. compensation ((1) – (5))/dividend ((1) – (4)) to shareholder | 928.94 | 850.00 |
| 7. shareholder income tax (compensation (35% × (6)), dividend (15% × (6))) | 325.13 | 127.50 |
| 8. shareholder FICA tax (7.65% × (6)) | 71.06 | 0.00 |
| 9. net shareholder proceeds ((6) – (7) – (8)) | $532.75 | $722.50 |

## b. Capital Structure

Because interest is generally deductible, profits earned on corporate debt capital are taxed at the corporate level only to the extent the profits exceed the interest cost. In contrast, because dividends are not deductible, profits earned on equity capital are fully taxed at the corporate level. Thus, the capital structure of a corporation plays an important role in determining the size of the corporate income tax base. As previously described, the use of debt or equity and the receipt of a financial return in the form of interest, dividends, or capital gain also have an important effect on the taxation of the owners of the firm.

The tax law has had great difficulty differentiating between debt and equity. In 1969, Congress authorized the Treasury to develop regulations in this area to consider (among other factors): (1) the existence of a written unconditional promise to pay on demand or on a specified date a sum certain in money at a fixed rate of interest, (2) whether the instrument is subordinated to or has preference over any debt of the corporation, (3) the issuer's debt to equity ratio, (4) whether the instrument is convertible into stock, and (5) the relationship between holdings of the issuer's stock and holdings of the instrument in question. See I.R.C. § 385(a) and (b). In response, Treasury issued three drafts of regulations attempting to distinguish debt from equity. The task of devising workable rules to make this distinction, however, proved elusive, and Treasury ultimately withdrew all of the regulations.

In the absence of regulations, taxpayers and the IRS generally look to judicial opinions and other authorities to determine whether an instrument will be treated as debt or equity for tax purposes. An example of judicial guidance is the Third Circuit's opinion in Fin Hay Realty Co. v. U.S., 398 F.2d 694, 696-97 (3d Cir. 1968), where the court identified the following possible factors:

> (1) the intent of the parties; (2) the identity between creditors and shareholders; (3) the extent of participation in management by the holder of the instrument; (4) the ability of the corporation to obtain funds from outside sources; (5) the "thinness" of the capital structure in relation to debt; (6) the risk involved; (7) the formal indicia of the arrangement; (8) the relative position of the obligees as to other creditors regarding the payment of interest and principal; (9) the voting power of the holder of the instrument; (10) the provision of a fixed rate of interest; (11) a contingency on the obligation to repay; (12) the source of the interest payments; (13) the presence or absence of a fixed maturity date; (14) a provision for redemption by the corporation; (15) a provision for redemption at the option of the holder; and (16) the timing of the advance with reference to the organization of the corporation. . . .

The court, however, cautioned that:

> neither any single criterion nor any series of criteria can provide a conclusive answer in the kaleidoscopic circumstances which individual cases present. . . .
>
> The various factors which have been identified in the cases are only aids in answering the ultimate question whether the investment, analyzed in terms of its economic reality, constitutes risk capital entirely subject to the fortunes of the corporate venture or represents a strict debtor-creditor relationship. Since there is often an element of risk in a loan, just as there is an element of risk in an equity interest, the conflicting elements do not end at a clear line in all cases. . . .

Thus, the determination is ultimately based on all of the facts and circumstances.

There have been a number of reform proposals to align more closely the tax treatment of debt and equity (and thus reduce or eliminate the importance of the proper classification). One set of proposals, discussed in part C of this chapter, involves integrating the corporate income tax system and thereby removing the possibility that some corporate-source income is taxed more than once. In this way, the tax difference between corporate debt and equity would be much reduced since income from both types of capital would generally bear only a single level of tax. The preferential rate provided in 2003 to the dividend income and long-term capital gain of individuals was a step towards this type of reform, although the capital gain preference (which is not limited to gain from investments in corporate stock) extends beyond that necessary to address the corporate double tax. Moreover, providing a tax preference for dividends still allows taxpayers to choose whether their share of corporate-source income should be subject to the corporate or investor tax rate.

Other proposals move in the opposite direction and would limit the tax advantages of debt financing. In other words, these proposals view the debt-equity problem as taxing corporate debt capital too lightly rather than corporate equity capital too heavily. These proposals tend to arise during periods when Congress perceives debt financing as causing a larger distortion, such as encouraging corporate acquisition activity or exposing corporations to excessive bankruptcy risk through overleveraging. The following excerpt, prepared during one such period, summarizes options for treating debt and equity more uniformly; the financial crisis of 2008 may herald the beginning of another such period.

> [T]he tax treatment of debt could be made less favorable by . . . limiting the deduction for interest on indebtedness. Possible limitations include the following: disallowing a flat percentage of all interest deductions; limiting the deduction for interest on debt in excess of a specific rate of return; limiting interest deductions based on inflation (interest indexing); disallowing interest deductions in excess of a specified percentage of income; disallowing corporate interest deductions in transactions that reduce corporate equity; and denying interest deductions in specified situations, such as acquisitions involving high risk, acquisitions involving borrowing against untaxed appreciation, or hostile acquisitions. . . .
>
> Proposals to more nearly conform the tax treatment of debt and equity by limiting interest deductions have been based on the notion that certain types of debt with high interest rates or equity features should be treated, in whole or in part, as equity. Other proposals have been based on the concept that debt issued for certain purposes (such as certain takeovers) does not serve a worthy public purpose and should be discouraged by disallowing an interest deduction. Others, such as indexing, have been based on the idea of more properly measuring economic income. Many of the proposals to limit interest deductions are subject to criticism as resulting in an improper measurement of income. Also, proposals to limit interest deductions have been criticized as causing a bias in favor of foreign persons who may deduct interest in computing income in their home country. Proposals to limit interest deductions also involve difficult issues relating to transitional rules and effective dates. . . . [Staff of Joint Committee on Taxation, Federal Income Tax Aspects of Corporate Financial Structures (1989), pp. 3-4.]

**Problem 3-1:** Study the following two hypotheticals involving Z corporation. Which alternative is the Board of Directors of the corporation more likely to adopt? In your view, does the choice raise tax issues that need to be addressed either legislatively or administratively? If so, try to fashion an appropriate solution.

Z has annual earnings (before taxes) of $1,500,000. It pays corporate taxes at a flat 33 percent rate. There are 100,000 shares outstanding of Z, which has almost no debt on its balance sheet.

*Alternative #1*: Inventor has been studying Z's line of business for some time and is convinced that, with a little bit of retooling and some new capital, Z can easily expand into a related line of business and improve its profitability. According to Inventor, Z should issue $6,000,000 in market-rate 12 percent bonds and use the new capital to expand into the related business. Inventor anticipates that the new capital will yield a 20 percent rate of profit (prior to taxes and return to investors), or an additional $1,200,000 in annual earnings. The Board prepares the following estimated annual income flow of the corporation before and after Inventor's plan to reveal an estimated $3.20 increase in earnings per share if the plan works as expected:

| *Income flow* | *Before* | *After* |
|---|---|---|
| Shareholders | $1,000,000 | $1,320,000 |
| Bondholders | 0 | 720,000 |
| Corp. income taxes | 500,000 | 660,000 |
| Total annual earnings | $1,500,000 | $2,700,000 |
| Total shares outstanding | 100,000 | 100,000 |
| Earnings per share | $10.00 | $13.20 |

*Alternative #2*[1]: Assume, in the alternative, that Investment Banker (IB) has been studying Z's balance sheet and has also developed a plan to boost its earnings per share. Unlike Inventor, however, IB's idea does not involve any change or expansion to Z's business. Pursuant to IB's plan, the corporation should issue $6,000,000 in market-rate 12 percent bonds and use the proceeds to buy back about 2/3 of the corporation's shares at a price of $90/share, an almost 30 percent premium over its current fair market value. The Board prepares the following estimated annual income flow of the corporation before and after IB's plan to reveal an estimated $5.29 increase in earnings per share:

1. This example is taken from American Law Institute, Tax Advisory Group Draft No. 18 (Nov. 3, 1988).

| *Income flow* | *Before* | *After* |
|---|---|---|
| Redeeming shareholders | $660,000 | 0 |
| Continuing shareholders | 340,000 | 520,000 |
| Bondholders | 0 | 720,000 |
| Corp. income taxes | 500,000 | 260,000 |
| Total annual earnings | $1,500,000 | $1,500,000 |
| Total shares outstanding | 100,000 | 34,000 |
| Earnings per share | $10.00 | $15.29 |

---

Congress has enacted a number of provisions restricting the availability of the interest deduction to corporate taxpayers in particular circumstances. In certain cases, the interest deduction is limited because the purported debt instrument too closely resembles equity. See I.R.C. §§ 163(*l*) (debt whose principal is repayable in stock of the issuer); 163(e)(5) and (i) (debt with yields significantly higher than risk-free borrowing rate); 279(a) and (b) (subordinated and convertible acquisition debt issued by corporation with debt-equity ratio in excess of threshold level). In other cases, the disallowed interest relates to debt that has been used to replace corporate equity. See I.R.C. § 172(b)(1)(E) and (h) (debt incurred in certain corporate equity reduction transactions). In still other circumstances, the interest deduction is restricted because it provides an arbitrage-type benefit after taking into account the preferential taxation of the return from the debt-financed investment. See I.R.C. §§ 163(j) (limiting deduction of interest paid to related persons who do not pay tax on the interest); 264 (denying interest on debt incurred or continued to purchase or carry tax-preferred life insurance and related contracts). In addition, Congress has authorized the Treasury Department to issue regulations adopting a bifurcated approach in the debt-equity area by treating a given instrument as part-debt and part-stock, and also made the issuer's characterization of an instrument at the time of its issue (as either stock or debt) generally binding on the issuer and all holders of the instrument. In general, a holder may deviate from that characterization for tax purposes only if it provides notice of the deviation. See I.R.C. § 385(a) and (c).

Another proposal would deny a deduction for the portion of interest that merely compensates the lender for the effect of inflation during the period of the loan. The theory is that the inflation component of interest represents the amount necessary to keep the lender whole after inflation is taken into account. Under this view, the inflation component is simply repayment of principal and thus should be nondeductible by the borrower and excludible by the lender. Because of the different tax situations of borrowers and lenders, the proposal would be expected to raise revenue.

Some debt-equity issues arise not because of the potentially ambiguous terms of the instrument or the circumstances of its issue but because of "creative" planning designed to make equity look like debt (or vice-versa). The following two IRS notices illustrate such planning. Notice 97-21 describes an attempt to disguise an interest that is economically equivalent to debt as equity. To understand the scheme, you should know that a real estate investment trust (REIT) is entitled to deduct any dividends paid to its owners. The deduction prevents the potential double taxation of profits earned through a REIT. The IRS has since promulgated regulations to deny the attempted tax advantage described in Notice 97-21. See Reg. § 1.7701(*l*)-3.

## Notice 97-21

1997-1 C.B. 407

... [C]ertain persons are engaging in multiple-party financing transactions to avoid taxes imposed by the Internal Revenue Code. These transactions are designed to allow a person (the "sponsor") to avoid tax on substantial amounts of income (or to shelter substantial amounts of other income) by using a conduit entity whose income tax treatment artificially allocates the conduit entity's income to participants that are not subject to federal income tax. ... An example of these transactions is as follows:

> A corporate sponsor forms a real estate investment trust or a foreign corporation (the "Company"). The Company issues two classes of stock. The corporate sponsor holds substantially all of the common stock of the Company. The other class (the "fast-pay preferred stock") is held by persons that are not subject to federal income tax (the "exempt participants"). The fast-pay preferred stock has limited voting rights and provides for preferred "dividends" equal to 13 percent of the stock's issue price each year for 10 years.
>
> The Company holds income-producing assets (such as one or more mortgage loans) that are the obligations of or guaranteed by the corporate sponsor or that are guaranteed by a federal agency. At all times during the first 10 years after the fast-pay preferred stock is issued, the Company is required to invest in assets that will produce income, and cash flows, at least equal to 101 percent of the dividends payable on the fast-pay preferred stock.
>
> During the first 10 years, the Company may also make distributions on its common stock. It is not, however, permitted to distribute more than 105 percent of its income in any year. Accordingly, it is not permitted to make any distributions representing a meaningful return of initial investment to the holders of the common stock during the first 10 years.
>
> In year 11, and thereafter, the fast-pay preferred stock provides for distributions in each year of 1 percent of its original issue price. As a result, after the first 10 years, the fair market value of the fast-pay preferred stock is substantially less than the amount for which the exempt participants purchased it.
>
> Beginning in year 11, the Company may be merged into another corporation without the separate approval of the exempt participants provided that the exempt participants receive a formula payment equal to the present value of the annual 1-percent dividend payments on the fast-pay preferred stock (computed using a discount rate of 10 percent). Otherwise the fast-pay preferred stock cannot be called by the Company.

As illustrated by this example, the fast-pay preferred stock performs economically much like a 10-year, self-amortizing debt instrument. That is, payments on the fast-pay preferred stock reflect in part recoveries of the amount originally invested by the exempt participants and in part a market yield on the unamortized portion of the original investment. The economic self-amortization of the fast-pay preferred stock is conceptually inconsistent with characterizing the full amount of each payment as a "dividend" (and thus as income on an investment). [This treatment of the full amount of the payment as a dividend causes substantially all the Company's income to be allocated to the exempt participants. If the fast-pay preferred stock were treated as a self-amortizing debt instrument, this result would not follow. — EDS.]

At the end of 10 years, the Company's obligation to make distributions on the fast-pay preferred stock will have virtually ceased, and substantially all of the net value of the Company will be represented by its common stock. Because only the current income of the Company will have been distributed during the first 10 years, the value of the Company's assets is unlikely to have declined significantly. Accordingly, the sponsor's investment in the Company economically performs like a zero-coupon investment, substantially increasing in value as the exempt participants' interest in the Company declines. If the Company makes the formula payment to the exempt participants after the initial 10-year period, the Company may be merged into or consolidated with a corporate sponsor or its affiliate. In the event of a merger, the corporate sponsor expects to receive substantially all of the Company's assets with the Company's high basis and to avoid recognizing any gain.

Thus, in the example, the corporate sponsor's expectation in investing in the Company is that it will realize a predictable economic benefit at the end of the 10-year period without ever incurring any tax liability for that benefit. Alternatively, if the principal asset of the Company is a debt instrument or other obligation issued by the sponsor, the sponsor could be viewed as attempting to use deductions from that debt instrument or obligation to shelter income, without ever having to recognize its share of the income that corresponds to those deductions. These expectations result from the parties' treatment of the full amount of the payments to the exempt participants as dividends. This treatment causes substantially all of the Company's income to be allocated to the exempt participants, even though a significant portion of that income inures economically to the sponsor.

## Notice 94-48

1994-1 C.B. 357

The Internal Revenue Service is aware of proposed transactions designed to provide corporations with significant tax advantages in satisfying their equity capital requirements. Although the details may vary, these transactions are intended to give the issuing corporations the tax benefits of issuing debt even though the corporations actually issue stock. In addition, the instruments are intended to be treated as equity for regulatory, rating agency, or financial accounting purposes.

One example involves X, a corporation, creating PRS, a partnership, to allow X to achieve its financing objectives. X contributes $20x to PRS in return for a limited partnership interest. GP, the general partner of PRS, contributes $5x to PRS. X or GP also may contribute additional capital to PRS. PRS then issues debt instruments (notes) to third-party investors for $80x. Of the $105x in capital raised by PRS, $100x is used to purchase newly issued preferred stock of X.

X intends to take the position that (a) the dividends it pays to PRS are not income to the extent that they are allocable to X because X, in effect, is paying a dividend to itself, and (b) it is entitled to deduct its distributive share of interest deductions for payments on the notes.

The Service believes that the overall substance of the arrangement as to X is simply an issuance of preferred stock. Accordingly, the deduction by X of an allocable portion of PRS's interest expense on the notes without an off-setting inclusion of dividend income by X is inappropriate. To allow X an interest deduction in this situation is the economic equivalent of affording X a deduction for a part of the dividends it pays on its preferred stock.

The existence of the partnership does not justify an interest deduction by X. Depending on the facts and circumstances, at least to the extent of all or part of X's interest in PRS, PRS may not be respected as a partnership for federal income tax purposes. Instead, PRS may be considered to be a mere financing arrangement used to facilitate the issuance of the X preferred stock.

Moreover, even if X were treated as having issued its share of the notes, the notes, in substance, would be non-recourse as to X and secured solely by the X preferred stock. Depending on all the facts and circumstances, the notes would be economically equivalent to debt instruments that are convertible into X preferred stock at the option of X and, as such, could be treated as equity for federal income tax purposes. . . .

Finally, even if PRS were respected as a partnership for federal income tax purposes and X were not required to include in income its distributive share of dividends that it pays to PRS, X's distributive share of the partnership interest deductions could be disallowed as a deduction to X because they relate to income that would not be taxable to X.

Although the position taken by the Service in any particular case depends on the specific facts of that case, it is anticipated that the Service will challenge transactions of the type described in this notice. Moreover, upon examination, the Service will scrutinize carefully any transaction designed to produce interest deductions with respect to a related issuance of stock.

### c. New Financial Products

Thus far, it might appear that the debt-equity problem is essentially one of line-drawing. In other words, there is a substantive difference between debt and equity, and the very difficult task of distinguishing between them requires consideration of a multitude of factors, including the terms of the specific instrument, the circumstances of its issue (such as the issuer's debt-equity ratio), and the characteristics of the parties to the transaction. The preceding two notices might be viewed as involving tax shelter transactions designed to exploit various loopholes in the tax law but not really raising debt-equity questions.

The following excerpt, however, suggests that there may be a more fundamental problem with the tax law's treatment of debt and equity. If, under finance theory, instruments characterized as "debt" by the tax law can be replicated in certain circumstances by instruments characterized as "equity," the distinctions under current law may be indefensible as a practical matter.

## Alvin C. Warren, Jr.
## U.S. Income Taxation of New Financial Products

88 J. Publ. Econs. 899 (2004)

### Fixed-Return Instruments

Although in theory an income tax might be based on changes in the values of assets, considerations of administrability, liquidity, and political acceptability have produced a tax that is generally triggered by certain events, usually known as realization events. As illustrated by the following example, the income tax nevertheless requires taxation of income prior to receipt of cash in the case of debt with fixed returns:

> Example 1. A corporation issues a bond that will pay the holder $133 in 3 years. No interest is payable on the obligation, which is therefore known as a zero coupon bond. An investor buys the bond from the issuing corporation for $100.

The bond in Example 1 is said to have *original issue discount* (OID) because the *stated redemption price at maturity* ($133) exceeds the issue price ($100). The difference is spread over the 3 years by first determining that rate of interest, known as the yield-to-maturity, which would compound the amount invested to the stated redemption price. In our example, the yield-to-maturity is 10% because $\$100 \times (1.1)^3 = \$133$, assuming annual compounding for simplicity, as we will throughout the paper. That yield is then applied annually to the compounded value of the investment, so $10 is taxable in year 1 ($0.1 \times \$100$), $11 in year 2 ($0.1 \times \$110$), and $12 in year 3 ($0.1 \times \$121$).

The rationale for this treatment is straightforward: the asset will increase in value to a known amount, and yield-to-maturity is a financially reasonable way to distribute that increase over time. . . .

### Contingent-Return Instruments

The foregoing treatment of original issue discount is to be contrasted with the taxation of an asset on which the returns are not fixed. The purchase, for example, of corporate stock on which no dividends are paid does not produce any income tax consequences until the stock is sold or otherwise disposed of. Once again, the rationale for this result is straightforward: whether or not there will be any gain or loss on the transaction is uncertain. In the absence of annual revaluation of all assets, imposition of the income tax has had to wait until the gain or loss is realized through sale or other disposition. This wait-and-see approach applies generally to assets with contingent, rather than fixed, returns, including forward contracts and options.

Because the last two categories of contracts are particularly important in the discussion that follows, a very brief review of their characteristics and current taxation may prove helpful. A *forward contract* is an executory agreement to sell a specified asset at a currently agreed price on a certain date in the future. (A forward contract that is standardized and traded on an exchange is usually known as a future). In general, no money changes hands at the time forward contracts are written, and there are no tax consequences until gain or loss is realized on performance or disposition of the contract.

Under an *option contract*, one party has the right, but not the obligation, to buy or sell a specified asset in the future for a price fixed at the time the contract is agreed to. The right to buy is generally known as a *call option*, and the right to sell is known as a *put option*. Unlike a forward contract, the party undertaking the obligation to buy or sell, the writer of the option, typically receives a payment, generally known as a *premium*, as consideration at the time the obligation is entered into.

The purchase of an option is usually treated as a capital expenditure, and there are generally no tax consequences to either party until its exercise or disposition. If the option lapses without exercise, the option writer is treated as if he had sold the option. If a call is exercised, the writer includes the premium in the amount realized on the sale of the asset, and the holder of the call includes the premium in the cost (or *basis* in the language of the tax code). If a put is exercised, the writer reduces basis by the amount of the premium, and the holder of the put reduces amount realized by the same amount. If an option is sold prior to exercise, gain or loss is recognized, with the nature of the gain generally determined by that of the underlying asset. . . .

To recapitulate, income is taxed annually on a yield-to-maturity basis on certain financial assets with fixed returns, whereas a wait-and-see approach has traditionally been applied to assets with contingent returns. Whatever one thinks of the fairness and efficiency consequences of this dual regime, it is workable only if the two categories of assets can be distinguished.

### Financial Equivalences

Financial theory suggests that the tax law distinction between fixed and contingent return assets is not tenable, because financial equivalences sometimes permit one category of asset to be replicated using the other. We will illustrate this possibility using the well-known concept of put-call parity. . . .

Consider the following four assets: (1) a share of stock that does not pay dividends, (2) a risk-free zero coupon bond, (3) a call option to buy a share of the specified stock, and, (4) a put option to sell a share. Of these four assets, only the second, the bond, is subject to taxation under the yield-to-maturity regime applicable to fixed returns. The return on the stock, call, and put is uncertain and therefore subject to wait-and-see income taxation.

There is, however, a fundamental relationship among these four assets that allows each to be restated in terms of the others, as long as adequately competitive markets exist for each. Suppose that the *strike price* at which the put and call can be exercised is the same as the amount payable in the future under the bond, and the date at which the put and call can be exercised is the same as the date on which the bond will be paid. The put-call parity theorem states that the values of the stock (S), bond (B), call (C), and put (P) on the exercise date must satisfy the following relationship, ignoring transactions costs and credit risks:

$$S + P = B + C$$

An investor who holds both a share of stock and a put at a strike price of K will at the date of exercise have assets worth S but no less than K, because he will exercise the put if S is less than K. Similarly, an investor who holds a bond that will pay K on the exercise date and a call at a strike price of K is guaranteed the value of K on that date; if S is then greater than K, he will exercise the call to receive stock with the value of S. If the stock plus a put must equal the bond plus a call on the exercise date, the two positions must also be equal in value before that date if there are competitive markets for each contract. Otherwise, an arbitrageur would sell the more expensive position and acquire the cheaper position to obtain a riskless windfall to the extent of the difference in value.

Put-call parity suggests that a synthetic share of nondividend-paying stock can be created by purchasing a zero coupon bond and a call, while writing a put:

$$S = B + C - P$$

Similarly, a synthetic zero coupon bond can be created by purchasing a share of stock, writing a call and buying a put:

$$B = S - C + P$$

At this point, the theoretical challenge presented by put-call parity to the income tax distinction between fixed and contingent returns should be apparent. If modern financial practice will permit the creation of a synthetic share of stock, an issuing corporation could achieve interest deductibility on the bond portion of the position, even though no such deductions are available for actual shares of stock. Synthetic debt, on the other hand, would avoid application of the OID provisions, because none of the components of the synthetic position would be taxed until realization.

Indeed, taxpayers could combine opposing positions in, say, actual and synthetic debt to eliminate any financial outcomes other than the interest deduction, which could be applied to defer taxes on other income.

## *NOTES*

1. *An example.* Suppose a corporation issues for $100 a zero-coupon bond promising to pay the holder $133 in three years' time. As explained in example 1 from the Warren article, this would be the equivalent of the corporation issuing a $100 bond bearing 10 percent interest compounded annually. Assuming that an annual compounding period is used to determine the tax consequences, the holder would have interest income, and the corporation would have an interest deduction, of $10, $11, and $12, respectively, in years 1, 2, and 3. See I.R.C. §§ 1272(a)(1), 163(e)(1).

Suppose, instead, the corporation issues a synthetic zero-coupon bond. Thus, a taxpayer acquires non-dividend-paying stock of the corporation for $100. In addition, in exchange for some premium, the corporation grants to the holder a right to sell the stock back to the corporation for $133 in three years' time. Finally, also in exchange for some premium, the holder grants to the corporation a right to repurchase the stock for $133 in three years' time. As the Warren article explains, this combination of stock, a put option owned by the holder, and a call option held by the corporation, is a synthetic zero-coupon bond. Aside from a difference in the two premiums and any other transaction costs, the synthetic bond also ensures that the holder will receive $133 in three years' time in exchange for his payment of $100, or the equivalent of a 10 percent yield compounded annually, the same as the zero-coupon bond. If the stock is worth less than $133 in three years' time, the holder would exercise his put option and sell the stock back to the corporation for $133, and the corporation's call option would lapse. Conversely, if the stock is worth more than $133 in three years' time, the corporation would exercise its call option and repurchase the stock for $133 and the put option would lapse. In either case, after ignoring again any difference in premiums and other transaction costs, the holder (and the corporation) would be assured of receiving (and paying) $133 in three years' time in exchange for initially paying (and receiving) $100. Under current law, as discussed in chapter nine, the holder of the synthetic bond in certain circumstances is required to take the redemption premium ($33) into income over the three year period under the same economic accrual principles as OID. See I.R.C. § 305(c); Reg. § 1.305-5(b). No deduction is allowed, however, to the issuer (because the redemption premium is treated as a constructive distribution and not interest).

2. *Exchange-traded notes.* An illustration of the difficult tax issues raised by new financial products concerns the proper tax treatment of "exchange traded notes" ("ETNs"). ETNs are securities in which the issuer promises to make a future payment to the holder equal to the issue price (net of the issuer's fee) plus or minus a return tied to some index, such as a stock index. The promise is not "principal

protected," meaning that the holder is not assured of getting back all of his initial investment; should the index fall sufficiently during the period the security is outstanding, the holder would suffer a loss from making the investment. The investor can hold the security until maturity and be redeemed by the issuer or sell the security on an exchange that trades them.

Unlike an index mutual fund or an exchange-traded fund, the issuer of an ETN does not necessarily own shares of the companies included in the index. The ETN issuer simply uses the rise and fall of the index as the barometer to determine the amount that must be repaid to the holder. By not acquiring and maintaining the portfolio of stocks included in the index, the ETN issuer potentially saves on transaction costs and can charge lower fees than a fund that actually owns those stocks. ETN issuers can also avoid the "tracking error" that occurs when the return from the portfolio of stocks owned is slightly different from the index return. On the other hand, since an ETN is unsecured debt of the issuer, there is credit risk to the instrument not found in an index mutual fund or exchange-traded fund. This credit risk became quite real during the economic crisis beginning at the end of 2008 when the financial stability of certain issuers suddenly came into serious question.

From the holder's standpoint, an investment in an ETN bears some similarity to the purchase of the portfolio of stocks included in the index or a mutual fund holding those stocks. In both of those situations, the holder's return is generally taxed either currently (upon distribution of dividends to the holder or the mutual fund) or upon realization (sale of the underlying stock by the holder or the mutual fund or sale of the mutual fund shares). The investment also loosely resembles a bond, including possibly an OID bond whose return is taxed currently to the holder, although unlike a typical bond, an ETN offers a contingent return with no principal protection. Currently, taxpayers generally assume that "wait-and-see" tax rules apply to the entire return from an ETN. Thus, they generally defer reporting any gains or losses until the instrument is redeemed or sold, at which point the entire return may be taxed as capital gain or loss. As you might imagine, the mutual fund industry is not happy with this tax development. In part because of this brewing conflict across different financial sectors, the IRS is examining how these instruments should be taxed. See Notice 2008-2, 2008-1 C.B. 252.

**Problem 3-2:** Consider how the following two transactions might be taxed:

(a) GE issues 100 shares of common stock to a taxpayer. The stock is trading at $10/share, and the taxpayer therefore pays GE $1,000 cash. The taxpayer automatically reinvests any dividends received in additional GE stock, and after five years, sells all of the shares back to GE for their fair market value at that time.

(b) Instead of issuing stock to the taxpayer, GE agrees to pay the taxpayer the total return, in terms of dividends and change in stock value, on

100 shares of its stock over the next five years. Thus, at the end of five years, GE will pay the taxpayer an amount equal to the taxpayer's initial payment to GE, any dividends distributed on 100 shares of stock during the five years, plus (or minus) any increase (or decrease) in value of the shares during the period. In exchange for this total return, the taxpayer pays GE $1,000 cash.

### d. Earnings Accumulation

Because a shareholder of a C corporation is generally taxed on corporate income only upon a realization event, another common strategy to reduce the impact of the double tax is for a corporation to accumulate its earnings rather than to pay them out as dividends. In that way, the shareholder-level tax on the corporation's earnings can at least be delayed until the shareholder realizes any gain upon a sale of corporate stock. But the efficacy of this strategy from a tax standpoint depends upon the relationship between: (1) the tax imposed on the income of the shareholder and corporation (specified $I_s$ and $I_c$ in the following tables), (2) the shareholder and corporation pre-tax rate of return on investments (specified $R_s$ and $R_c$), and (3) the tax imposed on a current versus a future distribution ($D_{cur}$ and $D_{fut}$). As the following tables show, if the rates in each relationship are identical, then the accumulation strategy provides no advantage to taxpayers, consistent with the "new" view of dividend taxation. If the rates in one or more of the relationships are different from one another, the accumulation strategy may be either favorable or unfavorable to taxpayers.

Consider first a situation where the rates in each relationship are identical. But for the temporary nature of investor-level tax rates, current law closely resembles this case in certain circumstances. Thus, assume that all shareholders are individuals whose income is taxed at a flat rate of 35 percent (the current maximum rate for individuals), all corporations are also taxed at a flat rate of 35 percent (the tax rate for most large corporations today), and the taxable income of individuals and corporations is determined in exactly the same way (almost true today). Next, assume that a current distribution (as a dividend) is taxed at a 15 percent rate (the current maximum rate for dividends received by individuals) and a future distribution is also fully taxed at a 15 percent rate. (This last assumption may or may not be true under current law. The 15 percent tax rate on dividends and long-term capital gain is due to expire after 2012. Also, if the future distribution is taxed as a capital gain, the taxable amount is only the gain portion of the distribution.) Finally, assume that the pre-tax rate of return for investments made by shareholders and corporations alike is 10 percent. **Table 3-2** shows the result under these assumptions if a corporation alternatively distributes currently its after-tax profits to its shareholders or retains such profits for one year and then makes a distribution of all accumulated amounts.

**Table 3-2**
**Accumulation vs. Current Distribution of Corporate Profits**

($I_C = I_S = 35\%$, $R_C = R_S = 10\%$, $D_{cur} = D_{fut} = 15\%$)

| | *current distribution* | *accumulation and distribution after one year* |
|---|---|---|
| 1. corporate pre-tax earnings | $1,000.00 | $1,000.00 |
| 2. corporate income tax | 350.00 | 350.00 |
| 3. current distribution | 650.00 | |
| 4. distribution tax | 97.50 | |
| 5. net amount to shareholder or corporation ((1) – (2) – (4)) | 552.50 | 650.00 |
| 6. (5) invested for one year | 55.25 | 65.00 |
| 7. income tax on (6) | 19.34 | 22.75 |
| 8. net amount to shareholder or corporation after one year ((5) + (6) – (7)) | 588.41 | 692.25 |
| 9. distribution tax | | 103.84 |
| 10. net after tax to shareholder ((8) – (9)) | $588.41 | $588.41 |

As you can see, the accumulation strategy provides no benefit in this case. This result might seem surprising since the accumulation delays payment of the shareholder-level tax for a year. But this advantage is offset by the fact that accumulation keeps all of the corporation's earnings within the "double tax" system of subchapter C for the year. If the corporation had instead made a distribution at the beginning of the year, its earnings would have escaped the corporate tax system, but at the price of an immediate shareholder-level tax.

The three assumed relationships in **table 3-2**, however, are key to this result. Although current law in certain circumstances nearly replicates these rate relationships, this congruence has not always held in the past and may well not hold in the future.

For example, assume the same facts as in **table 3-2** except that the issue arises after 2012 when the preferential dividend and long-term capital gain rates have expired. Assume therefore that a current distribution (as a dividend) is taxed at 35 percent and a future distribution is taxed at a long-term capital gain rate of 20 percent. (Assume again in this situation and all of the others that the future distribution tax of 20 percent applies to the entire amount of the distribution and not just to the gain portion.) **Table 3-3** shows the results of the same two scenarios under this alternative set of assumptions.

Under the assumptions in **table 3-3**, the accumulation strategy provides a benefit. By imposing a lower tax on a later distribution, the law has biased the corporation's distribution policy in favor of accumulation rather than current distribution. And the longer the accumulation, the greater the advantage. Throughout almost the entire tax history of this country, the rate relationship shown in **table 3-3** favoring deferred over current distributions has been the norm, and that rate

**Table 3-3**
**Accumulation vs. Current Distribution of Corporate Profits**

($I_C = I_S = 35\%$, $R_C = R_S = 10\%$, $D_{cur} = 35\%$, $D_{fut} = 20\%$)

| | *current distribution* | *accumulation and distribution after one year* |
|---|---|---|
| 1. corporate pre-tax earnings | $1,000.00 | $1,000.00 |
| 2. corporate income tax | 350.00 | 350.00 |
| 3. current distribution | 650.00 | |
| 4. distribution tax | 227.50 | |
| 5. net amount to shareholder or corporation ((1) – (2) – (4)) | 422.50 | 650.00 |
| 6. (5) invested for one year | 42.25 | 65.00 |
| 7. income tax on (6) | 14.79 | 22.75 |
| 8. net amount to shareholder or corporation after one year ((5) + (6) – (7)) | 449.96 | 692.25 |
| 9. distribution tax | | 138.45 |
| 10. net after tax to shareholder ((8) – (9)) | $449.96 | $553.80 |

relationship may return after 2012. Hence, the law has developed various rules to prevent corporations from accumulating their earnings unreasonably and to prevent shareholders from claiming they are entitled to pay only the preferential "future" distribution tax (i.e., the long-term capital gain tax) rather than the less preferential "current" distribution tax (i.e., the dividend tax). Note that if the relationship between the two distribution taxes were reversed, with a more favorable tax imposed on current rather than future distributions, then the law would bias corporations in favor of immediate distributions and against accumulations. This arguably is what occurred immediately after the dividend tax rate was *temporarily* reduced in 2003 to 15 percent.

Over the years, the corporate and individual *income* tax rates have also not necessarily been the same and seem likely to diverge again in the future. For example, under one reform proposal, the top corporate income tax rate would be reduced to 28 percent and (partly to fund the corporate rate reduction) the top individual income tax rate would be increased to 44 percent. **Tables 3-4** and **3-5** show the effect if those were the flat rates imposed on the income of corporations and individuals. **Table 3-4** assumes that current and future distributions are taxed identically, whereas **table 3-5** assumes a distribution tax rate relationship of 35 percent for current distributions and 20 percent for future ones.

As you can see, the law favors corporate accumulations in both situations. In the situation in **table 3-4**, taxing corporate income more favorably than shareholder income allows the corporation to earn a greater after-tax return than the shareholder, assuming an equivalent pre-tax return. Thus, it is advantageous for the corporation to retain and invest its earnings as long as possible. Although the advantage of

**Table 3-4**
**Accumulation vs. Current Distribution of Corporate Profits**

($I_C$ = 28%, $I_S$ = 44%, $R_C$ = $R_S$ = 10%, $D_{cur}$ = $D_{fut}$ = 15%)

| | *current distribution* | *accumulation and distribution after one year* |
|---|---|---|
| 1. corporate pre-tax earnings | $1,000.00 | $1,000.00 |
| 2. corporate income tax | 280.00 | 280.00 |
| 3. current distribution | 720.00 | |
| 4. distribution tax | 108.00 | |
| 5. net amount to shareholder or corporation ((1) − (2) − (4)) | 612.00 | 720.00 |
| 6. (5) invested for one year | 61.20 | 72.00 |
| 7. income tax on (6) | 26.93 | 20.16 |
| 8. net amount to shareholder or corporation after one year ((5) + (6) − (7)) | 646.27 | 771.84 |
| 9. distribution tax | | 115.78 |
| 10. net after tax to shareholder ((8) − (9)) | $646.27 | $656.06 |

**Table 3-5**
**Accumulation vs. Current Distribution of Corporate Profits**

($I_C$ = 28%, $I_S$ = 44%, $R_C$ = $R_S$ = 10%, $D_{cur}$ = 35%, $D_{fut}$ = 20%)

| | *current distribution* | *accumulation and distribution after one year* |
|---|---|---|
| 1. corporate pre-tax earnings | $1,000.00 | $1,000.00 |
| 2. corporate income tax | 280.00 | 280.00 |
| 3. current distribution | 720.00 | |
| 4. distribution tax | 252.00 | |
| 5. net amount to shareholder or corporation ((1) − (2) − (4)) | 468.00 | 720.00 |
| 6. (5) invested for one year | 46.80 | 72.00 |
| 7. income tax on (6) | 20.59 | 20.16 |
| 8. net amount to shareholder or corporation after one year ((5) + (6) − (7)) | 494.21 | 771.84 |
| 9. distribution tax | | 154.37 |
| 10. net after tax to shareholder ((8) − (9)) | $494.21 | $617.47 |

accumulation in **table 3-4** looks modest, the advantage will grow the longer the accumulation. The reverse is also true — in those few instances during our tax history when corporate income has been taxed less favorably than shareholder income, there has been an advantage to current distributions over retentions. (There is also an advantage to an S election in that situation if the corporation is eligible — do you

**Table 3-6**
**S and C Corporation Comparison**

($I_C = I_S = 35\%$, $R_C = R_S = 10\%$, $D_{cur} = D_{fut} = 15\%$)

| | *C corporation* | | |
|---|---|---|---|
| | *current distribution* | *accumulation and distribution after one year* | *S corporation* |
| 1. corporate pre-tax earnings | $1,000.00 | $1,000.00 | $1,000.00 |
| 2. corporate/shareholder income tax | 350.00 | 350.00 | 350.00 |
| 3. current distribution | 650.00 | | |
| 4. distribution tax | 97.50 | | |
| 5. net amount to shareholder or corporation ((1) − (2) − (4)) | 552.50 | 650.00 | 650.00 |
| 6. (5) invested for one year | 55.25 | 65.00 | 65.00 |
| 7. income tax on (6) | 19.34 | 22.75 | 22.75 |
| 8. net amount to shareholder or corporation after one year ((5) + (6) − (7)) | 588.41 | 692.25 | 692.25 |
| 9. distribution tax | | 103.84 | |
| 10. net after tax to shareholder ((8) − (9)) | $588.41 | $588.41 | $692.25 |

understand why?) **Table 3-5** shows that if a reduced future distributions tax is added to the picture, the advantage of corporate accumulation is even greater.

Finally, examination of tax planning choices would not be complete without some consideration of subchapter S. **Table 3-6** compares the results of an investment through an S and C corporation under the assumption that the rates in each relationship are identical. Not surprisingly, the S option is preferable to either C option (current distribution or retention). The intuition should be clear—although dividends and long-term capital gain are taxed preferentially to individuals under current law, some remnant of double taxation persists under subchapter C. The use of an S corporation eliminates this possibility.

**Table 3-7** shows, however, that subchapter S is not always an advantage. This table assumes that individual income is taxed at a flat rate of 44 percent whereas corporate income is taxed at a flat rate of 28 percent, the possible reform discussed earlier. Now, despite avoiding any double tax, an S corporation produces a result inferior to either of the C options. The principal reason is evident from line 2 of **table 3-7**. The $1,000 of pre-tax corporate income bears only a 28 percent, or $280 tax, if a C corporation is used, but a 44 percent, or $440 tax, if an S corporation is employed. This situation shows the sensitivity of passthrough entity owners to possible increases in *individual* income tax rates. C corporations benefit if corporate tax rates are reduced, but owners of partnerships, LLCs, S corporations, and sole proprietors, as well as high-income wage earners, will tend to resist such a change if it is funded by an increase in individual income tax rates.

**Table 3-7**
**S and C Corporation Comparison**

($I_C$ = 28%, $I_S$ = 44%, $R_C$ = $R_S$ = 10%, $D_{cur}$ = $D_{fut}$ = 15%)

| | *C corporation* | | |
|---|---|---|---|
| | *current distribution* | *accumulation and distribution after one year* | *S corporation* |
| 1. corporate pre-tax earnings | $1,000.00 | $1,000.00 | $1,000.00 |
| 2. corporate/shareholder income tax | 280.00 | 280.00 | 440.00 |
| 3. current distribution | 720.00 | | |
| 4. distribution tax | 108.00 | | |
| 5. net amount to shareholder or corporation ((1) – (2) – (4)) | 612.00 | 720.00 | 560.00 |
| 6. (5) invested for one year | 61.20 | 72.00 | 56.00 |
| 7. income tax on (6) | 26.93 | 20.16 | 24.64 |
| 8. net amount to shareholder or corporation after one year ((5) + (6) – (7)) | 646.27 | 771.84 | 591.36 |
| 9. distribution tax | | 115.78 | |
| 10. net after tax to shareholder ((8) – (9)) | $646.27 | $656.06 | $591.36 |

## *NOTE*

*AET and PHCT.* As previously mentioned, Congress has over the years tried to counteract the potential tax bias in favor of accumulation. The two principal methods were the enactment of the accumulated earnings tax (AET) (I.R.C. §§ 531 et seq.) and the personal holding company tax (PHCT) (I.R.C. §§ 541 et seq.). When applicable, these taxes are imposed on a corporation in addition to the corporate and shareholder income taxes. Thus, they may result in a third level of taxation on corporate-source income. No corporation is subject to both the AET and PHCT at the same time.

The AET applies to corporations (other than personal holding companies) that are "formed or availed of for the purpose of" avoiding the shareholder income tax "by permitting earnings and profits to accumulate instead of being divided or distributed." I.R.C. § 532(a). The AET is 15 percent of "accumulated taxable income," which is equal to the corporation's taxable income (with adjustments) reduced by the sum of (1) dividends paid (or treated as paid) for the taxable year and (2) the accumulated earnings credit. I.R.C. §§ 531 and 535(a). As a result of the accumulated earnings credit, a corporation may accumulate up to $250,000 of earnings and profits over its life (reduced to $150,000 for certain service corporations) without paying the AET; corporations other than mere holding and investment corporations may retain additional amounts for the reasonable needs of the business, such as funding the planned construction of a new manufacturing plant. I.R.C. § 535(c). A further accumulation beyond the reasonable needs of the business is indicative of the purpose to avoid the shareholder income tax (thus triggering the AET), unless the corporation proves the contrary by the preponderance of the evidence. I.R.C. § 533(a). Most disputes and planning involving the AET focus on the reasonable needs of the business, with the statute providing special substantive and burden of proof rules in sections 534 and 537.

The PHCT targets "incorporated pocketbooks," i.e., closely held corporations that may be serving as vehicles to avoid the shareholder-level tax. Unlike the AET, application of the PHCT depends on objective tests: (1) at least 60 percent of the corporation's "adjusted ordinary gross income" for the taxable year must be "personal holding company income" and (2) at some time during the last half of the taxable year, more than 50 percent in value of the corporation's outstanding stock must have been owned, directly or indirectly, by or for not more than five individuals. I.R.C. § 542(a). The first requirement generally limits the PHCT to corporations that derive most of their income from passive investments or the provision of personal services by significant shareholders. See I.R.C. §§ 542 and 543. This is the type of income that can be easily shifted from a shareholder to a corporation if tax advantageous. The second requirement (complete with constructive stock ownership rules in section 544) limits the PHCT's application to closely held entities where such an income-shifting strategy is most likely. The PHCT is equal to 15 percent of the corporation's "undistributed personal holding company income," which is equal to the corporation's taxable income (with adjustments) reduced by dividends paid (or treated as paid) for the taxable year. I.R.C. §§ 541 and 545(a). A deficiency dividend procedure in section 547 ensures that no corporation really need pay the PHCT; instead, the corporation may actually or constructively distribute the necessary amount to its shareholders (who will then pay a dividend tax). The corporation may be liable, however, for interest and penalties. See I.R.C. § 547.

The 15 percent rate of the AET and PHCT generally parallels the tax to shareholders had the accumulated corporate income been distributed to them as a dividend. Like the preferential rate for dividends, the 15 percent rate is scheduled to expire at the end of 2012; if it expires, the rate would revert to the maximum ordinary income tax rate for individuals.

## C. Reforming the Taxation of C Corporations

This part describes several possible reforms to the taxation of C corporations. Section one considers proposals to "integrate" the corporate and shareholder taxes and tax C corporation income only once. Because the corporate tax is largely a tax on public companies, section two examines proposals to redesign the tax to take advantage of the unique characteristics of such companies, such as the existence of financial reports prepared by independent auditors and readily available market prices for the company's shares. Finally, section three considers "traditional" reform of the corporate tax by broadening the tax base and reducing the tax rate.

## 1. *Corporate Integration*

### Staff of Joint Committee on Taxation, Present Law and Background Relating to Selected Business Tax Issues (2006)

The present law structure of a separate entity level tax on corporate income has long been recognized to create a variety of economic distortions. The two levels of tax on corporate form income (entity and individual level), as compared to the single individual level tax imposed on passthrough entities (S-corps, partnerships, LLCs), create a bias against the corporate form of organization; this in turn limits investors' access to publicly traded equity investment, which may impose a particular burden to smaller investors who are less likely to have significant access to equity investments in passthrough entities. To the extent that the two levels of tax impose a higher level of tax on investment generally, the incentive to save is reduced. The resulting increase in the cost of capital needed to finance new investment will lead to lower capital formation, thereby reducing future output and productivity. An additional distortion resulting from the present law corporate income tax rules is the incentive to finance new investments from debt rather than equity on account of the deductibility of interest payments on debt but no comparable deduction for dividends paid on equity. Overreliance on debt financing can increase bankruptcy risk. Finally, there may be incentives created for the retention of earnings in the corporation, which may lead to distortions in the allocation of capital to the extent that corporations with current earnings have less favorable investment opportunities than would their shareholders. In addition, present law results in considerable complexity and tax planning as taxpayers seek to structure the most tax-favorable form of doing business and providing returns to investors.

At the same time, proposals to eliminate separate corporate and shareholder levels of taxation (referred to as "corporate integration") involve significant policy decisions and can also produce considerable complexity. Under present law, although the Code provides rules for imposing separate tax at the corporate and at the shareholder level, this does not always result in actual payment of two levels of tax. In some cases, the amounts that are distributed to shareholders may have borne less than a full tax at the corporate level due to the operation of various deductions, deferrals, or other provisions that have reduced or eliminated corporate level tax. Also, in some cases, shareholders are tax-exempt, or the rate of tax the shareholder may pay is reduced due to capital gains treatment, the lower rates for dividends of individuals, the dividends-received deduction for corporations, step-up in basis of stock at death, or other provisions. Thus, under present law, the combined individual and corporate tax rates on corporate earnings that are distributed to shareholders may not be as great as two full levels of tax, and may be less than a single full level of tax. If a decision were made to increase corporate integration, policy decisions would need to be made regarding those situations in which at least one level of tax should be collected and at which level (corporate or shareholder) it should be collected. Complexity would be involved in coordinating the tax results at the entity and individual levels.

As one example, consider a corporation whose earnings are subject to little or no tax due to tax incentives or preferences for particular types of investment or business activities. Under present law, earnings of such a corporation distributed to taxable investors, or gains of such investors from retained earnings, may still be taxed to the investors at the "second level" of tax. In considering a form of corporate integration, decisions would have be made whether to collect at least one full level of tax or whether to pass through the tax benefits to investors. If the latter decision is made, issues may still arise regarding the appropriate investors to receive the benefit and how to treat situations where shares have changed hands between the time of the tax benefited activities and the time of the distribution. Present law rules for partnerships contain elaborate rules that attempt to prevent the misallocation of certain tax benefits to partners.

As another example, consider a corporation that conducts a business activity and that has tax-exempt shareholders. Under present law, the income from the business activity is taxed at the corporate level although the tax-exempt shareholders are not taxed on dividend income or capital gain from their investment. Under present law, the single-level-of-tax regimes do collect a business income tax from business activities, even when there are tax-exempt investors. Thus, if the tax-exempt corporate shareholders of a C corporation conducting a business were instead equity owners of a partnership or of an S corporation that conducted the same business, they would be subject to unrelated business income tax on their share of partnership or S corporation income from such business, whether or not distributed. In considering a form of corporate integration, a decision would have to be made whether to continue the present law approach that the presence of tax-exempt equity investors does not exempt business income from tax. . . .

## *NOTES AND QUESTIONS*

1. *Possible reasons for the corporate tax.* Evaluate the strength of the following reasons that have been articulated to preserve a separate entity-level tax on corporate income:

a. The corporate form of business organization offers investors special benefits, including well-established corporate governance and shareholder protection rules, limited liability, easy transferability of ownership interests, a centralized management structure, and perpetual life of the entity. It also often provides investors with liquid ownership interests and wider access to capital markets. The corporate income tax is the price that must be paid for all of the benefits obtained.

b. The sole proprietorship/partnership model of taxation is appropriate where the investors actively participate in the business and share a close unity of interest with the enterprise. A separate entity-level tax is justified where those features are not present.
c. A separate entity-level tax on corporate income helps to increase the progressivity of the federal income tax.
d. The corporate tax permits revenue to be collected on the share of corporate income allocable to tax-exempt and foreign shareholders who would be exempt from paying tax on such income.
e. Whether justified initially or not, the corporate income tax presently exists and has been capitalized in share prices. Hence, adopting an integrated system would simply result in unjustified windfalls to existing shareholders.
f. The corporate income tax produces substantial revenues. Integration will result in loss of those revenues, and will have to be offset by increases in other, perhaps less popular or efficient, taxes.
g. The corporate income tax protects the individual income tax. In the absence of a corporate income tax, income earned by a corporation might not be taxable to anyone until withdrawn from the corporation and distributed to shareholders.
h. Administrative problems make integration of the corporate and individual income taxes impractical for widely held corporate entities. A two-tier tax system is the only feasible way of taxing the income of such entities.

2. *Implementation questions.* There are four principal methods of achieving integration:

a. *Passthrough*—Under this approach, all corporations would be treated as passthrough entities in the same manner as S corporations and partnerships under current law. Corporate profits would be allocated and taxed to the shareholders as the income arises.

**Example 3-1:** Assume that corporation X has $200 in profits and is owned equally by shareholder A, who is in the 30 percent tax bracket, and shareholder B, who is in the 40 percent bracket. Under the passthrough method, the $200 of X profits would be allocated equally to A and B and they would pay current taxes of $30 and $40, respectively, on their shares of corporate income.

b. *Dividend exclusion*—This method retains the separate corporate income tax. However, distributions of profits (net of the corporate tax) to shareholders would generally be excluded from the recipient's income. The current 15 percent dividend tax rate is an example of a partial dividend exclusion approach. A more comprehensive version of this method, termed the "Comprehensive Business Income Tax" (or "CBIT") by the Treasury in 1992, would extend the same treatment to corporate debt and make the approach applicable to all businesses above a certain dollar size no matter how they are organized. Thus, all business income would generally be taxed at the entity level, without any deduction for either dividends or interest payments, and investors would be exempt from paying any tax on dividends and interest received.

**Example 3-2:** Assume the same facts as in **example 3-1** except that there is a flat 35 percent corporate income tax. Under the shareholder dividend exclusion method, the corporation would pay the 35 percent tax on its $200 of profits, or $70 in corporate tax. The remaining $130 in net profits would be received by the shareholders tax-free when distributed to them.

c. *Shareholder credit*—This approach retains the separate corporate income tax but would treat it largely as a withholding tax—a prepayment by the corporation of taxes on behalf of the shareholders in the same manner as the withholding of taxes by an employer on the wages paid to its employees. Upon a subsequent distribution of profits to the shareholders, they would pay tax on the amount distributed, grossed-up to reflect the withholding tax previously paid. They would also receive, however, a refundable credit for their share of the corporate tax paid on their behalf.

**Example 3-3:** Assume the same facts as in **examples 3-1** and **3-2**, that is, a 35 percent corporate tax and A and B in the 30 and 40 percent brackets, respectively. Under the shareholder credit approach, the $200 of corporate profits would initially bear a 35 percent tax of $70. A subsequent distribution of the corporation's $130 in after-tax profits would be treated for tax purposes as a $200 distribution, $100 each to A and B, to take into account the withholding tax previously paid. (This process is known as "grossing-up" the dividend to its pre-tax amount, the same method used when wages subject to withholding are paid and taxed. The wage earner must report the gross amount of wages as income, and not just the net amount received in each paycheck after any amounts withheld, and then obtains a credit for the amount of income tax withheld.) A and B would therefore owe $30 and $40 in taxes, respectively, on the $100 dividend deemed received by each. However, they each would be entitled to a $35 credit representing their respective shares of the corporate tax previously paid on their behalf. Hence, as a result of the distribution, A would be entitled to a $5 refund from the government, and B would owe only $5 in additional tax. A's refund would resemble the refund of taxes overwithheld on wage income.

d. *Dividends-paid deduction*—Under this approach, the corporate income tax would be retained but the corporation would be entitled to a deduction equal to the amount of profits distributed to its shareholders. The shareholders would be taxed on receiving the distribution of the profits. Thus, the tax treatment of dividends would be changed to resemble the current-law treatment of interest.

**Example 3-4:** Assume the same facts as **examples 3-1, 3-2,** and **3-3**. The corporation would or would not pay tax on the $200 profits depending upon whether the profits are distributed to the shareholders. If distributed, the $200 deduction would offset the $200 in corporate income, resulting in the corporation paying no tax. The $200 distribution would be taxable to A and B, who would pay $30 and $40 in taxes, respectively. On the other hand, if none or only part of the corporation's profits is distributed, the undistributed profits would remain taxable to the corporation under this method, while any profits distributed would be taxable to A and B.

3. *How should integration be implemented?* Compare the principal integration techniques just described from the standpoint of fairness, neutrality, and simplicity. How should each treat "preference income"—that is, economic income that, due to either a timing or exclusion provision or a preferential rate or credit in the Code, escapes part or all of the regular income tax? How would tax-exempt shareholders be treated under each technique? What should be the tax consequences under each method of a sale of corporate stock?

## 2. *Providing Greater Conformity Between Book and Taxable Income*

Since the corporate tax is basically a tax on public corporations, would it be feasible and advisable to require greater conformity between a corporation's calculation of "book" income determined for financial accounting purposes and taxable income used for tax purposes?

### Staff of Joint Committee on Taxation, Present Law and Background Relating to Corporate Tax Reform (2006)

... The Financial Accounting Standards Board ("FASB") establishes and interprets the financial accounting standards which govern U.S. Generally Accepted Accounting Principles ("GAAP") and which are used by publicly traded companies in compiling their annual reports filed with the SEC. The primary purpose of financial reporting is to provide information about a company to investors and creditors. By contrast, corporations calculate their taxable income in accordance with the Code. The primary purpose of tax accounting is to measure income for the purpose of levying the Federal income tax. The tax laws also have been used as instruments of social and fiscal policy. The Code generally requires that a corporation's taxable year and overall method of accounting conform to those used for financial reporting purposes. However, many specific differences are permitted (and, in some cases, required) between financial accounting and tax accounting.

### Common Book-Tax Differences

Many book-tax differences are caused by the timing of income or expense recognition under the two systems. Timing differences are often referred to as "temporary" differences because, over time, the total income and expense recognition with respect to these items will be the same under the two systems. For example, expenses are generally accrued under GAAP if they are probable and their amount can be reasonably estimated; in contrast, expenses generally are not deductible for tax purposes until all events have occurred which determine the fact of liability and the amount of the liability can be determined with reasonable accuracy. These general principles often result in the recognition of accrued expenses in earlier years for GAAP purposes than for tax purposes; however, eventually the same amount of expenses will be reported under both systems.

The treatment of capital costs is another prominent temporary difference; accelerated depreciation and expensing for small businesses generally result in deductions for capital costs being reflected in taxable income earlier than in book income. Other examples include bad debts, an estimate of which must be accrued for book purposes while no tax deduction is permitted until an account is actually written off, and nonqualified deferred compensation expenses, which are accrued as the employee earns them for book purposes but generally are not deductible for tax purposes until paid.

In addition to the temporary differences caused by the timing of income and expense recognition, some book-tax differences are caused by the inclusion of an item of income or expense for one system but not the other. These are referred to as "permanent differences." Permanent differences include the interest on tax-exempt bonds, nondeductible meals and entertainment expenses, fines and penalties, and compensation in excess of tax deductible limits, each of which is taken into account as income or expense in determining financial accounting income but not taxable income.

Book income and taxable income may also permanently differ as a result of the rules governing consolidated filing of financial reports and tax returns by related corporations. For tax purposes, only domestic subchapter C corporations owned at least 80 percent (determined by both voting power and value) by a parent corporation may be included in the parent corporation's consolidated filing. Financial accounting requires consolidation of subsidiaries in which the parent company has direct or indirect financial control, regardless of whether the subsidiaries are domestic corporations. Thus, consolidated financial statements generally include the income of foreign subsidiaries and controlled subsidiaries owned less than 80 percent by the parent. These entities are not included in the parent's consolidated tax return.

Some book-tax differences are the result of differing classification of balance sheet entries for book and tax purposes. For example, a financial instrument may be classified as either debt or equity for one system, with the opposite treatment under the other system. In such a case, payments on the instrument would be treated differently (for example, as interest payments or as dividend payments) in the calculation of book income and taxable income.

### Reporting of Book-Tax Differences to the IRS

Effective for tax years ending on or after December 31, 2004, the IRS requires corporations with total assets in excess of $10 million to file Schedule M-3, a detailed reconciliation between net income per financial statements and taxable income. The level of detail required by schedule M-3 is significantly greater than that required by Schedule M-1, which was required for years prior to the effective date of Schedule M-3. Treasury officials have suggested that the more detailed disclosure will help IRS auditors determine which book-tax differences deserve the most focus and also will have a deterrent effect on aggressive tax positions. . . .

### Fundamental Principles Creating Book-Tax Differences under Present Law

Book income and taxable income differ, in part, because of the different fundamental purposes they serve. The primary purpose of financial reporting is to provide information about a company to investors and creditors. Accordingly, the system of financial reporting values accuracy and conservatism. The system is tolerant of judgment and estimates in some cases, even though they might differ somewhat from one practitioner to the next, in an effort to present the most accurate picture of a company's financial position and income. [2]

The primary purpose of tax accounting is to measure income for the purpose of levying the income tax. The system favors objectivity, administrability, and consistency among taxpayers. For this reason, the use of judgment and estimates is generally avoided. The tax laws are also used as a fiscal and social policy tool, creating incentives for certain taxpayer behaviors which the Congress wishes to encourage. Such incentives, while serving what are considered to be important policy objectives, generally create deviations between book income and taxable income.

These differences of purpose between financial accounting and tax accounting were noted by Justice Blackmun in Thor Power Tool Company v. Comm'r [439 U.S. 522, 542-44 (1970)]:

> The presumption petitioner postulates is insupportable in light of the vastly different objectives that financial and tax accounting have. The primary goal of financial accounting is to provide useful information to management, shareholders, creditors,

2. It is thought that the judgment of a practitioner who is intimately familiar with a company's financial circumstances, even though it may not be exactly the same as another practitioner, may present a more accurate reflection of those circumstances than would the application of an objective rule.

and others properly interested; the major responsibility of the accountant is to protect these parties from being misled. The primary goal of the income tax system, in contrast, is the equitable collection of revenue; the major responsibility of the Internal Revenue Service is to protect the public fisc. Consistently with its goals and responsibilities, financial accounting has as its foundation the principle of conservatism, with its corollary that "possible errors in measurement [should] be in the direction of understatement rather than overstatement of net income and net assets." In view of the Treasury's markedly different goals and responsibilities understatement of income is not destined to be its guiding light. Given this diversity, even contrariety, of objectives, any presumptive equivalency between tax and financial accounting would be unacceptable.

This difference in objectives is mirrored in numerous differences of treatment. Where the tax law requires that a deduction be deferred until "all the events" have occurred that will make it fixed and certain, U.S. v. Anderson, 269 U.S. 422, 441 (1926), accounting principles typically require that a liability be accrued as soon as it can reasonably be estimated. Conversely, where the tax law requires that income be recognized currently under "claim of right," "ability to pay," and "control" rationales, accounting principles may defer accrual until a later year so that revenues and expenses may be better matched. Financial accounting, in short, is hospitable to estimates, probabilities, and reasonable certainties; the tax law, with its mandate to preserve the revenue, can give no quarter to uncertainty. This is as it should be. Reasonable estimates may be useful, even essential, in giving shareholders and creditors an accurate picture of a firm's overall financial health; but the accountant's conservatism cannot bind the Commissioner in his efforts to collect taxes. . . .

Finally, a presumptive equivalency between tax and financial accounting would create insurmountable difficulties of tax administration. Accountants long have recognized that "generally accepted accounting principles" are far from being a canonical set of rules that will ensure identical accounting treatment of identical transactions. "Generally accepted accounting principles," rather, tolerate a range of "reasonable" treatments, leaving the choice among alternatives to management. Such, indeed, is precisely the case here. Variances of this sort may be tolerable in financial reporting, but they are questionable in a tax system designed to ensure as far as possible that similarly situated taxpayers pay the same tax. If management's election among "acceptable" options were dispositive for tax purposes, a firm, indeed, could decide unilaterally—within limits dictated only by its accountants—the tax it wished to pay. Such unilateral decisions would not just make the Code inequitable; they would make it unenforceable.

### Discussion of Issues Related to Book-Tax Conformity

Reform proposals seeking to increase conformity between book and tax accounting may take various forms, including complete conformity, partial conformity, or the requirement that a corporation employ a certain book accounting method as a condition of employing that method for tax purposes.

One potential feature of these proposals which may be attractive is the creation of a "healthy tension" between a company's desire to have high book income and its desire to have low taxable income. Assuming this tension exists under any given proposal, management will be constrained in taking aggressive positions for either book or tax purposes, because such positions by definition will either cost the company additional tax dollars (in the case of aggressive book positions) or result in diminished book income (in the case of aggressive tax positions). In addition, the greater flexibility of the GAAP rules in allowing judgment and estimates might be deemed acceptable for the tax system because the tension serves to keep judgment calls balanced between potential overstatement and understatement of income. It has been suggested that book-tax conformity could be an effective tool in discouraging the use of corporate tax shelters. In 1999, a Treasury department report stated that eliminating the book-tax disparity would "significantly limit the allure and benefit of corporate tax shelters to public corporations." The staff of the Joint Committee on Taxation, in its report on the investigation of Enron Corporation and related entities, noted that the difference between tax and financial accounting created an incentive for the company to engage in such transactions.

In addition, book-tax conformity proposals may represent simplification and reduce compliance costs since the appropriate treatment of conformed items of income and loss would have to be determined only once, rather than two or more times (including potentially for the alternative minimum tax) under the current system.

Opponents of conformity proposals may argue that the differing fundamental principles on which the book and tax accounting systems are based, as discussed above, offer sufficient reason to maintain the status quo. Furthermore, the benefits of conformity may be limited by the existence of many potential circumstances under which the healthy tension does not exist because the company is not motivated to report higher book income. In these cases, companies may instead use the relative flexibility of GAAP rules to minimize book (and therefore taxable) income with no negative consequences.

One potential category of corporations not motivated to maximize financial accounting profits may be corporations which are not publicly traded and which do not rely on financial statements for borrowing purposes. In addition, some publicly traded corporations may not be motivated to maximize profits in particularly profitable years because they perceive steady earnings growth over a period of years as more valued by investors than a pattern of earnings which peaks and then falls. Still other public companies may view investor behavior as not driven by financial accounting net income. Because the primary purpose of GAAP is to convey information, a company's net income number may be less important than the overall package of information conveyed. In a book-tax conformity environment, corporations that choose accounting methods which minimize book and taxable income would be free to provide to investors supplemental information such as the amount by which net income would be higher if the alternative method were chosen. In some industries, even this may be seen as unnecessary because investors may rely more on other financial data (such as gross revenue) rather than net income.

On the other side of the healthy tension, proponents of book-tax conformity may see the desire to keep taxable income lower as moderating aggressive behavior in financial accounting. However, it should be noted that companies with large tax loss carryforwards may have little or no incentive to minimize current-year taxable income, freeing them to take aggressive accounting positions.

The consideration of book-tax conformity proposals requires judgments regarding the role of fiscal and social policy in the Federal tax law. Generally, economic and social incentives enacted by Congress in the Code result in book-tax differences because such policies represent departures from the GAAP goal of calculating income in the most accurate way for investors. Accordingly, whichever tax incentives remain untouched by a book-tax conformity proposal will necessarily be outside the scope of the proposal or will otherwise constitute an exception to the proposal.

A related consideration is the question of who would promulgate the rules governing calculation of a conformed book and taxable income. Proposals which levy a tax on financial accounting income, determined under GAAP, could be criticized for placing the determination of Federal revenues in the hands of FASB. Alternatively, proposals which rely on the Congress to set out new accounting standards to be used for both financial accounting and tax purposes would contradict decades of practice in the accounting and auditing fields, as sanctioned by the Securities and Exchange Commission.

## *NOTES*

1. *Book income adjustment.* In 1986, Congress enacted a book income adjustment that generally increased the corporate minimum tax base by one-half of the excess of book income over corporate minimum taxable income (determined without such adjustment). The goal was to increase conformity in the measurement of income used for book and tax purposes and reduce the likelihood that corporations reporting financial profits nevertheless pay little or no corporate tax. This adjustment proved controversial and was replaced after three years by a different adjustment based on the "adjusted current earnings" of the corporation, an amount not tied to financial reporting amounts. I.R.C. § 56(g).

2. *LIFO conformity.* As its name suggests, the last-in, first-out (LIFO) inventory accounting method allows taxpayers to compute their inventory costs based on the assumption that their most recently acquired goods are the first items sold. If the cost of goods increases over time, this approach permits taxpayers to defer reporting taxable income. A condition for using this method for tax purposes is its use for financial reporting purposes. I.R.C. § 472(c).

With the increasing amounts of cross-border investment by U.S. companies, the FASB is considering a proposal to replace U.S. GAAP rules with a set of international accounting standards known as the International Financial Reporting Standards, or "IFRS." Some members of the business community also support this possible change as a way to obtain somewhat more relaxed and flexible financial reporting rules. The LIFO conformity rule may play an important role in determining the fate of this policy change since the use of LIFO is not acceptable under IFRS. Thus, companies preparing their financial statements in accordance with IFRS would potentially face a large tax increase from loss of the ability to use the LIFO method for tax purposes. Such companies would have to report, generally over a four-year period, the accumulated amount of income deferred by LIFO, estimated to be about $90 billion for public firms as of 2007. The hardest hit firms would be those in the oil and gas industry and certain manufacturing sectors. No doubt, if IFRS is adopted without any modification to permit the continued use of LIFO for financial reporting purposes, there would be a strong push to repeal the LIFO conformity rule. Alternatively, as recommended by the Obama Administration in 2011, Congress might explicitly end use of the LIFO method for tax purposes, allowing the revenue increase to be counted for budget purposes.

3. *Increased public disclosures.* The new Schedule M-3 described in the JCT excerpt is an example of a disclosure-based solution to the problem of book-tax discrepancies. Some believe that the new schedule will provide the IRS with an improved roadmap for identifying questionable corporate tax return positions. Other disclosure-based proposals include public dissemination of corporate tax returns (or summaries of their key aspects), required inclusion of relevant tax return information in financial reports, and mandatory disclosure to the IRS of "uncertain tax positions" for which the taxpayer recorded a reserve for financial accounting purposes (see chapter four).

4. *A "change in market value" and "market capitalization" tax.* Two other corporate tax reform proposals also are premised on the corporate tax being largely a tax on public firms. A "change in market value" tax would treat the corporate tax base as the annual change in the market capitalization value of the firm during the year. See Joseph Bankman, A Market-Value Based Corporate Income Tax, 68 Tax Notes 1347 (1995); Michael Knoll, An Accretion Corporate Income Tax, 49 Stan. L. Rev. 1 (1996). Corporations would pay tax at some rate on increases in value during the year and would be entitled to deduct and carry forward, or potentially receive tax refunds (at some rate) for, decreases in value during the year. The theory is that both financial accounting income and, to a lesser extent, taxable income attempt to measure the "economic income" of the firm during the year, but the best (and by far easiest) method of doing that is to examine the change in value of the firm determined by public markets. Since corporate managers and shareholders presumably all want to enhance firm value, this proposal would preserve the "healthy tension" described in the previous excerpt between tax and book objectives by aligning the tax base with economic (and book) objectives without introducing the complications noted in the excerpt. Under this proposal, accountants and financial accounting rules would remain necessary to help capital markets determine value accurately, but the need for tax recordkeeping, reporting, and planning would be largely eliminated.

The "change in market value" proposal might present liquidity problems for some firms in meeting their tax obligations since change in value would not necessarily be commensurate with cash flow changes to the firm. On the other hand, the public nature of the firms means that they should have easy access to equity and debt capital that could be used to pay such liabilities. Another possibility is to allow the firms to pay their tax obligations in whole or in part through the issuance of their own securities. The proposal would also need to be integrated with the international tax obligations of many firms. Since change in market value would presumably reflect both domestic and foreign-source gains, firms should be entitled to credit against their corporate tax any income taxes paid to foreign countries. Policymakers would need to determine whether and how to limit this credit.

In contrast to the preceding proposal, which would focus on year-to-year *changes* in market value and thereby resemble an *income* tax, a "market capitalization" tax would require firms to pay tax on their market capitalization values determined each year (or more frequently), in the same manner as existing real or personal *property* taxes. The theory of this tax follows from the Tiebout model (see Charles Tiebout, A Pure Theory of Local Expenditures, 64 J. Pol. Econ. 416 (1956)), which imagines state and local governments competing with one another to provide public goods and services in the same manner as private market competition. The key to the Tiebout model is the real property tax, which operates as the "price" paid by residents of a particular jurisdiction for a particular set of government benefits and amenities made available only to residents of the jurisdiction. By moving, a taxpayer can choose the right price for the right package of benefits, and state and local governments can tailor what they offer in accordance with this "market." In the same way as the Tiebout model, the corporate market capitalization tax imagines firms as choosing between public and non-public status, with the tax representing the price for the benefits provided by the former status. Since the market capitalization tax would be imposed on the full value of the firm each year, and not just its change in value, it could raise the same amount of corporate tax revenue as under current law with a much lower tax rate. An estimate based on 2007 values projects the necessary tax rate to be less than one percent of market capitalization value. See Calvin H. Johnson, Replace the Corporate Tax with a Market Capitalization Tax, 117 Tax Notes 1082, 1085 (2007).

5. *Relationship to integration.* Possible reforms in the calculation of the corporate income tax base may or may not be accompanied by integration of the corporate- and shareholder-level taxes. Preservation of a separate shareholder-level tax in addition to the corporate tax would seem to be least consistent with the "change in market value" tax proposal since the corporate and shareholder tax bases would be virtually the same if there were no integration.

Corporate integration for public companies could also be achieved by imposing a "change in market value" tax (otherwise known as "mark-to-market") on shareholders and repealing the corporate tax altogether. Shareholders would report income and loss (presumably ordinary income and ordinary loss, without any preferential tax rate) each year based on the change in value of their shares in public companies during the year, regardless of whether such income and loss is realized. The liquidity problems this tax might cause for shareholders may lead one to conclude that it would be administratively easier to collect the tax from the corporation and repeal the shareholder-level tax instead.

6. *What about private corporations?* Corporate tax reforms based on the existence of readily ascertainable share values or reliable information provided in financial statements would not work well for private corporations. This problem could be resolved by a 1999 recommendation to reserve the corporate tax *exclusively* for public companies. Private firms, no matter how organized, would all be taxed as pass-through entities and would be given a choice similar to existing subchapters S and K. See American Law Institute, Federal Income Tax Project: Taxation of Private Business Enterprises, Reporters' Study (1999). Any reform distinguishing between public and private firms for tax purposes, however, must consider the potential distortive effects of such a line.

7. *What is the reason for the book-tax discrepancy?* Book income increased significantly more than corporate taxable income during the 1990s. Treasury Department, Approaches to Improve the Competitiveness of the U.S. Business Tax System for the 21st Century (2007), pp. 97-98. In addition to strong economic growth and book-tax differences (such as the disparate treatment of stock options), some attributed the book-tax disparity to increased use of corporate tax shelters. For example, one reported transaction during the 1990s involving the Enron Corporation was designed to generate almost $1 billion in tax deductions without any accompanying expense for book purposes. In addition, even though the approximately $330 million in tax savings from the deductions was not expected to arise until more than 16 years following the transaction, the corporation planned to begin increasing its book income by the anticipated tax savings immediately. See Staff of Joint Committee on Taxation, Report of Investigation of Enron Corporation and Related Entities Regarding Federal Tax and Compensation Issues, and Policy Recommendations (2003), Vol. I, p. 208 (Project Condor). More recent evidence indicates substantial variability in the book-tax difference from year to year.

### *3. Broadening the Corporate Income Tax Base*

"Traditional" tax reform of both individual and corporate income taxes involves a broadening of the tax base and reduction in tax rates. Broader, more comprehensive, tax bases are generally viewed as creating less distortion and inefficiency than narrower tax bases that attempt to favor or disfavor various activities and income. A broader base also generates increased revenue, which can be used to fund a reduction in the tax rate. Lower tax rates are generally considered less distortive in the choices between labor and leisure, savings and consumption, and the other margins along which the tax would apply. Lower *corporate* tax rates are sometimes viewed as particularly attractive in maintaining a competitive environment in the U.S. for international capital.

## Dept. of the Treasury, Business Taxation and Global Competitiveness (2007)

The current business tax base includes an array of special provisions that reduce taxes for particular types of activities, industries, and businesses. These provisions take the form of exclusions from income, deductions allowed or enhanced from what otherwise would be allowed, preferential tax rates, income deferral, and tax credits. Some of these provisions are intended to ease tax compliance and administration, such as allowing cash accounting for small corporations, but others were intended by Congress to encourage particular types of activity. The premise underlying many of the special provisions is that they promote activities that have spillover effects, or address various externalities or market failures. Unwarranted tax subsidies may lead to the misallocation of capital, as they encourage investment decisions based on tax characteristics rather than economic fundamentals, and generally reduce economic growth.

Together, these provisions substantially narrow the corporate tax base, which requires that tax rates be higher in order to raise the same tax revenue. For example, it is estimated that these special corporate tax provisions narrow the corporate tax base by roughly 25 percent. If the tax base were broadened by removing these special provisions, the top corporate tax rate of 35 percent could be reduced to 27 percent, or, as an alternative, about 40 percent of investment costs could be written off immediately (i.e., expensed) by all businesses. . . .

A primary effect of targeted tax incentives is to further encourage the activities that benefit from the favorable taxation. This expansion may occur at the expense of other economic activities, and the value of what is lost can exceed the value of what is gained, reducing the overall value of society's output of goods and services.

For example, consider an investment incentive targeted to widget production. Without the investment incentive, an investment in widgets would yield the same pre-tax rate of return as other investments, say 10 percent per year. The 10-percent rate of return is sufficient to cover taxes and provide investors their required after-tax rate of return, say 7 percent.

Now consider the effects of an investment incentive that cuts taxes on widget investments so that a 10 percent pre-tax return now yields 8 percent after taxes. Since other investments yield only 7 percent after taxes, investment funds will flow into widget production and out of other activities. Indeed, this presumably is the intention of the tax incentive. The expansion of the widget industry will reduce the pre-tax return available on widget investments as, for example, investments expand into less productive technologies. The declining pre-tax return will lower the after-tax return, and eventually expansion into widget investments will stop when the after-tax return falls to 7 percent, the same return as available elsewhere in the economy. However, when the expansion stops, widget investments will yield a pre-tax return that is below the 10 percent pre-tax return provided by other investments. Say the pre-tax return on widgets falls to 8 percent. In that case, society will have given up investments that earn 10 percent in exchange for investments that earn only 8 percent, for a net loss of 2 percent. If the additional economic activity encouraged by the special tax treatment is not warranted by, for example, spillover effects or externality considerations, the tax incentive would have reduced the productivity of the nation's stock of capital.

Tax incentives also may impose costs on society even when the tax incentive is unsuccessful in expanding the tax favored activity. If other taxes are raised to offset the revenue needed to cover the tax incentives, these other taxes introduce distortions of their own. In addition, taxpayers expend resources attempting to win favorable tax breaks. Such lobbying expenditures are a pure loss to society because their only effect is to transfer economic resources from one group to another.

Targeted tax incentives also add to the complexity of the tax system. Rules and regulations have to be established to ensure that the incentives are limited to their intended beneficiaries. Taxpayers have to spend time and money learning about tax incentives. The Internal Revenue Service (IRS) has to spend resources monitoring and enforcing the rules. Disputes invariably will arise between the taxing authority and taxpayers, and society will expend resources adjudicating these disputes.

The recently enacted domestic production activities deduction and the research and experimentation (R&E) credit serve as examples of the types of complexity that can be created by targeted tax incentives. The production deduction allows firms to claim a special additional deduction [equal to] 9 percent of qualified income. The deduction is . . . similar in effect to a reduction in the statutory tax rate, e.g., from 35 percent to 32 percent. . . .

The production deduction, however, is not universally available and is much more complicated than a simple, across-the-board cut in the tax rate. The deduction is subject to a number of limitations and restrictions and is only available for certain qualified activities of a business. As a result, the tax code and accompanying tax regulations must specify which activities of a business qualify for the deduction. For taxpayers, this requires a completely new set of accounting distinctions so that all revenue and expense can be attributed to qualified domestic production activities on an item-by-item basis. Property is typically includable while services are not; domestic activities are includable while foreign activities are not. Many firms have no business reason to track their activities in these ways, but now are subject to a tax requirement to do so. . . . [P]rovisions like the domestic production deduction are not unprecedented. Canada implemented a similar provision that was found to be complex and difficult to administer. As a result of those problems, the provision was repealed and replaced with a general tax rate cut.

While research and experimentation undoubtedly has positive externalities for the economy, the R&E credit has been one of the most controversial issues between taxpayers and the IRS. Much of this controversy arises from uncertainty over the interpretation of the statutory requirements for credit eligibility. The definition of eligible research is inherently difficult, and in audits of taxpayers the IRS is required to make technical judgments about whether an activity was directed to produce truly innovative products or processes. These audits create a burden for both the IRS and taxpayers. The credit also creates significant compliance costs. Businesses are required to maintain detailed records for the credit, which may differ from the types of records normally kept by its operational units. . . . While a subsidy to encourage private-sector investment in research may be viewed as desirable, the administrative difficulties erode the positive incentives the provision provides.

In addition to being targeted, many tax incentives are temporary. Temporary tax provisions create a number of problems. If the provisions actually are temporary, they have no long-term effect on economic decisions, which calls into question their rationale. They might do little more than alter the timing of investments and serve as a give-away to the tax favored activity. Temporary tax provisions add uncertainty to the tax system, and make it difficult for businesses to plan their future activities and investments effectively. Temporary tax provisions also encourage relatively large amounts of lobbying expenditures, as taxpayers continually seek to extend purportedly temporary tax incentives. The R&E credit is an example of a (seemingly permanent) temporary tax provision. It has been scheduled to expire on a regular basis since its inception in 1981, but actually lapsed for only a single one-year period.

Although targeted tax incentives may create economic distortions, in some instances their intended purpose is to correct economic distortions caused by a market failure. The R&E credit is an example of a targeted tax incentive that attempts to correct a market failure. Without a subsidy, the private market might not allocate enough resources to research because private inventors cannot reap the full benefit of their inventions. It can be difficult for inventors to charge all those who use or benefit from their invention. For example, an invention might be copied by others, or it might pave the way for further improvements. Because the inventor might not be able to collect the invention's full return, he has an insufficient incentive to conduct research and develop innovations. He foregoes investments in research that produce social benefits in excess of their private costs. A tax subsidy is one way to increase the return available to the private inventor, and correct for the failure of the private market to reward innovation sufficiently.

For purposes of addressing an externality like this, the tax system is a limited policy tool. The most significant limitation is that a substantial fraction of firms owe no corporate tax; the portion of corporations without annual tax liability has recently varied between 40 percent and 50 percent of the total number of corporations. Since tax preferences are non-refundable, they are of no immediate value to firms without taxable income.

It has been estimated that businesses spent approximately $40 billion complying with the tax code in 2004. While this is the total cost of compliance, the existence of special targeted tax provisions greatly complicates the tasks of complying with and administering the tax code. Eliminating these special provisions would reduce these compliance costs as well as opening opportunities for additional simplifications.

### Targeted Tax Preferences Forgo Government Tax Revenue and Cause Tax Rates To Be Higher for All Businesses

. . . [The following table] shows the revenue that could be raised over a 10-year period by repealing all corporate tax preference items effective January 1, 2008. The table itemizes all the preferences that, if eliminated, would raise more than $5 billion over a 10-year period, assuming the corporate tax would have a comprehensive income base with the same statutory tax rates as the current system. The estimates assume no transition rules except for accelerated depreciation, which is repealed only for investments made beginning in 2008.

**Special Provisions Reduce the Corporate Tax Base by up to 25 Percent**

| | *FY 2008-17;* | *$ Billions* |
|---|---|---|
| Baseline Corporate Income Tax Revenues, FY2008 Budget | | 3,711 |
| Major Preferences Under the Current Corporate Income Tax | | |
| Deduction for US production activities | | 210 |
| Exclusion of interest on state and local bonds | | 135 |
| Research and experimentation (R&E) tax credit | | 132 |
| Deferral of income from controlled foreign corporations | | 120 |
| Low income housing tax credit | | 55 |
| Exclusion of interest on life insurance savings | | 30 |
| Inventory property sales source rules exception | | 29 |
| Deductibility of charitable contributions | | 28 |
| Special ESOP rules | | 23 |
| Exemption of credit union income | | 19 |
| New technology credit | | 8 |
| Special Blue Cross/Blue Shield deduction | | 8 |
| Excess of percentage over cost depletion, fuels | | 7 |
| Other corporate preferences | | 27 |
| | Total | 831 |
| Additional Preference Under a Comprehensive Corporate Income Tax | | |
| Expensing and accelerated depreciation provisions | | 410 |
| Total Revenue from Preferences | | 1,241 |

The revenue forgone from the existence of corporate tax preferences comes at a significant cost to economic efficiency. If the revenue from tax preferences were used to lower the corporate tax rate, the rate could be lowered from 35 percent to 27 percent while producing approximately the same revenue. . . .

## *NOTES*

1. *Other corporate preferences.* Two other significant corporate preferences not listed in the table are repeal of the LIFO method of accounting (estimated to raise

about $80 billion over ten years) and the graduated corporate tax rates ($28 billion over ten years).

2. *Rate cuts versus expensing.* The Treasury report left open the possibility that revenue raised from base-broadening could be used to *either* reduce corporate tax rates *or* increase expensing of the cost of new tangible investment such as machinery and equipment. As between the two possibilities, the conventional wisdom is that expensing provides a greater "bang for the buck." Like a rate cut, expensing can provide a tax benefit that would eliminate any corporate tax on new, marginal investment. Either rate cuts or expensing could thus provide a powerful incentive to increase capital investment. Unlike expensing, however, the tax benefit from a rate cut would apply to the entire return from both old and new capital, including above-normal returns from inframarginal investments. Thus, in comparison to expensing, a rate cut would arguably have less impact because of revenue lost on existing investment or investment that would have been made without as large an incentive.

Despite these considerations, rate cuts might nevertheless be preferred over expensing. By limiting its incentive effect to new investment, expensing necessarily drives down the value of old capital. Businesses owning this old capital are unlikely to overlook this effect and may, therefore, take it into account in deciding the amount of their future investment. Thus, the incentive effect of expensing may be undermined to some extent by a loss of business confidence. A rate cut (but not expensing) also reduces the distortive effects of the tax system, such as the biases favoring debt over equity and passthrough entities over C corporations. A rate cut decreases the return from wasteful tax shelter activity; in contrast, expensing may create greater opportunities for tax shelters by producing negative tax rates when the investment is financed with debt. In addition, it is hard to design an expensing provision that is neutral across different types of investment. Finally, a rate cut is generally viewed as more likely than expensing to attract internationally mobile capital to the U.S., especially capital producing above-normal returns. From the standpoint of influencing where an investment will occur, a rate cut's application to the *entire* return from inframarginal investment provides a stronger incentive for relocation than expensing (which exempts only the normal return). Indeed, the experience in industrial countries outside the U.S. has been increasingly to finance corporate rate cuts with *lower* depreciation allowances, which are less relevant to the location of high-profit international investments. For the same reason, a rate cut would likely be more successful than expensing in reducing the incentive of taxpayers to engage in purely tax-structured income-shifting transactions.

3. *Taxation of outbound investment.* U.S. corporations are generally taxed on their worldwide income. In contrast, a foreign corporation is generally not taxed by the U.S. unless it has income effectively connected with a U.S. trade or business or certain U.S.-source investment-type income. This combination of rules has long encouraged U.S. corporations to conduct their business activities outside the U.S. through a foreign subsidiary, preferably one subject to little or no foreign tax. In general, subpart F limits the tax advantage if the subsidiary is classified as a "controlled foreign corporation" (CFC) (meaning that it is controlled by certain U.S.

shareholders) and the subsidiary's income is considered "subpart F income" (representing certain types of income for which deferral of U.S. taxation is not permitted). The subpart F income of a CFC is taxed to its U.S. shareholders as the income is earned; other income of the CFC (and any income of a foreign subsidiary not qualifying as a CFC) is generally not taxed by the U.S. until the income is repatriated to the U.S. As noted in Table 2.1 of the Treasury excerpt, the deferred taxation of a portion of a CFC's income has an estimated revenue loss of $120 billion over ten years.

A base-broadening objective might support repeal of deferral and its replacement with current taxation of all income earned by a CFC. Such a change would be consistent with an economic efficiency norm known as "capital export neutrality" (CEN), a goal of taxing all income of U.S. taxpayers the same, no matter where the income is generated. Supporters of CEN argue that it removes any tax bias from a U.S. taxpayer's decision to invest at home or abroad and, if abroad, in which foreign country. Repeal of deferral, however, would violate a different economic efficiency norm known as "capital import neutrality" (CIN). Adherents of CIN contend that to be competitive, U.S. taxpayers investing in a given location should face the same tax consequences as investors from other countries who are investing in the same location. CIN, therefore, would generally support *no* U.S. taxation of foreign investment; all investors in a given location should face only taxes imposed by the host country (the country where the investment takes place). Current law, by taxing currently some but not all of the income of a CFC, achieves essentially a middle ground that does not fully satisfy either CEN or CIN.

In 2011, the Obama Administration proposed an important refinement to current law's middle-ground approach. The Administration supported retention of the basic compromise under current law, but urged that certain U.S. interest deductions allocable to any foreign income not currently taxed by the U.S. should be similarly deferred. The deferred deductions would be allowed upon the repatriation of the foreign income and imposition of U.S. tax on such income. This proposal is analogous to other anti-tax arbitrage provisions in the Code that limit or deny deductions for expenses allocable to tax-preferred or tax-exempt income.

# Chapter 4

# Substance vs. Form

Beginning with this chapter, we turn to the taxation of various transactions between corporations and their investors and between one corporation and another. The taxation of corporate transactions is the principal concern of the subchapter C rules and a core part of most corporate tax practices.

This chapter introduces you to perhaps the most difficult and important question in the taxation of corporate transactions: under what circumstances are the tax consequences of a transaction determined by its "substance" as opposed to its "form"? As you will learn in succeeding chapters, the subchapter C rules are highly form-oriented. The rules often specify in exquisite detail the tax consequences of complying with a particular set of requirements or steps. Yet the courts (and the IRS) repeatedly remind taxpayers that merely following the form and conditions set out in the law may not be enough to qualify for the desired tax consequences. What more is needed? When is literal compliance with the law not enough? Unfortunately, as you might suspect, there are no clear answers to these questions. It is important, however, to begin to think about these matters at the outset. We will return to these issues again and again throughout the rest of this course.

The importance of these issues was heightened in 2010 when Congress, after more than a decade of debate, codified the "economic substance" doctrine in section 7701(o). This doctrine has been one of the principal tools enabling a court to look beyond the form of a transaction to its substance. In addition to clarifying the meaning of the common law doctrine, Congress enacted a sizable, strict liability penalty on any underpayment attributable to a violation of the doctrine.

Part A of this chapter introduces you to some of the general principles the courts have laid out in this area, often in response to government efforts to prevent tax avoidance. Part B then reviews the principal additional steps the government has taken outside of litigation to combat tax avoidance. Part C concludes with a discussion of the new legislative provision.

## A. Judicial Principles

As we will see throughout this book, courts have articulated and applied a "substance-over-form" principle in a variety of different ways. Unfortunately, the courts have not always been consistent in their formulations. Confusingly, even the terminology varies—courts sometimes use different labels when referring to the same approach and use the same label when referring to different approaches. Courts also employ different tests to determine whether to uphold a particular substance-over-form argument, and apply the tests to the facts in different ways.

One common term used by the courts is to conclude that a particular transaction is a "sham." This conclusion sometimes results from a court's finding that a particular set of facts didn't really happen, or didn't happen in the manner claimed by the parties. In this sense, the claimed facts and purported transaction are "fake." In his dissent in Knetsch v. U.S., 364 U.S. 361, 370 (1960), Justice Douglas seemed to be thinking of this type of case when he referred to a court not respecting a transaction that is "hocus-pocus." Other courts sometimes refer to this type of case as a "sham in fact." If a court determines that a transaction didn't really happen, then not surprisingly, it refuses to allow the tax consequences that would have arisen if the transaction had taken place.

An example of a fake transaction occurred during the late 1970s when some taxpayers, in order to obtain tax savings, began investing in year-end "straddle transactions" designed to produce offsetting gain and loss positions. The strategy was for the taxpayer to sell the loss position in the current year but to hold the gain position into the succeeding year before selling. The taxpayer claimed that this strategy resulted in a deferral of tax and conversion of ordinary income into capital gain. In some cases, taxpayers appear to have claimed the purported tax benefits from the transactions without actually doing them, presumably to avoid incurring the transaction costs for what were essentially meaningless investments. Not surprisingly, the tax benefits in these cases were disallowed. See Forseth v. Comm'r, 85 T.C. 127, 164-66 (1985), aff'd, 845 F.2d 746 (7th Cir. 1988); cf. Dewees v. Comm'r, 870 F.2d 21, 28-29 (1st Cir. 1989).

The term "sham," however, is not used only in this limited sense. In *Knetsch*, the taxpayer purchased long-term annuity bonds from an insurance company with the proceeds of debt borrowed from that company and secured by the bonds. Much of the interest paid on the debt was also borrowed from the insurance company. Because the taxpayer prepaid the interest and was not taxed currently on the return from the bonds, he claimed that his net out-of-pocket expenses of about $90,000 from the transactions produced interest deductions of almost $300,000 and tax savings of over $230,000. The majority agreed with the lower court's conclusion that the circular flow of funds between the taxpayer and insurance company made the claimed payment of interest a "sham," and therefore denied the tax consequences asserted by the taxpayer. The interest, in effect, was not really paid by the taxpayer because most of it had been loaned to him by the same party that purportedly received the interest. Justice Douglas disagreed, arguing that in contrast to "hocus-pocus," the taxpayer's steps had actually taken place—there were real borrowings and real purchases with the proceeds—and therefore the taxpayer's position should have been respected. The tax consequences of a "sham transaction" in the sense used in *Knetsch* are sometimes determined through application of the "step-transaction doctrine." This principle permits a court to collapse the formally independent steps of a transaction in order to determine what really happened and, therefore, what tax consequences are appropriate.

The difference between an entirely fabricated transaction and one whose steps are actually undertaken but completely circular may be fairly small. In either case, it is quite easy to see how a fact-finder might conclude that because "nothing really happened" or "no transaction really occurred," the tax consequences flowing from the purported transaction should be disallowed. But courts apply substance-over-form principles, and sometimes use the term "sham" very loosely in this context, to disallow tax claims in circumstances outside these two narrow situations.

For example, in Goldstein v. Comm'r, 364 F.2d 734 (2d Cir. 1966), in order to shelter income from winning the Irish Sweepstakes, the taxpayer undertook the same basic transactions as the ones involved in *Knetsch*. The transactions, however, were not carried out with the same counterparty; because the taxpayer borrowed money from two commercial banks to purchase some Treasury notes, there was no circular flow of funds. The Second Circuit respected as real the borrowing of money, the purchase of Treasury notes, and the prepayment of interest. Nevertheless, it denied the taxpayer's claimed interest deduction because the transaction had "no substance or purpose aside from the taxpayer's desire to obtain the tax benefit." The court indicated that an interest deduction should be permitted only where funds are borrowed for a "purposive activity," meaning an activity whose purpose is not merely tax avoidance. Id. at 741. Other explanations offered by courts to deny a taxpayer's position even when a transaction really occurs include the taxpayer's failure to have a profit motive, bear a sufficient level of risk, or have a realistic chance of earning a pre-tax profit. When "sham" is used loosely to refer to these types of transactions (sometimes also described as a "sham in substance"), the sham analysis may overlap with other doctrines resting on substance-over-form principles, such as "economic substance" or "business purpose." Thus, a transaction found to lack "economic substance" and/or a sufficient "business purpose" may also sometimes be termed a "sham" or "sham in substance," with the result that the claimed tax consequences are not respected.

The following case, *Gregory v. Helvering*, remains the most influential decision in the tax law of substance versus form. As the note following the case indicates, there were actually three very interesting opinions in the case. The trial court (Board of Tax Appeals) held for the taxpayer based on an approach suggesting a limited role of courts to find the facts and apply the literal terms of the tax statute to those facts. This decision was reversed on appeal, and Judge Learned Hand's majority opinion for the Second Circuit ultimately became the blueprint for the Supreme Court's holding in favor of the government.

At the time of the *Gregory* case, Congress had determined that a particular transaction, now considered a "divisive reorganization," should not result in any immediate tax consequences to the participants in the transaction. We will take up in chapter twelve the current law of divisive reorganizations and the theory behind their tax treatment. For now, simply examine closely the rather crude statutory language that Congress used at that time to define the covered transaction, and then consider the transaction undertaken by Mrs. Gregory. Why did she not receive the tax consequences specified in the statute?

## Gregory v. Helvering

293 U.S. 465 (1935)

Mr. Justice SUTHERLAND delivered the opinion of the Court.

Petitioner in 1928 was the owner of all the stock of United Mortgage Corporation. That corporation held among its assets 1,000 shares of the Monitor Securities Corporation. For the sole purpose of procuring a transfer of these shares to herself in order to sell them for her individual profit, and, at the same time, diminish the amount of income tax which would result from a direct transfer by way of dividend, she sought to bring about a "reorganization" under section 112(g) of the Revenue Act of 1928. . . . To that end, she caused the Averill Corporation to be organized under the laws of Delaware on September 18, 1928. Three days later, the United Mortgage Corporation transferred to the Averill Corporation the 1,000 shares of Monitor stock, for which all the shares of the Averill Corporation were issued to the petitioner. On September 24, the Averill Corporation was dissolved, and liquidated by distributing all its assets, namely, the Monitor shares, to the petitioner. No other business was ever transacted, or intended to be transacted, by that company. Petitioner immediately sold the Monitor shares for $133,333.33. She returned for taxation, as capital net gain, the sum of $76,007.88, based upon an apportioned cost of $57,325.45. Further details are unnecessary. It is not disputed that if the interposition of the so-called reorganization was ineffective, petitioner became liable for a much larger tax as a result of the transaction.

The Commissioner of Internal Revenue, being of opinion that the reorganization attempted was without substance and must be disregarded, held that petitioner was liable for a tax as though the United corporation had paid her a dividend consisting of the amount realized from the sale of the Monitor shares. In a proceeding before the Board of Tax Appeals, that body rejected the commissioner's view and upheld that of petitioner. 27 B.T.A. 223. Upon a review of the latter decision, the Circuit Court of Appeals sustained the commissioner and reversed the board, holding that there had been no "reorganization" within the meaning of the statute. 69 F.(2d) 809. . . .

Section 112 of the Revenue Act of 1928 deals with the subject of gain or loss resulting from the sale or exchange of property. Such gain or loss is to be recognized in computing the tax, except as provided in that section. The provisions of the section, so far as they are pertinent to the question here presented, follow:

> Sec. 112(g). Distribution of Stock on Reorganization. If there is distributed, in pursuance of a plan of reorganization, to a shareholder in a corporation a party to the

> reorganization, stock or securities in such corporation or in another corporation a party to the reorganization, without the surrender by such shareholder of stock or securities in such a corporation, no gain to the distributee from the receipt of such stock of securities shall be recognized. . . .
>
> (i) Definition of Reorganization. As used in this section . . .
>
> (1) The term "reorganization" means . . . (B) a transfer by a corporation of all or a part of its assets to another corporation if immediately after the transfer the transferor or its stockholders or both are in control of the corporation to which the assets are transferred. . . .

It is earnestly contended on behalf of the taxpayer that since every element required by the foregoing subdivision (B) is to be found in what was done, a statutory reorganization was effected; and that the motive of the taxpayer thereby to escape payment of a tax will not alter the result or make unlawful what the statute allows. It is quite true that if a reorganization in reality was effected within the meaning of subdivision (B), the ulterior purpose mentioned will be disregarded. The legal right of a taxpayer to decrease the amount of what otherwise would be his taxes, or altogether avoid them, by means which the law permits, cannot be doubted. . . . But the question for determination is whether what was done, apart from the tax motive, was the thing which the statute intended. The reasoning of the court below in justification of a negative answer leaves little to be said.

When subdivision (B) speaks of a transfer of assets by one corporation to another, it means a transfer made "in pursuance of a plan of reorganization" of corporate business; and not a transfer of assets by one corporation to another in pursuance of a plan having no relation to the business of either, as plainly is the case here. Putting aside, then, the question of motive in respect of taxation altogether, and fixing the character of the proceeding by what actually occurred, what do we find? Simply an operation having no business or corporate purpose — a mere device which put on the form of a corporate reorganization as a disguise for concealing its real character, and the sole object and accomplishment of which was the consummation of a preconceived plan, not to reorganize a business or any part of a business, but to transfer a parcel of corporate shares to the petitioner. No doubt, a new and valid corporation was created. But that corporation was nothing more than a contrivance to the end last described. It was brought into existence for no other purpose; it performed, as it was intended from the beginning it should perform, no other function. When that limited function had been exercised, it immediately was put to death.

In these circumstances, the facts speak for themselves and are susceptible of but one interpretation. The whole undertaking, though conducted according to the terms of subdivision (B), was in fact an elaborate and devious form of conveyance masquerading as a corporate reorganization, and nothing else. The rule which excludes from consideration the motive of tax avoidance is not pertinent to the situation, because the transaction upon its face lies outside the plain intent of the statute. To hold otherwise would be to exalt artifice above reality and to deprive the statutory provision in question of all serious purpose.

Judgment affirmed.

## *NOTES AND QUESTIONS*

1. *The lower court opinions.* The Board of Tax Appeals thought the issue in the case was whether Averill's existence should be respected, given the purpose it served and its short life. The Board refused to ignore the corporation, and held for the taxpayer:

> As long as corporations are recognized before the law as if they were creatures of substance, there is nothing to distinguish this corporation from innumerable others, whether they be devised to achieve temporary tax reduction or some other legitimate end. Congress has not left it to the Commissioner to say, in the absence of fraud or other compelling circumstance, that the corporate form may be ignored in some cases and recognized in others. Whatever can be said of the wisdom of recognizing the corporate device, the taxing statutes have so plainly accepted it and provided the detailed methods of taxing its transactions, that to disregard it in a case like this would vary the time, method and amount of tax which the statute imposes. [27 B.T.A. 223, 225 (1932).]

Furthermore, the Board justified a limited judicial role in interpreting the tax statute:

> A statute so meticulously drafted must be interpreted as a literal expression of the taxing policy, and leaves only the small interstices for judicial consideration. The general legislative plan apparently was to recognize the corporate entity and, in view of such recognition, to specify when the gains or losses would be recognized and upon what basis they should be measured. We may not destroy the effectiveness of this statutory plan by denying recognition to the corporation and thus preventing consideration of its transactions. [Id. at 225-26.]

Writing for the Second Circuit, Judge Learned Hand agreed with the Board in respecting Averill's existence:

> We do not . . . agree fully with the way in which the Commissioner treated the transaction; we cannot treat as inoperative the transfer of the Monitor shares by the United Mortgage Corporation, the issue by the Averill Corporation of its own shares to the taxpayer, and her acquisition of the Monitor shares by winding up that company. The Averill Corporation held a juristic personality, whatever the purpose of its organization; the transfer passed title to the Monitor shares and the taxpayer became a shareholder in the transferee. All these steps were real. . . . [69 F.2d 809, 811 (2d Cir. 1934).]

Nevertheless, the court reversed the Board and held for the government:

> We agree with the Board and the taxpayer that a transaction, otherwise within an exception of the tax law, does not lose its immunity, because it is actuated by a desire to avoid, or, if one choose, to evade, taxation. Any one may so arrange his affairs that his taxes shall be as low as possible; he is not bound to choose that pattern which will best pay the Treasury; there is not even a patriotic duty to increase one's taxes. . . . Therefore, if what was done here, was what was intended by section 112(i)(1)(B),* it is of no consequence that it was all an elaborate scheme to get rid of income taxes, as it certainly was. Nevertheless, it does not follow that Congress meant to cover such a transaction, not even though the facts answer the dictionary definitions of each term used in the statutory definition. It is quite true, as the Board has very well said, that as the articulation of a statute increases, the room for interpretation must contract; but the meaning of a sentence may be more than that of the separate words, as a melody is more than the notes, and no degree of particularity can ever obviate recourse to the setting in which all appear, and which all collectively create. The purpose of the section is plain enough; men engaged in enterprises—industrial, commercial, financial, or any other—might wish to consolidate, or divide, to add to, or subtract from, their holdings. Such transactions were not to be considered as "realizing" any profit, because the collective interests still remained in solution. But the underlying presupposition is plain that the readjustment shall be undertaken for reasons germane to the conduct of the venture in hand, not as an ephemeral incident, egregious to its prosecution. To dodge the shareholders' taxes is not one of the transactions contemplated as corporate "reorganizations." [Id. at 810-11.]

As we have seen, the Supreme Court affirmed the Second Circuit and, in the process, tracked much of Judge Hand's opinion.

2. *The Court's holding.* In finding for the government, does the Supreme Court respect or reject the form of the taxpayer's transaction? If form was respected, what was the basis for the Court's holding?

3. *Business purpose.* Was there a nontax business purpose for the taxpayer's transaction? Does your answer depend upon how one describes her transaction? Why was a business purpose needed in the first place?

4. *Role of tax avoidance purpose or motive.* Both appellate court opinions make clear that the existence of a tax avoidance purpose or motive on the part of the taxpayer is not by itself damning. As Judge Hand put it, "there is not even a patriotic duty to increase one's taxes." These words and the similar ones used by the Supreme Court are recited over and over again by taxpayers in defense of their tax positions (as well as by courts when they uphold a taxpayer's claim) even though, as we have seen, the principle stated in the appellate court opinions was pure dicta. At the end of the day, Mrs. Gregory lost her case. Moreover, despite the principle articulated by both courts, is it so clear that her tax avoidance purpose was irrelevant to the outcome?

---

* [Quoted in the Supreme Court opinion.]

5. *Role of legislative intent. Gregory* is sometimes viewed as a case that turned on legislative intent. The Court initially says "the question for determination is whether what was done, apart from the tax motive, was the thing which the statute intended" and then answers its question, "the transaction upon its face lies outside the plain intent of the statute." Unfortunately, the Court does not provide guidance regarding how such intent was (or should be) determined. Textualists question the propriety of "looking behind the words of the statute" in part because of the difficulty of ascertaining the true intent of the legislature. Legislators don't vote on Committee Reports and rarely read or write them; should such legislative material therefore be given any special effect? More broadly, some are skeptical about a court's reliance upon legislative intent because of concern that, in the guise of judicial interpretation, a court may simply substitute its judgment for that of the legislature.

The counterargument is that the bare words in a statute are necessarily an imperfect way for a legislature to convey the rule it wishes to impose in a particular situation. Thus, the "law" is more than such words; they must be interpreted in the context in which they were intended. Under this view, when application of a statute to a particular set of facts is clear, a court should not resort to nonstatutory guidance. But if application of a statute to a set of facts is ambiguous and Congressional intention is clear, a court should interpret the statute consistent with that intention. Almost 25 years after his majority opinion for the Second Circuit in *Gregory*, Judge Hand was still supportive of the use of nonstatutory sources to aid in the interpretation of statutes:

> The literal meaning of the words of a statute is seldom, if ever, the conclusive measure of its scope. Except in rare instances statutes are written in general terms and do not undertake to specify all the occasions that they are meant to cover; and their "interpretation" demands the projections of their expressed purpose upon occasions not present in the minds of those who enacted them. [Gilbert v. Comm'r, 248 F.2d 399, 411 (2d Cir. 1957).]

6. *Mrs. Gregory's transaction today.* Because of the current preferential tax rate applicable to dividend income received by individuals, Mrs. Gregory would not need to undertake the same tax planning today to have her income taxed at a long-term capital gain rate. On the other hand, current law might give rise to an issue that did not exist at the time of Mrs. Gregory's case—namely, the possible taxation of United upon its distribution of the Averill stock to her. We discuss this possibility in chapter twelve.

7. *The fruits of* Gregory. *Gregory* has been used as authority in virtually all substance versus form cases in which a taxpayer's claimed tax consequences are denied. It has been used, for example, to support all of the different ways in which courts have concluded that a transaction is a "sham," and is generally viewed as the source of the "business purpose" and "economic substance" doctrines. As noted above, the case has also been used in the opposite way, to justify a holding in favor of the taxpayer because the "mere" tax avoidance objective of the taxpayer is

not determinative. The following case is just one example of contemporary judicial thinking on the question of substance versus form. By way of background, you should know that insurance companies commonly enter into agreements with reinsurance companies to spread further the risks assumed by the insurance company. Under the applicable tax laws, however, the income of the Bermuda reinsurance company (OPL) involved in the following case was subject to income taxation only by Bermuda, and not by the U.S., as long as it maintained no more than a minimal business presence in the U.S. Unlike the U.S., however, Bermuda does not impose any corporate income taxes.

## United Parcel Service of America, Inc. v. Commissioner

254 F.3d 1014 (11th Cir. 2001)

Cox, Circuit Judge:

. . . [United Parcel Service of America, Inc. (UPS)], whose main business is shipping packages, had a practice in the early 1980s of reimbursing customers for lost or damaged parcels up to $100 in declared value. Above that level, UPS would assume liability up to the parcel's declared value if the customer paid $.25 per additional $100 in declared value, the "excess-value charge." If a parcel were lost or damaged, UPS would process and pay the resulting claim. UPS turned a large profit on excess-value charges because it never came close to paying as much in claims as it collected in charges, in part because of efforts it made to safeguard and track excess-value shipments. This profit was taxed; UPS declared its revenue from excess-value charges as income on its 1983 return, and it deducted as expenses the claims paid on damaged or lost excess-value parcels.

UPS's insurance broker suggested that UPS could avoid paying taxes on the lucrative excess-value business if it restructured the program as insurance provided by an overseas affiliate. UPS implemented this plan in 1983 by first forming and capitalizing a Bermuda subsidiary, Overseas Partners, Ltd. (OPL), almost all of whose shares were distributed as a taxable dividend to UPS shareholders (most of whom were employees; UPS stock was not publicly traded). UPS then purchased an insurance policy, for the benefit of UPS customers, from National Union Fire Insurance Company. By this policy, National Union assumed the risk of damage to or loss of excess-value shipments. The premiums for the policy were the excess-value charges that UPS collected. UPS, not National Union, was responsible for administering claims brought under the policy. National Union in turn entered a reinsurance treaty with OPL. Under the treaty, OPL assumed risk commensurate with National Union's, in exchange for premiums that equal the excess-value payments National Union got from UPS, less commissions, fees, and excise taxes.

Under this plan, UPS thus continued to collect $.25 per $100 of excess value from its customers, process and pay claims, and take special measures to safeguard valuable packages. But UPS now remitted monthly the excess-value payments, less claims paid, to National Union as premiums on the policy. National Union then collected its commission, excise taxes, and fees from the charges before sending the rest on to OPL as payments under the reinsurance contract. UPS reported neither revenue from excess-value charges nor claim expenses on its 1984 return, although it did deduct the fees and commissions that National Union charged.

The IRS determined a deficiency in the amount of the excess-value charges collected in 1984, concluding that the excess-value payment remitted ultimately to OPL had to be treated as gross income to UPS. . . . Following a hearing, the tax court agreed with the IRS.

. . . The [tax] court's analysis proceeded . . . under the substantive-sham or economic-substance doctrines. . . . The conclusion was that UPS's redesign of its excess-value business warranted no respect. Three core reasons support this result, according to the court: the plan had no defensible business purpose, as the business realities were identical before and after; the premiums paid for the National Union policy were well above industry norms; and contemporary memoranda and documents show that UPS's sole motivation was tax avoidance. The revenue from the excess-value program was thus properly deemed to be income to UPS rather than to OPL or National Union. The court also imposed penalties.

UPS now appeals, attacking the tax court's economic-substance analysis and its imposition of penalties. The refrain of UPS's lead argument is that the excess-value plan had economic substance, and thus was not a sham, because it comprised genuine exchanges of reciprocal obligations among real, independent entities. The IRS answers with a before-and-after analysis, pointing out that whatever the reality and enforceability of the contracts that composed the excess-value plan, UPS's postplan practice equated to its preplan, in that it collected excess-value charges, administered claims, and generated substantial profits. The issue presented to this court, therefore, is whether the excess-value plan had the kind of economic substance that removes it from "shamhood," even if the business continued as it had before. . . . We agree with UPS that this was not a sham transaction. . . .

I.R.C. §§ 11, 61, and 63 together provide the Code's foundation by identifying income as the basis of taxation. . . . [T]hese sections come with the gloss, analogous to that on other Code sections, that economic substance determines what is income to a taxpayer and what is not. . . . This economic-substance doctrine, also called the sham-transaction doctrine, provides that a transaction ceases to merit tax respect when it has no "economic effects other than the creation of tax benefits." . . . Even if the transaction has economic effects, it must be disregarded if it has no business purpose and its motive is tax avoidance. See . . . Frank Lyon Co. v. U.S., 435 U.S. 561, 583-84 (1978) (one reason requiring treatment of transaction as genuine was that it was "compelled or encouraged by business or regulatory realities"); Gregory v. Helvering, 293 U.S. 465, 469 (1935) (reorganization disregarded in part because it had "no business or corporate purpose").

The kind of "economic effects" required to entitle a transaction to respect in taxation include the creation of genuine obligations enforceable by an unrelated party. . . . The restructuring of UPS's excess-value business generated just such obligations. There was a real insurance policy between UPS and National Union that gave National Union the right to receive the excess-value charges that UPS collected. And even if the odds of losing money on the policy were slim, National Union had assumed liability for the losses of UPS's excess-value shippers, again a genuine obligation. A history of not losing money on a policy is no guarantee of such a future. Insurance companies indeed do not make a habit of issuing policies whose premiums do not exceed the claims anticipated, but that fact does not imply that insurance companies do not bear risk. Nor did the reinsurance treaty with OPL, while certainly reducing the odds of loss, completely foreclose the risk of loss because reinsurance treaties, like all agreements, are susceptible to default.

The tax court dismissed these obligations because National Union, given the reinsurance treaty, was no more than a "front" in what was a transfer of revenue from UPS to OPL. As we have said, that conclusion ignores the real risk that National Union assumed. But even if we overlook the reality of the risk and treat National Union as a conduit for transmission of the excess-value payments from UPS to OPL, there remains the fact that OPL is an independently taxable entity that is not under UPS's control. UPS really did lose the stream of income it had earlier reaped from excess-value charges. UPS genuinely could not apply that money to any use other than paying a premium to National Union; the money could not be used for other purposes, such as capital improvement, salaries, dividends, or investment. These circumstances distinguish UPS's case from the paradigmatic sham transfers of income, in which the taxpayer retains the benefits of the income it has ostensibly forgone. . . . Here that benefit ended up with OPL. There were, therefore, real economic effects from this transaction on all of its parties.

The conclusion that UPS's excess-value plan had real economic effects means . . . that it is not per se a sham. But it could still be one if tax avoidance displaced any business purpose. The tax court saw no business purpose here because the excess-value business continued to operate after its reconfiguration much as before. This lack of change in how the business operated at the retail level, according to the court, betrayed the restructuring as pointless.

It may be true that there was little change over time in how the excess-value program appeared to customers. But the tax court's narrow notion of "business purpose"—which is admittedly implied by the phrase's plain language—stretches the economic-substance doctrine farther than it has been stretched. A "business purpose" does not mean a reason for a transaction that is free of tax considerations. Rather, a transaction has a "business purpose," when we are talking about a going concern like UPS, as long as it figures in a bona fide, profit-seeking business. . . . This concept of "business purpose" is a necessary corollary to the venerable axiom that tax-planning is permissible. See Gregory v. Helvering, 293 U.S. 465, 469 (1935) ("The legal right of a taxpayer to decrease the amount of what otherwise would be his taxes, or altogether avoid them, by means which the law permits, cannot be doubted."). The Code treats lots of categories of economically similar behavior differently. For instance, two ways to infuse capital into a corporation, borrowing and sale of equity, have different tax consequences; interest is usually deductible and distributions to equity holders are not. There may be no tax-independent reason for a taxpayer to choose between these different ways of financing the business, but it does not mean that the taxpayer lacks a "business purpose." To conclude otherwise would prohibit tax-planning.

The case law, too, bears out this broader notion of "business purpose." Many of the cases where no business purpose appears are about individual income tax returns, when the individual meant to evade taxes on income probably destined for personal consumption; obviously, it is difficult in such a case to articulate any *business* purpose to the transaction. See, e.g., *Gregory*, 293 U.S. at 469 (purported corporate reorganization was disguised dividend distribution to shareholder); Knetsch v. U.S., 364 U.S. 361, 362-65 (1960) (faux personal loans intended to generate interest deductions). . . . Other no-business-purpose cases concern tax-shelter transactions or investments by a business or investor that would not have occurred, *in any form*, but for tax-avoidance reasons. . . . By contrast, the few cases that accept a transaction as genuine involve a bona fide business that — perhaps even by design — generates tax benefits. See, e.g., *Frank Lyon*, 435 U.S. at 582-84 (sale-leaseback was part of genuine financing transaction, heavily influenced by banking regulation, to permit debtor bank to outdo its competitor in impressive office space); Jacobson v. Comm'r, 915 F.2d 832, 837-39 (2d Cir. 1990) (one of many cases finding that a bona fide profit motive provided a business purpose for a losing investment because the investment was not an obvious loser ex ante).

The transaction under challenge here simply altered the form of an existing, bona fide business, and this case therefore falls in with those that find an adequate business purpose to neutralize any tax-avoidance motive. True, UPS's restructuring was more sophisticated and complex than the usual tax-influenced form-of-business election or a choice of debt over equity financing. But its sophistication does not change the fact that there was a real business that served the genuine need for customers to enjoy loss coverage and for UPS to lower its liability exposure.

We therefore conclude that UPS's restructuring of its excess-value business had both real economic effects and a business purpose, and it therefore under our precedent had sufficient economic substance to merit respect in taxation. It follows that the tax court improperly imposed penalties and enhanced interest on UPS for engaging in a sham transaction. [The court remanded the decision to the tax court to consider the IRS's alternative arguments.]

RYSKAMP, District Judge, dissenting:

I respectfully dissent. Although I agree with the majority's recitation of the facts as well as its interpretation of the applicable legal standard, I find that its reversal of the tax court is contrary to the great weight of the evidence that was before the lower court. The majority, as well as the tax court below, correctly finds that the question before the Court is whether UPS's insurance arrangements with [National Union (NUF)] and OPL are valid under the sham-transaction doctrine. Under the sham-transaction doctrine, UPS's transaction ceases to merit tax respect when it has no "economic effects other than the creation of tax benefits," . . . or has no business purpose and its sole motive is tax avoidance. . . . Thus the question before the Court is not strictly whether UPS had a tax avoidance motive when it formulated the scheme in question, but rather whether there was some legitimate, substantive business reason for the transaction as well. There clearly was not.

. . . [T]he evidence in this case overwhelmingly demonstrates that UPS's reinsurance arrangement with NUF and OPL had no economic significance or business purpose outside of UPS's desire to avoid federal income tax, and was therefore a sham transaction. First, the tax court based its decision upon evidence that the scheme in question was subjectively motivated by tax avoidance. For example, the evidence showed that tax avoidance was the initial and sole reason for the scheme in question, that UPS held off on the plan for some time to analyze tax legislation on the floor of the United States House of Representatives, and that a letter sent to AIG Insurance from UPS detailing the scheme claimed that AIG would serve in merely a "fronting" capacity and would bear little or no actual risk. The evidence thus showed that this scheme was hatched with only tax avoidance in mind.

Second, the tax court based its decision on overwhelming evidence that UPS's scheme had no real economic or business purpose outside of tax avoidance. For example, the evidence showed that NUF's exposure to loss under the plan (except in the very unlikely event of *extreme* catastrophe) was infinitesimal, and that UPS nevertheless continued to fully bear the administrative costs of the EVC program. NUF was only liable for losses not covered by another insurance policy held by UPS, yet UPS still collected the EVCs and deposited the money into UPS bank accounts, still processed EVC claims, and continued to pay all EVC claims out of UPS bank accounts (while collecting the accrued interest for itself). All NUF really did in the scheme was collect over $1 million in fees and expenses before passing the EVC income on to OPL, which was of course wholly owned by UPS shareholders. In essence, NUF received an enormous fee from UPS in exchange for nothing.

Moreover, the tax court systematically rejected every explanation of the scheme put forth by UPS. UPS claimed that the scheme was meant to avoid violation of state insurance laws, yet the evidence showed no real concern for such laws and that in fact UPS was well aware that federal preemption of these state laws likely made its old EVC plan legal. UPS claimed that it intended OPL to become a full-line insurer someday, yet the evidence showed that it was nevertheless unnecessary to specifically use *EVC income* for such a capital investment. UPS claimed that elimination of the EVC income allowed it to increase its rates, yet one of its own board members testified that this explanation was untrue. I also note that UPS's claim that OPL was a legitimate insurance company fails in light of the fact that OPL was charging a substantially inflated rate for EVCs. Evidence in the tax court showed that in an arms-length transaction with a legitimate insurance company, EVC rates would have been approximately half those charged by UPS (and in turn passed on to OPL), providing further evidence that the transaction was a sham. In sum, UPS failed to show any legitimate business reason for giving up nearly $100 million in EVC income in 1984.

For these reasons, I would affirm the holding of the tax court and find that UPS's arrangement with NUF and OPL was a sham transaction subject to federal tax liability.

## *NOTES AND QUESTIONS*

1. *The "economic substance" doctrine.* As you can tell from this opinion, there has been considerable judicial development of the substance versus form inquiry since *Gregory.* A principal test now used by the courts is the "economic substance" doctrine. Unfortunately, the precise meaning of this doctrine has varied from court to court. The doctrine generally involves both an "objective" inquiry—does a transaction have a sufficient nontax economic effect?—and a "subjective" inquiry—does the transaction have an adequate business purpose apart from the avoidance of taxes? In deciding whether to respect a transaction for tax purposes, courts have been divided concerning whether both inquiries—or just one of them—must be answered in the affirmative. In *UPS*, the Eleventh Circuit fell squarely into the former, "conjunctive" camp when it stated that "[e]ven if the transaction has economic effects, it must be disregarded if it has no business purpose and its motive is tax avoidance." 254 F.3d at 1018. In contrast, in ACM Partnership v. Comm'r, 157 F.3d 231, 247 (3d Cir. 1998), the Third Circuit took essentially a middle ground when it said that the two inquiries "do not constitute discrete prongs of a 'rigid two-step analysis,' but rather represent related factors both of which inform the analysis of whether the transaction had sufficient substance, apart from its tax consequences, to be respected for tax purposes."

Moreover, no consensus exists regarding the precise meaning of the economic substance tests. According to some courts, the objective test is flunked only if a transaction does not afford any possibility of the taxpayer earning a pre-tax profit. Other courts evaluate that test, however, based on whether the nontax economic consequences of a transaction are significant in comparison with the claimed tax consequences. The subjective, "business purpose," inquiry has generally been interpreted as requiring the existence of a *nontax-related* purpose although, as discussed further in note 3 below, *UPS* may represent a somewhat different view. In part to resolve these uncertainties, Congress codified the economic substance doctrine in section 7701(o), as discussed in part C.

2. *What was the economic effect in* UPS? According to the Eleventh Circuit, UPS's transaction had economic effect because it created genuine enforceable obligations affecting three unrelated parties: UPS, National Union, and OPL. Further, even if National Union played no role in the transaction other than as a mere conduit for transmission of the EVCs from UPS to OPL, the court stated that

> there remains the fact that OPL is an independently taxable entity that is not under UPS's control. UPS really did lose the stream of income it had earlier reaped from excess-value charges. UPS genuinely could not apply that money to any use other

> than paying a premium to National Union; the money could not be used for other purposes, such as capital improvement, salaries, dividends, or investment. [254 F.3d at 1019.]

Does this explanation provide support for the taxpayer's claim that the transaction had economic effect?

3. *What was UPS's business purpose for the transaction?* How does the Eleventh Circuit describe the business purpose requirement and UPS's compliance with it? Under the court's test, did Mrs. Gregory's transaction have a business purpose? Does satisfaction of each aspect of the economic substance doctrine depend in part on identifying exactly what the "transaction" is?

4. *COLI cases.* Cases involving the tax consequences of corporate-owned life insurance (COLI) raise the same issues presented in *Knetsch* and *Goldstein*. COLI is whole-life insurance purchased by corporations typically on the lives of their employees. The insurance premiums are commonly funded by a combination of (1) policy loans, secured by the equity build-up in the policy, that are obtained by the corporation from the insurance company, (2) policyholder dividends, (3) permissible withdrawals from the policy, and (4) a small amount of cash investment. Payment of interest on the loans is also usually funded from the same sources. The interest and other expenses generally exceed the yield from the insurance investment so that there is a negative pre-tax return. But because the return from the investment, either when earned or paid out as a death benefit, is generally not taxed and the taxpayer claims a deduction for the interest, the negative pre-tax return is converted into a positive return after taxes. Although section 264(a) generally disallows the deduction of interest in these circumstances, corporations have carefully tailored their COLI programs to satisfy an exception to that rule. Corporations often use the tax savings from these investments to fund other obligations, such as the cost of maintaining employee benefit programs.

In a series of COLI cases, courts have refused to allow taxpayers to deduct their interest. See Dow Chemical v. U.S., 435 F.3d 594 (6th Cir. 2006), rev'g 250 F. Supp. 2d 718 (E.D. Mich. 2003), cert. denied, 549 U.S. 1205 (2007); Am. Elec. Power v. U.S., 326 F.3d 737 (6th Cir. 2003), cert. denied, 540 U.S. 1104 (2004); In re CM Holdings, 301 F.3d 96 (3d Cir. 2002); Winn-Dixie v. Comm'r, 254 F.3d 1313 (11th Cir. 2001), cert. denied, 535 U.S. 986 (2002). The cases have generally affirmed the transactions as "real," and not factual shams, despite the same two-party fact pattern with circular cash flows that existed in *Knetsch*. Nevertheless, the courts have concluded that the transactions lacked economic substance and a nontax business purpose. The courts have made plain that a valid business purpose to use the tax savings (such as to fund employee benefit programs) is not enough; there must be a business purpose, aside from obtaining tax savings, for entering into the transactions themselves. See *Am. Elec. Power*, 326 F.3d at 744. Although corporations often have a valid business reason to insure the life of a key employee, the COLI programs have also included insurance on the lives of virtually the entire workforce, a practice known as "janitors' insurance." (Corporations purchased janitors' insurance to take advantage of a statutory exception to section 264(a), an exception that has since been limited to key persons. See I.R.C. § 264(e)(1). That legislative change is illustrative of a continuing cat-and-mouse game in this area in which Congress has repeatedly tightened exceptions that taxpayers were found to have exploited in unintended ways.)

5. *SILO and LILO cases.* Other recent cases applying economic substance and substance-over-form principles have addressed the tax consequences of SILO ("sale-in/lease-out") and LILO ("lease-in/lease-out") transactions. In a typical SILO deal, a foreign owner of business property transfers the property to a U.S. person and then leases the property back from that person. The transactions are generally designed to ensure that the pre-transaction economic rights of the parties with respect to the property remain essentially unchanged. For example, after the transaction is carried out, the original foreign owner typically retains full use of the property with generally the same benefits and risks as it had prior to the transaction. In general, the transaction's only real effects are: (1) to allow the new nominal U.S. owner of the property to claim net tax benefits, such as depreciation deductions, and (2) to compensate the original foreign owner for its participation. In some cases, the parties claim that the foreign person retains ownership of the property for foreign tax law purposes (even though the U.S. person is treated as the owner for U.S. tax law purposes). This claim potentially allows "double-dipping" in which *both* parties assert entitlement to depreciate the property (one for U.S. tax law purposes and one for foreign tax law purposes).

A typical LILO transaction is similar. In this deal, the foreign owner of business property leases the property (the "head lease") to a U.S. person, which subleases the property (the "sublease") back to the foreign person. The rights obtained by the U.S. person under the head lease are essentially transferred back to the foreign person under the sublease; thus, the two leases basically leave unaltered the pre-transaction rights and responsibilities of the parties with respect to the property. Although the sublease is typically for a shorter term than the head lease, reciprocal options ensure that the foreign person can continue to use the property with the same rights and responsibilities even after the sublease expires. The U.S. person makes a large prepayment of the rent due on the head lease, financed by borrowed money; repayment of that money plus interest is financed by the rental payments received from the foreign person on the sublease. After all the dust settles, the only changes from the pre-transaction arrangement are generally (1) the claiming of net tax benefits, such as a deduction for the rental payments, by the U.S. person, and (2) a cash payment to the foreign person for its participation.

As in the COLI cases, courts generally have denied the claimed tax benefits from SILO and LILO deals, even though the transactions were carefully structured to satisfy the letter of the law at the time. (The law has since been amended to remove some of the purported tax benefits. Before the change in law, taxpayers were reportedly involved in at least 400 SILO transactions alone, resulting in claimed tax deductions of over $35 billion.) In general, the courts have relied upon a factual sham analysis (concluding that the taxpayer was not a genuine purchaser or lessor of the property or an obligor on the purported debt) as well as the absence of economic substance and business purpose. In Wells Fargo v. U.S., 641 F.3d 1319 (Fed. Cir. 2011), aff'g 91 Fed. Cl. 35 (2010), the court relied on the "substance-over-form" doctrine (but apparently *not* the economic substance doctrine) to deny the taxpayer's claim and conclude that the taxpayer's transactions were "abusive tax shelters":

> [The] purely circular transactions . . . elevate form over substance. The only flow of funds between the parties to the transaction was the initial lump sum given to the tax-exempt entity as compensation for its participation in the transaction. From the tax-exempt entity's point of view, the transaction effectively ended as soon as it began. The benefits to Wells Fargo continued to flow throughout the term of the sublease, however, in the form of deferred tax payments. The third-party lender and its affiliate were also compensated for their participation, as were the creators and promoters of the transactions. These transactions were win-win situations for all of the parties involved because free money—in the form of previously unavailable tax benefits utilized by Wells Fargo—was divided among all parties. The money was not entirely "free," of course, because it was in effect transferred to Wells Fargo from the public fisc. [641 F.3d at 1329-30.]

See also BB&T Corp. v. U.S., 523 F.3d 461 (4th Cir. 2008) (LILO transaction) and AWG Leasing Trust v. U.S., 592 F. Supp. 2d 953 (N.D. Ohio 2008) (SILO transaction) (both decisions holding for the government based on factual sham analysis).

Interestingly, shortly before the Claims Court decision in *Wells Fargo*, the same court (but a different judge) upheld the validity of a LILO transaction. Consolidated Edison Co. v. U.S., 90 Fed. Cl. 228 (2009). Although the *Con Ed* transaction had numerous distinctive features, the basic economic arrangement and claimed tax benefits appear to have been similar to other LILO deals. In *Con Ed*, the court may have been influenced by the fact that the leased property (a Dutch energy generating facility) bore some relationship to the U.S. taxpayer's utility business (although the taxpayer did not use the facility in its business). This aspect may have made the case appear to be analogous to the situation in *UPS*. In addition, the court found that the particular facts did not suggest the same "manufactured" quality to the transaction often present in tax shelters (see Notice 2004-30 (infra p. 134)). It remains to be seen whether such factors are, and should be, important in applying new section 7701(o) and resolving substance-over-form cases.

6. Gitlitz. Recall that in *Gitlitz* (p. 15), the Supreme Court favored a literal interpretation of the tax statute even though it arguably produced a nonsensical result (which Congress subsequently reversed). Although *Gitlitz* did not involve a tax shelter, it may suggest how the current Court might be inclined to view the tax consequences of a shelter transaction whose validity turned on how literally the statute should be interpreted.

7. *Evaluation.* How would you compare the Eleventh Circuit's opinion in *UPS* with the Supreme Court's decision in *Gregory*? We will have more opportunities

in the rest of this course to consider additional applications of the substance versus form principle.

## B. Other Government Responses to Tax Avoidance

### 1. *Introduction*

Curbing tax avoidance through litigation and reliance on substance-over-form principles is time-consuming and resource-intensive. Continuing concern about corporate tax shelters has led the government to take certain additional steps to address tax avoidance, such as imposing disclosure and record-keeping requirements on taxpayers and their advisors. To appreciate the type of tax planning that has evoked this concern, read the following IRS Notice describing a simple subchapter S tax shelter that was the subject of a Congressional hearing. The next section then describes the government's other principal responses, aside from litigation, to stem tax avoidance.

**Notice 2004-30**

2004-1 C.B. 828

. . . [A]n S corporation, its shareholders, and an organization exempt from tax under § 501(a) and described in either § 501(c)(3) or § 401(a) of the Internal Revenue Code (such as a tax-qualified retirement plan maintained by a state or local government) (the exempt party) undertake the following steps. An S corporation issues, pro rata to each of its shareholders (the original shareholders), nonvoting stock and warrants that are exercisable into nonvoting stock. For example, the S corporation issues nonvoting stock in a ratio of 9 shares for every share of voting stock and warrants in a ratio of 10 warrants for every share of nonvoting stock. Thus, if the S corporation has 1,000 shares of voting stock outstanding, the S corporation would issue 9,000 shares of nonvoting stock and warrants exercisable into 90,000 shares of nonvoting stock to the original shareholders. The warrants may be exercised at any time over a period of years. The strike price on the warrants is set at a price that is at least equal to 90 percent of the purported fair market value of the newly issued nonvoting stock on the date the warrants are granted. For this purpose, the fair market value of the nonvoting stock is claimed to be substantially reduced because of the existence of the warrants.

Shortly after the issuance of the nonvoting stock and the warrants, the original shareholders donate the nonvoting stock to the exempt party. The parties to the transaction claim that, after the donation of the nonvoting stock, the exempt party owns 90 percent of the stock of the S corporation. The parties further claim that any taxable income allocated on the nonvoting stock to the exempt party is not subject to tax on unrelated business income (UBIT) under §§ 511 through 514 (or the exempt party has offsetting UBIT net operating losses). The original shareholders might also claim a charitable contribution deduction under § 170 for the donation of the nonvoting stock to the exempt party. In some variations of this transaction, the S corporation may issue nonvoting stock directly to the exempt party.

Pursuant to one or more agreements (typically redemption agreements, rights of first refusal, put agreements, or pledge agreements) entered into as part of the transaction, the exempt party can require the S corporation or the original shareholders to purchase the exempt party's nonvoting stock for an amount equal to the fair market value of the stock as of the date the shares are presented for repurchase. In some cases, the S corporation or the original shareholders guarantee that the exempt party will receive the fair market value of the nonvoting stock as of the date the stock was given to the exempt party if that amount is greater than the fair market value on the repurchase date.

Because they own 100 percent of the voting stock of the S corporation, the original shareholders have the power to determine the amount and timing of any distributions made with respect to the voting and nonvoting stock. The original shareholders exercise that power to cause the S corporation to limit or suspend distributions to its shareholders while the exempt party purportedly owns the nonvoting stock. For tax purposes, however, during that period, 90 percent of the S corporation's income is allocated to the exempt party and 10 percent of the S corporation's income is allocated to the original shareholders. The transaction is structured for the original shareholders to exercise the warrants and dilute the shares of nonvoting stock held by the exempt party, or for the S corporation or the original shareholders to purchase the nonvoting stock from the exempt party at a value that is substantially reduced by reason of the existence of the warrants. In either event, the exempt party will receive a share of the total economic benefit of stock ownership that is substantially lower than the share of the S corporation income allocated to the exempt party.

... The transaction described in this notice is designed to artificially shift the incidence of taxation on S corporation income away from taxable shareholders to the exempt party. In this manner, the original shareholders attempt to avoid paying income tax on most of the S corporation's income over a period of time. The Service intends to challenge the purported tax benefits from this transaction. . . .

## *NOTES*

1. *Some keys to the shelter*. The objective of the transaction described in Notice 2004-30 was to allocate most of the taxable income of the S corporation to parties who would not have to pay tax on such income, while preserving most of the economic benefit of the income for the corporation's taxable shareholders. As claimed by the shelter promoters, some of the keys to the validity of the plan

were: (1) disregard of the nonvoting stock as an impermissible second class of stock (I.R.C. § 1361(c)(4)); (2) disregard of the warrants as an impermissible second class of stock because their terms satisfied a specific regulatory safe harbor (Reg. § 1.1361-1(*l*)(4)(iii)(A) and (C)); and (3) asserted ability of the tax-exempt shareholder to avoid paying tax on its allocable share of the S corporation income, even though such income constituted unrelated business taxable income (I.R.C. § 512(e)). The promoters also had to assure participants that the various prearranged steps to the shelter would survive scrutiny under the step transaction doctrine and not be recharacterized under substance-over-form principles.

2. *The manufactured nature of the shelter.* As disclosed in the Congressional hearing on the shelter, the shelter promoters used a variety of techniques, including cold-calling prospective customers, to identify S corporations with enough income to make participation in the tax shelter worthwhile. They also went to considerable lengths to solicit participation on the part of a special class of tax-exempt entities that the promoters believed could avoid paying tax on the S corporation income allocated to them. The promoters then tried to pair up the solicited S corporations and exempt parties so as to create an appearance that their connection was reasonable. For example, shareholders of S corporations operating in a given location made contributions of stock to exempt entities active in the same location. The promoters suggested that clients take various other steps to ensure that the tax shelter would not adversely affect the business operations of the S corporation. For instance, to protect an S corporation from business competitors who might try to take advantage of the fact that newly issued stock would at least temporarily be held by an outsider (the tax-exempt shareholder), promoters suggested that participants change the name of their companies to hide involvement in the shelter from their competitors.

3. *Listed transactions.* The purpose of the Notice was to alert taxpayers that the described transaction and any substantially similar transaction constituted a "listed transaction." The significance of this classification is discussed in the following section.

## 2. *Disclosure and Related Requirements to Curb Tax Avoidance*

The perceived proliferation of tax avoidance transactions led the government to develop a new strategy to supplement traditional enforcement efforts and litigation. The strategy attempts to discourage participation in a tax shelter before it becomes widespread and requires a major commitment of limited government enforcement resources. In addition to being costly, litigation is sometimes criticized as producing ad hoc and untimely results for the tax system. Even if a court resolves the consequences of a particular tax shelter in the government's favor, the decision may provide little help in deterring promoters and taxpayers from developing and entering into a later generation of shelters.

The new strategy entails giving prompt notice to the public of specific tax avoidance transactions, such as the one set forth in Notice 2004-30. Transactions that are the same or substantially similar to the described transaction are known as "listed transactions." The notice describes the government's position with respect to these transactions and alerts taxpayers to the likelihood that the government will challenge the claimed tax consequences. In addition to the transaction described in Notice 2004-30, the transactions described in Notice 2002-65 (p. 22) and Notice 97-21 (p. 83) as well as the LILO and SILO transactions and others discussed in subsequent chapters, are all examples of listed transactions.

The key to implementing the government's anti-shelter strategy is the creation of a "web of disclosure" and certain record-keeping requirements affecting taxpayers and certain advisors. The requirements enable the IRS to identify early the nature of potentially questionable transactions and their participants, as well as to determine how extensively a particular tax strategy has been disseminated. The information not only forms the basis for issuance of a listed transaction notice but also increases the awareness of taxpayers and their advisors that their involvement in a questionable transaction will likely be detected.

Taxpayers must disclose on their tax returns their participation in a "reportable transaction," which includes: (1) any listed transaction; (2) transactions offered to the taxpayer under conditions of confidentiality and for which the taxpayer has paid a minimum fee; (3) transactions promising the taxpayer a refund of fees in the event all or a portion of the intended tax benefits from the transaction are not sustained; (4) transactions resulting in certain claimed losses in excess of threshold amounts; and (5) certain "transactions of interest" that have the potential for tax avoidance and have been previously identified by the IRS. Reg. § 1.6011-4(a) and (b). The IRS has broad authority to expand or contract the list of required disclosures, and has already identified a number of common transactions resulting in claimed losses that need not be disclosed. As part of the disclosure requirement, taxpayers must maintain copies of all material documents relating to their involvement in a reportable transaction until expiration of the applicable statute of limitations for asserting a deficiency resulting from the taxpayer's participation in the transaction. Reg. § 1.6011-4(g)(1).

Full disclosure by taxpayers is fostered in several ways. First, taxpayers who fail to make a required disclosure must pay a penalty. I.R.C. § 6707A(a)-(c). In addition, taxpayers owing a deficiency resulting from their participation in a listed transaction or a non-listed reportable transaction with a significant tax avoidance purpose are more likely to be liable for a penalty; a higher, strict liability penalty may be imposed if the transaction was not disclosed. I.R.C. §§ 6662A and 6664(d). If a taxpayer fails to disclose participation in a listed transaction, the statute of limitations for assessing any resulting tax deficiency is tolled until one year after the IRS obtains information about the taxpayer's involvement. I.R.C. § 6501(c)(10). Finally, certain public companies must include in their SEC filings information about tax penalties imposed as a result of the company's participation in certain reportable transactions, including the penalty for failing to disclose a listed transaction on the company's tax return. I.R.C. § 6707A(e).

The web of disclosure extends also to any "material advisor" with respect to a reportable transaction. The term "material advisor" is defined broadly to include any person providing "material aid, assistance, or advice with respect to organizing, managing, promoting, selling, implementing, insuring, or carrying out any reportable transaction," but only if such person derives gross income above certain threshold amounts from its involvement. I.R.C. § 6111(b)(1). In general, to be a material advisor, a person must provide an oral or written statement relating to a tax aspect of a transaction that causes the transaction to be a reportable transaction, and the statement must be provided to a person who must disclose the transaction, such as the taxpayer or another material advisor. Reg. § 301.6111-3(b)(2)(i) and (ii)(A). Thus, a material advisor generally includes a promoter or organizer who develops a reportable transaction as well as an attorney who advises such persons regarding the tax aspects of the transaction, assuming the gross income threshold is exceeded. Material advisors are required to file information returns with the IRS describing the reportable transaction and the claimed tax benefits. I.R.C. § 6111(a). Failure to make the required disclosure results in a penalty. I.R.C. § 6707.

Finally, each material advisor to a reportable transaction must maintain, and make available to the IRS upon request, a list of advisees, including the advisee's identifying information, circumstances of involvement in the transaction, amount invested, and claimed tax consequences from the transaction. Persons need not be listed if they entered into a listed transaction or transaction of interest more than six years before the transaction was identified by published guidance. Each material advisor must also list the name of other known material advisors. I.R.C. § 6112; Reg. § 301.6112-1(b)(2) and (2)(i). The list must be maintained for seven years following the earlier of the date the material advisor last made a statement relating to the transaction or the date the transaction was last entered into. Reg. § 301.6112-1(d). Failure to make this list available to the IRS within 20 days of request also results in a penalty. I.R.C. § 6708.

## *NOTES*

1. *Circular 230.* Circular 230 (31 C.F.R. Part 10) contains the rules governing the practice of taxpayer representatives before the Treasury Department, including the IRS. Recent amendments to Circular 230 address the content of opinions provided to taxpayers who engage in certain tax avoidance transactions. In certain cases, these opinions may be used by taxpayers to help avoid the imposition of penalties in the event their tax claims are not upheld. Circular 230 provides that any "covered opinion," generally defined as any written advice (including electronic communications such as e-mails) concerning the federal tax issues arising from a listed transaction and certain other tax avoidance transactions, must satisfy certain minimum standards. In general, a covered opinion must: (1) identify and consider all relevant facts and not be based on unreasonable factual assumptions; (2) relate the applicable law to the relevant facts and not assume the favorable resolution of any

significant federal tax issue; and (3) state with reasons the likelihood of the taxpayer's success (both overall and with respect to each significant federal tax issue) or explain why such a conclusion cannot be reached. 31 C.F.R. § 10.35(b)(2)(i) and (c). If, based strictly on the merits (and without taking into account the audit lottery or the possibility of a favorable settlement), the opinion fails to reach a "more likely than not" conclusion (more than 50 percent probability) concerning likelihood of success with respect to any significant federal tax issue, the opinion must state that it cannot be used for the purpose of avoiding penalties that may be imposed on the taxpayer. Id., § 10.35(c)(3)(ii) and (iii) and (e)(4). (This requirement is one of the reasons for the common, broad disclaimer appearing as a legend of e-mail messages and other correspondence prepared by tax professionals.) Certain written advice, including advice not prepared in connection with a taxpayer's taking a position on a tax return, or that does not resolve a federal tax issue in the taxpayer's favor, is excluded from these requirements. Id., § 10.35(b)(2)(ii)(C) and (E). Practitioners who violate these requirements may be censured, suspended, disbarred from practicing before the IRS, or required to pay monetary penalties, depending upon the nature of the violation.

2. *Other developments principally affecting public companies.* Other recent developments, principally affecting public companies, may also change the calculus of whether such companies engage in tax avoidance transactions.

a. *Schedule M-3.* As described in chapter three, Schedule M-3 generally must be filed with the income tax return of any corporation with assets of at least $10 million. This schedule requires a detailed reconciliation of differences in a corporation's computation of its book and taxable income and increases the likelihood that the IRS will discover aggressive or questionable tax return positions.
b. *FASB Interpretation No. 48 (FIN 48).* Under FIN 48 (codified in FASB Accounting Standards Codification (ASC) 740-10), a company must determine that it is more likely than not (more than 50 percent probability) that a tax position, such as a claimed tax deduction or credit, will be sustained in order for the position to be taken into account for financial accounting purposes. The determination must be made under the assumption that the IRS will examine the tax position and have full knowledge of all relevant information. FIN 48 makes it more likely that aggressive or questionable tax positions will provide no immediate financial accounting benefits.
c. *Tax accrual work papers.* Current IRS policy is to allow its examiners to request the tax accrual work papers of taxpayers only if they have claimed tax benefits from a listed transaction; a broader request is permissible if the listed transaction was not disclosed or the taxpayer engaged in multiple such transactions. Ann. 2002-63, 2002-2 C.B. 72 (announcing the IRS's "policy of restraint"); Ann. 2010-76, 2010-2 C.B. 432 (generally expanding policy of restraint to include work papers connected to required disclosure of uncertain tax positions (see note d. below)). Tax accrual work papers contain the taxpayer's analysis of its potential tax liability if tax positions taken by the

taxpayer are identified and challenged by the IRS. The analysis, which may lay out the taxpayer's estimate of success and potential dollar exposure with respect to each of its tax reporting positions, is necessary to calculate the amount of any tax liability reserve for purposes of the taxpayer's financial statements. Thus, the work papers may identify the taxpayer's own assessment of "soft spots" in the taxpayer's tax return. The work papers are commonly shared with the taxpayer's independent auditors who are responsible under the securities laws for certifying the information on the taxpayer's financial statements. A broad disclosure of work papers to the IRS might undermine the taxpayer's candid relationship with its auditors.

In U.S. v. Textron, 577 F.3d 21 (1st Cir. 2009), cert. denied, 130 S. Ct. 3320 (2010), aff'g in part and rev'g in part 507 F. Supp. 2d 138 (D.R.I. 2007), the First Circuit agreed with the lower court that the taxpayer waived its attorney-client privilege and the section 7525 tax advice privilege when it voluntarily disclosed the work papers to its independent auditors. The First Circuit further concluded that the taxpayer's work-product privilege did not bar disclosure of the work papers to the IRS (which had made the request based on evidence that the taxpayer had engaged in nine SILO transactions). The District Court had found that, but for the possibility of litigation with the IRS and a determination adverse to the taxpayer, there would have been no need to prepare the work papers and create a tax liability reserve. The lower court concluded that the work papers were prepared "because of" the prospect of litigation and were therefore protected by the work-product doctrine. The First Circuit disagreed, finding that the doctrine focuses on materials prepared "for use" in litigation, and that there was no evidence the work papers had been "prepared for such a use or would in fact serve any useful purpose for Textron in conducting litigation if it arose." 577 F.3d at 30. Rather, the work papers were prepared to satisfy the taxpayer's obligations under the securities laws. The court noted that the taxpayer would have been required to prepare the work papers even if the chance of litigation on any issue was remote. In response to the taxpayer's contention that disclosure of the documents would be unfair, the court responded:

> [T]ax collection is not a game. Underpaying taxes threatens the essential public interest in revenue collection. If a blueprint to Textron's possible improper deductions can be found in Textron's files, it is properly available to the government *unless* privileged. Virtually all discovery against a party *aims* at securing information that may assist an opponent in uncovering the truth. Unprivileged IRS information is equally subject to discovery. [Id. at 31 (emphasis in original).]

See also U.S. v. El Paso Co., 682 F.2d 530 (5th Cir. 1982), cert. denied, 466 U.S. 944 (1984) (concluding that work-product protection is available only if primary motivating reason for work papers was to prepare for future litigation); but cf. U.S. v. Deloitte, LLP, 610 F.3d 129 (D.C. Cir. 2010) (concluding that protection is available as long as one of several uses of work papers includes the prospect of litigation).

d. *Disclosure of uncertain tax positions.* To improve the efficiency of IRS tax audits, certain corporations are required to disclose their uncertain tax positions on their tax returns. Reg. § 1.6012-2(a)(4). The disclosure, which is intended to dovetail the analysis already required by FIN 48, must include a concise description of each uncertain tax position for which the taxpayer recorded a reserve for financial accounting purposes. The concise description must include all of the relevant facts affecting the tax treatment of the position; the information must reasonably be expected to apprise the IRS of the identity of the tax position and the nature of the issue. The corporation need not, however, disclose the rationale for an uncertain tax position or the nature of the uncertainty. To help the IRS determine the materiality of the disclosed positions, the corporation must also rank the positions based on the amount of reserve recorded for the position (without revealing the specific amount reserved for it) and identify those positions for which the reserve amount exceeds ten percent of the aggregate reserve for all tax positions. Corporations having assets of at least $100 million and issuing audited financial statements must comply with this new reporting requirement for taxable years beginning in 2010. Over a five year period, the asset threshold for reporting purposes is reduced to $10 million. Ann. 2010-75, 2010-2 C.B. 428.

## C. Codification of Economic Substance Doctrine

After more than a decade of debate, Congress in 2010 codified the economic substance doctrine; it also enacted a strict liability penalty to be added to any tax underpayment attributable to a violation of the doctrine (or any "similar rule of law"). Read I.R.C. §§ 7701(o), 6662(a), (b)(6), and (i), and 6664(a), (c)(1) and (2), and the following legislative description of the new provision.

### Staff of Joint Committee on Taxation, Technical Explanation of the Revenue Provisions of the "Reconciliation Act of 2010," as Amended (2010)

The provision clarifies and enhances the application of the economic substance doctrine. Under the provision, new section 7701(o) provides that in the case of any transaction[1] to which the economic substance doctrine is relevant, such transaction

1. The term "transaction" includes a series of transactions.

is treated as having economic substance only if (1) the transaction changes in a meaningful way (apart from Federal income tax effects) the taxpayer's economic position, and (2) the taxpayer has a substantial purpose (apart from Federal income tax effects) for entering into such transaction. The provision provides a uniform definition of economic substance, but does not alter the flexibility of the courts in other respects.

The determination of whether the economic substance doctrine is relevant to a transaction is made in the same manner as if the provision had never been enacted. Thus, the provision does not change present law standards in determining when to utilize an economic substance analysis.[2]

The provision is not intended to alter the tax treatment of certain basic business transactions that, under longstanding judicial and administrative practice are respected, merely because the choice between meaningful economic alternatives is largely or entirely based on comparative tax advantages. Among these basic transactions are (1) the choice between capitalizing a business enterprise with debt or equity; (2) a U.S. person's choice between utilizing a foreign corporation or a domestic corporation to make a foreign investment; (3) the choice to enter a transaction or series of transactions that constitute a corporate organization or reorganization under subchapter C; and (4) the choice to utilize a related-party entity in a transaction, provided that the arm's length standard of section 482 and other applicable concepts are satisfied. Leasing transactions, like all other types of transactions, will continue to be analyzed in light of all the facts and circumstances. As under present law, whether a particular transaction meets the requirements for specific treatment under any of these provisions is a question of facts and circumstances. Also, the fact that a transaction meets the requirements for specific treatment under any provision of the Code is not determinative of whether a transaction or series of transactions of which it is a part has economic substance.

The provision does not alter the court's ability to aggregate, disaggregate, or otherwise recharacterize a transaction when applying the doctrine. For example, the provision reiterates the present-law ability of the courts to bifurcate a transaction in which independent activities with non-tax objectives are combined with an unrelated item having only tax-avoidance objectives in order to disallow those tax-motivated benefits.

*Conjunctive analysis*—The provision clarifies that the economic substance doctrine involves a conjunctive analysis—there must be an inquiry regarding the objective effects of the transaction on the taxpayer's economic position as well as an inquiry regarding the taxpayer's subjective motives for engaging in the transaction. Under the provision, a transaction must satisfy both tests, i.e., the transaction must change in a meaningful way (apart from Federal income tax effects) the taxpayer's economic position and the taxpayer must have a substantial non-Federal-income-tax

---

2. If the realization of the tax benefits of a transaction is consistent with the Congressional purpose or plan that the tax benefits were designed by Congress to effectuate, it is not intended that such tax benefits be disallowed. . . .

purpose for entering into such transaction, in order for a transaction to be treated as having economic substance. This clarification eliminates the disparity that exists among the Federal circuit courts regarding the application of the doctrine, and modifies its application in those circuits in which either a change in economic position or a non-tax business purpose (without having both) is sufficient to satisfy the economic substance doctrine.[3]

*Non-Federal-income-tax business purpose*—Under the provision, a taxpayer's non-Federal-income-tax purpose for entering into a transaction (the second prong in the analysis) must be "substantial." For purposes of this analysis, any State or local income tax effect which is related to a Federal income tax effect is treated in the same manner as a Federal income tax effect. Also, a purpose of achieving a favorable accounting treatment for financial reporting purposes is not taken into account as a non-Federal-income-tax purpose if the origin of the financial accounting benefit is a reduction of Federal income tax.

*Profit potential*—Under the provision, a taxpayer may rely on factors other than profit potential to demonstrate that a transaction results in a meaningful change in the taxpayer's economic position or that the taxpayer has a substantial non-Federal-income-tax purpose for entering into such transaction. The provision does not require or establish a minimum return that will satisfy the profit potential test. However, if a taxpayer relies on a profit potential, the present value of the reasonably expected pre-tax profit must be substantial in relation to the present value of the expected net tax benefits that would be allowed if the transaction were respected. Fees and other transaction expenses are taken into account as expenses in determining pre-tax profit. In addition, the Secretary is to issue regulations requiring foreign taxes to be treated as expenses in determining pre-tax profit in appropriate cases.

*Personal transactions of individuals*—In the case of an individual, the provision applies only to transactions entered into in connection with a trade or business or an activity engaged in for the production of income.

*Other rules*—No inference is intended as to the proper application of the economic substance doctrine under present law. The provision is not intended to alter or supplant any other rule of law, including any common-law doctrine or provision of the Code or regulations or other guidance thereunder; and it is intended the provision be construed as being additive to any such other rule of law.

As with other provisions in the Code, the Secretary has general authority to prescribe rules and regulations necessary for the enforcement of the provision.

*Penalty for underpayments and understatements attributable to transactions lacking economic substance*—The provision imposes a new strict liability penalty under section 6662 for an underpayment attributable to any disallowance of claimed tax

---

3. The provision defines "economic substance doctrine" as the common law doctrine under which tax benefits under subtitle A with respect to a transaction are not allowable if the transaction does not have economic substance or lacks a business purpose. Thus, the definition includes any doctrine that denies tax benefits for lack of economic substance, for lack of business purpose, or for lack of both.

benefits by reason of a transaction lacking economic substance, as defined in new section 7701(o), or failing to meet the requirements of any similar rule of law. [4] The penalty rate is 20 percent (increased to 40 percent if the taxpayer does not adequately disclose the relevant facts affecting the tax treatment in the return or a statement attached to the return). An amended return or supplement to a return is not taken into account if filed after the taxpayer has been contacted for audit or such other date as is specified by the Secretary. No exceptions (including the reasonable cause rules) to the penalty are available. Thus, under the provision, outside opinions or in-house analysis would not protect a taxpayer from imposition of a penalty if it is determined that the transaction lacks economic substance or fails to meet the requirements of any similar rule of law. . . .

## *NOTES*

1. *Scope of section 7701(o).* The Code and regulations are already replete with anti-tax-avoidance provisions applicable in specific cases. Section 7701(o) may be viewed as imposing a substance-over-form principle broadly throughout the tax law, even outside the areas and circumstances in which the principle has traditionally been invoked. Many tax shelter claims have involved the unanticipated consequences of interactions of different portions of the law; section 7701(o) presumably will now be available to determine whether those consequences will be respected.

A broad provision, of course, runs the risk of affecting too many transactions, including ones whose tax advantages are fully intended by Congress. The statute, for the most part, is silent as to its scope. Other than excluding certain personal transactions of individuals, the statute leaves to the courts to determine whether the doctrine is "relevant" and should be applied. Indeed, the determination of relevance is to be made as if the provision had never been enacted. The Joint Committee explanation identifies a few transactions that should generally be immune from challenge under the new provision. Given the "unofficial" nature of this legislative history, many have urged the IRS to compile and publish "angel lists" of permissible transactions in regulations. The ambiguous scope of the new provision relates not only to whether the doctrine is relevant in a particular case, but also to the specific doctrines to which it applies. For example, what precisely is the relationship between the "economic substance doctrine" (as defined in section 7701(o)(5)(A) and explained by the Joint Committee (n. 3)) and the various substance-over-form doctrines (such as the sham transaction, step transaction, and business purpose doctrines)? Traditionally, the two-prong economic substance test incorporates certain of the substance-over-form doctrines, thereby compounding the potential confusion.

---

4. It is intended that the penalty would apply to a transaction the tax benefits of which are disallowed as a result of the application of the similar factors and analysis that is required under the provision for an economic substance analysis, even if a different term is used to describe the doctrine.

Compilation of an angel list would be a monumental task and might even contravene the intended prophylactic effect of the new statute. In Notice 2010-62, 2010-2 C.B. 411, the IRS provided interim guidance on how it intends to apply the new provision:

> [T]he IRS will continue to analyze when the economic substance doctrine will apply in the same fashion as it did prior to the enactment of section 7701(o). If authorities, prior to the enactment of section 7701(o), provided that the economic substance doctrine was not relevant to whether certain tax benefits are allowable, the IRS will continue to take the position that the economic substance doctrine is not relevant to whether those tax benefits are allowable. The IRS anticipates that the case law regarding the circumstances in which the economic substance doctrine is relevant will continue to develop. Consistent with section 7701(o)(5)(C), codification of the economic substance doctrine should not affect the ongoing development of authorities on this issue. The Treasury Department and the IRS do not intend to issue general administrative guidance regarding the types of transactions to which the economic substance doctrine either applies or does not apply.

2. *Penalties*. The penalty structure accompanying section 7701(o) furnishes an important reason for the demand for increased certainty. In general, tax underpayments attributable to a violation of the provision are subject to a 40 percent penalty, which is reduced to 20 percent only if the taxpayer adequately discloses the challenged transaction. I.R.C. § 6662(a), (b)(6), and (i). Moreover, the strict liability penalty is not abated, for example, if there was reasonable cause for the underpayment and the taxpayer acted in good faith. I.R.C. § 6664(c)(1) and (2). As a practical matter, this means that taxpayers cannot be shielded from the penalty even if they obtain appropriate advice of counsel prior to carrying out the transaction. Proponents of a tough, strict liability penalty argue that it enhances the deterrent effect of codifying the doctrine, discouraging all but the most audacious taxpayers from entering into questionable transactions. Opponents assert, however, that a penalty has a useful deterrent effect only when the activity triggering the penalty is reasonably clear. Otherwise, the penalty may operate erratically, deterring some legitimate business activity and potentially punishing innocent violators. Congress presumably did not intend to require taxpayers to engage in transactions in the *least* tax-efficient manner possible in order to avoid the penalty. A tough penalty may also backfire; the IRS and the courts may be reluctant to assert and apply the economic substance doctrine if they know that such a penalty would automatically follow.

The penalty applies if the taxpayer's claimed tax benefits are disallowed by reason of section 7701(o) or for failing to meet the requirements of any "similar rule of law." I.R.C. § 6662(b)(6). According to the Joint Committee's explanation (n. 4), a similar rule of law includes one resulting from "application of the similar factors and analysis that is required under the provision for an economic substance analysis, even if a different term is used to describe the doctrine." In addition to potentially implicating various common-law substance-over-form doctrines, the description could conceivably encompass statutory and regulatory anti-avoidance provisions. Furthermore, because courts sometimes list alternative rationales for their holdings, it may be difficult to determine which specific rule of law has been violated in any given case.

The uncertain scope of both section 7701(o) and the penalty creates the possibility of the new provision being used strategically by the IRS as a bargaining chip in settlement negotiations. Courts may be hard pressed to ignore the economic substance doctrine if the IRS raises it. Yet, if the position is raised and considered, the penalty significantly increases the stakes of the disagreement. The IRS's interim guidance in Notice 2010-62, as well as its announced plan to centralize the decision-making process for asserting the doctrine (and penalty), are intended to moderate such concerns, but it remains to be seen how the law will evolve.

3. *Other broad anti-tax-avoidance provisions.* Other tax provisions that carry out a broad anti-tax-avoidance function (but are narrower than section 7701(o)) include sections 269, 482, 446. Another notable example is the section 701 anti-abuse regulation in the partnership area.

a. *Section 269.* This provision potentially applies if, in general, any person or persons acquire control of a corporation (meaning at least 50 percent of the voting power or value of the corporation), or a corporation acquires property from another corporation with a transferred basis (such as pursuant to a "reorganization," discussed in chapter eleven). In either case, if the principal purpose of the acquisition was tax avoidance by securing the benefit of a deduction, credit, or other allowance that the acquirer would not otherwise enjoy, the IRS may disallow such tax benefit. This provision has been applied in cases where the purpose of a corporate acquisition is to acquire a favorable tax attribute, such as the target corporation's net operating loss carryforwards. A limiting feature of the provision is the requirement that "the" principal purpose of the acquisition must be tax avoidance, which is a high standard to prove.

b. *Section 482.* This provision authorizes the IRS to reallocate tax items among commonly controlled organizations if the reallocation is necessary "to prevent evasion of taxes or clearly to reflect the income" of such organizations. This provision is most commonly applied to reallocate tax items between commonly controlled U.S. and foreign entities.

c. *Section 446(b).* This provision grants broad authority to the IRS to compute taxable income using a method of accounting that "clearly reflect[s] income."

d. *Reg. § 1.701-2(b).* The partnership anti-abuse regulation authorizes the IRS to recast a partnership transaction for tax purposes if (1) a principal purpose of the transaction is "to reduce substantially the present value of the partners' aggregate federal tax liability" and (2) the tax savings is accomplished "in a manner that is inconsistent with the intent of subchapter K." Thus far, despite the potentially expansive language, the regulation has not had much effect in litigated cases.

4. *Rules vs. standards.* Codification of the economic substance doctrine revives the debate between rules and standards and whether it makes more sense to address tax avoidance through a somewhat nebulous standard rather than a specific rule. An example of a specific rule in the tax area is a provision permitting the recovery of capital expenditures based upon an assumed recovery period and rate of recovery. An example of a standard in the same situation would be a provision authorizing taxpayers to deduct a reasonable estimate of the economic depreciation from capital expenditures suffered during the year.

Rules are generally thought to be more costly to develop than standards. In the depreciation example, assuming a policy determination to permit a tax allowance equal to economic depreciation, a rule requires considerable effort to determine the appropriate period and rate of recovery for many different classes of capital investments. In contrast, a standard essentially externalizes that cost by obliging each taxpayer to make a case-by-case determination.

From the standpoint of the tax system as a whole, however, rules may be cheaper to implement and enforce. Once made, a rule simplifies the upfront compliance task for each taxpayer and also reduces the costs necessary to resolve controversies after-the-fact. The case-by-case determination required by a standard likely results in more, and more difficult, disputes after the fact than had the taxpayer been required to comply with a rule.

Rules also permit less discretion than a standard, both at the initial stage of compliance and at later stages when disputes must be resolved. Rules, therefore, are sometimes viewed as more consistent with the tax policy principle of treating similarly situated taxpayers similarly.

The comparative advantage of a rule over a standard, however, may be primarily important in the taxation of *common* transactions involving many repeat activities undertaken by numerous taxpayers. In the case of *uncommon* transactions, the advantages may be exactly the opposite. The more unlikely a transaction is, the less worthwhile it may be to incur the high upfront costs of crafting an appropriate tax rule. It thus may be preferable to provide a more open-ended standard initially, wait for the uncommon transaction to occur (if it ever does), and then determine the precise tax treatment after the fact. Moreover, uncommon transactions may give rise to less concern about discretion and the failure to tax similarly situated taxpayers in similar ways; since the transactions are, by definition, uncommon, they do not involve many similarly situated taxpayers. If this common/uncommon distinction is valid, then it may help to justify use of a broad anti-tax-avoidance or substance-over-form standard, rather than a rule, to combat tax avoidance transactions. Although tax shelters may often include common individual steps, they may combine these steps in uncommon ways and therefore may appropriately be viewed as uncommon transactions. Thus, it may be more efficient to allow shelter transactions to be subject to a somewhat nebulous standard at the outset, with the precise tax ramifications of the transaction determined only in retrospect.

5. *A look ahead.* Section 7701(o) potentially affects the tax consequences of every transaction examined in this course. Thus, you should be sure to keep this provision in mind as we delve into the details of subchapter C.

# Chapter 5

# Ordinary Distributions

This chapter examines the tax consequences of an ordinary distribution of cash or property by a corporation to its shareholders with respect to its stock. For tax purposes, an "ordinary distribution" should be distinguished from a *redemption distribution*, in which the shareholder typically surrenders some stock in the transaction, and a *liquidating distribution*, in which the corporation completely liquidates. (Those two topics are considered in chapters six and ten, respectively.) The requirement that the transaction be "with respect to the stock" of the distributing corporation distinguishes an ordinary distribution from a corporate payment to a shareholder who is acting in a nonshareholder capacity, such as a debtholder or employee of the corporation.

As you gradually learn how specific corporate transactions are taxed, try to keep in mind alternative ways of achieving the parties' economic objectives. You will soon discover that the numerous rules in subchapter C often unavoidably overlap one another, thereby creating the possibility that a given economic result reached in different ways may have different tax consequences. The goal of the tax planner is to figure out how to obtain the most beneficial tax outcome that will be respected by the IRS and the courts. Meanwhile, the goal of the policymaker is to try to make as consistent as possible the tax consequences of similar transactions, an objective that helps to explain much reform in subchapter C.

Parts A and B describe the shareholder- and corporate-level tax consequences, respectively, of an ordinary distribution by a C corporation. Part C then briefly revisits S corporations and considers the tax treatment of ordinary distributions by such corporations if they have a prior history as a C corporation.

## A. Shareholder-Level Consequences

Read I.R.C. §§ 301(a)-(c), 316(a), 61(a)(7). The portion of an ordinary distribution qualifying as a dividend must be included in the gross income of the distributee. For tax purposes, however, the term "dividend" does not have the same meaning as in corporate law. Rather, an ordinary distribution is treated as a dividend for tax purposes only to the extent the distribution is made out of the current or accumulated earnings and profits ("E&P") of the distributing corporation. The purpose of E&P is to determine whether a distribution constitutes a realization of the distributee shareholder's prior, untaxed enrichment or a mere return of capital. The portion of a distribution in excess of E&P is treated as a tax-free return of the distributee's basis in the stock with respect to which the distribution is made, with any additional amount taxed as gain from the sale of such stock. These rules apply to distributions of cash or property (other than stock of the distributing corporation and rights to acquire such stock). See I.R.C. § 317(a). (The tax treatment of distributions of stock and stock rights of the distributing corporation is examined in chapter nine.) The distributee obtains a basis in any property distributed equal to its fair market value at the time of the distribution. I.R.C. § 301(d).

### 1. *Earnings and Profits*

As just described, E&P is critical to determine the tax treatment of an ordinary distribution. Surprisingly, however, the term is not defined in the statute or regulations. The following ruling provides some guidance on the meaning of E&P.

## Rev. Rul. 2009-25

2009-2 C.B. 365

. . . When is interest that is disallowed as a deduction under § 264(a)(4) of the Internal Revenue Code ("Disallowed Interest") taken into account in determining earnings and profits?

FACTS

A, an individual, holds a paid-up life insurance contract on his own life. Upon the death of A, the death benefit under the contract ($500) is payable to the beneficiary named in the contract.

X is a calendar year subchapter C corporation unrelated to A. On the first day of Year 1, X purchases A's life insurance contract for $100 in a transaction that is not described in § 101(a)(2)(A) or (B), and names itself the beneficiary under the contract.

On the first day of Year 1, X borrows $100 at seven percent simple interest per annum to purchase the life insurance contract. The interest on the loan is unconditionally payable at the end of Year 1 and Year 2 and the interest was in fact paid at the end of Year 1 and Year 2. But for its disallowance under § 264(a)(4), X could deduct seven dollars of interest on the loan in both Year 1 and Year 2 under § 163.

Other than the initial purchase price, the interest on the loan is the only amount X incurs in connection with the contract.

A dies on the first day of Year 3, and X receives the $500 death benefit under the life insurance contract. Pursuant to § 101(a)(2), X includes $386 in gross income ($500 (death benefit) – ($100 (amount paid for the contract) + $14 (Disallowed Interest deductions in Year 1 and Year 2))).

## LAW AND ANALYSIS

Section 101(a)(1) provides that except as otherwise provided in § 101(a)(2), (d), (f), and (j), gross income does not include amounts received (whether in a single sum or otherwise) under a life insurance contract, if such amounts are paid by reason of the death of the insured.

Section 101(a)(2) generally provides that in the case of a transfer for valuable consideration, by assignment or otherwise, of a life insurance contract or any interest therein, the amount excluded from gross income by § 101(a)(1) shall not exceed an amount equal to the sum of the actual value of such consideration and the premiums and "other amounts" subsequently paid by the transferee. The term "other amounts" includes interest paid or accrued by the transferee on indebtedness with respect to the contract or any interest therein if such interest paid or accrued is not allowable as a deduction by reason of § 264(a)(4).

Section 163(a) generally provides that a deduction is allowed for all interest paid or accrued within the taxable year on indebtedness.

Section 264(a)(4) generally provides that no deduction shall be allowed for any interest paid or accrued on any indebtedness with respect to one or more life insurance policies owned by the taxpayer covering the life of any individual, or any endowment or annuity contracts owned by the taxpayer covering any individual.

Earnings and profits are a measure of economic income, or a corporation's capacity to pay dividends. . . .

> "In general, the computation of earnings and profits of a corporation . . . is based upon reasonable accounting concepts that take into account the economic realities of corporate transactions as well as those resulting from the application of tax law. Thus, losses and expenses that are disallowed as a deduction for Federal income tax purposes, charitable contributions in excess of the limitation provided therefore [sic], and other items that have actually depleted the assets of the corporation, even though not reflected in the income computations, are allowed as deductions in computing earnings and profits." Rev. Rul. 75-515, 1975-2 C.B. 117, obsoleted by Rev. Rul. 2003-99, 2003-2 C.B. 388. . . .

See also Rev. Rul. 71-165, 1971-1 C.B. 111 ("An expense of an accrual basis corporation that under the Code is never an allowable deduction in computing taxable income usually is reflected in earnings and profits in the year to which it is attributable, except where the Code specifically provides that the corporation's earnings and profits shall not be reduced by any amount which is not allowable as a deduction in computing its taxable income."). . . . Because Disallowed Interest depletes the assets of a corporation at the time the interest would be allowed as a deduction but for its disallowance under § 264(a)(4), earnings and profits are also reduced in that year. Accordingly, X in both Year 1 and Year 2 reduces its earnings and profits by the seven dollars of Disallowed Interest.

In Year 3, X receives the $500 death benefit under the life insurance contract purchased from A and, under § 101(a)(2), excludes from gross income an amount representing the $14 of Disallowed Interest.

Items excluded from gross income generally increase earnings and profits. See § 1.312-6(b). Furthermore, even though the Disallowed Interest in Year 1 and Year 2 actually depletes the amount of earnings available for distribution, X previously reduced its earnings and profits by the Disallowed Interest in each of those years. Section 1.312-6(d) ("A loss sustained for a year before the taxable year does not affect the earnings and profits of the taxable year."); Rev. Rul. 76-299, 1976-2 C.B. 211 ("A capital loss carryover does not affect the earnings and profits of the taxable year in which it is used because the loss giving rise to the carryover is reflected in the accumulated earnings and profits at the beginning of the taxable year of the carryover"). Reducing earnings and profits in Year 3 by the amount of Disallowed Interest taken into account under § 101(a)(2) would cause an unwarranted double reduction of earnings and profits and, therefore, is not permitted. . . .

Although X in Year 3 includes in its gross income only $386 of the $500 death benefit because of the applicable offsets under § 101(a)(2) (including the $14 of Disallowed Interest), X includes $400 ($500 (the death benefit) less $100 (the amount X pays for the contract)) in its earnings and profits in Year 3.

## HOLDING

Disallowed Interest under § 264(a)(4) reduces earnings and profits for the taxable year in which the interest would have been allowable as a deduction but for its disallowance under § 264(a)(4). It does not further reduce earnings and profits when the death benefit is received under a life insurance contract.

## *NOTE*

*Calculating E&P.* As the ruling explains, E&P generally refers to the economic profits of a corporation and is somewhat similar to, but not the same as, the concept of "earned surplus" used for corporate law purposes. As a practical matter, the usual way to compute E&P is to adjust the corporation's taxable income to take into account differences between taxable and economic income. Skim I.R.C. § 312(k)(1) and (n). For example, to determine E&P, taxable income must generally be increased by untaxed items of economic income and decreased by nondeductible economic expenses. Corporations must use the same method of accounting (including realization principles) to compute both E&P and taxable income. Read Reg. § 1.312-6(a) and (b) and do the following problem.

**Problem 5-1:**

(a) In computing E&P, what adjustments (if any) must be made to a corporation's taxable income to take into account the following items:
 (i) Tax-exempt bond interest.
 (ii) Life insurance proceeds excluded from income under section 101.
 (iii) Entertainment expenses that cannot be adequately substantiated.
 (iv) A criminal fine paid as a result of a violation of the securities laws.
 (v) Accelerated depreciation properly claimed for tax purposes.

(b) A sole shareholder contributes $100 in the formation of a corporation. Assume that over a period of time (and without making any distributions), the corporation: (i) has $200 of taxable profits; (ii) pays corporate tax of $50; (iii) earns $100 of tax-exempt income; and (iv) invests $100 in a piece of land that is currently worth $400. If, at this point, it is permissible under state law for the corporation to borrow and make an ordinary distribution of $650, how is the shareholder taxed?

---

A distribution is a dividend if there is sufficient current *or* accumulated E&P. "Current" E&P refers to the corporation's E&P in the year of the distribution. In general, current E&P is considered first, and if there is enough current E&P, determined as of the close of the taxable year in which the distribution occurs and without diminution for the amount of the distribution, to "cover" the amount of the distribution, then the entire distribution is a dividend and the accumulated E&P (or any accumulated deficit in E&P) is ignored. I.R.C. § 316(a)(2); Reg. § 1.316-1(e) (ex.1), -2(a). The following ruling describes how much of a distribution is a dividend if current E&P (determined as just described) is insufficient to cover the distribution.

## Rev. Rul. 74-164

1974-1 C.B. 74

. . . X corporation and Y corporation each using the calendar year for Federal income tax purposes made distributions of $15,000 to their respective shareholders on July 1, 1971, and made no other distributions to their shareholders during the taxable year. The distributions were taxable as provided by section 301(c) of the Internal Revenue Code of 1954.

*Situation 1.* At the beginning of its taxable year 1971, X corporation had earnings and profits accumulated after February 28, 1913, of $40,000. It had an operating loss for the period January 1, 1971 through June 30, 1971, of $50,000 but had earnings and profits for the entire year 1971 of $5,000.

*Situation 2.* At the beginning of its taxable year 1971, Y corporation had a deficit in earnings and profits accumulated after February 28, 1913, of $60,000. Its net profits for the period January 1, 1971 through June 30, 1971, were $75,000 but its earnings and profits for the entire taxable year 1971 were only $5,000.

*Situation 3.* Assume the same facts as in *Situation 1* except that X had a deficit in earnings and profits of $5,000 for the entire taxable year 1971.

*Situation 4.* Assume the same facts as in *Situation 1* except that X had a deficit in earnings and profits of $55,000 for the entire taxable year 1971.

Section 301(a) and 301(c) of the Code provides, in part, that: (1) the portion of a distribution of property made by a corporation to a shareholder with respect to its stock which is a dividend (as defined in section 316), shall be included in the shareholder's gross income; (2) the portion of the distribution which is not a dividend shall be applied against and reduce the adjusted basis of the stock; and (3) the portion which is not a dividend to the extent that it exceeds the adjusted basis of the stock and is not out of increase in value accrued before March 1, 1913, shall be treated as gain from the sale or exchange of property.

Section 316(a) of the Code provides that the term "dividend" means any distribution of property made by a corporation to its shareholders out of its earnings and profits accumulated after February 28, 1913, or out of its earnings and profits of the taxable year computed as of the close of the taxable year without diminution by reason of any distribution made during the year, and *without regard to the amount of earnings and profits at the time the distribution was made.*

Section 1.316-2(a) of the Income Tax Regulations provides, in part, that in determining the source of a distribution, consideration should be given first, to the earnings and profits of the taxable year; and second, to the earnings and profits accumulated since February 28, 1913, only in the case where, and to the extent that, the distributions made during the taxable year are not regarded as out of the earnings and profits of that year.

Applying the foregoing principles, in *Situation 1*, the earnings and profits of X corporation for the taxable year 1971 of $5,000 and the earnings and profits accumulated since February 28, 1913, and prior to the taxable year 1971, of $40,000 were applicable to the distribution paid by it on July 1, 1971. Thus, $5,000 of the distribution of $15,000 was paid from the earnings and profits of the taxable year 1971 and the balance of $10,000 was paid from the earnings and profits accumulated since February 28, 1913. Therefore, the entire distribution of $15,000 was a dividend within the meaning of section 316 of the Code.

In *Situation 2* the earnings and profits of Y corporation for the taxable year 1971 of $5,000 were applicable to the distribution paid by Y corporation on July 1, 1971. Y corporation had no earnings and profits accumulated after February 28, 1913, available at the time of the distribution. Thus, only $5,000 of the distribution by Y corporation of $15,000 was a dividend within the meaning of section 316 of the Code. The balance of such distribution, $10,000 which was not a dividend, applied against and reduced the adjusted basis of the stock in the hands of the shareholders, and to the extent that it exceeded the adjusted basis of the stock was gain from the sale or exchange of property.

In the case of a deficit in earnings and profits for the taxable year in which distributions are made, the taxable status of distributions is dependent upon the amount of earnings and profits accumulated since February 28, 1913, and available at the dates of distribution. In determining the amount of such earnings and profits, section 1.316-2(b) of the regulations provides, in effect, that the deficit in earnings and profits of the taxable year will be prorated to the dates of distribution.

Applying the foregoing to *Situations 3* and *4* the distribution paid by X corporation on July 1, 1971, in each situation was a dividend within the meaning of section 316 of the Code to the extent indicated as follows:

*Situation #3*

| | |
|---|---|
| Accumulated Earnings and Profits (E&P) 1/1 | $40,000 |
| E&P deficit for entire taxable year ($5,000) Prorate to date of distribution 7/1 (1/2 of $5,000) | (2,500) |
| E&P available 7/1 | $37,500 |
| Distribution 7/1 ($15,000) | (15,000) taxable as a dividend |
| E&P deficit from 7/1 - 12/31 | (2,500) |
| Accumulated E&P balance 12/31 | $20,000 |

*Situation #4*

| | |
|---|---|
| Accumulated E&P 1/1 | $40,000 |
| E&P deficit for entire taxable year ($55,000) Prorate to date of distribution 7/1 (1/2 of $55,000) | (27,500) |
| E&P available 7/1 | $12,500 |
| Distribution 7/1 ($15,000) | (12,500) taxable as a dividend |
| E&P deficit from 7/1 to 12/31 | (27,500) |
| Accumulated E&P balance 12/31 | $(27,500) |

### *NOTES AND QUESTIONS*

1. *Is proration correct?* Read carefully Reg. § 1.316-2(a)-(c). Was it proper for the IRS to prorate the E&P deficit in *Situations 3* and *4*? Why or why not?

2. *Multiple distributions.* If multiple distributions are made on the same class of stock in a given year, current E&P is allocated pro rata to each distribution based upon the amount of the distribution. For example, if four $10,000 distributions are

made by a corporation in a year in which its current E&P, determined as of the end of the taxable year without diminution for the distributions, is $24,000, then $6,000 ($10,000/$40,000 × $24,000) of each distribution is treated as out of current E&P. Any accumulated E&P is then allocated to each distribution in the chronological order of the distribution beginning with the earliest. Reg. § 1.316-2(b) and (c). Thus, in the example, if the corporation also has $4,000 of accumulated E&P, then all of the first $10,000 distribution is a dividend (representing a distribution of $6,000 current and $4,000 accumulated E&P) but only $6,000 of each subsequent distribution is a dividend.

If multiple distributions are made on different classes of stock, the IRS's position is to allocate current E&P based on the distribution priority of each class under the corporate charter. Rev. Rul. 69-440, 1969-2 C.B. 46. For example, suppose a corporation in a given year makes a $10,000 distribution on a senior class of stock and a $5,000 distribution on a more junior class of stock. If the corporation's current E&P as of the close of the taxable year is $12,000, the entire $10,000 distribution on the senior class is treated as out of current E&P, but only $2,000 of the $5,000 distribution on the junior class is so treated. It is unclear whether the allocation of accumulated E&P to multiple distributions on different classes of stock also follows their distribution priority or is instead based on the chronological order of the distributions.

3. *Origin of the "nimble dividend" rule.* The rule treating a distribution as a dividend if it is out of either current or accumulated E&P (sometimes referred to as the nimble dividend rule) originated in 1936 as a relief measure for taxpayers. In that year, Congress approved a corporate tax on undistributed profits, generally measured by a corporation's income less any dividends distributed. Some corporations wished to avoid the tax by distributing a dividend but, because of losses incurred in prior years, had accumulated deficits in E&P. Therefore, under the law in existence at the time, such distributions could not qualify as dividends for tax purposes. Accordingly, Congress changed the law to its present form, thereby allowing a corporation with sufficient current E&P to distribute a dividend.

Some might argue that the nimble dividend rule is inappropriate because it treats a distribution by a corporation with positive current E&P, but an overall E&P deficit (after taking into account the positive current amount), as a taxable distribution of profits rather than a nontaxable return of capital. On the other hand, allowing current E&P to fund a dividend simplifies the law. A rule looking only to accumulated E&P would in theory require corporations to keep track of their E&P over their entire history. This task may be complicated, especially if a corporation has previously been involved in a merger or division and therefore either succeeded to the E&P of, or had a portion of its E&P allocated to, another corporation.

The tax law determination of a dividend is made independently of characterization of the distribution under state corporate law. See Jaques v. Comm'r, 935 F.2d 104, 107-08 (6th Cir. 1991) (constructive distribution exceeding amount of corporate surplus, and therefore not qualifying as a dividend under state law, nevertheless qualified as a tax law dividend because of sufficient E&P); U.S. v. Lesoine, 203

F.2d 123, 125-26 (9th Cir. 1953) (same). As a practical matter, however, state law rules limiting the permissible amount of an ordinary distribution mean that such a distribution will generally also qualify as a tax-law dividend. See, e.g., 8 Del. Code Ann. § 170(a) (2009) (limiting state-law dividend to amount in corporate surplus or current-year or prior-year profits); N.Y. Bus. Corp. Law § 510(b) (Consol. 2009) (same).

4. *Tax law determination of "dividend" controls.* In Boulware v. U.S., 552 U.S. 421 (2008), the defendant was charged with criminal tax evasion resulting from his failure to report taxable income when he diverted funds from his controlled corporation for the benefit of both his girlfriend and wife. The defendant sought to introduce evidence that the corporation had no E&P in the relevant years. The government contended that such evidence was not relevant in the criminal tax case unless the defendant first established that a nontaxable return-of-capital distribution was intended, something the defendant had not shown. The Court rejected the government's position and concluded that the existence of a tax deficiency, one of the necessary elements of the crime, is determined by the tax law. In the absence of corporate E&P, and assuming that the amount deemed distributed was with respect to the defendant's stock in the corporation and did not exceed his basis in that stock, there would have been no tax deficiency. On remand, the trial court's refusal to admit the defendant's proffer of evidence was sustained (and the conviction was reinstated) because the proffer was only a legal opinion and did not suffice to establish the defendant's claim. The proffer failed to show that the constructive payment to the defendant was "with respect to his stock" and that defendant's stock basis exceeded the payment. U.S. v. Boulware, 558 F.3d 971 (9th Cir. 2009), cert. denied, 130 S. Ct. 737 (2009).

5. *Importance of E&P for international tax purposes.* For reasons previously mentioned, the computation of a U.S. corporation's E&P is generally of only limited significance. Nevertheless, the amount of E&P of a foreign subsidiary of a U.S. corporation may be quite important for various reasons. See, e.g., I.R.C. §§ 902(a) and (c)(1) (foreign subsidiary's E&P affects amount of U.S. corporation's foreign tax credit); 952(c)(1)(A) (foreign subsidiary's E&P affects how much U.S. corporation is currently taxed on subsidiary's foreign-source income).

## 2. *Taxation of Dividends Received by Shareholders Who Are Individuals*

Dividends (as defined in section 316(a)) received by shareholders must be included in their ordinary income. Individuals, however, are presently entitled to pay tax on "qualified dividend income" at a maximum rate of 15 percent. This preferential rate is scheduled to expire at the end of 2012; should it expire, dividends would revert to being taxed at ordinary income tax rates. Qualified dividend income generally includes any dividend received from a U.S. corporation as well as one from a foreign corporation if it (1) is incorporated in a U.S. possession, (2) is generally eligible for benefits under a comprehensive tax treaty with the U.S., or (3) has shares that are readily tradable on a U.S. securities market. I.R.C. § 1(h)(11)(B)(i) and (C)(i) and (ii).

Although an individual's qualified dividend income is currently taxed at the same rate as long-term capital gain, the two types of income are not treated exactly the same. Current law continues to limit the deductibility of capital losses against qualified dividend income (as well as any other ordinary income) to, generally, $3,000 per year even though capital losses may generally be applied to offset capital gains without limit. See I.R.C. § 1211(b). The capital loss limitation discourages "cherry-picking"; taxpayers with both unrealized capital gains and losses may not realize just their losses and apply them without limit to shelter their qualified dividend income (and any other ordinary income). As illustrated in **problem 5-2**, below, Congress added one other rule to prevent the conversion of short-term capital gain (generally taxed like ordinary income) into long-term capital gain.

Read I.R.C. §§ 1(h)(1)(C), (3), (11)(A), 1211(b), 1222(7) and (11) very carefully and then do **problem 5-2** to see if you can figure out Congress's handiwork in carrying out these policy objectives. The problem requires you to delve into a portion of section 1(h) of the Code, a notoriously difficult provision to understand. One reason the provision is so confusing is that it specifies a slightly different preferential rate for several different types of income earned by individuals and provides a larger preference for taxpayers in lower brackets. **Problem 5-2** avoids some of the confusion by focusing on an individual who has just capital gain (and loss) and dividend income, and is not entitled to a larger preference. In reading and applying these provisions, note that "net capital gain" is different from "adjusted net capital gain," and that neither is exactly the same as "net long-term capital gain."

**Problem 5-2:**

(a) Tom has $20,000 of long-term capital gain, $15,000 of long-term capital loss, and $10,000 of qualified dividend income. How much income will be taxed at a maximum rate of 15 percent? Assume that if section 1(h)(1) is applicable to Tom, the only applicable subparagraph is section 1(h)(1)(C).

(b) Same as (a) except that his long-term capital loss is $25,000, not $15,000.

*NOTES*

1. *Amount of distribution and impact of liabilities.* Under section 301(b), the amount of a distribution is equal to the cash plus the fair market value of any property distributed, generally reduced by the amount of any liabilities assumed by the shareholder in the transaction or to which the distributed property is subject. For example, if $100 of property is distributed by a corporation to a shareholder but the property is

subject to a $30 liability, the amount distributed under section 301(b) is generally treated as $70; that amount is then tested under section 301(c) as a dividend, return of basis, or capital gain to the distributee. The regulations try to make sure that the amount of a liability taken into account under this provision is consistent with the economic effect of the liability transfer. For instance, if, following the distribution in the foregoing example, the $30 liability remains an obligation of the corporation and it is expected that the corporation, rather than the shareholder, will satisfy the liability, then the amount distributed will be treated as $100 rather than $70. See Reg. § 1.301-1(g) (taking liability into account only if it is assumed by the shareholder within the meaning of section 357(d)). Congress enacted section 357(d) (examined in chapter seven) in response to a notorious tax shelter known as the "Bond and Option Sales Strategy," or "BOSS," which tried to take advantage of situations where the amount of a liability taken into account for tax purposes did not match its economic effect. See Notice 99-59, 1999-2 C.B. 761. The BOSS shelter spawned a number of variations, some of which are discussed in chapter seven.

2. *Tax treatment of nondividend distributions to shareholders owning different classes or blocks of stock.* For purposes of section 301(c)(2) and (3), each class of stock is considered separately. Thus, if a shareholder owns shares in different classes of stock of a corporation, a distribution with respect to one class will be treated as a return of basis or gain based solely on the shareholder's basis in the shares of that class. Basis in shares of any other class is disregarded. For shares of stock within a given class, proposed regulations treat each share as a separate investment, following the rule in Johnson v. U.S., 435 F.2d 1257 (4th Cir. 1971). Prop. Reg. § 1.301-2. Accordingly, if a shareholder owns different blocks of stock—shares acquired at different times for different prices—of the same class, a distribution with respect to that class must be allocated pro rata to each share in the class held by the shareholder. Therefore, a shareholder may recognize gain under section 301(c)(3) from distributions on her low-basis shares even though she still has unrecovered basis in her high-basis shares (after taking into account the distribution). For example, suppose a shareholder owns two blocks of common stock, the first with a $1/share basis and the second with a $5/share basis. If the shareholder receives a $2/share distribution on the common stock and the distributing corporation has no current or accumulated E&P, the shareholder recognizes $1/share gain from the distribution on the low-basis block, but recognizes no gain from the distribution on the high-basis block (which has a remaining basis of $3/share).

### 3. *Taxation of Dividends Received by Corporate Shareholders*

Section 1(h) only applies to the taxation of individuals and trusts and estates. A corporate shareholder therefore is not entitled to the preferential rate on qualified dividend income. Corporate shareholders, however, are subject to some special rules including a deduction for all or a portion of their dividends received.

### a. Dividends-Received Deduction

Read I.R.C. §§ 243(a), (b)(1) and (2), (c); and 1504(a)(1) and (2). Corporations are generally entitled to deduct 70, 80, or 100 percent of the dividends they receive, depending upon the amount of stock the corporation owns in the distributing corporation. The usual explanation for this deduction is that it prevents corporate-source income from being taxed more than once at the corporate level and potentially more than twice altogether.

> **Example 5-1:** Assume that all tax rates are a flat 33 percent and that shareholder A owns all of the stock of corporation X, which in turn owns all of the stock of corporation Y. If Y earns $100 of taxable income, it must pay $33 in corporate tax and can therefore distribute at most $67 in net after-tax profits to X. If there were no dividends-received deduction, X would have to pay approximately $22 in income tax on receipt of the $67 dividend and would therefore be able to distribute at most $45 to A. If X distributed that amount, A would have to pay a $15 tax on the $45 of dividend income and end up with $30 after taxes. The total tax burden of $70, or 70 percent of the income earned by Y, would represent two levels of corporate tax on the same income and three levels of tax altogether. The dividends-received deduction prevents this result by permitting X to deduct all or a substantial portion of any dividends received from Y, thereby eliminating all or most of the $22 tax payable by X in the example.

One unintended consequence of the section 243 deduction, however, is a corporate strategy known as "dividend-stripping" or "dividend capture":

> **Example 5-2:** P corporation purchases the shares of T corporation for $30/share. Shortly after the purchase, T pays a substantial dividend to its shareholders of $5/share, with the consequence that T's share value falls to about $25/share after the dividend. Because of the dividends-received deduction, P need include in income only a fraction of the $5/share dividend. Yet if it sells its T shares after the distribution and has sufficient capital gains to shelter, P can obtain full benefit of the $5/share capital loss recognized on sale of the shares. Recall also that corporate taxpayers like P do not receive a capital gains preference. See I.R.C. § 1201(a). Thus, the capital loss potentially offsets capital gains taxable at the full statutory rate.

Read I.R.C. § 246(c)(1), (2) and (4) and the following case, which describe some of the provisions enacted to prevent dividend-stripping. Section 1059, briefly discussed after the case, deals more directly with the problem.

*NOTE*

*Another unintended effect?* Some analysts have suggested that the dividends-received deduction may encourage corporate acquisition activity. Consistent with the "new view" of dividend taxation discussed in chapter three, this analysis assumes that, as stated in U.S. v. Phellis, 257 U.S. 156, 171-72 (1921), the price of corporate stock capitalizes to some extent the future shareholder taxes that would be due upon a later distribution out of corporate solution of earnings accumulated at the time the stock is acquired. Under this assumption, corporate stock may be a bargain for *corporate* buyers whose tax liability on a distribution is reduced by reason of the dividends-received deduction. For example, assume the same facts as in **example 5-1** (including flat tax rates of 33 percent), except that after corporation Y earns the $100 in taxable income, pays a corporate tax of $33, and accumulates the remaining after-tax profits of $67, corporation X *purchases* the stock of Y. Suppose the price of the Y stock is $45, reflecting in part the anticipated 33 percent tax ($22) that would arise upon distribution of the $67 accumulation to a shareholder who is an individual. If X acquires Y for $45 and then obtains a $67 distribution from Y without paying any tax because of the dividends-received deduction, the acquisition would increase X's assets by $22 (presumably resulting in an increase in the price of *X's* stock). The jury is still out on whether the dividends-received deduction has the effect of encouraging corporate acquisitions. The key questions are whether, and to what extent, future shareholder taxes are capitalized in share price.

## The Progressive Corp. v. United States

970 F.2d 188 (6th Cir. 1992)

MILBURN, Circuit Judge.

. . . [T]he principal issues are (1) whether Progressive's simultaneous purchases of a stock and a put option on the same stock resulted in a holding period of zero under § 246(c)(3) [1] so that Progressive did not meet the 16-day [2] holding period prescribed in § 246(c)(1)(A) and thus failed to qualify for the "dividends received" deduction otherwise allowed corporate taxpayers by § 243, and (2) whether Progressive's purchase of a stock and the simultaneous, or nearly simultaneous, sale of deep-in-the-money call options resulted in a holding period of zero under § 246(c)(3) so that Progressive did not meet the 16-day holding period prescribed in § 246(c)(1)(A) and thus failed to qualify for the dividends received deduction established by § 243. For the reasons that follow, we reverse and remand. . . .

Like most insurance companies, Progressive maintained an active investment portfolio, and one of the strategies Progressive used in trading for its own portfolio is

1. [Now codified in section 246(c)(4)(A), but referred to throughout this opinion as section 246(c)(3).]

2. [Now 46 days.]

called a "forward conversion." A forward conversion consists of three substantially contemporaneous transactions. The first is the purchase of a block of common stock ("stock" or "underlying stock"). The second is the purchase of a put option [3] on a similar quantity of the same stock as was purchased. The third consists of the selling of a call option [4] on a similar quantity of the same stock. An example offered by the parties of such a tripartite forward conversion is as follows:

> [Taxpayer] acquires 100 shares of the common stock of the Company A for $49.00 per share on Day 1. Also on Day 1, [taxpayer] purchases for $200.00 the right to put 100 shares of Company A stock to a third party at a price of $50.00 per share on or before Day 91. [Taxpayer] also sells for $300.00 a call on 100 shares of Company A common stock which entitles a third party to purchase from it the 100 shares of Company A stock at a price of $50.00 per share on or before Day 91.

. . . The purpose of such a forward conversion strategy was to hedge the stock purchase. Thus, if the price of the underlying stock stayed below the exercise price of the options as of the exercise date, Progressive would exercise its put option and sell the stock at the exercise price. If the price of the stock rose above the exercise price, the holder of the call option on the stock would almost certainly exercise his call option and require Progressive to sell the stock at the exercise price.

During 1981 and 1982, Progressive employed this forward conversion strategy and received substantial stock dividends which it included in income. During those years, § 243 provided that a corporate taxpayer could claim a "dividends received" deduction for 85 percent of the dividends it received from domestic corporations. Another provision of the code, § 246(c)(1)(A), provided that the dividends received deduction would be allowed only if the stock paying the dividends had been held by the taxpayer for at least sixteen days. Moreover, § 246(c)(3) set up certain rules for determining whether the taxpayer had held the underlying stock long enough to qualify for the deduction. In relevant part it provided:

> The holding periods determined under the preceding provisions of this paragraph shall be appropriately reduced (in the manner provided in regulations prescribed by the Secretary) for any period (during such holding periods) in which the taxpayer has the option to sell, is under a contractual obligation to sell, or has made (and not closed) a short sale of, substantially identical stock or securities.

Although Progressive held options to sell (put options) substantially identical stock to that which it owned for the entire period of its ownership of the stock,

3. A put option is an option to sell a stock at a particular price on or before a specified date. Having bought a put option, the buyer has the right to sell the stock at the set price (called the "exercise" or "strike" price) at any time before the expiration of the option.

4. A call option is an option to buy a stock at a given price on or before a specified date. The seller of a call option is obligated to sell the designated stock at a particular price if the buyer of the option elects to exercise it on or before the specified date.

it claimed dividends received deductions for $1,026,899 in 1981 and $3,655,193 for 1982.

In a second kind of strategy distinct from its forward conversion strategy, Progressive bought stock before its ex-dividend date [5] and at the same time, or shortly thereafter, sold an in-the-money call option on the stock it had purchased. [6] Employing this second strategy during 1980, 1981, and 1982, Progressive received dividends of approximately $97,000 and claimed a dividends received deduction for each of those years.

Following an audit in 1985, the Internal Revenue Service disallowed the dividends received deductions Progressive had claimed. The deductions with respect to the forward conversion transactions were disallowed because, under section 246(c)(3), the put options held by Progressive concurrently with its ownership of the stock in question effectively reduced the holding period of the stock to less than sixteen days, *i.e.*, zero. Similarly, as to Progressive's second strategy of selling simultaneous in-the-money call options, the IRS determined that the dividends received deductions should be disallowed because the call options were so deep-in-the-money that they were the equivalent of obligations to sell the stock and that, as such, they, too, reduced the relevant holding period to zero pursuant to section 246(c)(3).

Following the disallowance of its deductions, Progressive filed a tax refund action on December 21, 1988. The district court granted Progressive's motion for summary judgment because it thought that Reg. § 1.246-3(d)(2) was controlling and that it required a taxpayer to be short of the stock before the holding period stopped running. Ruling that Progressive was never in a "short position" because at all times it actually owned the stock it bought or sold options on, the district court concluded that Progressive had held its stock long enough to qualify for the dividends received deductions it had taken. This timely appeal followed.

. . . The district court held that Progressive was entitled to the dividends received deductions with respect to its forward conversion strategy because a regulation issued by the Secretary of the Treasury, § 1.246-3(d)(2), should be read to require that the taxpayer actually be short the stock before the holding period is tolled. In so doing, the court focused on the following introductory sentence of the regulation:

> (2) Special rules. Section 246(c) requires that the holding periods determined thereunder shall be appropriately reduced for any period that the taxpayer's stock holding

---

5. The ex-dividend date of a stock is the date on which the stock is first sold without the right to receive a previously declared dividend. Usually this is the business day following the distribution of a dividend. The purpose of buying stock shortly before its ex-dividend date is to position oneself as a holder of the stock in order to receive a dividend.

6. A call option is in-the-money if the exercise price of the option is below the market trading price of the stock on the day the option was issued. Thus, if a stock sold for $50 a share, a call option entitling a third party to buy that stock for $45 prior to a given date would be referred to as an in-the-money call option. A call option is deep-in-the-money if the exercise price is well below the market trading price on the date the option is issued.

> is *offset* by a corresponding *short position resulting from an option to sell*, a contractual obligation to sell, or a short sale of, substantially identical stock or securities. (Emphasis added).

This regulation was expressly authorized by Congress in the text of section 246(c)(3), and the district court held that the regulation should be "deemed legislative and therefore binding on a court." Because Progressive actually owned the underlying stock at all times during which it also held a put option on the stock, the district court reasoned that Progressive was never in a "short position" within the meaning of the regulation. It therefore concluded that "Progressive was justified in relying on the regulation . . . ," and that the deductions were properly taken.

The governing statute, § 246(c)(3), does not use the phrase "short position." It states flatly that the "holding periods . . . shall be appropriately reduced . . . for any period . . . in which the taxpayer has an option to sell. . . ." The statute thus requires that the period during which the stock is held must be reduced day for day by any period during which the taxpayer also has an option to sell a similar amount of the same stock. Thus, the statute fits the factual situation in this case clearly and exactly. . . . The plain language of a statute determines the meaning of the statute. . . .

Progressive succeeded in diverting the district court's attention from the statute to the regulation issued pursuant to the statute, *viz.*, § 1.246-3(d)(2), and creating confusion by arguing that the phrase used only in the regulation, "short position," results in the addition of a requirement that the taxpayer actually be short of the given stock (by not owning it) before the statutory holding period is to be reduced. Without an analysis of the statute or a finding that it was in some way ambiguous, the district court went directly to the regulation and engaged in a construction of a phrase found in the regulation, but not in the statute. It was error to rely on such an interpretation of the regulation without first finding that the statute itself was ambiguous.

It is obvious that the statute, in its parenthetical language, does delegate to the Secretary of the Treasury the power to provide by regulation the "manner" in which the holding periods "shall be appropriately reduced. . . ." That delegation, however, does not purport to authorize the Secretary to abrogate the express terms of the statute, which provide that the holding period shall be reduced where the taxpayer has a concurrent option to sell the same stock. Beyond its introductory sentence, the body of the regulation purports only to describe how the holding periods should be calculated when the amount of stock actually owned by a corporation differs from the amount of stock comprehended in one of the three "short positions" described in the statute, *i.e.*, holding a put option, being obligated on a call option, or having actually sold the same stock short. The regulation in no way modifies the express terms of the statute, nor could it lawfully do so. Treasury regulations cannot be given a construction that will violate the language of the statute they implement. . . .

Even if the district court had properly resorted to the regulation for assistance in interpreting the statute, the interpretation given the regulation by the district court is internally inconsistent. The district court held that the regulation allowed the holding period to run, despite the holding of offsetting put options, as long as the taxpayer actually owned an equivalent amount of the underlying stock. Thus, according to the district court, the holding period would be reduced only when the corporate taxpayer was actually short the stock in question, *i.e.*, when it did not own that stock. If the taxpayer does not own the stock, however, it will not receive any dividends to which the deduction at issue might apply. Thus, no corporation in a "short position" as defined by the district court would ever receive a dividend in the first place. This makes nonsense out of the very idea of a *holding* period. . . .

Wherever possible, courts should read regulations to be consistent with the statutes that authorize them, and a construction that thwarts the statute which the regulation implements is impermissible. . . . Thus, the statute requires that the holding period in this case be reduced by the period of time during which Progressive held put options on the same stock it owned, and, because it held put options on the same stock it owned at all times during its ownership, the holding period was zero, and Progressive was not entitled to the dividends received deductions it took.

. . . [A]s to the second strategy involving the simultaneous purchase of stock and sale of in-the-money call options, the government did not file a cross-motion for summary judgment, and instead asked the district court to decide whether the in-the-money call options sold by Progressive in connection with its second strategy were so deep-in-the-money, *i.e.*, so far below the market trading price on the day they were sold, that each was the equivalent of "a contractual obligation to sell" within the meaning of the statute. It argued that the very low exercise price made it virtually certain that the purchasers of the call options would exercise them, thus obligating Progressive to sell the stock. Because of its resolution of this case, the district court never addressed the question of whether the in-the-money call options sold by Progressive were so deep-in-the-money that they should be treated as contractual obligations to sell the stock for purposes of calculating holding periods under section 246(c).

There is authority to support the government's argument in this regard. Rev. Rul. 80-238, 1980-2 C.B. 96, issued in 1980 and applicable to the years here in question, explains that the selling of a call option at-the-money (where the exercise price is the current market price) or out-of-the-money (where the exercise price is above the current market price) does not reduce the taxpayer's holding period for the underlying stock under section 246(c). It goes on to explain, however, that the situation is different where in-the-money call options are involved.

> Such considerations, however, are not applicable to "in-the-money" call options, that is, call options that are sold with a striking price below the market price of the underlying stock on the date that the option is written, since in such a situation the exercise of such options may be virtually guaranteed and the element of risk is either greatly reduced or eliminated.

1980-2 C.B. at 96. This court has held that revenue rulings "are entitled to great deference, and have been said to 'have the force of legal precedents unless unreasonable or inconsistent with the provisions of the Internal Revenue Code'." . . .

. . . [T]his matter should be remanded to the district court for a determination of whether the call options sold by Progressive were so deep-in-the-money as to be the equivalents of the contractual obligations to sell mentioned in section 246(c)(3). . . .

## *NOTES AND QUESTIONS*

1. *Money machine?* Examine closely the terms of the "tripartite forward conversion" example provided by the court at the beginning of its opinion. Is there anything odd about this example? If transaction costs are disregarded, what happens to the taxpayer if on or before Day 91, the price of the stock either rises to $55/share or falls to $45/share? Has the taxpayer created a money machine?

2. *The importance of market risk.* As described in *Progressive*, corporations must hold dividend-paying stock longer than 45 days in order to be eligible for the dividends-received deduction. This rule uses market risk to discourage corporations from engaging in purely tax-motivated investment strategies such as dividend-stripping. Consistent with this purpose, the holding period is tolled during periods the corporation hedges its investment in the underlying stock and therefore is not bearing real market risk. I.R.C. § 246(c)(4). Several partially overlapping rules carry out this objective; the broadest, as prescribed by regulations, tolls the holding period whenever the taxpayer diminishes its risk of loss with respect to the underlying stock by holding an offsetting position in "substantially similar or related property." I.R.C. § 246(c)(4)(C). In general, property is considered substantially similar or related to the underlying stock if the fair market values of the property and stock primarily reflect the same firm, industry, or economic factors (such as interest rates or commodity prices), and changes in the value of the stock are reasonably expected to vary directly or inversely with changes in the value of the property. Reg. § 1.246-5(b)(1). Thus, the stock of two corporations, even though in the same industry, would not ordinarily be considered substantially similar or related to one another if the change in value in one stock would not reasonably be expected to approximate the change in the value of the other. On the other hand, if the primary asset of both corporations is a particular commodity (such as gold), and changes in value of one stock have historically approximated changes in value of the other, the two stocks may be considered substantially similar or related to one another. Reg. § 1.246-5(d) (ex. 1 and 2). The regulations delineate the circumstances in which a position in a broader, more diversified investment, such as a stock index fund, should be considered substantially similar or related to a portfolio of stock investments held by the taxpayer.

3. *Economic substance?* As explained by the Sixth Circuit, the District Court simply misread the statute in this case. Suppose, however, neither the statute nor the

regulations had specifically addressed the consequences of Progressive's investment strategy. Would the forward conversion strategy have passed muster under section 7701(o)? Apart from federal income taxes, did Progressive have a "substantial purpose" for entering into the transaction(s) and was the company's economic position changed in a "meaningful way" as a result of the transaction(s)? Or is the economic substance doctrine not "relevant" in the first instance?

4. *Dividends from only certain distributing corporations qualify.* Consistent with its underlying purpose, the dividends-received deduction is generally available only with respect to dividends distributed by taxable U.S. corporations. I.R.C. §§ 243(a), 246(a)(1). In general, only to that extent is the deduction needed to prevent more than one U.S. corporate tax being imposed on corporate-source income. Dividends from certain foreign corporations are eligible for the dividends-received deduction if, in general, the dividends are from earnings taxed by the U.S. or previously accumulated by a taxable U.S. corporation. I.R.C. §§ 243(e), 245. If the dividends are from earnings that have been taxed by a foreign country, then a U.S. corporate recipient of the dividend is deemed, under certain circumstances, to have paid the foreign tax, entitling the recipient to claim the foreign tax credit. I.R.C. §§ 902(a), 901(a). This provision is aimed at a different form of double taxation, one involving the taxation of the same income by two different countries.

5. *Section 301(e) and premature dividends-received deductions.* In calculating its E&P, a corporation must make adjustments to its taxable income to ensure that E&P better reflects the corporation's economic income. For example, a corporation that defers reporting taxable income from an installment sale must calculate E&P as if the installment method were not used. See I.R.C. §§ 312(n)(5), 453(a) and (c). In general, these adjustments make it more likely that a distribution from such a corporation will qualify as a dividend for tax purposes. For corporate shareholders of the distributing corporation, however, the adjustments also make it more likely that they will be entitled to a dividends-received deduction. Arguably, such a deduction may be premature; the deduction is intended to prevent more than one corporate tax being imposed on corporate-source income, yet the distributing corporation may not yet have paid any corporate tax because of the deferral provision. Read I.R.C. § 301(e). This provision represents a crude attempt to prevent a premature dividends-received deduction in this type of situation. What practical problems do corporations face in attempting to comply with this provision?

### b. Special Treatment of "Extraordinary Dividends"

A more direct response to dividend-stripping is the rule relating to extraordinary dividends. Read I.R.C. § 1059(a)-(d). In general, if a corporation receives an "extraordinary dividend" with respect to stock held for two years or less at the time the dividend is announced, the corporation must reduce its basis in such stock by the portion of the dividend not taxed by reason of the dividends-received deduction. The corporation must recognize gain to the extent the nontaxed portion of the dividend exceeds the corporation's basis in the stock. An extraordinary dividend is generally any dividend equaling or exceeding five percent of the corporation's basis in preferred stock or ten percent of its basis in any other stock. For this purpose, certain dividends received during a consecutive 85-day period (or within one year) must be aggregated.

A corporate shareholder's receipt of an extraordinary dividend is analogous to a shareholder's receipt of a dividend from an S corporation. In each case, the goal of the tax law is generally to prevent taxing at the shareholder level income that has previously been taxed. The extraordinary dividend rule borrows from passthrough tax principles by requiring a stock basis reduction equal to the portion of the dividend that is not taxed. Cf. I.R.C. § 1367(a)(2)(A).

The analogy between passthrough tax principles and the extraordinary dividend rule, however, is imperfect. In a passthrough tax system, income earned by the business entity is passed through to the owners with a resulting increase in the basis in their ownership interests. See I.R.C. §§ 1367(a)(1) (increase to basis in S corporation stock), 705(a)(1) (increase to basis in partnership interest). Thus, a subsequent tax-free distribution of the earnings must similarly reduce the same basis. See I.R.C. §§ 1367(a)(2)(A), 705(a)(2). In contrast, except in the case of corporations filing a consolidated return, income earned by a C corporation does not increase a corporate shareholder's basis in the stock of the distributing corporation; thus, an across-the-board reduction in such basis in the case of any dividend to a corporate distributee would be inappropriate. The analogy holds, however, in circumstances where a corporate shareholder's stock basis *does* reflect the corporate earnings that are distributed, such as when a corporate shareholder acquires stock in a corporation with accumulated earnings that are subsequently distributed. The conditions in section 1059 that limit the provision to large dividends distributed on stock held for a fairly short period can be understood as restricting the reach of the rule to this type of case.

The analogy to passthrough tax principles also explains why an extraordinary dividend generally does not include a "qualifying dividend" within the meaning of section 243(b). See I.R.C. § 1059(e)(2). A "qualifying dividend" is one received by a corporation from another corporation that is a member of the same affiliated group. As described in chapter fourteen, corporate members of an affiliated group filing a consolidated return are generally already taxed under passthrough tax principles. For example, members of such a group must generally adjust their basis in the shares of other members to ensure that no more than one level of corporate tax is imposed on the group's income. The extraordinary dividend rules are therefore generally not needed for dividends between members of an affiliated group.

The preferential rate for qualified dividend income also creates a possible dividend-stripping advantage for shareholders who are individuals. They, too, could potentially receive dividends taxed at a preferential rate and then use the offsetting loss to shelter income taxed at the full rate. To be eligible for qualified dividend treatment, individuals must generally hold their stock for over 60 days and otherwise satisfy the same holding period requirements applicable to the dividends-received deduction. I.R.C. § 1(h)(11)(B)(iii). In addition, rather than requiring individuals who receive extraordinary dividends to reduce the basis in their stock—a requirement few shareholders would likely understand and comply with—the law simply treats any resulting capital loss from sale of the stock on which the extraordinary dividend is distributed as long-term rather than short-term. This treatment applies regardless of the shareholder's holding period in the stock at the time of disposition, but is limited to the amount of the extraordinary dividend treated as qualified dividend income. See I.R.C. § 1(h)(11)(D)(ii). It remains to be seen how well taxpayers comply with this rule.

**Problem 5-3:**

(a) On March 1, X corporation purchased 1,000 shares of GM's cumulative preferred stock for $30,000. On August 1 of the same year, GM announced that it anticipated it would have its first profitable year in five years, and that it would pay to record owners of its cumulative preferred stock as of September 1 a dividend of $10 per share. This dividend represented back dividends for the prior three years. What are the tax consequences to X when it receives the dividend later in September?
(b) Same as (a), except that the shares were purchased for $6,000.
(c) Read I.R.C. § 1059(d)(6). Based upon your understanding of the theory behind the tax treatment of extraordinary dividends, try to explain the reason for this exception.

### c. Debt-Financed Portfolio Stock

As **example 5-3** below illustrates, if a corporation's ownership of dividend-paying stock is debt-financed, the combination of the dividends-received and interest deductions may produce a form of tax arbitrage similar to that involved in *Knetsch*, *Goldstein*, and the COLI cases, all previously discussed in chapter four:

> **Example 5-3:** In the absence of taxes, it would ordinarily not make sense to borrow funds at a pre-tax interest rate of 12 percent in order to purchase shares of a corporation providing a pre-tax dividend return of 10 percent (and no possibility of appreciation in such shares). Yet if the purchaser is a corporation entitled to a dividends-received deduction, the transaction might make sense. For example, if tax rates are a flat 33 percent, the after-tax cost of the transaction is reduced to 8 percent (12% × (1-.33)) because of the interest deduction. Meanwhile, if the corporate purchaser is entitled to a 70 percent dividends-received deduction, the after-tax return is equal to 9 percent (10% × (1- (.33 × .30))).

Read I.R.C. § 246A(a), (c)(1) and (2), and (d). In general, Congress's response to the tax arbitrage problem is to deny a dividends-received deduction to the extent the investment in the stock paying the dividend is debt-financed. This limitation on the dividends-received deduction only applies to investments in "portfolio stock," defined generally to exclude ownership of stock possessing at least 50 percent of the vote and value of the distributing corporation, or at least 20 percent of the vote and value of such corporation if five or fewer corporate shareholders own at least 50 percent of such stock. I.R.C. § 246A(c)(2). The 100 percent dividends-received deduction is specifically not subject to the limitation. I.R.C. § 246A(b)(1). The Achilles' heel of this provision is the required showing that debt be "directly attributable" to the portfolio stock investment. I.R.C. § 246A(d)(3). The following ruling interprets this condition in three situations. **Problem 5-4**, which follows the ruling, then tests your understanding of Congress's response to this arbitrage problem.

## Rev. Rul. 88-66

1988-2 C.B. 34

. . . In the three situations described below, is an indebtedness "directly attributable to investment in the portfolio stock" within the meaning of section 246A(d)(3) of the Internal Revenue Code? . . .

*Situation 1.* X corporation owned portfolio stock, as defined in section 246A(c)(2) of the Code, as well as certain other liquid assets, including cash, that it had on hand to meet its reasonably anticipated business needs. X acquired a new facility to meet the needs of its growing business and borrowed to finance its acquisition, rather than selling its portfolio stock and other liquid assets. X's portfolio stock was not used as collateral for the loan, which was secured by the new facility. It was customary to use a mortgage loan for such acquisitions, and there were no other factors indicating such loan was obtained to facilitate the continued carrying of the portfolio stock.

*Situation 2.* Y corporation was engaged in the active conduct of a business. Y intended to begin construction of a new plant within the next 18 months and wished to finance the plant using long-term debt. Because the market conditions were favorable for a debt offering, Y issued its debt in advance of the planned construction and temporarily invested the proceeds it received in portfolio stock, as defined in section 246A(c)(2) of the Code.

*Situation 3.* Z Bank was wholly owned by, and filed a consolidated return with, Parent holding company. Z Bank was chartered in state A, which precludes banks from investing in stock. Z Bank received deposits from its customers in the ordinary course of its business and not for the specific purpose of purchasing portfolio stock as defined in section 246A(c)(2) of the Code. Z Bank made a loan to Parent, so that Parent could invest the loan proceeds in portfolio stock, and Parent made this investment. There were no other circumstances demonstrating a direct connection between the deposits received by Z Bank and the funds that it loaned to Parent which Parent invested in portfolio stock. . . .

Section 246A(a) of the Code provides that, in the case of any dividend on debt-financed portfolio stock, there shall be substituted for the percentage which would otherwise be used in determining the deduction allowable under section 243, 244, or 245(a) a percentage equal to the product of—

> (1) 70 percent (80 percent in the case of any dividend from a 20-percent owned corporation as defined in section 243(c)(2)), and
> (2) 100 percent minus the average indebtedness percentage.

Section 246A(c)(1) of the Code provides that the term "debt financed portfolio stock" means any portfolio stock if at some time during the base period there is portfolio indebtedness with respect to such stock.

Section 246A(c)(2) of the Code provides that the term "portfolio stock" means any stock of a corporation unless the taxpayer owns at least 50 percent (20 percent if 50 percent is owned by 5 or fewer corporate shareholders) of the total voting power and value of the stock of the corporation.

Section 246A(d)(3)(A) of the Code provides that the term "portfolio indebtedness" means any indebtedness directly attributable to investment in the portfolio stock.

The legislative history of section 246A of the Code indicates that Congress was concerned that the conjunction of the dividends received deduction and the interest deduction could result in the avoidance of substantial corporate-level taxes on corporate earnings. H.R. REP. NO. 432, 98TH CONG., 2D SESS., PT. 2, 1180-81 (1984). Therefore, section 246A was enacted to reduce the dividends received deduction where indebtedness is directly attributable to investment in portfolio stock.

The legislative history provides that the "directly attributable" requirement is satisfied if there is a direct relationship between the debt and an investment in stock. Congress decided against incorporating an allocation or apportionment formula or a fungibility concept; thus, section 246A does not apply merely because of the existence of outstanding commercial paper that is issued as part of an ongoing cash management program or deposits received by a depository institution in the ordinary course of its business. *Id.*

However, where indebtedness is clearly incurred for the purpose of *acquiring* portfolio stock or otherwise is directly traceable to the acquisition, the indebtedness constitutes portfolio indebtedness. For example, any non-recourse loan secured in whole or in part with portfolio stock is portfolio indebtedness. . . . Further, section 246A of the Code is also applicable where the indebtedness is directly attributable to the *carrying* of portfolio stock. For example, section 246A applies if portfolio stock is acquired by a corporation using its equity, and later the corporation borrows money using the portfolio stock as security, if the purchaser could reasonably have been expected to sell the portfolio stock rather than incur the indebtedness. H.R. CONF. REP. NO. 861, 98TH CONG., 2D SESS. 813 (1984), 1984-3 (Vol. 2) C.B. 1, 67.

Portfolio indebtedness is not required to be that of the holder of the dividend paying stock and may exist in the controlled group situation. Thus, for example, section 246A of the Code can apply where one member of an affiliated group incurs the portfolio indebtedness and another member of the group acquires the stock. H.R. Rep. No. 432 at 1181.

## HOLDINGS

*Situation 1.* The debt incurred to finance the acquisition of a new facility is not indebtedness directly attributable to investment in portfolio stock because there is no direct relationship between the debt and the carrying of the portfolio stock. Although the mortgage permits the corporation to acquire its new facility without disposing of its portfolio stock investment or other assets, that debt is not allocated under an apportionment formula or a fungibility concept for purposes of determining what constitutes portfolio indebtedness. Under the circumstances, it is not reasonable to expect the borrower would have sold the stock to raise the proceeds for the acquisition in lieu of obtaining the mortgage loan.

*Situation 2.* The debt issued to finance the construction of the new plant the proceeds from which are temporarily invested in portfolio stock is indebtedness directly attributable to investment in portfolio stock. The fact that this is a temporary investment does not change the result, because section 246A of the Code does not rely on the ultimate purpose for the indebtedness if it is clear that the loan proceeds were actually used to buy portfolio stock.

*Situation 3.* Parent's investment in portfolio stock using the proceeds of the loan from Bank Z does not make the loan from Bank Z indebtedness directly attributable to investment in portfolio stock. Absent circumstances that demonstrate a direct relationship between outside group indebtedness and the investment in portfolio stock, the intercompany loans do not trigger the application of section 246A of the Code. This is because, in the consolidated return context, intercompany loans generally create a wash for federal income tax purposes and do not create the potential for tax avoidance that section 246A was designed to prevent. Thus, because the only outside indebtedness of the Parent-Bank group consists of deposits received by Bank Z in the ordinary course of business and there is no direct relationship between this outside indebtedness and the portfolio stock purchase, there is no indebtedness directly attributable to investment in portfolio stock subject to section 246A.

## *NOTES*

1. *Protecting the policy of the dividends-received deduction.* In addition to curbing tax arbitrage, section 246A might be explained as protecting the policy of the dividends-received deduction. The deduction prevents imposition of more than one corporate-level tax if corporate-source income is distributed through tiers of

corporate owners to the ultimate shareholders of the enterprise. Implicit in the deduction policy is the assumption that the earnings will pass through each tier of corporations as a non-deductible distribution. That assumption is not satisfied, however, when a corporate investor receives a dividend on portfolio stock and passes through that income as deductible interest rather than a nondeductible distribution. In this situation, allowing a dividends-received deduction to the corporate investor would potentially have the effect of eliminating *all* corporate tax (rather than merely one level of corporate tax) on the stream of corporate-source income. Hence, a provision such as section 246A is needed to prevent the dividends-received deduction from undermining the corporate tax.

2. *Interest deduction versus the dividends-received deduction.* In other cases where the combination of a claimed interest deduction and some other tax preference produces an unintended double tax benefit, the approach of the law is to disallow the interest deduction, as exemplified by *Knetsch*, *Goldstein*, and the COLI cases. Section 246A takes the opposite approach by leaving the interest deduction intact but curtailing instead the provision creating the tax preference. Presumably, Congress chose this approach because of the uncertainty in determining the amount of the tax preference and, therefore, the extent of the double tax benefit. For example, a debt-financed corporate acquisition of stock on which few, if any, dividends are paid does not produce the arbitrage benefit that section 246A seeks to curb. Thus, a rule limiting the interest deduction of a corporation acquiring such stock might be too broad.

One situation where the interest deduction, rather than the dividends-received deduction, may need to be limited is when the borrowing and the ownership of portfolio stock is not carried out by the same corporation. For example, suppose corporation X borrows money to acquire 80 percent of the stock of corporation Z and Z invests in portfolio stock. As Rev. Rul. 88-66 indicates, section 246A might apply to this situation if X's debt can be shown to be directly attributable to Z's portfolio stock investment. But a rule denying a portion of Z's dividends-received deduction might be unfair to the other shareholders of Z who have not made debt-financed acquisitions. Although section 246A(f) authorizes regulations that would disallow the interest deduction or provide "other appropriate treatment" in this circumstance, no such regulations have been issued.

3. *Short sales.* In a short sale, a taxpayer sells shares borrowed from another shareholder. Typically, the taxpayer is obligated to return the borrowed shares plus make payments, analogous to interest, during the period the short sale remains open; these payments are ordinarily deductible as long as the short sale is open for a sufficiently long period. Cf. I.R.C. § 263(h). Thus, a corporate taxpayer that both invests in dividend-paying stock and sells short other stock may obtain the same tax arbitrage benefit that section 246A attempts to prevent. Under current law, if the stock sold short is substantially similar or related to the underlying dividend-paying stock investment, a corporate taxpayer is barred from deducting any dividends received on the underlying investment. I.R.C. § 246(c)(1)(B). If the stock sold short is not substantially similar or related to the underlying stock investment, the

dividends-received deduction may still be reduced, but only if the short sale proceeds are directly attributable to investment in portfolio stock. I.R.C. § 246A(d)(3)(B).

4. *A successful application of section 246A.* In H Enterprises International v. Comm'r, 75 T.C.M. 1948 (1998), aff'd per curiam, 183 F.3d 907 (8th Cir. 1999), a subsidiary corporation borrowed funds and distributed a portion of the proceeds to the "investment divisions" of its parent corporation. The court found that other than investment returns, the cash distribution was the only significant source of funds for the investment divisions. The divisions invested their money in dividend-paying stock. The court held that section 246A applied to disallow the dividends-received deduction of the parent. The fact that one corporation (the subsidiary) borrowed the money and another corporation (the parent) invested in the dividend-paying stock and claimed the dividends-received deduction was not fatal to the government's position.

5. *And an unsuccessful application.* In OBH, Inc. v. U.S., 397 F. Supp. 2d 1148 (2005), the taxpayer, formerly known as Berkshire Hathaway and managed by Warren Buffett, borrowed funds and contributed the proceeds to its wholly-owned insurance subsidiary as a way to increase the subsidiary's capital and net worth. Once contributed, however, the proceeds were commingled with the subsidiary's other funds including money earned from its active business operations. The IRS agent, who first became aware of the taxpayer's business plans from a Forbes Magazine article, spent *three years* developing the tax case in an effort either to trace the debt proceeds to the insurance company's purchase of dividend-paying stock, or to show that the taxpayer's dominant purpose in incurring the debt was to purchase dividend-paying stock. In one instance, the agent attempted to trace the debt proceeds through 154 separate securities transactions in order to match the debt with the purchase of dividend-paying stock. The court found, however, that the agent's tracing method contained so many arbitrary assumptions regarding the use of proceeds as to constitute a "fungibility" approach prohibited by the legislative history of section 246A. The court therefore refused to deny the subsidiary's dividends-received deduction pursuant to section 246A. In reaching its conclusion, the court recognized that it was "virtually impossible" for the Service to apply the provision successfully to companies like Berkshire that engaged in numerous investment transactions, but stated that it is up to Congress rather than the courts to expand the provision's scope.

6. *Possible formula approach?* As noted in Rev. Rul. 88-66, the legislative history of section 246A indicates Congressional rejection of a formula approach or fungibility concept in determining whether debt is directly attributable to investment in portfolio stock. Section 7701(f) of the Code, however, provides separate authority for the Treasury to issue regulations to prevent the avoidance of tax provisions "which deal with the linking of borrowing to investment . . . through the use of related persons, pass-thru entities, or other intermediaries." In Ann. 2004-44, 2004-1 C.B. 957, the Treasury requested public comment regarding the possible adoption of a pro rata allocation rule in the regulations under section 7701(f) and application of such regulations for purposes of section 246A.

**Problem 5-4:**

(a) On February 25, corporation X purchases 1,000 shares of IBM stock for a total cost of $100,000. X finances 60 percent of the acquisition by borrowing $60,000 from Local Bank. Subsequently, IBM distributes a $2/share quarterly dividend to all shareholders of record as of May 15, including X. (The prior dividend was distributed to holders of record as of February 15.) Throughout the period, the full amount of X's debt remains outstanding. Determine the tax consequences of the dividend to X.

(b) Would the result in (a) change if X borrowed the money, contributed $100,000 to corporation Y, its wholly-owned subsidiary, and had Y make the investment in IBM stock?

## B. Corporate-Level Consequences

Prior to 1984, corporations generally did not recognize any gain or loss on the distribution of property to their shareholders. Nonrecognition treatment constituted a major gap in the corporate tax base and much tax planning was designed to take advantage of it. The nonrecognition rule is generally attributed to the following case, one of the most famous in the corporate tax law. As we will see in chapter ten, the holding of the case and its ultimate legislative reversal in 1984 (for ordinary distributions) and 1986 (for liquidating distributions) helped to shape much of the tax law dealing with corporate acquisitions and liquidations. The specific facts of the case, however, dealt with an ordinary distribution.

### General Utilities & Operating Co. v. Helvering

296 U.S. 200 (1935)

Mr. Justice McReynolds delivered the opinion of the Court.

[On] January 1, 1927, petitioner, General Utilities, a Delaware corporation, acquired 20,000 shares (one-half of total outstanding) common stock [of] Islands Edison Company, for which it paid $2,000. Gillet & Company owned the remainder.

During January, 1928, Whetstone, president of Southern Cities Utilities Company, contemplated acquisition by his company of all Islands Edison common stock. He discussed the matter with Lucas, petitioner's president, also with Gillet & Co. The latter concern agreed to sell its holdings upon terms acceptable to all. But Lucas pointed out that the shares which his company held could only be purchased after distribution of them among stockholders, since a sale by it would subject the realized profit to taxation, and when the proceeds passed to the stockholders there would be further exaction. Lucas had no power to sell, but he, Gillet, and Whetstone were in accord concerning the terms and conditions under which purchase of all the stock might become possible — "it being understood and agreed between them that petitioner would make distribution of the stock of the Islands Edison Company to its stockholders and that counsel would prepare a written agreement embodying the terms and conditions of the said sale, agreement to be submitted for approval to the stockholders of the Islands Edison Company after the distribution of said stock by the petitioner."

Petitioner's directors, [on] March 22, 1928, considered the disposition of the Island Edison shares. Officers reported they were worth $1,122,500, and recommended an appreciation on the books to that figure. Thereupon a resolution directed this change; also

> "that a dividend in the amount of $1,071,426.25 be and it is hereby declared on the Common Stock of this Company payable in Common Stock of The Islands Edison Company at a valuation of $56.12-1/2 a share, out of the surplus of the Company arising from the appreciation in the value of the Common Stock of The Islands Edison Company held by this Company, viz., $1,120,500.00, the payment of the dividend to be made by the delivery to the stockholders of this Company, pro rata, of certificates for the Common Stock of The Islands Edison Company held by this Company at the rate of two shares of such stock for each share of Company Stock of this Corporation."

Accordingly, 19,090 shares were distributed amongst petitioner's thirty-three stockholders and proper transfers to them were made upon the issuing corporation's books. It retained 910 shares.

After this transfer, all holders of Islands Edison stock sold to Southern Cities Utilities Company at $56.12-1/2 per share. Petitioner realized $46,346.30 net profit on 910 shares and this was duly returned for taxation. There was no report of gain upon the 19,090 shares distributed to stockholders.

The Commissioner of Internal Revenue declared a taxable gain upon distribution of the stock in payment of the dividend declared March 22d, and made the questioned deficiency assessment. . . . [The Board of Tax Appeals] found:

> "The respondent has determined a deficiency in income tax in the amount of $128,342.07 for the calendar year 1928. The only question presented in this proceeding for redetermination is whether petitioner realized taxable gain in declaring a dividend and paying it in the stock of another company at an agreed value per share, which value was in excess of the cost of the stock to petitioner. . . . On March 26, 1928, the stockholders of the Islands Edison Company (one of which was petitioner, owning 910 shares) and the Southern Cities Utilities Company, entered into a written contract of sale of the Islands Edison Company stock. At no time did petitioner agree with Whetstone or the Southern Cities Utilities Company, verbally or in writing, to make sale to him or to the Southern Cities Utilities Company of any of said stock except the aforesaid 910 shares of the Islands Edison Company. . . .

> [The Commissioner's] theory is that upon the declaration of the dividend on March 22, 1928, petitioner became indebted to its stockholders in the amount of $1,071,426.25, and that the discharge of that liability by the delivery of property costing less than the amount of the debt constituted income. . . . The intent of the directors of petitioner was to declare a dividend payable in Islands Edison stock; their intent was expressed in that way in the resolution formally adopted; and the dividend was paid in the way intended and declared. We so construe the transaction, and . . . hold that the declaration and payment of the dividend resulted in no taxable income."

The Commissioner asked the Circuit Court of Appeals, Fourth Circuit, to review the Board's determination. He alleged: "The only question to be decided is whether the petitioner (taxpayer) realized taxable income in declaring a dividend and paying it in stock of another company at an agreed value per share, which value was in excess of the cost of the stock."

The court stated:

> "There are two grounds upon which the petitioner urges that the action of the Board of Tax Appeals was wrong: First, that the dividend declared was in effect a cash dividend and that the respondent realized a taxable income by the distribution of the Islands Edison Company stock to its stockholders equal to the difference between the amount of the dividend declared and the cost of the stock. Second, that the sale made of the Islands Edison Company stock was in reality a sale by the respondent (with all the terms agreed upon before the declaration of the dividend), through its stockholders who were virtually acting as agents of the respondent, the real vendor."

Upon the first ground, it sustained the Board. Concerning the second, it held that, although not raised before the Board, the point should be ruled upon.

> "When we come to consider the sale of the stock of the Islands Edison Company we cannot escape the conclusion that the transaction was deliberately planned and carried out for the sole purpose of escaping taxation. The purchaser was found by the officers of the respondent; the exact terms of the sale as finally consummated were agreed to by the same officers; the purchaser of the stock stated that the delivery of all the stock was essential and that the delivery of a part thereof would not suffice; the details were worked out for the express and admitted purpose of avoiding the payment of the tax and for the reason that the attorneys for the respondent had advised that unless some such plan was adopted the tax would have to be paid; and a written agreement was to be prepared by counsel for the respondent which was to be submitted to the stockholders; all this without the stockholders, or any of them, who were ostensibly making the sale, being informed, advised or consulted. Such admitted facts plainly constituted a plan, not to use the harsher terms of scheme, artifice or conspiracy, to evade the payment of the tax. For the purposes of this decision it is not necessary to consider whether such a course as is here shown constituted a fraud, it is sufficient if we conclude that the object was to evade the payment of a tax justly due the government.
>
> The sale of the stock in question was, in substance, made by the respondent company, through the stockholders as agents or conduits through whom the transfer

of the title was effected. The stockholders, even in their character as agents, had little or no option in the matter and in no sense exercised any independent judgment. They automatically ratified the agreement prepared and submitted to them."

A judgment of reversal followed.

Both tribunals below rightly decided that petitioner derived no taxable gain from the distribution among its stockholders of the Islands Edison shares as a dividend. This was no sale; assets were not used to discharge indebtedness.

The second ground of objection, although sustained by the court, was not presented to or ruled upon by the Board. The petition for review relied wholly upon the first point; and, in the circumstances, we think the court should have considered no other. Always a taxpayer is entitled to know with fair certainty the basis of the claim against him. Stipulations concerning facts and any other evidence properly are accommodated to issues adequately raised.

Recently (April, 1935) this court pointed out:

> "The Court of Appeals is without power, on review of proceedings of the Board of Tax Appeals, to make any findings of fact. The function of the court is to decide whether the correct rule of law was applied to the facts found; and whether there was substantial evidence before the Board to support the findings made. If the Board has failed to make an essential finding and the record on review is insufficient to provide the basis for a final determination, the proper procedure is to remand the case for further proceedings before the Board. And the same procedure is appropriate even when the findings omitted by the Board might be supplied from examination of the records." . . .

Here the court undertook to decide a question not properly raised. Also it made an inference of fact directly in conflict with the stipulation of the parties and the findings, for which we think the record affords no support whatever. To remand the cause for further findings would be futile. The Board could not properly find anything which would assist the Commissioner's cause.

The judgment of the court below must be reversed. The action of the Board of Tax Appeals is approved. . . .

## *NOTES AND QUESTIONS*

1. *What happened to the gain?* According to the Court, when the Islands Edison (IE) stock was sold to Southern Cities Utilities Company (SCUC), the taxpayer paid tax on its profit from sale of the 910 IE shares it had retained, but the taxpayer's shareholders did not pay tax on their sale of the 19,090 IE shares that had been distributed to them. Why not?

2. *What about* Gregory*?* Like *General Utilities*, *Gregory v. Helvering* (p. 120), decided by the same Justices just eleven months earlier, involved a sale of a corporate asset (the Monitor stock held by United Mortgage Corp.) and distribution of

proceeds. In each case, the transaction was structured to reduce the resulting income tax consequences. In *Gregory*, all three courts acknowledged this tax avoidance purpose; likewise, in *General Utilities*, the Fourth Circuit stated that "the transaction was deliberately planned and carried out for the sole purpose of escaping taxation." 74 F.2d at 976. How should the Court's unanimous holdings *against* the taxpayer in *Gregory*, but in *favor* of the taxpayer in *General Utilities*, be reconciled?

3. *Current law.* Read I.R.C. §§ 311(a) and (b)(1) and 301(d). The holding of *General Utilities* remains codified in section 311(a). In the case of ordinary distributions, however, the holding is largely reversed by section 311(b)(1). In general, on a distribution of appreciated property, a corporation must recognize gain as if it sold such property to the distributee for the property's fair market value. The *General Utilities* rule remains applicable if the distributed property is not appreciated (i.e., loss property) or an obligation of the distributing corporation. In addition, section 311(b)(1) is limited to distributions to which subpart A (I.R.C. §§ 301-307) applies. As a result, section 311(b)(1) is inapplicable to distributions pursuant to a liquidation or reorganization of the corporation. As explained in chapter ten, the current-law tax treatment of the distributing corporation in a corporate liquidation is similar to its treatment in an ordinary distribution. In contrast, as described in chapters eleven and twelve, a distribution pursuant to a reorganization largely remains a nonrecognition transaction to the distributing corporation.

4. *Impact of liabilities.* If the distributed property is encumbered by a liability or the shareholder assumes a corporate liability in connection with the distribution, and if the liability is greater than the fair market value of the property, the distributing corporation must recognize gain equal to the excess of the liability over the corporation's basis in the property distributed. I.R.C. §§ 311(b)(2), 336(b). The tax consequences are generally the same as if the corporation had sold the property for the same consideration to the distributee. The same result occurs even if the liability is nonrecourse. I.R.C. § 7701(g); Comm'r v. Tufts, 461 U.S. 300 (1983).

5. *Impact on E&P.* Read I.R.C. § 312(a) and (b). What adjustments, if any, must be made to a corporation's E&P (initially $100) if it distributes an asset with an adjusted basis of $25 and a fair market value of $60 to its shareholders? What if the value of the asset were only $10?

6. *Integration.* From a policy standpoint, do you think the *General Utilities* doctrine can be defended as a way to achieve partial integration of the corporate and shareholder income taxes? Explain.

> **Problem 5-5:** X corporation transfers appreciated property to an LLC in exchange for a ten percent interest in the LLC. Assume that the LLC is taxed as a partnership, neither X nor the LLC recognizes gain or loss on the transfer, and both X's basis in the LLC interest received and the LLC's basis in the properties received are equal to X's former basis in those properties. I.R.C. §§ 721(a), 722, and 723. Subsequently, X distributes its ten percent interest in the LLC to its shareholders in a transaction qualifying under section 301. What are the tax consequences of this transaction to X? Does your answer

depend upon who owns the other 90 percent of the LLC, how close in time the transfer and distribution are, and whether X has a business purpose for carrying out these steps?

## C. Distributions by S Corporations with E&P

We already examined in chapter two the tax consequences of distributions by S corporations with no E&P, that is, with no prior history as a C corporation. The rules are fairly straightforward; because no distinction is drawn between distributed and undistributed earnings of the corporation in determining the amount taxable to the corporation's shareholders, the actual distribution of earnings to the shareholders is generally a nontaxable event to them. It is simply a receipt of funds on which they have previously paid tax. It is only when the distribution reflects an amount *not previously included* in the shareholder's income that tax consequences can arise. Under what circumstances might there be such a distribution?

For shareholders of a corporation that has always maintained "S" status, *stock basis* is the account used to determine whether a distribution is a taxable one. I.R.C. § 1368(a) and (b). Why is that? Do you recall why *debt basis* is not available for this purpose?

For S corporations with accumulated E&P (and, therefore, a prior history as a C corporation), the taxation of distributions is more complicated. In part, this is because the election of S status by a C corporation does not affect the amount of the corporation's E&P. Thus, in years after the election, an S corporation will have two types of earnings: (1) those accumulated during its "S" years (which have been passed through to its shareholders and the distribution of which should generally be tax-free to them), and (2) those accumulated during its "C" years (the distribution of which should be taxable to shareholders under the section 301(c) rules). The tax consequences of a distribution by such a corporation therefore depend upon which pool of earnings is being distributed. As you will see in working through **problem 5-6**, below, the function of the "accumulated adjustments account" ("AAA") is generally to treat distributions by an S corporation as coming out of its S earnings before its C earnings. This stacking rule is ordinarily favorable to taxpayers because, for example, it delays treatment of the distribution as a dividend under sections 301(c)(1) and 316(a).

The complication of maintaining the AAA could be avoided if the election of S status by a C corporation (or a transaction in which an S corporation succeeds to a C corporation's E&P, such as in a reorganization) were treated as a taxable event to the shareholders that deemed all of the corporation's E&P to be distributed to them followed by a recontribution of that amount back to the corporation. If this rule were adopted, then there would no longer be any S corporations with undistributed E&P. Thus, any distribution by an S corporation could be taxed under the simpler set of rules applicable to S corporations without any C history. Of course, this change in the law might create a significant impediment against a corporation electing S status (or being acquired by an S corporation in a reorganization) once it has successfully operated as a C corporation. **Problem 5-6(c)**, below, explores whether a less dramatic policy change might eliminate the need for the AAA.

Review and read I.R.C. §§ 1366(a); 1367(a); 1368(a)-(d), (e)(1)(A) and (C), and (e)(2); 1371(a), (c)(1) and (3), (e)(1); and 1377(b), and do the following problem.

**Problem 5-6:** Mr. E forms X corporation as a C corporation with an initial capitalization of $1,000. During its first six years of operation, X accumulates E&P of $10,000. At the beginning of Year 7, X becomes an S corporation. X has $2,000 of net earnings in Year 7 and an additional $2,000 of net earnings in Year 8. In addition, exactly six months into Year 8, X distributes $6,000 cash to E.

(a) What are the tax consequences to E upon receipt of the $6,000 distribution?
(b) To make sure you understand the role of section 1368(c) and the AAA, answer question (a) based on the assumption that section 1368(c) is not in the statute and that the distribution is taxed only under the general rules of section 1368(a) and (b). How is the result different from your answer to question (a)?
(c) Are there other ways of stacking the earnings distributed by an S corporation with a prior C history to eliminate the need for the AAA? Try to articulate the rule that would implement each alternative. From a policy standpoint, would any of the alternatives be preferable to current law? Why or why not?
(d) Assume the same facts as in **problem 5-6**, except that the net earnings in Years 7 and 8 are all tax-exempt income. How is E taxed on receipt of the Year 8 distribution? See I.R.C. §§ 1366(a)(1)(A), 1367(a)(1)(A), and 1368(e)(1)(A). Do these rules require a shareholder such as E to pay tax on his share of the S corporation's tax-exempt income? Taking this example into account, what is the stacking rule carried out by section 1368(c) and the AAA?
(e) Do the Year 7 and 8 earnings (taxable or tax-exempt) of the corporation increase its E&P account? See I.R.C. § 1371(a) and (c). Explain the rationale for your conclusion.
(f) Can the AAA ever become a negative amount? How? What is the significance of a negative AAA? See Reg. § 1.1368-2(a)(3)(ii).
(g) Assume the same facts as in **problem 5-6**, except that the corporation has a $3,000 net loss during Year 8. What is the tax consequence to E of the $6,000 cash distribution occurring in the middle of Year 8? See I.R.C. §§ 1368(e)(1)(C), 1368(d) (flush language).

(h) Assume the same facts as in **problem 5-6**, except that there is no distribution during Year 8. Furthermore, on January 1 of Year 9, E sells 20 percent of his X corporation stock to Ms. F, a nonresident alien, for $8,000. Finally, during Year 9, X has no additional earnings and distributes $6,000 cash pro rata to E and F ($4,800 to E and $1,200 to F). What are the tax consequences to E and F upon receipt of their distributions in Year 9? See I.R.C. §§ 1361(b)(1)(C), 1362(d)(2), 1371(e)(1), and 1377(b)(1); Reg. § 1.1377-2(b) (last sentence).

(i) Assume the same facts as in **problem 5-6**, except that there is no distribution during Year 8, E sells 20 percent of his X stock to Ms. G (an eligible shareholder) on July 15 of Year 9 for $8,000, and X has taxable income of $2,000 in Year 9, of which $1,000 was earned before July 16 and $1,000 was earned after July 15. During Year 9, X distributes $5,000 cash to E on March 1 and $3,000 cash pro rata to E and G ($2,400 to E and $600 to G) on August 1. What are the tax consequences to E and G upon receipt of their distributions in Year 9? Assume that the election provided by Reg. § 1.1368-1(g)(2) is effectively made to treat Year 9 as two taxable years. See Reg. § 1.1368-1(g) and -3 (ex. 6).

## *NOTES AND QUESTIONS*

1. *Distributions in excess of AAA.* If multiple distributions are made in a taxable year and their total amount exceeds the amount in the AAA as of the end of the taxable year, a pro rata portion of AAA is allocated to each distribution based on the amount of the distribution. For example, if four $10,000 distributions are made by an S corporation in a year in which its AAA, determined as of the end of the taxable year without diminution for the distributions, is $24,000, then $6,000 ($10,000/$40,000 × $24,000) of each distribution is treated as out of AAA. Reg. § 1.1368-2(b), -3 (ex. 8). This rule is the same as the allocation of current E&P by a C corporation to multiple distributions during a year. Any accumulated E&P of the S corporation is then allocated to each distribution in the chronological order of the distribution beginning with the earliest. Reg. § 1.316-2(b) and (c).

2. *Distributions in loss years.* As illustrated by **problem 5-6(g)** above, the tax consequence of a distribution by an S corporation with accumulated E&P is determined without regard to losses incurred by the corporation in the year of distribution. This rule helps allow an S corporation to plan the tax consequences of its distributions even though the amount of the corporation's income or loss for the year is not yet known at the time of the distribution.

3. *Income exempt from tax (and related expenses).* As illustrated by **problem 5-6(d)** above, the AAA is not adjusted for tax-exempt income and related expenses of an

S corporation. Rev. Rul. 2008-42, 2008-2 C.B. 175, involved an S corporation that paid premiums on an insurance policy covering the life of its key employee. The corporation was the beneficiary of this policy. Because any death benefits would be excluded from the corporation's income (I.R.C. § 101(a)(1), (j)(1) and (2)(A)), the IRS concluded that any benefits received were in the nature of exempt income and therefore would not increase AAA. Therefore, even though the nondeductible premiums (see I.R.C. § 264(a)(1)) represented a section 1367(a)(2)(D) item, the premiums constituted an expense related to this exempt income and therefore did not reduce AAA.

4. *Federal tax attributable to C years.* The AAA is also not adjusted for any federal tax attributable to a taxable year in which an S corporation was a C corporation. I.R.C. § 1368(e)(1)(A). Based on your understanding of the purpose of the AAA, explain the reason for this provision.

5. *Corporate-level consequences.* Like a C corporation, an S corporation that distributes appreciated property to its shareholders recognizes gain on the distribution, and the gain is passed through to the corporation's shareholders. I.R.C. §§ 1371(a), 311(b)(1), 1366(a)(1) and (c). Since the gain passed through increases both stock basis and AAA, the shareholders are not taxed again upon distribution of the amount previously included in income. I.R.C. §§ 1367(a)(1), 1368(b)(1), (c)(1), and (e)(1)(A).

During periods when dividends are taxed less favorably than long-term capital gain, proper planning may be counterintuitive for an S corporation with accumulated E&P that contemplates distributing a long-term capital gain asset to its shareholders. Suppose, for example, that X corporation (an S corporation with a prior history as a C corporation) owns two such assets, each valued at $10 million, but with a basis of $9 million and $1 million, respectively. X plans to distribute one of the assets to its shareholders and is agnostic regarding which one. Assume that prior to the transaction, the shareholders have a zero basis in their stock, the AAA is also zero, and X has $20 million of accumulated E&P. If dividends are taxed less favorably than long-term capital gain, which asset should X distribute to minimize the overall tax consequences of the transaction? Why?

# Chapter 6

# Redemptions

## A. Introduction

This chapter concerns the tax treatment of a corporate redemption, a transaction very similar to an ordinary distribution. A redemption, also sometimes called a "share buyback" or "share repurchase," is a distribution by a corporation to a shareholder in exchange for some or all of the shareholder's stock in the corporation.

Although share repurchases have long been common transactions among closely held corporations, in the early 1980s public corporations began to use such transactions widely as an alternative means of distributing corporate earnings to shareholders. Between 1999 and 2004, the amount of corporate earnings distributed by the companies included in the S&P 500 stock index through share repurchases roughly equaled the amount those companies distributed as dividends. The amount of their share repurchases jumped in 2005 and 2006 to almost twice the amount of dividends, and in 2007, the amount increased further to almost $600 billion, or close to three times the amount of dividends. This shift occurred despite legislative changes enacted in 2003 that disproportionately reduced the tax rate on dividend income in comparison to capital gain from share repurchases.

Why do corporations make distributions via share buybacks rather than dividends? For closely held corporations (which may distribute few, if any, dividends), a share buyback provides a practical way to overcome the liquidity problem resulting from the nonmarketability of the corporation's shares. The buyback permits corporate assets to finance a change in the ownership of the corporation, such as one resulting from the death or retirement of a shareholder or a disagreement among the shareholders.

For public corporations, a standard explanation for the popularity of share buybacks is their greater flexibility compared to dividends. Under this view, the level of dividends is sacrosanct to investors and must therefore be sustained year after year, whereas a share buyback is more in the nature of a bonus that a corporation can pay out idiosyncratically in an unusually good year. Thus, transitory earnings are more likely to be distributed through stock repurchases, and the growth in the amount of such transactions may be attributable to increased earnings volatility. In addition, some companies may use share repurchases rather than dividends to help attain a particular earnings per share target or to prevent dilution of the value of stock options. Consistent with the "bonus" hypothesis, there is evidence of companies buying back their shares when their profits are good and their stock prices high. This evidence tends to contradict the view that a share buyback is a signal from inside management regarding the positive future prospects of the corporation and the undervalued nature of its stock.

Traditionally, there have also been tax explanations for the preference for buybacks. Both dividends and share repurchases result in a distribution of funds out of corporate solution. But if the share repurchase produces long-term capital gain for the shareholder and if such income is taxed more favorably than dividend income, then the share repurchase results in a lower tax cost than the dividend. Under certain assumptions, some portion of the tax savings might shift (in the form of a higher share price) to those shareholders who continue to own stock in the corporation following the repurchase. In other words, share buybacks may result in an increase in share price because of possible positive signals from management and tax savings.

Because of the traditional difference in the taxation of long-term capital gain and dividend income, current law goes to extraordinary lengths to try to determine which of these two tax consequences is appropriate for a given redemption. The law generally makes this determination by comparing the result of the redemption to that under two competing analogies — a sale or exchange of stock and an ordinary distribution. For the most part, the law focuses exclusively on the effect of the redemption to the *redeemed shareholder*; to that party, which analogous transaction does the redemption more closely resemble? The touchstone of this examination is the amount the shareholder's interest in the corporation is reduced as a result of the redemption. These rules exemplify a statutory "substance over form" approach, since the form of the transaction (an exchange) is disregarded in certain circumstances.

For example, a redemption of a shareholder's entire interest in a corporation is generally treated for tax purposes like a sale or exchange of stock (referred to as "exchange" treatment). From the shareholder's perspective, the redemption looks similar to a sale of stock to a third party or to the continuing shareholders of the corporation, either of which ordinarily results in exchange treatment. The key is the shareholder's reduced interest in the corporation as a result of each transaction; in the case of a complete redemption, the interest is terminated. On the other hand, a redemption of only a portion of a sole shareholder's interest in a corporation is generally treated for tax purposes like an ordinary distribution. In this case, the fact that the shareholder surrenders some shares in the transaction is viewed as a meaningless gesture — the shareholder continues as the sole owner of the corporation both before and after the transaction, so there is no change in interest. In between these two extremes are many possible variations, and the law tries (sometimes in excruciating detail) to specify the tax consequences of many of them as well. In general, the law ignores the *corporation's* perspective to the transaction, including the fact that both an ordinary distribution and a redemption, but not a sale or exchange of stock to a third party or to continuing shareholders, result in a distribution of assets out of corporate solution.

Because individuals are taxed (through 2012) very similarly on their dividend income and long-term capital gain, the overall tax stake of determining the appropriate analogy for a corporate redemption is much reduced. To be sure, exchange treatment of a redemption is still generally more favorable for individuals because it permits the taxpayer to reduce the taxable amount by the taxpayer's basis in the shares surrendered. Indeed, exchange treatment potentially allows the shareholder to claim a loss in the transaction, an outcome that is not possible if the redemption is treated as an ordinary distribution. Moreover, for corporate shareholders, the proper characterization of a redemption for tax purposes continues to be as important as ever. But these remaining stakes surely would not justify the existing complicated and extensive rules concerning the tax consequences of a redemption.

In fact, in important ways, the law now mostly operates as an attractive nuisance. Because of the traditional preference of individuals for exchange treatment of their redemptions, the law generally tilts away from that characterization and in favor of ordinary distribution treatment. But this means that corporate shareholders, which generally are subject to the same law and have the exact opposite preference, can easily take advantage of it, and they have. It seems clear that the tax law of corporate redemptions would be significantly simplified and reformed if there were confidence in the long-term continuity of current law's similar tax treatment of dividend income and long-term capital gain.

Part B of this chapter reviews the current-law rules for the taxation of redemptions. Because the tax law is quite detailed and specific, and because economically equivalent transactions involving distributions can often be carried out with or without a redemption or with a different order of steps, it is common for such transactions to be designed in a manner that minimizes their tax consequences. Part C considers the difficult question of when such tax planning is permissible and when it is impermissible.

Almost all of the illustrations included in this chapter involve redemptions carried out by closely held corporations, the type of situations that the law was principally designed to address. The same rules, however, also generally apply to redemptions by public corporations. The rules apply imperfectly in that situation since neither the public corporation nor the redeemed shareholder generally has the necessary information — the effect of the transaction on the shareholder's interest in the corporation after taking into account all other shareholder ownership changes resulting from the same transaction — to determine with certainty the tax consequences of the redemption. Indeed, since a redeemed shareholder selling public stock generally does not know the identity of the other party to the transaction, the shareholder may not even realize that the transaction is a redemption.

### *NOTE*

*Distributions to non-U.S. shareholders.* In general, non-U.S. shareholders continue to favor redemptions (which may produce tax-exempt capital gain) rather than dividends (taxed at 30 percent or a reduced rate by treaty).

## B. Taxation of Corporate Redemptions

### 1. *Shareholder-Level Consequences*

Read I.R.C. §§ 302(a), (b), (d) and (f) and 317(b). In general, a corporate redemption is treated as a distribution "in part or full payment in exchange for the stock" redeemed if one of the alternative circumstances specified in section 302(b), usually referred to as "safe harbors," is satisfied. "Exchange" characterization enables shareholders to recover basis in the transaction and to report any gain or loss as long-term capital gain or loss if the stock surrendered is a capital asset held for over one year. I.R.C. §§ 1001(a), 1222(3). In the absence of exchange treatment, the redemption is treated as an ordinary distribution subject to section 301. I.R.C. § 302(d). As described in chapter five, a section 301 distribution is a dividend to the extent of the distributing corporation's current or accumulated E&P.

Three of the safe harbors authorizing exchange treatment under section 302 describe redemptions that resemble a sale of stock from the shareholder's perspective. The remaining safe harbor in section 302, section 302(b)(4), concerns a redemption in partial liquidation of the distributing corporation. As we will see, this safe harbor turns on the consequences of the redemption to the distributing corporation rather than the redeemed shareholder. Another provision, section 303, authorizes exchange treatment of redemptions to pay certain taxes and expenses resulting from the death of the shareholder whose stock is redeemed. The following sections describe some of the details relating to these provisions.

#### a. Constructive Ownership Rules

In deciding whether a redemption looks more like a sale of stock or an ordinary distribution to the shareholder being redeemed, current law applies an extensive set of "constructive ownership" rules to try to identify the true economic interest of the shareholder in the corporation both before and after the transaction. These rules, which also apply for certain other tax purposes (but only if specifically cross-referenced), treat a taxpayer as owning stock that is actually owned by someone else if they have a sufficiently close relationship. Thus, the rules represent a further effort to determine tax consequences based on substance rather than form. Where there are several relationships among the shareholders that might justify attribution, it is important to remember that any given shareholder cannot end up owning, directly and indirectly, more than 100 percent of the corporation in question. Thus, a useful general approach is to examine each shareholder separately and determine how much of the stock actually owned by others is treated as owned by the shareholder in question. Read I.R.C. §§ 302(c)(1) and 318 and do the following problems:

**Problem 6-1:** A, B, C, D, and E own X Corporation in the following manner:

A— 10 shares
B— 20 shares
C— 30 shares
D— 40 shares
E— 50 shares
150 shares total

A and B are both sons of C, A by blood and B by adoption. C is the son of D, and C also has an option to purchase five of D's shares. E is the Estate of Mother, who was the mother of A and B and wife of C. The beneficiaries of Mother's Estate are A, B, C, and F, each 25 percent beneficiaries. F is the sister of A and B, and the daughter of C and Mother. How many shares of X Corporation does each of these parties own, either directly or indirectly, by reason of section 318?

**Problem 6-2:**

(a) Individuals Q and R each owns 50 percent of corporation Y. Y owns 70 percent of corporation Z. R also owns 100 percent of corporation T. Determine the actual and constructive ownership of the following, after application of the section 318 constructive ownership rules:
   (i) The proportion of Z owned by individual Q;
   (ii) The proportion of T owned by individual Q;
   (iii) The proportion of T owned by corporation Z;
   (iv) The proportion of Y owned by corporation T;
   (v) The proportion of Z owned by corporation T.
(b) Same as the above, except that Y corporation is an S corporation, and it is owned 40 percent by Q, 40 percent by R, and 20 percent by individual S. Answer the same questions as above.

## b. Substantially Disproportionate Redemptions

As described in the following ruling, a "substantially disproportionate" redemption qualifies for exchange treatment. Read I.R.C. § 302(a) and (b)(2). In general, this test requires the redemption to result in some significant reduction in the redeemed shareholder's interest in the corporation following the redemption, and the law provides a mostly bright-line, numerical basis for determining whether the test has been met. In addition, to qualify as a substantially disproportionate redemption, the redeemed shareholder must own immediately after the redemption less than 50 percent of the total combined voting power of all classes of stock entitled to vote.

## Rev. Rul. 81-41

1981-1 C.B. 121

. . . Can a redemption of voting preferred stock qualify as a substantially disproportionate redemption under section 302(b)(2) of the Internal Revenue Code, even though the redeeming shareholder, as a result of not owning any common stock either directly or constructively, is unable to have a reduction in common stock ownership?

. . . A domestic corporation, X, had outstanding 5,100 shares of voting common stock and 4,900 shares of voting preferred stock. Except for minor limitations of local law, the common and preferred stock have equal voting rights. Each share of common and preferred stock has one vote in electing directors. The preferred stock is entitled to a cumulative nine percent annual dividend and is not a participating stock. All the preferred stock is owned by A, who is the founder of X and the board chairman. The preferred stock is not section 306 stock within the meaning of section 306(c) of the Code. A holds no common stock in X, either directly or constructively within the meaning of section 318 of the Code. The common stock in X is widely held by persons unrelated to A.

In accord with a request from A, X redeemed 2,000 shares of the preferred stock for cash. Thus, A's vote in X was reduced from 49 percent immediately before the redemption to 36.25 percent immediately after the redemption (2,900 shares still held by A divided by 8,000 shares then outstanding). There was no plan or intent for X to redeem any of the stock held by shareholders other than A.

. . . Section 302(a) of the Code provides that if a corporation redeems its stock and if paragraph (1), (2), (3), or (4) of section 302(b) applies to the redemption, the redemption shall be treated as a distribution in part or full payment in exchange for the stock. Section 302(b)(2) states as a general rule that section 302(a) shall apply to a redemption if the distribution is substantially disproportionate with respect to the shareholder. Under section 302(b)(2)(C) a distribution is substantially disproportionate if:

> (i) the ratio which the voting stock of the corporation owned by the shareholder immediately after the redemption bears to all of the voting stock of the corporation at such time,
>
> is less than 80 percent of—
>
> (ii) the ratio which the voting stock of the corporation owned by the shareholder immediately before the redemption bears to all of the voting stock of the corporation at such time.
>
> For purposes of this paragraph, no distribution shall be treated as substantially disproportionate unless the shareholder's ownership of the common stock of the corporation (whether voting or nonvoting) after and before redemption also meets the 80 percent requirement of the preceding sentence . . .

Section 302(b)(2) does not apply to a redemption unless immediately after the redemption the shareholder owns less than 50 percent of the total combined voting power of all classes of stock entitled to vote. Section 302(b)(2)(B). Finally, section 302(b)(2) does not apply to a redemption made pursuant to a plan the purpose or effect of which is a series of redemptions resulting in a distribution that in the aggregate is not substantially disproportionate with respect to the shareholder. Section 302(b)(2)(D).

In the present case, A owned 49 percent of the voting stock of X prior to the redemption. Eighty percent of 49 percent is 39.2 percent. Because A owned 36.25 percent of the voting stock of X after the redemption, the first "80 percent test" of section 302(b)(2)(C) is satisfied. In addition, because A owned only 36.25 percent of the voting stock of X after the redemption, the limitation of section 302(b)(2)(B) is met. Also, because this redemption was not part of a plan to redeem other stock of X, the provisions of section 302(b)(2)(D) are not violated. The question remaining is whether the second "80 percent test" of section 302(b)(2)(C), which concerns the ownership of common stock, has to be satisfied even though A owned no common stock either directly or constructively.

The Senate Finance Committee Report accompanying the enactment of section 302 states:

> Paragraph (2) of subsection (b) sets forth a general rule that if the redemption is substantially disproportionate, it will be treated as a sale under subsection (a), if the other conditions described in the paragraph are met. *It is intended that the general rule shall apply with respect to a redemption of preferred stock (other than section 306 stock) as well as common stock.* S. REP. NO. 1622, 83D CONG., 2D SESS. 234 (1954). (Emphasis added.)

Moreover, section 1.302-3 of the Income Tax Regulations states that section 302(b)(2) of the Code only applies to a redemption of both voting stock and other stock, but does not apply to the redemption solely of nonvoting stock. Therefore, both the legislative history and the regulations accompanying section 302(b)(2) indicate that the provision should apply to the redemption of voting preferred stock.

In the same report, the Senate Finance Committee does make two statements that a substantially disproportionate redemption requires a reduction in the redeemed shareholder's ownership of common stock in the redeeming corporation. However, the context of the first of these statements (S. REP. NO. 1622 at 44-45) indicates that this requirement is a safeguard against abuse where the redeeming shareholder holds common stock. Similarly, the second statement (S. REP. NO. 1622 at 234) views this requirement as meaning, "it is necessary that the shareholder's ownership of voting or nonvoting common stock (that is, his participating interest) in the corporation also be reduced by the percentage required with respect to voting stock." These statements indicate that in the case of a redeeming shareholder owning two or more classes of stock, one of which is common stock, the shareholder may not retain or improve his or her "participating" interest in the corporation (while having a substantially disproportionate reduction in his or her voting interest) and still claim the protection of the section 302(b)(2) safe-harbor. To conclude otherwise would permit a "bail-out" of corporate earnings at capital gains rates without a sacrifice of the shareholder's economic interest in the corporation. See U.S. v. Davis, 397 U.S. 301, 313 (1970). Thus, these statements (indicating that section 302(b)(2) requires a reduction in common stock ownership) are addressed to situations where the redeeming shareholder owns common stock, and are not addressed to situations where the redeeming shareholder does not own any common stock.

In the present case, A owns no common stock either directly or constructively. Therefore, the additional "safeguard" provided by the second "80 percent test" of section 302(b)(2)(C) is inapplicable to A.

## HOLDING

A redemption of voting preferred stock can qualify as a substantially disproportionate redemption under section 302(b)(2) even though the redeeming shareholder does not experience a reduction in common stock ownership, if the shareholder owns no common stock either directly or constructively.

## *NOTE*

*Step-transaction principles*. Section 302(b)(2)(D) provides that a redemption will not be treated as substantially disproportionate if it is pursuant to a plan to carry out a series of redemptions that result in the redemption not being substantially disproportionate (in the aggregate) to the taxpayer. In Rev. Rul. 85-14, 1985-1 C.B. 92, the minority shareholders of a closely held corporation were required to tender their shares back to the corporation in the event they ceased being actively involved in the corporation's business. One such shareholder informed the majority shareholder of his plan to resign from the company. Based on that information, the majority shareholder had a portion of his own shares redeemed prior to the resignation and complete redemption of the minority shareholder. Standing by itself, the partial redemption of the majority shareholder qualified as a substantially disproportionate redemption under section 302(b)(2). But taking into account both transactions, the partial redemption of the majority shareholder did not qualify. The IRS applied section 302(b)(2)(D) to conclude that the majority shareholder's redemption was not substantially disproportionate. Although there was no joint plan between the majority and minority shareholders to carry out the redemptions together, the IRS indicated that "a 'plan' for purposes of section 302(b)(2)(D) need be nothing more than a design by a single redeemed shareholder to arrange a redemption as part of a sequence of events that ultimately [produces a result not satisfying the section 302(b)(2) tests]."

Read I.R.C. § 302(a) and (b)(2) and Reg. § 1.302-3, and do the following problem:

**Problem 6-3:** Corporation V, which is owned entirely by unrelated individuals J, K, and L, has three classes of stock outstanding: voting common stock, a class of voting preferred stock, and a class of nonvoting preferred stock. Each share of the voting preferred stock has the same voting rights as one share of the common stock. J owns 200 shares each of the common stock and the voting preferred stock. K owns 100 shares of each of the three classes of stock. L owns 100 shares of the nonvoting preferred stock. Assuming that V has a sufficient amount of E&P, determine the tax consequences to the shareholder of each of the following alternatives:

(a) V redeems 100 shares each of J's common stock and voting preferred stock. Would your conclusion change if you knew that there were issued, but not outstanding, 200 additional shares of voting preferred stock that V held as treasury stock?
(b) V redeems 20 shares of K's common stock, 80 shares of his voting preferred stock, and 50 shares of his nonvoting preferred stock. Would your conclusion change if the class of nonvoting *preferred* stock were actually nonvoting *common* stock with approximately the same per share value as the class of voting common stock?
(c) V redeems 50 shares each of K's common stock, voting preferred stock, and nonvoting preferred stock. Would your conclusion change if you knew that as part of the same plan, V will redeem 100 shares of J's common stock six months after the redemption of K's stock?
(d) V redeems 50 shares of L's nonvoting preferred stock.
(e) Same as (d), except that L owned voting preferred stock, and it is that stock that is redeemed. Would your conclusion change if L also owned one share of common stock that was also redeemed? Suppose the one share of common stock was not redeemed?

## c. Redemptions Terminating the Shareholder's Interest

In general, a redemption that terminates the redeemed shareholder's interest in a corporation also qualifies for exchange treatment. In the case of a redemption by a family-owned corporation, however, it is common for the stock owned by the remaining shareholders to be attributed to the redeemed shareholder, thereby potentially negating the claimed termination of interest. To provide relief in this common circumstance, the law permits taxpayers to waive the family attribution rules if certain specified conditions are met. Read I.R.C. § 302(a), (b)(3), and (c), Reg. § 1.302-4(c)-(g), and the following materials.

## Lynch v. Commissioner

801 F.2d 1176 (9th Cir. 1986)

Cynthia Holcomb Hall, Circuit Judge:

. . . Taxpayers, William and Mima Lynch, formed the W.M. Lynch Co. on April 1, 1960. The corporation issued all of its outstanding stock to William Lynch (taxpayer). The taxpayer specialized in leasing cast-in-place concrete pipe machines. He owned the machines individually but leased them to the corporation which in turn subleased the equipment to independent contractors.

On December 17, 1975 the taxpayer sold 50 shares of the corporation's stock to his son, Gilbert Lynch (Gilbert), for $17,170. Gilbert paid for the stock with a $16,000 check given to him by the taxpayer and $1,170 from his own savings. The taxpayer and his wife also resigned as directors and officers of the corporation on the same day.

On December 31, 1975 the corporation redeemed all 2300 shares of the taxpayer's stock. In exchange for his stock, the taxpayer received $17,900 of property and a promissory note for $771,920. Gilbert, as the sole remaining shareholder, pledged his 50 shares as a guarantee for the note. In the event that the corporation defaulted on any of the note payments, the taxpayer would have the right to vote or sell Gilbert's 50 shares.

In the years immediately preceding the redemption, Gilbert had assumed greater managerial responsibility in the corporation. He wished, however, to retain the taxpayer's technical expertise with cast-in-place concrete pipe machines. On the date of the redemption, the taxpayer also entered into a consulting agreement with the corporation. The consulting agreement provided the taxpayer with payments of $500 per month for five years, plus reimbursement for business related travel, entertainment, and automobile expenses. In February 1977, the corporation and the taxpayer mutually agreed to reduce the monthly payments to $250. The corporation never withheld payroll taxes from payments made to the taxpayer.

After the redemption, the taxpayer shared his former office with Gilbert. The taxpayer came to the office daily for approximately one year; thereafter his appearances dwindled to about once or twice per week. When the corporation moved to a new building in 1979, the taxpayer received a private office.

In addition to the consulting agreement, the taxpayer had other ties to the corporation. He remained covered by the corporation's group medical insurance policy until 1980. When his coverage ended, the taxpayer had received the benefit of $4,487.54 in premiums paid by the corporation. He was also covered by a medical reimbursement plan, created the day of the redemption, which provided a maximum annual payment of $1,000 per member. Payments to the taxpayer under the plan totaled $96.05.

. . . We must decide whether the redemption of the taxpayer's stock in this case is taxable as a dividend distribution under 26 U.S.C. § 301 or as long-term capital gain under 26 U.S.C. § 302(a). Section 302(a) provides that a corporate distribution of property in redemption of a shareholder's stock is treated as a sale or exchange of such stock if the redemption falls within one of four categories described in section 302(b). If the redemption falls outside of these categories, then it is treated as a dividend distribution under section 301 to the extent of the corporation's earnings and profits.[1]

Section 302(b)(3) provides that a shareholder is entitled to sale or exchange treatment if the corporation redeems all of the shareholder's stock. In order to determine whether there is a complete redemption for purposes of section 302(b)(3), the family attribution rules of section 318(a) must be applied unless the requirements of section 302(c)(2) are satisfied. Here, if the family attribution rules apply, the taxpayer will be deemed to own constructively the 50 shares held by Gilbert (100% of the corporation's stock) and the transaction would not qualify as a complete redemption within the meaning of section 302(b)(3).

Section 302(c)(2)(A) states in relevant part:

> In the case of a distribution described in subsection (b)(3), [the family attribution rules in] section 318(a)(1) shall not apply if—
>
> (i) immediately after the distribution the distributee has no interest in the corporation (including an interest as officer, director, or employee), other than an interest as a creditor. . . .

The Commissioner argues that in every case the performance of post-redemption services is a prohibited interest under section 302(c)(2)(A)(i), regardless of whether the taxpayer is an officer, director, employee, or independent contractor.

The Tax Court rejected the Commissioner's argument, finding that the services rendered by the taxpayer did not amount to a prohibited interest in the corporation. In reaching this conclusion, the Tax Court relied on a test derived from Lewis v. Comm'r, 47 T.C. 129, 136 (1966) (Simpson, J., concurring):

> Immediately after the enactment of the 1954 Code, it was recognized that section 302(c)(2)(A)(i) did not prohibit office holding *per se*, but was concerned with a retained financial stake in the corporation, such as a profit-sharing plan, or in the creation of an ostensible sale that really changed nothing so far as corporate management was concerned. Thus, in determining whether a prohibited interest has been retained under section 302(c)(2)(A)(i), we must look to whether the former stockholder has either retained a financial stake in the corporation or continued to control the corporation and benefit by its operations. In particular, where the interest retained is not that of an officer, director, or employee, we must examine the facts and circumstances to determine whether a prohibited interest has been retained under section 302(c)(2)(A)(i). . . .

1. On the date of the redemption, W.M. Lynch Co. had accumulated earnings and profits of $315,863, and had never paid a dividend.

After citing the "control or financial stake" standard, the Tax Court engaged in a two-step analysis. First, the court concluded that the taxpayer was an independent contractor rather than an employee because the corporation had no right under the consulting agreement to control his actions. . . . Second, the court undertook a "facts and circumstances" analysis to determine whether the taxpayer had a financial stake in the corporation or managerial control after the redemption. Because the consulting agreement was not linked to the future profitability of the corporation, the court found that the taxpayer had no financial stake. . . . The court also found no evidence that the taxpayer exerted control over the corporation. . . . Thus, the Tax Court determined that the taxpayer held no interest prohibited by section 302(c)(2)(A)(i). . . .

We reject the Tax Court's interpretation of section 302(c)(2)(A)(i). An individualized determination of whether a taxpayer has retained a financial stake or continued to control the corporation after the redemption is inconsistent with Congress' desire to bring a measure of certainty to the tax consequences of a corporate redemption. We hold that a taxpayer who provides post-redemption services, either as an employee or an independent contractor, holds a prohibited interest in the corporation because he is not a creditor.

The legislative history of section 302 states that Congress intended to provide "definite standards in order to provide certainty in specific instances." S. REP. NO. 1622, 83D CONG., 2D SESS. 233. . . . "In lieu of a factual inquiry in every case, [section 302] is intended to prescribe specific conditions from which the taxpayer may ascertain whether a given redemption" will qualify as a sale or be treated as a dividend distribution. H. R. REP. NO. 1337, 83D CONG., 2D SESS. 35. . . . The facts and circumstances approach created by the Tax Court undermines the ability of taxpayers to execute a redemption and know the tax consequences with certainty.

The taxpayer's claim that the Senate rejected the mechanical operation of the House's version of section 302 is misleading. The Senate did reject the House bill because the "definitive conditions" were "unnecessarily restrictive." S. REP. NO. 1622, 83D CONG., 2D SESS. 44. . . . However, the Senate's response was to add paragraph (b)(1) to section 302, which reestablished the flexible, but notoriously vague, "not essentially equivalent to a dividend" test. This test provided that all payments from a corporation that were not essentially equivalent to a dividend should be taxed as capital gains. The confusion that stemmed from a case-by-case inquiry into "dividend equivalence" prompted the Congress to enact definite standards for the safe harbors in section 302(b)(2) and (b)(3). The Tax Court's refusal to recognize that section 302(c)(2)(A)(i) prohibits all noncreditor interests in the corporation creates the same uncertainty as the "dividend equivalence" test.

The problem with the Tax Court's approach is apparent when this case is compared with Seda v. Comm'r, 82 T.C. 484 (1984). In *Seda*, a former shareholder, at his son's insistence, continued working for the corporation for two years after the redemption. He received a salary of $1,000 per month. The Tax Court refused to hold that section 302(c)(2)(A)(i) prohibits the retention of employment relations *per se*, despite the unequivocal language in the statute. . . . Instead, the court applied the facts and circumstances approach to determine whether the former shareholder retained a financial stake or continued to control the corporation. The Tax Court found that the monthly payments of $1,000 constituted a financial stake in the corporation. . . . This result is at odds with the holding in *Lynch* that payments of $500 per month do not constitute a financial stake in the corporation. . . . The court also found in *Seda* no evidence that the former shareholder had ceased to manage the corporation. . . . Again, this finding is contrary to the holding in *Lynch* that the taxpayer exercised no control over the corporation after the redemption, even though he worked daily for a year and shared his old office with his son. . . . *Seda* and *Lynch* thus vividly demonstrate the perils of making an *ad hoc* determination of "control" or "financial stake."

[The court's discussion of Cerone v. Comm'r, 87 T.C. 1 (1986), is omitted. In *Cerone*, the Tax Court concluded, after a lengthy analysis, that the redeemed shareholder retained a financial stake in the corporation (and, therefore, a prohibited interest) because he drew an annual salary that was $2,400 higher than the taxpayer's salary in *Seda* and was employed by the corporation for a longer period after the redemption.]

Although the Tax Court reached the correct result in *Cerone*, its approach undermines the definite contours of the safe harbor Congress intended to create with sections 302(b)(3) and 302(c)(2)(A)(i). Whether a taxpayer has a financial stake according to the Tax Court seems to depend on two factors, length of employment and the amount of salary. Length of employment after the redemption is irrelevant because Congress wanted taxpayers to know whether they were entitled to capital gains treatment on the date their shares were redeemed. . . . As for the amount of annual salary, the Tax Court's present benchmark appears to be the $12,000 figure in *Seda*. Salary at or above this level will be deemed to be a financial stake in the enterprise, though the $6,000 annual payments in this case were held not to be a financial stake. There is no support in the legislative history of section 302 for the idea that Congress meant only to prohibit service contracts of a certain worth, and taxpayers should not be left to speculate as to what income level will give rise to a financial stake.

In this case, the taxpayer points to the fact that the taxpayers in *Seda* and *Cerone* were employees, while he was an independent contractor. On appeal, the Commissioner concedes the taxpayer's independent contractor status. We fail to see, however, any meaningful way to distinguish *Seda* and *Cerone* from *Lynch* by differentiating between employees and independent contractors. All of the taxpayers performed services for their corporations following the redemption. To hold that only the employee taxpayers held a prohibited interest would elevate form over substance. The parenthetical language in section 302(c)(2)(A)(i) merely provides a subset of prohibited interests from the universe of such interests, and in no way limits us from finding that an independent contractor retains a prohibited interest. Furthermore, the Tax Court has in effect come to ignore the parenthetical language. If employment relationships are not prohibited interests *per se*, then the taxpayer's status as an employee or independent contractor is irrelevant. What really matters under the Tax Court's approach is how the taxpayer fares under a facts and circumstances review of whether he has a financial stake in the corporation or managerial control. Tax planners are left to guess where along the continuum of monthly payments from $500 to $1000 capital gains treatment ends and ordinary income tax begins.

... [W]e conclude that those who provide post-redemption services, whether as independent contractors or employees, hold an interest prohibited by section 302(c)(2)(A)(i) because they are more than merely creditors. ... We believe that any attempt to define prohibited interests based on the level of control leads to the same difficulties inherent in making a case-by-case determination of what constitutes a financial stake.[2]

... Taxpayers who wish to receive capital gains treatment upon the redemption of their shares must completely sever all noncreditor interests in the corporation.[3] We hold that the taxpayer, as an independent contractor, held such a noncreditor interest, and so cannot find shelter in the safe harbor of section 302(c)(2)(A)(i). Accordingly, the family attribution rules of section 318 apply and the taxpayer fails to qualify for a complete redemption under section 302(b)(3). The payments from the corporation in redemption of the taxpayer's shares must be characterized as a dividend distribution taxable as ordinary income under section 301. ...

## *NOTES AND QUESTIONS*

1. *Tax planning.* According to the court, the corporation's principal business was to lease equipment from the taxpayer and then sublease the same equipment to unrelated third parties. This business activity, combined with flexibility in determining the amount of compensation paid to the taxpayer and his son, presumably enabled the corporation to accumulate whatever income amounts it wished each year, including modest amounts qualifying for low corporate tax brackets.

---

2. Determining the existence of control is particularly difficult in the context of a family-held corporation. The exercise of control often will not be obvious because a parent may influence a child, and hence corporate decisionmaking, in myriad ways. Our rule that the provision of services is a prohibited interest eliminates the need to make a speculative inquiry into whether the parent still controls the corporation after the redemption. Of course, no rule could or should prohibit post-redemption parent-child communication concerning the management of the corporation.

3. Our definition of a prohibited interest still leaves an open question as to the permissible scope of a creditor's interest under section 302(c)(2)(A)(i). *See, e.g.*, Reg. § 1.302-4(d) (a creditor's claim must not be subordinate to the claims of general creditors or in any other sense proprietary, *i.e.*, principal payments or interest rates must not be contingent on the earnings of the corporation).

The taxpayer argues that some creditor relationships might result in an "opportunity to influence" as great or greater than any officer, director, or employee relationship. He cites Rev. Rul. 77-467, 1977-2 C.B. 92 which concluded that a taxpayer who leased real property to a corporation, after the corporation redeemed his shares, held a creditor's interest under section 302(c)(2)(A)(i). While the taxpayer here may be correct in his assessment of a creditor's "opportunity to influence" a corporation, he overlooks the fact that Congress specifically allowed the right to retain such an interest.

The redemption may then have represented the taxpayer's effort to withdraw the low-taxed corporate-source income at a favorable shareholder tax rate.

2. *Interest as creditor.* The rule prohibiting retention (and acquisition for a ten-year period) of certain non-creditor interests following the redemption is designed to ensure that the apparent separation of the redeemed shareholder from the corporation is bona fide. Only in that circumstance is the taxpayer allowed to avoid the normal implication of a family member retaining control of the company after the redemption. From this perspective, it is somewhat curious that the court focuses in some detail on minor matters such as the specific terms of the taxpayer's post-redemption consulting arrangement, the frequency of his office visits, and his coverage under the company's health insurance plan, but makes scant mention, other than in footnote 3, of the retained "creditor's" interest. The note received by the taxpayer, secured by all of the company's stock, obligated the company to pay him virtually the entire value of the company (determined as of the time of the redemption). Read Reg. § 1.302-4(d). Do you think this retained interest would escape being treated as a prohibited interest? What additional facts would be helpful to resolve that question?

3. *No directors.* Similar to the facts in *Lynch*, the taxpayer in Rev. Rul. 59-119, 1959-1 C.B. 68, was completely redeemed in exchange for a series of installment payments. The taxpayer sought to include his representative as a member of the corporation's board of directors in order to oversee corporate compliance with the conditions of the buyout and thereby protect the taxpayer's interest as creditor. The IRS ruled that any such director, even one with limited duties and power, would violate the condition of section 302(c)(2)(A)(i). According to the IRS, the desired oversight could be achieved without violating that condition by having the taxpayer's representative attend the board meetings but not in the capacity of a director, officer, or employee.

4. *Section 302(b)(5).* The second sentence of section 302(b)(5) is a convoluted way of reminding taxpayers that the section 302(b) safe harbors are alternate ways of achieving exchange treatment of a redemption. I.R.C. § 302(a). Thus, if a redeemed shareholder satisfies a safe harbor in addition to section 302(b)(3), the shareholder may obtain exchange treatment without complying with a condition that is only applicable to the latter provision. For example, suppose that prior to a redemption, the taxpayer owns 40 percent of a corporation, the taxpayer's son owns 20 percent, and an unrelated party owns the remaining 40 percent. A redemption of the taxpayer's entire interest in the corporation would potentially qualify under section 302(b)(3) only if the taxpayer satisfies the conditions to waive the attribution from his son, including the prohibition against acquiring certain non-creditor interests in the corporation during the ten years following the distribution. Even if family attribution is not waived, however, the redemption qualifies under section 302(b)(2), which does not contain that condition. Thus, in order to obtain exchange treatment, the taxpayer need not satisfy the condition under section 302(b)(3).

5. *Ten-year lookback rules.* In addition to prohibiting the acquisition of certain interests during the ten years following the redemption, the waiver of family

attribution is also conditioned on certain transfers not having occurred during the ten years prior to the redemption. Read I.R.C. § 302(c)(2)(B). Is either of the lookback rules applicable to *Lynch*? Why or why not? What would have been the consequence of a violation of either rule? The following ruling provides some background about the lookback rules.

## Rev. Rul. 77-293

1977-2 C.B. 91

. . . Corporation X had 120 shares of common stock outstanding, all of which were owned by A, its president. A's son, B, had been employed by X for many years as its vice-president and general assistant to the president. Realizing that the future successful operation of X required a thorough knowledge of its operation, products lines, and customer needs, A had trained and supervised B in all phases of the business so that upon A's retirement B would be able to assume responsibility for managing the business.

As part of A's plan to retire from the business and to give ownership of the business to B, A gave 60 shares of X stock to B as a gift, and not as consideration for past, present, or future services. Shortly thereafter, A resigned and B assumed the position of chairman of the board and president of X. X redeemed the remaining 60 shares of stock owned by A in exchange for property. Immediately after the redemption, A was not an officer, director, or employee of X and no longer had any interest in X. A's gift of stock to B was for the purpose of giving B complete ownership and control of X. The earnings and profits of X exceeded the amount of the distribution in redemption of the X stock. . . .

Section 302(c)(2)(A) of the Code provides that for purposes of section 302(b)(3), 318(a)(1) will not apply if (i) immediately after the distribution the distributee has no interest in the corporation (including an interest as an officer, director, or employee), other than an interest as a creditor, (ii) the distributee does not acquire any such interest (other than stock acquired by bequest or inheritance) within ten years from the date of such distribution, and (iii) the distributee files an agreement to notify the district director of any acquisition of any such interest in the corporation. However, pursuant to section 302(c)(2)(B)(ii), the provisions of section 302(c)(2)(A) are not applicable if any person owns (at the time of the distribution) stock the ownership of which is attributable to the distributee under section 318(a) and such person acquired any stock in the corporation, directly or indirectly, from the distributee within the ten-year period ending on the date of the distribution, unless such stock so acquired from the distributee is redeemed in the same transaction. However, section 302(c)(2)(B)(ii) will not apply if the disposition by the distributee did not have as one of its principal purposes the avoidance of Federal income tax.

The structure and legislative history of section 302 of the Code make it clear that the purpose of section 302(c)(2)(B) is not to prevent the reduction of capital gains through gifts of appreciated stock prior to the redemption of the remaining stock of the transferor, but to prevent the withdrawal of earnings at capital gains rates by a shareholder of a family controlled corporation who seeks continued control and/or economic interest in the corporation through the stock given to a related person or the stock he retains. Application of this provision thus prevents a taxpayer from bailing out earnings by transferring part of the taxpayer's stock to such a related person and then qualifying the redemption of either the taxpayer's stock or the transferee's stock as a complete termination of interest by virtue of the division of ownership thus created and the availability of the attribution waiver provisions.

Tax avoidance within the meaning of section 302(c)(2)(B) of the Code would occur, for example, if a taxpayer transfers stock of a corporation to a spouse in contemplation of the redemption of the remaining stock of the corporation and terminates all direct interest in the corporation in compliance with section 302(c)(2)(A), but with the intention of retaining effective control of the corporation indirectly through the stock held by the spouse. Another example, which would generally constitute tax avoidance within the meaning of this provision, is the transfer by a taxpayer of part of the stock of a corporation to a spouse in contemplation of the subsequent redemption of the transferred stock from the spouse. . . .

Whether one of the principal purposes of an acquisition or disposition of stock is tax avoidance within the meaning of section 302(c)(2)(B) of the Code can be determined only by an analysis of all of the facts and circumstances of a particular situation. Here, the gift of X stock by A was to B who is active and knowledgeable in the affairs of the business of X and who intends to control and manage the corporation in the future. The gift of stock was intended solely for the purpose of enabling A to retire while leaving the business to B. Therefore, the avoidance of Federal income tax will not be deemed to have been one of the principal purposes of the gift of stock from A to B, notwithstanding the reduction of the capital gains tax payable by A as a result of the gift of appreciated stock prior to the redemption.

Accordingly, if A files the agreement specified in section 302(c)(2)(A)(iii) of the Code, the redemption by X of its stock from A qualifies as a termination of interest under section 302(b)(3). . . .

## *NOTE*

*The ambivalent statute.* This ruling illustrates the highly ambivalent nature of the statute in determining the tax consequences of a redemption. Initially, the statute provides that a redeemed shareholder is entitled to exchange treatment if the redemption terminates the shareholder's interest in the corporation. I.R.C. § 302(a), (b)(3). The statute then reverses course and disqualifies the shareholder from that safe harbor if the remaining shareholders are family members whose ownership of stock is attributed to the redeemed shareholder. I.R.C. §§ 302(c)(1), 318(a). Family attribution is permitted to be waived, however—

thereby potentially reviving the safe harbor and exchange treatment of the redeemed shareholder—provided such shareholder does not retain or acquire within the ten years following the redemption certain non-creditor interests in the corporation, and complies with certain procedural requirements. I.R.C. § 302(c)(2)(A). But the waiver option is blocked, and the safe harbor is again unavailable, if certain transfers of stock took place within the ten years *prior to* the redemption. I.R.C. § 302(c)(2)(B). Finally, the safe harbor is revived once again, and exchange treatment of the redemption is allowed, if one of the principal purposes of the transfers within the prior ten years was not the avoidance of federal income tax. I.R.C. § 302(c)(2)(B) (flush language).

It is perhaps little wonder that the fourth and fifth iterations of this layered structure of rules have essentially been read out of the Code. For example, in Rev. Rul. 77-293, the IRS indicates that the purpose of section 302(c)(2)(B) is "to prevent the withdrawal of earnings at capital gains rates by a shareholder of a family controlled corporation who seeks continued control and/or economic interest in the corporation through the stock given to a related person." Yet, that purpose is explicitly the function of section 302(c)(2)(A) without regard to a transfer of interest within the prior ten years. Thus, both the IRS and the courts have interpreted the "no tax avoidance purpose" condition liberally to negate the application of section 302(c)(2)(B) in many circumstances. The ruling leaves open the possibility that a tax avoidance purpose might be found (and therefore section 302(c)(2)(B) would remain operative) if the family successor to the redeemed shareholder were not active and knowledgeable in the affairs of the business prior to the redemption.

Review I.R.C. §§ 302(a), (b)(3), (c), (d), and 318 and Reg. § 1.302-4(c)-(g), and do the following problems. **Problem 6-6** requires you to consider the waiver of family attribution rules in the context of a redemption of an interest held by an entity, such as a partnership, trust, estate, or corporation. Under what circumstances might the *family* attribution rules be important for that type of redemption?

**Problem 6-4:** Dinky, Inc. was organized 40 years ago by Dad to engage in the manufacture and production of miniature toys. About 15 years ago, when Junior graduated from business school, Dad convinced Junior to join him in the business. At that time, Dad gave Junior 10 shares of the common stock of the corporation; Dad retained the remaining 90 shares. Dad plans to retire from the business and leave it all to Junior, who has established himself as a capable successor. Assuming that Dad's basis in his Dinky stock is $100,000, consider the tax consequences of each of the following alternatives. Explain any actions that should be taken to achieve the optimal tax result in a given situation.

(a) Dinky redeems all of Dad's stock for $900,000 cash.
(b) Dinky redeems 85 shares of Dad's stock for $850,000 cash.
(c) Same as (b), except that two years after the redemption, Dinky redeems the remaining five shares of Dad's stock for $50,000 cash.

Is this result fair? What else might you argue as a result of this redemption?

(d) Same as (a), except that a portion of the consideration paid by Dinky is in the form of a note, the interest rate of which is linked to the prime rate.
(e) Same as (d), except that the amount to be paid by Dinky varies, depending upon the future profitability of the corporation.
(f) Same as (a), except that after the redemption, Dad remains as director of a wholly-owned subsidiary of Dinky specializing in the manufacture of toy soldiers.
(g) Same as (a), except that two years after the redemption, Junior negotiates a merger of Dinky, Inc. into Mammoth, Inc., a national toy manufacturing company, and as part of the deal, Junior and Dad are both asked to serve as members of Mammoth's Board of Directors.

**Problem 6-5:** Father owns all of the stock of Techco, a corporation engaged in a high-tech line of business. Father has built the business from scratch, and it has been very successful. Son is engaged to be married in one year's time, when Son will graduate from law school and start his career as a civil rights lawyer. Father would like to make Son a large cash gift of $20,000 at that time, as Son's wedding present. Consider the tax consequences of each of Father's following alternative plans:

(a) Techco distributes $20,000 cash to Father out of its sizable cash surplus. Father will use the funds to make the cash gift to Son.
(b) Techco redeems two percent of Father's stock in exchange for $20,000 cash. Father will use the funds for his gift to Son.
(c) Father gives Son stock representing two percent of Techco. On the wedding day, Techco redeems Son's stock, paying him $20,000 cash.

**Problem 6-6:** Rudolph owns 50 percent of the stock of P Corporation. The other half is owned by the Estate of his deceased mother, Jill. Rudolph's father (and Jill's husband), Jack, is the sole beneficiary of Jill's Estate. P has substantial earnings and profits. Each 50 percent interest in P is worth $550,000. Rudolph's basis in his P stock is $10,000; the Estate's interest had a fair market value of $500,000 on the date of Jill's death. Determine the tax consequences of the following alternatives:

(a) P redeems all of the stock held by Jill's Estate.
(b) Same as (a), except that Rudolph's sister, Annie, is also a beneficiary of Jill's Estate.

(c) Same as (a), except that Jack and Rudolph are co-beneficiaries of Jill's Estate. What actions might the parties take in order to have the redemption taxed in a more favorable way?

(d) Same as (a), except that five years before the redemption, Jack gave Rudolph all of the stock in P Corporation that Rudolph now owns.

### d. Redemptions Not Essentially Equivalent to a Dividend

A redemption that is "not essentially equivalent to a dividend" also qualifies for exchange treatment. Read I.R.C. § 302(a) and (b)(1). Obviously, this label is not very helpful in distinguishing between redemptions that should or should not be treated as ordinary distributions. Read Reg. § 1.302-2 and the following materials to see how this phrase has been interpreted.

#### United States v. Davis

397 U.S. 301 (1970)

Mr. Justice MARSHALL delivered the opinion of the Court.

In 1945, taxpayer and E. B. Bradley organized a corporation. In exchange for property transferred to the new company, Bradley received 500 shares of common stock, and taxpayer and his wife similarly each received 250 such shares. Shortly thereafter, taxpayer made an additional contribution to the corporation, purchasing 1,000 shares of preferred stock at a par value of $25 per share.

The purpose of this latter transaction was to increase the company's working capital and thereby to qualify for a loan previously negotiated through the Reconstruction Finance Corporation. It was understood that the corporation would redeem the preferred stock when the RFC loan had been repaid. Although in the interim taxpayer bought Bradley's 500 shares and divided them between his son and daughter, the total capitalization of the company remained the same until 1963. That year, after the loan was fully repaid and in accordance with the original understanding, the company redeemed taxpayer's preferred stock.

In his 1963 personal income tax return taxpayer did not report the $25,000 received by him upon the redemption of his preferred stock as income. Rather, taxpayer considered the redemption as a sale of his preferred stock to the company—a capital gains transaction under § 302 of the Internal Revenue Code of 1954 resulting in no tax since taxpayer's basis in the stock equaled the amount he received for it. . . . According to the Commissioner [of Internal Revenue], the redemption of taxpayer's stock was essentially equivalent to a dividend and was thus taxable as ordinary income under §§ 301 and 316 of the Code. . . . The District Court ruled in [the taxpayer's] favor. . . . The Court of Appeals held that the $25,000 received by taxpayer was "not essentially equivalent to a dividend" within the meaning of that phrase in § 302(b)(1) of the Code because the redemption was the final step in a course of action that had a legitimate business (as opposed to a tax avoidance) purpose. . . . We reverse.

. . . [U]nder [§§ 301 and 316,] a distribution is includable in a taxpayer's gross income as a dividend out of earnings and profits to the extent such earnings exist.[4] . . . The basic question in this case is whether the . . . legitimate business motivation [for the $25,000 distribution] qualifies [it] under § 302(b)(1) of the Code. Preliminarily . . . we must consider the relationship between § 302(b)(1) and the rules regarding the attribution of stock ownership found in § 318(a) of the Code.

. . . [T]axpayer admits that paragraphs (2) and (3) [of section 302(b)] do not apply. . . . [T]axpayer agrees that for the purposes of §§ 302(b)(2) and (3) the attribution rules of § 318(a) apply and he is considered to own the 750 outstanding shares of common stock held by his wife and children in addition to the 250 shares in his own name.

Taxpayer, however, argues that the attribution rules do not apply in considering whether a distribution is essentially equivalent to a dividend under § 302(b)(1). According to taxpayer, he should thus be considered to own only 25 percent of the corporation's common stock, and the distribution would then qualify under § 302(b)(1) since it was not pro rata or proportionate to his stock interest, the fundamental test of dividend equivalency. *See* Treas. Reg. § 1.302-2(b). However, the plain language of the statute compels rejection of the argument. In subsection (c) of § 302, the attribution rules are made specifically applicable "in determining the ownership of stock for purposes of this section." Applying this language, both courts below held that § 318(a) applies to all of § 302, including § 302(b)(1). . . .

[I]t was necessary that the attribution rules apply to § 302(b)(1) unless they were to be effectively eliminated from consideration with regard to §§ 302(b)(2) and (3) also. For if a transaction failed to qualify under one of those sections solely because of the attribution rules, it would according to taxpayer's argument nonetheless qualify under § 302(b)(1). We cannot agree that Congress intended so to nullify its explicit directive. We conclude, therefore, that the attribution rules of § 318(a) do apply; and, for the purposes of deciding whether a distribution is "not essentially equivalent to a dividend" under § 302(b)(1), taxpayer must be deemed the owner of all 1,000 shares of the company's common stock.

. . . After application of the stock ownership attribution rules, this case viewed most simply involves a sole stockholder who causes part of his shares to be redeemed by the corporation. We conclude that such a redemption is always "essentially equivalent to a dividend" within the meaning of that phrase in § 302(b)(1)[5]. . . .

---

4. . . . Taxpayer makes no contention that the corporation did not have $25,000 in accumulated earnings and profits.

5. Of course, this just means that a distribution in redemption to a sole shareholder will be treated under the general provisions of § 301, and it will only be taxed as a dividend under § 316 to the extent that there are earnings and profits.

The predecessor of § 302(b)(1) came into the tax law as § 201(d) of the Revenue Act of 1921, 42 Stat. 228:

> "A stock dividend shall not be subject to tax but if after the distribution of any such dividend the corporation proceeds to cancel or redeem its stock at such time and in such manner as to make the distribution and cancellation or redemption essentially equivalent to the distribution of a taxable dividend, the amount received in redemption or cancellation of the stock shall be treated as a taxable dividend. . . ."

Enacted in response to this Court's decision that pro rata stock dividends do not constitute taxable income, Eisner v. Macomber, 252 U.S. 189 (1920), the provision had the obvious purpose of preventing a corporation from avoiding dividend tax treatment by distributing earnings to its shareholders in two transactions — a pro rata stock dividend followed by a pro rata redemption — that would have the same economic consequences as a simple dividend. Congress, however, soon recognized that even without a prior stock dividend essentially the same result could be effected whereby any corporation, "especially one which has only a few stockholders, might be able to make a distribution to its stockholders which would have the same effect as a taxable dividend." H.R.REP. NO. 1, 69TH CONG., 1ST SESS. 5. In order to cover this situation, the law was amended to apply "(whether or not such stock was issued as a stock dividend)" whenever a distribution in redemption of stock was made "at such time and in such manner" that it was essentially equivalent to a taxable dividend. Revenue Act of 1926, § 201(g), 44 Stat. 11.

This provision of the 1926 Act was carried forward in each subsequent revenue act and finally became § 115(g)(1) of the Internal Revenue Code of 1939. Unfortunately, however, the policies encompassed within the general language of § 115(g)(1) and its predecessors were not clear, and there resulted much confusion in the tax law. At first, courts assumed that the provision was aimed at tax avoidance schemes and sought only to determine whether such a scheme existed. . . . Although later the emphasis changed and the focus was more on the effect of the distribution, many courts continued to find that distributions otherwise like a dividend were not "essentially equivalent" if, for example, they were motivated by a sufficiently strong nontax business purpose. . . . There was general disagreement, however, about what would qualify as such a purpose, and the result was a case-by-case determination with each case decided "on the basis of the particular facts of the transaction in question." . . .

By the time of the general revision resulting in the Internal Revenue Code of 1954, the draftsmen were faced with what has aptly been described as "the morass created by the decisions." . . . In an effort to eliminate "the considerable confusion which exists in this area" and thereby to facilitate tax planning, H. R. REP. NO. 1337, 83D CONG., 2D SESS. 35 (1954) the authors of the new Code sought to provide objective tests to govern the tax consequences of stock redemptions. Thus, the tax bill passed by the House of Representatives contained no "essentially equivalent" language. Rather, it provided for "safe harbors" where capital gains treatment would be accorded to corporate redemptions that met the conditions now found in §§ 302(b)(2) and (3) of the Code.

It was in the Senate Finance Committee's consideration of the tax bill that § 302(b)(1) was added, and Congress thereby provided that capital gains treatment should be available "if the redemption is not essentially equivalent to a dividend." Taxpayer argues that the purpose was to continue "existing law," and there is support in the legislative history that § 302(b)(1) reverted "in part" or "in general" to the "essentially equivalent" provision of § 115(g)(1) of the 1939 Code. According to the Government, even under the old law it would have been improper for the Court of Appeals to rely on "a business purpose for the redemption" and "an absence of the proscribed tax avoidance purpose to bail out dividends at favorable tax rates." . . . However, we need not decide that question, for we find from the history of the 1954 revisions and the purpose of § 302(b)(1) that Congress intended more than merely to re-enact the prior law.

In explaining the reason for adding the "essentially equivalent" test, the Senate Committee stated that the House provisions "appeared unnecessarily restrictive, particularly, in the case of redemptions of preferred stock which might be called by the corporation without the shareholder having any control over when the redemption may take place." S. REP. NO. 1622, 83D CONG., 2D SESS. 44 (1954). This explanation gives no indication that the purpose behind the redemption should affect the result. Rather, in its more detailed technical evaluation of § 302(b)(1), the Senate Committee reported as follows:

> "The test intended to be incorporated in the interpretation of paragraph (1) is in general that currently employed under section 115(g)(1) of the 1939 Code. Your committee further intends that in applying this test for the future . . . the inquiry will be devoted solely to the question of whether or not the transaction by its nature may properly be characterized as a sale of stock by the redeeming shareholder to the corporation. For this purpose the presence or absence of earnings and profits of the corporation is not material. Example: X, the sole shareholder of a corporation having no earnings or profits causes the corporation to redeem half of its stock. Paragraph (1) does not apply to such redemption notwithstanding the absence of earnings and profits." S. REP. NO. 1622, *supra*, at 234.

The intended scope of § 302(b)(1) as revealed by this legislative history is certainly not free from doubt. However, we agree with the Government that by making the sole inquiry relevant for the future the narrow one whether the redemption could be characterized as a sale, Congress was apparently rejecting past court decisions that had also considered factors indicating the presence or absence of a tax-avoidance motive. At least that is the implication of the example given. Congress clearly mandated that pro rata distributions be treated under the general rules laid down in §§ 301 and 316 rather than under § 302 and nothing suggests that there should be a different result if there were a "business purpose" for the redemption. Indeed, just the opposite inference must be drawn since there would not likely be a tax-avoidance purpose in a situation where there were no earnings or profits. We conclude that the Court of Appeals was therefore wrong in looking for a business purpose and considering it in deciding whether the redemption was equivalent to a dividend. Rather, we agree with the Court of Appeals for the Second Circuit that "the business purpose of a transaction is irrelevant in determining dividend equivalence" under § 302(b)(1). . . .

Taxpayer strongly argues that to treat the redemption involved here as essentially equivalent to a dividend is to elevate form over substance. Thus, taxpayer argues, had he not bought Bradley's shares or had he made a subordinated loan to the company instead of buying preferred stock, he could have gotten back his $25,000 with favorable tax treatment. However, the difference between form and substance in the tax law is largely problematical, and taxpayer's complaints have little to do with whether a business purpose is relevant under § 302(b)(1). It was clearly proper for Congress to treat distributions generally as taxable dividends when made out of earnings and profits and then to prevent avoidance of that result without regard to motivation where the distribution is in exchange for redeemed stock.

We conclude that that is what Congress did when enacting § 302(b)(1). If a corporation distributes property as a simple dividend, the effect is to transfer the property from the company to its shareholders without a change in the relative economic interests or rights of the stockholders. Where a redemption has that same effect, it cannot be said to have satisfied the "not essentially equivalent to a dividend" requirement of § 302(b)(1). Rather, to qualify for preferred treatment under that section, a redemption must result in a meaningful reduction of the shareholder's proportionate interest in the corporation. Clearly, taxpayer here, who (after application of the attribution rules) was the sole shareholder of the corporation both before and after the redemption, did not qualify under this test. . . .

Mr. Justice DOUGLAS, with whom THE CHIEF JUSTICE and Mr. Justice BRENNAN concur, dissenting.

I agree with the District Court . . . and with the Court of Appeals . . . that respondent's contribution of working capital in the amount of $25,000 in exchange for 1,000 shares of preferred stock with a par value of $25 was made in order for the corporation to obtain a loan from the RFC and that the preferred stock was to be redeemed when the loan was repaid. For the reasons stated by the two lower courts, this redemption was not "essentially equivalent to a dividend," for the bona fide business purpose of the redemption belies the payment of a dividend. As stated by the Court of Appeals:

> "Although closely-held corporations call for close scrutiny under the tax law, we will not under the facts and circumstances of this case, allow mechanical attribution rules to transform a legitimate corporate transaction into a tax avoidance scheme." . . .

When the Court holds it was a dividend, it effectively cancels § 302(b)(1) from the Code. This result is not a matter of conjecture, for the Court says that in the case of closely held or one-man corporations a redemption of stock is "always" equivalent to a dividend. I would leave such revision to the Congress.

## *NOTES AND QUESTIONS*

1. *Understanding Congress's intent.* Proposed regulations issued in 2009 clarify the tax consequences of a redemption that is taxed under section 301 but is not a dividend (because the distributing corporation has no or insufficient E&P). In that situation, the redeemed shareholder is allowed to offset against the amount of the distribution the shareholder's basis in any stock belonging to the same class as the shares redeemed. I.R.C. § 301(c)(2); Prop. Reg. § 1.302-5(a)(1). Thus, suppose a taxpayer owns all 1,000 shares of corporation X with a basis of $1/share. X, which has no E&P, redeems 500 of the shares for $1,000. Assuming that the redemption is taxed under section 301 and all 1,000 shares are of the same class, the taxpayer would be entitled to offset the $1,000 distribution with the taxpayer's entire $1,000 basis in all of the shares held, not merely the $500 basis in the shares actually redeemed. Taxpayer would therefore report no gain or loss from the transaction.

If this rule were the law in 1954 when the Senate committee report was prepared, how would it have affected the meaning of the example in the report that is so critical to the Court's analysis? Under this assumption, did the Court interpret the example correctly?

2. *Loan?* The Court does not really respond to the taxpayer's final argument—namely, that if he had made a subordinated loan to his company (rather than purchasing preferred stock) and then was repaid the loan, he would not have had any tax consequences. How would you respond?

## Patterson Trust v. United States

729 F.2d 1089 (6th Cir. 1984)

KRUPANSKY, Circuit Judge.

. . . Prior to 1969, Henry Patterson, Sr. was the sole shareholder and chief executive officer of Puritan. In 1969, he gave forty shares of Puritan stock to each of his children—John, Hank and Ellen. At the time, Ellen was married to Bill Hicks (Hicks), who, along with Hank, was employed by Puritan. Henry Patterson retained 200 shares of Puritan stock.

Bill Hicks was apparently a skilled business manager, while Hank Patterson (Hank) lacked effectiveness. Through the years, a bitter tension between Hicks and Hank developed, resulting in numerous altercations, one of which ended with Hank's hospitalization. At one point, John Patterson (John) participated in the management of the business but, because of the Hank-Hicks rivalry, John resigned and pursued a teaching career.

At trial, there was testimony that Henry Patterson desired that Hicks operate the company after Patterson's retirement. . . . He designated Hicks to act as Puritan's president and general manager in his absence. Patterson . . . died in November 1971.

In June 1971, Hicks presented the Puritan directors with a demand for an increase in salary and a proposal that they place all of the Puritan shares in a voting trust which Hicks would then control. The directors demurred and Hicks resigned. He immediately staged a slowdown of Puritan employees and persuaded the company's most substantial commercial accounts to demand that Puritan rehire him. Within ten days of Hicks' resignation, Puritan was on the verge of collapse. John, who had since returned to the business, contacted Hicks and negotiated a five-year employment contract with him.

Hicks' contract provided an increased salary, a profit sharing arrangement, and a five-year option to acquire eighty shares of Puritan stock. Hicks acquired five of those shares and his option on the remaining seventy-five shares remained open. At the same time, Hank also received a five-year contract.

During the ensuing five years, Puritan performed well but problems between Hank and Hicks became increasingly aggravated; Hank, John, and Ella Patterson, their mother, often were at odds with Hicks and his wife, Ellen.

In the spring of 1976, the Patterson estate was closed. Henry Patterson had placed his 200 shares of Puritan stock in the Henry T. Patterson Trust (Trust) with his widow, Ella, as the beneficiary with the power to appoint the corpus at her death. Following the closing of the estate, the Puritan stock was thus distributed:

| | |
|---|---|
| Henry T. Patterson Trust | 200 shares |
| Ella Patterson | 25 shares |
| Hank Patterson | 40 shares |
| John Patterson | 40 shares |
| Ellen (Patterson) Hicks | 40 shares |
| Bill Hicks | 5 shares |
| Lester Winkler | 6 shares |

Hicks devised a two-step plan whereby he and his wife could obtain control of Puritan. First, Puritan would redeem the Trust shares and, following the redemption, Hicks would exercise his option and acquire an additional seventy-five shares. As a result, Hicks and his spouse would own 120 shares and the remaining shareholders would control only 111 shares, thus Hicks would acquire a controlling interest in Puritan.

The Reeves Bank, as Trustee, determined that if it refused to redeem the shares, Hicks would leave the company and eventually the Trust corpus would be worthless. Thus, acting in what it perceived as the best interests of the Trust and the beneficiary, the Reeves Bank determined to accept the proposed redemption.

On April 2, 1976, the directors were presented with the proposal. The Trustee reported that it would be in Ella's best interest to redeem the shares and invest the proceeds. . . . Following the redemption, on July 7, 1976 Hicks exercised his option and purchased seventy-five shares of Puritan stock from the company. . . .

The Trust reported the transaction as a capital gains sale. Upon review, the Commissioner determined that the amount received by the Trust in the redemption, $190,000.00, was a dividend taxable as ordinary income under § 301. . . . The district court rejected the Trust's argument that the transaction amounted to a termination of its interest in Puritan, but accepted the Trust's alternative argument that the transaction was not essentially equivalent to a dividend and was therefore entitled to capital gains treatment. . . .

As explicated by the Supreme Court [in *Davis*], § 302(b)(1) provides that corporate distributions which do not alter the shareholder's "relative economic interests or rights" will be taxed as a dividend, regardless of the form or nomenclature given the transactions. The test is to examine the change in the taxpayer's relationship to the corporation; § 302(b)(1) is satisfied, under this test, if the examination establishes a "meaningful reduction" of the taxpayer's relative interests or rights in the company. . . . [T]he starting point must be a comparison of the Trust's relative holdings prior to and after the redemption. As in *U.S. v. Davis, supra*, this comparison requires application of the attribution statutes.

Briefly stated, the 1954 Code provided that a trust constructively owned its shares plus the shares held by the beneficiary, including those shares which § 318 attributed to the beneficiary. §§ 302(c), 318.

Applying this statute, it is readily apparent that prior to the redemption, the Trust constructively owned 345 shares of the Puritan company, computed from its own shares (200), Ella's holdings (25), and the shares owned by Ella's children (John-40, Hank-40, Ellen Hicks-40). Following the redemption, the Trust's constructive holdings were reduced to 145 shares (25 owned by Ella, 120 held by her children). Only 11 other shares remained actually outstanding (Hicks-5, Winkler-6); therefore, the Trust held 345/356 shares, or 97%, before and 145/156 shares, or 93%, immediately after the redemption.

When the district court made this comparison it included the seventy-five option shares held by Hicks. Accordingly, the district court determined that the Trust held 80% of the company before redemption (345/431), and 62.8% after redemption (145/231). Because the Trust no longer controlled the company after the redemption (holding less than two-thirds of the stock), the district court concluded that the "meaningful reduction" test had been satisfied. The district court included the Hicks option in its calculations pursuant to the plain language of the attribution statute, § 318(a)(4), which stated [emphasis added]:

> If *any* person has an option to acquire stock, such stock shall be considered as owned by such person.

On appeal, the Government urges that § 318(a)(4) actually applies only to the taxpayer or to individuals whose shares are otherwise attributable to the taxpayer. The Government would therefore greatly narrow the scope of § 318(a)(4). Under the Government's view of the statute, the Trust's ownership interest in Puritan was reduced only 4% as a result of the redemption, from 97 to 93%, which, it contends, was not meaningful as a matter of law.

... [T]he Government invites this court to examine the legislative history of § 318(a)(4) and conclude that "any person" actually means only those "parties in the line of attribution".... The Government relies on the commentary in the "Detailed Discussion of Bill" portion of the Senate Report relative to § 318(a)(3) [currently effective as § 318(a)(4)]. The commentary describes the operation of the relevant portions of the attributive statute in the following manner:

> **§ 318. Constructive Ownership of Stock**
>
> This section describes the area in which although in fact transactions related to stock ownership are in connection with a specific individual, ownership of stock is deemed to be in the hands of persons other than the person directly involved. Thus, for the purpose of determining whether a redemption of stock qualifies as a disproportionate redemption ... consideration is given not only to the stock held by such person but also to stock owned by members of his family....
>
> The area of constructive ownership includes members of the family, persons having interests in ... trusts, ... such ... trusts, ... and stock held under an option.
>
> In the family area (sec. 318(a)(1)) an individual is deemed to own stock owned by his parents, his children, and his grandchildren.... In the case of trusts, ... the beneficiary or grantor is deemed to own his proportionate interest in the stock owned by the trust or estate and the trust or estate is deemed to own all of the stock owned by its beneficiaries or grantors.
>
> In any of the cases *above described* where stock, though not owned, is subject to an option, the holder of such option is deemed to own such stock (sec. 318(a)(3)). S. REP. NO. 1622, 83D CONG., 2D SESS. 45 (1954) [emphasis added].

The Government urges that as a result of the commentary's apparent limitation of the option attribution rule to "the cases above described," "the Senate indicated its intent that § 318(a)(3) (now § 318(a)(4)) should be limited to parties in the line of attribution." The Internal Revenue Service has consistently followed the reasoning herein argued by the Government, *see, e.g.*, Rev. Rul. 68-601, and the tax court has adopted the Service's view as well.... However, only two appeals courts have addressed the issue and they, without analysis, adopted diverse positions.

In Friend v. U.S., 345 F.2d 761 (1st Cir. 1965), the First Circuit's *dictum* indicated that that court believed that "Congress intended that section to apply only where options are held by the person whose shares are being redeemed." ... In Sorem v. C.I.R., 334 F.2d 275, 280 (10th Cir. 1964), the court, again without analysis, applied the plain language of the options attribution provision of § 318(a), and rejected the Government's view.

The Government argues that this court should defer to the Service's consistently-applied interpretation of the Code. However, while it is axiomatic that where statutory language remains vague even when illuminated by the legislative history, the construction offered by the agency charged with the enforcement of the statute will often be accorded dispositive weight, it is an equal principle that the agency may not so interpret the statute as to controvert its plain and unambiguous language. Except in "rare and exceptional circumstances," . . . such as where Congress "expressly indicates" its intent that the plain meaning of the statutory language be avoided, . . . unambiguous statutory language "is to be regarded as conclusive." . . .

Instantly, the Government asserts only the commentary of the Senate Report, reprinted above, as support for its construction of "any person" in § 318(a)(4). The commentary falls short of a clear indication by Congress that the natural impact of the statutory language under review should be restrained. Accordingly, the district court appropriately included the option shares held by Hicks in determining the Trust's relative holdings prior to and following redemption.

It should be noted that, even if the Hicks shares were excluded, on the instant record the district court would have been entitled to enter the factual finding that the transaction under review was not essentially equivalent to a dividend and was therefore properly claimed as a capital gain. "The question whether a distribution in redemption of stock . . . is not essentially equivalent to a dividend . . . depends upon the facts and circumstances of each case." § 1.302-3(b); *U.S. v. Davis, supra.* Obviously, one of the pertinent facts would be the relative holdings of the taxpayer as computed under § 318's constructive stock ownership provisions, § 1.302(b), *U.S. v. Davis*; however, neither statutory enactment nor judicial construction would support the proposition that the resulting comparative calculation would become the exclusive and dispositive fact. In this case, the redemption effected "a change in the relative economic interests or rights" of all the stockholders of the Puritan company. Therefore, despite the fact that—excluding operation of § 318(a)(4)—the Trust's relative holdings fell only 4% after redemption, under the unique facts and circumstances of this case, such was a "meaningful reduction" and the distribution was therefore not a dividend. . . .

## *NOTES AND QUESTIONS*

1. *Waiver of family attribution.* Since all of the Trust's shares were redeemed, could the Trust have obtained exchange treatment under section 302(a) and (b)(3) by satisfying the conditions necessary to waive family attribution?

2. *Planning with options.* The court dismissed the government's interpretation of section 318(a)(4) as not supported by a plain reading of the statute. The government was concerned that option shares, if attributed to a person out of the line of attribution of the distributee, could be used opportunistically by distributees to satisfy one of the section 302(b) safe harbors. But the government's proposed rule was too narrow because if option shares are attributed to a person *in* the distributee's line of attribution, they may be used opportunistically by distributees to *avoid* section 302(b) when they represent "stormy" harbors. The *Heinz* case (infra

p. 238) and Notice 2001-45 (infra p. 236) illustrate these possibilities. Thus, to avoid a potentially abusive use of the option rule, it might be necessary to rewrite section 318(a)(4) completely so that option shares are attributed only when the terms of the option make exercise likely. It would be difficult (and complicated) to devise a rule that could not be gamed.

3. *Meaningful reduction?* Both courts concluded that, after the option shares held by Hicks were taken into account in determining the effect of the redemption on the Trust's ownership interest, the resulting reduction in the Trust's interest from 80 to 62.8 percent constituted a meaningful reduction. Moreover, at the end of its opinion, the Sixth Circuit even suggested that a reduction in the Trust's interest from 97 to 93 percent would also have qualified as a meaningful reduction. What aspects of the transaction might tend to undermine each conclusion?

4. *Family discord.* Was it proper to attribute Ellen's shares through Ella to the Trust? The family attribution rules are based on a paradigm that family members are in harmony with one another and have common economic interests. But suppose this assumption is not true and there is hostility between the relevant family members. Does *Davis* leave open the possibility of avoiding family attribution if sufficient family discord can be demonstrated? Compare Robin Haft Trust v. Comm'r, 510 F.2d 43, 48 (1st Cir. 1975) (yes) with David Metzger Trust v. Comm'r, 693 F.2d 459, 465-68 (5th Cir. 1982) (no).

5. *Redemptions by public corporations.* The following two rulings involve redemptions by public corporations. What special problems do such redemptions present?

## Rev. Rul. 76-385

1976-2 C.B. 92

Corporation X, a family corporation, owned all of the stock of corporation Y. X and Y both owned a small number of shares of stock of corporation Z. Z's stock is listed on the New York Stock Exchange. It has outstanding one class of stock consisting of 28 million shares of common stock.

Pursuant to a settlement of Federal antitrust litigation, Z agreed to divest itself of certain property owned by it. In accordance with this agreement, Z offered to distribute the property to its shareholders in redemption of shares of their Z stock. The offer was accepted by a portion of the Z shareholders, including Y. However, X did not accept the offer. In redemption of Y's stock in Z, Z distributed to Y a portion of the property required to be divested with a fair market value equal to the fair market value of the Z stock surrendered by Y. Although the redemption terminated Y's actual ownership of stock of Z, Y still is considered as owning the Z stock owned by X after the redemption through the application of the constructive ownership of stock rules of section 318(a)(3)(C) of the Code, which section 302(c) makes applicable to section 302. Thus, when the stock constructively owned by Y is considered, calculations indicate that the redemption reduced Y's percentage of ownership of the stock of Z from .0001118 percent to .0001081 percent. Based on this reduction, the percentage of stock of Z owned by Y after the redemption was 96.7 percent of the percentage of stock owned by Y before the redemption. . . .

In U.S. v. Davis, 397 U.S. 301 (1970), the Supreme Court of the United States held that a redemption must result in a meaningful reduction of the shareholder's proportionate interest in the corporation in order to qualify as not essentially equivalent to a dividend within the meaning of section 302(b)(1) of the Code and that the business purpose of the redemption is irrelevant to this determination. The Supreme Court further held that section 318(a) applies for the purpose of determining whether a distribution is "not essentially equivalent to a dividend" under section 302(b)(1).

One purpose for the enactment of section 302(b)(1) of the Code was to provide capital gain treatment for redemptions of stock held by certain minority shareholders, especially minority holders of preferred stock who exercise no control over corporate affairs. *See* S. Rep. No. 1622, 83rd Cong., 2d Sess. 44-45 (1954).

The redemption in the instant case falls within the category of redemptions Congress intended to exclude from dividend treatment through the enactment of section 302(b)(1) of the Code since the redemption involves a minority shareholder whose relative stock interest in Z is minimal and who exercises no control over the affairs of Z. In addition, as a result of the redemption, Y experienced a reduction of its voting rights, its right to participate in current earnings and accumulated surplus, and its right to share in net assets on liquidation. Thus, under the facts and circumstances of the instant case, the redemption qualifies under section 302(b)(1).

Accordingly, the redemption was not essentially equivalent to a dividend within the meaning of section 302(b)(1) of the Code and, therefore, qualified as an exchange under section 302(a). *See also* Rev. Rul. 75-512, 1975-2 C.B. 112, in which a redemption of a minority shareholder's interest in a closely held corporation resulting in a 19 percent reduction in its interest was not essentially equivalent to a dividend.

## Rev. Rul. 81-289

1981-2 C.B. 82

X corporation has outstanding 1,000,000x shares of voting common stock which are widely held and publicly traded. X has approximately 1,000x shareholders, none of whom owns a significant amount of the X common stock. In an isolated transaction and not as part of a periodic redemption plan, X offered to purchase from its shareholders 25,000x shares of its common stock at the rate of $20x per share. Approximately 10 percent of X's shareholders tendered stock for redemption. X redeemed a total of 20,000x shares of its stock pursuant to the tender offer. Individual A, who owned 2,000x shares of X stock at the time of the tender offer, surrendered 40x shares for redemption. Accordingly, A's proportionate interest in X was .2 percent (2,000x shares divided by 1,000,000x shares) before the tender offer and remained .2 percent (1,960x shares divided by 980,000x shares) after the tender offer. A was not related to any other shareholder of X within the meaning of section 318.

. . . The existence and size of a reduction in proportionate interest that results from a redemption is important because the relationships of the shareholders and the continued exercise of control and participation in the earnings and assets by those shareholders whose stock is redeemed may render essentially meaningless any differences between the redemption and an ordinary dividend distribution. For example, after applying the constructive ownership of stock rules of section 318 of the Code in *Davis*, the taxpayer owned all of the redeeming corporation's stock both before and after the redemption with the result that the distribution was precisely pro rata and, thus, essentially equivalent to a dividend.

. . . In the present situation the redemption did not result in any reduction of A's right to vote, to participate in current earnings and accumulated surplus, or to share in the corporation's net assets on liquidation. Thus, this redemption with regard to A does not satisfy the meaningful reduction standard and does not qualify as an exchange within the meaning of section 302(a) and (b)(1) of the Code.

## *NOTES AND QUESTIONS*

1. *Proper reading of legislative history?* In Rev. Rul. 76-385, the IRS based its conclusion in part on its understanding of the purpose of section 302(b)(1):

> One purpose for the enactment of section 302(b)(1) of the Code was to provide capital gain treatment for redemptions of stock held by certain minority shareholders, especially minority holders of preferred stock who exercise no control over corporate affairs. *See* S. Rep. No. 1622, 83rd Cong., 2d Sess. 44-45 (1954).

The cited portion of the Senate report is as follows:

> While the House bill set forth definite conditions under which stock may be redeemed at capital-gain rates, these rules appeared unnecessarily restrictive, particularly, in the case of redemptions of preferred stock which might be called by the corporation without the shareholder having any control over when the redemption may take place. Accordingly, your committee follows existing law by reinserting the general language indicating that a redemption shall be treated as a distribution in part or full payment in exchange for stock if the redemption is not essentially equivalent to a dividend.

Did the IRS interpret the Senate report correctly?

2. *What is going on in Rev. Rul. 76-385?* Why does the IRS conclude in Rev. Rul. 76-385 that such a minute change in interest constitutes a "meaningful

reduction"? On the other hand, why didn't corporation X agree to have its Z shares redeemed?

3. *Practical problems.* In Rev. Rul. 81-289, corporation X offered to buy back 2.5 percent of its shares (25,000x/1,000,000x) but ended up redeeming only two percent (20,000x/1,000,000x), the same portion that A tendered to the corporation (40x/2,000x). Suppose that X had ended up redeeming only 1.5 percent of its shares (15,000x/1,000,000x). Would this fact have changed the tax consequences of the redemption to A? To the corporation? What practical problems do redemptions by public corporations present?

### e. Partial Liquidations

Certain redemptions constituting a partial liquidation of the distributing corporation also entitle the distributee to exchange treatment. Read I.R.C. § 302(a), (b)(4) and (e). Unlike the rest of section 302(b), application of this provision does not depend upon the extent to which the redemption reduces the distributee's interest in the corporation. Indeed, section 302(b)(4) may be available even though the distributee's interest is not reduced at all. Do you see what portion of the statute supports that conclusion? For the same reason, it is possible to qualify for section 302(b)(4) even though there is no actual redemption, *i.e.*, the shareholders do not surrender any shares in the distribution. Would it be possible to satisfy any of the other safe harbors in the absence of some shareholder surrendering some shares in the distributing corporation?

What constitutes a "partial liquidation"? In general, the statute defines it as a distribution that is not essentially equivalent to a dividend (determined at the corporate rather than shareholder level) and that occurs pursuant to a plan within a certain timeframe of adoption of the plan. The following ruling provides a little more insight.

**Rev. Rul. 60-322**

1960-2 C.B. 118

. . . M corporation has 3,800 shares of common stock, par value of 10x dollars per share, of which 200 shares are held in the treasury. The balance sheet indicates accumulated earnings of 1,500x dollars.

The corporation was engaged in the business of buying raw skins and tanning and selling the leather to a certain segment of the leather trade. It showed consistent profits until two years ago when the demand therefor suffered a serious, if not a permanent, decline. In an effort to revitalize the business, the corporation changed over to buying raw skins of another kind and tanning and selling the leather to another segment of the leather trade. However, the situation did not improve with the result that continuing losses were incurred and a large inventory of 5,000x dollars was accumulated.

Early in the year under consideration, M corporation determined that further purchases should be curtailed and inventories liquidated. Pursuant to this policy, the inventory was reduced to 3,000x dollars. In doing so, the corporation had sustained substantial operating losses. However, in view of the depressed state of the market and the grim future prospects, the process of liquidating its inventory is expected to be continued and the operations will be carried on at a modified basis with purchases kept at a minimum. In this manner, it is felt that the operating losses can be minimized and if the business decline continues, then a complete liquidation will eventually be voted by the stockholders. Accordingly, the M corporation proposes to redeem a portion of its stock with cash from the sale of United States Series G bonds and from the proceeds of the inventories being liquidated in the ordinary course of business. . . .

Where a corporation has earnings available, in order for the distribution of assets by it to its shareholders to be treated as a partial liquidation, the distribution must result from a genuine contraction of the business of the corporation. *See* Joseph W. Imler v. Comm'r, 11 T.C. 836, *acq.*, 1949-1 C.B. 2. . . . In the instant case, the earnings and profits of prior years were retained in the corporation and resulted in building up a large inventory and investment of funds in Government bonds.

Under the foregoing set of facts, it is held that neither the sale of investments nor the sale of a large part of the inventory in the ordinary course of business constitutes a genuine contraction of the business of the corporation. Accordingly, the proposed distribution of cash for the portion of the stock of M corporation to be redeemed will not constitute a distribution in partial liquidation. . . . The provisions of section 301 will apply to this distribution and, accordingly, the distribution will be taxed as a dividend to the extent provided in section 316.

## *NOTES AND QUESTIONS*

1. *Genuine contraction of the business.* The *Imler* case, cited with approval by the ruling as an example of a qualifying partial liquidation, involved a corporation that discontinued certain unprofitable lines of business and reduced its operations due to a fire. The distribution of the discontinued assets (or proceeds from their sale) plus the portion of the corporation's working capital attributable to the discontinued business, was pursuant to a genuine contraction of the business and, therefore, not essentially equivalent to a dividend distribution. In contrast, as Rev. Rul. 60-322 illustrates, a mere sale and distribution of excess assets of a corporate business does not qualify as a genuine contraction. For advance ruling purposes, the IRS ordinarily requires a distribution to result in at least a 20 percent reduction in gross revenues, net fair market value of assets, and employees before it will rule on the existence of a partial liquidation. See Rev. Proc. 2008-3, 2008-1 C.B. 110. As a practical matter, because of the ambiguous nature of the genuine corporate

contraction standard, most qualifying partial liquidations satisfy the somewhat brighter-line safe harbor set forth in section 302(e)(2) and (3). Under that rule, a distribution qualifies as a partial liquidation if it terminates one of at least two qualified trades or businesses of the corporation, meaning generally a trade or business actively conducted for at least five years. The statute prevents an indirect distribution of excess assets from qualifying under section 302(b)(4) by imposing the five-year requirement and also disregarding trades or businesses acquired in a taxable transaction during the five years. I.R.C. § 302(e)(3). The concept of a qualified trade or business arises again in connection with the taxation of divisive reorganizations, a topic addressed in chapter twelve.

2. *Corporate distributees.* The partial liquidation rule does not apply to corporate distributees. See I.R.C. § 302(b)(4)(A). Does this condition disadvantage corporations? How is a corporation taxed if it receives a distribution that qualifies as a partial liquidation? Read I.R.C. § 1059(e)(1)(A)(i).

3. *Policy.* Why do distributions in partial liquidation of the distributing corporation entitle the distributee to exchange treatment? At this point in the course, that question cannot be easily answered. The reason, however, should become clearer once we examine in chapter ten the tax treatment of shareholders in a *complete* liquidation of the distributing corporation.

#### f. Section 303

Read I.R.C. § 303(a). When an owner of a closely held corporation dies, a common problem for the estate is the need to finance funeral and administration expenses and any estate and inheritance taxes that may be due. Because of the attribution rules, even a complete redemption of the estate's stock in the corporation may be taxed as an ordinary distribution if the beneficiaries of the estate are the continuing owners of the corporation. Section 303(a) is a relief provision that allows the estate under certain circumstances to obtain exchange treatment for a redemption distribution not exceeding the amount of certain taxes imposed on the estate and its funeral and administration expenses. Because the estate generally obtains a stepped-up basis in the corporation's stock under section 1014(a), this provision can potentially result in significant tax savings.

### 2. *Corporate-Level Consequences*

Review I.R.C. § 311(a) and (b)(1). As described in chapter five, a corporation generally recognizes gain upon an ordinary distribution of appreciated property. The same rule applies in the case of a redemption distribution even if the shareholder obtains exchange treatment of the distribution under section 302(a), since the distribution will still be one "to which subpart A applies," i.e., sections 301-307. If a corporation redeems its stock by distributing its note to the redeemed shareholder (the facts in *Lynch*, p. 194), there could be an issue regarding whether the corporation recognizes gain, since the note would constitute "property" (within the meaning of section 317(a)) and the corporation would ordinarily have a zero basis in its own note. The parenthetical in section 311(b)(1)(A), however, makes clear that the corporation does not recognize gain on distribution of its own note. If a corporation distributes its own stock (or rights to acquire such stock) to its shareholder in exchange for other stock of the corporation held by the shareholder, the transaction is not treated as a redemption. I.R.C. § 317(a) and (b). Instead, the stock-for-stock exchange would likely be a nonrecognition transaction under section 1036(a) or as an "E" reorganization (recapitalization) (see chapter eleven).

Read I.R.C. § 312(a) and (n)(7). What impact does a redemption have on corporate E&P? Does the effect on E&P suggest that a "sale or exchange of stock" or an "ordinary distribution" is the better analogy for such a transaction?

**Problem 6-7:** Q Corporation has two equal unrelated shareholders, A and B, and the following balance sheet:

| *Assets* | | *Liabilities and Capital* | |
|---|---|---|---|
| Cash | 120 | Liabilities | 100 |
| Plant | 80 (FMV = 130) | Paid-in capital | 50 |
| | | Retained earnings (= E&P) | 50 |
| Total | 200 | Total | 200 |

Q completely redeems B's one-half interest for $75 cash and then it sells the plant for $130. Determine the amount of Q's E&P immediately after each of these events. Do you think the outcome after each event is correct? Why or why not?

## *NOTES*

1. *Compliance?* Section 312(n)(7) only applies if the redemption is treated as an exchange to the redeemed shareholder under section 302(a) or 303. In certain cases, however, such as share repurchases carried out by public corporations, the corporation may not know the tax consequences of the redemption to the shareholder.

2. *Stock reacquisition expenses.* Ordinary distributions are not deductible by the distributing corporation but, prior to 1986, there was limited authority that a distribution in redemption of stock might be deductible in extraordinary circumstances. See Five Star Manufacturing Co. v. Comm'r, 355 F.2d 724 (5th Cir. 1966), rev'g 40 T.C. 379 (1963) (redemption to prevent liquidation of corporation and to preserve viability of its business was deductible). In 1986, Congress added section 162(k),

which generally denies any deduction by a corporation for amounts paid in connection with the reacquisition of its stock. The rule applies not only to amounts paid for the repurchase but also to certain expenses incurred in connection with the repurchase, such as legal, accounting, brokerage, and appraisal fees. The rule treats such amounts as nonamortizable capital expenditures. The provision specifically does not apply to interest expense or amortizable amounts properly allocable to indebtedness, such as interest incurred on debt used to finance the stock repurchase or loan fees connected to such debt. Section 162(k) was added to clarify that certain "greenmail" payments by a corporation — amounts paid to buy out shareholders in order to thwart an attempted hostile takeover of the corporation — are not deductible, but the rule is not limited to that specific situation. (The recipients of greenmail payments must pay a special 50 percent tax on their gain or income from the transaction. See I.R.C. § 5881.)

In certain circumstances, section 404(k)(1) authorizes a corporation to deduct amounts paid to redeem stock held by an Employee Stock Ownership Plan (ESOP) (a type of retirement trust funded with the corporation's stock for the benefit of the corporation's employees) if the redemption proceeds are distributed by the ESOP to beneficiaries of the plan. There is a split among the Circuits regarding whether section 162(k) trumps this provision. Compare Boise Cascade v. U.S., 329 F.3d 751 (9th Cir. 2003) (allowing deduction) with General Mills v. U.S., 554 F.3d 727 (8th Cir. 2009), Nestle Purina Petcare Co. v. Comm'r, 594 F.3d 968 (8th Cir. 2010), cert. denied, 131 S. Ct. 86 (2010), and Conopco v. U.S., 572 F.3d 162 (3d Cir. 2009) (disallowing deduction). The regulations now specifically prohibit a deduction in this situation. Reg. § 1.162(k)-1.

3. *Effect of state law.* As in the case of ordinary distributions, the tax consequences of a redemption are not dependent upon the state-law characterization of the transaction. See Wentworth v. Comm'r, 510 F.2d 883 (6th Cir. 1975) (complete redemption of taxpayer's interest was taxable event even though it was determined in hindsight that redemption caused corporation to be insolvent and therefore violated state law).

### 3. *Redemptions by S Corporations*

As we have seen, section 1368 sets forth the shareholder-level tax consequences of a distribution from an S corporation to which section 301(c) would apply (including a redemption distribution taxable to the distributee under section 301 by reason of section 302(d)). Because the rules of subchapter C generally also apply to S corporations, see I.R.C. § 1371(a), redemptions by S corporations that satisfy one of the section 302(b) safe harbors qualify for exchange treatment. Work through the following **problem 6-8** to see whether a shareholder who is partially redeemed by an S corporation without any prior C history generally has the same tax preference as a shareholder partially redeemed by a C corporation.

**Problem 6-8:** Unrelated individuals A, B, and C own 60 shares each of Z corporation, representing all of its outstanding stock. Each shareholder has a $12,000 basis in her stock, and Z has always been an S corporation. If, for nontax purposes, it is equally acceptable to all parties for Z to distribute to A $6,400 (in exchange for 16 of her shares) or $6,800 (for 17 shares), which transaction should be carried out? Why?

How does a redemption affect the AAA and E&P of an S corporation with a prior C history? Read I.R.C. §§ 1368(e)(1)(B) and 1371(c)(2) and Reg. § 1.1368-2(d)(1). Does it matter if the redemption is treated as an ordinary distribution under section 301? See Reg. § 1.1368-2(a)(3)(iii) and (5)(iii) and (v), and -3 (ex. 9).

**Problem 6-9:** X is a calendar-year S corporation with two equal, unrelated shareholders, A and B. At the beginning of the taxable year, A's basis in her X stock is $1,100 and X has $1,000 of E&P and $1,500 of AAA. During the year, X has taxable income of $500. On March 15, X distributes $600 to each shareholder. On December 31, X redeems all of A's stock for $1,200. What are the tax consequences of these transactions to X and A?

## C. Tax Planning Involving Corporate Redemptions

Because it is often possible to carry out a particular transaction involving a distribution in a variety of different ways, it is common for such transactions to be designed in a manner that minimizes their tax consequences. This part considers when such tax planning is considered permissible and, indeed, sanctioned by the tax authorities, and when the planning is viewed as impermissible. As you read through these materials, try to determine what guidance they provide to corporate tax planners.

### Grove v. Commissioner

490 F.2d 241 (2d Cir. 1973)

KAUFMAN, Chief Judge:

... Philip Grove received an engineering degree in 1924 from Rensselaer Polytechnic Institute ["RPI"], a private, tax-exempt educational institution. During the Depression, he founded what is now Grove Shepherd Wilson & Kruge, Inc. and at all times since has controlled a majority of its shares. The balance of the Corporation's shares, with the exception of those held by RPI, are owned by officers and employees of the Corporation or their relatives.

The Corporation's business is building airfields, highways, tunnels, canals, and other similar heavy construction projects in both the United States and foreign countries. These projects usually involve the investment of large sums of money over an extended period of time and involve a high degree of risk. Since, in this industry, contract payments normally are made only after specified levels of progress are achieved, a firm must always commit substantial amounts of its own funds, whether borrowed or internally generated, to a project. Moreover, a company can determine an acceptable contract price based only on its best estimate of the cost to complete the project. A bad "guess" or unforeseen contingency may require a firm to complete a project while incurring a loss. Not surprisingly, the mortality rate in this industry is high. To protect against such adverse developments, successful firms seek to maintain liquidity by holding ample cash or other assets easily converted to cash. One method of conserving cash, adopted by the Corporation, is to retain all earnings and refrain from paying dividends.

. . . RPI, like all universities and colleges, pursued its alumni with a wide variety of contribution plans. One plan employed "life income funds," and its terms were simple. An alumnus would make a gift of securities to RPI and retain a life interest in the income from the donated securities. Whatever dividends and interest were paid during the donor's life would belong to the donor, while any capital appreciation would inure to RPI. Upon the death of the donor, RPI would obtain full title to the securities.

In 1954, Dr. Livingston Houston, RPI's president, suggested to Grove that he make a gift under the "life income funds" plan. Grove explained that his only significant holdings were shares of his own corporation, but expressed a willingness to donate some of these shares under the plan, with certain qualifications. The Corporation, he stated, could not agree to any obligation or understanding to redeem shares held by RPI. This condition, of course, stemmed from a fear that RPI might seek redemption at a time when the Corporation was hard pressed for cash, which, as we have noted, was an asset crucial to a company in the heavy construction business. Moreover, since Grove at that time was unsure of RPI's money-management qualifications, he further conditioned his gift on a requirement that if RPI disposed of the shares, any proceeds would be invested and managed by an established professional firm.

RPI found these terms acceptable and on December 30, 1954, Grove made an initial gift of 200 shares, valued at $25,560. A letter accompanying the donation set forth the conditions we have recited. Moreover, in addition to retaining an interest in the income from the gift for his life, Grove specified that in the event he should predecease his wife Harriet, she would receive the income until her death.

On the same day, the Corporation and RPI signed a minority shareholder agreement. RPI agreed not to "sell, transfer, give, pledge or hypothecate, or in any way dispose of the whole or any part of the common stock of the Corporation now or hereafter owned . . . until (RPI) shall have first offered the Corporation the opportunity to purchase said shares upon the terms and conditions hereinafter provided." The redemption price was established at book value of the shares as noted on the Corporation's most recent certified financial statement prior to the offer. Pursuant to the contract, the Corporation was "entitled (but not obligated) to purchase all or any part of the shares of stock so offered." If the Corporation did not exercise its option to purchase within sixty days, RPI could transfer the shares to any other party and the Corporation's right of first refusal would not subsequently attach to such transferred shares.

The 1954 gift was the first in a series of annual contributions to RPI by Grove. From 1954 to 1968, Grove donated to RPI between 165 and 250 shares of the Corporation each year, reaching a cumulative total of 2,652 shares, subject to terms substantially similar to those noted earlier.

Generally, RPI offered donated shares to the Corporation for redemption, between one and two years after they were donated by Grove. The transactions followed a similar pattern. On each occasion, the Finance Committee of RPI's Board of Trustees first authorized the sale of specific shares of the Corporation. RPI's treasurer or controller would then write to Sidney Houck, the Corporation's treasurer, informing him of RPI's desire to dispose of the shares. Upon receipt of this letter, Houck would call a special meeting of the Corporation's board of directors to consider whether or not to exercise the Corporation's right of first refusal. The Board would adopt a resolution authorizing redemption and Houck would so inform RPI's financial officer, enclosing a company check for the amount due. By return mail, RPI would forward the appropriate stock certificate to the Corporation for cancellation.

At the time of the first redemption, in December, 1955, RPI opened an investment account at . . . Merrill Lynch. . . . The account was captioned "Rensselaer Polytechnic Institute (Philip H. Grove Fund) Account." In accordance with Grove's wishes concerning the management of disposition proceeds, RPI authorized Merrill Lynch to act directly upon investment recommendations made by Scudder, Stevens, & Clark, Grove's personal investment adviser. RPI deposited the proceeds of each redemption transaction into this account which, pursuant to Scudder, Stevens & Clark's instructions, were generally invested in securities of large corporations whose shares traded on organized stock exchanges. Merrill Lynch paid the income from these investments to RPI on a monthly basis. RPI, in turn, made quarterly remittances to Grove, accompanied by an analysis of all account transactions.

On his personal income tax return for 1963, Grove reported as taxable income dividends of $4,939.28 and interest of $2,535.73 paid to him by RPI from the Merrill Lynch account. For 1964, Grove reported $6,096.05 in dividends and $3,540.81 in interest. The Commissioner, however, assessed deficiencies in Grove's taxable income for these years, asserting that Grove "realized additional dividends in the amounts of $29,000 and $25,800 in 1963 and 1964, respectively, as the result of the redemption of stock by Grove Shepherd Wilson & Kruge, Inc." . . .

The Commissioner's view of this case is relatively simple. In essence, we are urged to disregard the actual form of the Grove-RPI-Corporation donations and redemptions and to rewrite the actual events so that Grove's tax liability is seen in a wholly different light. Support for this position, it is argued, flows from the Supreme

Court's decision in Comm'r v. Court Holding Co., 324 U.S. 331 (1945), which, in language familiar to law students, cautions that "the incidence of taxation depends upon the substance of a transaction. . . . To permit the true nature of a transaction to be disguised by mere formalisms, which exist solely to alter tax liabilities, would seriously impair the effective administration of the tax policies of Congress." . . . In an effort to bring the instant case within this language, the Commissioner insists that whatever the appearance of the transactions here under consideration, their "true nature" is quite different. He maintains that Grove, with the cooperation of RPI, withdrew substantial funds from the Corporation and manipulated them in a manner designed to produce income for his benefit. In the Commissioner's view, the transaction is properly characterized as a redemption by the Corporation of Grove's, not RPI's shares, followed by a cash gift to RPI by Grove. This result, it is said, more accurately reflects "economic reality."

The Commissioner's motives for insisting upon this formulation are easily understood once its tax consequences are examined. Although Grove reported taxable dividends and interest received from the Merrill Lynch account on his 1963 and 1964 tax returns, amounts paid by the Corporation to redeem the donated shares from RPI were not taxed upon distribution. If, however, the transactions are viewed in the manner suggested by the Commissioner, the redemption proceeds would be taxable as income to Grove. Moreover, because the redemptions did not in substance alter Grove's relationship to the Corporation — he continued throughout to control a majority of the outstanding shares — the entire proceeds would be taxed as a dividend payment at high, progressive ordinary-income rates, rather than as a sale of shares, at the fixed, and relatively low, capital gains rate. . . .

Clearly, then, the stakes involved are high. . . . Here, our aim is to determine whether Grove's gifts of the Corporation's shares to RPI prior to redemption should be given independent significance or whether they should be regarded as meaningless intervening steps in a single, integrated transaction designed to avoid tax liability by the use of mere formalisms.

The guideposts for our analysis are well marked by earlier judicial encounters with this problem. "The law with respect to gifts of appreciated property is well established. A gift of appreciated property does not result in income to the donor so long as he gives the property away absolutely and parts with title thereto before the property gives rise to income by way of sale." . . . As noted below by the Tax Court, the Commissioner here "does not contend that the gifts of stock by (Grove) to RPI in 1961 and 1962 were sham transactions, or that they were not completed gifts when made." If Grove made a valid, binding, and irrevocable gift of the Corporation's shares to RPI, it would be the purest fiction to treat the redemption proceeds as having actually been received by Grove. The Tax Court concluded that the gift was complete and irrevocable when made. The Commissioner conceded as much and we so find.

It is argued, however, that notwithstanding the conceded validity of the gifts, other circumstances establish that Grove employed RPI merely as a convenient conduit for withdrawing funds from the Corporation for his personal use without incurring tax liability. The Commissioner would have us infer from the systematic nature of the gift-redemption cycle that Grove and RPI reached a mutually beneficial understanding: RPI would permit Grove to use its tax-exempt status to drain funds from the Corporation in return for a donation of a future interest in such funds.

We are not persuaded by this argument. . . . The [Tax Court] . . . specifically found that "there was no informal agreement between (Grove) and RPI that RPI would offer the stock in question to the corporation for redemption or that, if offered, the corporation would redeem it." . . . It cannot seriously be contended that the Tax Court's findings here are "clearly erroneous" and no tax liability can be predicated upon a nonexistent agreement between Grove and RPI or by a fictional one created by the Commissioner.

Grove, of course, owned a substantial majority of the Corporation's shares. His vote alone was sufficient to insure redemption of any shares offered by RPI. But such considerations, without more, are insufficient to permit the Commissioner to ride roughshod over the actual understanding found by the Tax Court to exist between the donor and the donee. . . .

Nothing in the December, 1954, minority shareholder agreement between the Corporation and RPI serves as a basis for disturbing the conclusion of the Tax Court. Although the Corporation desired a right of first refusal on minority shares — understandably so, in order to reduce the possibility of unrelated, outside ownership interests — it assumed no obligation to redeem any shares so offered. In the absence of such an obligation, the Commissioner's contention that Grove's initial donation was only the first step in a prearranged series of transactions is little more than wishful thinking grounded in a shaky foundation. . . .

We are not so naive as to believe that tax considerations played no role in Grove's planning. But foresight and planning do not transform a non-taxable event into one that is taxable. Were we to adopt the Commissioner's view, we would be required to recast two actual transactions — a gift by Grove to RPI and a redemption from RPI by the Corporation — into two completely fictional transactions — a redemption from Grove by the Corporation and a gift by Grove to RPI. Based upon the facts as found by the Tax Court, we can discover no basis for elevating the Commissioner's "form" over that employed by the taxpayer in good faith. "Useful as the step transaction doctrine may be in the interpretation of equivocal contracts and ambiguous events, it cannot generate events which never took place just so an additional tax liability might be asserted." . . . In the absence of any supporting facts in the record we are unable to adopt the Commissioner's view; to do so would be to engage in a process of decision that is arbitrary, capricious and ultimately destructive of traditional notions of judicial review. We decline to embark on such a course. . . .

OAKES, Circuit Judge (dissenting):

Review of the tax consequences of a business transaction requires consideration of the economic realities of the entire transaction. . . . Whether a transaction should be viewed as two or more steps or as one integrated transaction may result in entirely different tax consequences. . . .

Here, as I see it, the form of the transaction was two-step: a gift of stock followed by a redemption of the stock by the donor controlled corporation. The substance of the transaction, however, was a payment out of corporate earnings and profits to a charity designated by the donor who retained a life interest in the gift.

The factors which distinguish the RPI-Grove transactions from other charitable donations of securities and which persuade me to treat this as an integrated transaction are two: first, the gifts made by the Groves were of stock in a closed corporation that was inevitably redeemed annually; second, by virtue of retaining a life income from the reinvested proceeds and by retaining a measure of control over how those proceeds should be reinvested (by designating the investment adviser who was also the Groves' personal adviser), the Groves were able to achieve a bail-out from their non-dividend-paying closed corporation. . . .

## *NOTES AND QUESTIONS*

1. *The current IRS position.* The IRS has stopped trying to recharacterize gifts of stock to charities followed by redemptions of the charity's interest as, in effect, a distribution to the donor, except in those cases where the charitable donee is legally bound or can be compelled by the corporation to surrender its shares for redemption. See Rev. Rul. 78-197, 1978-1 C.B. 83. The facts in *Grove*, however, arguably presented a more complex question because less than the entire interest in the stock was given away. Should the Commissioner have made more of this fact before the court? Under current law, a deduction is generally not allowed for a gift to a charity of a partial interest in property, such as the remainder interest in *Grove*, because of the difficulty determining the value of the interest given away. I.R.C. § 170(f)(3). The value of a remainder interest, for example, depends upon the rights exercised by the holder of the life estate. Exceptions to section 170(f)(3) are provided in cases where valuation is feasible and in certain other situations.

2. *Impact of section 7701(o).* What impact, if any, would section 7701(o) have on the tax consequences of this transaction if it were to arise today? Assume that a taxpayer in Grove's situation regularly contributes to a charity a *complete* interest in shares of his company (which shares are periodically redeemed in the manner described in the case) so that the transaction does not run afoul of section 170(f)(3). Will the tax consequences of the transaction be respected?

3. *Bailouts.* The class of transactions illustrated by *Grove* are commonly referred to as "bailouts" in the tax literature. A "bailout" is a transaction in which corporate E&P is distributed (or bailed out) without imposition of the normal dividend tax. Traditionally, bailouts included transactions taxing the distributee at a preferential long-term capital gain rate (rather than the tax rate on dividends).

*Grove* illustrates how a bailout can be accomplished with a *zero* tax imposed on the amount distributed. As the following case illustrates, this result is possible even in the absence of a tax-exempt distributee.

## Zenz v. Quinlivan

213 F.2d 914 (6th Cir. 1954)

GOURLEY, District Judge.

. . . Appellant is the widow of the person who was the motivating spirit behind the closed corporation which engaged in the business of excavating and laying of sewers. Through death of her husband she became the owner of all shares of stock issued by the corporation. She operated the business until remarriage, when her second husband assumed the management. As a result of a marital rift, separation, and final divorce, taxpayer sought to dispose of her company to a competitor who was anxious to eliminate competition.

Prospective buyer did not want to assume the tax liabilities which it was believed were inherent in the accumulated earnings and profits of the corporation. To avoid said profits and earnings as a source of future taxable dividends, buyer purchased part of taxpayer's stock for cash. Three weeks later, after corporate reorganization and corporate action, the corporation redeemed the balance of taxpayer's stock, purchasing the same as treasury stock which absorbed substantially all of the accumulated earnings and surplus of the corporation.

. . . The question . . . presented is not whether the overall transaction, admittedly carried out for the purpose of avoiding taxes, actually avoided taxes which would have been incurred if the transaction had taken a different form, but whether the sale constituted a taxable dividend or the sale of a capital asset. . . .

The basic precept underlying the capital gains theory of taxation as distinguished from ordinary income tax is the concept that a person who has developed an enterprise in which earnings have been accumulated over a period of years should not be required to expend the ordinary income tax rate in the one year when he withdraws from his enterprise and realizes his gain.

Common logic dictates that a fair basis of measuring income is not determined upon the profits on hand in the year of liquidation but is properly attributable to each year in which the profits were gained.

We cannot concur with the legal proposition enunciated by the District Court that a corporate distribution can be essentially equivalent to a taxable dividend even though that distribution extinguishes the shareholder's interest in the corporation. To the contrary, we are satisfied that where the taxpayer effects a redemption which completely extinguishes the taxpayer's interest in the corporation, and does not retain any beneficial interest whatever, that such transaction is not the equivalent of the distribution of a taxable dividend as to him. . . .

The statutory concept of dividend is a distribution out of earnings and profits, and normally it is proportionate to shares and leaves the shareholder holding his shares as his capital investment. . . .

Complete and partial liquidations are treated for the purpose of the statute, as sales with a consequent measure of gain or loss, even though the proceeds may to some extent be derived from earnings. . . .

The use of corporate earnings or profits to purchase and make payment for all the shares of a taxpayer's holdings in a corporation is not controlling, and the question as to whether the distribution in connection with the cancellation or the redemption of said stock is essentially equivalent to the distribution of a taxable dividend under the Internal Revenue Code and Treasury Regulation must depend upon the circumstances of each case.

Since the intent of the taxpayer was to bring about a complete liquidation of her holdings and to become separated from all interest in the corporation, the conclusion is inevitable that the distribution of the earnings and profits by the corporation in payment for said stock was not made at such time and in such manner as to make the distribution and cancellation or redemption thereof essentially equivalent to the distribution of a taxable dividend. . . .

## *NOTES AND QUESTIONS*

1. *Is the law flawed? Zenz* exposes what may be a fundamental flaw in the tax law of corporate redemptions. Taxing certain redemptions like a sale of stock to a third party because the two transactions resemble one another to the redeemed shareholder overlooks the different *corporate* consequences of the transactions. In a sale of stock to a third party, there is no change in the amount of corporate E&P. In contrast, a sale of stock back to the corporation may deplete the amount of corporate E&P. Thus, it is not clear that these two transactions should be taxed alike. Conversely, the similar impact on corporate E&P of a redemption and an ordinary distribution perhaps leads to the conclusion that those two transactions should have similar tax consequences. *Zenz* shows how easily taxpayers have been able to take advantage of tax rules that fail to treat similar transactions in similar ways. Does section 7701(o) now trump this type of planning?

2. *Bootstrap acquisitions.* The *Zenz* transaction is commonly referred to as a "bootstrap" acquisition because the purchase price is financed in part by the assets of the corporation being acquired. A bootstrap acquisition has traditionally been a favorite way to structure a buyout since it permits a withdrawal of E&P at a preferential long-term capital gain rate. In other words, a plain vanilla stock redemption can be viewed as resulting in a bailout. As illustrated by *Zenz*, even under current law where the dividend income and long-term capital gain of individuals are taxed alike, it may still be advantageous to structure a buyout as a bootstrap acquisition if the shares redeemed were recently inherited. Under current law, the transaction drains out most, but not all, of the corporation's E&P. See I.R.C. § 312(n)(7).

3. *Order of the steps*. In *Zenz*, the government argued that the order of the steps should be reversed with the distribution to the taxpayer treated as preceding her stock sale to the third party. If the redemption had preceded the stock sale, it presumably would have been taxed like an ordinary distribution. The government asserted that the taxpayer and her buyer had employed a "circuitous approach" to carry out their transaction in order to drain the corporation of its E&P without anyone paying the normal tax on dividends. The court rejected the government's characterization and approved the taxpayer's tax position, which was at least consistent with the formal order of steps that she undertook.

In Rev. Rul. 75-447, 1975-2 C.B. 113, the Service agreed to permit the *Zenz* result even when the taxpayer undertakes the formal order of steps incorrectly. The ruling interprets *Zenz* as concluding that the actual sequence of a redemption and sale "is irrelevant as long as both events are clearly part of an overall plan." In other words, if the overall plan is to terminate a shareholder's interest in a corporation or to carry out a substantially disproportionate reduction in such interest, compliance with that objective will be measured by comparing the shareholder's interest before and after *both events*, regardless of the order in which they occur.

A variation on the *Zenz* transaction occurs when the seller or buyer is a corporation. In that case, the parties may try to structure the transaction to include a pre-purchase or post-purchase distribution qualifying as a dividend so that the corporate seller or buyer can claim the dividends-received deduction. The parties must be aware of the possible application of section 1059 to their transaction. In this area, the IRS sometimes continues to assert that the order of the steps should be reversed so that a transaction, which in form is a dividend to a corporate shareholder followed by a sale of the shareholder's remaining interest, should be treated in substance as a sale of the shareholder's entire interest with or without a subsequent distribution to the buyer. Compare TSN Liquidating Corp. v. U.S., 624 F.2d 1328 (5th Cir. 1980) (form of transaction respected) with Waterman Steamship Corp. v. Comm'r, 430 F.2d 1185 (5th Cir. 1970), cert. denied, 401 U.S. 939 (1971) (transaction successfully recharacterized by IRS as straight sale of stock). The following ruling illustrates another possible way for the IRS to challenge the tax consequences of bootstrap acquisitions.

## Rev. Rul. 69-608

1969-2 C.B. 42

Advice has been requested as to the treatment for Federal income tax purposes of the redemption by a corporation of a retiring shareholder's stock where the remaining shareholder of the corporation has entered into a contract to purchase such stock.

Where the stock of a corporation is held by a small group of people, it is often considered necessary to the continuity of the corporation to have the individuals enter into agreements among themselves to provide for the disposition of the stock of the corporation in the event of the resignation, death, or incapacity of one of them. Such agreements are generally reciprocal among the shareholders and usually provide that on the resignation, death, or incapacity of one of the principal shareholders, the remaining shareholders will purchase his stock. Frequently such agreements are assigned to the corporation by the remaining shareholder and the corporation actually redeems its stock from the retiring shareholder.

Where a corporation redeems stock from a retiring shareholder, the fact that the corporation in purchasing the shares satisfies the continuing shareholder's executory contractual obligation to purchase the redeemed shares does not result in a distribution to the continuing shareholder provided that the continuing shareholder is not subject to an existing primary and unconditional obligation to perform the contract and that the corporation pays no more than fair market value for the stock redeemed.

On the other hand, if the continuing shareholder, at the time of the assignment to the corporation of his contract to purchase the retiring shareholder's stock, is subject to an unconditional obligation to purchase the retiring shareholder's stock, the satisfaction by the corporation of his obligation results in a constructive distribution to him. The constructive distribution is taxable as a distribution under section 301. . . .

If the continuing shareholder assigns his stock purchase contract to the redeeming corporation prior to the time when he incurs a primary and unconditional obligation to pay for the shares of stock, no distribution to him will result. If, on the other hand, the assignment takes place after the time when the continuing shareholder is so obligated, a distribution to him will result. While a pre-existing obligation to perform in the future is a necessary element in establishing a distribution in this type of case, it is not until the obligor's duty to perform becomes unconditional that it can be said a primary and unconditional obligation arises.

The application of the above principles may be illustrated by the situations described below.

*Situation 1*

A and B are unrelated individuals who own all of the outstanding stock of corporation X. A and B enter into an agreement that provides in the event B leaves the employ of X, he will sell his X stock to A at a price fixed by the agreement. The agreement provides that within a specified number of days of B's offer to sell, A will purchase at the price fixed by the agreement all of the X stock owned by B. B terminates his employment and tenders the X stock to A. Instead of purchasing the stock himself in accordance with the terms of the agreement, A causes X to assume the contract and to redeem its stock held by B. In this case, A had a primary and unconditional obligation to perform his contract with B at the time the contract was assigned to X. Therefore, the redemption by X of its stock held by B will result in a constructive distribution to A. . . .

*Situation 2*

A and B are unrelated individuals who own all of the outstanding stock of corporation X. An agreement between them provides unconditionally that within ninety days of the death of either A or B, the survivor will purchase the decedent's stock of X from his estate. Following the death of B, A causes X to assume the contract and redeem the stock from B's estate.

The assignment of the contract to X followed by the redemption by X of the stock owned by B's estate will result in a constructive distribution to A because immediately on the death of B, A had a primary and unconditional obligation to perform the contract.

*Situation 3*

All of the stock of X corporation was owned by a trust that was to terminate in 1969. Individuals A and B were the beneficiaries of the trust. Since B was the trustee of the trust, he had exclusive management authority over X through his control of the board of directors. In 1966, A paid to B the sum of 25x dollars and promised to pay an additional 20x dollars to B in 1969 for B's interest in the corpus and accumulations of the trust plus B's agreement to resign immediately as supervisor of the trust and release his control over the management of the corporation. The actual transfer of the stock held in trust was to take place on termination of the trust in 1968. In 1969, X reimbursed A for the 25x dollars previously paid to B, paid 20x dollars to B, and received the X stock held by B.

For all practical purposes, A became the owner of B's shares in 1966. Although naked legal title to the shares could not be transferred until the trust terminated in 1968, B did transfer all of his beneficial and equitable ownership of the X stock to A in exchange for an immediate payment by A of 25x dollars and an unconditional promise to pay an additional 20x dollars upon termination of the trust. The payment by X of 20x dollars to B and 25x dollars to A in 1969 constituted a constructive distribution to A in the amount of 45x dollars. . . .

*Situation 4*

A and B owned all of the outstanding stock of X corporation. A and B entered into a contract under which, if B desired to sell his X stock, A agreed to purchase the stock or to cause such stock to be purchased. If B chose to sell his X stock to any person other than A, he could do so at any time. In accordance with the terms of the contract, A caused X to redeem all of B's stock in X.

At the time of the redemption, B was free to sell his stock to A or to any other person, and A had no unconditional obligation to purchase the stock and no fixed liability to pay for the stock. Accordingly, the redemption by X did not result in a constructive distribution to A. . . .

*Situation 5*

A and B owned all of the outstanding stock of X corporation. An agreement between A and B provided that upon the death of either, X will redeem all of the X stock owned by the decedent at the time of his death. In the event that X does not redeem the shares from the estate, the agreement provided that the surviving shareholder would purchase the unredeemed shares from the decedent's estate. B died and, in accordance with the agreement, X redeemed all of the shares owned by his estate.

In this case A was only secondarily liable under the agreement between A and B. Since A was not primarily obligated to purchase the X stock from the estate of B, he received no constructive distribution when X redeemed the stock.

*Situation 6*

B owned all of the outstanding stock of X corporation. A and B entered into an agreement under which A was to purchase all of the X stock from B. A did not contemplate purchasing the X stock in his own name. Therefore, the contract between A and B specifically provided that it could be assigned by A to a corporation and that, if the corporation agreed to be bound by the terms, A would be released from the contract.

A organized Y corporation and assigned the stock purchase contract to it. Y borrowed funds and purchased all of the X stock from B pursuant to the agreement. Subsequently Y was merged into X and X assumed the liabilities that Y incurred in connection with the purchase of the X stock and subsequently satisfied these liabilities.

The purchase by Y of the stock of X did not result in a constructive distribution to A. Since A did not contemplate purchasing the X stock in his own name, he provided in the contract that it could be assigned to a corporation prior to the closing date. A chose this latter alternative and assigned the contract to Y. A was not personally subject to an unconditional obligation to purchase the X stock from B. . . .

*Situation 7*

A and B owned all of the outstanding stock of X corporation. An agreement between the shareholders provided that upon the death of either, the survivor would purchase the decedent's shares from his estate at a price provided in the agreement. Subsequently, the agreement was rescinded and a new agreement entered into which provided that upon the death of either A or B, X would redeem all of the decedent's shares of X stock from his estate.

The cancellation of the original contract between the parties in favor of the new contract did not result in a constructive distribution to either A or B. At the time X agreed to purchase the stock pursuant to the terms of the new agreement, neither A nor B had an unconditional obligation to purchase shares of X stock. The subsequent redemption of the stock from the estate of either pursuant to the terms of the new agreement will not constitute a constructive distribution to the surviving shareholder.

## *NOTES AND QUESTIONS*

1. *Form over substance?* The fact patterns presented in Rev. Rul. 69-608 illustrate that, despite the "substance-over-form" doctrine, the form of corporate transactions is often dispositive. Make sure that you understand the fine distinctions being drawn in the ruling to justify the different tax consequences in the various factual situations. For example, how are situations 4 and 6 different from situation 1? What might you suggest to shareholders who find themselves in situation 2?

2. *Tax-free redemption in connection with a divorce.* Litigation involving Joann and John Arnes and their wholly-owned corporation, Moriah, illustrates how overlapping tax rules may result in a tax-free redemption even though there is neither a tax-exempt shareholder in the transaction nor one who has recently inherited the redeemed stock. Pursuant to a divorce property settlement, Moriah redeemed Joann's half interest in the corporation for $450,000. Joann contended that this transaction was tax-free to her under section 1041(a), which provides for the nonrecognition of gain or loss on transfers of property between spouses or former spouses if incident to a divorce. Regulations in effect at the time permitted certain transfers to a third party, such as Joann's transfer of stock to Moriah, to qualify as a direct transfer to a former spouse like John, for purposes of section 1041, if the transfer to the third party was "on behalf of" the former spouse. In that situation, the regulations treated John as receiving the stock from Joann and then transferring it to Moriah. The Ninth Circuit agreed with Joann's position and therefore held that she did not recognize any gain or loss in the transaction:

> John Arnes had an obligation to Joann Arnes that was relieved by Moriah's payment to Joann. That obligation was based in their divorce property settlement, which called for the redemption of Joann's stock. Although John and Joann were the sole stockholders in Moriah, the obligation to purchase Joann's stock was John's, not Moriah's. Furthermore, John personally guaranteed Moriah's note to Joann. Under Washington law, Joann could sue John for payment without suing Moriah. . . . Thus, John was liable, with Moriah, for the payments due Joann.
>
> We hold that Joann's transfer to Moriah did relieve John of an obligation, and therefore constituted a benefit to John. Joann's transfer of stock should be treated as a constructive transfer to John, who then transferred the stock to Moriah. The $450,000 was paid to Joann by Moriah on behalf of John. The transfer of $450,000 from the corporate treasury need not escape taxation, if we hold, as we do, that Joann is not required to recognize any gain on the transfer of her stock, because it is subject to section 1041. The tax result for Joann is the same as if she had conveyed the property directly to John. [Joann C. Arnes v. U.S., 981 F.2d 456, 459 (9th Cir. 1992).]

The government responded to this defeat by asserting a tax deficiency against John Arnes. According to the government, if the redemption of Joann's stock was made on behalf of John, then the redemption constituted a constructive distribution to John under the authority of Rev. Rul. 69-608. This result was the clear implication of the Ninth Circuit's decision in Joann's case, and the same court would hear any appeal of John's case. However, a divided Tax Court (10-7) disagreed, exercising a rare opportunity to, in effect, reverse the court that would hear the appeal from its decision. The Tax Court found that the Ninth Circuit panel in Joann's case had overlooked a prior Ninth Circuit authority, Edler v. Comm'r, 727 F.2d 857 (9th Cir. 1984), holding that a taxpayer in John's situation did *not* receive a constructive distribution. In *Edler*, the taxpayer's primary obligation to acquire his former wife's stock was modified by a nunc pro tunc order making the corporation the primary obligor and the taxpayer only secondarily obligated. The Ninth Circuit concluded in *Edler* that the redemption of the former wife's stock therefore did not constitute a constructive distribution to the taxpayer. According to the Tax Court, John Arnes' case was even stronger than the taxpayer's case in *Edler* because from the inception of the divorce proceeding, Moriah, and not John, was obligated to acquire Joann's stock. Hence, John had no "primary and unconditional obligation" to acquire Joann's stock and therefore did not receive a constructive distribution. The court found situation 5 in Rev. Rul. 69-608 to be "directly analogous" to John's case. See John A. Arnes v. Comm'r, 102 T.C. 522, 528 (1994). The IRS did not appeal this decision. As a result, neither Joann nor John had to pay any tax upon the distribution of $450,000 from their closely held corporation.

Regulation § 1.1041-2 now tries to provide a regulatory solution to the *Arnes* problem. In general, the regulation provides flexibility to the parties, common in the divorce area, to determine who should be taxed on the distribution, provided that *someone* is taxed. Thus, under the general rules, the spouse who is redeemed (the "transferor spouse") is taxed in the redemption unless the other spouse ("the non-transferor spouse") is treated as receiving a constructive distribution under general tax principles, including the "primary and unconditional obligation" test set out in Rev. Rul. 69-608. If the nontransferor spouse is treated as receiving a constructive distribution, then the transferor spouse is deemed to transfer the redeemed shares to the nontransferor spouse in a section 1041 transaction followed by a taxable redemption of those shares held by the nontransferor spouse. In short, under the general rules, one spouse or the other is taxed in a redemption depending upon application of constructive distribution principles. Finally, the parties may reverse these outcomes despite application of those principles if they expressly so provide in a written agreement or divorce or separation instrument. The agreement must specify consistent tax treatment by both parties.

Even with the regulatory guidance, it still seems possible for the two parties to take inconsistent positions and potentially whipsaw the government. The regulations require the parties to take consistent positions if they seek to reverse the outcome of the general rules. But if they agree to abide by the general rules, generally meaning application of the "primary and unconditional obligation" test in Rev. Rul. 69-608, they conceivably could litigate separately and take inconsistent positions with respect to the application of that test. Thus, in the future, the spouse in Joann's situation could claim that the test dictates a constructive distribution to her former spouse. Hence, under the regulation, the spouse in Joann's situation would be absolved of any tax liability. Meanwhile, the spouse in John's situation could argue in a subsequent case that the test does *not* result in a constructive distribution to him, and if he prevails, he would also be absolved from taxation by the regulation. Presumably, the Commissioner will try to make sure the position of both parties is considered in the same proceeding.

3. Golson *rule*. Under the *Golson* rule, the Tax Court "will follow a Court of Appeals decision which is squarely in point where appeal from the case under consideration lies to that Court of Appeals and to that court alone," even though the Tax Court would decide differently if appeal were to a different circuit. Golson v. Comm'r, 54 T.C. 742, 757 (1970), aff'd without discussion of this issue, 445 F.2d 985 (10th Cir. 1970), cert. denied, 404 U.S. 940 (1971). In John Arnes' case, the Tax Court concluded that the Ninth Circuit's decision in Joann's case did not bind the Tax Court under the *Golson* rule because Joann's case involved the tax consequences to her under section 1041, not whether John received a constructive distribution. Further, John was not a party to Joann's case and possibly had a position adverse to hers.

4. *More constructive redemptions*. Suppose a shareholder (such as a majority owner) of a corporation transfers property to a corporate employee in consideration of services provided by the employee to the corporation. The regulations treat this transaction as if the shareholder transferred the property to the corporation as a contribution of capital followed by the corporation's transfer of the property to the employee, taxable under section 83. Any amount paid by the employee to the shareholder for the property is treated as paid to the corporation and then distributed to the shareholder in a transaction to which section 302 applies. Reg. § 1.83-6(d)(1). Thus, the transaction could result in the shareholder receiving a dividend.

5. *Disappearing basis*. If a distribution in redemption of stock is treated as an ordinary distribution and not as a sale or exchange of stock, what happens to the shareholder's basis in the stock redeemed? Read Reg. § 1.302-2(c). The potential problem of the basis shifting to other shares of the same or a different taxpayer is illustrated by the last two materials in this chapter.

## Notice 2001-45

2001-2 C.B. 129

. . . The transaction involves the use of the attribution rules of § 318 of the Internal Revenue Code and § 1.302-2(c) of the Income Tax Regulations to increase the basis of stock owned by a taxpayer (the "Taxpayer") that claims a loss upon disposition of that stock. In the transaction, there is a redemption of stock that is owned by a person (other than the Taxpayer) that is not subject to U.S. tax or is otherwise indifferent to the Federal income tax consequences of the redemption. Purportedly as a result of the application of the attribution rules of § 318, the redemption of stock is claimed to be a dividend under § 301 rather than a payment in exchange for stock under § 302(a). A variety of devices, often including options, is employed to treat the redeemed shareholder as owning stock in the redeeming corporation owned or treated as owned by the Taxpayer under the attribution rules of § 318. The attribution of ownership of such shares purportedly prevents the redemption of stock from reducing the redeemed shareholder's ownership interest in the redeeming corporation, thereby causing the redemption to be treated as a dividend.

As a result of the redemption, the Taxpayer takes the position that under § 1.302-2(c) all or a portion of the basis of the redeemed stock is added to the basis of stock in the redeeming corporation that the Taxpayer owns. The Taxpayer then sells the stock and claims a loss.

Variations on the transaction include (1) the use of the transaction to reduce income or gain (rather than generate loss) and (2) the transfer of the stock (the basis of which was purportedly increased by reason of the redemption) to an entity in a carryover basis exchange, followed by either a sale of the entity interest or a sale of the stock by the entity.

. . . Section 1.302-2(c) provides that when an amount received in a redemption of stock is treated as a distribution of a dividend, "proper adjustment" of the basis of the remaining stock will be made with respect to the stock redeemed. Example 2 of § 1.302-2(c) illustrates a proper adjustment where the entire amount received in redemption of the stock held by one spouse is treated as a dividend because the redeemed spouse is treated as owning stock held by the other spouse. In that example, the basis of the stock of the nonredeemed spouse is properly increased by the basis of the stock of the redeemed spouse.

It is the position of the Service and the Treasury that such an adjustment is not proper in every case in which the redeemed shareholder retains no stock in the redeeming corporation. The example in the regulations is premised on the concept that an adjustment is appropriate where the redeemed spouse is required to include the full redemption proceeds as a dividend in gross income that is subject to U.S. tax and such spouse retains no stock to which the basis of the redeemed stock could attach.

The Service intends to disallow losses claimed (or to increase taxable income or gains) in the transactions described in this Notice to the extent a taxpayer derives a tax benefit that is attributable to stock basis purportedly shifted from the redeemed shares. Depending on the facts of the particular case, reasons for disallowance may include, but are not limited to, the following: (1) the redemption does not result in a dividend (and consequently there is no basis shift) because, viewing the transaction as a whole, the redemption results in a reduction of interest in the redeeming corporation to which § 302(b) applies; (2) the basis shift is not a "proper adjustment" as contemplated by § 1.302-2(c); and (3) there is no attribution of stock ownership or basis shift because the steps taken to achieve those results are transitory and serve no purpose other than tax avoidance. . . .

*NOTES*

1. *Listed transaction and penalties.* The I.R.S. notice further identifies the possible penalties that may be imposed on the taxpayer, promoter, tax return preparer, and others who are involved in such a transaction and specifies that it and any substantially similar one is a "listed transaction." The significance of this designation was discussed in chapter four.

2. *Deferred loss.* Proposed regulations issued in 2009 restrict the shifting of basis in redeemed stock where the redemption is treated as an ordinary distribution. The proposal treats any unrecovered basis that cannot be shifted to other shares of the redeemed taxpayer in the same class as the redeemed shares as a deferred loss of the taxpayer. The loss would generally be allowed on the earlier of the date (1) events occur that would have caused the redemption to satisfy section 302(b)(1), (2), or (3) had the events occurred at the time of the redemption, or (2) all classes of stock of the redeeming corporation become worthless within the meaning of section 165(g). Prop. Reg. § 1.302-5(a)(3)(i), (b)(4)(i). For example, suppose A and B, husband and wife, own all of the shares of corporation X and A is completely redeemed in a transaction taxable under section 301. Under the proposed regulations, A's unrecovered basis in the redeemed shares does not shift to B but rather remains with A in the form of a deferred loss. A may claim the loss upon the earlier of certain later events, such as a divorce between A and B, a complete redemption of B's interest in X, or a determination that the X stock is worthless. The proposal may create some administrative difficulties since the redeemed shareholder may not know when or whether subsequent events have occurred that would permit the deferred loss to be claimed.

## H.J. Heinz Company v. United States

76 Fed. Cl. 570 (2007)

ALLEGRA, J.

[In 1983, Heinz Co., a Pennsylvania food products manufacturer, organized HCC as a Delaware subsidiary to undertake financing activities previously carried out directly by Heinz. HCC's principal activity was to borrow money from outside lenders and lend the same money to Heinz's operating subsidiaries. The purpose for forming the new Delaware subsidiary was to minimize the state income tax liability on profits earned from the financing activities. Because HCC had no office or employees of its own (with Heinz management essentially making all of the decisions for its subsidiary), Pennsylvania state tax officials questioned Heinz as early as 1984 whether the separate existence of HCC should be respected, or whether the two companies should simply be treated as a single Pennsylvania entity for state tax purposes. Tax officials from other states also questioned whether in view of HCC's structure, income tax should be paid to their states as a result of certain of its other financing activities. This controversy and uncertainty continued throughout the period of the transaction described below. During the years at issue, Heinz, HCC, and Heinz's other subsidiaries all joined together to file a consolidated return for federal income tax purposes with Heinz, as the common parent of the group, responsible for the group's tax liability.

In late 1994, HCC purchased on the open market 3.5 million shares of Heinz common stock for approximately $129 million plus $2 million in transaction costs. HCC borrowed much of the money needed for the purchase. In January, 1995, HCC sold 3.325 million of the Heinz shares back to Heinz in exchange for a zero coupon note (the "Note") that promised to pay the holder about $197 million in seven years' time. In addition, beginning three years after issuance and continuing until maturity, the Note was convertible into 3.51 million shares of Heinz common stock. According to Goldman Sachs, Heinz's investment banker, the Note, including its conversion privilege, was "reasonably valued" at $130.5 million when issued, or the same value as the shares bought back by Heinz. The purchase by HCC and share buyback by Heinz occurred during a period that Heinz was regularly engaged in purchasing its own common stock on the open market for various corporate purposes.

In May 1995, HCC sold its remaining 175,000 Heinz shares to AT&T for about $7 million in cash. Thus, HCC's short-term investment in Heinz stock produced about a $6.5 million profit ($130.5 million note plus $7 million cash less $131 million purchase price and transaction costs). In addition, during the period it held the Heinz stock, HCC received about $1.7 million in Heinz dividends and paid an unspecified amount of borrowing costs.

Because of the conversion privilege obtained by HCC when its Heinz shares were bought back by Heinz, the taxpayer took the position that the redemption should be treated as a dividend from Heinz to HCC which, under the consolidated income tax regulations, was not taxable to HCC. Dividend characterization followed from the fact that, as a result of attribution from holding the option, HCC's interest in Heinz actually *increased* following the redemption. See I.R.C. § 318(a)(4). The taxpayer therefore claimed that HCC's basis in the shares sold back to Heinz shifted over to HCC's remaining 175,000 shares in Heinz. Thus, the sale of those shares to AT&T resulted in a $124 million capital loss ($7 million amount realized less $131 million total basis). This loss was carried back to offset significant capital gains realized by the group in 1992-94.]

. . . If plaintiff is correct, transactions that, for financial accounting purposes, produced more than a $6 million profit, yielded, for tax purposes, a loss of over $124 million. Understanding how this might be the case requires a review of how the Code treats some intercorporate transactions.

. . . The parties agree that the 3,325,000 shares that Heinz obtained from HCC had a basis in HCC's hands of $124.2 million. Heinz asserts that it "redeemed" these shares with the Note within the meaning of section 317(b) of the Code, which provides that "stock shall be treated as redeemed by a corporation if the corporation acquires its stock from a shareholder in exchange for property, whether or not the stock so acquired is cancelled, retired, or held as treasury stock." Defendant admits that *if* a true redemption occurred, it would be treated as a dividend under section 302(d) of the Code. It further admits that *if* a true redemption occurred, and a dividend arose under section 302(d), the transfer of stock from HCC to Heinz did not reduce the former's equity position in the latter, so that the basis HCC had in the 3,325,000 shares would shift to HCC's remaining 175,000 shares. And defendant acknowledges that *if* this shifting in basis occurred, HCC was entitled to deduct a huge capital loss upon the subsequent sale of those 175,000 shares to AT&T.

In the tax law, "if" is a colossal word. Should the transaction in which Heinz acquired the 3,325,000 shares actually be considered a redemption within the meaning of section 317(b)? If it is not, plaintiffs essentially concede that HCC's basis in the 3,325,000 shares did not shift to its remaining stock and that the subsequent sale of the latter stock did not produce a loss. In arguing for this result, defendant makes several points. First, it contends that no redemption occurred under section 317(b) because Heinz did not exchange property for the stock within the meaning of that section. Second, defendant asseverates that even if the transaction technically qualified as a "redemption" within the meaning of section 317(b), the transaction should not be treated as such because it lacked economic substance and had *no bona* fide business purpose other than to produce tax benefits; it was, in a word, a sham. Finally, it asserts that under the so-called "step transaction doctrine," the purchase of the stock by HCC and the exchange of the stock for the Note should be merged together and viewed as a direct purchase of the stock by Heinz. . . .

Section 317(b) presupposes that the individual or corporation receiving property from the redeeming corporation, in fact, possesses the stock being redeemed. In arguing that this requirement was not met here, defendant asserts that HCC had a transitory interest in the Heinz shares that should not be respected for tax purposes because it did not have the benefits and burdens of that ownership. . . .

In the case *sub judice*, several factors suggest that HCC's ownership of the Heinz stock was more than notional. HCC incurred significant indebtedness to generate the funds that were used to purchase the Heinz stock on the market, indebtedness that was not guaranteed by its parent. Further, unlike in other cases, HCC received dividends on the stock during the period of its possession. . . . And HCC, and not Heinz, bore the risk of loss and the opportunity for gain as to the value of the Heinz stock it possessed — indeed, from the time that it obtained the Heinz stock between August and November of 1994, to the time it sold it in January of 1995, the stock appreciated, a fact that was reflected in the purchase price in the parties' agreement. Moreover, while the evidence on this point is a bit mixed, on balance, it appears that HCC was under no preexisting obligation to distribute or disgorge any profits it received — either in the form of dividends received, gain realized on the sale, or otherwise — to its parent. . . . Accordingly, and setting aside, briefly, other substance-over-form considerations, it appears preliminarily that HCC possessed the burdens and benefits associated with the Heinz stock and, to that extent, the later redemption qualified under section 317(b). . . .

Plaintiffs have the burden of proving that the portion of the transaction in question that saw HCC acquire shares and then transfer them to Heinz had both a business purpose and economic substance. As to the former, plaintiffs assert that HCC acquired the stock as an investment and to add "substance" to its operations for state tax law purposes. Both claims have decidedly hollow rings.

Plaintiffs' assertion that HCC acquired the Heinz stock for investment purposes finds cosmetic support in the relevant corporate minutes, which mention this as a reason for approving the acquisition. However, any notion that this claim was authentic is belied, *inter alia*, by the testimony of Mr. Crowe, a Heinz vice president and its chief tax advisor, who admitted that, before HCC purchased any Heinz stock, Heinz planned on redeeming all but a small portion of that stock, with the residue stock being left with HCC only as part of a plan to produce the desired carryback losses. Indeed, as will be described in greater detail below, HCC had already hired Goldman Sachs to design the Note that would be exchanged for the Heinz stock at least six weeks before it acquired its first share. Moreover, the record suggests that HCC could not have reasonably viewed its temporary holding of the Heinz stock as a *bona fide* short-term investment. For one thing, the investment fundamentals of the transaction were all wrong — HCC acquired that stock on the open market at the then current price even though it knew that, unless the stock was registered, it would have to sell it in a private placement at a discount (which is what occurred). Moreover, HCC not only had to borrow funds and pay interest to effectuate this purchase, but incurred nearly $2 million in other expenses and fees in making the purchases, even though Heinz and HCC both knew that all but a small portion of the stock would be redeemed within a matter of months. Ironically, the most damning testimony on this point came from plaintiffs' expert, Mr. Hatton. In explaining why he believed that it was not a foregone conclusion that HCC would exercise the stock conversion feature in the Note, Mr. Hatton emphasized how poorly Heinz's stock had fared in the three years prior to the transaction, noting that Heinz had "drastically underperformed the market." Mr. Hatton further testified that the actual increases that occurred in Heinz's stock value in the three years following the issuance of the Note were "unforeseen," adding that during this bull market period, Heinz "still underperformed versus the S&P 500."

Lastly, HCC could not "invest" in the Heinz stock and also fully participate in the Heinz stock repurchase program. The main purpose of that program — to reacquire common shares to be held in the Heinz treasury to deal with stock options, preferred stock conversions and other corporate purposes — could not be accomplished so long as HCC held the Heinz stock in its treasury as an "investment," a fact verified by several witnesses. Moreover, unlike the shares held in its treasury, Heinz was obligated to pay dividends on the shares held by HCC, undercutting the impact that the repurchase would have on its equity standing. Of course, this was not a problem as the record indicates that, *ab initio*, plaintiffs had every intention of making sure that the shares ended up with the parent. For this and the others reasons discussed above, the court rejects the notion that a non-tax business purpose was served here by having HCC "invest" in its parent's stock.

Perhaps sensing this outcome, plaintiffs' banner assertion at trial was that HCC purchased the Heinz stock to bolster its "substance" as a Delaware-based corporation, so as to lessen the likelihood that it would be disregarded by state taxing officials. There are at least four major flaws in this assertion.

First, nothing in the record suggests that anyone associated with Heinz thought, at the time, that HCC's purchase of the Heinz stock would improve its stature as a Delaware holding company—there is no hint of this in the Heinz and HCC corporate minutes, the Heinz internal working papers, the series of memoranda prepared by Heinz tax officials detailing the steps that should be taken to bolster HCC's status, and even the documents discussing the Heinz stock purchase itself. Nothing whatsoever. It is thus fair to conclude that this claim is of relatively recent vintage, a fact that undercuts its legitimacy. Second, the record reveals that Heinz officials knew or should have known that the stock purchase would not improve HCC's status in prior taxable years. By the time the stock acquisitions began in 1994, HCC had been operating either out of a desk drawer or with a single employee for a number of years and the debate over its operations already was coming to a head, with various states—among them, Pennsylvania, Connecticut, New York and North Carolina—already having challenged its status as a separate company. Internal documents tellingly reveal that Heinz officials knew full well that there was nothing that they could do in 1994 or 1995 to limit their exposure for prior taxable years, with Mr. Crowe, Heinz's primary tax manager, soberly stating that "[n]othing can be done about the lack of substance in prior years" and that "[w]e must simply hope that our luck holds." Third, the record demonstrates that Heinz officials knew or should have known that the stock acquisition would not improve HCC's status in fiscal year 1995 or thereafter. In fact, they knew that there very likely would not be such subsequent years because, according to testimony, Heinz was contemporaneously planning to have HCC cease its Delaware lending operations, such as they were.

Overall, it strains credibility to imagine that, with state officials around the country actively pursuing the misuse of Delaware holding companies and with HCC already the target of various audits, Heinz officials seriously believed that having HCC act as a conduit, in purchasing and reselling its parent stock within the same fiscal year, would be viewed by state taxing officials as adding much of anything to HCC's "substance." Plaintiffs have not explained how they derived this conclusion—perhaps because they did not derive it at the time—nor have they cited a single case or authority suggesting that the transaction should have been the least bit helpful. Instead, they rely solely upon the self-serving and conclusory testimony of various Heinz executives, views that simply cannot be squared with the record. Indeed, at the time of the stock transaction, HCC already owned billions of dollars of Heinz-related debt and stock—holdings that apparently gave the Heinz tax professionals no solace. Over more than a decade, those tax professionals argued that HCC should take a more active role in managing its own affairs, have employees and be charged by Heinz for services being rendered—steps that Heinz officials ignored for many years and never fully adopted. Yet, plaintiffs would have this court believe that the same Heinz officials readily embraced a step never mentioned by those same tax professionals to combat a problem that had already matured, and with virtually no hope that the steps taken would have any salutary impact. In light of the objective evidence (or, in plaintiff's case, the lack thereof), it is far more believable that the Heinz officials never seriously entertained this thought, let alone reasonably so.

This court will not don blinders to the realities of the transaction before it. Stripped of its veneer, the acquisition by HCC of the Heinz stock had one purpose, and one purpose alone — producing capital losses that could be carried back to wipe out prior capital gains. There was no other genuine business purpose. As such, under the prevailing standard, the transaction in question must be viewed as a sham — a transaction imbued with no significant tax-independent considerations, but rather characterized, at least in terms of HCC's participation, solely by tax-avoidance features. The tax advantage sought by Heinz via this sham must be denied.

[The court further found that after applying "step transaction doctrine" principles, "HCC's ownership of the Heinz stock must be ignored, with Heinz being viewed as having acquired that stock on the market."]

Once it is determined that the purchase by Heinz of its stock from HCC did not qualify as a redemption within the meaning of section 317(b), the rest of the pieces of the puzzle readily fall into place. Because, under both the sham and step transaction doctrines, Heinz cannot be viewed as having obtained the stock from HCC in a transaction that qualified as a redemption under section 317(b) of the Code, the transfer of the 3,325,000 shares to Heinz did not cause a dividend to arise under section 302(d) of the Code. As such, the reattribution rules of Treasury Regulation § 1.302-2(c) were not triggered here and HCC's basis in the 175,000 shares it retained was not increased by the cost basis of the shares it relinquished. It follows, *a fortiori*, that the sale of the retained shares did not produce the capital losses claimed, making the loss carrybacks in question inappropriate.

### III. CONCLUSION

A Heinz promotion from the late 1950s and early 1960s touted its tomato ketchup by stating — "It's Red Magic Time!" But no amount of magic, red or otherwise, can hide the meat of the transactions in question, the connective tissues and gristle of which have been revealed by the multi-tined substance-over-form doctrine. *Sans sa sauce*, it becomes plain that plaintiffs' transaction simply was not "the thing which the statute intended." *Gregory*, 293 U.S. at 469. . . .

## *NOTES AND QUESTIONS*

1. *So what happened?* By the end of its opinion, the court finds that "the pieces of the puzzle readily fall into place." 76 Fed. Cl. at 593. But according to the court,

what exactly happened in this transaction? And which statutory provision is the court referring to when it states that the "transaction simply was not the thing which the statute intended"? Id. Does *Gregory* really provide support for the court's holding?

2. *Extraordinary dividend?* Read I.R.C. § 1059(e)(1)(A). In general, this rule applies to any redemption of stock that is not pro rata to all shareholders or that would not have been treated as a dividend but for the application of the option-attribution rule. In either case, any resulting dividend is treated as an extraordinary dividend to which section 1059(a) applies without regard to the period the redeemed shareholder held the stock. In *Heinz*, if the dividend to HCC had been treated as an extraordinary dividend subject to section 1059(a), it would have eliminated the subsequently claimed capital loss on the sale to AT&T.

So why didn't the government prevail on this straightforward, though technical, argument? One reason may have been section 1059(e)(2), which provides that an extraordinary dividend does not include any "qualifying dividend," within the meaning of section 243. Under section 243(b), a qualifying dividend is generally one between two corporations that are members of the same affiliated group. Because Heinz and HCC were members of such a group, the dividend technically qualified as a "qualifying dividend" and, therefore, perhaps did not constitute an extraordinary dividend. The potential conflict between section 1059(e)(1) and (2) has now been resolved in the regulations in favor of the former provision, but that resolution was not in effect for the taxable years involved in the *Heinz* case. See Reg. § 1.1059(e)-1(a) and (c).

Section 1059(e)(2) is generally designed to prevent a section 1059 basis reduction in cases where the same basis reduction is already mandated through the consolidated return regulations. Thus, if a dividend is distributed between members of an affiliated group filing a consolidated return, the recipient corporation must generally reduce its basis in the stock of the distributing corporation without regard to section 1059. See Reg. § 1.1502-32(b)(2)(iv) and (3)(v). Importantly, however, this rule does not apply to dividends distributed by the common parent corporation of the group (like Heinz) to one of its subsidiaries (like HCC). Therefore, from a policy standpoint, it would seem that section 1059(e)(2) should not have barred application of section 1059(a) with respect to Heinz's buyback of its stock held by HCC.

3. *More planning with options.* The option-attribution portion of section 1059(e)(1)(A) was added by Congress in 1997 in response to a widely publicized redemption by the Dupont corporation of its shares held by the Seagram corporation. Like the transaction in *Heinz*, the redemption by Dupont included an option granted to Seagram to purchase shares in Dupont in the future, and that option was key to the taxpayer's claim that the redemption should properly be characterized as a dividend. We examine certain other aspects of the Seagram-Dupont transaction in chapter eleven.

# Chapter 7

# Transfers to Controlled Corporations

This chapter concerns the taxation of transfers of property to corporations controlled by the transferor(s). Since 1921, such transactions have been treated under certain circumstances as "nonrecognition events," i.e., transactions in which the transferors do not recognize gain or loss. Rather, any gains or losses realized but not recognized in the transaction are preserved for later recognition. This rule facilitates the formation of corporate businesses and reflects a policy judgment that certain transfers merely change the form, and not the substance, of property ownership. The paradigmatic example is a transfer of property by a shareholder to a corporation wholly owned by the shareholder, such as the incorporation of a sole proprietorship. The tax treatment of these transactions previews the taxation of a broader class of nonrecognition events that are referred to as "reorganizations" and examined in chapters eleven and twelve.

In contrast to how certain property transfers *to* corporations are taxed, distributions of property *by* corporations to shareholders, including distributions to shareholders in control of the corporation, are generally treated as taxable events in which gain (and, in certain circumstances, loss) is recognized by the corporation. Although such distributions may also merely change the form and not the substance of property ownership, they are not granted similar nonrecognition treatment because of the practical difficulty of preserving for later recognition the amounts not recognized in the transaction. For example, appreciated property held by a C corporation is subject to two possible future taxes, at the corporate and shareholder levels. If gain is not recognized upon a distribution of the property out of corporate solution, then at least one of those future taxes would ordinarily be lost. As discussed in chapters five and six, current law avoids this problem by generally taxing both the corporation and the shareholder in a nonliquidating distribution, and chapter ten describes a similar result when the corporation liquidates.

Property transfers by shareholders to corporations do not encounter the same problem of potentially escaping tax. Indeed, if property enters a "double-tax" world, any pre-incorporation gain or loss not recognized in the transaction can be preserved *twice*, in the hands of both the shareholder-transferor and the corporate transferee, and current law generally follows that approach. As is common in the tax law, this goal is achieved by preserving after the transaction the transferor's basis in the property transferred. Such basis generally becomes both the corporate transferee's basis in the property transferred and the shareholder-transferor's basis in any corporate stock received in exchange for the property.

The pre-incorporation gain or loss not recognized in the transaction is preserved twice to make sure it does not escape taxation. Subsequent to the transfer, there may be a realization event by either the shareholder (through disposition of the corporate stock) or the corporation (through disposition of the property transferred). Current law ensures that either disposition will result in the recognition of the preserved amount of gain or loss. Unfortunately, there is no subsequent reconciliation of these amounts for C corporations to prevent double taxation of the pre-incorporation amounts. The possible doubling-up of pre-incorporation *losses* has long been a potentially attractive feature of these transactions and is now specifically restricted. Thus, under current law, gain, but not necessarily loss, is preserved twice.

Part A describes the basic tax rules when property is transferred by shareholders to corporations. As you will see, even though the policy objective of treating certain of these transactions as nonrecognition events is fairly straightforward, implementation of this goal raises a host of issues. Part B then examines how these transactions are taxed in the common circumstance where liabilities are included as part of the transfer. The possible doubling-up of losses, and changes in the timing of those losses, have created tax shelter opportunities, and part B details the anatomy of one prominent shelter involving liabilities.

## A. Transfers of Property by Shareholders to Corporations

Read I.R.C. §§ 351(a) and (d), 368(c), and 7701(a)(1) and Reg. § 1.351-1(a)(1) and (2), -1(b). Section 351(a) provides for the nonrecognition of gain or loss upon certain transfers of property to a corporation controlled by the transferor(s) in exchange for stock of the corporation. As you review the following materials describing the principal issues raised by this provision, consider which issues are a necessary consequence of any statutory line-drawing and which derive from specific policy choices made in section 351(a).

### 1. *The Required Transfer of "Property"*

#### James v. Commissioner

53 T.C. 63 (1969)

SIMPSON, Judge:

. . . The petitioners William A. James and Beryl N. James are husband and wife, and the petitioners C. N. Talbot and Lula E. Talbot are husband and wife. . . . For many years, Mr. James was a builder, real estate promoter, and developer. . . .

On January 12, 1963, Mr. and Mrs. Talbot entered into an agreement with Mr. James for the promotion and construction of a rental apartment project, consisting of not less than 50 apartments, the project to conform to Federal Housing Administration (FHA) standards. The agreement provided that on completion of the project the parties would form a corporation to take title to the project. The voting stock in such corporation was to be distributed one-half to the Talbots and one-half to Mr. James. . . . The Talbots agreed to transfer to the corporation the land on which the apartment project was to be built, such land to be the only asset contributed by the Talbots to the venture. Mr. James agreed "to promote the project . . . and . . . (to) be responsible for the planning, architectural work, construction, landscaping, legal fees, and loan processing of the entire project." . . .

After the execution of the January 12 agreement, Mr. James began negotiations to fulfill his part of the contract. He made arrangements with an attorney and an architectural firm to perform the work necessary to meet FHA requirements — development of legal documents, preparation of architectural plans, and the like; and he obtained from United Mortgagee Service Corp. (United Mortgagee), a lender, its agreement to finance the project and a commitment by FHA to insure the financing. . . .

On August 8, 1963, the FHA issued to United Mortgagee a commitment for the insurance of advances in the amount of $850,700 to Chicora Apartments, Inc., for the apartment project sponsored by Mr. James and the Talbots. On August 27, 1963, United Mortgagee sent Mr. James a draft of a proposed agreement to make a first mortgage loan of $850,700 on the Chicora Apartment project in accordance with Mr. James' application for such loan. . . .

On November 5, 1963, Chicora Apartments, Inc. (Chicora), was granted, upon application of Messrs. Talbot and James, a corporate charter, stating its authorized capital stock to consist of 20 no-par common shares. On the same date, the land on which the apartment project was to be constructed was conveyed to Chicora by Mrs. Talbot in consideration for 10 shares of stock. . . . Chicora's board of directors determined that on the date of this conveyance the value of the real property so transferred was $44,000. Also on November 5, 1963, 10 shares of stock were issued to Mr. James. The minutes of a meeting of Chicora's board of directors held on that date state that those 10 shares were issued to Mr. James in consideration of his "transfer" to the corporation of the "following described property":

1. FHA Commitment issued pursuant to Title 2, Section 207 of the National Housing Act, whereby the FHA agrees to insure a mortgage loan in the amount of $850,700.00, on a parcel of land in Myrtle Beach, South Carolina . . . provided 66 apartment units are constructed thereon . . .
2. Commitment from United Mortgagee Servicing Corp., agreeing to make a mortgage loan on said property in the amount of $850,700.00 and also commitment from said mortgagee to make an interim construction loan in an identical amount.
3. Certain contracts and agreement which W. A. James over the past two years have (sic) worked out and developed in connection with the architectural and construction services required for said project.

4. The use of the finances and credit of W. A. James during the past two years (and including the construction period) in order to make it possible to proceed with the project.

Thus, as a result of these transactions, Chicora had outstanding all 20 of its authorized shares of stock.

On November 6, 1963, the FHA issued to Chicora its commitment . . . in the amount of $850,700. Under FHA regulations, this commitment could not be issued to an individual, but was required to be issued to a corporation. . . .

The apartment project was built by W. A. James Construction Co. Construction was begun in late 1963 or early 1964, and the buildings were completed and occupancy begun on or about July 28, 1964. . . .

Both Mr. and Mrs. James and Mr. and Mrs. Talbot deemed their receipt of Chicora common stock to be in return for a transfer of property to a controlled corporation under section 351. Accordingly, neither family reported any income from such receipt on their respective income tax returns for 1963. In his statutory notice of deficiency, the respondent determined that Mr. James received such stock, with a value of $22,000, for services rendered and not in exchange for property, and thus received taxable income in that amount. He further determined that the Talbot's transfer of property to Chicora did not meet the requirements of section 351, with the result that they should have recognized a long-term capital gain of $14,675—the difference between $7,325, the basis of the land transferred, and $22,000, the value of the stock received.

## OPINION

The first, and critical, issue for our determination is whether Mr. James received his Chicora stock in exchange for the transfer of property or as compensation for services. The petitioners argue that he received such stock in consideration of his transfer to Chicora of the FHA and United Mortgagee commitments and that such commitments constituted "property" within the meaning of section 351. The respondent does not appear to challenge the petitioners' implicit assertion that Mr. James was not expected to render future services to the corporation in exchange for the issuance of stock to him. Although the accuracy of this assertion is subject to some question, the state of the record is such that we must decide the issues as the parties have presented them. Thus, the sole question on this issue is whether Mr. James' personal services, which the petitioners freely admit were rendered, resulted in the development of a property right which was transferred to Chicora, within the meaning of section 351.

Section 351(a) provides, in pertinent part:

> (a) GENERAL RULE.—No gain or loss shall be recognized if property is transferred to a corporation . . . by one or more persons solely in exchange for stock or securities in such corporation and immediately after the exchange such person or persons are in control (as defined in section 368(c)) of the corporation. For purposes of

> this section, stock or securities issued for services shall not be considered as issued in return for property.

The second sentence of this subsection was first included in the statute as a part of the 1954 Code, although it is said merely to restate the case law. . . . In explaining the second sentence, the House Ways and Means Committee stated:

> In accordance with this provision, such stock or securities received by a person who has rendered or will render services to the transferee corporation would be fully taxable as compensation upon receipt. Your committee does not intend, however, to vitiate the remaining portion of the transaction, through application of this provision. (H.R. Rep. No. 1337, 83d Cong., 2d Sess., p. A117 (1954).)

According to the petitioners' argument, Mr. James, as a result of the services performed by him, acquired certain contract rights which constituted property and which he transferred to Chicora. The fact that such rights resulted from the performance of personal services does not, in their view, disqualify them from being treated as property for purposes of section 351. In support of this position, the petitioners refer to situations involving the transfer of patents and secret processes. . . .

It is altogether clear that for purposes of section 351, not every right is to be treated as property. The second sentence of such section indicates that, whatever may be considered as property for purposes of local law, the performance of services, or the agreement to perform services, is not to be treated as a transfer of property for purposes of section 351. Thus, if in this case we have merely an agreement to perform services in exchange for stock of the corporation to be created, the performance of such services does not constitute the transfer of property within the meaning of section 351.

Although patents and secret processes — the product of services — are treated as property for purposes of section 351, we have carefully analyzed the arrangement in this case and have concluded that Mr. James did not transfer any property essentially like a patent or secret process; he merely performed services for Chicora. In January of 1963, he entered into an agreement to perform services for the corporation to be created. He was to secure the necessary legal and architectural work and to arrange for the financing of the project, and these were the services performed by him. Although he secured the services of the lawyer and the architect, they were paid for by the corporation. He put in motion the wheels that led to the FHA commitment, but it was not a commitment to him — it was a commitment to United Mortgagee to insure a loan to Chicora, a project sponsored by Mr. James. It was stipulated that under the FHA regulations, a commitment would not be issued to an individual, but only to a corporation. Throughout these arrangements, it was contemplated that a corporation would be created and that the commitment would run to the corporation. The petitioners rely heavily on the claim that Mr. James had a right to the commitment, that such right constituted property, and that such right was transferred to the corporation in return for his stock. However, the commitment was not his to transfer; he never acquired ownership of the commitment — he could not and did not undertake to acquire such ownership. The evidence as to the commitment by United Mortgagee to make a loan for the construction of the project is somewhat incomplete, but since all the parties knew that a corporation was to be formed and that the FHA commitment would be made to that corporation, it seems clear that there was no commitment to loan to Mr. James the funds necessary for the construction of the project. Thus, throughout these arrangements, Mr. James never undertook to acquire anything for himself; he was, in accordance with his agreement with the Talbots, making the preliminary arrangements for the construction of the apartment project. The enterprise would be operated, once the initial steps were completed, by a corporation, Chicora, and everything that was done by him was done on behalf of the contemplated corporation. In these circumstances, it seems clear that Mr. James received his share of the stock in the corporation in return for the services performed by him and that he did not transfer any property, within the meaning of section 351, to the corporation. . . .

The facts of this case are substantially similar to those in U.S. v. Frazell, 335 F.2d 487 (C.A. 5, 1964). . . . In that case, the taxpayer, a geologist, investigated certain oil and gas properties to be acquired by a joint venture, and he was to receive an interest in the joint venture. However, before any transfer was made to him, a corporation was formed to take over the assets of the joint venture, and part of the stock was transferred to the taxpayer. It was not clear whether the taxpayer acquired an interest in the joint venture which was then exchanged for his share of the stock or whether he acquired the stock directly in exchange for the services performed by him. The court found that, in either event, the taxpayer received compensation for his services. If he received the stock in return for the services performed by him, such stock was taxable as compensation; and he did not transfer any property to the corporation within the meaning of section 351. . . .

The next question is whether the Talbots are taxable on the gain realized from the exchange of their land for Chicora stock. Section 351(a) applies only if immediately after the transfer those who transferred property in exchange for stock owned at least 80 percent of Chicora's stock. Sec. 368(c). Since Mr. James is not to be treated as a transferor of property, he cannot be included among those in control for purposes of this test. . . . The transferors of property, the Talbots, did not have the required 80-percent control of Chicora immediately after the transfer, and therefore, their gain must be recognized. This result is inconsistent with the apparent meaning of the second sentence from the committee report, but the statutory scheme does not permit any other conclusion. . . .

## *NOTES AND QUESTIONS*

1. *Transfers of "property."* Section 351 is limited to transfers of "property" in exchange for stock and specifically does not apply to the receipt of stock for services. The prohibition applies to both past and future services rendered to the issuing corporation. Reg. § 1.351-1(a)(1)(i). The service-provider must generally recognize ordinary income equal to the fair market value of the stock received and, depending upon the nature of the compensation, the issuing corporation may either deduct the

value of the stock or treat it as a capital expenditure. I.R.C. § 83(a), (h); Reg. § 1.83-6(a)(4). The IRS disregards the provision of services that are merely ancillary and subsidiary to the transfer of property in a qualifying section 351 transaction. See Rev. Rul. 64-56, 1964-1 C.B. 133.

2. *What is "property"?* The definition of "property" contained in section 317(a) only applies for purposes of part 1 of subchapter C (I.R.C. §§ 301-318); there is no statutory or regulatory definition of the term for purposes of section 351. A sometimes difficult question is whether rights created from services, such as "know-how" or related intangible rights, have sufficiently matured to qualify as "property" rather than the provision of services. As illustrated by *James*, a further issue is whether any property rights created through the services of the transferor represent rights belonging to the transferor that are transferred to the transferee in a section 351 transaction.

Hempt Bros., Inc. v. U.S., 490 F.2d 1172 (3d Cir. 1974), cert. denied, 419 U.S. 826 (1974), involved the incorporation of an entire business previously owned and operated by a cash-basis partnership. The taxpayer (the corporate transferee) contended that one of the assets transferred in the incorporation — an account receivable — did not constitute "property" for purposes of section 351. Although the taxpayer's position would have required the partnership to recognize gain on the transfer of the zero-basis receivable, an IRS challenge of that transaction was likely barred by the statute of limitations. Meanwhile, the taxpayer's position would also have produced a fair market value basis in the receivable that would have offset the taxpayer's income upon collection of the amount due. The court concluded that the receivable qualified as property for purposes of section 351.

Suppose Mr. James was a cash method taxpayer who performed services for Chicora in exchange for its promise to pay him in the future. Could he then have transferred his receivable to the corporation in exchange for stock and obtained nonrecognition treatment in that transaction?

3. *Transfer of income rights and tax benefit rule.* In *Hempt Bros.*, supra, the court also concluded that assignment of income principles generally do not trump section 351. Thus, a cash-basis transferor is generally not taxed upon transfer of an income right to a corporation in connection with a qualifying section 351 transaction, either at the time of the transfer or upon collection of the income, at least where the income right is transferred as part of its associated business and there is a valid business purpose for the transfer. The IRS has acquiesced in this result under these circumstances. See Rev. Rul. 80-198, 1980-2 C.B. 113. In addition, the tax benefit rule generally does not override section 351 to tax the transferor when a previously deducted item, such as a bad debt reserve of an accrual basis transferor, is included in the transfer. See Nash v. U.S., 398 U.S. 1 (1970); Rev. Rul. 78-280, 1978-2 C.B. 139 (approving *Nash* and specifying required basis adjustments to prevent double benefit).

4. *Transfers to investment companies.* A transfer of property does not qualify for nonrecognition treatment under section 351 if it is made to an investment company. I.R.C. § 351(e)(1). In general, this rule disqualifies certain transfers that result in a

diversification of the transferor's interest, and is consistent with the policy of excluding from the scope of section 351 transactions that effect a substantive change in the transferor's property ownership. See Reg. § 1.351-1(c)(1)(i).

5. *Impact on non-service-providers.* As shown in *James*, whether a taxpayer has provided property or services to a corporation may affect the tax consequences of non-service-providers in the same transaction, such as the Talbots. Read carefully Reg. § 1.351-1(a)(2) (ex. 3). Is the conclusion of this example consistent with the holding in *James*? How would you reconcile the two?

## 2. *The "Control" Requirement*

### Kamborian's Estate v. Commissioner

469 F.2d 219 (1st Cir. 1972)

ALDRICH, Senior Circuit Judge.

[The taxpayers were four individuals who collectively owned about 76 percent of the stock of X corporation. Two of the individuals were also trustees of a trust that owned about 13 percent of the X stock (50,000 shares). Taxpayers also owned all of the stock of Y corporation. For bona fide business reasons, X acquired all of the Y stock from the taxpayers in exchange for 22,871 shares of X common stock, some of which was nonvoting. In the same exchange, the trust purchased an additional 418 X shares from X for cash. These two transactions increased the taxpayers' combined holdings in X to 77.3 percent and reduced the trust's interest to just under 13 percent, notwithstanding its purchase. However, the combined holdings of taxpayers and the trust remained in excess of 80 percent, and taxpayers took the position that the transactions were both tax-free exchanges under section 351. The Commissioner disagreed, claiming that the "control" group should be limited to the taxpayers as the former owners of the Y stock. In refusing to include the trust's purchase, the Commissioner relied, in part, upon Reg. § 1.351-1(a)(1)(ii).]

... The Tax Court ruled in favor of the Commissioner ... and taxpayers ... make a frontal attack on the regulation, urging us to hold it invalid as going beyond what they claim is a plain and positive statute.

We start with the general proposition expressed in section [1001(c)] of the Code:

> Except as otherwise provided in this subtitle, on the sale or exchange of property the entire amount of the gain or loss, determined under section 1001, shall be recognized.

Section 351 provides: ...

> (a) General Rule.—No gain or loss shall be recognized if property is transferred to a corporation by one or more persons solely in exchange for stock or securities in such corporation and immediately after the exchange such person or persons are in control (as defined in section 368(c)) of the corporation.

"Control" is defined in section 368(c) as the possession of 80% of the stock of the transferee corporation.

Taxpayers' brief contains a wistful aside that there is involved a large tax and only a small discrepancy. We are not moved, legally or emotionally, by this fact. But in order to avoid any overfall therefrom, we will imagine another case that would have to be decided against the government if taxpayers are correct and all arranged transactions, regardless of their purpose or their connection with one another, are to be viewed as a single exchange. Let us suppose that P owns 10% and S 90% of the stock of W, and P owns all of the stock of Z. If P transfers his Z stock to W for further W shares, ending up with a 30% interest, it is obviously not a tax-free exchange. But if P induces S to buy, contemporaneously, one share of W stock for cash the present petitioners would say that P and S are to be considered jointly as exchanging property, and since together they owned over 80% of the transferee corporation, P may claim the statutory exception.

Our analysis does not lead to such a result. By the term "property [that] is transferred," the statute contemplates a single transaction, even though, as it goes on to recognize, there may be a number of transferors or participants. What is a transaction must be determined in the light of the statutory purpose, lest taxpayers be allowed to frustrate that purpose by manipulation of clearly taxable exchanges. *Cf.* Knetsch v. U.S., 364 U.S. 361, 365-366 (1960); Goldstein v. Comm'r, 364 F.2d 734, 740-742 (2d Cir. 1966), *cert. denied* 385 U.S. 1005. We stated that purpose long ago in speaking of the predecessor of section 351, which contains no presently material variance.

> "It is the purpose of Section 112(b)(5) to save the taxpayer from an immediate recognition of a gain, or to intermit the claim of a loss, in certain transactions where gain or loss may have accrued in a constitutional sense, but where in a popular and economic sense there has been a mere change in the form of ownership and the taxpayer has not really 'cashed in' on the theoretical gain, or closed out a losing venture." Portland Oil Co. v. Comm'r, 109 F.2d 479, 488 (1st Cir. 1940), *cert. denied* 310 U.S. 650.

Thus in our hypothetical, considering P alone, there was not a "mere change in the form of ownership." Before the transaction P "owned" Z corporation, since he owned 100% of its stock. After the transaction his ownership of Z was reduced to 30% because he held only a 30% interest in W, the transferee corporation. In keeping with "economic sense" a taxpayer may be allowed a certain amount of slack. This has been ruled to be 20%; and had P ended with an 80% interest in W, and thus of Z, his ownership of the latter would not be thought to be materially changed. Sec. 368(c). But where P does not own that 80% it can be permissible to consider transfers by other owners only if those transfers were, in economic terms, sufficiently related to P's to make all of the transfers parts of a single transaction.

It is possible that a valid association may exist even when different types of property are transferred to the transferee corporation by different transferors.

Thus in Halliburton v. Comm'r, 78 F.2d 265 (9th Cir. 1935), funds contributed by other parties were found to be as necessary to the overall purpose of the transaction as was the exchange by the litigating taxpayers. In our P and S case, however, there is no economic connection, and hence no basis for regarding the two transfers as parts of one transaction, and hence of considering P and S as a unit in terms of control. If a taxpayer were able, so simply, to effect a concatenation and say that the statute applied to him, the statute would be meaningless.

The instant case presents no better claim of a connection in an economic sense. The four shareholders of Y decided it would be advantageous to merge Y with X. Finding themselves short of the requirements for tax-free treatment, they persuaded a shareholder of X, who was a complete stranger to Y, to make a token purchase of X shares. Other than the fact that the trust's participation was incorporated into the acquisition agreement, there was no relation between the exchange of Y shares and this very minor purchase. The trust transferred no Y shares. The cash it contributed to X—$5,000 for 418 shares of a corporation with nearly 400,000 shares outstanding—could have had no significant impact on X's ability to conduct its business. The trustees' desire to help the Y stockholders avoid taxes, warrantably found by the Tax Court to have been the primary motive for the trust's purchase, cannot be used to make a single transaction out of otherwise unrelated transfers. . . .

## *NOTES AND QUESTIONS*

1. *"Control" held by a "control group."* As explained by the court (quoting from *Portland Oil*), a requirement that the transferee corporation be controlled by the transferor in a qualifying section 351 transaction flows from a policy objective of limiting the nonrecognition provision to mere changes in the form of property ownership. For purposes of section 351, "control" is defined in section 368(c) to refer to stock possessing at least 80 percent of the total combined voting power of all classes of stock entitled to vote and at least 80 percent of the total number of shares of all other classes of stock. Rev. Rul. 59-259, 1959-2 C.B. 115, explains that the latter condition is met only if the taxpayer owns at least 80 percent of *each class* of non-voting stock.

Section 351 is not limited, however, to property transfers carried out by just one person. Nonrecognition treatment is also potentially available to two or more persons who transfer property to a corporation in the same transaction. Even if no single person ends up with as much as 80 percent of the stock of the corporate transferee, each person may receive nonrecognition treatment if they collectively end up with the necessary control. The concept of a "control group," which permits the incorporation of ventures owned by more than one person to be tax-free, may in certain circumstances conflict with the policy objective of limiting section 351 transactions to transfers constituting a mere change in form of property ownership. A transaction may be tax-free to all transferors even though each of them has exchanged an independent, wholly-owned property interest for a fractional interest in a much larger venture.

The concept of a control group requires a determination of which transfers should be considered together. In *Kamborian's Estate*, the court indicated that there should be some "economic connection" between the various transfers, but there is no such condition in the statute or regulations. (If such a condition were included, how would it be defined and enforced?) Instead, the regulations merely focus on the timing of the transfers — they need not be simultaneous, but must proceed pursuant to previously defined rights "with an expedition consistent with orderly procedure." Reg. § 1.351-1(a)(1) (fifth sentence). Case law has interpreted this requirement quite liberally. See Portland Oil Co. v. Comm'r, 109 F.2d 479, 488-89 (1st Cir. 1940), cert. denied, 310 U.S. 650 (1940) (treating together, for purposes of the predecessor to section 351, transfers that were 28 days apart and pursuant merely to a non-binding mutual understanding).

Control need not be obtained as a result of the transfers; the control group merely needs to be *in control* of the transferee immediately after the exchange. This requirement opens up the possibility, illustrated in *Kamborian's Estate*, of a person with a preexisting interest in the transferee accommodating other parties by joining their transfers of property to the transferee. Regulation § 1.351-1(a)(1)(ii), the provision whose validity was upheld in *Kamborian's Estate*, authorizes the disregard of transferors who receive stock that is of relatively small value compared to the value of their preexisting holding, if the primary purpose of the transfer is to qualify the exchange of other transferors under section 351. The same provision applies to transferors who receive stock of relatively small value compared to the value of services performed by the transferor for the transferee; this prevents otherwise excluded service-providers from being included within the control group through the additional transfer of a small property interest. The IRS defines "of relatively small value" to mean less than ten percent of the value of the purported transferor's preexisting holding in the transferee (or the value of services performed for the transferee). Rev. Proc. 77-37, 1977-2 C.B. 568, 570.

2. *Control "immediately after the exchange."* The requirement that the transferors be in control of the transferee immediately after the exchange presents the oft-litigated question of whether dispositions of stock subsequent to the exchange should be considered. For example, in Intermountain Lumber Co. v. Comm'r, 65 T.C. 1025 (1976), the court held (at the behest of the taxpayer) that section 351(a) did not apply to a transfer of property to a corporation in exchange for all of the corporation's stock. The court concluded that, in determining whether the transferor had control immediately after the exchange, the existence of a prearranged plan resulting in the transferor losing control over the corporation had to be taken into account.

The absence of any comparable requirement regarding the period property must be held *prior to* a purported section 351 transaction provides tax planning opportunities. For example, assume that G has a binding obligation to transfer to H one-half of the stock of a new corporation that is about to be formed. If G transfers property to a corporation in exchange for all of its stock and then transfers half of the stock to H pursuant to the binding agreement, the property transfer to the corporation may not qualify under section 351 based on the holding in *Intermountain Lumber*. If section 351 is inapplicable, G may have to recognize gain or loss on the entire property interest transferred to the corporation. Suppose, instead, G transfers a half-interest in the property to H prior to the formation of the corporation, followed by a joint transfer by G and H of their respective half-interests in the property to a corporation in exchange for all of its stock. Although the transfer of the half-interest in the property to H may be taxable to G (with roughly the same tax consequence as the transfer of half the stock to H under the original plan), the joint transfers to the corporation by G and H may qualify under section 351. If so, G would not have to recognize any gain or loss on the transfer of the half-interest in the property directly to the corporation.

Rev. Rul. 2003-51, 2003-1 C.B. 938, involved a taxpayer who lost control over the corporate transferee as a result of a subsequent *nontaxable* transfer of the transferee's stock. The taxpayer transferred a business to a wholly-owned corporation and then immediately thereafter transferred the transferee's stock to another corporation in exchange for all of its stock. As a result of the two steps, which were undertaken pursuant to a prearranged binding agreement, the taxpayer created a holding company structure in which the taxpayer's original business was held by the subsidiary corporation. As is evident, the transaction appeared to change merely the form of the taxpayer's property interest. Because there is no attribution rule applicable to section 351 that would treat the taxpayer as retaining control over the subsidiary corporation through attribution from the holding company, however, there was a technical violation of the control requirement. The IRS held that since the second transfer qualified under section 351, the first transfer should not be treated as inconsistent with that provision despite this technical violation.

In general, in the case of a corporate transferor of property in a purported section 351 transaction, a subsequent distribution by such transferor of the transferee's stock is not taken into account in determining whether the transferor(s) have control of the transferee immediately after the transfer. I.R.C. § 351(c)(1). These steps may be part of a qualifying divisive reorganization, discussed in chapter twelve.

3. *Service-providers and control.* As shown in *James* (p. 246), a person who merely provides services to the corporate transferee is generally not included as a member of the control group. Thus, any stock received by such person may not be counted in determining whether the control requirement is met. A different result may occur, however, if the person provides services to someone else. For example, suppose D transfers property to a new corporation that issues one-half of its stock to each of D and E, and the stock issued to E represents compensation for services previously rendered by E *to D*. Does section 351 apply to this transaction?

See Reg. § 1.351-1(b)(1) and (2) (ex. 1). Would it matter if, prior to the transaction, D had a binding obligation to compensate E in this manner?

4. *S corporations.* Section 351 applies to property transfers to both C and S corporations. The special tax rules applicable to S corporations, however, sometimes interact with section 351 in unusual ways. Consider the application of the "accommodation transferor" rule discussed in *Kamborian's Estate* to the following situation. A and B own equal shares of Z corporation, which is and has always been an S corporation. The corporation is worth $600 and each shareholder has a $100 basis in her stock. The parties agree for C to become a one-third shareholder in the corporation by transferring $300 worth of property (in which C has a $50 basis) to Z for Z stock. Prior to C's transfer, Z distributes $100 cash pro rata to each of A and B. The three individuals then make simultaneous transfers to Z in exchange for Z stock: C transfers her property and A and B each transfers $100. What are the tax consequences of these transactions to the parties?

5. *Overlap.* Neither the facts of *Kamborian's Estate* nor the court's hypothetical example resembles an incorporation transaction. Rather, each might more accurately be described as an *acquisition* by one corporation of another. Yet apparently, section 351 might apply to each transaction, and would have applied, if the facts had been slightly different. The taxation of the *Kamborian's Estate* transaction under other provisions is considered in chapters eight (concerning certain transfers of stock involving commonly controlled corporations) and eleven (concerning nondivisive reorganizations).

### 3. *"Solely for Stock" Requirement*

Section 351(a) applies to transfers of property solely in exchange for stock of the corporate transferee. What happens if, in addition to such stock, the transferor also receives money or other (nonqualifying) property, generally referred to as "boot"? In that case, the transferor must recognize any gain (but not loss) realized, but only up to the amount of money plus the fair market value of any property received. Read I.R.C. § 351(b) and the following ruling. At the time of the ruling, a taxpayer recognized long-term capital gain or loss if she sold or exchanged a capital asset held for over six months.

## Rev. Rul. 68-55

1968-1 C.B. 140

. . . Corporation Y was organized by [corporation] X and A, an individual who owned no stock in X. A transferred 20x dollars to Y in exchange for stock of Y having a fair market value of 20x dollars and X transferred to Y three separate assets and received in exchange stock of Y having a fair market value of 100x dollars plus cash of 10x dollars. In accordance with the facts set forth in the table below if X had sold at fair market value each of the three assets it transferred to Y, the result would have been as follows:

| | *Asset I* | *Asset II* | *Asset III* |
|---|---|---|---|
| Character of asset | Capital asset held more than 6 months | Capital asset held not more than 6 months | Section 1245 property |
| Fair market value | $22x | $33x | $55x |
| Adjusted basis | 40x | 20x | 25x |
| Gain (loss) | $18x | $13x | $30x |
| Character of gain or loss | Long-term capital loss | Short-term capital gain | Ordinary income |

The facts in the instant case disclose that with respect to the section 1245 property the depreciation subject to recapture exceeds the amount of gain that would be recognized on a sale at fair market value. Therefore, all of such gain would be treated as ordinary income under section 1245(a)(1) of the Code.

Under section 351(a) of the Code, no gain or loss is recognized if property is transferred to a corporation solely in exchange for its stock and immediately after the exchange the transferor is in control of the corporation. If section 351(a) of the Code would apply to an exchange but for the fact that there is received, in addition to the property permitted to be received without recognition of gain, other property or money, then under section 351(b) of the Code gain (if any) to the recipient will be recognized, but in an amount not in excess of the sum of such money and the fair market value of such other property received, and no loss to the recipient will be recognized.

The first question presented is how to determine the amount of gain to be recognized under section 351(b) of the Code. The general rule is that each asset transferred must be considered to have been separately exchanged. . . . Thus, for purposes of making computations under section 351(b) of the Code, it is not proper to total the bases of the various assets transferred and to subtract this total from the fair market value of the total consideration received in the exchange. Moreover, any treatment other than an asset-by-asset approach would have the effect of allowing losses that are specifically disallowed by section 351(b)(2) of the Code.

The second question presented is how, for purposes of making computations under section 351(b) of the Code, to allocate the cash and stock received to the amount realized as to each asset transferred in the exchange. The asset-by-asset approach for computing the amount of gain realized in the exchange requires that for this purpose the fair market value of each category of consideration received must be separately allocated to the transferred assets in proportion to the relative fair market values of the transferred assets. . . .

Accordingly, the amount and character of the gain recognized in the exchange should be computed as follows:

| | *Total* | *Asset I* | *Asset II* | *Asset III* |
|---|---|---|---|---|
| Fair market value of asset transferred | $110x | $22x | $33x | $55x |
| Percent of total fair market value | — | 20% | 30% | 50% |
| Fair market value of Y stock received in exchange | $100x | $20x | $30x | $50x |
| Cash received in exchange | 10x | 2x | 3x | 5x |
| Amount realized | $110x | $22x | $33x | $55x |
| Adjusted basis | — | 40x | 20x | 25x |
| Gain (loss) realized | — | ($18x) | $13x | $30x |

Under section 351(b)(2) of the Code the loss of 18x dollars realized on the exchange of Asset Number I is not recognized. Such loss may not be used to offset the gains realized on the exchanges of the other assets. Under section 351(b)(1) of the Code, the gain of 13x dollars realized on the exchange of Asset Number II will be recognized as short-term capital gain in the amount of 3x dollars, the amount of cash received. Under sections 351(b)(1) and 1245(b)(3) of the Code, the gain of 30x dollars realized on the exchange of Asset Number III will be recognized as ordinary income in the amount of 5x dollars, the amount of cash received.

## *NOTES*

1. *Securities and nonqualified preferred stock of the transferee.* The "solely for stock" requirement represents an additional condition to distinguish a qualifying section 351 transaction from a *sale* of the transferred property in which the transferor must recognize gain or loss. The statute has been amended to narrow the type of consideration that qualifies for nonrecognition treatment under section 351. Formerly, a transfer of property in exchange for *securities* of the transferee (generally, a long-term debt instrument) qualified for such treatment, but this is no longer permitted. (The regulations have not been fully updated to reflect this change. See, e.g., Reg. § 1.351-1(a)(1).) In addition, a transfer in exchange for "nonqualified preferred stock" ("NQPS") of the transferee is generally taxed as if the transferor received boot, and not stock, on the theory that such preferred stock represents a more secure form of investment than the property transferred. See I.R.C. § 351(g). In general, NQPS refers to preferred stock with certain debt features such as a put option by the holder, a call option by the issuer that is either mandatory or likely to be exercised, or a debt-like rate of return.

The legislative history indicates that until the regulations provide otherwise, NQPS continues to be treated as "stock" for other purposes in section 351. To illustrate the significance of this rule, suppose that A transfers property to corporation X in exchange for 90 percent of its common stock, and B owns all of X's nonvoting NQPS, acquired in an unrelated transaction. For purposes of determining whether A's transfer qualifies under section 351, the NQPS is treated as X stock. Hence, A's transfer fails to satisfy section 351, since A does not control X immediately after the exchange. If, in exchange for property, B acquires the NQPS in the same transaction as A's, then section 351(a) applies to A's transfer. Since B receives no qualifying property, however, B's transfer falls outside of section 351(a) and therefore B must recognize gain or loss. I.R.C. §§ 351(g)(1)(A), 1001. If B receives some of X's common stock in addition to the NQPS, then B would be taxed under section 351(b); the NQPS would be treated as boot and B would recognize gain (but not loss). I.R.C. § 351(g)(1)(B).

2. *Stock rights and contingent stock.* For purposes of section 351, a right to acquire stock, such as a stock option, is generally treated as boot and not stock. Reg. § 1.351-1(a)(1) (last sentence). However, a right to receive stock that is contingent upon the occurrence or nonoccurrence of a specified future event, such as the satisfaction of an earnings target after the transfer of property to a corporation, may be treated in certain circumstances as "stock" for purposes of section 351. In contrast to a holder of a stock option, a transferor receiving contingent stock need take no positive action nor provide any additional consideration in order to receive additional stock of the transferee. The IRS treats contingent stock as stock for purposes of section 351 so long as the holder's rights are not assignable and cannot ripen into anything other than additional stock of the transferee. See Hamrick v. Comm'r, 43 T.C. 21 (1964), acq. in result only, 1966-1 C.B. 2; Rev. Rul. 66-112, 1966-1 C.B. 68.

3. *Asset-by-asset (or "tracing") versus "aggregate" approaches.* Rev. Rul. 68-55 illustrates an asset-by-asset or tracing approach in allocating boot received by the transferor to each of the properties transferred in order to determine the amount and character of the gain recognized. There is, however, generally no similar allocation of the stock received by the transferor to each of multiple properties transferred. Although such stock is received without the recognition of gain or loss in a qualifying section 351 transaction, the transferor's basis and holding period in the stock depend upon the properties transferred. In general, under section 358(a), the transferor's basis in any stock received in a section 351 transaction is the same as the transferor's basis in the property transferred. In addition, under section 1223(1), the transferor obtains a "tacked" holding period in the stock received (equal to the transferor's holding period in the property transferred), but only if the property is a capital asset or section 1231 property. (The transferor obtains a new or "fresh" holding period in stock received in exchange for any other property.) In determining the transferor's basis and holding period in stock received in a section 351 transaction, an "aggregate" approach rather than a tracing method is generally used.

To illustrate, assume that in a qualifying section 351 transaction, A transfers an account receivable (FMV of $40, basis to A of $0) and land (FMV of $60, basis to A of $90) to corporation X in exchange for all ten shares of X. The land is a capital asset held by A for two years; the account receivable is a section 1221(a)(4) asset. If current law used a tracing method, then A would hold after the exchange four X shares (representing the portion of such shares allocable to the account receivable) with a basis of $0 and a new holding period. In the remaining six X shares, A would have a basis of $90 ($15/share basis) and a holding period of two years. In contrast, under the aggregate approach currently followed, A would hold all ten shares with an aggregate basis of $90 ($9/share basis) and with a split holding period (40 percent of each share would have a zero holding period and 60 percent would have a two-year holding period). See Rev. Rul. 85-164, 1985-2 C.B. 117. The aggregate approach provides fewer planning opportunities for taxpayers compared to the tracing approach. The aggregate approach is also used if the transferor receives stock of different classes, although the aggregate basis in the properties transferred must be allocated between the classes of stock received based on the relative fair market values of the stock in each class. Reg. § 1.358-2(b)(2).

### 4. *Preservation of Gain or Loss Not Recognized in Section 351 Transaction*

Gain or loss not recognized in a section 351 transaction is deferred for future recognition by generally preserving the transferor's basis in any property transferred in both the transferee's basis in such property and the transferor's basis in any stock received. I.R.C. §§ 358(a), 362(a). These general rules must be adjusted, however, to take into account any boot received and gain recognized in the transaction. If boot is received, the transferor obtains a basis in the boot equal to its fair market value. I.R.C. § 358(a)(2). As a result, the total amount of the transferor's preserved basis—the transferor's aggregate basis in any properties transferred—must be reduced by the fair market value of any boot plus the amount of money received; only the remaining amount is available to be allocated to the transferor's basis in stock of the transferee. I.R.C. § 358(a)(1)(A). At the same time, any gain recognized in the transaction need not be preserved for future recognition. This goal is achieved by increasing (by the amount of gain recognized) both the transferor's basis in the stock received and the transferee's basis in the property transferred. See I.R.C. §§ 358(a)(1)(B), 362(a).

A further adjustment is required to prevent a section 351 transaction from doubling up certain pre-incorporation losses of the transferor. Under section 362(e)(2), if the transferee's aggregate basis in property transferred by a given transferor in a section 351 transaction exceeds the aggregate fair market value of such property immediately after the transaction, then the transferee's basis must be reduced by such excess. Under this rule, a transferor may still be able to double up pre-incorporation losses in individual items of property transferred so long as there is no *net* doubling up of losses after taking into account all of the properties transferred by the transferor in the transaction (and any gain recognized). Any required reduction in basis must be allocated to individual assets in proportion to the amount of built-in loss in such asset at the time of the transfer. In providing this limitation, Congress was ambivalent regarding whether the transferee's basis (in properties transferred) or the transferor's basis (in stock received) should be reduced. In general, the transferee must reduce basis but the parties may jointly elect to have the transferor reduce stock basis instead.

Read I.R.C. §§ 358(a) and (b)(1), 362(a) and (e)(2), 1001(a) - (c), 1032, 1223(1) and (2), 7701(a)(42) - (45), and Reg. § 1.358-2(b), and do the following problem:

**Problem 7-1:**

(a) Jones, the sole shareholder of T Corporation, transfers to T two parcels of land (both capital assets held by Jones for two years), Gainacre (FMV = $10,000, basis = $5,000) and Lossacre (FMV = $10,000, basis = $12,000), and some inventory (a section 1221(a)(1) asset) (FMV = $5,000, basis = $2,000), in exchange for T common stock worth $15,000, T preferred stock worth $5,000, and $5,000 cash. Assume that the preferred stock is not "nonqualified preferred stock." Determine the tax consequences of the transaction to all parties.

(b) Same as (a), except that Jones's basis in Lossacre was $20,000 immediately prior to the transfer to T.

(c) Assume that just prior to the transfers described in (b), Smith owned all of T's stock, valued at $100,000. As part of the same transaction as Jones's transfers, Smith contributed $5,000 cash to T in exchange for additional T stock.

(d) Same as (c), except that Smith and Jones are married to each other.

*NOTES*

1. *Limiting loss duplication and importation.* In Shell Petroleum, Inc. v. U.S., 102 A.F.T.R.2d (RIA) 5085 (S.D. Tex. 2008), involving a year prior to the effective date of section 362(e)(2), the court held that losses were doubled up upon the transfer in a section 351 transaction of certain oil and gas property that had depreciated in value. In reaching its decision, the court considered the statute as well as the business purpose and economic substance doctrines; relying in part on *UPS* (p. 125), it distinguished *Coltec* (infra p. 287). Although not discussed in the case, section 269 authorizes the disallowance of tax benefits resulting from certain corporate acquisitions if the principal purpose of the acquisition is tax avoidance; section 269 has also traditionally played a role in policing the doubling-up of built-in losses. See Reg. § 1.269-3(c)(1).

A separate rule, which applies in lieu of section 362(e)(2) if both are applicable, reduces the transferee's basis in contributed property in the case of certain nonrecognition transfers when the transferee, but not the transferor, is subject to U.S. tax. I.R.C. § 362(e)(1). The specific case Congress had in mind was the transfer of property with a built-in loss by a person not subject to U.S. tax, such as certain foreign corporations, to a taxable U.S. person. Since recognition of the loss by the transferor would not have resulted in any U.S. tax benefit, Congress did not want any such benefit to be created in the hands of the transferee. Like section 362(e)(2), this provision only applies in cases where the transferee's aggregate basis in property transferred in the transaction exceeds the fair market value of such property immediately after the transaction. The provision applies to section 351 transactions as well as certain other tax-free transfers that preserve basis.

2. *Zero basis problem.* The application of sections 1032 and 351 in transactions involving parent and subsidiary corporations can potentially produce anomalous results. For example, if P corporation issues stock for cash and contributes the cash to its subsidiary (S corporation), P recognizes no gain or loss under section 1032(a) and P's basis in its S stock is increased by the amount of cash. Suppose, instead, P contributes its stock to S, which then sells the P stock for cash. Although this alternative produces the same economic result as the first transaction, it may have different tax consequences. Since corporations generally have a zero basis in their own stock, P's contribution of its stock to S, if qualifying under section 351, would generally leave P's basis in its S stock unchanged. I.R.C. § 358(a). Further, because S would generally receive the P stock with a zero basis (I.R.C. § 362(a)) and section 1032 provides a nonrecognition result only when a corporation transfers its *own* stock, S's disposition of the P stock may be a taxable event. The *Lessinger* case (infra p. 271) illustrates a similar zero-basis problem when a taxpayer's debt obligation is transferred in a section 351 transaction.

The flaw illustrated by this example is the preservation of a built-in gain in the hands of both P (in the S stock) and S (in the P stock) when P contributes its stock to S in a section 351 transaction. As we have seen, the statutory objective is generally to preserve twice any built-in amount of the transferor in the property transferred. In this case, however, there is no built-in amount of the transferor (P) in the property transferred (P stock) since section 1032(a) allows P to transfer such property without recognizing gain or loss. Hence, there is no reason for any gain or loss to be preserved in the hands of P or S immediately following the transaction.

The IRS permits a subsidiary to dispose of its parent's stock without the recognition of gain or loss in certain triangular reorganizations (discussed in chapter eleven) or where the subsidiary essentially acts as a conduit for the disposition of such stock by the parent. See Reg. § 1032-2 and -3. The zero basis problem persists, however, in other cases. See Rev. Rul. 2006-2, 2006-1 C.B. 261 (indicating that problem remains under study). One possible solution would be to give corporations a fair market value, rather than zero, basis in their own shares. Because this rule would violate the fundamental tax principle that "basis" represents amounts of previously taxed income, it would need to be accompanied by additional rules to prevent the creation of non-economic tax losses. For example, if a parent corporation transfers its stock to a subsidiary in a nontaxable transaction and the subsidiary sells the stock after it has declined in value, it might be necessary to prevent the subsidiary from recognizing a loss upon such sale.

3. *Taxation of boot to controlled corporation and transferor.* If the controlled corporation exchanges boot consisting of appreciated property in a section 351 transaction, it must recognize gain as if it distributed the boot to the transferor-shareholder in a nonliquidating distribution. I.R.C. §§ 351(f), 311(a), (b)(1). Thus, it generally makes no difference to the controlled corporation whether it distributes appreciated property to its shareholders or exchanges such property in a section 351 transaction. These alternatives may, however, make a difference to the transferor-shareholder. As previously noted, if boot is received in a section 351 transaction, the shareholder must recognize any gain realized but not in excess of the boot received. I.R.C. § 351(b). Further, the gain may qualify as long-term capital gain. In contrast, boot received as part of an ordinary distribution is a dividend to the extent of the corporation's E&P. I.R.C. §§ 301, 316. The regulations offer the unhelpful guidance that boot received in connection with a section 351 transaction is taxable under section 301 if it "has the effect of the distribution of a taxable dividend." Reg. § 1.351-2(d). In general, the test is whether payments received by the shareholder-transferor represent fair consideration for the property transferred in the section 351 transaction. Any amounts received in excess of fair consideration may be vulnerable to characterization as a dividend. In Davis v. U.S., 255 F.2d 48 (6th Cir. 1958), the court held that a cash distribution received by a taxpayer four years after he made a qualifying section 351 transfer constituted boot in that transaction, and not a dividend, because the cash reflected an agreed adjustment to the terms of the initial exchange.

4. *Is section 351 elective?* Since the tax consequences of a section 351 transaction are mandatory only if its conditions are satisfied, taxpayers can avoid the consequences by not meeting the required conditions. Reasons to avoid section 351 include (1) recognizing a loss by the transferor, (2) obtaining a higher basis in the transferred property to the transferee, and (3) freezing the amount of pre-incorporation gain that is taxed at favorable rates. An example of the third situation would be an investor who transfers an appreciated real estate parcel in a taxable transaction to a controlled corporation engaged in property development to ensure that gains arising prior to the transfer are taxed at a favorable capital gains rate. See Bradshaw v. U.S., 683 F.2d 365 (Ct. Cl. 1982). The IRS closely scrutinizes attempted "sales" to make sure that they do not, in fact, qualify as section 351 transactions.

## 5. *Contributions to Capital*

In Rev. Rul. 70-291, 1970-1 C.B. 168, the IRS concluded that if shareholders surrender to the issuing corporation a pro rata portion of their stock in exchange for no consideration, they should be taxed as if they made a contribution to the capital of such corporation, resulting in tax consequences closely analogous to those of a section 351 transaction. In the following case, the Supreme Court held that the same result should arise even though the stock surrender is not pro rata.

## Commissioner v. Fink

483 U.S. 89 (1987)

Justice POWELL delivered the opinion of the Court.

The question in this case is whether a dominant shareholder who voluntarily surrenders a portion of his shares to the corporation, but retains control, may immediately deduct from taxable income his basis in the surrendered shares.

. . . Respondents Peter and Karla Fink were the principal shareholders of Travco Corporation, a Michigan manufacturer of motor homes. Travco had one class of common stock outstanding and no preferred stock. Mr. Fink owned 52.2 percent, and Mrs. Fink 20.3 percent, of the outstanding shares. Travco urgently needed new capital as a result of financial difficulties it encountered in the mid-1970's. The Finks voluntarily surrendered some of their shares to Travco in an effort to "increase the attractiveness of the corporation to outside investors." Mr. Fink surrendered 116,146 shares in December 1976; Mrs. Fink surrendered 80,000 shares in January 1977. As a result, the Finks' combined percentage ownership of Travco was reduced from 72.5 percent to 68.5 percent. The Finks received no consideration for the surrendered shares, and no other shareholder surrendered any stock. The effort to attract new investors was unsuccessful, and the corporation eventually was liquidated. On their 1976 and 1977 joint federal income tax returns, the Finks claimed ordinary loss deductions totaling $389,040, the full amount of their adjusted basis in the surrendered shares. The Commissioner of Internal Revenue disallowed the deductions. He concluded that the stock surrendered was a contribution to the corporation's capital. Accordingly, the Commissioner determined that the surrender resulted in no immediate tax consequences, and that the Finks' basis in the surrendered shares should be added to the basis of their remaining shares of Travco stock.

In an unpublished opinion, the Tax Court sustained the Commissioner's determination for the reasons stated in Frantz v. Comm'r, 83 T.C. 162, 174-182 (1984), *aff'd*, 784 F.2d 119 (CA2 1986). In *Frantz* the Tax Court held that a stockholder's non pro rata surrender of shares to the corporation does not produce an immediate loss. The court reasoned that "this conclusion . . . necessarily follows from a recognition of the purpose of the transfer, that is, to bolster the financial position of [the corporation] and, hence, to protect and make more valuable [the stockholder's] retained shares." . . . Because the purpose of the shareholder's surrender is "to decrease or avoid a loss on his overall investment," the Tax Court in *Frantz* was "unable to conclude that [he] sustained a loss at the time of the transaction." . . . "Whether [the shareholder] would sustain a loss, and if so, the amount thereof, could only be determined when he subsequently disposed of the stock that the surrender was intended to protect and make more valuable." . . . The Tax Court recognized that it had sustained the taxpayer's position in a series of prior cases. . . . But it concluded that these decisions were incorrect, in part because they "encourage[d] a conversion of eventual capital losses into immediate ordinary losses." . . .

In this case, a divided panel of the Court of Appeals for the Sixth Circuit reversed the Tax Court. . . . The court concluded that the proper tax treatment of this type of stock surrender turns on the choice between "unitary" and "fragmented" views of stock ownership. Under the "fragmented view," "each share of stock is considered a separate investment," and gain or loss is computed separately on the sale or other disposition of each share. . . . According to the "unitary view," "the stockholder's entire investment is viewed as a single indivisible property unit," and a sale or disposition of some of the stockholder's shares only produces "an ascertainable gain or loss when the stockholder has disposed of his remaining shares." . . . The court observed that both it and the Tax Court generally had adhered to the fragmented view, and concluded that "the facts of the instant case [do not] present sufficient justification for abandoning" it. . . . It therefore held that the Finks were entitled to deduct their basis in the surrendered shares immediately as an ordinary loss, except to the extent that the surrender had increased the value of their remaining shares. The Court of Appeals remanded the case to the Tax Court for a determination of the increase, if any, in the value of the Finks' remaining shares that was attributable to the surrender.

Judge Joiner dissented. Because the taxpayers' "sole motivation in disposing of certain shares is to benefit the other shares they hold[,] . . . viewing the surrender of each share as the termination of an individual investment ignores the very reason for the surrender." . . . He concluded: "Particularly in cases such as this, where the diminution in the shareholder's corporate control and equity interest is so minute as to be illusory, the stock surrender should be regarded as a contribution to capital." . . .

We . . . reverse.

. . . It is settled that a shareholder's voluntary contribution to the capital of the corporation has no immediate tax consequences. § 263; § 1.263(a)-2(f). Instead, the shareholder is entitled to increase the basis of his shares by the amount of his basis in the property transferred to the corporation. § 1016(a)(1). When the shareholder later disposes of his shares, his contribution is reflected as a smaller taxable gain or a larger deductible loss. This rule applies not only to transfers of cash or tangible property, but also to a shareholder's forgiveness of a debt owed to him by the corporation. § 1.61-12(a). Such transfers are treated as contributions to capital even if the other shareholders make proportionately smaller contributions, or no contribution at all. The rules governing contributions to capital reflect the general principle that a shareholder may not claim an immediate loss for outlays made to benefit the corporation. We must decide whether this principle also applies to a controlling shareholder's non pro rata surrender of a portion of his shares.[1]

. . . The Finks contend that they sustained an immediate loss upon surrendering some of their shares to the corporation. By parting with the shares, they gave up an ownership interest entitling them to future dividends, future capital appreciation,

1. The Finks concede that a pro rata stock surrender, which by definition does not change the percentage ownership of any shareholder, is not a taxable event. *Cf.* Eisner v. Macomber, 252 U.S. 189 (1920) (pro rata stock dividend does not produce taxable income).

assets in the event of liquidation, and voting rights.[2] Therefore, the Finks contend, they are entitled to an immediate deduction. §§ 165(a) and (c)(2). In addition, the Finks argue that any non pro rata stock transaction "give[s] rise to immediate tax results." For example, a non pro rata stock dividend produces income because it increases the recipient's proportionate ownership of the corporation. By analogy, the Finks argue that a non pro rata surrender of shares should be recognized as an immediate loss because it reduces the surrendering shareholder's proportionate ownership.

Finally, the Finks contend that their stock surrenders were not contributions to the corporation's capital. They note that a typical contribution to capital, unlike a non pro rata stock surrender, has no effect on the contributing shareholder's proportionate interest in the corporation. Moreover, the Finks argue, a contribution of cash or other property increases the net worth of the corporation. For example, a shareholder's forgiveness of a debt owed to him by the corporation decreases the corporation's liabilities. In contrast, when a shareholder surrenders shares of the corporation's own stock, the corporation's net worth is unchanged. This is because the corporation cannot itself exercise the right to vote, receive dividends, or receive a share of assets in the event of liquidation.

. . . A shareholder who surrenders a portion of his shares to the corporation has parted with an asset, but that alone does not entitle him to an immediate deduction. Indeed, if the shareholder owns less than 100 percent of the corporation's shares, any non pro rata contribution to the corporation's capital will reduce the net worth of the contributing shareholder.[3] A shareholder who surrenders stock thus is similar to one who forgives or surrenders a debt owed to him by the corporation; the latter gives up interest, principal, and also potential voting power in the event of insolvency or bankruptcy. But, as stated above, such forgiveness of corporate debt is treated as a contribution to capital rather than a current deduction. The Finks' voluntary surrender of shares, like a shareholder's voluntary forgiveness of debt owed by the corporation, closely resembles an investment or contribution to capital. *See* B. Bittker & J. Eustice, Federal Income Taxation of Corporations and Shareholders ¶ 3.14, p. 3-59 (4th ed. 1979) ("If the contribution is voluntary, it does not produce gain or loss to the shareholder"). We find the similarity convincing in this case.

---

2. As a practical matter, however, the Finks did not give up a great deal. Their percentage interest in the corporation declined by only 4 percent. Because the Finks retained a majority interest, this reduction in their voting power was inconsequential. Moreover, Travco, like many corporations in financial difficulties, was not paying dividends.

3. For example, assume that a shareholder holding an 80 percent interest in a corporation with a total liquidation value of $100,000 makes a non pro rata contribution to the corporation's capital of $20,000 in cash. Assume further that the shareholder has no other assets. Prior to the contribution, the shareholder's net worth was $100,000 ($20,000 plus 80 percent of $100,000). If the corporation were immediately liquidated following the contribution, the shareholder would receive only $96,000 (80 percent of $120,000). Of course such a non pro rata contribution is rare in practice. Typically a shareholder will simply purchase additional shares.

The fact that a stock surrender is not recorded as a contribution to capital on the corporation's balance sheet does not compel a different result. Shareholders who forgive a debt owed by the corporation or pay a corporate expense also are denied an immediate deduction, even though neither of these transactions is a contribution to capital in the accounting sense.[4] Nor are we persuaded by the fact that a stock surrender, unlike a typical contribution to capital, reduces the shareholder's proportionate interest in the corporation. This Court has never held that every change in a shareholder's percentage ownership has immediate tax consequences. Of course, a shareholder's receipt of property from the corporation generally is a taxable event. §§ 301, 316. In contrast, a shareholder's transfer of property to the corporation usually has no immediate tax consequences.

The Finks concede that the purpose of their stock surrender was to protect or increase the value of their investment in the corporation. They hoped to encourage new investors to provide needed capital and in the long run recover the value of the surrendered shares through increased dividends or appreciation in the value of their remaining shares. If the surrender had achieved its purpose, the Finks would not have suffered an economic loss. In this case, as in many cases involving closely held corporations whose shares are not traded on an open market, there is no reliable method of determining whether the surrender will result in a loss until the shareholder disposes of his remaining shares. Thus, the Finks' stock surrender does not meet the requirement that an immediately deductible loss must be "actually sustained during the taxable year." § 1.165-1(b).

Finally, treating stock surrenders as ordinary losses might encourage shareholders in failing corporations to convert potential capital losses to ordinary losses by voluntarily surrendering their shares before the corporation fails. In this way shareholders might avoid the consequences of § 165(g)(1), which provides for capital-loss treatment of stock that becomes worthless. Similarly, shareholders may be encouraged to transfer corporate stock rather than other property to the corporation in order to realize a current loss.

We therefore hold that a dominant shareholder who voluntarily surrenders a portion of his shares to the corporation, but retains control, does not sustain an immediate loss deductible from taxable income. Rather, the surrendering shareholder must reallocate his basis in the surrendered shares to the shares he retains. The shareholder's loss, if any, will be recognized when he disposes of his remaining shares. A reallocation of basis is consistent with the general principle that "payments made by a stockholder of a corporation for the purpose of protecting his interest therein must be regarded as [an] additional cost of his stock," and so cannot be deducted immediately. Our holding today is not inconsistent with the settled rule that the gain or loss on the sale or disposition of shares of stock equals the difference

4. It is true that a corporation's stock is not considered an asset of the corporation. A corporation's own shares nevertheless may be as valuable to the corporation as other property contributed by shareholders, as treasury shares may be resold. This is evidenced by the fact that corporations often purchase their own shares on the open market.

between the amount realized in the sale or disposition and the shareholder's basis in the particular shares sold or exchanged. § 1001(a). We conclude only that a controlling shareholder's voluntary surrender of shares, like contributions of other forms of property to the corporation, is not an appropriate occasion for the recognition of gain or loss. . . .

[The concurring and dissenting opinions are omitted.]

## *NOTES AND QUESTIONS*

1. *Tax consequences of capital contributions by shareholders.* If a shareholder transfers property to a corporation without receiving any consideration in exchange, the tax consequences to the corporate transferee are generally the same as in a qualifying section 351 transaction. The corporation generally does not recognize any income in the transaction and takes a transferred basis in the property contributed, increased by any gain recognized to the transferor. See I.R.C. §§ 118(a), 362(a)(2). The consequences to the transferor are slightly less clear. If the transferor is the sole shareholder of the transferee, the IRS's position is that the transaction qualifies under section 351 despite the absence of an exchange. In that case, the issuance of additional stock by the corporate transferee would be a "meaningless gesture." See Rev. Rul. 64-155, 1964-1 C.B. 138; Lessinger v. Comm'r, 872 F.2d 519, 522 (2d Cir. 1989) (infra p. 271). Section 351 should also apply even if there is more than one shareholder so long as each shareholder contributes an amount that is pro rata to the shareholder's interest. If the transferor is not a sole shareholder and the contribution is not pro rata, the transaction might nevertheless be recharacterized as an exchange of property for stock of the transferee. For example, the transferor might be treated as constructively receiving stock of the transferee and then transferring such stock to one of the other shareholders. Cf. Reg. § 1.351-1(b)(1) and (2) (ex. 1). Alternatively, the contribution might be viewed as an additional payment for the transferor's prior receipt of stock of the transferee. If the contribution is recharacterized as part of an exchange, the transferor's recognition of gain or loss would depend upon whether section 351 is satisfied. The transferor's basis in the transferee's stock should be increased by the amount of money plus the basis of any property contributed, adjusted for any gain or loss recognized in the transfer to the corporation. As explained in *Fink*, a shareholder is ordinarily not entitled to deduct the amount of a capital contribution. See Reg. § 1.263(a)-2(f).

2. *Some alternatives.* If the character of the loss had not been important, was there an alternative way for the Finks to obtain an immediate loss in this case? What would have been the tax consequences if they had sold a portion of their stock to the minority shareholders of the corporation in exchange for a nominal amount of consideration? Or, if the minority shareholders were unwilling to cooperate, could the Finks simply have sold their stock back to the corporation for a nominal amount? How would this transaction have been taxed? Cf. I.R.C. §§ 302, 267(a)(1) and (b)(2).

3. *Economic loss?* The majority of the Court was apparently influenced by the fact that "[i]f the surrender had achieved its purpose, the Finks would not have suffered an economic loss." Should that have been a relevant factor? Why or why not?

4. *The stock surrender and plan to raise new capital.* Exactly why did the taxpayers surrender their shares? As found by the trial court, the plan was to have Travco raise additional capital by issuing 700,000 shares of preferred stock convertible 2:1 into common stock. To increase the attractiveness of this new issue of stock, the taxpayers first surrendered enough shares so that the total number of outstanding shares of common stock of the corporation fell below 1.4 million. This step ensured that the holder of the convertible preferred would own over 50 percent of the common stock upon conversion. The understanding from the outset was that if an outside buyer for the preferred shares could not be found, the taxpayers and their mother would purchase the new issue of stock. As it happened, an outside buyer did not surface, and two months after the non pro rata stock surrender, the taxpayers and their mother bought all of the preferred stock. Do these additional facts make you more or less sympathetic to the taxpayers' tax claims?

5. *Two surrenders.* As stated in the Court's opinion, Mr. Fink surrendered his shares in December 1976 and Mrs. Fink surrendered hers in January 1977. Why do you think they surrendered their stock at different times?

6. *Capital contributions by nonshareholders.* Section 118(a) also excludes from a corporation's income certain capital contributions made by nonshareholders. An example would be land or other property contributed by a governmental unit or civic group to induce a corporation to locate its business in a particular community. Reg. § 118-1. The corporation obtains a zero basis in any property contributed; if money is contributed, the corporation must reduce its basis in other property. I.R.C. § 362(c).

## B. Assumption of Liabilities

### *1. Basic Rules*

Suppose that as part of a qualifying section 351 transaction, the controlled corporation also assumes a liability of the transferor. Is the liability assumption treated like the payment of boot to the transferor in the transaction? The answer, in general, is "no." Read I.R.C. § 357(a). This answer might at first seem surprising since a liability assumption by the transferee can achieve the same economic result as a borrowing by the transferee to finance an actual payment of boot to the transferor. For this reason, the general rule is reversed—and a liability assumption is treated as boot—where the transferor's principal purpose is tax avoidance or not a bona fide business purpose. Read I.R.C. § 357(b).

A further exception generally requires a transferor to recognize gain to the extent any liabilities assumed exceed the aggregate basis of the properties transferred.

Read I.R.C. § 357(c)(1). If both sections 357(b) and 357(c) apply, the tax avoidance exception controls. The following case involves application of section 357(c) to a very simple fact pattern. Do you think the court interpreted the law correctly?

## Lessinger v. Commissioner

872 F.2d 519 (2d Cir. 1989)

[Sol Lessinger operated an accrual basis sole proprietorship engaged in the wholesale distribution of metal fasteners. The factor that had provided working capital to the proprietorship refused to continue lending funds to it so long as it remained a noncorporate entity because, under New York law, the factor could charge a higher interest rate on loans to corporations. As a result, Lessinger transferred the proprietorship to a preexisting corporation that he wholly owned. At the time, the proprietorship had a negative net worth of $255,000. The principal creditor of the corporation, Marine Midland Bank, requested Lessinger to execute a promissory note for this amount to the corporation and he did so. The note then served as collateral for the bank's loan to the corporation.

All parties agreed that the transaction qualified under section 351 even though no stock was issued to Lessinger, since he already owned all of the shares of the corporate transferee. The Tax Court concluded, however, that Lessinger recognized gain under section 357(c)(1) to the extent the liabilities assumed by the corporation exceeded Lessinger's basis in the assets transferred. In so holding, the Tax Court disregarded Lessinger's note because (1) the note lacked the normal indicia of debt (there was no due date, a promise to pay interest, or any security) and (2) Lessinger's basis in his own note was zero in any event so that the taxable amount under section 357(c)(1) was unchanged. The Second Circuit's opinion reversing the Tax Court is excerpted below.]

OAKES, Chief Judge:

. . . We believe, however, that a due date, interest, and security are not necessary to characterize Lessinger's obligation to his corporation as debt, and that his obligation was binding. The promissory note he signed . . . , which the corporation endorsed to Marine Midland as collateral for a loan, is significant because it shows that Marine Midland depended on his personal responsibility. And, in general, it is obvious that the creditors of the corporation continued to do business with it on the strength of the taxpayer's personal credit. . . . Lessinger received consideration when he gave his promise to the corporation, and we have no doubt that any court would enforce that promise to protect the corporate creditors if the corporation failed, even in the absence of alter ego liability. We conclude that the taxpayer's obligation to the corporation was real, not artificial.

We now turn to the Tax Court's second reason for ignoring the debt. The Tax Court quoted Alderman [v. Comm'r, 55 T.C. 662 (1971),] which, like our case, involved the incorporation of an accrual basis proprietorship with a negative net worth. In *Alderman*, the Tax Court disregarded the taxpayers' personal promissory note to their corporation because

> [t]he Aldermans incurred no cost in making the note, so its basis to them was zero. The basis to the corporation was the same as in the hands of the transferor, *i.e.*, zero. Consequently, the application of section 357(c) is undisturbed by the creation and transfer of the personal note to the corporation.

55 T.C. at 665. . . . *Alderman* purported to follow the literal language of the Tax Code. Section 357(c) does support the *Alderman* court's reliance on the concept of basis, but the statutory language is not addressed to a transaction such as Lessinger's, where the transferor's obligation has a value to the transferee corporation. The *Alderman* court did not consider the value of the obligation to the transferee.

Section 357(a) provides that generally, the corporation's assumption of the transferor's liabilities should cause no recognition of gain. . . . Subsection (c)(1) then provides an exception:

> (c) Liabilities in excess of basis
> (1) In general
> In the case of an exchange—
> (A) to which section 351 applies, . . .
> if the sum of the amount of the liabilities assumed, plus the amount of the liabilities to which the property is subject, exceeds the total of the *adjusted basis* of the property transferred pursuant to such exchange, then such excess shall be considered as a gain. . . .

I.R.C. § 357(c) (emphasis added). In general, then, the "adjusted basis" of the property transferred is crucial to the calculation.

"Basis," as used in tax law, refers to assets, not liabilities. Section 1012 provides that "[t]he basis of property shall be the cost of such property, except as otherwise provided." Liabilities by definition have no "basis" in tax law generally or in section 1012 terms specifically. The concept of "basis" prevents double taxation of income by identifying amounts that have already been taxed or are exempt from tax. . . . The taxpayer could, of course, have no "basis" in his own promise to pay the corporation $255,000, because that item is a liability for him. We would add parenthetically that to this extent *Alderman* was correct in describing the taxpayers' note there. But the corporation should have a basis in its obligation from Lessinger, because it incurred a cost in the transaction involving the transfer of the obligation by taking on the liabilities of the proprietorship that exceeded its assets, and because it would have to recognize income upon Lessinger's payment of the debt if it had no basis in the obligation.[5] Assets transferred under section 351 are taken by

5. Our approach requires acceptance of the fact that section 362(a), which requires a carryover basis for "property" transferred in nonrecognition transactions under section 351, cannot be applied to the corporation's valuation of its receivable from the taxpayer. The purpose of . . . section 362 . . . generally

the corporation at the transferor's basis, to which is added any gain recognized in the transfer. § 362(a). Consideration of "adjusted basis" in section 357(c) therefore normally does not require determining whether the section refers to the "adjusted basis" in the hands of the transferor-shareholder or the transferee-corporation, because the basis does not change. But here, the "basis" in the hands of the corporation should be the face amount of the taxpayer's obligation. We now hold that in the situation presented here, where the transferor undertakes genuine personal liability to the transferee, "adjusted basis" in section 357(c) refers to the transferee's basis in the obligation, which is its face amount.

Yet the Commissioner says that to reverse the Tax Court would, as *Alderman*, 55 T.C. at 665, suggested, "effectively eliminate section 357(c) from the Internal Revenue Code." Would it? The question of substance is whether the taxpayer in fact realized a gain from the transaction. He certainly did not do so by a cancellation of his indebtedness. If there was any cancellation, it was illusory: While his trade creditors at the time of the incorporation may have been paid off (or their accounts rolled over as a result of sales and payments by the corporation and further advances of credit by the trade creditors), the taxpayer's indebtedness to the corporation itself continued (except to the extent he paid it off). If Lessinger had a "gain" from the incorporation, it did not show up in his personal balance sheet, let alone by way of economic benefit in his pocket.

The purpose of section 357(c) is to provide a limited exception to section 351's nonrecognition treatment that operates, as the Commissioner reminds us here, "where the transferor realized economic benefit which, if not recognized, would otherwise go untaxed." Brief at 27 (quoting Focht v. Comm'r, 68 T.C. 223, 235 (1977)). Section 351 was intended to allow changes in business form without requiring the recognition of income. The transferor-shareholder recognizes income only to the extent that he receives boot in the form of money or other property. § 351(b). In 1938, the Supreme Court held that under the predecessor of section 351, . . . any assumption of liability by the transferee would be considered a payment of money or property to the transferor, causing the transferor to recognize income. U.S. v. Hendler, 303 U.S. 564 (1938). Congress reacted immediately by enacting . . . the predecessor of section 357(a), which provided that the assumption of a liability should *not* be considered the payment of property or money and should not provoke the recognition of gain.

Congress did not add section 357(c), which requires the recognition of gain when liabilities exceed assets, until 1954, when a House committee referred to the section as an "additional safeguard[ ] against tax avoidance not found in existing law." . . . The House and Senate committees that approved section 357(c) both cited a single example of a transaction that the section was intended to govern: If a

---

is to defer recognition of gain or loss. . . . In Lessinger's transaction, there simply were no gains or losses to be deferred. The excess of liabilities over assets (which Lessinger's promise to the corporation remedied) was caused by the proprietorship's insolvency — the excess of current payables over current receivables — rather than by unrecognized gain in any asset's basis.

taxpayer transfers property with an adjusted basis of $20,000 subject to a $50,000 mortgage, he should recognize $30,000 gain. . . . While some have argued that section 357(c) was designed to avoid a negative basis, its application in the Congress's example is also quite reasonable. The transferor, who has already benefited by depreciating the property or holding it while its value appreciates, has income because he will never have to pay the mortgage. Forcing the taxpayer in our case to recognize a gain, however, would be contrary to Congress's intent because it would tax a truly phantom gain, because his liability to the corporation, as we have said, was real, continuing, and indirectly, at least, enforceable by the corporation's creditors. . . .

Section 357(c) was amended in 1978 to solve a problem that had forced the courts to fashion delicate constructions of the section's language in order to conform with legislative intent. A cash basis transferor has no basis in accounts receivable. The Tax Court originally held that such a transferor would have to recognize gain if, after counting her accounts payable as transferred liabilities, liabilities exceeded assets. This analysis meant that the owner of almost any ongoing business transferred liabilities exceeding assets when incorporating. The Tax Court later developed an approach that excluded accounts payable from liabilities, after this court and the Court of Appeals for the Ninth Circuit announced different interpretations that achieved this result. Congress added section 357(c)(3) in 1978, and it now excludes from subsection (c)(1) "a liability the payment of which . . . would give rise to a deduction." This history, while not directly relevant to Lessinger,[6] is instructive. In Bongiovanni [v. Comm'r, 470 F.2d 921, 924 (2d Cir. 1972),] "a too literal reading of the words of the statute [would have] produce[d] an inequitable result which cannot be allowed to stand," and "Congress certainly could not have intended such an inequitable result especially in light of its expressed purposes in enacting Sections 351 and 357(c)," *id.* at 925. We find those words equally applicable here.

We conclude that our holding will not "effectively eliminate section 357(c)." Lessinger experienced no enrichment and had no unrecognized gains whose recognition was appropriate at the time of the consolidation. Any logic that would tax him would certainly represent a "trap for the unwary." Lessinger could have achieved incorporation without taxation under the Commissioner's theory by borrowing [$255,000] cash, transferring the cash to the corporation . . . , and later causing the corporation to buy his promissory note from the lender (or pay it off in consideration of his new promise to pay the corporation). If taxpayers who transfer liabilities exceeding assets to controlled corporations are willing to undertake genuine personal liability for the excess, we see no reason to require recognition of a gain, and we do not believe that Congress intended for any gain to be recognized. . . .

6. Section 357(c)(3) is inapplicable because Lessinger's proprietorship was on the accrual basis. None of the liabilities would have produced deductions if paid by the transferor because those expenses had been previously deducted when they were entered in the proprietorship's records. . . .

## *NOTES AND QUESTIONS*

1. *Circular analysis?* The Second Circuit correctly observes that a lender ordinarily has a basis in a note or debt instrument provided by a debtor. To a lender, the debt instrument is an asset that entitles the lender to receive repayment of principal under certain terms. We have previously seen in chapter two how a shareholder-lender's basis in debt issued by an S corporation-debtor entitles the shareholder to take into account losses passed through by the corporation. See I.R.C. § 1366(d)(1)(B). As the court notes, the lender's basis in debt is the reason why the lender ordinarily has no tax consequences upon repayment of principal.

The court concludes, however, that the term "adjusted basis" used in section 357(c)(1) refers to the *corporate transferee's* basis in the debt rather than the transferor's. Read that provision closely in conjunction with section 362(a). We have previously seen that the corporate transferee's basis in property transferred in a section 351 transaction depends in part upon the amount of gain recognized by the transferor in the transaction. Under the court's analysis, does the amount of the transferor's gain depend in part upon the corporate transferee's basis? Is there a way out of this loop?

Admittedly, section 357 is not a model of clarity. Read section 357(a) closely to make sure you understand exactly who the "taxpayer" and "another party to the exchange" are in a typical section 351 transaction. Your answers should then help you to understand which party may recognize gain as a result of section 357(c)(1).

2. *How should the transaction have been taxed?* The court states that "Lessinger received consideration when he gave his promise to the corporation." What consideration is the court referring to? If the statement is correct, what does it imply about the tax consequences of the transaction to Lessinger? Recall that the corporate transferee was a preexisting corporation wholly owned by Lessinger. Does it matter that the corporation had retained earnings from its business activities prior to the transaction? What role, if any, should Lessinger's note have played in determining the tax consequences of the transaction to him?

3. *Required transfer of net value.* Proposed regulations would exclude from section 351 treatment transactions in which there is no net value transferred to a corporation, such as where the liabilities assumed by the corporate transferee exceed the fair market value of the properties transferred. Prop. Reg. § 1.351-1(a)(1)(iii). According to the IRS, transactions in which no net value is transferred resemble sales and should not receive nonrecognition treatment. Had this rule been in effect, would it have changed the outcome in *Lessinger*? See footnote 5 of the opinion and I.R.C. § 357(c)(1)(A).

4. *Do borrowers have basis in their own notes?* In Peracchi v. Comm'r, 143 F.3d 487 (9th Cir. 1998), the Ninth Circuit indicated that the Second Circuit's approach in *Lessinger* was "untenable," but nevertheless reached essentially the same result in a different way. *Peracchi* involved a transfer by a taxpayer to his wholly-owned corporation of some real estate encumbered by liabilities greater than the taxpayer's

basis in the property. (It is unclear whether the liabilities also exceeded the fair market value of the property.) To avoid recognizing gain under section 357(c)(1), the taxpayer executed a promissory note promising to pay his corporation an amount greater than the excess of liabilities over basis. Although the taxpayer did not make any payments on the note until after the IRS's audit had begun and the corporation made no effort to enforce the terms of the note, the court concluded that the note was bona fide and that the taxpayer had a basis in it equal to its face amount. Accordingly, there was no section 357(c)(1) gain to be recognized.

In analyzing the significance of the promissory note, the court acknowledged that the debtor and creditor were under common control and that the taxpayer had paid "imperfect attention" to his obligations under the note. Nevertheless, the court was persuaded that because of the possibility of bankruptcy, the note represented real, additional investment by the taxpayer in his corporation:

> Without the note, no matter how deeply the corporation went into debt, creditors could not reach Peracchi's personal assets. With the note on the books, however, creditors can reach into Peracchi's pocket by enforcing the note as an unliquidated asset of the corporation.
>
> The key . . . is to ask whether bankruptcy is significant enough a contingency to confer substantial economic effect on this transaction. If the risk of bankruptcy is important enough to be recognized, Peracchi should get basis in the note: He will have increased his exposure to the risks of the business—and thus his economic investment in [his corporation]—by [the face amount of the note]. If bankruptcy is so remote that there is no realistic possibility it will ever occur, we can ignore the potential economic effect of the note as speculative and treat it as merely an unenforceable promise to contribute capital in the future. [143 F.3d at 493.]

The dissenting judge described the majority's conclusion as a form of magic "that would have made Merlin envious. The taxpayer has created something—basis—out of nothing." Id. at 497.

---

Read I.R.C. §§ 357(a)-(c), 358(a) and (d), and 362(a), and then test your understanding of current law by doing **problem 7-2**.

**Problem 7-2:**

(a) Mr. A transfers Blackacre to X corporation, which is wholly owned by him. A's basis in Blackacre is $50 and the property is subject to a $20 recourse mortgage. In the transaction, X issues $80 of common stock to A and assumes the liability. Absent section 357, what would be the tax consequences of this transaction?

(b) What are the tax consequences under current law? What is the rationale for the result? What is the role of section 358(d)? What happens to the gain that would be recognized by A but for section 357(a)?

(c) Same as (b), except that the amount of the mortgage is $60 and X issues only $40 stock to A. What is the rationale for this result?
(d) Same as (c), except that in the same transaction, A transferred Whiteacre (fair market value $20 and basis $10) to X in exchange for an additional $20 of X stock. See Reg. § 1.357-2(a).
(e) Same as (c), except that the amount of the mortgage is $40 and X also assumes $20 of A's accounts payables. A, a cash-basis taxpayer, had incurred the liabilities in the ordinary course of business in exchange for certain services provided to A. What is the rationale for this result? What happens to the gain that would be recognized by A but for section 357(a)?
(f) Same as (e), except that A was an accrual-basis taxpayer.
(g) Ms. B purchased Whiteacre for $30,000 cash five years ago. It is now worth $100,000 and she still owns it outright. B would like to incorporate Whiteacre in her wholly-owned corporation, Landco, and B is also in need of $20,000 cash. In lieu of transferring Whiteacre to Landco for $80,000 of additional Landco stock and $20,000 cash, B decides on the following plan: first, B goes to Local Bank and borrows $20,000 cash, pledging Whiteacre as collateral. Second, B transfers Whiteacre to Landco in exchange for $80,000 of Landco stock and Landco's assumption of the liability. Finally, Landco pays off the debt to Local Bank. What are the tax consequences of this transaction? How would your answer change if the amount of cash needed by B and transferred to her in the manner indicated was $40,000 and not $20,000?
(h) Same as (g), except that B borrowed the entire purchase price when she first acquired Whiteacre for $30,000. At the time of B's transfer of the property to Landco, $15,000 of the purchase money mortgage is still outstanding. In the transaction, Landco assumes the $15,000 liability and the $20,000 liability created in the manner described in question (g), and issues $65,000 of additional Landco stock to B. What are the tax consequences of this transaction? See Reg. § 1.357-1(c).

## 2. *Anatomy of a Tax Shelter*

The tax rules relating to liabilities included in a transfer of property to a controlled corporation (as well as similar rules applicable to transfers to partnerships) have spawned various tax shelters, and this has led to tax litigation as well as administrative and legislative changes. To help you gain a better understanding of what tax shelters are, how they develop, and what their impact may be on the tax system, as well as what the state of the law is today, this section describes the anatomy of one prominent shelter involving a section 351 transaction.

As is not uncommon, the story begins with a basic inconsistency in the manner in which the tax law treats two similar transactions. Consider the following two examples:

> **Example 7-1:** Ms. A transfers property worth $100 and with a $50 basis to corporation X in exchange for $80 of X stock and $20 cash. Immediately after the transfer, A controls X (within the meaning of section 368(c)).

> **Example 7-2:** Same as **example 7-1** except that the property is encumbered by a recourse liability of $20. In exchange for the property, X issues $80 of stock and assumes the liability.

In **example 7-1**, A must recognize gain of $20, the amount of the boot received. In contrast, thanks to section 357(a), A would ordinarily not have to recognize any gain in **example 7-2**. It is not hard to come up with a scenario where the two examples are economic equivalents. Nevertheless, unless section 357(b) comes into play, the two tax outcomes are different.

As discussed briefly in *Lessinger*, section 357(a) was enacted in response to the government victory in U.S. v. Hendler, 303 U.S. 564 (1938). In *Hendler*, the government prevailed upon the Supreme Court to hold that the assumption by a corporate transferee of certain liabilities was the equivalent of boot received by the transferor, requiring the transferor to recognize gain. But this victory backfired since the statute of limitations had already run on many of the transfers that were now taxable based on the Court's holding. Meanwhile, the gain that should have been recognized in those taxable transfers justified an increase in the corporate transferee's basis in the property received, producing greater depreciation deductions and losses and smaller amounts of gain than would have occurred under pre-*Hendler* law. See I.R.C. § 362(a). Thus, the immediate outcome of the case was a reduction in the tax liabilities of many corporations. Facing this prospect, the government sought assistance from Congress, which proceeded to enact section 357(a), effectively reversing the government's victory in *Hendler*.

The events following *Hendler* may be only a partial explanation for the Congressional reversal. After all, Congress could have reversed *Hendler* but also codified its rule on a *prospective* basis. Prospective codification should have adequately protected the fisc since any tax benefits gained by corporate transferees would ordinarily have been more than offset by increased tax collections from the transferors. Under this approach, the *Hendler* rule could have been made part of the law on a going-forward basis.

Thus, a more satisfactory explanation is that section 357(a)—which restored the government's pre-*Hendler* policy position—embodies the preferred policy outcome, one that is fully consistent with the policy behind section 351(a). If we think of corporation X in **example 7-2** as being no more than A's alter-ego, it is not hard to justify a nontaxable result in that example. In that case, the corporation's assumption of the debt may be little different from A's continuing to be liable for it; indeed, in many situations, A might remain secondarily liable on the debt (for example, in the capacity of a guarantor). Under this view, "nothing really happens" when A transfers property to X subject to a liability that is assumed by X, and therefore, the tax result should be in accordance with that economic reality.

When section 357(a) applies, the gain not recognized in the transaction is preserved in the hands of both the transferor and the corporate transferee, consistent with the general pattern of section 351 transactions. In **example 7-2**, A's basis in the $80 of X stock she received is $30 and X's basis in the $100 of property received is $50. See I.R.C. §§ 358(a)(1) and (d)(1), 362(a). In each case, there is preserved $50 of built-in gain, the same amount of gain realized but not recognized by A in the transaction.

A decision to avoid negative basis necessitated the enactment of section 357(c)(1). Suppose, for example, A's basis in the property in **example 7-2** had been only $10 instead of $50. In that case, if A were still not required to recognize any gain in the transfer, it would not be possible to preserve the $90 of unrecognized gain in the $80 of X stock she receives without giving her a negative basis in such stock. Accordingly, section 357(c)(1) requires A to recognize $10 gain in this situation, the amount by which the liability ($20) exceeds A's basis in the property transferred ($10). The remaining $80 of gain is preserved by giving her a zero basis in the $80 worth of stock.

The court in *Lessinger* also explains some of the controversy that developed in reaction to section 357(c)(1) and that eventually led to enactment of section 357(c)(3). The problematic scenario involved the incorporation of a cash-basis service business whose assets and liabilities consisted mainly of zero-basis account receivables as well as account payables. If the payables were treated as liabilities, section 357(c)(1) resulted in many of those incorporations being taxable events to the party incorporating the business. This result seemed inconsistent with the underlying policy rationale behind sections 351 and 357(a). Moreover, since incurrence of the payable had not yet provided any tax benefit to the cash-basis taxpayer, it was arguably inappropriate to treat "relief" of that payable (by reason of its assumption by the taxpayer's controlled corporation) as an income-recognition event to the taxpayer. After several courts struggled to resolve this controversy in an equitable way, Congress stepped in and enacted section 357(c)(3). Under section 357(c)(3), a liability that would give rise to a deduction if paid by the transferor and has not created or increased basis in any property, such as an account payable of a cash-basis taxpayer, is not treated as a liability for purposes of section 357(c)(1). Accordingly, the transferor would not recognize any gain in the problematic scenario described above.

It is important to understand how section 357(c)(3) achieves its objective. First, it accelerates the transferor's tax benefit from the liability by giving the transferor immediate basis credit for the liability even though it has not yet been paid. See I.R.C. § 358(a) and (d)(1) and (2). In addition, when the corporate transferee pays off the liability, the transferee may be entitled to claim a deduction of that amount.

See Rev. Rul. 80-198, 1980-2 C.B. 113. If so, the liability in effect provides a double tax benefit. An example illustrating both effects may be helpful:

> **Example 7-3:** A, a cash-basis taxpayer, incorporates her sole proprietorship at a time when the only assets and liabilities of the business consist of $100 in account receivables and $20 in account payables. In exchange, she receives $80 worth of her corporation's stock.

As a cash-basis taxpayer, her basis in the receivables is zero. Thus, but for section 357(c)(3), A would have to recognize $20 gain in the transaction, the amount by which the payables ($20) exceed her basis in the property transferred ($0). In addition, she would obtain a zero basis in the $80 of stock received and the corporation would take a $20 basis in the $100 of receivables. I.R.C. §§ 358(a)(1) and (d), 362(a). Of the $100 gain realized in the incorporation, $20 would be recognized and the remaining $80 would be preserved in the hands of both the corporation and the shareholder.

Now contrast the result after taking section 357(c)(3) into account. If the payable is not treated as a liability, then A does not recognize any gain in the incorporation. But she is still given basis credit for the payable because there is no required reduction in her stock basis on account of the payable. I.R.C. § 358(a) and (d)(1) and (2). Her basis in the $80 stock received is therefore still zero, thereby preserving only $80 of gain in her hands. In effect, she has been allowed to deduct the $20 payable immediately in the incorporation, thus reducing her $100 of gain in the receivable prior to the transfer to $80 of preserved future gain in the corporation's stock after the transfer. In addition, under certain circumstances, the $20 payable may also be deducted when the corporation pays it off, in which case the liability will have produced two tax benefits.

It should now be evident that section 357(c)(3), a provision that arguably reflects a sound policy decision, contains the seeds of a possible tax shelter. For large C corporations to take advantage of the possible sheltering opportunity, however, one other important link was necessary, since such corporations are generally ineligible to use the cash method of accounting for tax purposes. See I.R.C. § 448(a) and (b). Thus, an obligation other than an account payable incurred by a cash-method taxpayer had to be involved in the transaction. The following ruling provided the necessary link that tax shelters ultimately exploited.

## Rev. Rul. 95-74

1995-2 C.B. 36

### ISSUES

(1) Are the liabilities assumed by *S* in the § 351 exchange described below liabilities for purposes of §§ 357(c)(1) and 358(d)?

(2) Once assumed by *S*, how will the liabilities in the § 351 exchange described below be treated?

## FACTS

Corporation *P* is an accrual basis, calendar-year corporation engaged in various ongoing businesses, one of which includes the operation of a manufacturing plant (the Manufacturing Business). The plant is located on land purchased by *P* many years before. The land was not contaminated by any hazardous waste when *P* purchased it. However, as a result of plant operations, certain environmental liabilities, such as potential soil and groundwater remediation, are now associated with the land.

In Year 1, for bona fide business purposes, *P* engages in an exchange to which § 351 of the Internal Revenue Code applies by transferring substantially all of the assets associated with the Manufacturing Business, including the manufacturing plant and the land on which the plant is located, to a newly formed corporation, *S*, in exchange for all of the stock of *S* and for *S*'s assumption of the liabilities associated with the Manufacturing Business, including the environmental liabilities associated with the land. *P* has no plan or intention to dispose of (or have *S* issue) any *S* stock. *S* is an accrual basis, calendar-year taxpayer.

*P* did not undertake any environmental remediation efforts in connection with the land transferred to *S* before the transfer and did not deduct or capitalize any amount with respect to the contingent environmental liabilities associated with the transferred land.

In Year 3, *S* undertakes soil and groundwater remediation efforts relating to the land transferred in the § 351 exchange and incurs costs (within the meaning of the economic performance rules of § 461(h)) as a result of those remediation efforts. Of the total amount of costs incurred, a portion would have constituted ordinary and necessary business expenses that are deductible under § 162 and the remaining portion would have constituted capital expenditures under § 263 if there had not been a § 351 exchange and the costs for remediation efforts had been incurred by *P*.

## LAW AND ANALYSIS

*Issue 1:* Section 351(a) provides that no gain or loss shall be recognized if property is transferred to a corporation solely in exchange for stock and immediately after the exchange the transferor is in control of the corporation.

Section 357(a) provides a general rule that a transferee corporation's assumption of a transferor's liability in a § 351 exchange will not be treated as money or other property received by the transferor. Section 357(b) provides an exception to the general rule of § 357(a) when it appears that the principal purpose of the transferor in having the liability assumed was avoidance of Federal income tax on the exchange or, if not such purpose, was not a bona fide business purpose.

Section 357(c)(1) provides a second exception to the general rule of § 357(a). Section 357(c)(1) provides that if the sum of the liabilities the transferee corporation assumes and takes property subject to exceeds the total of the adjusted basis of the property the transferor transfers to the corporation pursuant to the exchange, then the excess shall be considered as gain from the sale or exchange of the property.

For purposes of applying the exception in § 357(c)(1), § 357(c)(3)(A) provides that a liability the payment of which would give rise to a deduction . . . is excluded. This special rule does not apply, however, to any liability to the extent that the incurrence of the liability resulted in the creation of, or an increase in, the basis of any property. Section 357(c)(3)(B).

Section 358(a)(1) provides that in a § 351 exchange the basis of the property permitted to be received under § 351 without the recognition of gain or loss shall be the same as that of the property exchanged, decreased by (i) the fair market value of any other property (except money) received by the transferor [and] (ii) the amount of any money received by the transferor, . . . and increased by . . . the amount of gain to the transferor which was recognized on such exchange. . . .

Section 358(d)(1) provides that where, as part of the consideration to the transferor, another party to the exchange assumed a liability of the transferor, such assumption (in the amount of the liability) shall, for purposes of § 358, be treated as money received by the transferor on the exchange. Section 358(d)(2) provides that § 358(d)(1) does not apply to any liability excluded under § 357(c)(3).

The legislative history of § 351 indicates that Congress viewed an incorporation as a mere change in the form of the underlying business and enacted § 351 to facilitate such business adjustments generally by allowing taxpayers to incorporate businesses without recognizing gain. Section 357(c)(1), however, provides that the transferor recognizes gain to the extent that the amount of liabilities transferred exceeds the aggregate basis of the assets transferred.

A number of cases concerning cash basis taxpayers were litigated in the 1970s with respect to the definition of "liabilities" for purposes of § 357(c)(1), with sometimes conflicting analyses and results. In response to this litigation, Congress enacted § 357(c)(3) to address the concern that the inclusion in the § 357(c)(1) determination of certain deductible liabilities resulted in "unforeseen and unintended tax difficulties for certain cash basis taxpayers who incorporate a going business."

Congress concluded that including in the § 357(c)(1) determination liabilities that have not yet been taken into account by the transferor results in an overstatement of liabilities of, and potential inappropriate gain recognition to, the transferor because the transferor has not received the corresponding deduction or other corresponding tax benefit. To prevent this result, Congress enacted § 357(c)(3)(A) to exclude certain deductible liabilities from the scope of § 357(c), as long as the liabilities had not resulted in the creation of, or an increase in, the basis of any property (as provided in § 357(c)(3)(B)).

While § 357(c)(3) explicitly addresses liabilities that give rise to deductible items, the same principle applies to liabilities that give rise to capital expenditures as well. Including in the § 357(c)(1) determination those liabilities that have not yet given rise to capital expenditures (and thus have not yet created or increased basis) with respect to the property of the transferor prior to the transfer also would result in an overstatement of liabilities. Thus, such liabilities also appropriately are excluded in determining liabilities for purposes of § 357(c)(1).

In this case, the contingent environmental liabilities assumed by *S* had not yet been taken into account by *P* prior to the transfer (and therefore had neither given rise to deductions for *P* nor resulted in the creation of or increase in, basis in any property of *P*). As a result, the contingent environmental liabilities are not included in determining whether the amount of the liabilities assumed by *S* exceeds the adjusted basis of the property transferred by *P* pursuant to § 357(c)(1).

Due to the parallel constructions and interrelated function and mechanics of §§ 357 and 358, liabilities that are not included in the determination under § 357(c)(1) also are not included in the § 358 determination of the transferor's basis in the stock received in the § 351 exchange. Therefore, the contingent environmental liabilities assumed by *S* are not treated as money received by *P* under § 358 for purposes of determining *P*'s basis in the stock of S received in the exchange.

*Issue 2:* In Holdcroft Transp. Co. v. Comm'r, 153 F.2d 323 (8th Cir. 1946), the Court of Appeals for the Eighth Circuit held that, after a transfer pursuant to the predecessor to § 351, the payments by a transferee corporation were not deductible even though the transferor partnership would have been entitled to deductions for the payments had the partnership actually made the payments. The court stated generally that the expense of settling claims or liabilities of a predecessor entity did not arise as an operating expense or loss of the business of the transferee but was a part of the cost of acquiring the predecessor's property, and the fact that the claims were contingent and unliquidated at the time of the acquisition was not of controlling consequence.

In Rev. Rul. 80-198, 1980-2 C.B. 113, an individual transferred all of the assets and liabilities of a sole proprietorship, which included accounts payable and accounts receivable, to a new corporation in exchange for all of its stock. The revenue ruling holds, subject to certain limitations, that the transfer qualifies as an exchange within the meaning of § 351(a) and that the transferee corporation will report in its income the accounts receivable as collected and will be allowed deductions under § 162 for the payments it makes to satisfy the accounts payable. In reaching these holdings, the revenue ruling makes reference to the specific congressional intent of § 351(a) to facilitate the incorporation of an ongoing business by making the incorporation tax free. The ruling states that this intent would be equally frustrated if either the transferor were taxed on the transfer of the accounts receivable or the transferee were not allowed a deduction for payment of the accounts payable.

The present case is analogous to the situation in Rev. Rul. 80-198. For business reasons, *P* transferred in a § 351 exchange substantially all of the assets and liabilities associated with the Manufacturing Business to *S*, in exchange for all of its stock, and *P* intends to remain in control of *S*. The costs *S* incurs to remediate the land would have been deductible in part and capitalized in part had *P* continued the Manufacturing Business and incurred those costs to remediate the land. The congressional intent to facilitate necessary business readjustments would be frustrated by not according to *S* the ability to deduct or capitalize the expenses of the ongoing business.

Therefore, on these facts, the Internal Revenue Service will not follow the decision in *Holdcroft*. ... Accordingly, the contingent environmental liabilities assumed from *P* are deductible as business expenses under § 162 or are capitalized under § 263, as appropriate, by *S* under *S*'s method of accounting (determined as if *S* has owned the land for the period and in the same manner as it was owned by *P*).

## HOLDINGS

(1) The liabilities assumed by *S* in the § 351 exchange described above are not liabilities for purposes of § 357(c)(1) and § 358(d) because the liabilities had not yet been taken into account by *P* prior to the transfer (and therefore had neither given rise to deductions for *P* nor resulted in the creation of, or increase in, basis in any property of *P*).

(2) The liabilities assumed by *S* in the § 351 exchange described above are deductible by *S* as business expenses under § 162 or are capital expenditures under § 263, as appropriate, under *S*'s method of accounting (determined as if *S* has owned the land for the period and in the same manner as it was owned by *P*).

## LIMITATIONS

The holdings described above are subject to § 482 and other applicable sections of the Code and principles of law, including the limitations discussed in Rev. Rul. 80-198, 1980-2 C.B. 113 (limiting the scope of the revenue ruling to transactions that do not have a tax avoidance purpose).

---

Taken at face value, Rev. Rul. 95-74 would seem to be a perfectly reasonable application of section 357(c)(3) to an accrual-basis taxpayer's liability that has not yet been deducted (or added to basis) at the time of its assumption by the corporate transferee in connection with the incorporation of the associated business. However, to one scouring the Code for a possible tax advantage—and oblivious to its clear, concluding admonition—the ruling revealed an opportunity.

## Notice 2001-17

2001-1 C.B. 730

The Internal Revenue Service and the Treasury Department have become aware of certain types of transactions, described below, that are being marketed to taxpayers for the purpose of accelerating and, in some cases, duplicating tax deductions. This notice is intended to alert taxpayers and their representatives that the losses generated by such transactions are not properly allowable for federal income tax purposes. This notice also alerts taxpayers and their representatives of certain responsibilities that may arise from participation in such transactions.

. . . These transactions take several forms but, in all cases, involve the transfer of a high basis asset (i.e., an asset with a basis that approximates its fair market value) to a corporation purportedly in exchange for stock of the transferee corporation, and the transferee corporation's assumption of a liability (such as a liability for deferred compensation or other deferred employee benefits or an obligation for environmental remediation) that the transferor has not yet taken into account for federal income tax purposes. The transferor typically remains liable on the underlying obligation. The basis and fair market value of the transferred asset, which may be a security of another member of the same affiliated group of corporations, are generally only marginally greater than the present value of the assumed liability. Therefore, the value of the stock of the transferee received by the transferor is minimal relative to the basis and fair market value of the asset transferred to the transferee corporation.

The transaction is purported to qualify as an exchange under § 351 of the Internal Revenue Code, with the intent that the basis of the stock that the transferor receives from the transferee corporation will be equal to the basis of the transferred asset, unreduced by the liability assumed by the transferee corporation. Under § 358(a), a transferor's basis in stock received in a § 351 exchange is equal to the transferor's basis in property exchanged for such stock, subject to certain adjustments, including a reduction for any money or other property received by the transferor. Under § 358(d)(1), liabilities assumed by the transferee corporation are treated as money received by the transferor. Under certain circumstances, however, liabilities assumed by a transferee corporation in a § 351 exchange are not treated as money received by the transferor and thus do not reduce the basis of the stock received in the exchange. See § 358(d)(2); § 357(c)(3).

The transferor typically sells the stock of the transferee corporation for its fair market value within a relatively short period of time after the purported § 351 exchange and claims a tax loss in an amount approximating the present value of the liability assumed by the transferee corporation. . . . In addition to the transferor's purported loss on the sale of the stock of the transferee corporation, the transferee corporation may claim a § 162 deduction with respect to payments on the liability.

Taxpayers assert several business purposes for these transactions. However, the Service and the Treasury are not aware of any case in which a taxpayer has shown a legitimate non-tax business reason to carry out the combination of steps described above. Moreover, the Service and the Treasury believe that any business purposes taxpayers may assert for certain aspects of these transactions are far outweighed by the purpose to generate deductible losses for federal income tax purposes.

ANALYSIS

Depending on the facts of the particular case, the Service intends to disallow losses claimed by the transferor with respect to these transactions. For transfers after October 18, 1999, the Service will assert that such losses are disallowed because the transferor's basis in the stock received is reduced under § 358(h) (reducing stock basis by the amount of certain liabilities).

For transfers on or before October 18, 1999, as well as for transfers after October 18, 1999, that are not subject to § 358(h), the Service will disallow such losses for one or more reasons, including but not limited to the following: (1) that the purported § 351 exchange lacks sufficient business purpose to qualify as a § 351 exchange; (2) that the transfer of the asset to the transferee corporation is not, in substance, a transfer of property in exchange for stock within the meaning of § 351, but instead is either an agency arrangement for the transferor or simply a payment to the transferee for its assumption of a liability; (3) that the purported § 351 exchange constitutes an acquisition of control of the transferee corporation for the principal purpose of tax avoidance within the meaning of § 269(a) and thus the purported loss should be disallowed under § 269(a); (4) that the principal purpose of the transferee's assumption of the liability was a purpose to avoid federal income tax or was not a bona fide business purpose within the meaning of § 357(b)(1), and thus the assumption of the liability should be treated as money received by the transferor that reduces its basis in the transferee stock; . . . (6) that the purported loss on the sale of the stock of the transferee corporation is not a bona fide loss actually sustained by the transferor, as required by § 1.165-1(b); and (7) that the overall transaction lacks sufficient economic substance to be respected for federal income tax purposes.

In addition, any deduction claimed by a transferee corporation for payments on a liability assumed in a transaction similar to that described above may, depending on the facts of the particular case, be subject to disallowance on one or more of several possible grounds, including that the payments are not for ordinary and necessary business expenses of the transferee corporation. Rev. Rul. 95-74, 1995-2 C.B. 36, which addressed the treatment of certain environmental liabilities assumed by a transferee of a manufacturing business, does not apply to the deductibility by the transferee of liabilities assumed in a transaction of the type described in this notice because Rev. Rul. 95-74 dealt with liabilities assumed by a transferee corporation in connection with the transfer of substantially all the assets associated with the operation of a manufacturing business to the transferee corporation in a transaction that qualified as a § 351 exchange.

The Service may impose penalties on participants in these transactions, or, as applicable, on persons who participate in the promotion or reporting of these transactions, including the accuracy-related penalty under § 6662, the return preparer penalty under § 6694, the promoter penalty under § 6700, and the aiding and abetting penalty under § 6701. . . .

*NOTES*

1. *Widespread use.* The "contingent liability shelter" described in Notice 2001-17 and a virtually identical one involving transfers by partners to partnerships were widely marketed by major accounting firms and other promoters during the late 1990s when many corporations had sizable amounts of capital gains to shelter. Enron engaged in the contingent liability transaction *twice* between the time of Rev. Rul. 95-74 and Notice 2001-17.

2. *Settlement initiative.* In 2002, to reduce the strain these cases placed on the tax system, the IRS announced a settlement initiative to resolve disputes involving contingent liability transactions not yet in, or designated for, litigation. See Rev. Proc. 2002-67, 2002-2 C.B. 733. In general, the initiative provided eligible taxpayers with two different ways to settle their tax disputes. One option allowed taxpayers to deduct 25 percent of the claimed capital loss but generally on the condition that they include the same amount as ordinary income over the succeeding 15 years. The purpose for the income inclusion was to prevent the potential doubling-up of the tax benefit since the procedure left open the possible future deduction of the assumed liability by the corporate transferee. The IRS agreed to waive penalties of those taxpayers agreeing to this option. The other option allowed taxpayers to deduct between 10 and 50 percent of the claimed capital loss, the exact amount to be determined through "baseball" style arbitration in which the arbitrator is required to select either the taxpayer's or the IRS's arbitration offer. This option also left the manner of the required income inclusion and possible application of penalties up to the arbitrator. Under either option, the IRS agreed not to challenge the deductibility of the taxpayer's transaction costs. Reportedly, the settlement initiative was not accepted by many taxpayers. The following case is one of the first of the disputes to be resolved by the courts on the merits.

## Coltec Industries, Inc. v. United States

454 F.3d 1340 (Fed. Cir. 2006), cert. denied, 549 U.S. 1206 (2007)

DYK, Circuit Judge.

In 1996, Coltec Industries, Inc. ("Coltec") reported a capital loss of approximately $378.7 million on its consolidated tax return. This loss was generated by Coltec's selling of high-basis stock for a relatively low price. . . . We conclude that, although Coltec's claimed capital loss fell within the literal terms of the statute, the transaction that created the high basis in the stock lacked economic substance and therefore must be disregarded for tax purposes. . . .

In 1996 Coltec was a publicly traded company with numerous subsidiaries. In that year, Coltec sold one of its businesses, Holley Automotive, Inc., for a gain of approximately $240.9 million. Coltec then met with its tax advisors at Arthur Andersen LLP to discuss, among other things, strategies to offset this gain. Arthur Andersen proposed a transaction that had been used in the past to generate capital losses. The transaction essentially involved three steps. First, the parent company would reorganize a dormant subsidiary into a special purpose entity. Second, the parent would transfer property and contingent liabilities to the newly reorganized subsidiary in exchange for stock in that subsidiary. Finally, the parent would sell the stock to a third-party for a nominal sum. The parent would treat its basis in the stock as equal to the property it transferred to the subsidiary but not reduced by the liabilities the subsidiary assumed. The parent would then suffer a significant loss from the sale of the stock because the sale price of the stock would be drastically lower than its basis.

Coltec found Arthur Andersen's proposal appealing. For one thing, Coltec had contingent liabilities, namely asbestos liabilities, which were a prerequisite for this type of transaction. . . . Coltec was at risk from the asbestos problem, as one of its subsidiaries, "Garlock," and one of Garlock's subsidiaries, "Anchor," had both previously manufactured or distributed asbestos products. . . .

Coltec decided to implement the Arthur Andersen proposal, and has admitted that tax avoidance was one of its reasons for doing so. Coltec's first step was to rename one of its dormant subsidiaries, "Garrison." Coltec caused Garrison to issue 99,800 shares of common stock and 1,300,000 shares of Class A stock to Coltec in exchange for a payment of $13,998,000. In a separate transaction, Garrison issued 100,000 shares of common stock to Garlock (representing approximately a 6.6% interest in Garrison), and assumed all the managerial responsibilities for handling the asbestos related claims against Garlock. Garrison also assumed, and agreed to indemnify Garlock against, all losses and liabilities incurred in connection with asbestos-related claims against Garlock. Garlock transferred to Garrison all outstanding Anchor stock, certain records and insurance policies relating to asbestos liabilities, and furniture. Garlock also transferred to Garrison a promissory note from one of its other subsidiaries, Stemco, Inc., in the amount of $375 million.[7] . . . [T]he $375 million amount was calculated to cover the estimated future asbestos liabilities of Garlock, including the Anchor liabilities. . . . Thus, Garrison assumed responsibility for Garlock's potential asbestos liabilities in exchange for a promissory note in the amount of approximately $375 million.

The third and final step involved Garlock's sale of its newly-acquired Garrison stock. On December 20, 1996, as previously contemplated, Garlock sold all of its 100,000 shares of Garrison stock to two banks for $500,000. The amount received was only slightly greater than half the transaction costs for establishing Garrison. As a condition of this sale, Coltec agreed to indemnify the banks against any veil-piercing claims for asbestos liabilities. Coltec, after this transaction, continued to own 93% of Garrison.

---

7. Stemco was indebted to Garlock, but rather than have Stemco transfer the promissory note directly to Garlock, Garlock had Stemco transfer the note to Garrison. The reason for utilizing a note from another entity was so that Garlock's basis in the note would be $375 million rather than zero. If Garlock had issued its own promissory note to Garrison, then Garlock's basis in that note would be treated as zero by the IRS because Garlock incurred no cost in making the note.

In its consolidated tax return for 1996, Coltec asserted that Garlock's basis in the Garrison stock was $379.2 million (representing the $375 million Stemco note plus the other property given to Garrison valued at approximately $4 million, but not reduced by the liabilities assumed by Garrison). Thus Garlock claimed to suffer a $378.7 million loss when it sold the stock for only $500,000. This $378.7 million loss more than offset Coltec's gains for that tax year. The unused loss was carried forward to offset gain in future tax years. Significantly, the loss was recognized only for tax purposes and not for book purposes, and the loss was not reported on the taxpayer's public financial reports.

. . . The government contended that the loss should be disallowed because Garlock was not entitled to the claimed basis for the Garrison stock. The government offered three separate theories. First, the government argued that the contingent asbestos liabilities were not excluded from "money received" treatment by § 358(d)(2), because § 357(c)(3) was inapplicable, as it refers to liabilities which would "give rise to a deduction" and the contingent liabilities here would not "give rise to a deduction." Second, the government argued that the transaction in which Garlock transferred a $375 million note to Garrison in exchange for the assumption of the asbestos liabilities had an improper purpose and should thus result in "money received" treatment under the statutory anti-abuse provision. Finally, the government argued that the transaction in which the note was exchanged for the liability assumption should be disregarded under the general economic substance doctrine with the result that the basis would not be increased by the amount of the Stemco note.

The Court of Federal Claims, after a bench trial, rejected the government's three arguments. The court held that the liabilities would "give rise to a deduction" under § 357(c)(3). The court also determined that that transaction should not result in "money received" treatment under § 357(b)(1), the statutory anti-abuse provision, because the principal purpose of the transaction was not tax avoidance; rather, it was a bona fide business purpose. The Court of Federal Claims finally rejected the government's alternative argument under the general economic substance doctrine, concluding that the doctrine was unconstitutional as a violation of separation of powers. The court went on to hold alternatively that the doctrine did not apply to the present case because the transaction had a bona fide business purpose. . . .

## DISCUSSION

We find nothing in the literal terms of the statute that required Garlock to reduce its basis in the stock by the amount of liabilities assumed by Garrison. However, we conclude that the Court of Federal Claims erred in rejecting the long-standing economic substance doctrine and in its application of that doctrine. The underlying transaction between Garlock and Garrison, in which a $375 million note was transferred to Garrison in exchange for the assumption of the contingent asbestos liabilities, had no meaningful economic purpose, save the tax benefits to Coltec. As such, that transaction must be ignored for tax purposes.

[The court's explanation that "contingent liabilities" are included within the term "liability" as used in section 358(d), is omitted.]

Consequently, under the general rule, the liabilities assumed by Garrison would be treated as "money received" by Garlock. Thus under the general rule [of section 358(d)(1)], Garlock's basis in its newly acquired Garrison stock would be decreased by the amount of the contingent liabilities assumed by Garrison.

However, there is an exception to this general rule for calculating basis. Section 358(d)(2) provides that § 358(d)(1) "shall not apply to the amount of any liability excluded under section 357(c)(3)." . . . The government asserts that the liabilities at issue do not fall under § 358(d)(2)'s exception. The government's argument requires that we consider the interaction of four code provisions: sections 358(d)(2), 357(c)(3), 357(c)(1), and 357(b)(1).

### i. Application of § 357(c)(3)

. . . The parties first dispute whether the liabilities here "would give rise to a deduction" as § 357(c)(3) requires. The government contends that the liability is not the kind that "would give rise to a deduction" under § 357(c)(3) because § 357(c)(3) only applies where the transferor (here Garlock) transferred *both* a liability and the underlying business that generated that liability. Because Garlock transferred its asbestos liabilities but kept its core business, the government urges that the liabilities do not fall within the scope of § 357(c)(3). It is true that the central purpose of § 357(c)(3) was to protect taxpayers who transferred the assets of their business along with liabilities of their business (such as accounts payable) from having to recognize gain if the liabilities exceeded the assets. The theory was that the transferor corporation should not have to recognize gain when it had lost the tax deduction that would flow from payment of the liabilities. However, we find the government's interpretation to be inconsistent with the plain language of § 357(c)(3). Nothing in the plain language of § 357(c)(3) limits the liabilities excludable to only those that were transferred along with an underlying business.

Accordingly, we conclude that § 357(c)(3) does not limit excludable liabilities to only those that were transferred with an underlying business, and that the liabilities here satisfy the "would give rise to a deduction" requirement. In so holding, we join the only other court of appeals to have considered this exact issue. *See* Black & Decker Corp. v. U.S., 436 F.3d 431, 437 (4th Cir. 2006). . . .

### ii. Applicability of § 357(b)(1)'s Anti-Abuse Provision

. . . Basically, § 357(c)(1) sets forth a gain-recognition calculation where one of the variables is the "amount of liabilities assumed." Section 357(c)(3) excludes certain liabilities from this gain-recognition calculus.

However, § 357(c)(1) does not apply when an exchange triggers § 357(b)(1)'s anti-abuse provision. 26 U.S.C. § 357(c)(2). Section 357(b)(1)'s anti-abuse provision applies where liabilities are assumed principally for tax avoidance purposes or lack a bona fide business purpose. . . .

When it applies, the effect of § 357(b)(1) is two-fold. First, it supplants § 357(c)(1) and requires that assumed liabilities be treated as "money received" for purposes of § 351(b), so that the full amount of gain must be recognized to the extent of liabilities assumed rather than merely (as (c)(1) requires) the amount that liabilities exceed basis. Second, it eliminates the § 357(c)(3) exclusion. In other words, § 357(c)(3)'s exclusion may be rendered inapplicable by (b)(1) if there is a principal tax avoidance purpose or an absence of bona fide business purpose.

The government argues that the transaction here falls within § 357(b)(1) because the principal purpose behind the assumption of liabilities by Garrison was to avoid taxes or was otherwise not a bona fide business purpose. Although neither § 358(d)(2) nor § 357(c)(3) (the sections directly involved here) makes a direct reference to § 357(b)(1) (the anti-abuse provision), the government argues that: § 357(c)(3) refers to § 357(c)(1); § 357(c)(1) can only apply when § 357(b)(1) does not apply; and that therefore, § 357(c)(3) cannot apply where § 357(b)(1) applies.

We disagree with the government's construction of these code provisions. These code provisions are not a model of statutory draftsmanship. The real question is what is meant by § 358(d)(2) when it refers to a "liability excluded under section 357(c)(3)." This could have two possible meanings. It could mean that a liability is excluded "under section 357(c)(3)" if—looking at § 357(c)(3) in a vacuum—the liability is of the type excluded from the § 357(c)(1) calculation. On the other hand, it could mean that the liability is "excluded" only if it is actually excluded from gain recognition under § 357(c)(1) by operation of § 357(c)(3)—that is, if the (c)(3) exclusion is meaningful because § 357(c)(1) is operative and not overridden by § 357(b)(1). In essence, the taxpayer urges the former interpretation, and the government urges the latter interpretation. We think the taxpayer's interpretation is the better of the two.

In construing statutory provisions, we appropriately consult dictionaries in use at the time the statute was enacted. The use of the term "under" in § 358(d)(2) suggests limiting consideration to (c)(3) itself since the dictionary definition of "under" in this context is "required by" or "in accordance with." In other words, the dictionary definition of the term "under" suggests looking only to the operation of § 357(c)(3) itself. The section says nothing about excluding liabilities from gain recognition. It deals only with excluding liabilities from the § 357(c)(1) computation. Moreover, we think that Congress likely would have done one of the following if it wished § 357(b)(1) to apply in this situation. On the one hand, it could have made explicit reference to the basis provision of § 358 in § 357(b)(1); instead that section refers only to treating an assumption of liabilities as "money received" for "purposes of section 351 or 361" (which deal only with gain recognition and not basis reduction). Alternatively, Congress could have made explicit reference to § 357(b)(1) in § 358(d)(2) if it intended to require that § 358(d)(2) apply only if § 357(c)(3)'s exclusion was not rendered inoperative by § 357(b)(1). In other words, if Congress wanted the operation of § 357(b)(1) to preclude the benefit of

§ 358(d)(2), it could have said in § 358(d)(2) something like, "§ 358(d)(1) shall not apply to the amount of any assumed liability excluded under § 357(c)(3) *unless the assumption involved a prohibited purpose described in § 357(b)(1)*." (The added underscored language would achieve the supposedly desired result.)

We thus conclude that if the liability is excluded by § 357(c)(3) standing alone, then § 358(d)(2)'s exception may be invoked. It does not matter whether the anti-abuse provision of § 357(b)(1) applies and overrides the actual operation of § 357(c)(1). The interpretation we adopt in this respect is identical to the interpretation adopted by the Fourth Circuit in *Black & Decker*, though we reach this result by a somewhat different interpretive path. We therefore conclude that the liabilities fall within § 357(c)(3); that § 357(b)(1) is not relevant here; and that § 358(d)(2) excludes the liabilities from "money received" treatment. The consequence is that under the literal terms of the statute the basis of Garlock's Garrison stock is increased by the Stemco note and is not reduced by the assumed contingent asbestos liabilities. Ultimately, the taxpayer would not be disqualified from claiming the capital loss.

II

Having concluded that Garlock's loss from the sale of its Garrison stock falls within the literal terms of the statute, we now turn to the government's argument under the general economic substance doctrine. We must first consider the Court of Federal Claims' holding that "the use of the economic substance doctrine to trump mere compliance with the Code would violate the separation of powers." That holding is untenable. In rejecting the economic substance doctrine, the court failed to follow binding precedent of the Supreme Court and this court and its predecessor court, the Court of Claims.

Over the last seventy years, the economic substance doctrine has required disregarding, for tax purposes, transactions that comply with the literal terms of the tax code but lack economic reality. This principle has its roots in several Supreme Court cases. . . . The economic substance doctrine has also been repeatedly applied by our predecessor court. . . . There can be no question that the Court of Federal Claims is required to follow the precedent of the Supreme Court, our court, and our predecessor court, the Court of Claims.

Despite acknowledging that "the [Supreme] Court has decided tax cases invoking [the economic substance] doctrine," the Court of Federal Claims chose not to follow this precedent because "[a] careful reading of *other* cases cited by the Government[] . . . reveals that the Court resolved the tax question at issue first by looking to the Code and utilized doctrinal language only to further support its conclusion." We fail to see how the existence of other Supreme Court cases that do not rely on the doctrine undermine the authority of those that do. . . .

Even if we were to assume that the decisions of the Supreme Court and our predecessor court recognizing the economic substance doctrine are not binding, we cannot agree that the doctrine is somehow unconstitutional. Even Coltec makes no effort to defend this proposition on appeal. The Court of Federal Claims has cited no authority supporting its determination that the doctrine is unconstitutional. . . .

The economic substance doctrine represents a judicial effort to enforce the statutory purpose of the tax code. From its inception, the economic substance doctrine has been used to prevent taxpayers from subverting the legislative purpose of the tax code by engaging in transactions that are fictitious or lack economic reality simply to reap a tax benefit. In this regard, the economic substance doctrine is not unlike other canons of construction that are employed in circumstances where the literal terms of a statute can undermine the ultimate purpose of the statute. The Supreme Court has explicitly held that when the judiciary goes beyond the literal language of a statute in order to give effect to its purpose, the separation of powers is not violated. . . . Here, the economic substance doctrine is merely a judicial tool for effectuating the underlying Congressional purpose that, despite literal compliance with the statute, tax benefits not be afforded based on transactions lacking in economic substance. We conclude that there is no basis for holding the economic substance doctrine unconstitutional.

### III

Although the Court of Federal Claims found the economic substance doctrine unconstitutional, it went on to hold that the doctrine was inapplicable in any event, relying on the findings that it made in connection with the statutory tax avoidance test. A review of that determination requires us to consider the basic principles of the economic substance doctrine, as well as its applicability to this case. . . .

#### B. Application of the Economic Substance Doctrine

Under these principles, Coltec had the burden of proving that this transaction, which admittedly had a tax avoidance purpose, had an economic reality. The Court of Federal Claims held that Coltec had met this burden. The ultimate conclusion as to business purpose is a legal conclusion, which we review without deference, and the underlying relevant facts are in large part undisputed.

In urging that the transaction had economic substance, Coltec focused particularly on its objective to make the company as a whole a more attractive acquisition target as well as on its objective to make other potential target companies view Coltec as a desirable acquirer. Coltec offered two arguments for why the liabilities-note transaction had economic substance in this context: (1) because the creation of Garrison to manage the asbestos liabilities would make Coltec more attractive and (2) because the transaction would add a barrier to veil-piercing claims against Coltec. Neither of these theories suggests that the transaction at issue has economic substance.

The first asserted business purpose focuses on the wrong transaction — the creation of Garrison as a separate subsidiary to manage asbestos liabilities. Coltec contends that the transaction had an economic purpose because, by having a separate corporation like Garrison manage Garlock's asbestos liabilities, Coltec became more attractive. . . . The Court of Federal Claims also found that "[T]he management and minimization of [the asbestos] liabilities were essential to the continued viability of Anchor and potentially Garlock. *Therefore, the conversion of these businesses into corporate form* was clearly to serve a *bona fide* business purpose."

The government does not dispute that the transfer of management activities may have had economic substance. The transfer of management activities, however, is not the transaction at issue. Here . . . we must focus on the transaction that gave the taxpayer a high basis in the stock and thus gave rise to the alleged benefit upon sale. That transaction is Garrison's assumption of Garlock's asbestos liabilities in exchange for the $375 million note. Coltec admits that "Garrison received the Stemco note in exchange for assuming Garlock's asbestos liabilities." It is this exchange that provided Garlock with the high basis in the Garrison stock, this exchange whose tax consequence is in dispute, and therefore it is this exchange on which we must focus.

The transfer of the liabilities in exchange for the note is separate and distinct from the fact that Garrison took a managerial role in administering the asbestos liabilities, as demonstrated by the fact that Garrison *managed* another entity's asbestos liabilities (Anchor's liabilities) without actually *assuming* Anchor's liabilities. The taxpayer has not demonstrated any business purpose to be served by linking Garrison's assumption of the liabilities to the centralization of litigation management.

Coltec's second argument for why the transaction has economic substance — that the transaction was designed to strengthen Coltec's position against potential veil-piercing claims — focuses on the appropriate transaction but is also unavailing. Coltec argues, and the Court of Federal Claims agreed, that the transfer of the liabilities for the note was designed to strengthen Coltec's core business from veil-piercing claims, because Garrison would serve as another corporate layer between asbestos claimants and Coltec. Coltec correctly points out that the asbestos liabilities of subsidiary companies such as Garlock frequently exceeded the assets of those companies, and that plaintiffs in asbestos liability cases routinely sought to pierce the corporate veil to reach the assets of parent companies. Understandably, this was a matter of considerable concern to parent companies such as Coltec. The problem is that there is no objective basis for suggesting that the assumption of these liabilities by another subsidiary (in this case Garrison) would in any way ameliorate this veil-piercing problem.

In this respect, Coltec relied entirely on the testimony of various Coltec executives about the veil-piercing benefits that they perceived from the Garlock-Garrison transaction. . . . These subjective views of Coltec's executives, even if credited, as they were by the Court of Federal Claims, are insufficient to establish economic substance. As we have discussed, economic substance is measured from an objective, reasonable viewpoint, not by the subjective views of the taxpayer's corporate officers. Looking at the transaction objectively, there is no basis in reality for the idea that a corporation can avoid exposure for past acts by transferring liabilities to a subsidiary.

The transfer of the liabilities for the note could only strengthen Coltec's defense against veil-piercing if third parties would be obligated to pursue Garrison instead of Garlock. It is perfectly clear that the transaction had no such result. We are not aware of, nor has Coltec brought to our attention, any authority suggesting otherwise. Nor has Coltec pointed to testimony from any third party that there could be such a benefit. The Court of Federal Claims made no such finding, and even Coltec concedes that Garrison's assumption of Garlock's asbestos liabilities did not actually shield Garlock or Coltec from direct liability, conceding that "Coltec could not, of course, effect a release of Garlock's liabilities to third parties."

Thus the transaction here could only affect relations among Coltec and its own subsidiaries — it has absolutely no affect on third party asbestos claimants. . . . We therefore see nothing indicating that the transfer of liabilities in exchange for the note effected any real change in the "flow of economic benefits," provided any real "opportunity to make a profit," or "appreciably affected" Coltec's beneficial interests aside from creating a tax advantage. Garrison's assumption of Garlock's liabilities in exchange for the Stemco note served no purpose other than to artificially inflate Garlock's basis in its Garrison stock. That transaction must be disregarded for tax purposes. When that transaction is disregarded, the basis in the Garrison stock is unaffected by the Stemco note/assumed liability exchange. . . .

## *NOTES AND QUESTIONS*

1. *When is the economic substance doctrine relevant?* The *Coltec* decisions present two opposing views concerning the role of the economic substance doctrine and its "relevance" to future transactions potentially subject to section 7701(o). The trial court urged that the doctrine be invoked very sparingly because

> [t]he public must be able to rely on clear and understandable rules established by Congress to ascertain their federal tax obligations. If federal tax laws are applied in an unpredictable and arbitrary manner, albeit by federal judges for the "right" reasons in the "right case," public confidence in the Code and tax enforcement system will be further eroded. [62 Fed. Cl. 716, 755 (2004).]

Balanced against the trial court's concern, however, is the effect on public confidence if taxpayers are allowed to reduce their tax liabilities through use of egregious tax shelters.

In contrast to the trial court, the Federal Circuit explained that

> [t]he economic substance doctrine represents a judicial effort to enforce the statutory purpose of the tax code. From its inception, the economic substance doctrine has been used to prevent taxpayers from subverting the legislative purpose of the tax code by engaging in transactions that are fictitious or lack economic reality simply to reap a tax benefit. In this regard, the economic substance doctrine is not unlike other canons of

> construction that are employed in circumstances where the literal terms of a statute can undermine the ultimate purpose of the statute. . . . Here, the economic substance doctrine is merely a judicial tool for effectuating the underlying Congressional purpose. . . . [454 F.3d at 1353-54.]

In characterizing the doctrine as merely a tool of statutory interpretation, the Federal Circuit unfortunately provides little guidance on when and how frequently it should be raised. Was it necessary to invoke the doctrine in *Coltec*? Did the Federal Circuit perhaps feel obligated to address the economic substance issue once the government raised it and the trial court made its novel assertion that use of the doctrine violated separation of powers?

2. *Deduction of asbestos liabilities?* If Garrison satisfied the asbestos liabilities assumed in the transaction, would it be entitled to deduct those expenses? What is the answer based on the discussion of issue 2 in Rev. Rul. 95-74?

3. Black & Decker. As mentioned in *Coltec*, another contingent liability case decided about the same time is Black & Decker v. U.S., 436 F.3d 431 (4th Cir. 2006), *aff'g in part and rev'g in part* 340 F. Supp. 2d 621 (D. Md. 2004). In that case, the taxpayer transferred to its controlled subsidiary $561 million in cash and also had the subsidiary assume the taxpayer's contingent liability to provide health care benefits for the taxpayer's employees. The contingent liability was valued at $560 million so that when the taxpayer subsequently sold the stock of the subsidiary for $1 million, it claimed a $560 million capital loss. The trial judge was apparently quite taken by the transaction, referring to it at a bench conference as "a thing of grace and beauty . . . a wonderful transaction," and stating, "I now [understand] why my former tax partners got paid so much." The judge denied the government's summary judgment motion that the statute precluded the claimed capital loss, and granted the taxpayer's summary judgment motion that as a matter of law, the transaction was not a sham and should be respected for tax purposes. Like the Federal Circuit in *Coltec*, the Fourth Circuit affirmed the trial judge's conclusion that the statute did not bar the capital loss. The court, however, found that there remained genuine issues of material fact to be resolved regarding whether the transaction was a sham, and therefore reversed that portion of the trial court opinion and remanded the case for trial. In December 2007, the parties announced that they had settled their dispute. According to news reports, the settlement required Black & Decker to pay the government about $50 million in 2008, or less than 30 percent of the amount the company had apparently reserved for the contingent additional tax liability (plus interest) if the company's position were not respected.

4. *Legislative fixes.* The contingent liability shelter illustrates the importance of matching as closely as possible the tax consequences of a transaction with its economic effect. This objective has been particularly difficult to achieve when liabilities are involved in a transaction because the economic effect of a liability transfer—that is, the amount of the economic obligation actually transferred from one party to another—may be hard to determine. In the contingent liability shelter, the entire liability transferred apparently became an obligation of the

corporate transferee because the value of the transferee's stock was reduced by the full amount of the liability. Yet, at least as found by the courts in *Black & Decker* and *Coltec*, sections 357(c)(3) and 358(d)(2) permitted the liability to be disregarded for tax purposes, so that there was no required matching reduction in the transferor's basis in the stock of the transferee. The result of the mismatch was the huge claimed capital loss upon disposition of the stock.

Read I.R.C. § 358(h). This provision was enacted in direct response to the contingent liability shelter. If, after application of the rest of section 358 (including section 358(a)(1) and (d)), the transferor's basis in the transferee stock exceeds its fair market value, such basis must be reduced (but not below fair market value) by the amount of any liability assumed by the transferee in the transaction. For this purpose, the term "liability" is defined broadly to include any fixed or contingent obligation to make a payment. Subject to regulatory override, no basis reduction is required if the liability assumption occurs in connection with a transfer of the trade or business, or substantially all of the assets, with which the liability is associated. The regulations have since removed the second exception contained in section 358(h)(2)(B) relating to liability assumptions in connection with a transfer of substantially all the assets. Reg. § 1.358-5.

In contrast to the contingent liability cases, certain earlier shelters were built upon the opposite claim that the liability amount to be taken into account for tax purposes exceeded the economic effect of transferring the liability. For example, under prior law, section 357 also applied to transfers of property "subject to" a liability (even though the liability was not expressly assumed by the transferee). Certain taxpayers transferred property subject to a liability and claimed that the full amount of the liability had to be taken into account for tax purposes even though less than the full amount was actually assumed by the transferee. An example is a section 351 transfer of an asset (with basis and value of $60,000) encumbered by a $100,000 nonrecourse liability (with the remaining security for the debt retained by the transferor). If the asset transferred was treated as "subject to" the full $100,000 liability, then that full amount arguably had to be taken into account under section 357 even though it exceeded the economic burden actually assumed by the transferee (the $60,000 value of the only asset received by the transferee that was encumbered by the liability). Under that interpretation, the transferor arguably had to recognize $40,000 gain under section 357(c); if the transferor was not subject to U.S. tax, however, there was no resulting U.S. tax liability. At the same time, the corporate transferee arguably obtained a basis of $100,000 in the transferred asset (still only worth $60,000), allowing the transferee to claim a large tax loss upon subsequent disposition of the asset.

Read I.R.C. §§ 357(a) and (d), 362(d). The statute has also been amended to try to stop these shelters and more closely match the tax and economic consequences of a liability transfer. Congress amended section 357(a) to limit that provision to liabilities expressly assumed (or treated as assumed) by the corporate transferee. Section 357(d) defines the amount of a liability that is treated as assumed for purposes of sections 357, 358(d) and (h), 362(d), and certain other provisions dealing with reorganizations. For recourse liabilities, the amount is generally the portion of the liability the transferee has agreed to and is expected to satisfy, whether or not the transferor's liability is relieved. Nonrecourse liabilities are generally treated as assumed if an asset subject to the liability is also transferred. If there are, however, additional nontransferred assets subject to the same nonrecourse liability, the amount treated as assumed must be reduced by the lesser of (1) the amount the owner of such nontransferred assets has agreed to and is expected to satisfy, or (2) the fair market value of such nontransferred assets. These same rules apply in determining how much of a liability should be taken into account in a corporate distribution where the distributee assumes a liability or takes property subject to a liability. See I.R.C. § 301(b)(2); Reg. § 1.301-1(g).

Section 362(d)(1) bars the corporate transferee from receiving a basis in any property transferred greater than its fair market value by reason of gain recognized to the transferor under section 357. Further, section 362(d)(2) limits the transferee's basis in any property received where the transferor is not subject to U.S. tax and the transferee assumes a nonrecourse liability that is also secured by assets not transferred to the transferee. In that case, for purposes of determining the transferee's basis, the gain recognized by the transferor is determined as if the transferee assumed only a ratable share of the nonrecourse liability (determined by relative fair market values of the transferred and nontransferred properties).

Application of these new rules will depend upon the facts and circumstances of the transactions. Since incorrect tax results may arise if the amount of a liability taken into account for tax purposes is *either* too much *or* too little relative to the economic effect of the liability transfer, transactions involving liabilities will likely remain a perilous area for the tax system.

# Chapter 8

# Redemptions Involving Related Corporations

Suppose a shareholder owns a controlling interest in two different corporations and transfers the stock of one of them (the "issuing corporation") to the other (the "acquiring corporation") in exchange for some consideration. How should the transaction be taxed? Although the transaction is simple, as we shall see, determining its proper tax consequences is not.

The *form* of the transaction is a sale of stock by the shareholder to the acquiring corporation. But the *substance* of the transaction may be a corporate distribution because the net effect of the transaction is a flow of funds out of corporate solution. Alternatively, the transaction might be taxed under section 351 if the shareholder has control (as defined in section 368(c)) of the acquiring corporation immediately after the transfer. Each of these characterizations produces different tax consequences.

Section 304, the subject of this chapter, generally treats this transaction as a corporate distribution for tax purposes in order to protect the potential dividend consequences to the shareholder. As discussed in connection with the taxation of corporate redemptions (chapter six), the currently comparable tax treatment to individuals of dividend income and long-term capital gain make this purpose much less important than in the past. Because corporate shareholders may prefer dividend characterization of the transaction, however, section 304 may be used by such taxpayers opportunistically, and some recent litigation and legislation have addressed these strategies.

The theory of section 304 is straightforward: because of the overlapping ownership interest in the two corporations, they should be treated for tax purposes as if they were really one. Thus, a sale of stock of the issuing corporation to the acquiring corporation should be taxed like a redemption by a single distributing corporation. The rules of section 302 apply in determining whether the redemption is treated as an exchange under section 302(a) or a distribution under section 301.

But as so often happens when form is disregarded for tax purposes, the reconstruction of the transaction introduces a host of difficult interpretive questions, and much of the evolution of the law has involved a gradual resolution of those questions. For example, under current law, the hypothetical redemption is treated as made by the *acquiring corporation*, perhaps because it appears to be the source of the funds leaving corporate solution. I.R.C. § 304(a)(1). Yet the tax consequences of this redemption turn, under section 302, on the shareholder's before-and-after interest in the *issuing corporation*. I.R.C. § 304(b)(1). This approach is understandable—given that the transaction generally does not result in any change to the shareholder's interest in the acquiring corporation—but it departs from the usual application of section 302. Finally, if the redemption is treated as a section 301 distribution, the E&P of *both* corporations is used to determine whether the distribution is a dividend. I.R.C. § 304(b)(2).

Transactions potentially affected by section 304 arise in two patterns, which are controlled by different portions of that provision. The example described thus far, where one or more persons has a controlling interest in two different corporations, is referred to as a "brother-sister acquisition" and is governed by section 304(a)(1). Another pattern involves a transfer by a shareholder of stock of a corporation (the "issuing corporation") to an acquiring corporation that is controlled by the issuing corporation; this pattern is commonly referred to as a "parent-subsidiary acquisition" and is governed by section 304(a)(2). (As we shall see, even the distinction between these two patterns is often not sharp once the constructive ownership rules are taken into account.) Corollary rules, including the definition of "control" and the application of constructive ownership rules, apply to both types of transactions. The balance of this chapter describes the tax consequences of transactions falling into one of these two patterns.

## A. Brother-Sister Acquisitions

Read I.R.C. § 304(a)(1), (b)(1) and (2), and (c). In a brother-sister acquisition, one or more persons controlling each of two corporations transfers stock in one of them to the other in exchange for property. The transaction is treated for tax purposes as a distribution in redemption of the stock of the acquiring corporation. Unlike certain provisions (such as section 357(b)) that recharacterize transactions for tax purposes based upon the taxpayer's purpose or intent, section 304 generally relies upon objective tests. The statute defines "control" quite expansively, and also applies liberalized constructive ownership rules, to try to ensure the provision is broad enough to identify all cases where two nominally separate corporations should be treated, in substance, as one. The following ruling illustrates the basic application of section 304(a)(1).

### Rev. Rul. 71-563

1971-2 C.B. 175

... A, an individual, owns 100 shares of corporation X which is all the outstanding stock of X. B, the son of A, owns all the outstanding stock of Corporation

Y. A sold 25 shares of stock of X to Y for cash. The purchase price of the X stock was its fair market value. The earnings and profits of Y exceeded the amount of cash paid by Y to A for the X stock.

Section 304(a)(1) . . . provides that for purposes of section 302 and section 303 of the Code, if one or more persons are in control of each of two corporations and in return for property, one of the corporations acquires stock in the other corporation from the person so in control, then such property shall be treated as a distribution in redemption of the stock of the corporation acquiring such stock. . . .

Section 304(c)(1) of the Code provides that for purposes of section 304 of the Code control means the ownership of stock possessing at least 50 percent of the total combined voting power of all classes of stock entitled to vote, or at least 50 percent of the total value of shares of all classes of stock.

Section 304(c)(2) of the Code makes section 318(a) of the Code (relating to the constructive ownership of stock) applicable to section 304 of the Code, with certain modifications not here relevant, for the purposes of determining control under section 304(c)(1) of the Code. Section 318(a)(1)(A) of the Code provides, in pertinent part, that an individual is considered as owning the stock owned, directly or indirectly, by his children.

Section 318(a)(2)(C) of the Code provides, in pertinent part, that if 50 percent or more in value of the stock in a corporation is owned, directly or indirectly, by any person, such person is considered as owning the stock owned, directly or indirectly, by such corporation, in that proportion which the value of the stock which such person so owns bears to the value of all the stock in such corporation.

A actually owned 100 percent of the stock of X before the transaction and by the application of section 318(a)(1)(A) of the Code, A is considered to have owned all of the stock of Y before the transaction. Accordingly, since Y acquired the stock of X for cash from a person (A) in control of both the issuing corporation (X) and the acquiring corporation (Y), the transaction is considered to be an acquisition of stock by a related corporation within the meaning of section 304(a)(1) of the Code and thus a redemption of the stock of Y, the acquiring corporation. . . .

Under section 1.304-2(a) . . . the amount received by A is treated as a distribution of property under section 302(d) of the Code unless the distribution is to be treated as received in exchange for stock pursuant to section 302(a). . . . Section 302(a) of the Code is applicable if the requirements of section 302(b) of the Code are satisfied.

Section 304(b)(1) of the Code provides that the applicability of section 302(b) of the Code is determined by reference to the stock of the issuing corporation, X. Through the application of section 318(a)(2)(C) of the Code, B owns the 25 shares of the stock of X held by Y. The ownership by B of the 25 shares of the stock of X is attributed to A by reason of application of section 318(a)(1)(A) of the Code. Therefore, after the transaction A still owns 100 percent of X and there is no complete termination of A's interest in the stock of X within the meaning of section 302(b)(3) of the Code nor is there a substantially disproportionate redemption within the meaning of section [302(b)(2)] of the Code.

The "not essentially equivalent to a dividend" test of section 302(b)(1) of the Code cannot be met since there has been no meaningful reduction in A's proportionate interest in the stock of X as a result of the transaction. In determining the existence of a meaningful reduction, the constructive ownership rules of section 318 of the Code are applied. . . .

The inapplicability of . . . section 302(a) of the Code results in the amount received by A being treated, pursuant to section 302(d) of the Code, as a distribution to which section 301 of the Code applies. Accordingly, the distribution is treated as a dividend to A from Y under section 301(c)(1) and section 316 of the Code. . . .

## *NOTES AND QUESTIONS*

1. *Tax consequences if redemption treated as section 301 distribution.* Statutory amendments to section 304(a)(1) and (b)(2) that postdate Rev. Rul. 71-563 and the existing regulations explain exactly which stock of the acquiring corporation is deemed redeemed, and the resulting tax consequences of the transaction, if the redemption is treated as a section 301 distribution to the shareholder transferring issuing corporation stock. In that case, the transferor is treated as transferring the issuing corporation stock to the acquiring corporation in exchange for stock of the latter corporation in a hypothetical section 351 transaction. As a result, the transferor's basis in the issuing corporation stock is preserved in both the transferor's basis in the acquiring corporation stock deemed received and the acquiring corporation's basis in the issuing corporation stock that is transferred. I.R.C. §§ 358(a), 362(a); Prop. Reg. § 1.304-2(a)(3). The acquiring corporation stock deemed received by the transferor is then treated as redeemed by the acquiring corporation. The redemption, taxed under section 301, is treated as a dividend to the extent of the E&P of both the acquiring and issuing corporations. I.R.C. § 304(b)(2). If the redemption leaves the transferor with unrecovered basis in the redeemed stock, the unrecovered amount increases the transferor's basis in any other stock in the acquiring corporation. Reg. §§ 1.302-2(c) (ex. 1); 1.304-2(c) (ex. 1 (last sentence)). If, as in the facts of Rev. Rul. 71-563, the transferor does not actually own any stock in the acquiring corporation, then there is the same potential "disappearing basis" problem discussed in connection with Notice 2001-45 (p. 236) and the notes thereafter. The transferor may be able to claim the basis as a loss at some point in the future. Prop. Reg. § 1.302-5(a)(3)(i), (b)(4)(i). Alternatively, it is possible that the unrecovered amount would simply increase the transferor's basis in any *issuing* corporation stock still owned after the transaction. In a portion not reproduced, Rev. Rul. 71-563 reached that conclusion, although based on an earlier version of the statute.

2. *Tax consequences if redemption treated as section 302(a) exchange.* If the deemed redemption is treated as an exchange to the transferor under section 302(a), the transferor's basis and holding period in the stock deemed redeemed is the same as her basis and holding period in the issuing corporation stock actually transferred. Prop. Reg. § 1.304-2(a)(5). Thus, the amount and character of her gain

or loss is the same as if she were treated as having exchanged her stock in the issuing corporation. Prop. Reg. § 1.304-2(c) (ex. 1); cf. Reg. § 1.304-2(a) (11th and 14th sentences) (reaching same result, although based on prior version of statute). The acquiring corporation obtains a cost basis in the issuing corporation stock acquired. Prop. Reg. § 1.304-2(a)(5); cf. Reg. § 1.304-2(c) (ex. 3 (last sentence)) (reaching same result, although based on prior version of statute); S. Rep. No. 99-313, 99th Cong., 2d Sess. 1048 (1986) (treating acquiring corporation as purchasing issuing corporation stock).

3. *Property*. Neither section 304(a)(1) nor section 304(a)(2) applies unless the transferor receives "property" in the transaction, defined in section 317(a) to include any property (including money) but not stock of the distributing corporation and rights to acquire such stock. In a brother-sister acquisition, the acquiring corporation is treated as the distributing corporation; thus, if the transferor receives only stock of the acquiring corporation, the transferor does not receive property and the transaction is not recharacterized by section 304. If, on the other hand, the transferor receives both stock of the acquiring corporation and property, the transaction may be taxed under section 304 and the stock received is taken into account in determining whether the transferor has control over the acquiring corporation. I.R.C. § 304(c)(2). Even if section 304 applies, however, only the property received is taxed under section 304; section 1001 (or, possibly, section 351) governs the treatment of any stock received. In a parent-subsidiary acquisition, the identity of the "distributing corporation" is more ambiguous; this issue is addressed in *Bhada* (infra p. 310).

4. *"Control" and constructive ownership rules*. "Control" for purposes of section 304 means stock possessing at least 50 percent of the voting power *or* value of a corporation. I.R.C. § 304(c)(1). As illustrated by Rev. Rul. 71-563, constructive ownership rules apply both to determine the existence of control and to ascertain whether the redemption should be taxed as an exchange or a section 301 distribution. In determining control, the section 318(a) constructive ownership rules are broadened to increase the amount of attribution between shareholders and corporations. Shareholders are attributed a portion of the stock owned by their corporations (equal to the shareholder's percentage interest (by value) in the corporation) if the shareholder owns at least five percent (by value) of the corporation. I.R.C. §§ 304(c)(3)(B)(i), 318(a)(2)(C). Corporations are attributed stock owned by their shareholders based on a three-part test. Corporations are deemed to own all of the stock owned by any shareholder who owns at least 50 percent of the value of the corporation. If a shareholder owns at least five percent of the value (but less than 50 percent), the corporation is deemed to own only a portion of the shareholder's stock based on the shareholder's percentage interest (by value) in the corporation. I.R.C. §§ 304(c)(3)(B)(ii), 318(a)(3)(C). Finally, there is no attribution from shareholders owning less than five percent of the value of the corporation. Thus, a public corporation is not treated as constructively owning the stock of another public corporation merely because the two corporations have a common shareholder, as long as such shareholder owns less than five percent (by value) of each corporation.

The same section 318(a) constructive ownership rules are broadened even further for purposes of testing the redemption under section 302. Shareholders are attributed a portion of the stock owned by their corporations (equal to the shareholder's percentage interest (by value) in the corporation) without regard to the size of the shareholder's interest in the corporation. Further, corporations are attributed *all* of the stock owned by their shareholders without regard to the shareholder's interest in the corporation. I.R.C. §§ 304(b)(1) (second sentence), 318(a)(2)(C) and (3)(C). Thus, for purposes of testing the tax consequences of a redemption under section 302, a public corporation is treated as owning stock of another public corporation if they have a common shareholder (even one holding only a *de minimis* interest).

Test your understanding of sections 304(c)(1) and (3) and 318(a) by determining which persons (if any) have control (as defined in section 304(c)(1)) of either corporation X or Y (or both) in the following alternative circumstances:

a. T owns 50 percent of the value (but only 40 percent of the voting power) of X and T's son owns 50 percent of the voting power (but only 35 percent of the value) of Y.
b. Corporation M owns 70 percent of the value of both corporations N and Y. Corporation N owns 70 percent of the value of corporation X.
c. Same as (b), except that M owns 40 percent of the value of N.

5. *E&P and deemed acquiring and issuing corporations.* Under section 304(b)(2), the E&P of both the acquiring and issuing corporations is taken into account in determining whether a section 304(a) transaction is taxable as a dividend. The regulations permit the E&P of certain other corporations (termed the "deemed acquiring corporation" or "deemed issuing corporation") also to be taken into account if, in general, a principal purpose of the taxpayer is to avoid section 304 applying to those other corporations. See Temp. Reg. § 1.304-4T.

For example, suppose a shareholder owns a controlling interest in corporations X and Y, and both corporations have substantial amounts of E&P. If the shareholder transfers X stock to Y in exchange for property and the transaction is recharacterized under section 304 as a section 301 distribution, the E&P of X and Y is counted in determining how much of the distribution is a dividend. Suppose that, in order to avoid that result, the shareholder first transfers all of the X stock to newly formed T corporation (which has no E&P) in exchange for all of the stock of T. In addition, the shareholder arranges for Y corporation to form a new wholly-owned subsidiary, Z corporation (which also has no E&P) and to capitalize Z with enough cash to purchase the stock of T. Finally, the shareholder transfers the stock of T to Z in exchange for the cash. This transaction has the same economic effect as a transfer of X stock to Y. However, even if the transaction is recharacterized under section 304 as a section 301 distribution, none of the distribution would be taxed as a dividend if the only E&P considered were that of Z (the acquiring corporation) and T (the issuing corporation), since neither of them has any E&P. Under the regulations, the

E&P of both Y (which is the deemed acquiring corporation) and X (the deemed issuing corporation) may also be taken into account if, in general, a principal purpose of the use of T and Z was to avoid having section 304 apply to X and Y.

6. *More than one transferor.* A brother-sister acquisition occurs if persons who collectively control the issuing and acquiring corporations transfer issuing corporation stock to the acquiring corporation in exchange for property. The purpose of this provision is to make section 304(a)(1) potentially applicable to transfers by persons acting in concert even though no single transferor controls both corporations (and, therefore, section 304(a)(1) would not be applicable if each transfer were considered independently). The principal question in these "control group" cases, similar to the inquiry in a section 351 transaction, is whether the transfers should be considered as connected to one another. In general, the transfers need not be simultaneous but must be related to one another based on all of the facts and circumstances. If supported by the facts and circumstances, the regulations allow transfers taking place in "one or more years" to be treated as related. Reg. § 1.304-2(b).

Suppose that, as a result of the constructive ownership rules, more than one person separately controls both the issuing and acquiring corporations but only one of them transfers issuing corporation stock to the acquiring corporation in exchange for property. The *Merrill Lynch* case that follows (on remand from the Second Circuit, see Merrill Lynch & Co. v. Comm'r, 386 F.3d 464 (2d Cir. 2004), aff'g and remanding 120 T.C. 12 (2003)) addressed the tax consequences of this fact pattern in a brother-sister acquisition. The case involved a series of transactions to facilitate sale of ML Capital Resources (ML Capital), a wholly-owned subsidiary of Merrill Lynch & Co., Inc. (Merrill Parent), which was the parent corporation of an affiliated group of corporations filing a consolidated return. To retain within the affiliated group certain of ML Capital's businesses operated through its wholly-owned subsidiaries, ML Capital first sold the stock of such subsidiaries (the "issuing corporations") to certain other wholly-owned subsidiaries of Merrill Parent (the "acquiring corporations") for cash, which was then distributed to Merrill Parent. (The sales by ML Capital are referred to as "cross-chain sales.") Merrill Parent then sold the stock of ML Capital to a buyer outside of the affiliated group.

The taxpayer and the government agreed that the tax consequences of the cross-chain sales were controlled by section 304(a)(1) since ML Capital controlled (directly and indirectly) both the issuing and acquiring corporations and transferred stock in the issuing corporations to the acquiring corporations for property. The taxpayer argued that, under section 304(a)(1) and (b)(1), the cash received by ML Capital should be treated as a dividend because the transaction did not change ML Capital's direct and indirect interest in the issuing corporations. The taxpayer preferred "dividend" characterization because, under the consolidated return regulations then in effect, the dividend increased Merrill Parent's basis in the stock of ML Capital, thereby increasing the amount of loss recognized by Merrill Parent on the subsequent sale of ML Capital. (The regulations have since been changed. See also I.R.C. § 304(b)(4).) In 2003, the Tax Court rejected the taxpayer's claim for dividend characterization. Instead, it held that the cash payment should be treated as a redemption qualifying under section 302(a) and (b)(3) because there was a "firm and fixed plan" at the time of the cross-chain sales to terminate ML Capital's interest in the issuing corporations (through the subsequent sale of ML Capital outside of the affiliated group). In 2004, the Second Circuit affirmed in part but remanded the case to consider a novel argument that the taxpayer raised for the first time on appeal—namely, that Merrill Parent was the relevant shareholder for purposes of the section 302 tests.

## Merrill Lynch & Co. v. Commissioner

131 T.C. 293 (2008)

MARVEL, J.

... Section 304(a)(1) recharacterizes the sale proceeds of subsidiary stock sold by one corporation to another of its commonly controlled corporations as a distribution in redemption of the acquiring corporation's stock and requires that the tax consequences of the distribution be determined under sections 301 and 302. Under section 302(a), a redemption of stock is treated as a distribution in exchange for stock if it meets any of the tests provided in section 302(b). If none of the section 302(b) tests is met, the redemption is treated as a dividend under section 301. Sec. 302(d). The termination of interest test of section 302(b)(3) mandates exchange treatment "if the redemption is in complete redemption of all of the stock of the corporation owned by the shareholder." In the application of this and all other tests under section 302(b), section 304(b)(1) requires that any determination as to whether the acquisition is to be treated as a distribution in exchange for stock must be made by reference to the stock of the issuing corporation.

The parties disagree on whether for purposes of section 304 Merrill Parent as well as ML Capital Resources is considered a shareholder whose continuing interest in the issuing corporations must be tested under section 302(b)(3). On appeal petitioner contended for the first time that because Merrill Parent's ownership interest in the issuing corporations was not completely terminated within the meaning of section 302(b)(3) by the sale of ML Capital Resources' stock outside the affiliated group, petitioner has properly reported the proceeds of the sale as dividends. Petitioner makes the same argument on remand. Petitioner's argument rests on the following: (1) Immediately before the cross-chain sales, the acquiring corporations were wholly owned subsidiaries of Merrill Parent; (2) under the attribution rules of section 318, ownership of the issuing corporations was also attributed to Merrill Parent through its ownership of ML Capital Resources; and (3) after the sale of ML Capital Resources, Merrill Parent continued constructively to own 100 percent of the stock of the issuing corporations through its ownership of the acquiring corporations.

Petitioner relies on section 304(a)(1) to support its position that the section 302(b)(3) termination of interest test applies to Merrill Parent's constructive ownership of the issuing corporations' stock. According to petitioner, the specific reference in section 304(a)(1)(B) to "person (or persons) so in control" requires the interests of *all* persons in control to be considered in applying section 302(b)(3). Petitioner asserts that under section 318, Merrill Parent constructively owned 100 percent of the stock of the issuing corporations both before and after the cross-chain sales. Sec. 304(c)(3). Petitioner concludes that because the sale of ML Capital Resources did not affect Merrill Parent's constructive ownership of the stock of the issuing corporations, the complete termination required under section 302(b)(3) did not occur, and the proceeds of the cross-chain sales were properly characterized as dividends.

Respondent contends that ML Capital Resources is the shareholder whose interest in the issuing corporations must be tested under section 302(b)(3) and that because Merrill Parent's sale of the stock of ML Capital Resources must be integrated with the cross-chain sales of the stock of the issuing corporations, the interest of ML Capital Resources in the issuing corporations was completely terminated under section 302(b)(3). To support his position, respondent argues that section 304(a)(1) explicitly refers to the corporation that receives property in exchange for its stock in the issuing corporation. Respondent also asserts that the regulations promulgated under section 304 clearly identify the interest of the transferor-shareholder as the relevant interest to be examined under the section 302(b)(3) test.

We must decide, therefore, whether Merrill Parent's continuing constructive ownership interest in the issuing corporations after the cross-chain sales must be taken into account in analyzing the tax consequences under sections 304(a)(1) and 302(b)(3) of ML Capital Resources' 1987 sale of stock in the issuing corporations to the acquiring corporations. In making this determination, we start by interpreting section 304(a)(1). In interpreting a statute, we begin with the language of the statute itself. . . . If the language of the statute is plain and unambiguous, we generally apply the statute in accordance with its terms. . . . Whether the statute is ambiguous is determined by reference to the language of the statute, the specific context in which that language is used, and the broader context of the statute as a whole. . . . If the statute is ambiguous or silent, we may look to the statute's legislative history to determine congressional intent and to resolve any ambiguity. . . .

While section 304(a)(1)(A) refers to "one or more persons" and section 304(a)(1)(B) refers to "person (or persons) so in control," section 304(a)(1) makes clear that the person or persons in control must also be transferors of issuing corporation stock who receive property in exchange for their transferred stock. Accordingly, under section 304, the persons in control must *actually* receive property in exchange for the transfer of their issuing corporation stock to warrant the redemption analysis in section 302. The references to "persons" in section 304(a), when read in conjunction with section 304(c)(1) and (3), merely indicate that the interests of more than one person may be combined through attribution of stock ownership in order to meet the requisite control required for the application of section 304(a)(1). The constructive ownership rules of section 318 are thus independent of the transfer and receipt requirements of section 304(a).

Because sections 302 and 304 operate to determine the tax consequences to the *recipient* of a corporate distribution, it necessarily follows that the rules set forth in sections 302 and 304 apply only to the shareholder who, in exchange for stock, actually receives the proceeds of a cross-chain sale. The position that the section 302(b) tests may be applied to a shareholder who indirectly or constructively holds stock but has neither transferred any stock nor received the proceeds of the stock sale cannot be reconciled with the language and structure of section 304(a)(1).

The regulations promulgated under section 304 also confirm that the section 302(b) tests apply only to the person or persons who actually transfer stock in the issuing corporation to the acquiring corporation in consideration for property. Section 1.304-2(a) provides as follows:

> (a) If a corporation, in return for property, acquires stock of another corporation from one or more persons, and the person or persons from whom the stock was acquired were in control of both such corporations before the acquisition, then such property shall be treated as received in redemption of stock of the acquiring corporation. . . . As to *each person transferring stock*, the amount received shall be treated as a distribution of property under section 302(d), unless as to such person such amount is to be treated as received in exchange for the stock under the terms of section 302(a) or section 303. . . . [Emphasis added.]

Although the regulation acknowledges that more than one person may be in control of both corporations within the meaning of section 304, it clearly recognizes that the person or persons in control must also have transferred stock in exchange for property. According to the regulation, only a person who has transferred stock in exchange for property is subject to the provisions of section 302. Section 1.304-2(c) (ex. 4), illustrates this distinction as follows:

> Corporation X and corporation Y each have outstanding 100 shares of common stock.. H, an individual, W, his wife, S, his son, and G, his grandson, each own 25 shares of stock of each corporation. H sells all of his 25 shares of stock of corporation X to corporation Y. Since both before and after the transaction H owned directly and constructively 100 percent of the stock of corporation X, and assuming that section 302(b)(1) is not applicable, the amount received by him for his stock of corporation X is treated as a dividend to him to the extent of the earnings and profits of corporation Y.

In the example more than one person was considered to be in control of each corporation and their interests were aggregated to determine control for purposes of section 304, but the section 302(b) tests were applied only to the shareholder who actually transferred stock to the commonly controlled corporation in exchange for property. Nothing in the statute or the regulations "commands" that the interests of *all* persons in control be tested under sections 304(a)(1) and 302(b), as petitioner contends.

. . . ML Capital Resources was the only "person" who transferred any stock to the acquiring corporations in the cross-chain sales, and ML Capital Resources was the only shareholder that received property from the acquiring corporations in exchange for stock in the issuing corporations. Consequently, ML Capital Resources is the only shareholder whose interest in the issuing corporations must be tested under the provisions of section 302(b)(3). Because the interest of ML Capital Resources in the issuing corporations was completely terminated upon its sale outside of the affiliated group, the redemption shall be treated as a distribution in exchange for stock. Secs. 304(a)(1), 302(b)(3). . . .

### *NOTE*

*Extraordinary dividend.* An amount treated as a dividend to a corporate transferor as a result of section 304(a) generally constitutes an extraordinary dividend taxed under section 1059(a) without regard to the period the transferor held the stock of the distributing corporation. I.R.C. § 1059(e)(1)(A)(iii)(II). Thus, the untaxed portion of the dividend (the amount equal to the dividends-received deduction) reduces the transferor's basis in the distributing corporation's stock, and any reduction in excess of such basis is taxed as gain. For this purpose, only the transferor's basis in the distributing corporation's stock that is deemed redeemed pursuant to section 304(a) is taken into account. Id. (last sentence); Prop. Reg. § 1.304-2(c) (ex. 3(ii)). For example, suppose corporation W transfers X stock to corporation Y for $100 and that amount is treated under section 304(a) as a dividend, entitling W to an 80 percent dividends-received deduction. Under section 1059(e)(1)(A)(iii)(II), W must reduce its basis in the Y stock deemed redeemed by $80 (the untaxed portion of the dividend). If W's basis in the X stock transferred to Y was $20, W's basis in the Y stock deemed received (and then redeemed) was also $20. I.R.C. §§ 304(a)(1) (2d sentence), 358(a)(1). W must, therefore, reduce its basis in such Y stock to zero and recognize $60 gain from the sale of such stock. As illustrated by this example, the purpose of extraordinary dividend treatment is to eliminate the advantage to corporate transferors of receiving dividend treatment under section 304(a).

## B. Parent-Subsidiary Acquisitions

Read I.R.C. § 304(a)(2). In a parent-subsidiary acquisition, a shareholder transfers the stock of one corporation (the "issuing corporation") to another (the "acquiring corporation") in exchange for property, and the issuing corporation controls the acquiring corporation. The transaction is treated for tax purposes as a distribution in redemption of the stock of the issuing corporation. The following case illustrates the application of section 304(a)(2).

## Bhada v. Commissioner

89 T.C. 959 (1987), aff'd, 892 F.2d 39 (6th Cir. 1989)

NIMS, J.

... The issue ... is whether the shares of International common stock received by petitioners in exchange for McDermott common stock constitute "property" within the meaning of section 304(a)(2)(A).

... McDermott, Inc. (McDermott), was a Delaware corporation at all relevant times. From 1959 until December 10, 1982, McDermott was the parent corporation to a group of corporations hereinafter referred to as the McDermott Group. From 1959 until December 10, 1982, McDermott International, Inc. (International), was a wholly-owned subsidiary of McDermott and a controlled foreign corporation within the meaning of section 957.

... International made an offer to exchange cash and shares of its own stock (International Common) for shares of the common stock of McDermott (McDermott Common). ...

International acquired 30 million shares of McDermott Common for which it gave $10,500,000 and 30 million shares of International Common. As a result of the exchange, International held approximately 68 percent of the voting power in McDermott, and former holders of McDermott Common who participated in the exchange held approximately 90 percent of the voting power in International.

Petitioners ... tendered to International 26 shares of McDermott Common and received in return 26 shares of International Common and $9.10 in cash. ...

If [I.R.C. § 304(a)(2)] applies to the December, 1982, transaction, the International Common and cash received by petitioners must be treated as a distribution in redemption of their stock in McDermott, and it will be necessary to apply section 302 to determine the character of the amounts received by petitioners in International Common and cash. The parties have agreed that the cash received by petitioners is property for purposes of section 304(a)(2) and that if section 304 does not apply to the International Common received by petitioners, the tax consequences of the receipt of that stock will then be governed by section 1001. [1]

Section 304 does not apply to the International Common received by petitioners unless this stock was "property" for purposes of section 304(a)(2). The term "property" is defined in section 317(a), which provides:

> For purposes of this part, the term "property" means money, securities, and any other property; except that such term does not include stock in the corporation making the distribution (or rights to acquire such stock).

---

1. Section 351 does not apply in this case because of the failure to meet the 80 percent control requirement of section 351. Although the former McDermott shareholders owned 90 percent of the total voting power in International after the December, 1982, exchange, they did not own at least 80 percent of the total of all other classes of stock of International. McDermott at all relevant times owned all of the shares of a class of nonvoting preferred stock of International. Respondent speculates that if section 304 does not apply to the December, 1982, transaction, the former shareholders of McDermott will suffer no adverse tax consequences and will in many cases recognize a loss for tax purposes.

The receipt of stock of a corporation which is not stock of the distributing corporation is "property." . . .

Respondent argues that the true nature of the transaction between International and petitioners was an exchange of International Common for McDermott Common rather than a distribution by International of its stock in exchange for McDermott Common. It is respondent's position that the term "distribution" in section 317(a) refers only to a distribution by a corporation with respect to its stock to its shareholders in their capacity as shareholders. Because International gave its stock to McDermott's shareholders and not to its own shareholders, respondent maintains that there was no distribution as defined in section 317(a). We disagree.

The terms "property" and "distribution" are defined in section 317 for purposes of Part I of Subchapter C of the Internal Revenue Code. . . . Respondent finds support for his definition of the term "distribution" by asserting that the term "distribution" as it appears in every section in Part I of Subchapter C refers to a distribution by a corporation to its shareholders in relation to its stock. However, in section 304 itself Congress has used the term "distribution" in its generic sense. Section 304(b)(3)(A) provides, "Except as otherwise provided in this paragraph, subsection (a) (and not section 351 and not so much of sections 357 and 358 as relates to section 351) shall apply to any property received in a distribution described in subsection (a)."

At first glance, it is difficult to determine whether the term distribution in section 304(b)(3)(A) refers to the distribution of property by the acquiring corporation to shareholders of the parent corporation that triggers the application of section 304 or to the hypothetical redemption distribution by the parent to its own shareholders that follows when section 304(a)(2) applies. This ambiguity is resolved, however, by section 304(b)(3)(B), which provides in pertinent part:

> (B) CERTAIN ASSUMPTIONS OF LIABILITY, ETC.—
>
> (i) IN GENERAL.—In the case of an acquisition described in section 351, subsection (a) shall not apply to any liability—
>
> (I) assumed by the acquiring corporation, or
>
> (II) to which the stock is subject,
>
> if such liability was incurred by the transferor to acquire the stock. For purposes of the preceding sentence, the term "stock" means stock referred to in paragraph (1)(B) or (2)(A) of subsection (a).

Section 304(b)(3)(B) provides that in a transaction described in both sections 304(a) and 351, section 304(a) does not apply to certain liabilities assumed by the acquiring corporation or to which the stock is subject. The reference to the assumption of liabilities by the acquiring corporation indicates that section 304(b)(3)(B) refers to the actual transaction, *i.e.*, the distribution of property by the acquiring corporation to shareholders of another corporation rather than the hypothetical redemption under section 304(a). Because section 304(b)(3)(B) refers to the actual transaction that triggers section 304, we can only conclude that section 304(b)(3)(A) also refers to the actual transactions when it uses the term distribution. Accordingly, the term distribution in section 317(a) does not exclusively refer to a distribution by a corporation to its shareholders with respect to its stock.

From this it follows that International "distributed" its own stock to petitioners in the December, 1982, exchange and that such stock is not to be deemed property. This is because the International Common was the stock of the corporation making the distribution, it was not property, and section 304 does not apply.

Respondent contends, however, that section 304(b)(3)(B) refers to actual transactions but that section 304(b)(3)(A) refers to the hypothetical redemption that occurs when section 304 applies. Respondent reasons that section 304(b)(3)(B) concerns liabilities assumed (a much more difficult matter to express in terms of the hypothetical transaction), whereas the conflict between sections 304 and 351 does not arise until after the hypothetical redemption distribution comes into play. We decline to adopt respondent's reading of the statute. Neither section 304(b)(3)(B) nor section 304(b)(3)(A) applies unless there is a conflict between sections 304 and 351. Respondent's analysis assumes that there is no relationship between sections 304(b)(3)(B) and 304(b)(3)(A). The language of the statute does not support respondent's position nor does anything in the legislative history suggest such a contorted reading of the statute.

Paragraph (3) was added to section 304(b) . . . to resolve the problems raised by transactions that literally fall within the provisions of both sections 304 and 351. . . . Section 351 provides that no gain or loss shall be recognized if property is transferred to a corporation by one or more persons solely in exchange for stock or securities in that corporation and immediately after the exchange the persons who transferred the property are in control of the corporation. For the purposes of section 351, "control" means ownership of stock possessing at least 80 percent of the total combined voting power of all classes of stock entitled to vote and at least 80 percent of the total number of shares of all other classes of stock of the corporation. . . . If property is received in addition to stock by persons transferring property to the corporation in a transaction to which section 351 applies, gain must be recognized but only to the extent of the amount of money received plus the fair market value of any other property received. Section 351(b). In other words, the property received in a section 351 transaction is treated as a sale or exchange rather than a dividend and may qualify for capital gain or loss treatment.

Before section 304(b)(3) was enacted, it was possible for taxpayers to avoid the application of section 304 to property received in addition to stock in an exchange of stock for stock of a related corporation if they met the 80 percent control requirement of section 351. . . . To prevent such a circumvention of section 304, Congress enacted section 304(b)(3). The Conference Report explains:

> The conference agreement extends the anti-bailout rules of sections 304 and 306 of present law to the use of corporations, including holding companies, formed or availed of to avoid such rules. Such rules are made applicable to a transaction that, under present law, otherwise qualifies as a tax-free incorporation under section 351.

> Section 351 generally will not apply to transactions described in section 304. Thus, section 351, if otherwise applicable, will generally apply only to the extent such transaction consists of an exchange of stock for stock in the acquiring corporation. . . .

Thus, it appears from the Conference Report that Congress was concerned only with the treatment of property received in a transaction that fell under the provisions of both sections 304 and 351. Congress must have assumed that section 304 would not apply to the stock of the acquiring corporation received by the shareholders of the related corporation because the stock of the acquiring corporation in a section 304(a) transaction is not property.

. . . Our conclusion comports with the purpose of section 304(a)(2). Section 115(g)(2) of the Internal Revenue Code of 1939, from which section 304 is derived, was enacted in response to the decision in Rodman Wanamaker Trust v. Comm'r, 11 T.C. 365 (1948), *aff'd*, 178 F.2d 10 (3d Cir. 1949), in which the Court treated the cash received by the taxpayer from a subsidiary in return for shares of its parent's stock as proceeds of a sale rather than a dividend.

The Committee Reports reveal Congress' intent to prevent sale or exchange treatment in cases in which assets of a subsidiary are withdrawn from corporate solution in exchange for stock of its parent.

> In *Wanamaker* section 115(g) of the Internal Revenue Code of 1939 was held not to be applicable when a subsidiary corporation purchased the stock of its parent . . . , even though the effect was, in fact, identical with that which would have resulted if the parent had itself purchased the stock.
>
> If the stockholders of a corporation which owns all the stock of a subsidiary corporation obtain cash from that subsidiary, in effect they have received a dividend to the same extent as would be the case if the cash had been . . . distributed by the parent to the stockholders. . . .

In this case, the cash received by petitioners constitutes assets withdrawn from International in exchange for stock of its parent, McDermott, and the parties agree that section 304 applies to the cash. However, in receiving International Common in return for McDermott Common, petitioners did not withdraw assets from International or McDermott. The transaction resulted in a change in the ownership structure of the two corporations. Congress did not intend to prevent such a change in corporate ownership by enacting section 304. . . .

## *NOTES AND QUESTIONS*

1. *Tax consequences of parent-subsidiary acquisitions.* If section 304(a)(2) applies, the transaction is recharacterized as a constructive redemption by the issuing corporation and the transferor's before-and-after interest in such corporation determines whether the redemption is taxed under section 301 or as an exchange under

section 302(a). If the redemption is taxed as an exchange, the tax consequences to the transferor and the acquiring corporation are the same as if the transferor had sold the issuing corporation stock to the acquiring corporation in a taxable transaction. If the redemption is taxed under section 301, the amount received by the transferor is treated as a dividend to the extent of the E&P of both the acquiring and issuing corporations. Counterintuitively, the acquiring corporation's E&P is considered and reduced first. I.R.C. § 304(b)(2). If the redemption leaves the transferor with unrecovered basis in the issuing corporation stock deemed redeemed, the unrecovered amount increases the transferor's basis in any other issuing corporation stock owned by the transferor. Reg. § 1.304-3(a) (last sentence). If the transferor does not own any other issuing corporation stock following the transfer, then there is the same potential "disappearing basis" problem discussed in connection with Notice 2001-45 (p. 236) and the notes thereafter. The transferor may be able to claim the basis as a loss at some point in the future. Prop. Reg. § 1.302-5(a)(3)(i), (b)(4)(i). The acquiring corporation receives a cost basis in the issuing corporation stock acquired. See Rev. Rul. 80-189, 1980-2 C.B. 106.

2. *Overlap between section 304(a)(1) and (2).* Because the shareholder in a parent-subsidiary acquisition need not own any particular interest in the issuing corporation prior to the transaction, a transaction qualifying under section 304(a)(2) need not also qualify under section 304(a)(1). On the other hand, because of the constructive ownership rules, any transaction qualifying under section 304(a)(1) ordinarily also qualifies under section 304(a)(2). For example, if A owns 50 percent or more of the value of both corporations X and Y and transfers X stock to Y in exchange for property, the transaction satisfies section 304(a)(1). Because X constructively owns all of the Y stock owned by A as a result of sections 304(c)(3)(A) and 318(a)(3)(C), the transaction also satisfies section 304(a)(2).

Where there is overlap between sections 304(a)(1) and (2), the latter provision has priority. I.R.C. § 304(a)(1) (flush language). Taken literally, however, section 304(a)(1) would then apply to almost no transactions. As a result, it is generally believed that a transaction that satisfies section 304(a)(1) and also satisfies section 304(a)(2) only as a result of the constructive ownership rules, is taxed under the former provision. See Broadview Lumber Co. v. U.S., 561 F.2d 698, 709 (7th Cir. 1977) (adopting this interpretation); Reg. § 1.304-2(c) (illustrating "application of section 304(a)(1)" to certain transactions that would also qualify under section 304(a)(2) after constructive ownership rules are taken into account). For example, if A controls both corporations X and Y and transfers X stock to Y for property, and X does not actually control Y, then section 304(a)(1) applies to the transaction. If X actually controls Y, then section 304(a)(2) has priority over section 304(a)(1).

Can you think of a transaction that qualifies under section 304(a)(1) but does not qualify under section 304(a)(2) even after the constructive ownership rules are taken into account?

3. *Overlap with section 351.* As described in *Bhada*, the statute also generally resolves the potential overlap between sections 304(a) and 351 in favor of the former provision. I.R.C. § 304(b)(3)(A). Thus, any property received by a transferor in a

qualifying section 304(a) transaction is generally taxed under that provision, rather than under sections 351(b) and 357, even though the transferor controls (within the meaning of section 368(c)) the acquiring corporation immediately after the transaction. This provision is consistent with section 304(a)'s goal of protecting potential dividend consequences. If the acquiring corporation assumes a liability in the transaction (or acquires the issuing corporation stock subject to a liability), the tax consequences of the stock-acquisition indebtedness may be governed by sections 351(b) and 357 (rather than section 304(a)). The exception for stock-acquisition indebtedness applies only if the liability was incurred by the transferor to acquire the issuing corporation stock from an unrelated person (or a related person having no continuing interest in either corporation after the transaction). I.R.C. § 304(b)(3)(B)(i) and (iii).

4. *Corporate inversions.* The goal of the transaction described in *Bhada* was to invert the corporate structure so that International, which was previously a wholly-owned subsidiary of McDermott, ended up being owned directly by the former McDermott shareholders, and International ended up with a 68 percent interest in McDermott. The purpose of the inversion was to achieve tax savings. Under the pre-inversion structure, International was a "controlled foreign corporation" (CFC) of McDermott, which resulted in McDermott being taxed currently on the portion of International's income treated as "subpart F income." I.R.C. § 951(a)(1). Under the post-inversion structure, International was no longer a CFC and therefore that provision was not applicable. The law has since been changed to try to prevent the tax advantages of such inversions. I.R.C. §§ 1248(i), 7874.

5. *Importance of section 304 in international transactions.* As noted initially, section 304 has limited importance for U.S. individuals as long as dividend income and long-term capital gain are taxed comparably. Changes to section 1059 and the consolidated return regulations have also generally reduced the importance of dividend characterization under section 304 to corporate transferors. Section 304 remains important, however, in the international context when, for example, both the acquiring and issuing corporations are foreign subsidiaries of a U.S. parent corporation (and the foreign nature of the subsidiaries makes them ineligible to join in the parent's consolidated return). Since many foreign countries limit the distribution of dividends by corporations within their jurisdiction, a common technique to repatriate money from a foreign subsidiary is to carry out a transaction in which the stock of one subsidiary is acquired by another subsidiary in exchange for cash. Under foreign law, the form of this transaction is generally respected, thereby avoiding any foreign law limitations on dividend payments. For U.S. law purposes, however, the recharacterization of the transaction as a distribution under section 304, and the interplay between section 304 and other U.S. tax law provisions applicable to international transactions, may produce challenging interpretive and policy questions.

**Problem 8-1:** Alston owns 70 shares of X corporation with a basis of $50 per share and a holding period of five years. The remaining 30 X shares are owned by Higgins, a key employee of the company who is unrelated to Alston. Alston's son owns 25 shares of Y corporation. The remaining 75 Y shares are owned by P corporation. Alston and his two brothers each owns one-third of P. X and Y have E&P of $3,000 each and P has no E&P. Determine the tax consequences of the following transactions, including the effects of the transactions on the bases and E&P of the parties:

(a) Alston sells 50 X shares to Y for $5,000 ($100 per share). Assume that the fair market value of Y stock is $200 per share at this time.
(b) Same as (a), except that Alston sells 40 X shares to Y for $4,000.
(c) Same as (b), except that Y has a $3,000 deficit in E&P.
(d) Same as (b), except that Alston owned all of P corporation prior to the sale.

# Chapter 9

# Stock Distributions and Preferred Stock Bailouts

Chapter five described the tax consequences of an ordinary distribution of property made by a corporation with respect to its stock. For purposes of that transaction, however, the term "property" excluded stock of the distributing corporation and rights to acquire such stock. I.R.C. § 317(a). Part A of this chapter completes the analysis of ordinary distributions by considering the tax treatment of distributions of stock or stock rights of the distributing corporation with respect to its stock. Part B then briefly describes a provision addressing a tax avoidance technique — the "preferred stock bailout" — that grew out of the tax rules described in part A. Like much of section 304 (discussed in chapter eight), the importance of both the tax avoidance technique and Congressional response are significantly reduced as long as dividend income and long-term capital gain are taxed in a comparable fashion.

## A. Distributions of Stock or Stock Rights of the Distributing Corporation

In Eisner v. Macomber, 252 U.S. 189 (1920), the Supreme Court held that a pro rata distribution of stock of the distributing corporation to holders of the same class of stock was not income to the recipients within the meaning of the Sixteenth Amendment. In effect, the Court found that the distribution merely changed the form and not the substance of the shareholders' investment and therefore was not a taxable event. Most commentators generally agree that *Macomber* no longer represents a valid interpretation of the Sixteenth Amendment and that its holding is not required by the Constitution. Nevertheless, the Court likely reached a sound policy outcome with respect to a pro rata common-on-common or preferred-on-common stock distribution, at least where only one class of common stock is outstanding prior to the distribution and the stock distributed has no unusual features, such as conversion rights.

Read I.R.C. § 305(a)-(d). The holding of *Macomber* is reflected in section 305(a), which generally excludes from income a distribution of stock (or rights to acquire stock) of the distributing corporation. The balance of the provision, however, reverses that result in circumstances where the distribution results in more than a mere change in form of the shareholders' investment; thus, under section 305(b) and (c), certain actual or constructive distributions of stock (including stock rights) are treated as distributions of property to which section 301 applies. In general, a distribution of stock is taxable under section 301 if (1) any distributee may elect to receive property other than stock, or (2) the effect of the distribution is to increase the proportionate interest of certain shareholders in the assets or E&P of the distributing corporation. The following sections describe these two situations.

### 1. *Stock Distributions Subject to Shareholder Election to Receive Property Other Than Stock*

Under the principle of constructive receipt, a taxpayer who is entitled to receive income without substantial limitation is treated as having income even though it is not reduced to actual possession. See Reg. § 1.451-2(a). Section 305(b)(1) follows this principle by treating a distributee who has the right to receive property other than stock as receiving a section 301 distribution of property even though the right is not exercised and the distributee actually receives only stock. The key is the distributee's entitlement to receive property other than stock, and not the actual receipt of such other property. Of course, if the distributee actually elects to receive the property other than stock, then the distribution is taxable under section 301 without regard to section 305(b)(1).

Although section 305(b)(1) carries out the principle of constructive receipt, the rule extends beyond a mere application of that principle. If *any* shareholder has an option to receive property other than stock, then *all* shareholders receiving stock in the distribution, including those who do not have such an option, are treated as receiving a section 301 distribution. Reg. § 1.305-2(a)(5). As a practical matter, it may be fairly unusual for some, but not all, shareholders to have a right to receive property other than stock, given the general corporate law requirement to provide the same rights to all holders of a given class of stock. As the following ruling illustrates, however, the shareholder election need not be an explicit part of the distribution but may arise from the circumstances of the distribution itself. See Reg. § 1.305-2(a)(4).

## Rev. Rul. 83-68

1983-1 C.B. 75

. . . Bank is a member of the Federal Home Loan Bank of City *R* (FHLB of *R*). Section 6(c)(2) of the Federal Home Loan Bank Act (Bank Act), 12 U.S.C. section 1421, requires member banks to maintain a stock interest in a Federal Home Loan

Bank (FHLB) equal to a percentage of their net home loan mortgages and a fraction of their borrowings from the FHLB. Section 6(c)(1) of the Bank Act provides that a FHLB may, in its discretion and upon application of a member, retire any shareholdings of the member banks in excess of the amount required to be held under section 6(c)(2) of the Bank Act.

On May 1, 1981, FHLB of *R* declared a six percent stock dividend payable to all member banks on June 1, 1981. The dividend declaration notice stated that not all members need to hold additional stock, and such members may wish to retire any stock in excess of the required amount. Each member bank was advised that it could notify the FHLB of *R* that it wished to tender its excess shares for redemption. At least one of the member banks had the option to have all the shares it received as a stock dividend redeemed because it already held excess shares. In accordance with an established policy of the FHLB of *R*, all redemption requests were honored in full. The FHLB of *R* has not refused to redeem any stock in the last ten years and apparently will not refuse to redeem stock in the future, although such option would always be available.

## LAW AND ANALYSIS

Section 305(a) of the Code provides, generally, that gross income does not include the amount of any distribution of the stock of a corporation made by the corporation to its shareholders with respect to its stock, except as otherwise provided in section 305(b).

Section 305(b)(1) of the Code provides that section 305(a) will not apply to a distribution by a corporation of its stock, and the distribution will be treated as a distribution of property to which section 301 applies, if the distribution is, at the election of any of the shareholders (whether exercised before or after the declaration of the distribution), payable either (a) in its stock, or (b) in property.

Section 1.305-2(a)(2) . . . provides that an election within the meaning of section 305(b)(1) of the Code can arise whether the election is exercised or exercisable before or after the declaration of the distribution. Under section 1.305-2(a)(3), an election can arise if the declaration of the distribution provides for a distribution in one medium, unless the shareholder specifically requests payment in the other. Under section 1.305-2(a)(4), an election can arise from the circumstances of the distribution. And, under section 1.305-2(a)(5), an election can arise whether all or some of the shareholders have the election.

Rev. Rul. 76-258, 1976-2 C.B. 95, held that a distribution of preferred stock that is immediately redeemable at the option of a shareholder gives the shareholder an election to receive either stock or property within the meaning of section 305(b)(1) of the Code and therefore is treated as a distribution of property to which section 301 applies.

In the present case, the distribution was to be made in stock of the FHLB of *R*. However, at all times a member has the right under the Bank Act to request the redemption of all or part of its stock in the FHLB of *R* to the extent such stock constituted excess holdings. Although it is left to the discretion of the FHLB whether to redeem stock held by a member, it is an established policy of the FHLB of *R* to honor all redemption requests unless unusual circumstances exist.

Section 305(a) of the Code does not apply to at least a part of the present distribution because, in substance, some or all of the shareholders have an election to receive either stock or money. This is true even though the distribution was to be of stock unless the shareholder chose otherwise. It is also irrelevant for purposes of section 305 that only some members were eligible to have their stock redeemed, and that not all of those members chose to have the stock dividend redeemed.

Example 1 of section 1.305-2(b) of the regulations points out that the portion of a distribution of stock which is not subject to an election to receive property will be treated under section 305(a) of the Code, while the portion of the stock distributed which is subject to such an election will be treated, by reason of section 305(b)(1), as a distribution of property to which section 301 applies.

The amount taxable to a given member bank will be that portion of the stock dividend subject to the excess holding election by the member bank having the largest portion redeemable at its option. Thus, if all of the shares distributed to any member bank constitute excess holdings, the entire distribution will be taxable with respect to every member bank, regardless of whether any of the shares received constitute excess holdings to that bank. On the other hand, if the largest portion of the distribution redeemable is, for example, one half, then one half of the distribution will be taxable to each member bank, regardless of the relative numbers of shares redeemable.

## HOLDING

All the members of FHLB of *R* who received the stock dividend will be treated as having received a distribution to which section 301 of the Code applies by reason of the application of section 305(b)(1). In this instance, because at least one member bank had the option to cause redemption of the entire distribution, the distribution will be entirely taxable to all member banks. The amount of the distribution and the basis of the stock dividend received by the member banks . . . will be its fair market value in the hands of FHLB of *R* immediately before the distribution. . . .

### *NOTES*

1. *Pattern of approving redemption requests.* Rev. Rul. 83-68 illustrates the IRS's position that even if a shareholder is not provided with a put option entitling the shareholder to be redeemed anytime the shareholder so requests, a corporate pattern of approving such requests may effectively confer such right on the shareholder and thereby constitute an election to receive stock or other property. In

Colonial Savings Assn. v. Comm'r, 854 F.2d 1001 (7th Cir. 1988), cert. denied, 489 U.S. 1090 (1989), involving facts essentially identical to those in Rev. Rul. 83-68, the court disagreed with the IRS's conclusion. The court found that despite the pattern of approving redemptions, the discretion retained by the FHLB to grant approval was meaningful, given the Congressional purpose of having the FHLB maintain supervisory authority over its member banks. Therefore, the taxpayer-member bank did not effectively have an election to receive stock or other property. In Rev. Rul. 90-98, 1990-2 C.B. 57, the IRS reiterated its general position but stated that, because of the special supervisory role of the FHLB, it would no longer assert this position in the case of stock distributions to FHLB member banks.

2. *Optional dividend reinvestment plans.* Shareholders who, pursuant to an optional dividend reinvestment plan, choose to take their dividends in the form of stock of the distributing corporation rather than cash are treated by reason of section 305(b)(1) as receiving a property distribution to which section 301 applies. See Rev. Rul. 76-53, 1976-1 C.B. 89.

3. *No choice.* In Rev. Rul. 80-154, 1980-1 C.B. 68, a resolution declaring a cash distribution by a foreign corporation also required the proceeds of the distribution to be reinvested in additional stock of the distributing corporation. The IRS concluded that the transaction should be treated as a nontaxable distribution of stock under section 305(a). The absence of any effective right on the part of the shareholders to receive property other than stock made section 305(b)(1) inapplicable.

**Problem 9-1:** Determine the federal income tax consequences of the following transactions. In each case, assume that the corporation making the distribution has only a single class of common stock outstanding both before and after the distribution.

(a) Corporation X declares a distribution of two additional shares of common stock (worth $10 each on the date of the distribution) for each share of common stock held, except that, at the option of the shareholder, the shareholder is entitled to receive one share of common stock plus $9 cash for each share held. See Reg. § 1.305-2(b) (ex. 1). Would your answer change if you knew that X were a public corporation?

(b) In a given year, public corporation Y declares four quarterly distributions, each equal to $5/share. Each distribution is payable at the option of the shareholder in either cash or Y common stock. However, the maximum amount of cash that may be distributed in any distribution is equal to 20 percent of the total amount of the distribution. If shareholders in the aggregate elect to receive 20 percent or less of the total quarterly distribution in cash, then each shareholder is distributed the amount of cash or Y stock elected. If shareholders in the aggregate elect to receive more than 20 percent of the total quarterly distribution in cash, then the amount of cash distributed is reduced pro rata from the amount elected so that the total cash distribution exactly equals 20 percent of the total quarterly distribution. For example, if each shareholder elects to receive the entire amount of a quarterly distribution in cash, then each shareholder is distributed $1/share in cash and $4/share in Y stock for that quarter.

(i) Suppose that the shareholder notice of each distribution is accompanied by information provided by "reputable tax counsel" that no matter what the shareholder elects, the entire distribution will be taxable to the shareholder as a dividend. Does this fact affect your analysis of the tax consequences of the distributions?

(ii) Suppose that no shareholder is given a choice of receiving cash in lieu of stock in any of the distributions described in (b). Instead, three of the quarterly distributions are payable only in Y stock and one quarterly distribution is payable only in cash. Do the tax consequences of this alternate arrangement shed any light on how the distributions described in (b) should be taxed?

## 2. *Stock Distributions with Disproportionate Effect*

Review I.R.C. § 305(b)(2)-(5). The other exceptions to section 305(a) follow from the general theme that a stock distribution does not constitute a mere change in the form of the shareholders' investment if it has the effect of disproportionately increasing the rights of certain shareholders in the distributing corporation's assets or E&P. Hence, stock distributions with such disproportionate effect are treated as distributions of property under section 301. The Supreme Court articulated this principle in Koshland v. Helvering, 298 U.S. 441, 446 (1936) ("where a stock dividend gives the shareholder an interest different from that which his former stock holdings represented he receives income").

To determine whether a stock distribution has a disproportionate effect, it is necessary to consider both the nature of the stock interest distributed and the nature of the interests outstanding prior to the distribution. For example, a pro rata distribution of either common or nonconvertible preferred stock by a corporation with only a single class of common stock outstanding prior to the distribution does not result in any change in the relative interests of the shareholders. All of the stock certificates of each shareholder still represent the same interests in the corporation that existed prior to the distribution. Hence, these distributions are excluded from income under section 305(a).

If, instead, the distributing corporation has outstanding prior to a distribution both common stock and a class of nonconvertible preferred stock, the analysis of a stock distribution may change. If the preferred shareholders receive a cash distribution and the holders of common stock receive a pro rata distribution of additional common stock, there is still no change in the relative interests of the shareholders. The interest in the corporation of the common shareholders remains subordinate to that of the preferred shareholders, whose interest is unchanged by the distribution. Therefore, the distribution of common stock is excluded from income under section 305(a). Reg. § 1.305-3(e) (ex. 2). If, however, the preferred shareholders receive cash and the common shareholders receive a pro rata distribution of the *preferred* stock, the distribution changes the relative interests of the shareholders, since the holders of common stock now share in the preference formerly held exclusively by the holders of preferred stock. Thus, the distribution of preferred stock is treated as a distribution of property under section 301. Reg. § 1.305-3(e) (ex. 3).

Suppose there is a distribution of stock *to* preferred shareholders. As the regulations explain, the distinguishing feature of preferred stock for this purpose is the *limited* nature of the preference provided to its holders. Reg. § 1.305-5(a) (fourth sentence). Thus, a pro rata distribution of preferred stock to holders of such stock increases the amount of their preference over the common shareholders of the distributing corporation. Furthermore, a pro rata distribution of common stock to such shareholders increases their interest in the corporation by allowing them to share in the residual interest held exclusively by the common stockholders prior to the distribution. As a result, in general, any stock distribution *on* preferred stock is treated as a distribution of property under section 301. I.R.C. § 305(b)(4).

The broadest application of the "disproportionate effect" principle can be found in section 305(b)(2). Under that provision, if as a result of a distribution or series of distributions, some shareholders increase their proportionate interest in the distributing corporation's assets or E&P and other shareholders receive property (sometimes referred to as the "companion distribution"), any stock distribution is treated as a distribution of property under section 301. The regulations interpret these conditions quite liberally to encompass many possible scenarios, although there must generally be two distributions — one of stock and one of property — to two different groups of shareholders. If the distributions are separated by more than 36 months, they are presumptively treated as not connected and therefore not encompassed by section 305(b)(2) unless made pursuant to a plan. Reg. § 1.305-3(b)(4). If, however, the distributions are made within 36 months of one another, they may be treated as connected even in the absence of any plan. For example, if a corporation makes a regular stock distribution to one class of stockholders and a regular cash distribution to a second class of stockholders, section 305(b)(2) may apply to make the stock distribution taxable under section 301 even though the two sets of distributions are independent and unrelated. Reg. § 1.305-3(b)(2). In general, the companion distribution must be one to which section 301 applies. Reg. § 1.305-3(b)(3) (third sentence).

The importance of section 305(b)(2) is strengthened by section 305(c), which authorizes regulations that treat certain common corporate transactions as constructive distributions of stock to a shareholder whose proportionate interest in the assets or E&P of the corporation is increased by the transaction. Thus, assuming that the required companion distribution exists, section 305(b)(2) may apply. The following ruling illustrates the potential breadth of section 305(b)(2) and (c).

## Rev. Rul. 78-60

1978-1 C.B. 81

Advice has been requested whether . . . under section 305(b)(2) and (c) the shareholders who experienced increases in their proportionate interests in the redeeming corporation as a result of the stock redemptions will be treated as having received distributions of property to which section 301 applies.

Corporation Z has only one class of stock outstanding. The Z common stock is held by 24 shareholders, all of whom are descendants, or spouses of descendants, of the founder of Z.

In 1975, when Z had 6,000 shares of common stock outstanding, the board of directors of Z adopted a plan of annual redemption to provide a means for its shareholders to sell their stock. The plan provides that Z will annually redeem up to 40 shares of its outstanding stock at a price established annually by the Z board of directors. Each shareholder of Z is entitled to cause Z to redeem two-thirds of one percent of the shareholder's stock each year. If some shareholders choose not to participate fully in the plan during any year, the other shareholders can cause Z to redeem more than two-thirds of one percent of their stock, up to the maximum of 40 shares.

Pursuant to the plan of annual redemption, Z redeemed 40 shares of its stock in 1976. Eight shareholders participated in the redemptions. . . . [The ruling explains that, based on the percentage interest of each redeemed shareholder in the corporation before and after the redemption, no safe harbor in section 302(b) was applicable to the redemptions and therefore, by reason of section 302(d), the redemptions were all treated as section 301 distributions to the redeemed shareholders.]

Section 305(b)(2) of the Code provides that section 301 will apply to a distribution by a corporation of its stock if the distribution, or a series of distributions that includes the distribution, has the result of the receipt of property by some shareholders, and increases in the proportionate interests of other shareholders in the assets or earnings and profits of the corporation.

Section 305(c) of the Code authorizes regulations under which a redemption treated as a section 301 distribution will be treated as a section 301 distribution to any shareholder whose proportionate interest in the earnings and profits or assets of the corporation is increased by the redemption.

Section 1.305-7(a) . . . provides that a redemption treated as a section 301 distribution will generally be treated as a distribution to which sections 305(b)(2) and 301 of the Code apply if the proportionate interest of any shareholder in the earnings and profits or assets of the corporation deemed to have made the stock distribution is increased by the redemption, and the distribution has the result described in section 305(b)(2). The distribution is to be deemed made to any shareholder whose interest in the earnings and profits or assets of the distributing corporation is increased by the redemption.

Section 1.305-3(b)(3) of the regulations provides that for a distribution of property to meet the requirements of section 305(b)(2) of the Code, the distribution must be made to a shareholder in the capacity as a shareholder and must be a distribution to which section 301 [or one of several other specified sections] applies. A distribution of property incident to an isolated redemption will not cause section 305(b)(2) to apply even though the redemption distribution is treated as a section 301 distribution. . . .

The 16 shareholders of Z who did not tender any stock for redemption in 1976 experienced increases in their proportionate interests of the earnings and profits and assets of Z . . . as a result of the redemptions. Shareholders *B* and *X*, who surrendered small amounts of their stock for redemption in 1976, also experienced increases in their proportionate interests. The 1976 redemptions were not isolated but were undertaken pursuant to an ongoing plan of annual stock redemptions. Finally, the 1976 redemptions are to be treated as distributions of property to which section 301 of the Code applies.

Accordingly, *B*, *X* and the 16 shareholders of *Z* who did not participate in the 1976 redemptions are deemed to have received stock distributions to which sections 305(b)(2) and 301 of the Code apply. . . .

## *NOTES AND QUESTIONS*

1. *Tax consequences to shareholders who are not redeemed.* Rev. Rul. 78-60 illustrates the somewhat surprising result that shareholders who choose not to have any of their stock redeemed and therefore receive nothing directly may, nevertheless, have tax consequences. In this situation, the application of section 305(b)(2) and (c) backstops section 305(b)(1) and the principle of constructive receipt. All of the shareholders are taxed because they all had the right to have a portion of their stock redeemed and to receive property in exchange for their stock. Under the regulations, the shareholders who are not redeemed are treated as if they receive cash (in an amount that is pro rata to the amount actually received by the redeemed shareholders) and then reinvest such cash in additional stock (thereby increasing their proportionate interest in the corporation). Given the unexpected nature of this result, the regulations provide a key exception (mentioned in the ruling) that exempts "isolated redemptions" from this consequence. Reg. § 1.305-3(b)(3) (last sentence) and -3(e) (ex. 10). Thus, if the redemption of certain shareholders is treated as isolated, those shareholders who are not redeemed are *not* taxed under sections 305(b)(2) and 301 as a result of the increase in their proportionate interest in the corporation.

To illustrate the tax consequences when sections 305(b)(2) and 301 apply to shareholders who are not redeemed, assume that X corporation has only two shareholders, A and B, each with 30 shares, and B has 10 shares redeemed. Assume that prior to the redemption, X is worth $300, each share is therefore worth $5, and B receives $50 in the redemption. Finally, assume (perhaps unrealistically in this example) that the "isolated redemption" exception does not apply and that B's redemption is taxable under section 301. Section 305(c) treats this transaction as a constructive distribution of stock to A, whose proportionate interest in the corporation is increased by the transaction. Since B's redemption qualifies as a companion distribution, section 305(b)(2) treats the constructive stock distribution to A as a distribution of property under section 301. How much is the deemed property distribution?

Under Reg. § 1.305-3(e) (ex. 8), A first determines her interest in X following the transaction, which is 60 percent in this example (30 shares owned/50 total shares following redemption). A is treated as receiving the number of X shares necessary to achieve this percentage interest under the assumption that the redemption did not occur. Since X had 60 shares without the redemption, A would have had to receive a distribution of 15 shares, giving her a total of 45 shares, to achieve a 60 percent interest in X (45/75 = 60%). By reason of section 305(b)(2), A receives a distribution of property under section 301 equal to the fair market value of the 15 shares. Share value is determined by dividing the post-redemption value of X ($250) by the number of shares hypothetically outstanding without the redemption (75 shares), or $3.33/share. The 15 shares are therefore worth $50 (15 × $3.33), which is the amount of the section 301 distribution to A. In short, the tax consequences are determined as if A and B each received a pro rata distribution of $50 cash (without any redemption) followed by A's reinvestment of her $50 cash to purchase 15 additional shares of X (and to bring X's value back up to $250).

2. *Convertible instruments.* Actual or constructive stock distributions may have a disproportionate effect when the distributions affect either a convertible instrument or the stock (termed the "underlying stock") into which the instrument is convertible. Since the conversion feature links the convertible instrument to the underlying stock, a change made to one without a commensurate change made to the other may cause a shift in the ownership of the corporation.

For example, suppose the class A shares of a corporation are convertible into its class B shares on a 1:1 basis. A distribution of stock to the class B shareholders without any change to the conversion formula dilutes the interest of the class A shareholders and increases the proportionate interest of the class B shareholders. Thus, assuming that there is a companion distribution, the distribution of stock may be covered by section 305(b)(2). A disproportionate result can be avoided if the conversion formula is fully adjusted to reflect the stock distribution on the underlying stock. Reg. § 1.305-3(d)(1)(i) (first sentence). Similarly, a change in proportionate interests may occur if the convertible interest is a debt instrument, with interest paid on such instrument treated as a companion distribution for purposes of section 305(b)(2). I.R.C. § 305(d)(2); Reg. § 1.305-3(b)(3) (fourth sentence) and -3(e) (ex. 4).

Suppose, instead, without any stock distribution on the underlying stock, the conversion formula is increased to allow class A shareholders to convert each share of their stock into 1.5 shares of class B. This change in the conversion ratio increases the proportionate interest of the class A shareholders, and section 305(c) treats them as receiving a constructive stock distribution. Thus, assuming again the existence of a companion distribution, section 305(b)(2) may apply to treat the constructive stock distribution as a distribution of property under section 301. Reg. § 1.305-3(e) (ex. 6) and -7(a). The same result may occur if there is an increase to the conversion formula applicable to a debt instrument. See Rev. Rul. 75-513, 1975-2 C.B. 114. Section 305(b)(4), which does not require a companion distribution, applies if the increase in the conversion ratio relates to convertible *preferred* stock (other than an increase made solely to prevent dilution of the conversion right resulting from a distribution of stock on the underlying stock).

3. *Redemption premiums and section 305(e).* A redemption premium is the amount by which stock may be redeemed in excess of its issue price. In certain cases, a redemption premium may be treated as a constructive distribution of stock to the holder of the instrument. If one of the section 305(b) exceptions applies, the constructive distribution is treated as a section 301 distribution of property that is taken into account under economic accrual principles (like original issue discount) over the term of the instrument. I.R.C. §§ 305(c)(3), 1272(a); Reg. § 1.305-5(b)(1). More rigorous rules are provided for stock that must be redeemed as of a certain date or is subject to a put option entitling the holder to require the issuer to redeem the stock. Although reasonable redemption premiums are excepted from these rules, this exception is quite limited in the case of stock subject to a mandatory redemption or put option. I.R.C. § 305(c)(1); Reg. § 1.305-5(b)(1) and (2). In general, if stock is merely callable by the issuer and not subject to a mandatory redemption or put option, a redemption premium is treated as a constructive distribution only if a redemption pursuant to the call option is more likely than not to occur. Reg. § 1.305-5(b)(3)(i).

Section 305(e), dealing with "stripped preferred stock," presents a variation on the tax treatment of redemption premiums. Stripped preferred stock is preferred stock from which the dividend rights have been separated; it is therefore ordinarily sold for an amount less than its redemption price, with the difference being analogous to a redemption premium. Section 305(e)(1) and (4) require that a purchaser of such stock must report as ordinary income, under economic accrual principles applicable to instruments with original issue discount, the difference between the redemption price and the purchase price. Unlike the treatment of redemption premiums under section 305(c), the tax consequences under section 305(e) do not depend on whether any of the section 305(b) exceptions are satisfied. Moreover, section 305(e) results in ordinary income taxed at regular tax rates, not a constructive distribution of property under section 301, which may result in a dividend taxable at preferential rates.

4. *Section 305(b)(3) and (5).* Explain how these two provisions are or are not consistent with the general principle that a stock distribution with a disproportionate effect is treated as a distribution of property to which section 301 applies. See Reg. § 1.305-6(a).

5. *Tracking stock.* Section 305 only concerns the tax treatment of distributions of stock of the *distributing corporation*; the distribution of stock of any other corporation would ordinarily constitute a distribution of property and fall outside of

section 305. See I.R.C. § 317(a). Distributions of "tracking stock" stretch the meaning of this distinction. "Tracking stock" is stock that tracks the economic performance of only a portion of the issuing corporation, such as a division or a subsidiary of such corporation. If the stock tracks the performance of a subsidiary, a threshold question is whether such stock should be considered stock of the issuing corporation or its subsidiary. Resolution of this question is crucial in determining the potential applicability of section 305 to distributions of such stock. A further question is whether such stock should be considered "preferred stock," an important characterization for purposes of provisions such as section 305(b)(3)-(5). Currently, these questions are largely unresolved.

6. *Stock rights and poison pills.* The rules of section 305 apply equally to stock of the distributing corporation and rights to acquire such stock. I.R.C. § 305(d)(1). Rev. Rul. 90-11, 1990-1 C.B. 10, involved the distribution of certain rights (commonly referred to as "poison pill rights") entitling the distributees to acquire stock of the distributing corporation at discounted prices. Exercise of the rights, however, was contingent upon the occurrence of certain highly uncertain triggering events, such as a tender offer for majority control of the corporation. If a triggering event did not occur within a certain period of time, the rights expired. Given the remote and speculative nature of the rights, the IRS concluded that the distribution did not constitute a taxable event.

7. *Tax treatment of tax-free and taxable stock distributions.* In general, a shareholder who receives a tax-free distribution of stock ("new stock") under section 305(a) must allocate to the new stock a portion of her basis in the stock on which the distribution was received ("old stock") based on the relative fair market value of the old and new stock on the date of distribution. I.R.C. § 307(a); Reg. § 1.307-1. The distributee's holding period in the new stock includes the period she held the old stock. I.R.C. § 1223(4). The transaction has no effect on the distributing corporation's E&P. I.R.C. § 312(d)(1)(B).

In general, a shareholder who receives a taxable stock distribution, by reason of section 305(b), is treated as receiving a distribution of property under section 301 equal to the fair market value of the stock received. The distributee obtains a fair market value basis in the stock received (I.R.C. § 301(d)) and a fresh holding period. The distributing corporation, however, is not taxed under section 311 and its E&P is reduced by the fair market value of the stock distributed. Reg. § 1.312-1(d).

**Problem 9-2:** Determine the federal income tax consequences of the following transactions involving corporation Z.

(a) Z has both common and nonconvertible preferred stock outstanding. Z makes pro rata distributions of cash to the preferred stockholders and shares of a new class of preferred stock to the common stockholders. The rights provided by the new class of preferred stock are subordinate in all respects to those of the original class of preferred stock. See Reg. § 1.305-3(e) (ex. 3).

(b) Same as (a), except that in lieu of the distributions described, Z distributes pro rata nonconvertible preferred stock to both its common and preferred stockholders.
(c) Z has outstanding a single class of common stock and some debentures convertible into the stock under a fixed formula. During the year, Z pays interest on the debentures and distributes common stock pro rata to the holders of the common stock. See Reg. § 1.305-3(e) (ex. 4).
(d) Z has outstanding class A and class B common stock. Class A shares are convertible into class B shares on a 1:1 basis. However, the conversion ratio adjusts to increase the number of class B shares obtainable by a class A shareholder for each class A share in order to take into account any distribution of cash to the class B shareholders. In a given year, Z makes a pro rata distribution of cash to the class B shareholders and the conversion ratio is adjusted to take into account the cash distribution. See Reg. § 1.305-3(e) (ex. 7) and -7(b)(1).

**Review Problem 9-3:** This problem requires you to apply sections 301 and 302, as well as section 305. Unrelated individuals Alston and Bragan own 50 percent each (30 shares apiece) of Dodge Corporation. Each shareholder has a $1,200 total basis in his stock. Dodge is worth $6,000 (each share worth $100) and has sufficient E&P to cover any of the following proposed distributions. The parties would like to shift two-thirds control of the corporation to Bragan, with Alston retaining the remaining one-third interest. Determine the tax consequences of the following alternate methods of accomplishing this goal. Which produces the most favorable tax consequences? The least favorable?

(a) Dodge distributes $1,500 cash to Alston in redemption of 15 of his shares. Following the redemption, Alston still owns 15 shares of Dodge, which represent a one-third interest in the corporation, and Bragan still owns the other 30 shares, which represent the remaining two-thirds interest.
(b) Dodge distributes a total of $1,500 cash pro rata to Alston and Bragan, $750 to each. Following the distribution, Bragan uses his $750 to purchase 10 of Alston's shares, worth $75 per share following the distribution. After the purchase, Alston owns 20 shares of Dodge, representing a one-third interest, and Bragan owns the other 40 shares, representing a two-thirds interest.
(c) Alston sells 10 of his shares to Bragan for $1,000. Following the stock sale, Dodge distributes a total of $1,500 cash pro rata to the shareholders: two-thirds, or $1,000, to Bragan (which exactly reimburses him for the purchase price for the stock), and one-third, or $500, to Alston. Following the sale and distribution, Alston and Bragan have one-third and two-thirds interests in Dodge, respectively.

(d) Dodge distributes $1,500 cash to Alston and an equal amount, in the form of 30 additional shares, to Bragan. (After both distributions are taken into account, the 30 additional shares would be worth $1,500, one-third of $4,500.) After the distributions, Alston owns 30 shares (a one-third interest) and Bragan owns 60 shares (a two-thirds interest).

## B. Preferred Stock Bailouts

In Chamberlin v. Comm'r, 207 F.2d 462 (6th Cir. 1953), a closely held corporation with significant accumulated earnings distributed pro rata to its common stockholders shares of a new issue of preferred stock. Two days later, as a result of prior negotiations, all of the stockholders sold the preferred stock to two insurance companies for cash. The transactions were carried out to enable the shareholders to obtain the accumulated earnings of the corporation in the form of a capital gain rather than a taxable dividend. The corporation had the right to redeem the preferred stock immediately and was required to redeem it within seven and one-half years of the distribution.

The IRS argued that the distribution of the preferred stock was taxable to the shareholders, given the tax avoidance purpose of the transaction and the shifting of interests in the corporation following the sale of the preferred stock to the insurance companies. The Sixth Circuit disagreed. It found that the tax consequences of a stock distribution are determined at the time of the distribution, not at a subsequent time based on what the shareholders do with the distributed stock. In this case, the pro rata distribution of preferred stock on common stock did not change the pre-distribution interest of any shareholder. In addition, the cash received by the shareholders resulted from the sale to the insurance companies rather than a distribution by the corporation out of its E&P. The court recognized that a subsequent redemption of the preferred stock might effectively use corporate earnings to reimburse the insurance companies for the cash they paid to the shareholders. But the court refused to treat the insurance companies as mere conduits of the corporation's earnings "in the absence of a finding that [the preferred stock] was immediately or shortly thereafter redeemed at a premium." 207 F.2d at 471. Accordingly, the court held that the stock distributions were tax-free to the shareholders, who received capital gain treatment on the subsequent sale of their preferred stock.

Congress promptly passed section 306 to prevent the "preferred stock bailout" permitted by *Chamberlin*. Rather than treating the stock distribution as taxable (as argued by the IRS in that case), Congress decided to "taint" the stock distributed tax-free and then to tax a subsequent disposition of the tainted stock generally in the same manner as a dividend. A key aspect of the *Chamberlin* transaction was the use of *preferred* stock, since it enabled the shareholders to dispose of a portion of their interest in the corporation without affecting their underlying residual interest held prior to the transaction. Thus, in general, the stock that is tainted (and classified as "section 306 stock") is limited to preferred stock.

With both qualified dividend income and long-term capital gain currently taxed to individuals at a maximum 15 percent rate, the importance of section 306 is much reduced. As previously discussed, whether a taxpayer's income is a dividend or capital gain may still be important for purposes of basis recovery, capital loss limitations, and the dividends-received deduction. In addition, withholding taxes affecting foreign investors may arise in the case of dividends but not capital gains. The following sections briefly sketch the principal features of section 306.

### 1. *Definition of Section 306 Stock*

Read I.R.C. § 306(c). Section 306 affects the tax consequences of certain dispositions of "section 306 stock." In general, that term includes stock (other than common stock) received tax-free by a taxpayer (1) under section 305(a), (2) in a section 351 exchange if cash received in lieu of the stock would have been treated as a dividend (such as pursuant to section 304), or (3) in a nondivisive or divisive reorganization (discussed in chapters eleven and twelve) if the effect is substantially the same as a stock dividend. Also, the term generally includes stock (including common stock) whose basis is determined by reference to the basis of the taxpayer or any other person holding section 306 stock. Because section 306 is intended to prevent a bailout of corporate earnings that would otherwise be taxable as a dividend, "section 306 stock" specifically excludes stock no part of the distribution of which would have been a dividend if money had been distributed in lieu of the stock. I.R.C. § 306(c)(2). Thus, if a corporation has no E&P in the year of the distribution of stock, the distributed stock is not section 306 stock.

### 2. *Dispositions of Section 306 Stock*

Read I.R.C. § 306(a). The rules provide slightly different results depending upon how a taxpayer disposes of section 306 stock. If section 306 stock is redeemed, the amount realized is treated as a distribution to which section 301 applies. I.R.C. § 306(a)(2). Thus, the amount of the distributing corporation's E&P in the year of the redemption is crucial in determining the amount treated as a dividend.

In contrast, in the case of any other disposition of section 306 stock, a portion of the amount realized is treated as ordinary income taxable as a dividend for purposes of section 1(h)(11). I.R.C. § 306(a)(1)(A) and (D). Thus, such ordinary income may potentially be taxed at preferential rates applicable to qualified dividend income. The amount treated as ordinary income is the portion of the initial stock distribution that would have been a dividend had the corporation distributed cash in lieu of the section 306 stock. (If the taxpayer only disposes of a portion of her section 306 stock, then the ordinary income amount is proportionately reduced.) Thus, the amount of the corporation's E&P at the time of the stock distribution, rather than the subsequent disposition of such stock, is crucial. Any amount realized in excess of the amount treated as ordinary income is first a tax-free recovery of basis and then gain from the sale of stock. No loss is allowed. Rather, any unrecovered basis is generally added back to the taxpayer's basis in the common stock with respect to which the section 306 stock was distributed. I.R.C. § 306(a)(1)(B) and (C); Reg. § 1.306-1(b)(2) (ex. 2 and 3). A disposition other than by redemption does not affect the amount of the corporation's E&P. Reg. § 1.306-1(b)(1) (fourth sentence). As the following example illustrates, different tax consequences arise depending on the manner of disposing of section 306 stock.

**Example 9-1:** Taxpayer is distributed 100 shares of preferred stock (worth $5,000) by corporation X in a transaction qualifying for tax-free treatment under section 305(a). In the year of the distribution, the ratable portion of X's E&P attributable to the distribution is $3,000. Two years later, taxpayer disposes of all of the preferred stock for $10,000 when the taxpayer's basis in the stock is $1,000. In the year of the disposition, X's E&P is $20,000.

(a) Classification as section 306 stock—Taxpayer received a tax-free distribution of preferred stock when the distributing corporation had E&P. Therefore, the preferred stock qualifies as section 306 stock. I.R.C. § 306(c)(1)(A).
(b) Redemption—If the disposition of the section 306 stock is by way of redemption, then the entire $10,000 is taxed as a dividend based on the amount of X's E&P in the year of the redemption. I.R.C. §§ 306(a)(2), 301(c)(1), 316(a). Taxpayer's $1,000 basis in the redeemed stock is added back to the taxpayer's basis in its remaining X stock. Cf. Reg. §§ 1.306-1(b)(2) (ex. 2 and 3), 1.302-2(c).
(c) Other disposition—In the case of any nonredemption disposition of the preferred stock, only $3,000 of the amount realized is treated as ordinary income taxable as a dividend. This is the amount of the distribution that would have been taxable as a dividend if X had distributed $5,000 cash in lieu of the preferred stock. Taxpayer also has $1,000 basis recovery and $6,000 gain from the sale of the stock. If, in the year of the stock distribution, the ratable portion of X's E&P attributable to the distribution had been $20,000, then $5,000 (the value of the preferred stock at the time of the distribution) of the amount realized would be treated as ordinary income taxable as a dividend; the $4,000 in excess of basis would be gain from the sale of stock. I.R.C. § 306(a)(1).

### 3. *Exceptions*

Read I.R.C. § 306(b). Section 306 is intended to prevent the bailout of corporate earnings without appropriate dividend consequences by shareholders who retain a continuing interest in the corporation. Thus, if the disposition of section 306 stock results in a complete termination of the taxpayer's interest in the corporation (after application of section 318 constructive ownership rules), the disposition is not subject to section 306(a), since there is no potential bailout abuse. The consequences of section 306(a) are also called off in certain other circumstances, including dispositions of section 306 stock (1) pursuant to a partial or complete liquidation of the corporation (see chapters six and ten), (2) in a transaction in which gain or loss is not recognized (although the section 306 taint may continue in the hands of the transferee or carry over to other stock received by the taxpayer in the transaction), and (3) in a transaction that is not considered by the Treasury to be pursuant to a plan having as one of its principal purposes the avoidance of federal income tax.

# Chapter 10

# Taxable Corporate Acquisitions and Liquidations

Corporate acquisitions are carried out in several different ways. In a corporate asset sale, one corporation (commonly referred to as the *target corporation*) transfers its assets to another corporation (commonly referred to as the *acquiring* or *purchasing corporation*) after which the target may be completely liquidated. In a corporate stock sale, the target's shareholders transfer their target stock to an acquiring corporation and the target may be subsequently liquidated into the acquiring corporation. A third pattern, sometimes known as a shareholder asset sale, reverses the order of the steps of a corporate asset sale. In this transaction, the target's shareholders first completely liquidate the target, receive a distribution of its assets, and then transfer those assets to the acquiring corporation. As described in the note below, acquisitions also take place as a result of a merger.

Over the years, one major objective of the corporate tax law has been to provide identical tax consequences to an acquisition no matter how it is carried out. This goal has necessarily required consideration of the tax consequences of acquisitions and liquidations together, and this chapter follows suit. This chapter, however, only describes part of the story. It deals with *taxable* corporate acquisitions in which, in general, either the target corporation, the owners of the target corporation, or both, recognize gain or loss in the transaction. The tax treatment of *tax-free* (or, more precisely, *tax-deferred*) corporate acquisitions, generally referred to as "reorganizations," is described in chapter eleven.

A complete liquidation of a corporation is defined as one or a series of corporate distributions in redemption of all of the stock of the corporation pursuant to a plan. I.R.C. § 346(a). Thus, a liquidation for tax purposes terminates the separate existence of a corporate entity and may result in a withdrawal of assets from corporate solution. Any business conducted by the corporation, however, need not necessarily be wound up and terminated in the process. Following a complete liquidation of a corporation, its business may be continued by its former shareholders in either corporate or noncorporate form. Alternatively, if the liquidation takes place in connection with an acquisition, the liquidating corporation's business may be continued in the hands of the acquiring party.

Parts A and B of this chapter describe the shareholder- and corporate-level tax consequences, respectively, of taxable corporate acquisitions and liquidations. Part C concludes by considering the consequences of these transactions when either the target or acquiring corporation is an S corporation.

### *NOTE*

*Forward and reverse mergers.* A merger of the target into the acquiring corporation, with the latter surviving (a "forward merger"), is generally treated for tax purposes as a corporate asset sale by the target followed by its complete liquidation. Consideration paid to the target shareholders in the merger is treated as paid first to the target corporation (in exchange for its assets) and then distributed by the target to its shareholders in the complete liquidation. Rev. Rul. 69-6, 1969-1 C.B. 104. Another common acquisition pattern involves a merger of a subsidiary of the acquiring corporation *into* the target corporation, with the target surviving. Since the corporation that does not survive the merger (the "merged corporation") is a subsidiary of the acquiring corporation, this transaction is commonly described as a "reverse triangular merger." In the merger, the target shareholders receive consideration in exchange for all of their shares and the target becomes a wholly-owned subsidiary of the acquiring corporation. For tax purposes, assuming that the merged corporation's existence is transitory, the transaction is treated as a sale of target stock by the target shareholders to the acquiring corporation. Rev. Rul. 73-427, 1973-2 C.B. 301. When there are numerous target shareholders and the objective is to acquire all of the target stock, reverse triangular mergers have traditionally been more expedient than stock tender offers because only a majority or supermajority of the target's shareholders need approve the merger. Many states, however, have now adopted "share exchange" provisions to accomplish the same result even though the transaction is carried out as a tender offer. See Model Bus. Corp. Act §§ 11.03, 11.04, 11.07(b).

## A. Shareholder-Level Consequences

### 1. *In General*

The tax consequences to target shareholders of a taxable corporate acquisition generally follow from the form of the transaction. In a stock sale, shareholders who dispose of their target stock must generally recognize gain or loss. See I.R.C. § 1001. In contrast, because target shareholders are treated as taxpayers separate from their corporation, they generally do not recognize gain or loss in a corporate asset sale unless it is accompanied by a liquidation of, or other distribution from, the target corporation.

Read I.R.C. §§ 331 and 334(a). In a complete liquidation of a corporation, amounts distributed to the shareholders are treated as payments in exchange for their stock in the corporation and not section 301 distributions. As a result, shareholders must generally recognize gain or loss in the transaction and obtain a basis in any property distributed equal to its fair market value at the time of the distribution. If a liquidation of a target corporation is followed by a sale of the former target's assets, the shareholders recognize only post-liquidation gain or loss (if any) on the assets sold.

The tax consequences under section 331 may seem unsurprising since, from the shareholder's perspective, a complete liquidation may appear to be identical to any other disposition of the shareholder's stock. Indeed, section 331 serves a practical purpose when the selling shareholder does not know the buyer's identity. Following a corporate liquidation under section 331, however, the amount of the corporation's E&P is eliminated. In contrast, following a sale of a shareholder's stock to a third-party buyer, the amount of the corporation's E&P is generally left intact. Thus, at least in theory, it is not clear that these two transactions should be taxed alike. We previously saw the significance of this issue in the context of a complete redemption in *Zenz v. Quinlivan* (p. 228).

## *NOTES AND QUESTIONS*

1. *Required allocations.* If a shareholder acquires shares in two or more transactions, the shareholder must allocate any liquidating distribution to each block of stock in order to determine the amount and character of any gain or loss. See Reg. § 1.331-1(e). If the complete liquidation involves a series of distributions occurring in more than one taxable year, a further allocation is required. A shareholder may fully offset an amount distributed in a given year with her basis in a particular block of stock, but may not claim any loss until the final distribution is made. See Rev. Rul. 85-48, 1985-1 C.B. 126. Suppose, in year 1, a calendar-year taxpayer purchases 100 shares of X corporation for $2,000. On March 1 of year 5, the taxpayer purchases an additional 400 shares for $20,000. What are the income tax consequences to the taxpayer if, pursuant to a plan of complete liquidation of X, the taxpayer receives a distribution of $11,250 on both December 1 of year 5 and June 1 of year 6 in complete redemption of all of the taxpayer's stock?

2. *Partial liquidations.* Chapter six explained that certain redemptions in partial liquidation of the distributing corporation are treated as distributions in exchange for the distributee's stock. See I.R.C. § 302(b)(4) and (e). Although this result did not fit easily with the theory of section 302, it should be more understandable now that you know the tax treatment of complete liquidations under section 331(a).

3. *Liquidation-reincorporations.* A common fact pattern that presents a substance-over-form inquiry is a liquidation followed or preceded by a transfer of the liquidating corporation's assets to another corporation. The regulations indicate that this transaction may be recharacterized as a reorganization, discussed in chapter

eleven, with possible dividend consequences to the corporation's shareholders. See Reg. § 1.331-1(c).

## 2. *Liquidating Distributions to a Controlling Corporate Shareholder*

Read I.R.C. §§ 332(a) and (b), 334(b), 1504(a)(2), and 381(a). In contrast to the general treatment of shareholders, a controlling *corporate* shareholder generally does not recognize gain or loss upon receipt of a liquidating distribution from its subsidiary. These liquidations are sometimes referred to as "section 332" or "parent-subsidiary" liquidations. For this rule to apply, the parent corporation must own at least 80 percent of the voting power and value of its subsidiary throughout the period the plan of liquidation is adopted and distributions are made. In addition, the liquidation must either take place within a single taxable year or be pursuant to a plan of liquidation under which all distributions occur within a three-year period. As discussed in part B of this chapter, the liquidating corporation also generally does not recognize gain or loss in a section 332 liquidation. See I.R.C. § 337(a).

This nonrecognition exception was added to the law to facilitate the simplification of corporate structures and is justified because a parent-subsidiary liquidation, like a section 351(a) transaction, is a mere change in form and not substance. In addition, the liquidation reduces the possibility of more than one corporate-level tax being imposed on the same gain since the effect of the liquidation is to eliminate one of two corporate tiers of taxation. The liquidating subsidiary's basis in its assets and other tax attributes (including E&P) generally are preserved in the hands of the parent corporation. **Problem 10-1** illustrates the pre-transaction gain or loss that is *not* preserved following the transaction:

> **Problem 10-1:** P corporation has owned all of the stock of S corporation for over five years. P's basis in its S stock is $1,000, and S's aggregate basis in its assets (worth $3,000) is $400. P and S do not file a consolidated return. Determine the federal income tax consequences to P in the event S is completely liquidated and distributes all of its assets to P. Following the liquidation, what happens to the pre-transaction built-in gain in S's assets? To the pre-transaction built-in gain in the S stock held by P? Explain the rationale for these results.

### *NOTES AND QUESTIONS*

1. *Liquidating distribution to controlling noncorporate shareholder.* Unlike a liquidating distribution to a controlling corporate shareholder, a distribution to a *non*corporate shareholder who owns a controlling interest in the liquidating

corporation is taxed under the general rule of section 331. This transaction could also be viewed as a mere change in form rather than substance. Nevertheless, for reasons described in chapter seven, the entire transaction cannot be treated as a nonrecognition event, since one tier of potential taxation is eliminated. *Partial* nonrecognition treatment might be possible; for example, if the liquidating corporation recognized gain or loss, the shareholder could be allowed nonrecognition treatment (except to the extent of any cash distributed in excess of the shareholder's basis in the liquidating corporation's stock) contingent on the shareholder receiving an *exchanged* basis in any property distributed. Nevertheless, current law generally requires both the liquidating corporation and the noncorporate shareholder to recognize gain or loss in the transaction.

2. *Recognition of losses in complete liquidation despite related parties.* In general, no loss deduction is allowed upon a sale or exchange of property between related persons (including a corporation and an individual owning over 50 percent of the value of the corporation's stock). I.R.C. § 267(a)(1) and (b)(2). This general rule prevents the parties, because of their close relationship, from "manufacturing" a realization event and colluding to produce a tax "loss" without any economic loss. When losses are disallowed in such transactions, the transferee is generally permitted to use the disallowed loss to offset any gain upon a *subsequent* disposition of the property (to an unrelated party). I.R.C. § 267(d). The general loss disallowance rule, however, does not apply to any loss arising upon a complete liquidation of a corporation (including a distribution to a controlling noncorporate shareholder under section 331). I.R.C. § 267(a)(1) (second sentence). One reason for allowing loss recognition is that the property exchanged by a shareholder in a liquidation (i.e., the shareholder's stock in the liquidating corporation) is completely redeemed in the transaction. Therefore, if disposition of such stock in a liquidation produced a disallowed loss, there would be no later opportunity to claim the loss. But if the liquidating corporation and shareholder are related, loss recognition leaves the tax system vulnerable to the possible creation of a shareholder-level loss through a misvaluation of the distributed corporate property. If the parties collude to understate the value of distributed property, the shareholder may benefit by claiming an immediate loss in the liquidation at the cost of obtaining a lower-than-fair-market-value basis in such property under section 334(a).

The special rule in the second sentence of section 267(a)(1) applies to losses incurred by *either* the shareholder *or* the corporation in a complete liquidation. Part B of this chapter, however, describes other rules that limit the corporation's recognition of a loss in a liquidating distribution to a related person.

3. *No election.* The nonrecognition of gain or loss provided by section 332 is not elective. In what circumstances might a taxpayer prefer a parent-subsidiary liquidation *not* to qualify under section 332? How might that objective be achieved?

4. *Tax shelters and other tax avoidance transactions.* Sections 332(c) and (d) and 334(b)(1)(B) all provide exceptions to the general treatment of parent-subsidiary liquidations in special circumstances involving possible tax avoidance. In section 332(c), the liquidating subsidiary is a regulated investment company (RIC) or

real estate investment trust (REIT) that is generally entitled to deduct any dividends paid to its shareholders. I.R.C. §§ 852(b)(2)(D), 857(b)(2)(B). The dividends-paid deduction is the mechanism used to avoid double taxation of the income of the RIC or REIT; the trade-off for the deduction is generally taxation of the dividend to the shareholders. Section 332(c) therefore provides that if the liquidating distribution is treated as a deductible dividend by the RIC or REIT subsidiary, the distribution is not tax-free to the parent corporation under section 332(a). Section 332(d) concerns a liquidation into a parent corporation that is a foreign corporation. Congress denied application of section 332(a) (and section 331) to this transaction to prevent possible avoidance of withholding taxes when dividends are distributed by U.S. corporations to foreign persons. Finally, section 334(b)(1)(B) prevents a parent-subsidiary liquidation from being used to import a net built-in loss from a party not subject to U.S. tax. An example would be the liquidation of a foreign subsidiary with a net built-in loss into its U.S. parent corporation. The rule provides that the U.S. parent in that situation obtains a basis in the loss property equal to its fair market value at the time of the distribution.

5. *Insolvent subsidiaries*. Section 332(b) requires the liquidating distribution to be in complete cancellation or redemption of all of the parent's stock in its subsidiary. Under the regulations, the parent must receive at least partial payment for its stock in the subsidiary. Reg. § 1.332-2(b). Accordingly, the nonrecognition rule of section 332 does not apply if the subsidiary is insolvent at the time of the liquidation; the parent instead may be entitled to claim a worthless stock or bad debt deduction in such a transaction. Proposed regulations issued in 2005 would make section 332 inapplicable if the parent does not receive at least partial payment on *each class* of stock owned in a subsidiary. For example, if the parent owns both the common and preferred stock of its subsidiary and the subsidiary's assets are insufficient to satisfy fully the liquidation preference of the preferred stock, a liquidation of the subsidiary results in the parent receiving no consideration for its common stock. Under the proposed regulations, section 332 would not apply to this liquidation and the parent could therefore obtain a worthless stock deduction for its common stock. The distribution on the preferred stock would be taxable under section 331 unless that portion of the transaction qualified as a reorganization (chapter eleven). See Prop. Reg. § 1.332-2(b), (e) (ex. 2).

## B. Corporate-Level Consequences

Although the corporate-level tax treatment of acquisitions and liquidations was changed dramatically in 1986, the tax policy objective of achieving neutrality in the tax consequences of the different acquisition patterns has continued throughout. Because pre-1986 law is still referenced today and is helpful in understanding current law, this part begins with a brief review of prior law.

### 1. *Pre-1986 Law*

In Comm'r v. Court Holding Co., 324 U.S. 331 (1945), a closely held corporation called off at the last minute a planned sale of its only asset, a building. Instead, to avoid any corporate-level tax, the shareholders liquidated the corporation, received a distribution of the building, and sold it to the buyer on substantially the same terms as the original plan. Based on the rule in *General Utilities* (p. 175), the corporation claimed that it did not recognize gain or loss upon distributing the building in the liquidation. Although the liquidation was a taxable event to the shareholders, they obtained a basis in the building equal to its fair market value and therefore recognized no gain or loss upon the sale to the buyer. Writing for the Court, Justice Black agreed with the trial court's assessment that the corporation was still liable for a corporate tax:

> A sale by one person cannot be transformed for tax purposes into a sale by another by using the latter as a conduit through which to pass title. To permit the true nature of a transaction to be disguised by mere formalisms, which exist solely to alter tax liabilities, would seriously impair the effective administration of the tax policies of Congress. [324 U.S. at 334.]

Five years later, Justice Black again wrote for the majority in U.S. v. Cumberland Public Service Co., 338 U.S. 451 (1950). In that case, the shareholders of a closely held corporation offered to sell their shares to a buyer. The buyer countered with an offer to purchase the corporation's assets rather than its stock. To avoid the corporate-level tax that would arise upon such a sale, the shareholders instead substituted the same steps resulting in a shareholder asset sale that had been carried out in *Court Holding Co.* The Supreme Court once again upheld the fact-finder's determination, but this time in favor of the taxpayer's claim that the corporate-level tax had been successfully avoided. The Court distinguished *Court Holding Co.* by noting that the taxpayer there had negotiated a corporate asset sale, reached an oral agreement, and only then purported to call off the sale at the last minute to carry out a shareholder asset sale under substantially the same terms as the prior oral agreement. In *Cumberland*, the Court stated:

> [The decision in *Court Holding Co.*] does not mean that a corporation can be taxed even when the sale has been made by its shareholders following a genuine liquidation and dissolution. While the distinction between sales by a corporation as compared with distribution in kind followed by shareholder sales may be particularly shadowy and artificial when the corporation is closely held, Congress has chosen to recognize such a distinction for tax purposes. [338 U.S. at 454-55.]

The finding that a major motive of the taxpayer was to reduce taxes "does not bar this conclusion." Id. at 455.

Justice Black's suggestion that Congress was responsible for the state of the law perhaps overlooked to some extent the Court's own role as a result of its prior decision in *General Utilities*. But he was surely correct to recognize the "shadowy and artificial" distinction between a corporate and shareholder asset sale for many closely held corporations whose shareholders, officers, and employees are the same person or persons. Congress soon decided that the resulting state of the law was untenable and that a statutory fix was in order.

The basic choice for Congress was either to repeal the *General Utilities* doctrine and have the corporation recognize gain or loss in both situations or, alternatively, to allow the nonrecognition of gain or loss in certain liquidating corporate sales. Somewhat surprisingly, Congress in 1954 chose the latter course by enacting former section 337, which generally permitted the nonrecognition of gain or loss on sales carried out by a corporation within one year of its liquidation. Congress also enacted former section 336, which codified the *General Utilities* rule in a corporate liquidation. By granting nonrecognition treatment to certain sales even if made to an unrelated party for cash, former section 337 represented a dramatic departure from normative income tax principles. Unlike other nonrecognition provisions, former section 337 was not needed to avoid liquidity or valuation difficulties or to prevent abuse, and a qualifying sale unquestionably changed the taxpayer's underlying investment. Moreover, former sections 337 and 336 did not merely defer tax consequences; since purchasers obtained a cost basis in the property acquired, gains not recognized in the transaction escaped taxation forever. The principal exception to former sections 337 and 336 concerned property with certain recapture-type gains (i.e., gains attributable to certain prior depreciation deductions). Upon disposition of such property, the taxpayer was required to recognize the recapture gain (and treat it as ordinary income) notwithstanding the nonrecognition provisions. See I.R.C. §§ 1245(a), 1250(a).

Enactment of former sections 337 and 336 created parity in the tax consequences of corporate and shareholder asset sales and therefore avoided the "shadowy and artificial" distinction presented by *Court Holding Co.* and *Cumberland*. It potentially disadvantaged, however, a third way of carrying out the same acquisition — namely, the shareholder stock sale that was the taxpayers' original choice in *Cumberland*. The sale of all of the stock of a target corporation to a corporate buyer followed by a liquidation of the target into the buyer achieved the same economic outcome as either a corporate or shareholder asset sale to the buyer. But because liquidation of the target into the corporate buyer qualified under the predecessor to section 332, the shareholder stock sale followed by liquidation of the target resulted in the corporate buyer obtaining the target's historic basis in the assets distributed. See I.R.C. § 334(b)(1). In contrast, in either a corporate or shareholder asset sale, the buyer obtained a basis in the acquired assets equal to their fair market value at the time of acquisition.

There may be sound business reasons to prefer one acquisition technique over another even though each may achieve the same economic end result. For example, a shareholder asset sale is cumbersome if there are a multitude of shareholders with differing interests. Either type of asset sale may be infeasible if certain of the assets, such as licenses or contracts, are not readily transferable, and asset sales generally tend to be messier than stock sales. On the other hand, an acquisition of assets rather than stock may be better at insulating the buyer from the target corporation's liabilities, including those that are unknown at the time of the acquisition.

To neutralize the tax consequences of the different acquisition patterns, Congress enacted former section 334(b)(2) in 1954 (in addition to former sections 337 and 336). This rule codified the principles of Kimbell-Diamond Milling Co. v. Comm'r, 14 T.C. 74 (1950), aff'd per curiam, 187 F.2d 718 (5th Cir. 1951), cert. denied, 342 U.S. 827 (1951), which treated for tax purposes a sale of a target corporation's stock followed by liquidation of the target into the corporate buyer as a sale of the target's assets to the buyer. In general, under former section 334(b)(2), if a corporation acquired in a taxable transaction at least 80 percent of the stock of a target corporation and liquidated the target under section 332 pursuant to a plan adopted within two years of the acquisition, the corporation's basis in any property distributed in the liquidation was equal to the corporation's basis in its target stock (and not the target's historic basis in such assets). In summary, thanks to former sections 337, 336, and 334(b)(2), corporate asset sales, shareholder asset sales, and shareholder stock sales (followed by liquidation of the target) all generally enabled an acquiring corporation to obtain a fair market value basis in the target's assets. The principal tax consequence of each acquisition method was the recognition of gain or loss by the target corporation's shareholders (but not by the corporation). The main exception to nonrecognition at the corporate level was the required recognition by the target of certain recapture gains.

At the urging of some members of the corporate tax bar, Congress in 1982 replaced former section 334(b)(2) with section 338. The enactment of section 338 was intended to substitute an explicit election for the transactional one permitted by former section 334(b)(2), and thereby reduce the uncertainty of the tax consequences of the transaction. Section 338 also eliminated the required liquidation of the acquired target corporation under former section 334(b)(2), a superfluous step if the buyer wanted to continue the target's business in a separate corporate entity.

Read I.R.C. § 338(a). In its original enactment, the words "to which [former] section 337 applies" were included in section 338(a)(1) after the words "single transaction." Thus, if the conditions of the provision were satisfied, it allowed taxpayers to treat an acquired target corporation as if it had sold all of its assets to itself in a qualifying sale under former section 337. The effect was to permit the target to mark up (or down) the basis of its assets to fair market value without any corporate-level tax consequences (other than recognition of certain recapture gains). The provision's principal conditions, which remain in the law today, were an explicit election (specified in section 338(g)) and the required acquisition (referred to as a "qualified stock purchase") by a corporation of at least 80 percent of the voting power and value of the target corporation during a 12-month period in a transaction in which the selling target shareholders recognized gain or loss. Read I.R.C. § 338(d), (g), (h)(1), (2), and (3)(A). Importantly, a liquidation of the target corporation was (and is) *not* required.

In adopting section 338, Congress tried to limit the selectivity of tax consequences previously allowed in corporate acquisitions. As noted, under the law enacted in 1954, only corporate nonrecapture gains were permitted to escape taxation altogether. As a result, the strategy of taxpayers in structuring acquisitions was to realize all nonrecapture gains (but avoid recognizing them due to the 1954 changes) but *not* realize any recapture gains (and therefore avoid recognizing them as well). This cherry-picking behavior is similar to the selective realization under current law of accrued losses but not gains.

For example, suppose a target corporation owned two principal assets whose value exceeded basis: land and some previously depreciated machinery and equipment. Under prior law, a corporate liquidating sale of the machinery and equipment resulted in the recognition of ordinary recapture income by the target notwithstanding the existence of former section 337. In contrast, a liquidating sale of the land escaped taxation by reason of the same provision, with the purchaser obtaining a fair market value basis in the land. Taxpayers, therefore, tried to include the land, but not the machinery and equipment, in the liquidating sale; the latter assets were transferred to the buyer in a transaction not treated as a realization event to the transferor. The goal was to avoid recognizing the recapture gain, at the cost of the buyer obtaining a lower transferred basis in those assets.

The goal of the "consistency" rules under section 338 is to prevent such selectivity. Read I.R.C. § 338(e), (f), (h)(4), (5), and (6)(A). These rules attempt to ensure that in a given acquisition, the section 338(g) election is applicable to either all or none of the assets acquired. The complexity of acquisitions and corporate structures make this a difficult goal to implement, and the Code provisions reflect some of that difficulty. In their original form, the implementing regulations contained almost 20 pages on the consistency issue alone. As we shall see, repeal of the *General Utilities* doctrine in 1986 reduced the significance of the concern about selectivity and facilitated a major simplification of the consistency rules and section 338 generally.

## *NOTES*

1. *The* Court Holding Co. *doctrine. General Utilities* repeal has changed the stakes, but the "*Court Holding Co.* doctrine" remains alive and well. In a particular transaction, the doctrine may justify treating one person rather than another as the proper taxpayer. More generally, along with *Gregory v. Helvering*, *Court Holding Co.* is frequently cited for the proposition that, for tax purposes, substance governs over form.

2. *Importance of history.* As noted, a section 338(g) election is available only if a *corporation* makes a qualified stock purchase of the target corporation. These conditions follow directly from former section 334(b)(2) and the purpose of that provision. Former section 334(b)(2) was concerned with stock acquisitions in which a subsequent liquidation of the target into the acquiring party would qualify under section 332 (and therefore result in the acquiring party obtaining the target's historic asset basis). In general, this scenario arose only if the acquiring party was a corporation. Under current law, the requirement of a corporate purchaser no longer serves a policy objective; accordingly, the regulations indicate that a noncorporate purchaser may generally form a wholly-owned corporation prior to the transaction in order to meet this requirement. Reg. § 1.338-3(b)(1).

## 2. *Liquidations under Current Law*

In 1986, after "chipping away" at the rule for many years, Congress repealed the *General Utilities* doctrine with respect to liquidations. Read the following excerpt for some of the reasons. Do you find them persuasive?

### House Ways and Means Committee Report Relating to Tax Reform Act of 1986

H.R. Rep. No. 99-426, 99th Cong., 1st Sess. 281-82 (1985)

The committee believes that the *General Utilities* rule, even in the more limited form in which it exists today, produces many incongruities and inequities in the tax system. First, the rule may create significant distortions in business behavior. Economically, a liquidating distribution is indistinguishable from a nonliquidating distribution; yet the Code provides a substantial preference for the former. A corporation acquiring the assets of a liquidating corporation is able to obtain a basis in assets equal to their fair market value, although the transferor recognizes no gain (other than possibly recapture amounts) on the sale. The tax benefits may make the assets more valuable in the hands of the transferee than in the hands of the present owner. The effect may be to induce corporations with substantial appreciated assets to liquidate and transfer their assets to other corporations for tax reasons, when economic considerations might indicate a different course of action. Accordingly, the *General Utilities* rule may be responsible, at least in part, for the dramatic increase in corporate mergers and acquisitions in recent years. The committee believes that the Code should not artificially encourage corporate liquidations and acquisitions, and believes that repeal of the *General Utilities* rule is a major step towards that goal.

Second, the *General Utilities* rule tends to undermine the corporate income tax. Under normally applicable tax principles, nonrecognition of gain is available only if the transferee takes a carryover basis in the transferred property, thus assuring that a tax will eventually be collected on the appreciation. Where the *General Utilities* rule applies, assets generally are permitted to leave corporate solution and to take a stepped-up basis in the hands of the transferee without the imposition of a corporate-level tax.[1] Thus, the effect of the rule is to grant a permanent exemption from the corporate income tax.

---

Reversal of the *General Utilities* rule entailed repealing former sections 336 and 337 as well as all references to that version of those two sections, including the one formerly included in section 338(a). As we shall see, the reversal also prompted a

1. The price of this basis step up is, at most, a single, shareholder-level capital gains tax (and perhaps recapture, tax benefit, and other similar amounts). In some cases, moreover, payment of the capital gains tax is deferred because the shareholder's gain is reported under the installment method.

number of collateral changes, including enactment of new section 1374. Confusingly, Congress used the same Code sections (336 and 337) to carry out its new policy. Whereas former section 336(a) provided for the *non*recognition of gain or loss by a corporation making a liquidating distribution, current section 336(a) generally provides for the *recognition* of gain or loss in the same transaction as if the liquidating corporation sold (for fair market value) the distributed property to the distributee. Current section 336(d) limits the recognition of losses in certain circumstances, however, and current section 337 deals with the tax consequences to the liquidating corporation in a section 332 liquidation. These changes highlight the importance of knowing which version of sections 336 and 337 is being referenced at any given time.

Read I.R.C. §§ 336(a) - (d) and 337 and do the following problem. In each case, try to figure out the purpose of the particular rule.

**Problem 10-2:** Determine the tax consequences to all parties of each of the following alternative situations:

(a) X corporation has only two assets: a parcel of real estate (Blackacre) and portfolio stock in General Electric (GE). X purchased Blackacre 12 years ago and the stock eight years ago, both for cash. X adopts a plan of liquidation and, pursuant to such plan, distributes its assets pro rata to its five unrelated individual shareholders, A, B, C, D and E, each of whom owns 20 percent of X. At the time of the liquidation, the fair market value of Blackacre and the GE stock is $100,000 each. X has a $20,000 basis in Blackacre and a $150,000 basis in the stock.

(b) Same as (a), except that following adoption of the plan of liquidation, X sells the two assets at fair market value to unrelated buyers, and distributes the sales proceeds to its shareholders in liquidation.

(c) Same as (a), except that Blackacre is encumbered with a $120,000 mortgage at the time of the liquidation.

(d) Same as (a), except that at the time of the liquidation, X has only one shareholder, corporation M, and M receives both Blackacre and the GE stock in the liquidation.

(e) Same as (d), except that M is the University of Virginia, an educational institution qualifying under section 501(c)(3) of the Code.

(f) Same as (d), except that X owes M $20,000. Following adoption of the plan of liquidation but prior to the actual liquidation, X pays off M by transferring to M one-fifth of its GE stock.

(g) Same as (a), except that at the time of the liquidation, corporation M owns 60 percent of X, and individuals B and C (who are unrelated to each other and to M) own 20 percent each. Assume that, in addition to Blackacre and the GE stock, X has $50,000 cash. In the liquidation, X distributes the stock plus $50,000 to M and divides Blackacre evenly between B and C.

(h) Same as (a), except that the GE stock was acquired by X 18 months prior to the adoption of the plan of liquidation as a contribution to capital. At the time the GE stock was acquired, its fair market value was $120,000 and the transferor's basis in the GE stock was $150,000. Review I.R.C. § 362(e)(2). What basis did X obtain when it acquired the GE stock? Under what circumstances might section 336(d)(2)(A) limit the recognition of a loss by a liquidating corporation?

### 3. *Asset Acquisitions under Current Law*

With the repeal of *General Utilities* and former section 337, a corporate asset sale, even though carried out as part of a liquidation of the corporation, is generally a taxable transaction, with the buyer obtaining a cost basis in the assets acquired. I.R.C. §§ 1001, 1012. Since a corporate sale of an entire business is treated for tax purposes as a sale of each individual asset of the business and not the sale of a single capital asset (see Williams v. McGowan, 152 F.2d 570 (2d Cir. 1945)), an important question is the allocation of a lump-sum purchase price for the entire business to each of the business's assets. Such allocation potentially determines both the amount and character of the seller's income and the buyer's basis in the assets acquired. The same allocation issue arises upon a qualified stock purchase with a section 338(g) election; allocation of the purchase price to the individual assets of the target corporation determines the tax consequences of the deemed sale and repurchase by the target of its assets. The following case describes the tax effect given by some courts to an agreement between the parties allocating purchase price. The remaining materials in this section concern the question of how purchase price is allocated to intangible assets.

### *NOTE*

*Taxable mergers.* As previously noted, a forward merger of the target into the acquiring corporation, with the latter surviving, is generally treated for tax purposes as a transfer of the target's assets to the acquiring corporation followed by a complete liquidation of the target. Thus, if the merger is taxable (and not a "reorganization," described in chapter eleven), then the same issues described in this section will generally arise. If the acquiring corporation wants to acquire all of the target's assets, a merger may be more expedient than an asset acquisition. A potential disadvantage of a merger, however, is that the acquiring corporation succeeds to all of the target's liabilities by operation of law. To some extent, the liabilities can be kept separate from the acquiring corporation's assets by having the target merge into a subsidiary or LLC owned by the acquiring corporation. If the existence of the LLC is disregarded for tax purposes (see chapter three), a merger into an LLC owned by the acquiring corporation is treated the same as a direct merger into that corporation.

## a. Effect of Purchase Price Allocation Agreement

### Commissioner v. Danielson

378 F.2d 771 (3d Cir. 1967)

SEITZ, Circuit Judge

. . . The taxpayers were stockholders in Butler County Loan Company ("Loan"), which was engaged in the small loan business . . . in Butler, Pennsylvania. The husband of taxpayer, Helen Sherman, had been its successful manager until his death in 1958. Thereafter, one Shukis was brought in to run the business and was given an option to buy 100 shares of the Loan's stock. He later exercised an option to buy 10 shares.

In 1959, the stockholders decided to solicit offers to purchase what was then a declining business. On November 2, 1959, Thrift Investment Corporation ("Thrift") offered in writing to buy all the common stock of Loan for $374 per share and "our usual non-compete agreement in the Butler area." The amount of Thrift's offer was higher than it would otherwise have been because Thrift "passed on" to the selling stockholders part of the favorable tax benefits which it inferred would accrue to it because the amount paid over and above the actual value of the stock was amortizable.

All the stockholders but Shukis accepted Thrift's offer. He notified Thrift that he was exercising his option to buy 90 additional shares. He apparently was willing to sell only if he was treated as holding 100 shares. On the same day that it heard from Shukis, November 5, 1959, Thrift forwarded to the President of Loan copies of the proposed agreement of purchase and copies of the non-competition agreement. The proposed covenant not to compete restrained the stockholders from engaging in the small loan business around Butler, Pennsylvania for approximately six years. However, it permitted them to own stock of any small loan corporation. The agreement contained a blank, which was presumably to be filled in later, representing that part of the total consideration which was to be allocated to the covenant not to compete.

Because of Shukis' action, a dispute arose between him and the other stockholders. Nevertheless, the settlement was fixed for November 16, 1959. At that time all the stockholders were present along with representatives of Thrift. All the stockholders except Shukis had one attorney. He had his own counsel present.

Thrift made it clear, of course, that the stockholder dispute would not cause it to increase the offering price for all outstanding shares. Thus, the cost of issuing any additional shares to Shukis would have to be shouldered by the other stockholders. Protracted negotiations took place that day between Shukis and the other stockholders. They finally reached a settlement. Thrift thereupon completed the agreements with Shukis and then with the other stockholders, the taxpayers herein.

Thrift allocated $152 per share to the covenant not to compete and $222 to the contract for the sale of stock. These figures were inserted in the documents. Some question was then raised by the taxpayers as to the tax treatment they would receive on the $152 per share allocated to the covenant. As found by the Tax Court, the Thrift officials explained that the allocations were to Thrift's tax advantage but they did not tell the stockholders that they (the stockholders) would receive capital gains treatment. Nor did Thrift make any attempt to explain to the stockholders that such amounts would be taxable to them as ordinary income. After a brief discussion with their own attorney concerning the allocation, the stockholders here involved, on the advice of their own counsel, signed the documents. Each payment check from Thrift contained the notation that it represented the consideration for both the sale of the stock and the agreement not to compete.

Each taxpayer reported the entire amount received by him as proceeds from the sale of capital assets.[2] The Commissioner disallowed that portion which corresponded to the consideration recited in the covenant not to compete and issued a notice of deficiency. The taxpayers then petitioned for a redetermination of the deficiency. The Tax Court ruled in favor of the taxpayers on the present issue, thus permitting the consideration allocated to the covenants to be taxed at capital gains rates rather than as ordinary income. It found in effect that the taxpayers produced strong proof that the covenants were not realistically bargained for by the parties and that the amounts allocated thereto by Thrift were in reality that part of the purchase price of the stock which represented a premium on corporate receivables.

. . . The Commissioner argues here, as he did before the Tax Court, that where the parties to a transaction involving the sale of a business have entered into a written agreement spelling out the precise amount to be paid for a covenant not to compete, they should not then be permitted, for tax purposes, to attack such provision except in cases of fraud, duress or undue influence.

The taxpayers counter by saying that such an approach would dignify form at the expense of substance and that the substance of this transaction, as found by the Tax Court, shows that the amounts allocated in the agreements for the covenants had no independent basis in fact or arguable relationship with business reality.

We address ourselves to the soundness of the rule contended for by the Commissioner because we are satisfied that if it is basically not acceptable then the factual findings of the Tax Court would compel us to affirm its decision in favor of these taxpayers. We say this because we think we could not, on this record, disturb the Tax Court's findings that the covenants were not fully restrictive in view of the wording and also because these particular stockholders were not realistically in a position to compete. In contrast, if the Commissioner's proposed rule is accepted, the factual findings of the Tax Court would require us to reverse its decision. This is so because after Thrift first evidenced its intention to make an allocation to the covenants not to compete the taxpayers had almost two weeks in which to investigate the tax

2. Thrift amortized that part of the payment which had been allocated to the covenant not to compete and the Commissioner has preserved his position with respect to that matter, presumably pending this determination.

consequences. Nevertheless, they entered into the agreement on the advice of their own counsel. The present record does not reveal that the taxpayers lacked a full understanding of the terms of the agreement or that the purchaser engaged in fraud, duress, or undue influence. We do not understand either the Tax Court or the dissent to view the facts any differently.

. . . [W]e are not here involved with a situation where the Commissioner is attacking the transaction in the form selected by the parties. Where the Commissioner attacks the formal agreement the Court involved is required to examine the "substance" and not merely the "form" of the transaction. This is so for the very good reason that the legitimate operation of the tax laws is not to be frustrated by forced adherence to the mere form in which the parties may choose to reflect their transaction. Gregory v. Helvering, 293 U.S. 465 (1935); C.I.R. v. Court Holding Co., 324 U.S. 331 (1945). In contrast, the Commissioner here is attempting to hold a party to his agreement unless that party can show in effect that it is not truly the agreement of the parties. And to allow the Commissioner alone to pierce formal arrangements does not involve any disparity of treatment because taxpayers have it within their own control to choose in the first place whatever arrangements they care to make.

We turn, then, to a consideration of the principle advanced by the Commissioner. We begin by noting that the determination as to whether a covenant not to compete was actually executed is important, taxwise, both to the buyer and the seller. A tax challenge aside, the amount a buyer pays a seller for such a covenant, entered into in connection with a sale of a business, is ordinary income to the covenantor and an amortizable item for the covenantee. Indeed, the presumed tax consequences of the transaction may, as here, help to determine the total amount a purchaser is willing to pay for such a purchase. Therefore, to permit a party to an agreement fixing an explicit amount for the covenant not to compete to attack that provision for tax purposes, absent proof of the type which would negate it in an action between the parties, would be in effect to grant, at the instance of a party, a unilateral reformation of the contract with a resulting unjust enrichment. If allowed, such an attack would encourage parties unjustifiably to risk litigation after consummation of a transaction in order to avoid the tax consequences of their agreements. And to go behind the agreement at the behest of a party may also permit a party to an admittedly valid agreement to use the tax laws to obtain relief from an unfavorable agreement.

Of vital importance, such attacks would nullify the reasonably predictable tax consequences of the agreement to the other party thereto. Here the buyer would be forced to defend the agreement in order to amortize the amount allocated to the covenant. If unsuccessful, the buyer would lose a tax advantage it had paid the selling-taxpayers to acquire. In the future buyers would be unwilling to pay sellers for tax savings so unlikely to materialize.

Finally, this type of attack would cause the Commissioner considerable problems in the collection of taxes. The Commissioner would not be able to accept taxpayers' agreements at face value. He would be confronted with the necessity for litigation against both buyer and seller in order to collect taxes properly due. This is so because when the Commissioner tries to collect taxes from one party he may, as here, dispute the economic reality of his agreement. When the Commissioner turns to the other party, there will likely be the arguments that the first party, as here, received consideration for bearing the tax burden resulting from the sale and that the covenants did indeed have economic reality.

For these reasons we adopt the following rule of law: a party can challenge the tax consequences of his agreement as construed by the Commissioner only by adducing proof which in an action between the parties to the agreement would be admissible to alter that construction or to show its unenforceability because of mistake, undue influence, fraud, duress, etc. . . .

Therefore, the decision of the Tax Court which disallowed the Commissioner's assessments must be vacated. . . .

[The dissenting opinion of Chief Judge STALEY is omitted.]

## *NOTES AND QUESTIONS*

1. *The "strong proof" test.* As described by the Third Circuit, the Tax Court had followed the test of Ullman v. Comm'r, 264 F.2d 305 (2d Cir. 1959), which permitted a taxpayer to disregard the consequences of an allocation agreement upon producing "strong proof" that the allocation did not comport with economic reality. In *Danielson*, the Third Circuit concluded that this test had been satisfied because "the covenants were not fully restrictive . . . and also because these particular stockholders were not realistically in a position to compete." Nevertheless, the court held that the taxpayer was still bound by the terms of the agreement for the reasons stated. Do you think the *Danielson* rule is a fair and appropriate one? Unless a case is appealable to a Circuit that has adopted the *Danielson* rule, the Tax Court continues to apply the "strong proof" test.

2. *One-way street.* In general, the test adopted in *Danielson* binds the taxpayer, but not the Commissioner, to the terms of the allocation agreement. Since the parties are ordinarily in the best position to determine how much is paid for a particular asset, should the Commissioner also be bound by their agreement?

3. *Non-offsetting tax stakes to the parties.* If the tax advantage of an allocation to one party were always counterbalanced by an offsetting disadvantage to the other party, the government could serve as a neutral stakeholder and liberally respect the parties' agreement for tax purposes. Unfortunately, for a variety of reasons, the parties' interests are frequently not offsetting. For example, the absence of a corporate capital gains preference generally means that a particular allocation likely matters more to the buyer than to a corporate seller. In that case, an allocation agreement could be expected to reflect to some extent opportunistic behavior by the parties to maximize their collective tax benefits.

### b. Allocation of Purchase Price to Intangible Assets

One of the more contentious areas in corporate acquisitions has been the proper treatment of purchase price allocable to the intangible assets of a business. Intangible assets are generally more difficult to value than tangible assets. Moreover, prior to enactment of current section 197, goodwill and going concern value were treated for tax purposes as nondepreciable assets. Therefore, buyers generally tried to minimize the amount of purchase price allocated to goodwill and going concern value for tax purposes.

One allocation method formerly used by taxpayers was the "second-tier allocation" method. This approach first required an estimate of the goodwill and going concern value of an acquired business based on a capitalization of the excess earning capacity of the tangible assets of the business. Excess earning capacity was the amount by which the average actual earnings of the business during a valuation period exceeded an assumed rate of return on its tangible assets. These excess earnings, capitalized at an appropriate discount rate, were deemed to be the value of the goodwill and going concern value. If the total purchase price for a business exceeded the aggregate fair market value of each of the business's assets (including the estimated value of its goodwill and going concern value), the second-tier allocation approach allocated the premium amount to all of the assets of the business (other than cash or cash equivalents) in proportion to their relative fair market values, as illustrated by **example 10-1**:

> **Example 10-1:** Assume that a business consists of only the following assets: cash ($10*x*), building ($70*x*), equipment ($30*x*) and goodwill ($20*x*), for an aggregate value of all assets of $130*x*. Under the second-tier allocation method, if a buyer purchases the entire business for $190*x*, the $60*x* premium is spread among the building, equipment, and goodwill (but not the cash) in relation to their relative fair market values, with the following result:

| *assets* | *fair market value* | *2d-tier allocation* |
|---|---|---|
| cash | $10*x* | $10*x* |
| building | $70*x* | $105*x* |
| equipment | $30*x* | $45*x* |
| goodwill | $20*x* | $30*x* |
| total | $130*x* | $190*x* |

As illustrated, a potential advantage of this approach was to allocate an amount of purchase price to depreciable assets, such as the building and equipment, in excess of their estimated fair market value. For this reason, Congress in 1986 prohibited use of the second-tier allocation method in the case of any "applicable asset acquisition," defined as any transfer of assets constituting a trade or business in which, in general, the transferee's basis is determined only by reference to the consideration paid for the assets. Instead, it mandated use of the residual method required under section 338 when a taxpayer makes a qualified stock purchase, elects to treat the transaction as a deemed sale and repurchase of the target's assets, and therefore allocates the stock purchase price among all of the assets of the target. Read I.R.C. § 1060(a) and (c). Under the residual method, the amount allocated to goodwill or going concern value is equal to the residual amount (if any) of purchase price in excess of the fair market value of all of the other assets of the business. The following table compares the two allocation methods based on the facts of **example 10-1**:

| *assets* | *fair market value* | *2d-tier allocation* | *residual method* |
|---|---|---|---|
| cash | $10*x* | $10*x* | $10*x* |
| building | $70*x* | $105*x* | $70*x* |
| equipment | $30*x* | $45*x* | $30*x* |
| goodwill | $20*x* | $30*x* | $80*x* |
| total | $130*x* | $190*x* | $190*x* |

In applying the residual method, the "fair market value" of the assets of a business refers to the *gross* fair market value of each asset, unreduced by mortgages, liens, or other liabilities (see Reg. § 1.338-6(a)(2)).

**Example 10-2:** Suppose corporation P acquires corporation T's entire business, which consists of only the following assets: marketable securities (gross FMV $100,000 subject to a $40,000 liability), a building (gross FMV $500,000 subject to a $400,000 mortgage), and $40,000 cash. P pays $260,000 cash for the business and takes the property subject to all liabilities. The total amount realized by T on the sale of its assets, and P's total basis in the assets acquired, are each equal to the $260,000 cash *plus* the liabilities, or a total of $700,000. This total is allocated $40,000 to the cash, $100,000 to the securities, and $500,000 to the building. The remaining $60,000 is allocated to the goodwill and going concern value of the business.

Section 1060 specifically adopts the *Danielson* rule where the parties have entered into an allocation agreement. See I.R.C. § 1060(a) (second sentence); Reg. § 1.1060-1(c)(4).

In short, in contrast to the second-tier allocation method, the residual method allocates any "premium" paid for a business entirely to its goodwill and going concern value. That result occurs, however, only if intangible assets *separate and distinct from goodwill* cannot be identified. When businesses were commonly being acquired for premium prices, taxpayers discovered a whole host of intangible assets separate from goodwill and claimed that the cost of such assets could be amortized over their expected useful lives. In a 1991 report, the General Accounting Office found that taxpayers had identified almost 200 different types of intangibles separate from goodwill in all open tax years as of 1989, with total value allocated to such intangibles increasing from $45 billion in 1980 to $262 billion in 1987. Upon challenge by the IRS, these novel claims quickly clogged up the tax litigation pipeline because they involved very resource-intensive disputes regarding the value and useful life of intangible elements of a business previously considered part of its goodwill.

In Newark Morning Ledger Co. v. U.S., 507 U.S. 546 (1993), the government sought to shortcut the resolution of these controversies by obtaining a ruling that, as a matter of law, certain customer-based intangible assets were inseparable from goodwill and hence their cost could not be amortized. The case involved an allocation of about $68 million of the purchase price for a newspaper business to an intangible denominated the "paid subscribers" of the business, i.e., those persons who were subscribers of one of the papers as of the date of acquisition. The taxpayer further claimed that due to death, relocation, changing tastes, and other factors, the "paid subscribers" constituted a wasting asset whose cost could be amortized over its expected life. The taxpayer provided statistical evidence indicating that the life of the subscription lists ranged from 14 to 23 years.

Consistent with its litigation strategy, the government did not challenge the taxpayer's factual claims. Instead, it argued that the intangible denominated "paid subscribers" was indistinguishable from, and indeed represented the very essence of, goodwill, defined as "the expectancy of continued patronage." Because the then applicable regulations barred any amortization of goodwill, the cost of the paid subscribers was similarly nondeductible. The government further asserted that the paid subscribers constituted a nonwasting, self-regenerating "mass asset." Under this doctrine, the departure of certain subscribers was balanced by the addition of new subscribers, with the result that the value of the paid subscribers as a whole remained roughly constant over time. Indeed, the number of subscribers to the taxpayer's newspapers actually stayed about the same during the tax years in question.

The Court, however, concluded that the inquiry was essentially a factual one. The Court found that goodwill is not amortizable *because* its useful life cannot be ascertained with reasonable accuracy:

> It must follow that if a taxpayer can prove with reasonable accuracy that an asset used in the trade or business or held for the production of income has a value that wastes over an ascertainable period of time, that asset is depreciable under § 167, regardless of the fact that its value is related to the expectancy of continued patronage. The significant question for purposes of depreciation is not whether the asset falls "within the core of the concept of goodwill," . . . but whether the asset is capable of being valued and whether that value diminishes over time. [507 U.S. at 566.]

Given the government's failure to present contrary factual evidence based on its litigation strategy, the Court upheld the position of the taxpayer.

Congress moved expeditiously to avoid the morass of case-by-case litigation invited by *Newark Morning Ledger* (decided in 1993) and, as part of the 1993 Act, enacted current section 197. (Actually, Congress rarely moves *that* expeditiously. The proposed legislation had been under consideration for several years pending the Supreme Court's resolution of the issue. The Court's decision in favor of the taxpayer allowed the legislation to be scored as budget neutral, facilitating its passage.)

Read I.R.C. § 197(a) - (e). The statute generally mandates a 15-year amortization period for the cost of any intangible asset covered by that provision. Choice of a 15-year period was basically a compromise intended to maintain revenue neutrality. But it necessarily meant that the legislation produced both winners (taxpayers with intangibles whose useful lives exceeded 15 years or that were previously unamortizable) and losers (taxpayers with intangibles whose useful lives were less than 15 years). Among the notable losers are taxpayers who obtain a covenant not to compete in connection with a business acquisition. Such an intangible is explicitly covered by section 197 (I.R.C. § 197(d)(1)(E)) even though noncompete agreements seldom extend for as long as 15 years. In lieu of noncompete agreements, one might therefore expect some taxpayers to try to utilize other, uncovered forms of intangible assets, such as consulting agreements. Although section 197 applies to any arrangement having "substantially the same effect as a covenant not to compete," this rule may be difficult for the IRS to administer.

In addition to customer-based and other intangibles, "goodwill" and "going concern value" are explicitly *included* in the list of covered intangibles. I.R.C. § 197(d)(1)(A) and (B). In other words, amounts expended for goodwill and going concern value may also be amortized over a 15-year period. Why do you think Congress included those two items in the legislation? Was it a sound policy judgment?

The permissible amortization of goodwill and going concern value means that, in theory, all intangibles covered by section 197 could be included within the "residual" class of assets under section 1060. The regulations, however, continue to treat goodwill and going concern value as the only assets within the residual class, thus avoiding the need to determine the fair market value of those assets separately. The regulations divide the assets of a business into seven classes: (I) cash and cash equivalents, (II) certain actively traded personal property, (III) accounts receivables and similar items, (IV) inventory and property held primarily for sale to customers, (V) all other tangible and intangible assets not included in one of the other classes, including furniture and fixtures, land, buildings, and equipment, (VI) section 197 intangibles other than goodwill and going concern value, and (VII) goodwill and going concern value. Purchase price must be allocated dollar-for-dollar to each class of assets in the order listed, up to the total fair market value of the assets in the class. If an amount allocated to a particular class is less than the aggregate fair market value of the assets in that class, each asset is allocated an amount in proportion to its fair market value. Any purchase price not allocated to the first six classes is allocated to class VII. Reg. §§ 1.1060-1(a)(1), 1.338-6(b).

The law generally applies only to the capitalized costs of intangible assets *acquired* by the taxpayer, see I.R.C. § 197(c)(1)(A), and specifically excludes the costs of *creating* certain intangibles such as goodwill and going concern value. See I.R.C. § 197(c)(2); Reg. § 1.197-2(d)(2). Congress decided that "there is no need at this time to change the Federal income tax treatment of self-created intangible assets, such as goodwill that is created through advertising and other similar expenditures." H.R. REP. NO. 103-111, 103D CONG., 1ST SESS. 323 (1993). What does the Court's holding in *Newark Morning Ledger* imply with respect to the deductibility of expenses incurred to create goodwill, such as advertising costs? If a customer list is not simply one "mass asset" that more or less retains its value over time (or, indeed, increases in size and value over time), but rather consists of many separate, individual assets, some of which disappear while others are added, then how should costs incurred to add customers to the list be treated for tax purposes?

One interesting controversy concerned the effective date of the legislation. Because the new law was intended partly to reduce the cost of litigation, Congress wanted to bring cases already in the tax litigation pipeline within the ambit of the law. But Congress was unsure about how best to accomplish that goal. Should the new law be applied retroactively to transactions already undertaken? Should taxpayers be allowed to elect retroactive application? Or should taxpayers with cases under challenge be given a mandatory or optional settlement offer, such as a payment of a flat percentage of any asserted deficiency? Would such a settlement offer be problematic?

The final legislation generally applied the rules prospectively (to acquisitions after date of enactment), but then permitted taxpayers whose acquisitions took place after a specified date (but before the enactment date) to elect into the new rules. Taxpayers with controversies involving acquisitions prior to the specified pre-enactment date still had to litigate or settle with the IRS on a case-by-case basis. Congress urged the IRS "in the strongest possible terms" to expedite the settlement of cases not covered by the legislation. H. CONF. REP. NO. 103-213, 103D CONG., 1ST SESS. 239 (1993).

**Problem 10-3:**

(a) A taxpayer acquires a five-year covenant not to compete that is covered by section 197. When the covenant expires at the end of Year 5, what happens to the taxpayer's remaining basis in the asset? See I.R.C. § 197(f)(1); Reg. § 1.197-2(g)(1)(iii). What is the rationale for this result?

(b) A taxpayer acquires all of the assets of a target corporation and also pays consideration to the key executives of the target in exchange for their execution of noncompete agreements. Because both goodwill and a covenant not to compete that is entered into in connection with the acquisition of a business are included as "section 197 intangibles," the amount paid for each may be written off over a 15-year period. Is there, nevertheless, some reason for the parties to allocate the total consideration disproportionately to the noncompete agreement rather than to the goodwill of the acquired business?

*NOTES AND QUESTIONS*

1. *Anti-churning rules.* In enacting section 197, Congress included broad "anti-churning rules" which carve out certain intangible assets from coverage under the general rule. See I.R.C. § 197(c)(3) and (f)(9). Anti-churning rules are common features of provisions that are effective only for property placed in service or acquired after a certain date. See, e.g., I.R.C. § 168(f)(5). If the provision grants more favorable tax treatment (such as faster depreciation) only to such property, taxpayers have an incentive to engage in a "churning transaction" that converts ineligible property of the seller into eligible property of the buyer. In general, the key indicator of a churning transaction is some relationship between the buyer and seller such that the transaction does not meaningfully alter the parties' economic holdings.

2. *What noncompete agreements are covered by section 197?* Section 197(d)(1)(E) makes section 197 applicable to a covenant not to compete only if it is "entered into in connection with an acquisition (directly or indirectly) of an interest in a trade or business or substantial portion thereof." In Recovery Group v. Comm'r, ___ F.3d ___ (1st Cir. 2011), the court interpreted this ambiguous language as referring to covenants executed in connection with an acquisition of (1) *any portion* of the stock of a corporation engaged in a trade or business or (2) a substantial portion of the assets of a trade or business. In either situation, the purchase price would presumably reflect the value of all or a portion of the intangible assets of the trade or business (such as goodwill and going concern value). Thus, the transaction would potentially present the type of valuation dispute — how much purchase price should be allocated between the covenant and other intangibles — that section 197 was intended to avoid. Accordingly, the court held that section 197(d)(1)(E) applied to a covenant executed in connection with an acquisition of a stock interest (23 percent) even though the interest did not represent a "substantial portion" of the corporation's total stock. Hence, the purchase price applicable to the covenant had to be amortized over 15 years. Do you find the court's interpretation of this provision convincing?

## 4. *Stock Acquisitions under Current Law*

As previously described, pre-1986 law eventually achieved parity in the taxation of all three corporate acquisition patterns — a corporate asset sale, a shareholder asset sale, and a corporate stock sale (followed by liquidation of the target into the acquiring corporation). Under current law, with the repeal of *General Utilities*, corporate and shareholder asset sales are still taxed alike, although both are taxed more heavily than under pre-1986 law. Assuming that the target corporation is liquidated as part of the corporate asset sale, the transactions result in the recognition of gain or loss by both the target and its shareholders, with the acquiring corporation obtaining a fair market value basis in the acquired assets.

Current law, however, generally taxes the third acquisition pattern — a corporate stock sale — more favorably than the other two. If the corporation acquiring the stock of the target makes a section 338(g) election, then the consequences are identical to those of a corporate asset sale (followed by a liquidation) or a shareholder asset sale: the target shareholders recognize gain or loss on sale of their stock, and the target corporation recognizes gain or loss (and obtains a fair market value basis in its assets) upon the deemed sale and repurchase of its assets. But in the case of a corporate stock sale, the result is *elective*. If the section 338(g) election is not made, then the transaction ordinarily has no corporate-level tax consequences. Therefore, the corporate tax is at least temporarily avoided at the cost of the target retaining its historic basis in its assets. For most taxpayers, this trade-off is generally worthwhile. In summary, under current law, a corporate stock sale without a section 338(g) election generally produces more favorable tax consequences than either a corporate or shareholder asset sale.

Nevertheless, a section 338 election *is* generally desirable on a sale of target stock if the target is owned by a parent corporation holding at least 80 percent of the voting power and value of the target's stock. Absent a section 338 election, the parent's sale of its target stock ordinarily results in the recognition of gain or loss even though there is no change in the basis of the target's assets. Therefore, the transaction results in one corporate tax (on the parent's gain or loss in its target stock) while continuing to preserve another corporate tax on the same income (the target's gain or loss in its assets). By contrast, the parties could eliminate the corporate tax on the stock sale by having the target first liquidate into its parent under section 332; if the parent then transfers the former target assets to the buyer, only the corporate tax on the asset sale is triggered (with a corresponding change in asset basis). (The same result could be achieved if the target first sells its assets directly to the buyer and then liquidates into its parent under section 332.)

Read I.R.C. § 338(h)(10). Like section 332, section 338(h)(10) seeks to reduce the possibility of more than one corporate tax being imposed on the same income. Thus, if a parent corporation sells its target stock to an acquiring corporation and the section 338(h)(10) election is made, the parent does not recognize gain or loss on sale of the stock but the target is deemed to sell and repurchase its assets. In general, the election produces the same tax consequences as if the target were liquidated under section 332 and the target's assets were then sold by the parent. Consistent with the general requirement of section 338, the section 338(h)(10) election is available only if a corporation makes a qualified stock purchase of the target corporation. Reg. § 1.338(h)(10)-1(c)(1).

In virtually all other stock purchases qualifying under section 338, a section 338 election is not desirable. It is important, therefore, not to make an inadvertent election. The "consistency" rules (I.R.C. § 338(e) and (f)) provide for the possibility of a deemed election. The repeal of the *General Utilities* doctrine, however, greatly reduced the need for consistency rules. Accordingly, the regulations have been rewritten to severely limit the scope of these rules. In general, they apply only in cases where the target has a controlling corporate shareholder, i.e., exactly the cases where a section 338 election is ordinarily desirable. In addition, if an election is not made but the consistency rules are otherwise violated, the consequence is *not* a deemed election. Rather, the acquiring party must simply take a transferred basis in any asset acquired (even though gain is recognized by the selling party). See Reg. § 1.338-8(a)(1), (2), and (4).

## *NOTES AND QUESTIONS*

1. *Selling consolidated group.* Under section 338(h)(10), the target must be a member (other than the parent) of the "selling consolidated group" at the time of the acquisition, and it is the members of that group that do not recognize gain or loss upon disposition of the target's stock. See I.R.C. § 338(h)(10)(A) and (B); Reg. § 1.338(h)(10)-1(b)(1) and (d)(5)(iii). In general, this condition requires a corporation to own at least 80 percent of the voting power and value of the target corporation, the same requirement for a section 332 liquidation. I.R.C. §§ 1501, 1504(a)(1)(B)(ii) and (2). Despite the nomenclature, the selling consolidated group need not file a consolidated return.

2. *The section 338(g) and 338(h)(10) elections.* These elections are separate and have similar, but not identical, tax consequences. As a result of either election, the target corporation is bifurcated and the "old" target is deemed to transfer all of its assets to the "new" target in a taxable transaction. If a section 338(h)(10) election is made, however, the old target is then generally deemed to liquidate. Reg. §§ 1.338-1(a)(1) (last sentence), 1.338(h)(10)-1(d)(4)(i). Because of the target's membership in the selling consolidated group, this liquidation ordinarily qualifies under section 332. Thus, the target's tax attributes, such as its E&P and net operating loss carry-overs, survive in the hands of the group. I.R.C. § 381(a)(1). This result is the same as if the target had actually liquidated under section 332 as part of a transfer of its assets to the buyer. The tax liability from the deemed asset sale by the old target is the responsibility of the seller. I.R.C. § 338(h)(10)(A); Reg. §§ 1.338(h)(10)-1(d)(3)(i), 1.1502-6(a). If a section 338(h)(10) election is made with respect to a target corporation, the section 338(g) election is also deemed made. Reg. § 1.338(h)(10)-1(c)(4). The regulations applicable to a section 338(g) transaction apply unless trumped by the regulations under section 338(h)(10). Reg. § 1.338(h)(10)-1(a).

In contrast, if a section 338(g) (but no section 338(h)(10)) election is made, the target's tax attributes are generally terminated. Reg. § 1.338-1(b)(1). This is the same result as if the target had transferred its assets and liquidated pursuant to section 331. Also, the tax liability from the deemed asset sale by the old target is the responsibility of the buyer. Reg. § 1.338-1(b)(3)(i). The section 338(g) election is made only by the acquiring corporation; by contrast, both that corporation and the selling consolidated group must make a section 338(h)(10) election since it affects the consequences of both parties. Reg. § 1.338(h)(10)-1(c)(3). If neither section 338 election is made in connection with a stock acquisition, the target retains its tax attributes and its asset basis remains unchanged.

3. *When a section 338(g) election may be advantageous (and a section 338(h)(10) election may be disadvantageous).* One unusual situation where a section 338(g) election may remain attractive is if the target corporation has expiring net operating losses. In that case, the expiring losses may offset any gain recognized by the target as a result of the election, while any resulting increase in the target's basis in its assets increases its future deductions. In other words, the section 338(g) election would have the effect of "freshening up" the target's expiring losses. A decision to elect section 338(g) should be made carefully, however, since the election terminates any losses not used by the target in the transaction. A section 338(g) election may also be advantageous if the target is a foreign corporation not subject to U.S. tax. In that case, the election may increase the target's basis in its assets without any U.S. tax consequences and may also eliminate undesired attributes of the target, including the amount of its E&P.

A section 338(h)(10) election may be disadvantageous if the selling consolidated group's potential gain on sale of its target stock is small relative to the target's potential gain on the deemed sale of assets if an election were made. This might arise, for example, if the selling consolidated group previously had acquired the target stock when the target held appreciated assets.

4. *Section 336(e).* As noted, both sections 338(h)(10) and 332 carry out a policy of preventing the imposition of more than one corporate tax on the same income. Once proposed regulations are finalized, section 336(e) will extend this policy to other dispositions by a parent of its target stock, including sales and distributions not qualifying under section 338(h)(10). See Prop. Reg. § 1.336-1(a) and (b)(1) - (5), -2(a) and (b)(1).

5. *Is parity possible?* With the repeal of *General Utilities*, is it possible any longer to achieve parity in the tax consequences of corporate asset and stock acquisitions? How might such a goal be achieved?

6. *Use of intermediaries.* With sellers generally preferring to sell the stock of their corporations under current law (to avoid any corporate-level tax consequences) and buyers generally preferring to acquire the corporate assets (to obtain a cost basis in such assets), some taxpayers have utilized intermediaries to try to bridge the difference. The following notice describes one such plan that the IRS has identified as a tax shelter.

## Notice 2008-111

2008-2 C.B. 1299

. . . An Intermediary Transaction involves a corporation (T) that would have a Federal income tax obligation with respect to the disposition of assets the sale of which would result in taxable gain (Built-in Gain Assets) in a transaction that would afford the acquiror or acquirors (Y) a cost or fair market value basis in the assets. An Intermediary Transaction is structured to cause the tax obligation for the taxable disposition of the Built-in Gain Assets to arise, in connection with the disposition by shareholders of T (X) of all or a controlling interest in T's stock, under circumstances where the person or persons primarily liable for any Federal income tax obligation with respect to the disposition of the Built-in Gain Assets will not pay that tax (hereafter, the Plan). This plan can be effectuated regardless of the order in which T's stock or assets are disposed. A transaction is not an Intermediary Transaction for purposes of this Notice if there is neither any X nor any Y engaging in the transaction pursuant to the Plan. . . .

There are four components of an Intermediary Transaction, and a transaction must have all four components: . . .

1. A corporation (T) directly or indirectly (e.g., through a pass-through entity or a member of a consolidated group of which T is a member) owns assets the sale of which would result in taxable gain (T's Built-in Gain Assets) and, as of the Stock Disposition Date (as defined in component two), T (or the consolidated group of which T is a member) has insufficient tax benefits to eliminate or offset such taxable gain (or the tax) in whole. The tax that would result from such sale is hereinafter referred to as T's Built-in Tax. However, for purposes of this component, T will not be considered to have any Built-in Tax if, on the Stock Disposition Date, such amount is less than five percent of the value of the T stock disposed of in the Stock Disposition (as defined in component two). In determining whether T's (or the consolidated group's) tax benefits are insufficient for purposes of the first sentence, the following tax benefits shall be excluded: (i) any tax benefits attributable to a listed transaction under § 1.6011-4(b)(2), and (ii) any tax benefits attributable to built-in loss property acquired within 12 months before any Stock Disposition described in component two, to the extent such built-in losses exceed built-in gains in property acquired in the same transaction(s). All references to T in this notice include successors to T.
2. At least 80 percent of the T stock (by vote or value) is disposed of by T's shareholder(s) (X), other than in liquidation of T, in one or more related transactions within a 12 month period (Stock Disposition). The first date on which at least 80 percent of the T stock (by vote or value) has been disposed of by X in a Stock Disposition is the Stock Disposition Date.
3. Either within 12 months before, simultaneously, or within 12 months after the Stock Disposition Date, at least 65 percent (by value) of T's Built-in Gain Assets are disposed of (Sold T Assets) to one or more buyers (Y) in one or more transactions in which gain is recognized with respect to the Sold T Assets. . . .
4. At least half of T's Built-in Tax that would otherwise result from the disposition of the Sold T Assets is purportedly offset or avoided or not paid.

. . . A transaction that has all four components . . . is only an Intermediary Transaction with respect to a person that engages in the transaction pursuant to the Plan. A person engages in the transaction pursuant to the Plan if the person knows or has reason to know the transaction is structured to effectuate the Plan. Additionally, any X that is at least a 5% shareholder of T (by vote or value), or any X that is an officer or director of T, engages in the transaction pursuant to the Plan if any of the following knows or has reason to know the transaction is structured to effectuate the Plan: (i) any officer or director of T; (ii) any of T's advisors engaged by T to advise T or X with respect to the transaction; or (iii) any advisor of that X engaged by that X to advise it with respect to the transaction. . . . A person can engage in the transaction pursuant to the Plan even if it does not understand the mechanics of how the tax liability purportedly might be offset or avoided, or the specific financial arrangements, or relationships of other parties or of T after the Stock Disposition. . . .

*NOTES*

1. *An example.* Enbridge Energy Co. v. U.S., 553 F. Supp. 2d 716, aff'd, 2009-2 U.S.T.C. ¶ 50,737 (5th Cir. 2009) (unpubl. op.), illustrates the type of transaction targeted by the IRS in Notice 2008-111. In that case, a buyer agreed to acquire a target corporation but could not agree with the seller on the price. To break the impasse, the buyer's tax advisor suggested introduction of an intermediary corporation that would acquire all of the target stock, merge with the target, and then sell the former target's assets to the buyer. The intermediary's involvement was based on the economic agreement previously negotiated by the buyer and seller, and the steps involving the intermediary all took place within a few days. The plan also involved infusion of certain high-basis, low-value property into the intermediary after its acquisition of the target, with the loss arising upon disposition of this property being used to shelter the gain from the sale of the former target assets. Taken together, the transaction was an attempted end-run around *General Utilities* repeal: it sought to provide the buyer with a cost basis in the target's assets without payment of any corporate-level tax, and the anticipated tax savings bridged the economic gap between the buyer and seller. Applying *Court Holding Co.*, the court held that the intermediary should be disregarded and that the buyer should be treated as having purchased the target stock directly from the seller prior to a liquidation of the target. This characterization left the buyer with the target's historic basis in its assets, not a cost basis. The court also imposed penalties against the buyer. According to the court, the following facts were relevant in determining whether an intermediary should be respected (and weighed in favor of disregarding the intermediary):

> (1) whether there was an agreement between the principals to do a transaction before the intermediary participated; (2) whether the intermediary was an independent actor; (3) whether the intermediary assumed any risk; (4) whether the intermediary was brought into the transaction at the behest of the taxpayer; and (5) whether there was a non-tax avoidance business purpose to the intermediary's participation. [553 F. Supp. 2d at 730.]

2. *Background and effect of Notice.* Notice 2008-111 is a scaled-back version of earlier notices identifying an intermediary transaction as a "listed transaction," the consequences of which are described in chapter four. Corporate stock acquisitions

are commonly followed by sales of selected, unwanted assets of the target, with the asset purchaser obtaining a cost basis in the purchased assets. Taxpayers argued that either the asset purchaser or the stock seller may be unaware of tax structuring carried out by the other party (although this was clearly *not* the case in *Enbridge Energy*), and therefore should not be made subject to the disclosure requirements and possible penalties accompanying involvement in a listed transaction. The "plan" requirement in Notice 2008-111, and its general limitation only to persons who know or have reason to know that the transaction is structured to effectuate the plan, was added to the notice to avoid overbreadth.

3. *Other multi-step acquisitions.* In general, in characterizing multi-step acquisitions *not* involving an intermediary, the IRS has tried to protect the policy of section 338 and preserve the availability of the section 338(h)(10) election. For example, suppose that as part of a plan, a corporation acquires all of the stock of a target and the target subsequently liquidates into the acquiring corporation. Under the *Kimbell-Diamond* doctrine, the entire transaction might be recharacterized as an acquisition of the target's assets rather than its stock. In that event, the acquiring corporation might obtain a cost basis in the assets of the target without making any election under section 338 (and potentially without recognition of any corporate-level gain or loss). The IRS might also be whipsawed if integration of the steps allowed the target shareholders to claim that they do not recognize gain or loss because the transaction qualifies as a "reorganization" (see chapter eleven). See King Enterprises v. U.S., 418 F.2d 511 (Ct. Cl. 1969). To prevent these adverse consequences, the IRS concluded in Rev. Rul. 90-95, 1990-2 C.B. 67, that the two steps should be given independent significance: the first step should be treated as a qualified stock purchase (entitling the acquiring corporation to make a section 338 election with respect to the target), and the second step should be treated as a section 332 liquidation. Accord, Rev. Rul. 2008-25, 2008-1 C.B. 986 (see infra p. 426); see also Rev. Rul. 2001-46, 2001-2 C.B. 321 (no violation of section 338 policy where collapsing of steps does not result in acquiring corporation obtaining cost basis in target assets). The regulations further clarify that the first step will be given independent significance if it would entitle the parties to make a section 338(h)(10) election, and such election is made. If the election is not made, this special treatment is relaxed and the entire transaction will be characterized in a manner consistent with step-transaction and other pertinent doctrine. Reg. § 1.338(h)(10)-1(c)(2) and (e) (exs. 11-13).

## C. Taxable Acquisitions and Liquidations Involving S Corporations

### 1. *In General*

The tax consequences of taxable acquisitions and liquidations involving S corporations generally integrate the subchapter C rules described in this chapter with the subchapter S rules that ensure an S corporation's income is taxed only once. For example, in a complete liquidation, an S corporation recognizes gain or loss under section 336(a) as if it sold its property to its shareholders. This gain or loss, however, is passed through to the shareholders who report it and pay any tax. I.R.C. § 1366(a). The shareholders adjust their stock basis for the income or loss passed through (I.R.C. § 1367(a)), with the result that they are not taxed on the same income again upon receipt of the liquidating distribution (I.R.C. § 331(a)). The same consequences arise if an S corporation sells all of its assets to a buyer and then liquidates.

The sale of stock of an S corporation presents the same policy issue previously discussed in connection with section 338(h)(10). Absent a special rule, the selling shareholder would recognize gain or loss on such a sale even though the basis of the corporation's assets would remain unchanged. Thus, the transaction would result in one tax on the S corporation's income (the shareholders' gain or loss in their stock) while preserving a second tax on the same income (the corporation's gain or loss in its assets). In contrast, as just described, a sale of the S corporation's assets in connection with a liquidation of the corporation results in a single tax being imposed and the buyer obtaining a fair market value basis in those assets. As we saw, this inconsistency in the tax treatment of stock and asset acquisitions is the same one addressed by section 338(h)(10) when a parent corporation sells its stock in a target C corporation.

The regulations address these problems in the same way by permitting a section 338(h)(10) election to be made if a corporation makes a qualified stock purchase of an S corporation. If the election is made, the shareholders of the S target do not recognize gain or loss upon sale of their stock, but the S target is deemed to sell and repurchase its assets (and the resulting gain or loss passes through to the shareholders under section 1366). The old S target is then deemed to liquidate under section 331. In effect, the election results in a single tax being imposed on the S target's income, with asset basis changed to fair market value. See Reg. § 1.338(h)(10)-1(b)(4) and (5), (c)(1), (d)(3)-(5), and (e) (ex. 10). The target's S election continues in effect through the time of the section 338 deemed asset sale notwithstanding the target's ceasing to qualify for S status as a result of its acquisition by a corporation. See Reg. § 1.338(h)(10)-1(d)(3)(i). All of the target's shareholders, including those who do not sell their shares, must consent to the section 338(h)(10) election, since the tax consequences affect all shareholders. Reg. § 1.338(h)(10)-1(c)(3). As noted, the election is available only if the buyer is a corporation making a qualified stock purchase. If an S corporation sells stock in a subsidiary qualifying as a QSub, however, the same tax result can be obtained without any election and regardless of the buyer's status as a corporation or whether the acquisition satisfies any of the other section 338 conditions. The reason is that, since the separate existence of the QSub is disregarded, the transaction is treated as a sale by the S corporation of the QSub's assets. I.R.C. § 1361(b)(3)(C)(ii).

## 2. *The Built-In Gains Tax*

Because the income of an S corporation is taxed just once, taxpayers could easily use such corporations to circumvent the repeal of *General Utilities*. For example, suppose a C corporation with accrued, unrealized gains elects to be taxed as an S corporation. If the conversion from C to S status is not a taxable event, then the potential double taxation of the accrued C gains would be jeopardized. Following the conversion, any recognition of those gains by the S corporation would be subject to at most one tax.

In 1986, rather than making the C to S conversion a taxable event, Congress subjected S corporations to a tax (the "built-in gains tax" (I.R.C. § 1374)) on certain gains recognized during the ten-year period following the conversion. The built-in gains tax, calculated at the highest tax rate applicable to C corporations, is the principal exception to the rule (I.R.C. § 1363(a)) exempting an S corporation from paying tax. In general, the tax applies only to the accrued or built-in amount of gain in the corporation's assets at the time of the conversion, i.e., gain accrued while the entity was a C corporation. The maximum amount of gain potentially subject to the tax is the aggregate amount of net built-in gain in all of the corporation's assets at the time of conversion. Because of the built-in gains tax, taxpayers should document carefully the value and bases of all significant assets when a C corporation becomes an S corporation.

When an S corporation recognizes such built-in gain, it pays tax on the gain. The same gain also passes through to its shareholders (subject to a partial offset for the corporate-level tax) under the general rules of passthrough taxation. Thus, the built-in gain is immediately taxed twice. Consistent with the purpose of the tax, a corporation that has always been an S corporation (and therefore by definition has no net built-in gain from prior years as a C corporation) is generally exempt from the tax.

Read I.R.C. § 1374(a), (b)(1), (c), (d)(1)-(4) and (7)(A) and apply these rules to the following problem:

**Problem 10-4:** Y corporation, a C corporation, becomes an S corporation at the beginning of year 5 when it has the following assets:

| *Asset* | *Fair market value* | *Adjusted basis* |
|---|---|---|
| Blackacre | $1,000 | $200 |
| Whiteacre | $600 | $500 |
| Greenacre | $200 | $500 |
| Total | $1,800 | $1,200 |

In year 7, Y sells Whiteacre, recognizing a $100 gain. In year 9, Y sells Blackacre, recognizing a $1,000 gain. In year 11, Y sells Greenacre, recognizing a $400 loss.

(a) Assuming that Y had no other income or deductions in those years, determine the tax consequences of these sales to Y under section 1374.
(b) Suppose that the maximum corporate income tax rate in year 7 is 35 percent. How much income or loss must Y pass through to its shareholders in that year? See I.R.C. § 1366(f)(2). What adjustment, if any, is made to Y's AAA as a result of the year 7 sale? See I.R.C. § 1368(e)(1)(A). Explain the rationale for your answers.
(c) Do your answers in (a) and (b) result in Y and its shareholders being treated the same as if Y had remained a C corporation through the end of year 7? If not, how do the results under subchapter S differ from what would have occurred under subchapter C? How could subchapter S be changed to make the results more congruent? In your answer, assume that Y (had it remained a C corporation) would have been subject to the highest corporate income tax rate in year 7.

*NOTES AND QUESTIONS*

1. *REBIGs and REBILs.* Review carefully the definitions of a "recognized built-in gain" ("REBIG") and a "recognized built-in loss" ("REBIL") in section 1374(d)(3) and (4). Aside from the fact that one definition applies to gain property and the other to loss property, how do the definitions differ? What might be the policy rationale for any difference?

2. *Loss and credit carryforwards.* In general, no carryforward or carryback from a C corporation year to an S corporation year is allowed. See I.R.C. § 1371(b)(1). Certain net operating loss, capital loss, and business credit carryforwards from a C year may be used, however, to reduce the amount of the built-in gains tax of an S corporation. See I.R.C. § 1374(b)(2) and (3). What is the reason for this exception?

3. *Accrued income and deduction items.* Accrued items of income and expense that have not yet been included in income or deducted at the time of a corporation's conversion from C to S status are treated as built-in gains and losses for purposes of the built-in gains tax; thus, they are included in the calculation of the corporation's net unrealized built-in gain. See I.R.C. § 1374(d)(5).

4. *Recognition period.* The ten-year recognition period was temporarily reduced to seven years for gains recognized in 2009 and 2010 and to five years for gains recognized in 2011. I.R.C. § 1374(d)(7)(B).

5. *Anti-stuffing rule.* Assets acquired by a corporation before or during the recognition period for a principal purpose of avoiding the section 1374 tax are generally disregarded. Reg. § 1.1374-9.

6. *Additional safeguards for* General Utilities *repeal.* The same problem addressed by section 1374 potentially arises when a C corporation transfers its assets to an S corporation in a nonrecognition transaction and the transferee succeeds to the transferor's basis in the assets transferred. Examples would be a liquidation of a

C corporation into its S parent under sections 332(a) and 337(a) or an asset acquisition qualifying as a corporate reorganization. Section 1374(d)(8) makes the S corporation subject to the section 1374 tax on the net built-in gain in the assets at the time of the liquidation or acquisition (which initiates the recognition period). In this instance only, a corporation that has always been an S corporation may, nevertheless, be subject to the built-in gains tax.

There is a potential double-counting problem if, for example, a C corporation with a wholly-owned subsidiary converts to S status and subsequently liquidates the subsidiary in a section 332 liquidation. Prior to the conversion, the parent's gain in its subsidiary stock may be replicated by the subsidiary's gain in its assets. Following the conversion, section 1374 would preserve the first gain and, following the liquidation, section 1374(d)(8) would preserve the second gain. Thus, taken together, the provisions would preserve the pre-conversion possibility of more than one corporate-level tax being imposed on the same income. In this case, taxpayers are allowed to reduce the initial pool of net built-in gain subject to section 1374 (as a result of the conversion) by any overlapping built-in gain that becomes subject to section 1374 by reason of section 1374(d)(8). See Reg. § 1.1374-3(b)(1).

Section 1374 principles are also applied when a C corporation converts into, or is acquired in a nonrecognition transaction by, a regulated investment company ("RIC") or real estate investment trust ("REIT"), two other types of corporations whose income is generally taxed only once. The C corporation may elect instead to recognize gain or loss in the conversion or acquisition, but only if the election does not result in the recognition of a net loss. Reg. § 1.337(d)-7(a)(1) and (c)(1).

Finally, the acquisition of all or substantially all of the assets of a taxable corporation by a tax-exempt entity, or the conversion of a taxable corporation to tax-exempt status, present other possible ways in which corporate-level tax might be avoided. In general, under current law, either transaction results in the recognition of gain or loss by the taxable corporation. This rule is an extension of, and is generally subject to the same exceptions as, section 337(b)(2) when a corporation liquidates under section 332 into a tax-exempt parent corporation. Reg. § 1.337(d)-4(a)(1) and (2).

### 3. *Excess Passive Investment Income*

If an S corporation has accumulated E&P from prior C years and over 25 percent of its gross receipts are from passive investment income, the corporation is subject to a tax under section 1375 on a portion of its net passive investment income. In addition, the corporation's S status terminates if it continues to have such E&P and excess passive investment income for three consecutive years. In general, "passive investment income" includes only royalties, rents, dividends, interest, and annuities. Like the built-in gains tax, the section 1375 tax is calculated using the highest corporate tax rate under section 11. Read I.R.C. §§ 1362(d)(3)(A) and (C)(i), 1375(a) and (b).

These provisions were enacted when corporate income tax rates were considerably lower than the top income tax rates for individuals (and there was no preferential rate for dividend income). As a result, a common tax planning strategy was for corporations to accumulate their earnings in passive investments rather than make distributions. If C corporations did this excessively, they ran the risk of having to pay the personal holding company or accumulated earnings penalty taxes, described in chapter three. To avoid those taxes without making distributions out of E&P, some C corporations converted to S status. The rules relating to the excess passive investment income of S corporations were intended to prevent such maneuvers. The provisions have remained despite the different incentives of taxpayers under current law due to the closer relationship between corporate and individual income tax rates (and the preferential rate for dividends). If an S corporation is close to running afoul of these provisions, it can eliminate its E&P by electing to treat its distributions as coming first out of that account. I.R.C. § 1368(e)(3). The IRS also may waive the adverse consequences of the excess passive investment income provisions, generally under the condition that the S corporation distribute all of its E&P. I.R.C. §§ 1362(f), 1375(d).

# Chapter 11

# Nondivisive Reorganizations

This chapter begins our examination of a class of transactions known as "reorganizations" for tax purposes. Many reorganizations are similar to the transactions described in chapter ten and involve acquisitions of a target corporation's assets or stock by another corporation. If the transaction satisfies certain specific conditions, however, taxation of the target and its shareholders is deferred. Thus, reorganizations represent an important option for tax planners in determining how to structure transactions. This chapter concerns nondivisive reorganizations, which encompass both acquisitive transactions and certain nondivisive changes to a single corporation, such as a recapitalization or reincorporation in a different state. Chapter twelve describes the taxation of divisive reorganizations in which a single corporation is divided into two or more corporations.

Reorganizations have been part of the tax system since 1918. Part A of this chapter briefly explores why the reorganization rules were enacted in the first place, and part B then examines the definition of a reorganization for tax purposes. Classification of a transaction as a reorganization is the threshold inquiry for determining the tax consequences of the transaction to the participants, and so the meaning of that term is the most significant part of our study. It is important to recognize whether a particular fact pattern qualifies as a reorganization and, perhaps more importantly, how to structure a transaction to qualify as one or not, depending upon the objectives of the parties involved. Part C reviews the principal tax consequences of a reorganization to the taxpayers involved, and part D concludes with a final observation.

Unfortunately, as you will soon see, the law involving reorganizations has not evolved in the same uniform manner as that concerning taxable corporate acquisitions. In chapter ten, we saw that an important policy goal, both before and after repeal of the *General Utilities* doctrine, was to achieve parity in the tax consequences of the various acquisition patterns. Parity reduces the distortion of taxes by removing tax considerations from the business decision of how an acquisition should be carried out. In contrast, the reorganization definition, developed piecemeal over many years, generally subjects each acquisition pattern to a different set of qualifying conditions in order to receive nonrecognition treatment. Thus, tax considerations are often an important element in determining how a reorganization is structured. The reorganization area is ripe for reform.

Reorganizations can be complicated transactions and, by necessity, this chapter provides only a survey of the key concepts and consequences. Still, with a close study of the following cases and materials, you should be able to come away with a good understanding of this area of the law. As you read the cases, bear in mind who the parties are, what they are advocating, and why. Furthermore, always consider why a transaction was effected in the manner chosen, how the problems encountered by the parties might have been avoided, and which of several alternatives might be the preferred method of carrying out the transaction in the future.

## A. Origins of the "Reorganization" Concept

### Marr v. United States

268 U.S. 536 (1925)

Mr. Justice BRANDEIS delivered the opinion of the Court.

Prior to March 1, 1913, Marr and wife purchased 339 shares of the preferred and 425 shares of the common stock of the General Motors Company of New Jersey for $76,400. In 1916, they received in exchange for this stock 451 shares of the preferred and 2,125 shares of the common stock of the General Motors Corporation of Delaware which (including a small cash payment) had the aggregate market value of $400,866.57. The difference between the cost of their stock in the New Jersey corporation and the value of the stock in the Delaware corporation was $324,466.57. The Treasury Department ruled that this difference was gain or income under the Act of September 8, 1916. . . .

The exchange of securities was effected in this way. The New Jersey corporation had outstanding $15,000,000 of 7 percent preferred stock and $15,000,000 of the common stock; all shares being of the par value of $100. It had accumulated from profits a large surplus. The actual value of the common stock was then $842.50 a share. Its officers caused to be organized the Delaware corporation, with an authorized capital of $20,000,000 in 6 percent nonvoting preferred stock and $82,600,000 in common stock; all shares being of the par value of $100. The Delaware corporation made to stockholders in the New Jersey corporation the following offer for exchange of securities: For every share of common stock of the New Jersey corporation, five shares of common stock of the Delaware corporation. For every share of the preferred stock of the New Jersey corporation, one and one-third shares of preferred stock of the Delaware corporation. In lieu of a certificate for fractional shares of stock in the Delaware corporation, payment was to be made in cash at the rate of $100 a share for its preferred and at the rate of $150 a share for its common stock. On this basis all the common stock of the New Jersey corporation was exchanged and all the preferred stock except a few shares. These few were redeemed in cash. For acquiring the stock of the New Jersey corporation only $75,000,000 of the common stock of the Delaware corporation was needed. The remaining $7,600,000 of the authorized common stock was either sold or held for sale as additional capital should be desired. The Delaware corporation, having thus become the owner of all the outstanding stock of the New Jersey corporation, took a transfer of its assets and assumed its liabilities. The latter was then dissolved.

It is clear that all new securities issued in excess of an amount equal to the capitalization of the New Jersey corporation represented income earned by it; that the new securities received by the Marrs in excess of the cost of the securities of the New Jersey corporation theretofore held were financially the equivalent of $324,466.51 in cash; and that Congress intended to tax as income of stockholders such gains when so distributed. The serious question for decision is whether it had power to do so. Marr contends that, since the new corporation was organized to take over the assets and continue the business of the old, and his capital remained invested in the same business enterprise, the additional securities distributed were in legal effect a stock dividend; and that under the rule of Eisner v. Macomber, 252 U.S. 189, applied in Weiss v. Stearn, 265 U.S. 242, he was not taxable thereon as income, because he still held the whole investment. The Government insists that identity of the business enterprise is not conclusive; that gain in value resulting from profits is taxable as income, not only when it is represented by an interest in a different business enterprise or property, but also when it is represented by an essentially different interest in the same business enterprise or property; that, in the case at bar, the gain actually made is represented by securities with essentially different characteristics in an essentially different corporation; and that, consequently, the additional value of the new securities, although they are still held by the Marrs, is income. . . . In our opinion the Government is right.

. . . In the case at bar, the new corporation is essentially different from the old. A corporation organized under the laws of Delaware does not have the same rights and powers as one organized under the laws of New Jersey. Because of these inherent differences in rights and powers, both the preferred and the common stock of the old corporation is an essentially different thing from stock of the same general kind in the new. But there are also adventitious differences, substantial in character. A 6 percent nonvoting preferred stock is an essentially different thing from a 7 percent voting preferred stock. A common stock subject to the priority of $20,000,000 preferred and a $1,200,000 annual dividend charge is an essentially different thing from a common stock subject only to $15,000,000 preferred and a $1,050,000 annual dividend charge. The case at bar is not one in which after the distribution the stockholders have the same proportional interest of the same kind in essentially the same corporation. . . .

The separate opinion of Mr. Justice VAN DEVANTER, Mr. Justice MCREYNOLDS, Mr. Justice SUTHERLAND, and Mr. Justice BUTLER.

We think this cause falls within the doctrine of Weiss v. Stearn, 265 U.S. 242, and that the judgment below should be reversed. The practical result of the things done was but the reorganization of a going concern. The business and assets were not materially changed, and the stockholder received nothing actually severed from his original capital interest—nothing differing in substance from what he already had.

*Weiss v. Stearn* did not turn upon the relatively unimportant circumstance that the new and old corporations were organized under the laws of the same state, but upon the approved definition of income from capital as something severed therefrom and received by the taxpayer for his separate use and benefit. Here stockholders got nothing from the old business or assets except new statements of their undivided interests, and this, as we carefully pointed out, is not enough to create taxable income.

## *NOTES AND QUESTIONS*

1. *Nonrecognition treatment and deferral.* Under section 1001, except as otherwise provided, any gains or losses realized in a transaction must be recognized. The reorganization provisions, applicable to exchanges carried out by both the target corporation and its shareholders, represent one of the exceptions to this general rule. Other exceptions include sections 267, 1031, 1033, and 1041, as well as sections 332, 337, and 351 in the corporate tax area. When the reorganization exception applies, the basis rules preserve for later recognition any gains and losses realized but not recognized in the transaction.

2. *Why is there a reorganization exception? Marr* illustrates two possible explanations for a reorganization exception. One is substance-over-form: despite its form as an exchange of interests, a transaction that does not result in any substantive change in the taxpayer's investment should generally not have any tax consequences. This principle was arguably embodied in Weiss v. Stearn, 265 U.S. 242 (1924), cited by both the majority and the dissent in *Marr*, where the Court held that a taxpayer who exchanged securities in virtually the same transaction as that in *Marr* did not recognize gain or loss. Unlike in *Marr*, however, both the old and new corporations in *Stearn* were incorporated in the same state and had securities with the exact same characteristics. Justice Brandeis was persuaded that this factual difference was enough to make the *Stearn* holding not binding in *Marr*. The legislative history to the 1918 Act that enacted the first reorganization exception (applicable to taxable years after those involved in *Marr*) states a goal "to negative the assertion of tax in the case of certain purely paper transactions." S. REP. NO. 65-617, 65TH CONG., 3D SESS. 5 (1918). This language is at least suggestive of a substance-over-form rationale similar to that presented in *Stearn* and *Marr*, and (if so interpreted) would support a limited reorganization exception, depending upon which interests are treated as substantively equivalent. For example, the exchange of securities of two

corporations engaged in different business activities would presumably not qualify for nonrecognition treatment under this rationale.

The *Marr* dissent, however, offered a different reason in support of nonrecognition treatment. The dissent argued that the transaction did not result in the taxpayer receiving anything "for his separate use and benefit." In other words, as a result of the transaction, nothing was distributed to the taxpayer out of corporate solution. In *Stearn*, the Court had relied upon Eisner v. Macomber, 252 U.S. 189 (1920), which held that a pro rata stock dividend was not income in part based on the same reason. Importantly, however, the transactions in *Macomber*, *Stearn*, and *Marr* each involved only a single business enterprise, so there was also an argument that the transaction did not produce any substantive change in the taxpayer's investment. Broadly interpreted, the *Marr* dissent's argument might be used to justify not taxing any transaction in which assets remain in corporate solution, including an exchange of securities of two very different corporations. This consumption-tax rationale may also have played a role in the enactment of the initial reorganization statutes. In addition, although not discussed in *Marr*, the development and continuation of the reorganization exception may also have been influenced by a desire to provide tax relief to corporations and (later) to prevent them from recognizing accrued losses.

Read the first three sentences of Reg. § 1.368-1(b). Which possible rationale for the reorganization exception do the current regulations seem to encapsulate?

## B. Definition of a Nondivisive Reorganization

### 1. *Introduction*

Skim I.R.C. § 368(a). The current statute defines, sometimes in excruciating detail, what a "reorganization" is, and we will shortly review some of this material. The early statutes, however, were much less specific, and courts were soon obliged to determine whether a transaction constitutes a taxable "sale" or a nontaxable "reorganization." The courts responded by specifying that a reorganization must satisfy both the "continuity of interest" ("COI") and "continuity of business enterprise" ("COBE") doctrines. These doctrines have never been part of the statute but are now incorporated in the regulations; thus, they remain conditions for reorganization status, at least in those cases where a more stringent condition is not specified. In addition, as first articulated in *Gregory v. Helvering* (p. 120), a transaction must have a business purpose to qualify as a reorganization. This part begins with a review of these nonstatutory reorganization requirements. The remaining sections then describe the statutory conditions for reorganization status in the case of corporate asset acquisitions, corporate stock acquisitions, and other nondivisive corporate transactions.

The following example illustrates some of the stakes involved if a corporate asset acquisition qualifies as a reorganization:

> **Example 11-1:** T corporation transfers all of its assets to P corporation in exchange for P stock and boot. Following the exchange, T distributes the consideration received to its shareholders in exchange for their stock in T.

In general, as we saw in chapter ten, both T (in its transfer of assets) and T's shareholders (in their exchange of T stock) must recognize gain or loss in this transaction, absent the reorganization exception. The distribution is also a taxable event to T, although if T recognizes gain or loss on the asset transfer, it should obtain a fair market value basis in any consideration received from P and should therefore have little or no additional tax consequences as a result of the distribution. Both P and T's shareholders should obtain a fair market value basis in any property received.

If the transaction qualifies as a reorganization, however, the consequences are quite different. In that case, both T and P are treated as a "party to a reorganization" (I.R.C. § 368(b)(2)) and a plan of reorganization exists. Therefore, T does not recognize any gain or loss on the asset transfer and obtains an exchanged basis in the P stock and a fair market value basis in the boot. I.R.C. §§ 361(a) and (b)(1) and (2), 358(a). T also does not recognize any gain or loss on the distribution. I.R.C. § 361(c)(1) and (2). T's shareholders recognize gain (but not loss) limited to the fair market value of the boot, and obtain an exchanged basis in the P stock and a fair market value basis in the boot. I.R.C. §§ 354(a)(1), 356(a)(1), 358(a). Finally, P obtains a transferred basis in the T assets acquired. I.R.C. § 362(b) (first sentence). In summary, qualification of a transaction as a reorganization is important because it defers the tax consequences of any corporate-level and shareholder-level exchange in the transaction. These results may or may not be favorable, depending upon the parties involved and other factors. Part C of this chapter reviews these and the other tax consequences of a reorganization in somewhat more detail.

A word on terminology: reorganizations commonly involve the issuance of stock by a corporation, and many acquisitions use "triangular" structures in which the acquiring corporation (or surviving corporation in a merger) uses stock of a corporation in control of the acquiror as part or all of the consideration. For example, S corporation might acquire all of the assets of T corporation in exchange for stock in P corporation, where P owns all of the stock of S. In this example, S is the acquiring corporation and P is the "issuing corporation" because its stock is issued in the transaction. The regulations generally use the term "issuing corporation" to include the acquiring corporation except in triangular acquisitions, where the term refers to the corporation in control of the acquiring corporation. Reg. § 1.368-1(b) (fifth sentence). Unless necessary to avoid ambiguity, this chapter uses the same terminology although it may deviate somewhat from terms used in the statute and other authorities. In addition, in the reorganization area, "control" generally means at least 80 percent of the voting power of all classes of stock entitled to vote and at least 80 percent of the shares of each other class of stock. I.R.C. § 368(c); Rev. Rul. 59-259,

1959-2 C.B. 115. Certain other provisions (such as section 351) use this same test, but others (such as sections 304, 332, 337, 338, and 1504(a) (defining an affiliated group)) do not.

Finally, a cautionary note: the regulations provide that the specifications of the reorganization provisions are "precise" and that a transaction must satisfy both the specifications and their underlying assumptions in order to qualify as a reorganization. Reg. § 1.368-1(b) (10th and 11th sentences). We will see a number of examples of this mindset in the following materials. Thus, commit a foot fault in this area at your peril!

## 2. *Nonstatutory Requirements*

### a. Continuity of Interest (COI) Doctrine

In Cortland Specialty Co. v. Comm'r, 60 F.2d 937 (2d Cir. 1932), cert. denied, 288 U.S. 599 (1933), a corporate taxpayer transferred substantially all of its properties to another corporation in exchange for cash and short-term notes and claimed that because the transaction qualified as a reorganization, it did not recognize any gain or loss. The statute provided some support for the taxpayer's position, since it defined a reorganization quite loosely to include "a merger or consolidation (including the acquisition by one corporation of . . . substantially all the properties of another corporation)." Relying upon the language and purpose of the statute, the court identified additional requirements for a reorganization:

> Reorganization, merger, and consolidation are words indicating corporate readjustments of existing interests. They all differ fundamentally from a sale where the vendor corporation parts with its interest for cash and receives nothing more. . . . [W]e believe that the general purpose of [the state merger and consolidation statutes] has been to continue the interests of those owning enterprises, which have been merged or consolidated, in another corporate form. A sale of the assets of one corporation to another for cash without the retention of any interest by the seller in the purchaser is quite outside the objects of merger and consolidation statutes.
>
> [The tax statute defining a reorganization] must be interpreted in this setting. Its purpose was to relieve those interested in corporations from profits taxes in cases where there was only a change in the corporate form in which business was conducted without an actual realization of any gain from an exchange of properties. When describing the kind of change in corporate structure that permits exemption from these taxes, [the tax statute] does not disregard the necessity of continuity of interests under modified corporate forms. . . .
>
> In defining "reorganization," [the tax statute] gives the widest room for all kinds of changes in corporate structure, but does not abandon the primary requisite that there must be some continuity of interest on the part of the transferor corporation or its stockholders in order to secure exemption. Reorganization presupposes continuance of business under modified corporate forms. [60 F.2d at 939-40.]

The court concluded that the taxpayer's receipt of cash and short-term notes did not satisfy COI and therefore the reorganization exception was inapplicable. This same conclusion is now specifically reached in the regulations. Reg. § 1.368-1(b) (ninth sentence).

Subsequent decisions elaborated on the nature of the consideration satisfying COI. These cases developed a highly formalistic standard: "stock" of the issuing corporation, including nonvoting preferred stock, meets the requirement; anything else, including long-term bonds of the issuing corporation, does not. See Helvering v. Minnesota Tea Co., 296 U.S. 378 (1935) (voting trust certificates representing common stock of issuing corporation satisfies COI); John A. Nelson Co. v. Helvering, 296 U.S. 374 (1935) (nonvoting, redeemable preferred stock satisfies COI); LeTulle v. Scofield, 308 U.S. 415 (1940) (bonds do not qualify). No consideration was given in these early cases to the possible debt-like features of preferred stock or the possible equity-like features of interests other than stock.

The Supreme Court confronted the question of what constitutes equity in Paulsen v. Comm'r, 469 U.S. 131 (1985), involving a merger of a stock savings and loan association into a mutual savings and loan association, with the mutual company surviving. As a mutual company, the surviving company had no capital stock; the only persons with proprietary rights in the company were its depositors. Therefore, in the transaction, the shareholders of the stock company received passbook savings accounts and time certificates of deposit in the surviving company, the only "equity" interests of the company, which gave the holders the right to vote, receive dividends, and share in the assets of the surviving company upon its liquidation. The Court concluded that COI was not satisfied because the debt characteristics of the interests received greatly outweighed their equity characteristics. In so holding, the Court distinguished an IRS revenue ruling that concluded that a merger between two mutual companies may qualify as a reorganization (despite the same debt-like features of the consideration provided by the surviving mutual company in the transaction). As a result, at least for transactions involving nonstock entities, the Court's decision raises a question whether COI requires some *comparison* between the "equity interest" surrendered and the "equity interest" obtained in exchange.

In addition to the nature of the consideration received, courts have also addressed the quantity of stock that must be obtained in order to satisfy COI. In *Minnesota Tea Co.*, supra, the Court said that the qualifying consideration must represent "a substantial part of the value of the thing transferred." But in *John A. Nelson Co.*, supra, COI was met even though the stock transferred constituted only 38 percent of the consideration received, and the current regulations permit qualifying consideration constituting as little as 40 percent. Temp. Reg. § 1.368-1T(e)(2)(v) (ex. 1). In determining the necessary quantity of stock, courts (and the regulations) focus on the amount of stock received as a percentage of the value of the target corporation, not the issuing corporation. Thus, for example, an acquisition of a small corporation by a very large one (sometimes referred to as a "minnow" acquired by a "whale") may satisfy COI even though the target shareholders end up owning only a tiny fraction of the stock of the issuing corporation.

## *QUESTION*

*Corporate-shareholder linkage*. In *Paulsen*, the shareholders of the stock S&L received passbook savings accounts and certificates of deposit in exchange for their stock. It is perhaps reasonable to conclude, as the Court did, that the shareholders received cash equivalents and therefore should recognize gain or loss. But what *other* tax issue was resolved by the Court's holding? Was the resolution of that issue equally reasonable?

---

The next two cases elaborate on the COI doctrine and explain who must receive the qualifying consideration. Try to reconcile these cases and then review the subsequent material to understand how the regulations reconcile them.

## May B. Kass v. Commissioner

60 T.C. 218 (1973)

DAWSON, Judge:

[The Atlantic City Racing Association ("ACRA") was a corporation that operated a racetrack. To gain control over ACRA's business, the Levy and Casey families, who owned about ten percent of ACRA's stock, transferred all of their ACRA shares and cash to a new corporation, Track Associates, Inc. ("TRACK") in exchange for all of the shares of TRACK. TRACK then acquired for cash about 84 percent of the stock of ACRA and liquidated ACRA by means of an upstream merger of ACRA into TRACK. In the merger, all of the ACRA shareholders (other than TRACK) received shares of TRACK in exchange for their ACRA shares. The formation of TRACK, its acquisition of over 80 percent of the stock of ACRA for cash, and the subsequent liquidation of ACRA, all were undertaken to qualify the transaction for tax purposes as an acquisition of the ACRA assets under former section 334(b)(2). This provision (the predecessor to current section 338) enabled TRACK to obtain the equivalent of a cost basis in the ACRA assets.

Taxpayer was an ACRA shareholder who did not tender her shares to TRACK in the initial cash acquisition. Instead, by operation of law, she exchanged her ACRA shares for TRACK shares in the upstream merger. She contended that the merger qualified as a reorganization and therefore she did not recognize any gain or loss on the exchange. The issue came down to whether there was enough continuity of interest in the merger.]

... Reorganization treatment is appropriate when [TRACK]'s stock ownership in [ACRA] was not acquired as a step in a plan to acquire assets of [ACRA]:

[TRACK]'s stockholding can be counted as contributing to continuity-of-interest, so that since such holding represented more than 80 percent of the stock of [ACRA], the continuity-of-interest test would be met. Reorganization treatment is inappropriate when [TRACK]'s stock ownership in [ACRA] was purchased as the first step in a plan to acquire [ACRA]'s assets in conformance with the provisions of section 334(b)(2). [TRACK]'s stockholding could not be counted towards continuity-of-interest, so in the last example there would be a continuity-of-interest of less than 20 percent. (Less than 20-percent continuity would be significantly less continuity-of-interest than that allowed in John A. Nelson Co. v. Helvering, 296 U.S. 374 (1935).) In short, where [TRACK]'s stock interest is "old and cold," it may contribute to continuity-of-interest. Where [TRACK]'s interest is not "old and cold," the sale of shares by the majority of shareholders actually detracts from continuity-of-interest.

In petitioner's case, TRACK's stock in ACRA was acquired as part of an integrated plan to obtain control over ACRA's business. The plan called for, first, the purchase of stock and, second, the subsidiary-into-parent merger. Accordingly, continuity-of-interest must be measured by looking to all the pre-tender offer stockholders rather than to the parent (TRACK) and the nontendering stockholders only; and by that measure the merger fails and petitioner must recognize her gain. . . .

[P]etitioner makes the following arguments, which we will deal with separately.

*One*, the continuity-of-interest doctrine should not be applied because TRACK was formed by a few stockholders in ACRA in order to purchase the business and, in the process, to acquire a stepped-up basis for as many of the assets as possible via section 334(b)(2). "In effect, the situation was the same as the sale of stock by some shareholders to other shareholders." The petitioner meets herself coming, so to speak, when making this argument. Confronted with the problem of how to characterize the second event in the present two-event transaction, she contends that the transaction was a true statutory merger in both form and substance, at least insofar as she, a minority shareholder, was concerned. Now, confronted with the continuity-of-interest problem, she would have us treat the transaction in a manner inconsistent with the characterization previously given to the transaction, that of a merger. Furthermore, the parties to these events (the selling shareholders of ACRA, the organizers of TRACK, and the nontendering, nondissenting shareholders such as the petitioner) chose the steps that were followed.[1] To allow one of them in a separate proceeding to characterize the facts as being in substance something else would lay the groundwork for an enormous amount of "whipsawing" by and against both taxpayers and the Government.

1. We realize that in one sense petitioner was not privy to the plans of the Levys and the Caseys. In another sense — in the same way that all shareholders in a corporation play a part in major corporate decisions — she was a party to the choice of steps taken. Certainly she was informed of the events taking place.

*Two*, in applying the continuity-of-interest test, if it is applied, the purchase of stock by TRACK and the subsequent merger should not be viewed as steps in an integrated transaction because the choice of merger over liquidation as a second step had independent significance to the minority shareholders and either choice would have suited TRACK. By so arguing, the petitioner attempts in effect to avoid the step-transaction doctrine and thus to limit the application of the continuity-of-interest test. If the merger can be separated from the stock purchase, the continuity-of-interest test might be applicable only with regard to ACRA's shareholders at the time of the statutory merger, namely, the parent corporation, TRACK, and the minority shareholders, including petitioner. We note at least one flaw: The choice — liquidation or merger — did make a difference to TRACK. If it had liquidated ACRA, TRACK would not have received all of ACRA's assets. Some of the assets would have gone to the minority shareholders, and it would have had to have purchased them from these shareholders at an additional price. By choosing to merge ACRA into itself, it was able to avoid this and other problems.

*Three*, if the purchase and merger are to be viewed as parts of a single transaction for continuity and reorganization purposes, then the incorporation of TRACK should also be integrated into the transaction for section 351 purposes; thus the petitioner should be viewed as having participated in a tax-free section 351 transaction along with the Levys and Caseys. Briefly, the answer to this argument is that while the purchase and the merger were interdependent events, petitioner's exchange of ACRA stock for TRACK stock was not "mutually interdependent" with the incorporation transfers made by the Levys [and] Caseys. . . . This result merely illustrates the truism that the step-transaction doctrine, even when worded consistently . . . and applied to identical facts, may result in integration in one case and "separateness" in another case simply because the legal question to be answered has changed. . . .

*Four*, assuming that the continuity-of-interest test is applied, it is met where all 16 percent of the stockholders of ACRA exchanged their stock for a total of 35 percent of the stock of TRACK. The 16-percent figure (really 16.04 percent) is the sum of the percentage of ACRA stock transferred to TRACK at the time of TRACK's formation (10.22 percent) plus the percentage of ACRA stock exchanged for TRACK stock following the statutory merger (5.82 percent). Fortunately, we need not engage in a game of percentages since the continuity figure argued for by petitioner, 16 percent, is not "tantalizingly" high. The plain fact that more than 80 percent of the shareholders of ACRA sold out for cash is sufficient to prevent this merger from meeting the quantitative test [of COI]. . . .

Finally, we emphasize that the petitioner is not any worse off than her fellow shareholders who sold their stock. She could have also received money instead of stock had she chosen to sell or to dissent from the merger. The nonrecognition of a realized gain is always an important matter. We hold that petitioner is not entitled to such favorable treatment in this case. . . .

*QUESTIONS*

1. *The lesson of* Kass. What is the lesson to be learned from *Kass*? Why wasn't continuity of interest met in her case?

2. *Shareholder-shareholder linkage*. Assume that the students in the class represent all of the shareholders of T corporation and that a sufficient percentage of the class has approved a proposed merger of T into P corporation, with each student having a choice of receiving either P stock or cash as consideration. If you accept the P stock, how will you be taxed in the transaction? Will you thereby retain a continuing interest in the business and assets formerly held by T? Will your tax consequences nevertheless be affected by the choices made by your fellow students? Why? What is the rationale for this result? What might happen if most of the other students are "tax-indifferent," that is, they are not subject to U.S. taxes for one reason or another?

3. *The court's rationalization*. In *Kass*, the court defended its decision by emphasizing that Mrs. Kass "is not any worse off than her fellow shareholders who sold their stock." Is that a fair explanation? Why or why not? If you had been advising Mrs. Kass from the outset and had had the ability to restructure the deal, what might you have suggested to her?

## J.E. Seagram Corp. v. Commissioner

104 T.C. 75 (1995)

[On May 6, 1981, Dome Petroleum Ltd. (Dome) commenced a tender offer for approximately 20 percent of the common stock of Conoco, Inc. (Conoco), a corporation engaged in the oil and gas business. The tender offer was dramatically oversubscribed, so that by May 27, Dome announced that about 50 percent of the Conoco stock had been tendered pursuant to the offer. On June 1, Conoco agreed to buy out Dome's interest in Conoco in exchange for all of the stock of one of Conoco's valuable subsidiaries plus cash.

The effect of the Dome transaction was to "put into play" the stock of Conoco. Other potential buyers noted how receptive Conoco's shareholders appeared to be to an acquisition of the company. As a result, three different corporations, J.E. Seagram Corp. (Seagram), E.I. DuPont de Nemours & Co. (DuPont), and Mobil Corp. (Mobil), all proceeded to make a series of competing offers for the acquisition of Conoco.

Of the three competitors, the Conoco board favored DuPont and negotiated a two-step purchase and sale agreement with that corporation. According to the agreement, a newly-formed wholly-owned subsidiary of DuPont ("DuPont Tenderor") would first offer to acquire all of the stock of Conoco in exchange for either shares of DuPont or cash. Second, following consummation of the tender offer, there would be a squeeze-out merger of Conoco into Dupont Tenderor in which any

Conoco shares not acquired in the tender offer would be acquired. The obligation of DuPont Tenderor to go forward with the transaction was subject to several conditions, including (1) a minimum (at least 51 percent) of the Conoco shares being tendered in the initial step, (2) a maximum (40 percent) of cash being paid for the Conoco stock, and (3) various state and regulatory approvals being obtained.

Following execution of the agreement, the other suitors, Seagram and Mobil, continued their efforts to acquire Conoco. Eventually, however, thanks in part to an option granted to Dupont Tenderor to acquire some Conoco stock directly from Conoco, DuPont Tenderor succeeded in obtaining a majority of the Conoco shares. As of that time, Seagram had acquired about 32 percent of the Conoco shares for cash. Mobil's offers were all contingent on its receiving at least 51 percent of Conoco's shares, so it did not end up purchasing any of those shares.

In recognition of DuPont's victory and pursuant to the DuPont tender offer, Seagram tendered its Conoco shares to DuPont Tenderor in exchange for DuPont stock. Ultimately, DuPont Tenderor acquired 94 percent of the Conoco stock in the tender offer (including the 32 percent interest of Seagram) and the remaining 6 percent of that stock in the subsequent squeeze-out merger. The consideration paid by DuPont Tenderor for the Conoco stock in the two steps consisted of the following:

| Conoco SH | Interest sold | Consideration paid |
|---|---|---|
| Seagram | 32% | DuPont stock |
| Other Conoco SHs | 22% | DuPont stock |
| Other Conoco SHs | 46% | Cash |

Thus, a total of 54 percent of Conoco was acquired by DuPont Tenderor for DuPont stock.

In the exchange of Conoco stock for DuPont stock, Seagram realized a $530 million loss. Although it did not report the loss for financial accounting purposes, it claimed the loss on its tax return. When the Commissioner disallowed the loss, Seagram (the petitioner in this case) brought suit.]

NIMS, J.

. . . The ultimate issue for decision is whether, for tax purposes, petitioner had a recognized loss upon the exchange of its Conoco stock for DuPont stock. Whether such a loss is to be recognized depends upon the effect to be given section 354(a)(1) under the above facts. Section 354(a)(1) provides . . . "No gain or loss shall be recognized if stock or securities in a corporation a party to a reorganization are, in pursuance of the plan of reorganization, exchanged solely for stock or securities in such corporation or in another corporation a party to the reorganization." Thus, if DuPont, DuPont Tenderor, and Conoco were parties to a reorganization, and if the statutory merger of Conoco into DuPont Tenderor was in pursuance of a plan of reorganization, then no loss is to be recognized by petitioner upon the exchange of its Conoco stock for DuPont stock.

[The excerpt omits the court's conclusion that the two-step acquisition constituted a single integrated transaction (i.e., a merger) undertaken pursuant to a plan of reorganization.]

Petitioner also argues that even if the DuPont tender offer and merger were to be treated as an integrated transaction, the merger does not qualify as a reorganization because it fails the "continuity of interest" requirement.

... Petitioner is essentially arguing that because it acquired approximately 32 percent of [the Conoco] shares for cash pursuant to its own tender offer, and DuPont acquired approximately 46 percent of these shares for cash pursuant to *its* tender offer, the combined 78 percent of Conoco shares acquired for cash after the date of the Agreement destroyed the continuity of interest requisite for a valid reorganization. We think petitioner's argument, and the logic that supports it, miss the mark.

Pursuant to its two-step tender offer/merger plan of reorganization, DuPont acquired approximately 54 percent of the ... Conoco stock in exchange for DuPont stock, which included petitioner's recently acquired Conoco shares that it tendered pursuant to DuPont's tender offer. If the 54 percent had been acquired by DuPont from Conoco shareholders in a "one-step" merger-type acquisition, there would be little argument that continuity of interest had been satisfied.

... The parties stipulated that petitioner and DuPont, through their wholly owned subsidiaries, were acting independently of one another and pursuant to competing tender offers. Furthermore, there is of course nothing in the record to suggest any prearranged understanding between petitioner and DuPont that petitioner would tender the Conoco stock purchased for cash if petitioner by means of its own tender offer failed to achieve control of Conoco. Consequently, it cannot be argued that petitioner, although not a party to the reorganization, was somehow acting in concert with DuPont, which was a party to the reorganization. If such had been the case, the reorganization would fail because petitioner's cash purchases of Conoco stock could be attributed to DuPont, thereby destroying continuity.

The cases cited by petitioner in support of its argument that DuPont's plan of reorganization failed for lack of continuity of interest are not germane. ... In Superior Coach of Fla., Inc. v. Comm'r, [80 T.C. 895 (1983),] the majority shareholders of P purchased all of the shares of T and merged T into P. We held that the P shareholders' acquisition of the T stock was "inextricably interwoven" with the intent to effect the merger, and since the "historic shareholders" of T retained no proprietary interest in P, the merger did not qualify as a reorganization under section 368(a)(1)(A). In other words, the reorganization failed because the majority shareholders of P were acting on its behalf when they bought the T stock for cash, and there was no continuity of interest on the part of the acquired corporation's previous shareholders. In the case before us, DuPont's shareholders did not purchase Conoco stock for cash (or for any other consideration) to facilitate the merger, and except for approving the Plan of Reorganization and the merger did not act on DuPont's behalf. *Superior Coach of Fla., Inc.* is therefore not apposite on its facts.

Petitioner cites Yoc Heating Corp. v. Comm'r, 61 T.C. 168, 177 (1973) for the proposition that continuity requires looking at shareholders "immediately prior to the inception of the series of transactions" in an integrated transaction. Again, we look at the facts: R, the acquiring corporation, purchased for cash over 85 percent of the stock of O, and then caused O to transfer its assets, subject to its liabilities, to R's wholly owned subsidiary, N. N issued one share of its stock to R in exchange for every three shares of O held by R plus cash to be paid to the minority shareholders of O.

... We held ... that the acquisition by N of O's assets constituted a purchase under the "integrated transaction" (step transaction) doctrine, rather than a reorganization. ... *Yoc Heating*'s comparison of stock ownership immediately prior and immediately after the series of transactions is perfectly appropriate to the facts of that case, where the acquiring corporation acquired control of the target for cash and then effected the corporate combination, because the shareholders of O before the acquisition by R lacked the requisite continuing interest in the affairs of O after the acquisition.

... Respondent points out, correctly we believe, that the concept of continuity of interest advocated by petitioner would go far toward eliminating the possibility of a tax-free reorganization of any corporation whose stock is actively traded. Because it would be impossible to track the large volume of third party transactions in the target's stock, all completed transactions would be suspect. Sales of target stock for cash after the date of the announcement of an acquisition can neither be predicted nor controlled by publicly held parties to a reorganization. A requirement that the identity of the acquired corporation's shareholders be tracked to assume a sufficient number of "historic" shareholders to satisfy some arbitrary minimal percentage receiving the acquiring corporation's stock would be completely unrealistic. ...

In the "integrated" transaction before us petitioner, not DuPont, "stepped into the shoes" of 32 percent of the Conoco shareholders when petitioner acquired their stock for cash via the ... competing tender offer, held the 32 percent transitorily, and immediately tendered it in exchange for DuPont stock. For present purposes, there is no material distinction between petitioner's tender of the Conoco stock and a direct tender by the "old" Conoco shareholders themselves. Thus, the requirement of continuity of interest has been met.

Petitioner extended its tender offer even after DuPont had been tendered a "significant majority" of the outstanding shares of Conoco. ... [P]etitioner, in connection with its tender of its just-acquired Conoco stock, issued a press release quoting Edgar M. Bronfman, Seagram's chairman and CEO, as saying that Seagram's was pleased at the prospect of becoming "a large stockholder of the *combined DuPont and Conoco*." We also noted that petitioner did not report a loss on the exchange of its Conoco stock for DuPont stock for financial accounting purposes. Instead, petitioner ascribed its carrying cost for its Conoco stock to the DuPont stock. None of these acts is consistent with the recognized loss petitioner claimed on its tax return.

For the reasons stated in this Opinion, we hold that a loss cannot be recognized by petitioner on its exchange of Conoco stock for DuPont stock, made pursuant to the DuPont-Conoco plan of reorganization. . . .

## *NOTES*

1. *Epilogue*. Seagram appealed the Tax Court's decision to the Second Circuit but settled the matter prior to any further decision. The settlement was apparently on terms favorable to Seagram because of conflicting precedents regarding both the integration of the tender offer with the subsequent merger and the failure to integrate Seagram's purchase of Conoco stock into the transaction. The settlement, however, was not Seagram's last dispute with the tax authorities as a result of its attempt to acquire Conoco. By 1995 (about the time of the Tax Court's decision), Seagram had decided to dispose of its DuPont shares, then worth about $10 billion (including about $7 billion of gain). Rather than pay a 35 percent capital gains tax on the gain, Seagram arranged for DuPont to buy back its shares in a corporate redemption. The key was Seagram's retention of an option to repurchase a like number of DuPont shares. Seagram claimed that the option (and application of the option-attribution rule in section 318(a)(4)) meant that the transaction was a $10 billion dividend for which it was entitled to a dividends-received deduction. Cf. *Heinz* (p. 238) involving a similar claim to dividend treatment. Seagram's claim was challenged and settled, apparently again on terms favorable to Seagram. Section 1059(e)(1)(A)(iii) now bars Seagram's claim by expressly treating such a redemption as an extraordinary dividend; this provision was enacted in part in response to the Seagram-DuPont transaction.

2. Yoc Heating. The regulations have changed the result of a *Yoc Heating* transaction where there is a qualified stock purchase of a target corporation, no section 338 election is made, and the target's assets are subsequently transferred to the purchasing corporation (or a member of its affiliated group) in a transaction potentially qualifying as a reorganization. Reg. § 1.338-3(d). In that case, the transfer of the target's assets may qualify as a reorganization to each of those corporations notwithstanding the prior cash purchases of the target's stock as part of the overall acquisition. The purpose of the regulation is to prevent any change in the basis of the target's assets when there is a qualified stock purchase of the target but no section 338 election is made. As in *Kass*, however, qualification of the transaction as a reorganization to any other party, including a minority shareholder of the target, must take into account the effect on COI of prior cash purchases that were part of the overall plan.

3. *Step-transaction doctrine*. As illustrated by *Kass* and *Seagram*, reorganization cases frequently require application of the step-transaction doctrine. Because the conditions for reorganization status vary with the taxpayer's acquisition pattern,

there is a premium placed on identifying which pattern actually transpired, and the step-transaction doctrine is often invoked to make that determination. Three common formulations of the step-transaction doctrine are the "binding commitment," "mutual interdependence," and "end result" tests. The binding commitment test combines formally independent steps only if, at the time of the first step, there was a binding commitment to undertake the others. It is the test least likely to result in integration of steps. Under the mutual interdependence test, individual steps are collapsed if they are so interdependent as to be fruitless without the completion of all of them. Finally, under the end result test, separate steps with independent legal significance are, nevertheless, integrated if they were all intended from the outset to be undertaken in order to achieve a particular end result. In general, the end result test is the one most likely to combine nominally independent steps. Unfortunately, the law in this area is very uncertain; no settled understanding exists regarding when the step-transaction doctrine should be invoked, which test should be used, and how a test should be applied to a given set of facts.

4. *Other controversies. Kass* and *Seagram* concern the significance for COI purposes of events occurring prior to a potential reorganization. Other cases have raised similar questions with regard to events following a potential reorganization. Read Reg. § 1.368-1(e)(1), (3), (4) and (8) (exs. 1-5, 7-9), and the following excerpt from the preamble to the regulations to understand the resolution of these and other questions.

## T.D. 8760

1998-1 C.B. 803

. . . The purpose of the continuity of interest requirement is to prevent transactions that resemble sales from qualifying for nonrecognition of gain or loss available to corporate reorganizations. The final regulations provide that the COI requirement is satisfied if in substance a substantial part of the value of the proprietary interest in the target corporation (T) is preserved in the reorganization. A proprietary interest in T is preserved if, in a potential reorganization, it is exchanged for a proprietary interest in the issuing corporation (P), it is exchanged by the acquiring corporation for a direct interest in the T enterprise, or it otherwise continues as a proprietary interest in T. The issuing corporation means the acquiring corporation (as the term is used in section 368(a)), except that, in determining whether a reorganization qualifies as a triangular reorganization (as defined in section 1.358-6(b)(2)), the issuing corporation means the corporation in control of the acquiring corporation. However, a proprietary interest in T is not preserved if, in connection with the potential reorganization, it is acquired by P for consideration other than P stock, or P stock furnished in exchange for a proprietary interest in T in the potential reorganization is redeemed. All facts and circumstances must be considered in determining whether, in substance, a proprietary interest in T is preserved. . . .

The . . . final regulations permit former T shareholders to sell P stock received in a potential reorganization to third parties without causing the reorganization to fail to satisfy the COI requirement. Some commentators have questioned whether the regulations are consistent with existing authorities.

The COI requirement was applied first to reorganization provisions that did not specify that P exchange a proprietary interest in P for a proprietary interest in T. Supreme Court cases imposed the COI requirement to further Congressional intent that tax-free status be accorded only to transactions where P exchanges a substantial proprietary interest in P for a proprietary interest in T held by the T shareholders rather than to transactions resembling sales. . . .

None of the Supreme Court cases establishing the COI requirement addressed the issue of whether sales by former T shareholders of P stock received in exchange for T stock in the potential reorganization cause the COI requirement to fail to be satisfied. Since then, however, some courts have premised decisions on the assumption that sales of P stock received in exchange for T stock in the potential reorganization may cause the COI requirement to fail to be satisfied. McDonald's Restaurants of Illinois, Inc. v. Comm'r, 688 F.2d 520 (7th Cir. 1982). . . . The apparent focus of these cases is on whether the T shareholders intended on the date of the potential reorganization to sell their P stock and the degree, if any, to which P facilitates the sale. Based on an intensive inquiry into nearly identical facts, some of these cases held that as a result of the subsequent sale the potential reorganization did not satisfy the COI requirement; others held that satisfaction of the COI requirement was not adversely affected by the subsequent sale. The IRS and Treasury Department have concluded that the law as reflected in these cases does not further the principles of reorganization treatment and is difficult for both taxpayers and the IRS to apply consistently.

Therefore, consistent with Congressional intent and the Supreme Court precedent which distinguishes between sales and reorganizations, the final regulations focus the COI requirement generally on exchanges between the T shareholders and P. Under this approach, sales of P stock by former T shareholders generally are disregarded.

The final regulations will greatly enhance administrability in this area by both taxpayers and the government. The regulations will prevent "whipsaw" of the government, such as where the former T shareholders treat the transaction as a tax-free reorganization, and P later disavows reorganization treatment to step up its basis in the T assets based on the position that sales of P stock by the former T shareholders did not satisfy the COI requirement. See, e.g., *McDonald's Restaurants*, supra. In addition, this approach will prevent unilateral sales of P stock by former majority T shareholders from adversely affecting the section 354 nonrecognition treatment expected by former minority T shareholders.

. . . The IRS and Treasury Department believe that issues concerning the COI requirement raised by dispositions of T stock before a potential reorganization correspond to those raised by subsequent dispositions of P stock furnished in exchange for T stock in the potential reorganization. . . . Cf. J.E. Seagram

Corp. v. Comm'r, 104 T.C. 75 (1995) (sales of T stock prior to a potential reorganization do not affect COI if not part of the plan of reorganization). The final regulations provide that, for COI purposes, a mere disposition of T stock prior to a potential reorganization to persons not related to P is disregarded and a mere disposition of P stock received in a potential reorganization to persons not related to P is disregarded. . . .

[W]here the step transaction doctrine applies to link T stock purchases with later acquisitions of T, the final regulations provide that a proprietary interest in T is not preserved if, in connection with the potential reorganization, it is acquired by P for consideration other than P stock. Whether a stock acquisition is made in connection with a potential reorganization will be determined based on the facts and circumstances of each case. . . .

*NOTES*

1. *Required amount of stock consideration.* In order to obtain an advance IRS ruling that a proposed transaction qualifies as a reorganization, taxpayers must represent that qualifying stock consideration received in the transaction constitutes at least 50 percent of the value of the target corporation. Rev. Proc. 77-37, 1977-2 C.B. 568, 569 (§ 3.02). The regulations indicate, however, that 40 percent stock consideration is sufficient to satisfy COI, and the IRS has issued rulings consistent with that position. Temp. Reg. § 1.368-1T(e)(2)(v) (ex. 1). The percentage is determined in the aggregate and not on a shareholder-by-shareholder basis. Thus, some target shareholders may be completely cashed out in the transaction so long as a sufficient total amount of qualifying stock is received.

2. *Measuring date for purposes of COI.* Satisfaction of the quantitative test may be affected by changes in the value of the issuing and target corporations between the time an agreement is reached and the time the deal is closed, particularly where the agreement provides for fixed consideration:

> **Example 11-2:** An agreement is reached for the merger of T corporation into P corporation, with P surviving. In the merger, each T shareholder is entitled to receive one share of P stock (worth $100 at the time of the agreement) for every five shares of T stock surrendered (each T share is worth $20 at the time of agreement). T shareholders may elect instead to receive $20 cash for each T share, but no more than half of the T shares may be exchanged for cash. Thus, based on the relative values at the time of the agreement, at least half of the value of T must be exchanged for P stock, thereby ensuring COI. Assume that at closing, the value of each P share has fallen to $50, half of the T shares are exchanged for P shares pursuant to the 5-for-1 formula in the merger agreement (so that each T share is exchanged for the equivalent of $10 worth of P stock), and the other half of the T shares are exchanged for $20

cash per share. As a result, only one-third of the value of T ($10/$30) would be acquired for P stock, which may or may not satisfy COI.

The regulations provide for a "signing date rule" under which COI is tested based on the relative values as of the last business day before the agreement is signed, but only if the agreement provides for fixed consideration (as in **example 11-2**). Temp. Reg. § 1.368-1T(e)(2)(i). Thus, in **example 11-2**, COI would be satisfied. If there is no fixed consideration provided in the agreement, then COI is tested as of the closing date. The theory is that fixed consideration in the agreement makes the target shareholders subject to the economic fortunes of the issuing corporation as of the time of signing, so a signing date rule is appropriate. It is as if the target shareholders carried out their exchange at the time of the agreement, with subsequent fluctuations in value ignored as simply post-transaction events.

3. *COI when the target corporation is insolvent.* In general, COI is determined based solely on the consideration received by the shareholders of the target corporation and not its creditors. If the target is insolvent, however, certain of its creditors may effectively be holders of target equity. The regulations treat the most senior class of creditors of an insolvent target who receive issuing corporation stock in a potential reorganization (and any creditors with claims of equal priority) as equity holders of the target. The interest of each creditor in the group is bifurcated into target equity and debt based on the proportion of issuing corporation stock paid in the aggregate to the group. For example, if the value of a particular creditor's claim is $100 and the group receives issuing corporation stock equal to 25 percent of the total value of their claims, then the creditor is treated as owning $25 of target equity and $75 of target debt. Consistent with the "full priority" rule in bankruptcy, the regulations treat any target creditors with claims more junior to such group as holding target equity equal to the full value of their claims. Satisfaction of COI is determined based on the mix of stock and non-stock consideration received in exchange for the equity interests held by the target creditors and stockholders. Reg. § 1.368-1(e)(6) and (8) (ex. 10). This rule applies regardless of whether the transaction is carried out in a title 11 bankruptcy proceeding or similar case and even if the creditors take no steps to assert control over the insolvent target (other than agreeing to take stock in the potential reorganization). A transfer in a title 11 or similar case must satisfy certain special rules in order to qualify as a reorganization (termed a "G" reorganization). See I.R.C. § 368(a)(1)(G) and (3).

4. *"Net value" requirement.* The COI rules for insolvent corporations were part of a broader set of proposed regulations that would add a "net value" requirement for all acquisitive reorganizations. The theory is that a corporation without net value cannot be acquired for stock of another corporation and, therefore, any acquisition constitutes a sale rather than a reorganization. As proposed, a "net value" requirement would be imposed on both the target and issuing corporations in order for a transaction to qualify as a reorganization. In general, the value of the target's assets must exceed the sum of its liabilities plus any boot (not stock) paid by the acquiring

corporation in the transaction. This ensures that some stock consideration exists in the transaction. In addition, the value of the issuing corporation's assets must exceed its liabilities immediately after the exchange. Prop. Reg. § 1.368-1(f)(1)-(3).

**Problem 11-1:**

(a) How would *Kass* and *Seagram* be decided under the current regulations?
(b) Suppose that in *Seagram*, following its exchange of Conoco stock for DuPont stock, Seagram had subsequently sold its DuPont stock on the market for cash. If the current regulations had been applicable, would that additional step have affected COI? Would it have made a difference if the sale by Seagram were pursuant to a binding agreement entered into prior to the exchange with DuPont?
(c) Answer the same questions as in (b) under the alternative assumptions that (i) Seagram's DuPont stock is subsequently redeemed by DuPont for cash rather than sold on the market, or (ii) DuPont subsequently redeems for cash the stock purchased from Seagram on the market.

## b. Continuity of Business Enterprise (COBE) Doctrine

In addition to COI, a transaction must satisfy the continuity of business enterprise (COBE) doctrine in order to qualify as a reorganization. As the following excerpt from the preamble to the regulations explains, COBE is a necessary corollary to COI.

### T.D. 7745

1981-1 C.B. 134

... Continuity of business enterprise requires that the transferee (P) either continue the transferor's (T's) historic business or use a significant portion of T's historic business assets. P is not required to continue T's business. However, there must be significant use of T's historic business assets in P's business.

... A number of taxpayers submitting comments argued that the proposed regulation is inconsistent with the underlying policy of the reorganization provisions since it requires T's shareholders to recognize gain even though the shareholders continue their investment in corporate solution. They suggest that the appropriate time to tax T's shareholders is when they "cash in" their investment through a sale or other taxable disposition of the P stock received in the transaction. Similarly, they argue that it is inappropriate to require gain recognition at the shareholder level merely because of a change in asset composition at the corporate level.

Under the general rule of section 1001(c), an exchange of stock or securities requires recognition of gain or loss unless the exchange falls within the precise specifications of a nonrecognition provision in the Internal Revenue Code (Code). Nonrecognition is accorded only if the exchange satisfies the underlying purpose of the exception as well as the specific description of the excepted exchange. *See* § 1.1002-1(b). The relationship of the exchange to the venture or enterprise is always material. *Id.*

Section 1031 of the Code, which permits deferral of recognition on the exchange of certain property, expressly excludes an exchange of corporate stock or securities. Similarly, section 1036, which applies to an exchange of stock, permits deferral only when stock is exchanged for stock in the same corporation.

An exception to the general rule of gain or loss recognition is contained in the reorganization provisions . . . of the Code. As stated in § 1.1002-1(c), the underlying assumption of any tax-free exchange "is that the new property is substantially a continuation of the old investment still unliquidated" and, with respect to corporate reorganizations, nonrecognition results because "the new enterprise, the new corporate structure, and the new property are substantially continuations of the old still unliquidated." . . .

The courts have long recognized that a tax-free reorganization presupposes that T's shareholders retain a material proprietary interest in P (continuity of interest). . . . A necessary corollary to this continuity of interest requirement is that the interest retained represent a link to T's business or its business assets. The continuity of business enterprise requirement ensures that tax-free reorganizations effect only a readjustment of the T shareholders' continuing interest in T's property under a modified corporate form. *See* § 1.368-1(b). Absent such a link between T's shareholders and T's business or assets there would be no reason to require T's shareholders to retain a continuing stock interest in P. If the shareholders' link to T's business or its assets is broken by, for example, a sale of T's business to an unrelated party, as part of the overall plan of reorganization, the interest received in P is no different than an interest in any corporation. An exchange of stock without a link to the underlying business or business assets resembles any stock for stock exchange and, as such, is a taxable event. Thus, it is not enough that the shareholder's investment remains in corporate solution. . . .

## *NOTES*

1. *The COBE requirement.* Read Reg. § 1.368-1(d)(1)-(4) and (5) (exs. 1-9). COBE requires the issuing corporation after the acquisition to either continue a significant line of the target's historic business or use in a business a significant portion of the target's historic business assets. The regulations use a one-in-three test to define "significant"; continuation of at least one of three equal lines of businesses formerly conducted by the target corporation complies with COBE. Reg. § 1.368-1(d)(5) (ex. 1). The "use" of assets in a business is interpreted liberally to

include the mere holding of assets for backup purposes. Id. (ex. 2). Step-transaction principles apply to determine whether the target's business or assets are "historic" and whether the issuing corporation continues or uses them. Reg. § 1.368-1(d)(2)(iii) and (5) (exs. 3 and 5). The issuing corporation is treated as holding any businesses and assets of the target actually held by members of the issuing corporation's qualified group, which generally includes corporations controlled (within the meaning of section 368(c)) directly or indirectly by the issuing corporation. As a result, such holdings are aggregated for purposes of determining whether COBE is satisfied. Reg. § 1.368-1(d)(4)(i), (ii) and (5) (exs. 6 and 7). In certain circumstances, a partnership's holding of the target's businesses or assets is also attributed to the issuing corporation. Reg. § 1.368-1(d)(4)(iii) and (5) (exs. 8 and 9). These rules facilitate post-acquisition restructurings by the issuing corporation of the former target's businesses and assets.

2. *Preventing tax-deferred liquidation and diversification.* One consequence of COBE is to prevent certain liquidations or diversifications of a taxpayer's investment from qualifying as a reorganization. For example, the conversion of a target's operating business assets into cash and investment assets may disqualify a transaction from reorganization status because of the absence of COBE. Reg. § 1.368-1(d)(5) (exs. 3 and 4). Similarly, in Rev. Rul. 87-76, 1987-2 C.B. 84, T corporation was acquired by P corporation in a potential reorganization. Prior to the acquisition, T sold all of its historic business assets (consisting of an investment portfolio of corporate stocks and bonds) and reinvested the proceeds in the type of tax-free municipal bonds used in P's business. The IRS concluded that COBE was not satisfied since P neither continued T's historic business nor used a significant portion of T's historic assets. Sections 351(e) and 368(a)(2)(F) provide additional statutory safeguards against tax-deferred diversification.

3. *Policy.* As mentioned in the excerpt, commentators have questioned the underlying policy rationale of COBE. The main issue is whether a disposition of the target's assets (a corporate-level event) should have any tax consequence to the shareholders of the target. For example, in Rev. Rul. 87-76, discussed above in note 2, T's sale of its investment portfolio presumably resulted in the recognition of gain or loss by T. But because COBE was not satisfied and the transaction was, therefore, not a reorganization, the disposition of T's assets also had the consequence of triggering recognition by any T shareholders who exchanged their T stock for P stock in the transaction. This result is arguably contrary to the general treatment of a C corporation and its shareholders as separate and distinct taxpayers. For example, a sale by a corporation of its assets ordinarily has no tax consequences to its shareholders even though their investment is changed or diversified through the corporate action. We have previously seen this same objection to corporate-shareholder linkage in connection with COI. When COI is flunked (generally as a result of a shareholder-level event), it may have corporate-level tax consequences. Similarly, when COBE is flunked (generally as a result of a corporate-level event), it may have shareholder-level tax consequences.

COBE is sometimes also criticized because of its lock-in effect. Prior to or following a corporate combination qualifying as a reorganization, COBE may restrict the ability of the corporations to dispose of unwanted assets and maximize efficiency gains. Of course, if a disposition of over two-thirds of the target's businesses and assets is an essential part of the deal, the business purpose for the corporate combination itself may be called into question.

### c. Business Purpose Requirement

The regulations retain the requirement, first articulated in *Gregory v. Helvering* (p. 120), that a transaction have a business purpose to qualify as a reorganization. Read Reg. § 1.368-1(b) (second sentence) (requirement of "business exigencies"), -1(c) (tenth sentence) ("transaction . . . must be an ordinary and necessary incident of the conduct of the enterprise"), and -2(g) (third sentence) (transaction "must be undertaken for reasons germane to the continuance of the business of a corporation"). In addition, after explaining that a reorganization must be pursuant to a "plan of reorganization," the regulations state:

> A scheme, which involves an abrupt departure from normal reorganization procedure in connection with a transaction on which the imposition of tax is imminent, such as a mere device that puts on the form of a corporate reorganization as a disguise for concealing its real character, and the object and accomplishment of which is the consummation of a preconceived plan having no business or corporate purpose, is not a plan of reorganization. [Reg. § 1.368-1(c) (last sentence).]

This language echoes the Supreme Court's opinion in *Gregory*.

Although the existence of a business purpose is essential, its precise meaning is uncertain. "Reorganization" is a construct of the tax statute, intended to specify a particular set of tax consequences with respect to transactions carried out in certain ways. As a result, most reorganizations involve an important element of tax planning and attempted tax savings. On the other hand, the business purpose requirement connotes some purpose beyond mere tax reduction or avoidance. Thus, a qualifying transaction will ordinarily have some mix of tax and nontax purposes, with the function of the business purpose requirement being to provide a limit on the proper mix.

Interpretation of the business purpose requirement in the reorganization context raises the same fundamental questions discussed in chapter four and subsequent chapters concerning "economic substance" and substance-over-form principles generally. In reviewing the rest of this chapter, consider how taxpayers would fare if the tax benefits from a reorganization were challenged under section 7701(o). Would taxpayers be able to show that, not taking into account its federal income tax effects, a reorganization changes in a meaningful way their economic position and they have a substantial purpose for entering into it? Or is the economic substance doctrine simply not relevant to the classification of a transaction as a reorganization — as suggested in the Joint Committee's explanation (p. 142) — because the tax benefits of a reorganization are specifically intended by Congress? If this interpretation is correct, can it be reconciled with the fact that *Gregory* — generally viewed as the source of the economic substance doctrine — was a case involving the classification of a transaction as a reorganization?

### 3. *Asset Acquisitions Qualifying as Reorganizations*

This section describes the statutory conditions for reorganization status of three types of asset acquisitions (or transactions treated as asset acquisitions for tax purposes): (1) a merger of the target into the issuing corporation, (2) a forward triangular merger of the target into a subsidiary of the issuing corporation, and (3) an acquisition of substantially all of the properties of the target corporation by the issuing corporation or its subsidiary. Although these acquisitions generally accomplish the same economic goal, they must satisfy different conditions to qualify as reorganizations.

#### a. Merger of Target into Issuing Corporation

Read I.R.C. § 368(a)(1)(A). To qualify as an "A" reorganization, a transaction need only be a "statutory merger or consolidation" and satisfy the nonstatutory requirements previously discussed. The following ruling clarifies the meaning of "statutory merger or consolidation" for reorganization purposes.

## Rev. Rul. 2000-5

2000-1 C.B. 436

. . . Whether a transaction in which (1) a target corporation "merges" under state law with and into an acquiring corporation and the target corporation does not go out of existence, or (2) a target corporation "merges" under state law with and into two or more acquiring corporations and the target corporation goes out of existence, qualifies as a reorganization under § 368(a)(1)(A) of the Internal Revenue Code?

FACTS

Situation (1). A target corporation transfers some of its assets and liabilities to an acquiring corporation, retains the remainder of its assets and liabilities, and remains in existence following the transaction. The target corporation's shareholders receive stock in the acquiring corporation in exchange for part of their target corporation stock and they retain their remaining target corporation stock. The transaction qualifies as a merger under state X corporate law.

Situation (2). A target corporation transfers some of its assets and liabilities to each of two acquiring corporations. The target corporation liquidates and the target corporation's shareholders receive stock in each of the two acquiring corporations in exchange for their target corporation stock. The transaction qualifies as a merger under state X corporate law.

## DISCUSSION

The purpose of the reorganization provisions of the Code is to provide tax-free treatment to certain exchanges incident to readjustments of corporate structures made in one of the specified ways described in the Code. Section 1.368-1(b).... In 1921, Congress defined a reorganization as including "... a merger or consolidation (including the acquisition by one corporation ... of substantially all the properties of another corporation)." In 1934, Congress separated this rule into two distinct provisions. In the predecessor of current § 368(a)(1)(C), an "acquisition by one corporation ... of substantially all the properties of another corporation" continued to be a reorganization where payment was effectuated with the acquiror's voting stock. In the predecessor of current § 368(a)(1)(A), the terms "merger or consolidation" were qualified by requiring that they be "statutory" mergers and consolidations. The word "statutory" was added to the definition of a reorganization so that the definition "will conform more closely to the general requirements of [state] corporation law." ...

Historically, corporate law merger statutes have operated to ensure that "[a] merger ordinarily is an absorption by one corporation of the properties and franchises of another whose stock it has acquired. The merged corporation ceases to exist, and the merging corporation alone survives." ... Thus, unlike § 368(a)(1)(C), in which Congress included a "substantially all the properties" requirement, it was not necessary for Congress to explicitly include a similar requirement in § 368(a)(1)(A) because corporate law merger statutes contemplated an acquisition of the target corporation's assets by the surviving corporation by operation of law.

Compliance with a corporate law merger statute does not by itself qualify a transaction as a reorganization.... In addition to satisfying the requirements of business purpose, continuity of business enterprise and continuity of interest, in order to qualify as a reorganization under § 368(a)(1)(A), a transaction effectuated under a corporate law merger statute must have the result that one corporation acquires the assets of the target corporation by operation of the corporate law merger statute and the target corporation ceases to exist. The transactions described in Situations (1) and (2) do not have the result that one corporation acquires the assets of the target corporation by operation of the corporate law merger statute and the target corporation ceases to exist. Therefore, these transactions do not qualify as reorganizations under § 368(a)(1)(A).

In contrast with the operation of corporate law merger statutes, a divisive transaction is one in which a corporation's assets are divided among two or more corporations. Section 355 provides tax-free treatment for certain divisive transactions, but only if a number of specific requirements are satisfied. Congress intended that § 355 be the sole means under which divisive transactions will be afforded tax-free status and, thus, specifically required the liquidation of the acquired corporation in reorganizations under both §§ 368(a)(1)(C) and 368(a)(1)(D) in order to prevent these reorganizations from being used in divisive transactions that did not satisfy § 355. . . . No specific liquidation requirement was necessary for statutory mergers because corporate law merger statutes contemplated that only one corporation survived a merger. The transaction described in Situation (1) is divisive because, after the transaction, the target corporation's assets and liabilities are held by both the target corporation and acquiring corporation and the target corporation's shareholders hold stock in both the target corporation and acquiring corporation. The transaction described in Situation (2) is divisive because, after the transaction, the target corporation's assets and liabilities are held by each of the two acquiring corporations and the target corporation's shareholders hold stock in each of the two acquiring corporations.

## HOLDING

The transactions described in Situations (1) and (2) do not qualify as reorganizations under § 368(a)(1)(A). However, the transactions described in Situations (1) and (2) possibly may qualify for tax-free treatment under other provisions of the Code.

## *NOTES*

1. *Federal tax meaning of "statutory merger or consolidation."* For many years, the regulations defined a "statutory merger or consolidation" as simply any merger or consolidation effected pursuant to the "corporation laws of the United States or a State or Territory or the District of Columbia." This interpretation necessarily made the important federal tax classification of a "reorganization" dependent upon the vagaries of the corporation laws of those jurisdictions. Rev. Rul. 2000-5 represents an effort to back away from that dependence and to set out specific federal tax law conditions to qualify as a statutory merger or consolidation. Subsequent to the ruling, the Treasury amended its regulations to clarify that an "A" reorganization generally requires a transfer by operation of law of all of the assets and liabilities of a target corporation to a single issuing corporation with the target ceasing to exist following the transfer. Reg. § 1.368-2(b)(1)(ii). Thus, a divisive transaction such as

the one described in Rev. Rul. 2000-5, even though qualifying as a "merger" under an applicable corporate statute, does not constitute an "A" reorganization.

2. *Mergers involving disregarded entities.* The regulations take into account state law developments permitting mergers between an LLC and a corporation or between LLCs. As described in chapter three, a single-member LLC may be disregarded as a separate entity for federal tax purposes with its assets and liabilities treated as belonging to its sole owner. If a disregarded LLC is involved in a statutory merger, the transaction may violate the prohibition against divisive transactions. The same problem can arise even if a merger involves only corporations since a "qualified subchapter S subsidiary" may also qualify as a disregarded entity for federal tax purposes. See I.R.C. § 1361(b)(3).

For example, suppose a disregarded LLC is wholly owned by T corporation. A merger of the LLC with P corporation in which P succeeds to all of the assets and liabilities of the LLC (and the LLC's separate legal existence is terminated) may, nevertheless, constitute a divisive transaction since the LLC's assets and liabilities are treated just prior to the merger as merely a part of T's assets and liabilities. Further, T remains in existence immediately after the merger. Hence, the regulations provide that such a merger does not qualify as an "A" reorganization. See Reg. § 1.368-2(b)(1)(i), (ii), and (iii) (ex. 6).

On the other hand, suppose X corporation merges into a disregarded LLC wholly owned by Y corporation, with the LLC surviving. This transaction may qualify as an "A" reorganization so long as the LLC succeeds to all of the assets and liabilities of X, and X ceases to exist following the transaction. See Reg. § 1.368-2(b)(1)(iii) (ex. 2). In this case, the transaction is not divisive—all of X's assets and liabilities become part of a single acquiring corporation (Y) and X ceases to exist following the transaction. If, however, the LLC is wholly owned by an entity treated as a partnership for federal tax purposes or is itself treated as a partnership, the transaction does not qualify as an "A" reorganization. The reason is that the assets and liabilities of X must become the assets and liabilities of a single entity that is treated as a *corporation* for federal tax purposes. Id. (exs. 5, 7).

The potential qualification of a merger involving an LLC as an "A" reorganization is an important tax law development. Previously, a disadvantage of a "direct" merger of a target into the issuing corporation was the exposure of the latter's assets to the target's liabilities. As a result, it was much more common to carry out a triangular merger between the target and a subsidiary of the issuing corporation. However, as you will soon learn, triangular mergers have more stringent reorganization conditions than direct mergers. A merger of a target into a disregarded LLC of the issuing corporation thus has the benefit of being tested under the more lenient requirements for direct mergers while still achieving separation of the target's liabilities from the issuing corporation's assets.

3. *Post-acquisition restructuring.* Another way to limit exposure of the issuing corporation's assets to the target's liabilities is to transfer the target's assets and liabilities into a new subsidiary of the issuing corporation immediately after the

acquisition. Section 368(a)(2)(C) provides that a subsequent transfer of the target's assets to a corporation controlled by the issuing corporation does not disqualify the transaction as an "A" reorganization. This provision generally eliminates the potential "remote continuity" problem when target shareholders receive stock of a corporation (the issuing corporation) that does not end up having direct ownership of the target's assets or stock. Although the statute provides relief for only certain reorganizations and only with respect to dropdowns of target assets or stock, the regulations have expanded this relief. They generally protect *any* reorganization from disqualification *or recharacterization* as a result of one or more post-acquisition transfers (including certain distributions) of certain assets or stock (including, but not limited to, target assets or stock) as long as the transfer is to members of the issuing corporation's "qualified group" (as defined in the COBE regulations). Reg. § 1.368-2(k)(1). A qualified group generally includes any corporation controlled (within the meaning of section 368(c)) directly or indirectly by the issuing corporation and also effectively includes certain controlled partnerships. Reg. § 1.368-1(d)(4).

Reg. § 1.368-2(k)(1) thus provides a safe harbor against the application of the step-transaction doctrine in order to facilitate post-acquisition restructuring by the issuing corporation. The full implications of this rule have not yet been determined. It is informally referred to as the "First to the Finish Line" rule because it generally respects the first reorganization that is achieved in a transaction. To avoid undermining longstanding IRS positions that recharacterize certain transactions (which we will encounter shortly), the safe harbor does not apply if the post-acquisition transfer is in the form of a liquidating distribution.

4. *Mergers under non-U.S. statutes.* Finally, the regulations sanction a qualifying merger or consolidation pursuant to a non-U.S. statute. Reg. § 1.368-2(b)(1)(iii) (ex. 13). According to the Treasury, despite its longstanding requirement that an "A" reorganization must be effected under a domestic statute, there is no indication in the legislative history that Congress intended such a limitation.

## b. Forward Triangular Merger

A forward triangular merger is a merger of a target corporation into a subsidiary controlled by the issuing corporation, with the subsidiary surviving. This transaction has traditionally been a popular method of carrying out an acquisition because it separates the assets of the issuing corporation from the liabilities of the target, avoids the need to obtain merger approval from the issuing corporation's shareholders, and is generally simpler to transact than an asset acquisition. The statute permits a forward triangular merger to qualify as an "A" reorganization but only under certain conditions. Read I.R.C. § 368(a)(2)(D), Reg. § 1.368-2(b)(2), and the following excerpt explaining the genesis of this provision and its conditions.

## S. Rep. No. 90-1653

90th Cong., 2d Sess. 2-3 (1968)

Present law does not permit the exchange of the stock of the parent in the case of statutory mergers into a subsidiary. Nevertheless, essentially this same result indirectly can be obtained through the combination of two transactions: The first being the acquisition, by a statutory merger, of all of the assets of a corporation by a parent, and the second being the contribution of these assets by the parent to the subsidiary. . . .

[T]he use of the stock of the parent corporation is permitted in the case of [stock or asset acquisitions qualifying as reorganizations]. . . .

Apparently the use of a parent's stock in statutory mergers was not initially provided for because there was no special concern with the problem at the time of the adoption of the 1954 code. However, this is no longer true. The committee understands that a case has arisen in which it is desired to have an operating company merged into an operating subsidiary in exchange for the stock of the parent holding company. The committee agrees . . . that there is no reason why tax-free treatment should be denied in cases of this type where for any reason the parent cannot or, for business or legal reasons, does not want to acquire the assets (even temporarily) through a merger.

For the reasons set forth above . . . it is desirable to permit the use of the stock of the parent corporation in a statutory merger in acquiring a corporation in essentially the same manner as presently is available in the case of other tax-free acquisitions.

. . . The bill permits a corporation which is a controlled subsidiary of another corporation (*i.e.*, the parent holds 80 percent of the voting shares and 80 percent of the total number of shares of all other classes of stock of the subsidiary) to acquire tax free all the assets of a third corporation in a statutory merger in which stock of the *parent* corporation is exchanged for the stock of the transferor corporation. The amendment . . . provides that if a parent corporation controls a subsidiary corporation (*i.e.*, has the 80-percent control referred to above), then the acquisition of substantially all the properties of a corporation merged (in a statutory merger) into the subsidiary in exchange for the stock of the parent corporation is not to be disqualified as a type A reorganization if two conditions are met: (1) the merger insofar as the tax laws are concerned would have qualified as a type A reorganization had the merger been made into the parent instead of into the subsidiary, and (2) no stock of the subsidiary is used in the transaction. In addition, the definition of "a party to a reorganization" is modified to include a parent corporation in the case described (by adding a new sentence to sec. 368(b)).

The amendment does not alter or modify the present requirements of "business purpose" or "continuity of enterprise." It modifies the present "continuity of interest" requirement but only in that it permits the use of the stock of the parent in making the acquisition, instead of the stock of the subsidiary.

The amendment applies whether or not the parent corporation is formed immediately before the merger, in anticipation of the merger, or after preliminary steps were taken to merge directly.

## *NOTES AND QUESTIONS*

1. *Comparison with other acquisitive transactions.* The Senate report explains that a forward triangular merger is economically equivalent to a direct merger into the issuing corporation followed by a dropdown of the target's assets into a subsidiary of the issuing corporation. It is curious, therefore, that these two transactions must satisfy slightly different conditions to qualify as reorganizations. Section 368(a)(2)(D), but not section 368(a)(1)(A), requires a transfer of "substantially all" of the properties of the target corporation in the transaction, the same condition as in a "C" reorganization. Reg. § 1.368-2(b)(2) (fourth sentence). Since a merger is treated for tax purposes as transferring *all* of the target's assets (and liabilities) by operation of law, the principal significance of this condition is to introduce a step-transaction inquiry regarding the effect of dispositions of the target's assets in connection with the merger. The COBE requirement places a similar condition on both types of mergers but its test is generally more lenient than the "substantially all" test. In addition, as explored in note 3 below, the two types of reorganizations have slightly different rules regarding the consideration that may be used in the transaction. The Senate report also notes that other forms of triangular asset and stock acquisitions may qualify as reorganizations but, as we will see, their rules are also different from those governing forward triangular mergers.

2. *The "would have qualified" condition.* Suppose there is no statutory authority for a direct merger of the target corporation into the issuing corporation. Does that mean that a merger of the target into a subsidiary of the issuing corporation cannot qualify as a reorganization under section 368(a)(2)(D)?

3. *Permissible consideration.* What is the effect on reorganization status of the following consideration provided in a forward triangular merger? For purposes of this question, the "acquiring corporation" is the corporation surviving the merger and the "controlling corporation" is a corporation in control of the acquiring corporation.

a. Nonvoting preferred stock issued by the controlling corporation;
b. A 30-year bond issued by the controlling corporation;
c. Cash paid by either the controlling or acquiring corporations;
d. The assumption of certain target liabilities by the controlling or acquiring corporation;
e. Nonvoting common stock or voting preferred stock issued by the acquiring corporation;

f. A 20-year bond or six-month note issued by the acquiring corporation;
g. A 15-year debenture issued by the acquiring corporation that is convertible into voting common stock of that corporation.

4. *Post-merger liquidation of the corporation surviving the merger.* If, immediately following a forward triangular merger and as part of the overall plan, the corporation surviving the merger is liquidated into the issuing corporation, the transaction is treated as an asset acquisition by the issuing corporation. See Rev. Rul. 72-405, 1972-2 C.B. 217. Because the post-acquisition step is a liquidation, Reg. § 1.368-2(k)(1) does not prevent such recharacterization. This is potentially important since it means that the transaction must satisfy the generally more stringent conditions of a "C" reorganization in order to obtain nonrecognition treatment.

## c. Acquisition of Target's Assets

In 1921, Congress permitted certain corporate asset acquisitions, rather than just a merger or consolidation, to qualify as a reorganization. The initial statute, however, did not place any limitation on the type of consideration exchanged in the transaction, arguably permitting a transfer of assets for cash to qualify as a reorganization. This gap was addressed by the Second Circuit in Cortland Specialty Co. v. Comm'r, 60 F.2d 937 (2d Cir. 1932), cert. denied, 288 U.S. 599 (1933), the first case articulating the COI doctrine. To "remove[] the danger that taxable sales can be cast into the form of a reorganization," Congress amended the statute in 1934 to limit the permissible consideration to voting stock of the acquiring corporation. S. REP. NO. 73-558, 73RD CONG., 2D SESS. 16-17 (1934). Oddly, Congress has never addressed the same "gap" in the case of a merger or consolidation.

In carrying out an acquisition, a transfer of assets may be a practical necessity if there is no applicable merger statute. An asset acquisition also permits the parties to select the assets and liabilities to be included in the acquisition. In addition, unlike a merger, an acquisition of assets typically does not require approval to be obtained from the shareholders of the acquiring corporation. Asset acquisitions, however, tend to be more cumbersome than mergers and the conditions for reorganization status are more stringent.

Read I.R.C. § 368(a)(1)(C), (2)(B) and (G), and Reg. § 1.368-2(d). To qualify as a "C" reorganization, a target corporation must transfer substantially all of its properties to another corporation and distribute any consideration received, as well as any properties not transferred, in pursuance of the plan of reorganization (unless the distribution is waived by the Secretary). In addition, the target may generally receive only a limited amount of consideration other than voting stock of the acquiring corporation or a corporation in control of such corporation. The following materials describe the principal conditions for a "C" reorganization in somewhat more detail. Although the regulations now reverse *Bausch & Lomb* (infra p. 403), the case illustrates well how strictly courts have sometimes interpreted the statute in the past.

## Rev. Rul. 88-48

1988-1 C.B. 117

. . . If a transferor corporation sold 50 percent of its historic assets to unrelated parties for cash and immediately afterwards transferred to an acquiring corporation all of its assets (including the cash from the sale), did the subsequent transfer meet the "substantially all" requirement of section 368(a)(1)(C) of the Internal Revenue Code?

### FACTS

*X* and *Y* were unrelated corporations that for many years were engaged in the hardware business. *X* operated two significant lines of business, a retail hardware business and a wholesale plumbing supply business. *Y* desired to acquire and continue to operate *X*'s hardware business but did not desire to acquire the other business. Accordingly, pursuant to an overall plan, the following steps were taken. First, in a taxable transaction, *X* sold its entire interest in the plumbing supply business (constituting 50 percent of its total historic business assets) to purchasers unrelated to either *X* or *Y* or their shareholders. Second, *X* transferred all of its assets, including the cash proceeds from the sale, to *Y* solely for *Y* voting stock and the assumption of *X*'s liabilities. Finally, in pursuance of the plan of reorganization, *X* distributed the *Y* stock (the sole asset *X* then held) to the *X* shareholders in complete liquidation.

Except for the issue relating to the "substantially all" requirement, the transfer of assets from *X* to *Y* constituted a corporate reorganization within the meaning of section 368(a)(1)(C) of the Code.

### LAW AND ANALYSIS

Section 368(a)(1)(C) of the Code defines a corporate reorganization to include the acquisition by one corporation, in exchange solely for all or part of its voting stock, of substantially all the properties of another corporation.

Section 368(a)(1)(C) of the Code is intended to accommodate transactions that are, in effect, mergers, but which fail to meet the statutory requirements that would bring them within section 368(a)(1)(A). . . .

Congress intended that transactions that are divisive in nature not qualify under section 368(a)(1)(C) of the Code. . . . The enactment of section 368(a)(2)(G) indicates the continuing interest in furthering this underlying objective of preventing divisive "C" reorganizations.

Rev. Rul. 57-518, 1957-2 C.B. 253, concerns whether, in a "C" reorganization, assets may be retained to pay liabilities. The ruling states that what constitutes "substantially all" for purposes of section 368(a)(1)(C) of the Code depends on the facts and circumstances in each case. Rev. Rul. 57-518, 1957-2 C.B. 253 exemplifies the Service's longstanding position that where some assets are transferred to the acquiring corporation and other assets retained, then the transaction may be divisive and so fail to meet the "substantially all" requirement of section 368(a)(1)(C). . . .

In the present situation, 50 percent of the *X* assets acquired by *Y* consisted of cash from the sale of one of *X*'s significant historic businesses. Although *Y* acquired substantially all the assets *X* held at the time of transfer, the prior sale prevented *Y* from acquiring substantially all of *X*'s historic business assets. The transaction here at issue, however, was not divisive. The sale proceeds were not retained by the transferor corporation or its shareholders, but were transferred to the acquiring corporation. Moreover, the prior sale of the historic business assets was to unrelated purchasers, and the *X* shareholders retained no interest, direct or indirect, in these assets. Under these circumstances, the "substantially all" requirement of section 368(a)(1)(C) was met because all of the assets of *X* were transferred to *Y*.

## HOLDING

The transfer of all of its assets by *X* to *Y* met the "substantially all" requirement of section 368(a)(1)(C) of the Code, even though immediately prior to the transfer *X* sold 50 percent of its historic business assets to unrelated parties for cash and transferred that cash to *Y* instead of the historic assets.

### *NOTES AND QUESTIONS*

1. *What is "substantially all"?* There is no statutory definition of "substantially all." In 1954, the House proposed to replace the test with a bright-line, "80 percent of the properties" rule, but the Senate rejected the proposal, which was never enacted. In Rev. Rul. 57-518, 1957-2 C.B. 253, the IRS indicated that the nature and amount of any properties retained by a corporation and the purpose of the retention are all considered in determining whether substantially all the properties have been transferred. As explained in Rev. Rul. 88-48, the purpose of the "substantially all" test is to prevent divisive transactions from qualifying as "C" reorganizations. Thus, a failure to transfer some part of the target's business assets is more likely to violate this requirement than the retention of a small amount of cash or liquid assets in order to satisfy remaining target creditors. For advance ruling purposes, "substantially all" means at least 90 percent of the value of the net assets and at least 70 percent of the value of the gross assets of a corporation immediately prior to a transaction. Rev. Proc. 77-37, 1977-2 C.B. 568, 569.

2. *Unwanted assets.* The tax law is very formalistic in determining the consequences of retaining unwanted assets in connection with a purported "C" reorganization. To illustrate, suppose in Rev. Rul. 88-48, the X shareholders wanted to

retain the plumbing business after the transaction (rather than selling it to an unrelated third party) and to transfer only the hardware business to Y. One option would be for X to transfer the plumbing business to Newco (a newly formed subsidiary of X), distribute to its shareholders all of the Newco stock, and then transfer its remaining hardware business to Y. If these steps are treated under step-transaction principles as part of a single overall plan, they will be integrated to determine whether the transfer of the hardware business constitutes substantially all of the properties of X. In other words, X may be treated as still owning both businesses at the time of the transfer of the hardware business to Y. See Helvering v. Elkhorn Coal, 95 F.2d 732 (4th Cir. 1937), cert. denied, 305 U.S. 605 (1938). An alternate plan would be for X to transfer the *hardware* business to Newco, distribute to its shareholders all of the Newco stock, and then have Newco transfer the hardware business to Y. In this case, Newco will be treated as transferring substantially all of its properties to Y, notwithstanding the prior steps and X's continued ownership of the plumbing business. See Rev. Rul. 2003-79, 2003-2 C.B. 80 (conclusion based on implication of recent statutory amendment affecting divisive reorganizations). Chapter twelve considers the tax consequences of the rest of the transaction, including the transfer of assets to Newco and the distribution of Newco stock to the X shareholders.

3. *Comparison with COBE.* As interpreted by Rev. Rul. 88-48, the "substantially all" test is not exactly the same as the COBE doctrine. How might you change the facts in Rev. Rul. 88-48 to cause the transaction potentially to flunk COBE while still satisfying the substantially all requirement?

## Bausch & Lomb Optical Co. v. Commissioner

267 F.2d 75 (2d Cir. 1959)

MEDINA, Circuit Judge.

Petitioner Bausch & Lomb Optical Company, a New York corporation engaged in the manufacture and sale of ophthalmic products, on March 1, 1950 owned 9923 1/4 shares of the stock of its subsidiary Riggs Optical Company, or 79.9488% of the 12,412 outstanding shares of Riggs. In order to effectuate certain operating economies, Bausch & Lomb decided to amalgamate Riggs with itself. To this end on April 22, 1950 Bausch & Lomb exchanged 105,508 shares of its unissued voting stock for all of the Riggs assets. An additional 433 shares of Bausch & Lomb stock went to 12 Riggs' employees.

On May 2, 1950, according to a prearranged plan, Riggs dissolved itself, distributing its only asset, Bausch & Lomb stock, pro rata to its shareholders. Bausch & Lomb thus received back 84,347 of its own shares which became treasury stock, while 21,161 shares went to the Riggs minority shareholders.

The Commissioner determined that the substance of these transactions was that Bausch & Lomb received the Riggs assets partly in exchange for its Riggs stock and partly for its own stock, and that the gain which Bausch & Lomb realized upon the

Riggs "liquidation" was subject to tax. In other words, that Bausch & Lomb parted with 21,161 shares of its own voting stock, plus 9923 1/4 shares of its Riggs stock, for the transfer to it of all of the Riggs assets. Bausch & Lomb contends, however, that a "reorganization" was effected under [section 368(a)(1)(C)] and that it is therefore entitled to tax-free treatment. The Tax Court sustained the Commissioner's position and held that the acquisition of the Riggs assets and the dissolution of Riggs must be viewed together, and that the surrender by Bausch & Lomb of its Riggs stock was additional consideration. The Tax Court accordingly held that the Riggs assets were not obtained "solely for all or a part of its voting stock." We agree.

Bausch & Lomb concedes that to qualify as a "C" reorganization, it could not furnish any additional consideration over and above its own stock. . . . Moreover, Bausch & Lomb admits, as the correspondence and minutes of pertinent meetings plainly show, that the acquisition of the Riggs assets and the dissolution of Riggs were both part of the same plan. Nevertheless, Bausch & Lomb asserts that the exchange of the Riggs assets for its stock should be treated as separate and distinct from the dissolution. The argument runs to the effect that, if the two steps are viewed apart from one another, a "C" reorganization is effected.

Petitioner contends that, even if a qualification according to the literal terms of [section 368(a)(1)(C)] is not found, the amalgamation was in substance a "reorganization" because it has the attributes of one, including "continuity of interest" and business purpose. This is factually not quite true for, while the amalgamation may have been for genuine business reasons, the division into two steps served only to facilitate the liquidation of Riggs. It was considered easier to distribute Bausch & Lomb stock than distribute the Riggs assets. Hence the "business purpose" of dividing the liquidation into two steps lends no support to Bausch & Lomb's contention that in substance and actuality a reorganization was achieved. Moreover, the Congress has defined in [section 368(a)(1)(C)] how a reorganization thereunder may be effected, and the only question for us to decide, on this phase of the case, is whether the necessary requirements have been truly fulfilled. It is for the Congress and not for us to say whether some other alleged equivalent set of facts should receive the same tax free status.

Nor does the fact that Bausch & Lomb may well have desired to hold the 84,347 shares of its own voting shares as treasury stock change our opinion of the transaction as a whole.

Bausch & Lomb suggests that under our present holding even if it had but a 1% interest in Riggs, the requirement that the acquisition be "solely for . . . its voting stock" could defeat [section 368(a)(1)(C)] reorganization treatment. This hypothesis is a far cry from the facts disclosed in this record, and the lack of controlling interest surrounds it with a mist of unreality. In any event, it will be time to consider such a situation in all its aspects when, as and if it comes before us. We merely hold that the attempt to thwart taxation in this case by carrying out the liquidation process in two steps instead of one fell short of meeting the requirements of a "C" reorganization. . . .

Of course, the fact that Bausch & Lomb "could have" merged with Riggs and hence qualified the transaction as a reorganization under [section 368(a)(1)(A)] is beside the point. For reasons of its own it chose not to do so. This is clearly not an "A" reorganization.

Bausch & Lomb also claims that a tax-free liquidation was effected under [section 332], although it plainly lacked the necessary 80% of the voting stock. This belabored effort to claim ownership of the 51 shares of Riggs voting stock for which 12 of Riggs' employees had received credit on Riggs' books, so as to raise Bausch & Lomb's interest slightly above the 80% required . . . has nothing whatever to commend it. As found by the Tax Court, Bausch & Lomb never was the legal or equitable owner of these shares, there was never any agreement on the part of the employees to assign them to Bausch & Lomb, and the original stock purchase agreements of the Riggs employees provided that if Riggs should be reorganized and its business acquired by another corporation, a successor corporation would have the right to assume the contract and substitute its stock in the place of the Riggs' stock originally reserved under the stock purchase agreements. New arrangements were made later, in line with the provision of the original stock purchase agreements just referred to, and the employees received certain cash payments and the 433 shares of Bausch & Lomb stock mentioned in the opening part of this opinion. We find in the facts of this case no foundation whatever for the claim that a liquidation was effected under [section 332]. . . .

## *NOTES AND QUESTIONS*

1. *Planning around* Bausch & Lomb. Suppose that prior to its acquisition of the assets of Riggs, Bausch & Lomb (B&L) formed a new subsidiary, Newco, to acquire the Riggs assets in exchange for B&L voting stock. Immediately following the acquisition, Riggs distributes the B&L voting stock to its shareholders (B&L and the minority Riggs shareholders) in complete liquidation. How would this transaction have been taxed?

2. *If the facts had been just* slightly *different.* Consider how the *Bausch & Lomb* transaction would have been taxed under the court's reasoning if the following alternative facts had existed prior to the proposed combination of the two corporations:

a. B&L had owned 20 percent or less of Riggs.
b. B&L had owned 80 percent or more of Riggs.

3. *Current law.* Regulation § 1.368-2(d)(4) reverses the outcome of the *Bausch & Lomb* transaction under certain circumstances. Had this regulation been in effect, what would have been the tax consequences of the transaction under the following alternative facts:

a. B&L's ownership of its Riggs' stock was "old and cold," Riggs had no liabilities, and, instead of receiving 21,161 shares of B&L voting stock in the dissolution of Riggs, the minority Riggs shareholders received only 2,000 shares of B&L voting stock with the balance in cash; B&L furnished both the stock and cash when it acquired the Riggs' assets.

b. B&L acquired its Riggs' stock for cash as part of its plan to acquire the assets of Riggs.

**Problem 11-2:** T corporation has $1,100x gross assets and $1,000x liabilities outstanding. P corporation would like to acquire T for P voting stock in a "C" reorganization. Which of the following transactions is most likely to qualify as a reorganization? Why?

(a) T transfers $100x assets to P for P voting stock, and T retains the remaining $1,000x assets to pay off its creditors.
(b) T transfers $1,100x assets to P in exchange for $100x P voting stock and P's assumption of all of T's liabilities. See Reg. § 1.368-2(d)(1).
(c) T uses $1,000x of its assets to pay off its creditors, and then T transfers its remaining $100x assets to P for P voting stock.
(d) T transfers $1,100x assets to P for $100x P voting stock and $1,000x cash, and T then uses the cash to pay off its creditors.
(e) T transfers $1,100x assets to P for $1,100x P voting stock, and T pays off its creditors with $1,000x of the P stock. See I.R.C. §§ 368(a)(2)(G)(i), 361(c)(1) and (3).
(f) T transfers $1,100x assets to P for $1,100x P voting stock, T sells $1,000x of the stock for $1,000x cash, and T then uses the cash to pay off its creditors. See I.R.C. § 358(a)(1).

**Problem 11-3:** T corporation has $650x operating assets, $250x investment assets, $100x cash, and liabilities of $350x. Determine which of the following transactions involving the acquisition of T's assets by P corporation would constitute a reorganization. GP is a corporation that controls P. Assume in each case that the "distribution" requirement is met.

(a) P acquires all of T's operating assets for P voting stock worth $650x.
(b) Same as (a) except that the consideration consists of P voting stock worth $50x and GP voting stock worth $600x.
(c) P acquires all of T's assets in exchange for P voting stock worth $600x, P nonvoting stock worth $50x, and P's assumption of all of T's liabilities.
(d) Same as (c) except that all of the P stock is voting stock.
(e) P acquires all of T's assets in exchange for GP voting stock worth $650x and the assumption (partly by P and partly by GP) of all of T's liabilities.

### 4. *Stock Acquisitions Qualifying as Reorganizations*

This section describes the conditions for reorganization status of (1) an acquisition of a target corporation's stock by the issuing corporation or its subsidiary, and (2) a reverse triangular merger of a subsidiary of the issuing corporation into a target corporation, with the target surviving (discussed more fully later). In general, these two types of transactions represent alternate ways of acquiring the stock of a target corporation. A stock acquisition preserves the separate corporate existence of the target and, therefore, does not intermingle its assets and liabilities with those of the acquiring corporation. Other differences exist between a stock and asset acquisition, including a possible difference in state transfer tax liability. As the following material shows, the reorganization requirements for these two types of stock acquisitions differ from one another (as well as from those applicable to the types of asset acquisitions described in the previous section).

#### a. Acquisition of Target's Stock

Read I.R.C. § 368(a)(1)(B) and Reg. § 1.368-2(c). In a "B" reorganization, the issuing corporation (or its subsidiary) acquires stock of the target corporation solely for voting stock of the issuing corporation and, immediately after the acquisition, the acquiring corporation controls the target. The "B" reorganization does not have a "substantially all" requirement, which gives the target flexibility (within the parameters of COBE) to dispose of unwanted assets prior to the acquisition. Traditionally, a stock acquisition carried out through a tender offer to the target's shareholders has presented practical difficulties because of the "hold-up" potential if some of the shareholders are unwilling to exchange their stock. Many states have now adopted "share exchange" provisions to allow a tender offer to be approved by just a majority or supermajority of the target's shareholders. This added flexibility under corporate law is, however, a mixed blessing for tax purposes, since a "B" reorganization is generally subject to the most stringent conditions of any reorganization.

**Chapman v. Commissioner**

618 F.2d 856 (1st Cir. 1980)

LEVIN H. CAMPBELL, Circuit Judge.

. . . Appellees were among the more than 17,000 shareholders of the Hartford Fire Insurance Company who exchanged their Hartford stock for shares of the voting stock of International Telephone and Telegraph Corporation pursuant to a formal exchange offer from ITT dated May 26, 1970. On their 1970 tax returns, appellees did not report any gain or loss from these exchanges. Subsequently, the Internal Revenue Service assessed deficiencies. . . . The Tax Court, with five judges dissenting, granted appellees' motion for summary judgment, and the Commissioner of Internal Revenue filed this appeal.

The events giving rise to this dispute began in 1968, when the management of ITT, a large multinational corporation, became interested in acquiring Hartford as part of a program of diversification. In October 1968, ITT executives approached Hartford about the possibility of merging the two corporations. This proposal was spurned by Hartford, which at the time was considering acquisitions of its own. In November 1968, ITT learned that approximately 1.3 million shares of Hartford, representing some 6 percent of Hartford's voting stock, were available for purchase from a mutual fund. After assuring Hartford's directors that ITT would not attempt to acquire Hartford against its will, ITT consummated the $63.7 million purchase from the mutual fund with Hartford's blessing. From November 13, 1968 to January 10, 1969, ITT also made a series of purchases on the open market totalling 458,000 shares which it acquired for approximately $24.4 million. A further purchase of 400 shares from an ITT subsidiary in March 1969 brought ITT's holdings to about 8 percent of Hartford's outstanding stock, all of which had been bought for cash.

In the midst of this flurry of stock-buying, ITT submitted a written proposal to the Hartford Board of Directors for the merger of Hartford into an ITT subsidiary, based on an exchange of Hartford stock for ITT's $2 cumulative convertible voting preferred stock. Received by Hartford in December of 1968, the proposal was rejected in February of 1969. A counterproposal by Hartford's directors led to further negotiations, and on April 9, 1969 a provisional plan and agreement of merger was executed by the two corporations. While not unlike the proposal Hartford had earlier rejected, this plan was somewhat more favorable to Hartford's stockholders. The merger agreement was conditioned upon approval, as required under state law, by the shareholders of the two corporations and by the Connecticut Insurance Commissioner. In addition, Hartford had an unqualified right to terminate the agreement if it believed there was any likelihood that antitrust litigation would be initiated. Although such litigation in fact materialized, Hartford's board of directors pushed ahead with the merger, and in October 1969 a Justice Department motion to enjoin the merger was denied by the United States District Court for the District of Connecticut.

Meanwhile, on April 15, 1969, attorneys for the parties sought a ruling from the IRS that the proposed transaction would constitute a reorganization under Section 368(a)(1)(B) of the Internal Revenue Code of 1954, so that, among other things, gain realized on the exchange by Hartford shareholders would not be recognized, see 26 U.S.C. § 354(a)(1). By private letter ruling, the Service notified the parties on October 13, 1969 that the proposed merger would constitute a nontaxable reorganization, provided ITT unconditionally sold its 8 percent interest in Hartford to a third party before Hartford's shareholders voted to approve or disapprove the proposal. On October 21, the Service ruled that a proposed sale of the stock to Mediobanca, an Italian bank, would satisfy this condition, and such a sale was made on November 9.

On November 10, 1969, the shareholders of Hartford approved the merger, which had already won the support of ITT's shareholders in June. On December 13, 1969, however, the merger plan ground to a halt, as the Connecticut Insurance Commissioner refused to endorse the arrangement. ITT then proposed to proceed with a voluntary exchange offer to the shareholders of Hartford on essentially the same terms they would have obtained under the merger plan. After public hearings and the imposition of certain requirements on the post-acquisition operation of Hartford, the insurance commissioner approved the exchange offer on May 23, 1970, and three days later ITT submitted the exchange offer to all Hartford shareholders. More than 95 percent of Hartford's outstanding stock was exchanged for shares of ITT's $2.25 cumulative convertible voting preferred stock. The Italian bank to which ITT had conveyed its original 8 percent interest was among those tendering shares, as were the taxpayers in this case.

In March 1974, the Internal Revenue Service retroactively revoked its ruling approving the sale of Hartford stock to Mediobanca, on the ground that the request on which the ruling was based had misrepresented the nature of the proposed sale. Concluding that the entire transaction no longer constituted a nontaxable reorganization, the Service assessed tax deficiencies against a number of former Hartford shareholders who had accepted the exchange offer. Appellees, along with other taxpayers, contested this action in the Tax Court, where the case was decided on appellees' motion for summary judgment. For purposes of this motion, the taxpayers conceded that questions of the merits of the revocation of the IRS rulings were not to be considered; the facts were to be viewed as though ITT had not sold the shares previously acquired for cash to Mediobanca. The taxpayers also conceded, solely for purposes of their motion for summary judgment, that the initial cash purchases of Hartford stock had been made for the purpose of furthering ITT's efforts to acquire Hartford. . . .

Taxpayers advanced two arguments in support of their motion for summary judgment. Their first argument related to the severability of the cash purchases from the 1970 exchange offer. Because 14 months had elapsed between the last of the cash purchases and the effective date of the exchange offer, and because the cash purchases were not part of the formal plan of reorganization entered into by ITT and Hartford, the taxpayers argued that the 1970 exchange offer should be examined in isolation to determine whether it satisfied the terms of Section 368(a)(1)(B) of the 1954 Code. The Service countered that the two sets of transactions — the cash purchases and the exchange offer — were linked by a common acquisitive purpose, and that they should be considered together for the purpose of determining whether the arrangement met the statutory requirement that the stock of the acquired corporation be exchanged "solely for . . . voting stock" of the acquiring corporation. . . .

For purposes of the second argument, the taxpayers conceded *arguendo* that the 1968 and 1969 cash purchases should be considered "parts of the 1970 exchange offer reorganization." Even so, they insisted upon a right to judgment on the basis that the 1970 exchange of stock for stock satisfied the statutory requirements for a reorganization without regard to the presence of related cash purchases. The Tax

Court agreed with the taxpayers, holding that the 1970 exchange in which ITT acquired more than 80 percent of Hartford's single class of stock for ITT voting stock satisfied the requirements of Section 368(a)(1)(B), so that no gain or loss need be recognized on the exchange under Section 354(a)(1). The sole issue on appeal is whether the Tax Court was correct in so holding.

. . . Section 354(a)(1) . . . provides that gain or loss shall not be recognized if stock or securities in a corporation are, in pursuance of the plan of reorganization, exchanged solely for stock or securities in another corporation which is a party to the reorganization. . . . Section 354(a)(1) does not apply to an exchange unless the exchange falls within one of the six categories of "reorganization" defined in Section 368(a)(1). The category relevant to the transactions involved in this case is defined in Section 368(a)(1)(B):

> "(T)he term 'reorganization' means—
>
> (B) the acquisition by one corporation, in exchange solely for all or a part of its voting stock . . . of stock of another corporation if, immediately after the acquisition, the acquiring corporation has control of such other corporation (whether or not such acquiring corporation had control immediately before the acquisition)."

The concept of "control" is defined in Section 368(c) as "the ownership of stock possessing at least 80 percent of the total combined voting power of all classes of stock entitled to vote and at least 80 percent of the total number of shares of all other classes of stock of the corporation." Subsection (B) thus establishes two basic requirements for a valid, tax-free stock-for-stock reorganization. First, "the acquisition" of another's stock must be "solely for . . . voting stock." Second, the acquiring corporation must have control over the other corporation immediately after the acquisition.

The single issue raised on this appeal is whether "the acquisition" in this case complied with the requirement that it be "solely for . . . voting stock." It is well settled that the "solely" requirement is mandatory; if any part of "the acquisition" includes a form of consideration other than voting stock, the transaction will not qualify as a (B) reorganization. See Helvering v. Southwest Consolidated Corp., 315 U.S. 194, 198 (1942) ("'Solely' leaves no leeway. Voting stock plus some other consideration does not meet the statutory requirement."). The precise issue before us is thus how broadly to read the term "acquisition." The Internal Revenue Service argues that "the acquisition . . . of stock of another corporation" must be understood to encompass the 1968-69 cash purchases as well as the 1970 exchange offer. If the IRS is correct, "the acquisition" here fails as a (B) reorganization. The taxpayers, on the other hand, would limit "the acquisition" to the part of a sequential transaction of this nature which meets the requirements of subsection (B). They argue that the 1970 exchange of stock for stock was itself an "acquisition" by ITT of stock in Hartford solely in exchange for ITT's voting stock, such that after the exchange took place ITT controlled Hartford. Taxpayers contend that the earlier cash purchases of 8 percent, even if conceded to be part of the same acquisitive plan, are essentially irrelevant to the tax-free reorganization otherwise effected.

The Tax Court accepted the taxpayers' reading of the statute. . . . The plurality opinion stated its "narrow" holding as follows:

> "We hold that where, as is the case herein, 80 percent or more of the stock of a corporation is acquired in one transaction, in exchange for which only voting stock is furnished as consideration, the 'solely for voting stock' requirement of section 368(a)(1)(B) is satisfied."

The plurality treated as "irrelevant" the 8 percent of Hartford's stock purchased for cash, although the opinion left somewhat ambiguous the question whether the 8 percent was irrelevant because of the 14-month time interval separating the transactions or because the statute was not concerned with transactions over and above those mathematically necessary to the acquiring corporation's attainment of control.

II.

For reasons set forth extensively in section III of this opinion, we do not accept the position adopted by the Tax Court. Instead we side with the Commissioner on the narrow issue presented in this appeal, that is, the correctness of taxpayers' so-called "second" argument premised on an assumed relationship between the cash and stock transactions. As explained below, we find a strong implication in the language of the statute, in the legislative history, in the regulations, and in the decisions of other courts that cash purchases which are concededly "parts of" a stock-for-stock exchange must be considered constituent elements of the "acquisition" for purposes of applying the "solely for . . . voting stock" requirement of Section 368(a)(1)(B). We believe the presence of non-stock consideration in such an acquisition, regardless of whether such consideration is necessary to the gaining of control, is inconsistent with treatment of the acquisition as a nontaxable reorganization. It follows for purposes of taxpayers' second argument which was premised on the assumption that the cash transactions were part of the 1970 exchange offer reorganization that the stock transfers in question would not qualify for nonrecognition of gain or loss. . . .

III. A.

Having summarized in advance our holding, and its intended scope, we shall now revert to the beginning of our analysis, and, in the remainder of this opinion, describe the thinking by which we reached the result just announced. We begin with the words of the statute itself. The reorganization definitions contained in Section 368(a)(1) are precise, technical, and comprehensive. They were intended to define the exclusive means by which nontaxable corporate reorganizations could be effected. . . . In examining the language of the (B) provision, we discern two possible meanings. On the one hand, the statute could be read to say that a successful reorganization occurs whenever Corporation X exchanges its own voting stock for stock in Corporation Y, and, immediately after the transaction, Corporation X controls more than 80 percent of Y's stock. On this reading, purchases of shares for which any part of the consideration takes the form of "boot" should be ignored, since the definition is only concerned with transactions which meet the statutory requirements as to consideration and control. To take an example, if Corporation X bought 50 percent of the shares of Y, and then almost immediately exchanged part of its voting stock for the remaining 50 percent of Y's stock, the question would arise whether the second transaction was a (B) reorganization. Arguably, the statute can be read to support such a finding. In the second transaction, X exchanged only stock for stock (meeting the "solely" requirement), and after the transaction was completed X owned Y (meeting the "control" requirement).

The alternative reading of the statute — the one which we are persuaded to adopt — treats the (B) definition as prescriptive, rather than merely descriptive. We read the statute to mean that the entire transaction which constitutes "the acquisition" must not contain any nonstock consideration if the transaction is to qualify as a (B) reorganization. In the example given above, where X acquired 100 percent of Y's stock, half for cash and half for voting stock, we would interpret "the acquisition" as referring to the entire transaction, so that the "solely for . . . voting stock" requirement would not be met. We believe if Congress had intended the statute to be read as merely descriptive, this intent would have been more clearly spelled out in the statutory language.[2]

We recognize that the Tax Court adopted neither of these two readings. For reasons to be discussed in connection with the legislative history which follows, the Tax Court purported to limit its holding to cases, such as this one, where more than 80 percent of the stock of Corporation Y passes to Corporation X in exchange solely for voting stock. The Tax Court presumably would assert that the 50/50 hypothetical posited above can be distinguished from this case, and that its holding implies no view as to the hypothetical. The plurality opinion recognized that the position it adopted creates no small problem with respect to the proper reading of "the acquisition" in the statutory definition. In order to distinguish the 80 percent case from the 50 percent case, it is necessary to read "the acquisition" as referring to at least the amount of stock constituting "control" (80 percent) where related cash purchases are present. Yet the Tax Court recognized that "the acquisition" cannot always refer to the conveyance of an 80 percent bloc of stock in one transaction, since to do so would

2. For example, Congress could have used the word "any" rather than the word "the" before "acquisition" in the first line of the (B) definition. This would have tended to negate the implication that this definition prescribes the conditions a transaction *must* meet to qualify, rather than simply describing that part of a transaction which is entitled to the statutory tax deferral.

frustrate the intent of the 1954 amendments to permit so-called "creeping acquisitions."[3]

The Tax Court's interpretation of the statute suffers from a more fundamental defect, as well. In order to justify the limitation of its holding to transactions involving 80 percent or more of the acquiree's stock, the Tax Court focused on the *passage* of control as the primary requirement of the (B) provision. This focus is misplaced. Under the present version of the statute, the *passage* of control is entirely irrelevant; the only material requirement is that the acquiring corporation *have* control immediately after the acquisition. As the statute explicitly states, it does not matter if the acquiring corporation already has control before the transaction begins, so long as such control exists at the completion of the reorganization. Whatever talismanic quality may have attached to the *acquisition* of control under previous versions of the Code . . . is altogether absent from the version we must apply to this case. In our view, the statute should be read to mean that the related transactions that constitute "the acquisition," whatever percentage of stock they may represent, must meet both the "solely for voting stock" and the "control immediately after" requirements of Section 368(a)(1)(B). Neither the reading given the statute by the Tax Court, nor that proposed as the first alternative above, adequately corresponds to the careful language Congress employed in this section of the Code. . . .

## *NOTES AND QUESTIONS*

1. *The aftermath of* Chapman. Following the decision in *Chapman*, the IRS reached agreement with IT&T to settle the seven-year controversy over the tax status of IT&T's 1970 acquisition of Hartford. IT&T agreed to pay $18.5 million to the government, which in turn agreed not to pursue tax claims against former Hartford shareholders who exchanged their shares for IT&T shares in 1970 and consistently treated the exchange as nontaxable. The agreement permitted the government to continue litigation only against those former Hartford shareholders who treated the exchange as nontaxable in 1970 but who subsequently sold their IT&T stock and claimed a fair market value (as of 1970) basis in their stock in calculating their taxable gain or loss from the sale. The settlement ended all pending IT&T-financed and controlled tax litigation — more than 1,000 cases pending in the Tax Court and over 17,000 other cases pending in various stages of administrative appeal — instituted by former Hartford shareholders against the government.

3. . . . In the typical creeping acquisition situation, Corporation X acquires a portion of Corporation Y's stock, let us say 40 percent, for cash or other nonstock consideration. If (B) reorganizations were limited to those encompassing 80 percent or more of Y's stock in one transaction, X would thereafter be barred, as a practical matter, from acquiring the remainder of Y's shares in a tax-free (B) reorganization. The 1954 Code, however, clearly permits X to trade voting stock for 40 percent or more of Y's remaining stock so long as the stock acquisition is sufficiently separated from the prior cash purchase. . . . In these circumstances, therefore, "the acquisition" must be interpreted as referring to an amount of stock less than 80 percent.

2. *Did the court get it right?* What aspects of the legislative history might help shed light on the validity of the taxpayer's position in *Chapman*?

3. *The unforgiving nature of a "B" reorganization. Chapman* illustrates the difficulty in qualifying a transaction as a "B" reorganization. Moreover, in Turnbow v. Comm'r, 368 U.S. 337 (1961), the Supreme Court had previously held that if "B" status is flunked in a stock-for-stock exchange, then the gain in the exchange must be recognized *in full*, and not just to the extent of any boot received. In other words, the presence of *any* consideration in the transaction other than voting stock will cause the entire stock-for-stock exchange to be taxable. The following material describes some of the important areas in which the IRS has found that use of nonqualifying consideration does *not* violate the "solely for voting stock" test, although many of the distinctions drawn may be hard to defend.

a. *Acquiring interests other than target stock.* In Rev. Rul. 98-10, 1998-1 C.B. 643, the IRS concluded that debentures of the issuing corporation used to acquire debentures held by the target's bondholders did not cause an accompanying stock-for-stock exchange to violate the "solely for voting stock" requirement. Some target bondholders were also stockholders but a substantial portion of the debentures were held by persons who owned no stock. This fact was important because it ensured that the debentures issued by the issuing corporation represented the fair value of the target debentures alone, and were not indirect, nonqualifying consideration paid for target stock. See also Rev. Rul. 70-269, 1970-1 C.B. 82 (substitution of options to acquire issuing corporation stock for substantially identical options to acquire target stock did not violate solely test).
b. *Paying expenses solely and directly related to reorganization.* In Rev. Rul. 73-54, 1973-1 C.B. 188, an issuing corporation's use of nonqualifying consideration to pay expenses of the target corporation and its shareholders did not violate the "solely for voting stock" requirement where the expenses were solely and directly related to the reorganization. Qualifying expenses included legal, accounting, and appraisal fees, administrative costs directly related to the reorganization, security underwriting and registration fees, transfer taxes, and transfer agents' fees. Since these expenses were directly related to the reorganization, the ruling reasoned that the payment did not constitute consideration for the target's stock or property. The holding of this ruling is, however, limited. Expenses *not* treated as solely and directly related to the reorganization include shareholders' fees for investment or estate planning advice, state transfer taxes solely belonging to shareholders, and fees for legal, accounting, or investment advice pertaining to shareholder participation in the reorganization.
c. *Source other than issuing corporation (or members of its affiliated group).* In general, the "solely for voting stock" requirement is not violated if the source of any nonqualifying consideration is not the issuing corporation (or members of its affiliated group). Compare Rev. Rul. 70-172, 1970-1 C.B. 77

(distribution by target to its shareholder immediately prior to stock-for-stock exchange did not violate test) with Rev. Rul. 75-360, 1975-2 C.B. 110 (target's cash redemption prior to stock-for-stock exchange violated test where source of funds for the redemption could be traced to the issuing corporation). This distinction has been relied upon to allow cash payments to dissenting shareholders of the target corporation, but only if made by the target. See Rev. Rul. 68-285, 1968-1 C.B. 147 (payments by target did not violate test); Rev. Rul. 73-102, 1973-1 C.B. 186 (payments by issuing corporation violated test). See also Rev. Rul. 68-562, 1968-2 C.B. 157 (cash purchase of target stock by 90 percent individual shareholder of issuing corporation not acting on behalf of that corporation did not violate test); Rev. Rul. 85-139, 1985-2 C.B. 123 (cash paid by subsidiary of issuing corporation violated test).

d. *Payments in lieu of fractional shares*. Nonqualifying consideration paid in lieu of fractional voting shares of the issuing corporation, which does not represent separately bargained-for consideration, does not violate the "solely" test. See Rev. Rul. 66-365, 1966-2 C.B. 116.

4. *Creeping acquisitions*. Step-transaction principles determine the effect for "B" reorganization purposes of stock acquisitions taking place over a period of time. The regulations describe the possible integration of transactions occurring "over a relatively short period of time such as 12 months," and the possible separation of events that are 16 years apart. Reg. § 1.368-2(c). Assuming that a taxpayer would like to establish the existence of a "B" reorganization, under what circumstances might the taxpayer argue that nominally distinct stock acquisitions should be integrated or, alternatively, should be treated as separate transactions?

5. *Recharacterization*. In Rev. Rul. 67-274, 1967-2 C.B. 141, the IRS held that an acquisition of all of the target's stock followed by a liquidation of the target into the acquiring corporation as part of the overall plan constitutes an asset acquisition rather than a stock acquisition. Accordingly, reorganization status of the transaction depended upon satisfying the requirements for a "C" rather than "B" reorganization. Importantly, Reg. § 1.368-2(k)(1) does not prevent such recharacterization, since the subsequent step is a liquidation. Recharacterization as a purported "C" reorganization may be either a blessing (for example, because of the boot relaxation rule) or a curse (for example, because of the "substantially all" requirement).

**Problem 11-4:** P corporation would like to acquire all of the stock of T corporation. S corporation, a wholly-owned subsidiary of P, owns 25 percent of the T stock and the rest is owned by unrelated parties. As part of an overall plan to acquire T, S distributes its T stock to P and P acquires the remaining T stock solely for P voting stock. Does this transaction qualify as a "B" reorganization? Does it matter whether the distribution by S is an ordinary one, a redemption, or in liquidation of S?

### b. Reverse Triangular Merger

In a reverse triangular merger, a subsidiary of the issuing corporation is merged into the target corporation, with the target surviving. In the merger, the target shareholders receive consideration consisting of stock of the issuing corporation in exchange for all of their target shares, and the target becomes a wholly-owned subsidiary of the issuing corporation. This transaction is an alternate way of acquiring the stock of the target corporation and is treated under certain conditions as an "A" reorganization. Read I.R.C. § 368(a)(2)(E), Reg. § 1.368-2(j), and the following excerpt from the legislative history to understand the origin and initial conditions of section 368(a)(2)(E).

## S. Rep. No. 91-1533

91st Cong., 2d Sess. 2-3 (1970)

[U]nder [section 368(a)(2)(D)], corporation X . . . may be merged into corporation S (a subsidiary) in exchange for the stock in corporation P (the parent of S) in a tax-free statutory merger. However, if for business and legal reasons (wholly unrelated to Federal income taxation) it is considered more desirable to merge S into X (rather than merging X into S), so that X is the surviving corporation — a "reverse merger" — the transaction is not a tax-free statutory merger.

Although the reverse merger does not qualify as a tax-free statutory merger, it may, in appropriate circumstances, be treated as tax-free as a stock-for-stock reorganization (subparagraph (B)). However, in order to qualify as a tax-free stock-for-stock reorganization it is necessary that the acquisition be *solely* for voting stock and that no stock be acquired for cash or other consideration. Thus, if a small amount of the stock of X . . . is acquired for cash before the merger of S into X, there often may be doubt as to whether or not the transaction will meet the statutory requirements of a stock-for-stock reorganization.

The committee agrees with the House, that there is no reason why a merger in one direction (S into X in the above example) should be taxable, when the merger in the other direction (X into S), under identical circumstances, is tax-free. Moreover, it sees no reason why in cases of this type the acquisition needs to be made solely for stock. For these reasons the amendment makes statutory mergers tax-free in the circumstances described above.

. . . The bill amends the tax laws to permit a tax-free statutory merger of one corporation into another when stock of the corporation in control (here called the "controlling corporation") of the merged corporation is given in the transaction to the shareholders of the survivor corporation in exchange for their stock. Under the new provision (sec. 368(a)(2)(E)) such a statutory merger may be a tax-free reorganization if it meets several conditions.

First, the corporation surviving the merger must hold substantially all of its own properties and substantially all of the properties of the merged corporation (except stock of the controlling corporation distributed in the transaction).

Second, in the transaction, former shareholders of the surviving corporation must receive voting stock of the controlling corporation in exchange for an amount of stock representing control in the surviving corporation. Control for this purpose (defined in sec. 368(c)) means that the amount of stock in the surviving corporation surrendered for voting stock of the controlling corporation must represent stock possessing at least 80 percent of the total combined voting power (in the surviving corporation), and also stock amounting to at least 80 percent of the total number of shares of all other classes of stock (in the surviving corporation). If voting stock of the controlling corporation is used in the exchange to the extent described, additional stock in the surviving corporation may be acquired for cash or other property (whether or not from the shareholders who received voting stock). Of course, this additional stock in the surviving corporation need not be acquired by the controlling corporation.

The amendment applies not only when the only assets of the merged corporation are the nominal capital required to organize it and the stock of its parent which is to be used in the merger exchange but also when the corporation has substantial properties.

In discussions on this bill, the Treasury Department has expressed concern that the corporate reorganization provisions need review and modification. The committee in agreeing to this amendment does not intend to foreclose consideration of any substantive changes which the Treasury may propose in the corporate reorganization provisions in any future presentations. . . .

*NOTES*

1. *Comparison with other acquisitions.* Once again, Congress enacted a new category of reorganization with different conditions, despite its apparent appreciation of the economic similarities of the various acquisition patterns. Rather than simply relaxing the rigidity of a "B" reorganization, Congress created a new, "B"-equivalent, category with generally more relaxed requirements. Thus far, the sporadic attempts since 1970 to respond to the Senate committee's invitation to reform the reorganization provisions have been unsuccessful.

2. *Conditions.* As explained in the committee report, there are two principal conditions for a transaction to qualify as an "A" reorganization by reason of section 368(a)(2)(E). First, the surviving corporation after the merger must hold substantially all of its properties and those of the merged corporation. This requirement, determined separately for each of the two corporations, has the same meaning as in a "C" reorganization; thus, it introduces the same step-transaction inquiry regarding the effect of dispositions of property in connection with the merger. For purposes of

this test, stock of the issuing corporation and other property provided by that corporation to the merged corporation, pursuant to the plan of reorganization, are not taken into account. Reg. § 1.368-2(j)(3)(iii).

In addition, in the transaction, the target shareholders must surrender control of the target corporation solely for voting stock of the issuing corporation. The regulations interpret this condition as requiring both the passage of a controlling interest in the target pursuant to the merger and the existence of control of the target by the issuing corporation after the merger. Reg. § 1.368-2(j)(3)(i) and (ii), -2(j)(6) (exs. 4, 5, 8, 9). In contrast, as explained in *Chapman* (p. 407), the passage of control is irrelevant in a "B" reorganization; it merely requires the existence of control of the target by the acquiring corporation immediately after the acquisition (whether or not it had control prior to the acquisition). In general, whether there is a passage of control in a qualifying reverse triangular merger is determined based on the target stock outstanding immediately prior to the merger. If the target redeems a portion of its stock prior to the merger, such stock is ignored for purposes of determining whether control is surrendered in the merger. Reg. § 1.368-2(j)(6) (exs. 2, 3, 5).

3. *Creeping acquisitions.* The required passage of control in the merger means that certain creeping acquisitions cannot qualify as reorganizations under section 368(a)(2)(E). For example, if P corporation owns 21 percent of the stock of T corporation and such stock is "old and cold," P cannot satisfy section 368(a)(2)(E) if it acquires the rest of T in a reverse triangular merger. Reg. § 1.368-2(j)(6) (ex. 4). If, however, the 21 percent interest was acquired by P as part of a plan to acquire the rest of T through a reverse triangular merger, the 21 percent interest is treated as acquired in the merger. Therefore, the transaction may qualify under section 368(a)(2)(E). Rev. Rul. 2001-26, 2001-1 C.B. 1297.

4. *Subsidiary of issuing corporation.* The issuing corporation's subsidiary that is merged into the target corporation may be an existing corporation or one formed immediately prior to the merger. Reg. § 1.368-2(j)(5). If a transitory subsidiary is used, however, the transaction may qualify as either a "B" reorganization or an "A" by reason of section 368(a)(2)(E). Reg. § 1.368-2(j)(6) (exs. 4, 5). Since those two reorganization provisions impose different conditions, use of a transitory subsidiary increases the likelihood that the transaction will qualify as a reorganization. In addition, if a transaction involving a transitory subsidiary fails to qualify as a reorganization, it is treated as a taxable acquisition of target stock (with no corporate-level tax consequences). In contrast, if an existing subsidiary is used and the transaction fails to qualify as a reorganization, there may be corporate-level as well as shareholder-level consequences.

**Problem 11-5:** Analyze the following transactions to determine whether they qualify as reorganizations pursuant to section 368(a)(1)(A) and (2)(E).

(a) T corporation has a single class of common stock and a single class of nonvoting preferred stock outstanding. As part of a plan for P corporation to acquire T, T distributes cash to its preferred stockholders in complete redemption of their T stock. P then forms S, a new wholly-owned subsidiary, and capitalizes it with voting stock of P. S merges into T, with T surviving, and in the merger, the holders of the T common stock surrender all of their stock in exchange for the P voting stock formerly held by S. The surrendered T stock is cancelled and the stock of S held by P becomes T stock by operation of law. As a result of the transaction, P owns all of the stock of T, the former common stockholders of T own voting stock of P, and the former preferred stockholders of T are cashed out.

(b) Same as (a), except that the cash used to redeem the nonvoting preferred stock originates with P and is transferred by S to the T preferred stockholders as part of the merger.

(c) Same as (a), except that the nonvoting preferred stock of T is owned by P prior to the transaction. In the merger of S into T, with T surviving, the common stockholders of T surrender all of their stock solely for P voting stock.

(d) Same as (c), except that P acquired the nonvoting preferred stock of T 18 months prior to the merger, 20 percent for cash and 80 percent for P voting stock.

(e) Same as (a), except that following the merger but as part of the overall plan, T issues a new class of nonvoting preferred stock (with more favorable terms than the former class of such stock) to unrelated corporation Q for cash.

## Tribune Co. v. Commissioner

125 T.C. 110 (2005)

[This case concerns whether the 1998 acquisition of the legal publishing company, Matthew Bender ("Bender") by Reed Elsevier ("Reed"), a publishing and information enterprise, qualified as a reorganization. At the time of the acquisition, the Times Mirror Co., an L.A.-based news and information company, owned all of the stock of TMD (a holding company), which in turn owned all of the stock of Bender. Tribune is the successor-in-interest to Times Mirror. In simplified form, the acquisition involved the following steps:

(1) Reed capitalized a new corporation, MergerSub, with $1.375 billion cash in exchange for common stock and voting preferred stock of MergerSub. The common stock represented 95 percent of the value of MergerSub and had 20 percent of the total voting power. The voting preferred stock represented 5 percent of the value and 80 percent of the vote.

(2) Reed capitalized another corporation, MB Parent, by transferring the voting preferred stock of MergerSub received in step (1) to MB Parent in exchange for voting preferred stock of MB Parent.

(3) MergerSub then used its $1.375 billion in cash to purchase voting common stock of MB Parent from that company. This stock represented 20 percent of the voting power of MB Parent, with the other 80 percent held by Reed as a result of owning the voting preferred stock of MB Parent received in step (2).

(4) At that point, MergerSub merged with and into Bender, with Bender surviving. In the merger, in exchange for all of its shares in Bender, TMD received the voting common stock of MB Parent previously held by MergerSub. Pursuant to the merger, all of the shares of MergerSub were converted into shares of Bender and the shares of Bender surrendered by TMD were cancelled. Thus, as a result of the merger, TMD owned 100 percent of the common stock of MB Parent (representing 20 percent of the vote) and Reed owned 100 percent of the preferred stock of MB Parent (representing 80 percent of the vote). MB Parent owned 100 percent of the preferred stock of Bender (representing 80 percent of the vote) and Reed owned 100 percent of the common stock of Bender (representing 20 percent of the vote).

(5) Following the merger, MB Parent transferred the $1.375 billion received in step (3) to a wholly-owned LLC and Times Mirror was designated as the sole manager of the LLC. Under the agreement forming the LLC, the manager had the sole right and authority to manage the business of the LLC, including the determination of how the LLC's cash would be invested. Corporate documents connected with the acquisition indicated that the cash would be used primarily to repurchase shares of Times Mirror and to make corporate acquisitions desired by Times Mirror.

(6) The certificate of incorporation of MB Parent gave the holders of its preferred and common shares the power to elect four members and one member, respectively, of the Board of Directors. However, certain corporate actions, including certain actions relating to the LLC, had to be approved by a unanimous vote of the Board.

(7) Three parallel options existed with respect to the MB Parent preferred stock owned by Reed. All of the options were exercisable after 20 years, or earlier in certain circumstances, at a price equal to the issue price for the shares. At that time and for that price, TMD had an option to purchase the preferred stock from Reed, Reed had an option to sell the stock back to MB Parent, and MB Parent had an option to redeem the shares. The preferred stock of Bender held by MB Parent was also subject to three parallel options exercisable at the same time as the foregoing options and at a price equal to the issue price of the stock. Reed had an option to purchase the stock from MB Parent, MB Parent had an option to sell it back to Bender, and Bender had an option to redeem the stock. Each issue of preferred stock provided for a fixed, annual dividend yield of 5.5 percent while the stock remained outstanding.

(8) Following the acquisition, Times Mirror and the LLC consolidated for financial accounting purposes, and Reed and Bender did likewise.
(9) Prior to the transaction, TMD's basis in the shares of Bender was about $78 million. Thus, a taxable disposition of Bender by TMD would have resulted in about $1.3 billion of capital gain.]

COHEN, J.

. . . Times Mirror and its advisers intended that the Bender transaction qualify as a tax-free "reverse triangular merger" under section 368(a)(1)(A) and (2)(E). . . . [A] reverse triangular merger is a statutory merger in which the merged corporation (MergerSub) merges with and into the target corporation (Bender) in exchange for stock of a corporation (MB Parent), which, immediately prior to the merger, controlled the merged corporation.

Respondent contends that the Bender transaction does not qualify as a reverse triangular merger because TMD received more than qualifying stock of MB Parent and the transaction thus fails to satisfy the "exchange" requirement of section 368(a)(2)(E)(ii), that is: "in the transaction, former shareholders of the surviving corporation exchanged, for an amount of voting stock of the controlling corporation, an amount of stock in the surviving corporation which constitutes control of such corporation." Section 368(c) defines "control" as "the ownership of stock possessing at least 80 percent of the total combined voting power of all classes of stock entitled to vote and at least 80 percent of the total number of shares of all other classes of stock of the corporation." Respondent argues that TMD's gain on the Bender transaction is taxable unless the fair market value of qualifying consideration, the MB Parent common stock, was at least equal in value to a "controlled block" (80 percent) of Bender stock. The parties agree that this requirement means that the MB Parent common stock must have had a value of $1.1 billion for the transaction to qualify as a reverse triangular merger.

Alternatively, . . . petitioner argues that the Bender transaction qualifies under section 368(a)(1)(B). . . . Petitioner's alternative position would not require valuation of the MB Parent common stock. It would, however, require us to conclude that Times Mirror's control over the cash in the LLC was not part of the consideration received in the Bender transaction because it was not intended by Times Mirror or Reed to be a "separate asset."

Respondent argues that the Bender transaction did not qualify under section 368(a)(1)(B) because TMD did not exchange its Bender stock solely for voting stock. . . .

In form, at the conclusion of the Bender transaction, TMD was the holder of MB Parent common stock and no longer owned Bender common stock. Determination of whether the MB Parent common stock had a value of $1.1 billion or, in the alternative, whether the sole consideration exchanged for the Bender common stock was the MB Parent common stock requires a factual analysis of the totality of the Bender transaction. . . .

## CONSIDERATION FOR THE TRANSFER OF BENDER TO REED

For purposes of section 368, the basic factual determination to be made is whether, under the contractual arrangements, the consideration received by TMD, the formal "divestor" of Bender, from MB Parent, the formal "divestee," was, as petitioner contends, common stock of MB Parent worth at least $1.1 billion or whether, as respondent contends, the consideration received was title to the common stock plus effective control over $1.375 billion — the amount paid by Reed in the transaction. Certainly from the standpoint of Times Mirror, control of the funds was the most important asset received. From the standpoint of Reed, control of the Bender operations was the most important asset received. Neither TMD nor MB Parent had officers or employees. TMD had no operations independent of Times Mirror, and MB Parent had no operations independent of Reed. . . .

Under the combined terms of the management agreement [and other corporate documents], all incidents of ownership of the $1.375 billion were shifted to Times Mirror as of July 31, 1998.

Examination of the voting, dividend, redemption, and liquidation provisions of the documents . . . confirms respondent's view that only Times Mirror had a continuing economic interest in the cash, and only Reed had a continuing economic interest in Bender. The structure of MB Parent and the dividend provisions assured that any dividends paid to MB Parent from the operations of Bender would be paid to Reed as dividends on MB Parent's preferred stock. Moreover, when the structure was ultimately unwound, TMD would own MB Parent and the LLC and Reed would own Bender.

The foregoing factual analysis demonstrates that the consideration received by TMD . . . was not common stock in MB Parent but was control over the cash deposited in the LLC. . . . [P]etitioner asserts that the common stock and the management authority cannot be valued separately because it would have been unthinkable to transfer them separately. But this argument does not aid petitioner's case. Recognizing that no one would separately purchase either the common stock or the management authority confirms respondent's argument that common stock was not the only consideration for the transfer and that the common stock, viewed alone, did not have the value necessary for the transaction to qualify under the reorganization provisions of the Internal Revenue Code.

## VALUATION OF MB PARENT COMMON STOCK

Petitioner argues that Times Mirror and Reed "conclusively" agreed that the MB Parent common stock was worth $1.375 billion. In the context of the entire agreement, however, the description of the consideration in the merger agreement as common stock was merely a recital consistent with the intended tax effect. We have examined the corporate governing documents to determine whether the MB Parent common stock possessed the requisite value for purposes of section 368(c).

The factual analysis of the transaction compels the conclusion that the management authority over the cash in the LLC had far more value to Times Mirror than the MB Parent common stock and thus represented the bulk of the consideration. [The court's discussion of expert testimony on this issue is omitted. — EDS.]

It is . . . unlikely that the authority of Times Mirror under the management agreement would be separated from TMD's ownership of the MB Parent common stock in the real world. However, separation of the management authority from the putative holder of the cash is part of the structure adopted by Times Mirror so that it could maintain its position that the only consideration received by TMD in the Bender transaction was the MB Parent common stock. Times Mirror and its advisers created the scenario that makes it necessary to value the MB Parent common stock at least as a portion of the total consideration. To support its statutory argument, petitioner is asking us to give effect to a fictional separation of the MB Parent common stock transferred to TMD from the management authority transferred to Times Mirror.

. . . We need not determine actual value of the MB Parent common stock, only proportionate value, i.e., whether the stock represents 80 percent of the total consideration paid by Reed. It is possible to engage in interminable arguments about the reports of the various experts presented by the parties in this case. To do so, however, would serve no useful purpose, because it would not affect the commonsense conclusions that (1) the MB Parent common stock cannot be isolated and treated as the sole consideration transferred to TMD for its divestiture of Bender and (2) the common stock of MB Parent, objectively, had a value less than $1.1 billion and less than 80 percent of the $1.375 billion paid by Reed.

## PERTINENT PRECEDENTS

Respondent invites us to adopt a broad-based approach and apply the "spirit" of the reorganization provisions in order to deter the type of abuse that respondent perceives the Bender transaction to be. We need not and do not accept respondent's invitation. We are, however, mindful of the precedents and judicial homilies that support respondent's position.

. . . Respondent also relies on . . . West Coast Mktg. Corp. v. Comm'r, 46 T.C. 32 (1966), in which the sole stockholder and president of the taxpayer corporation desired to dispose of certain land. In order to qualify the disposition as a tax-free reorganization under sections 354(a)(1) and 368(a)(1)(B), a corporation, Manatee, was formed, and the subject land was transferred to Manatee in exchange for stock. The stock of Manatee was then transferred to the acquiring corporation in exchange for its stock. Thereafter, Manatee was liquidated. . . . [T]his Court acknowledged that the transaction fell literally within the reorganization provisions but held that "the tax consequences must turn upon the substance of the transaction rather than the form in which it was cast." Respondent argues that MB Parent in the instant case is comparable to the intermediary corporation in *West Coast Mktg. Corp.* in that it had no business, no offices, and no employees, and it served no purpose other than to create the form necessary to support a claim for tax-free reorganization treatment.

. . . We agree with respondent that this case is . . . like *West Coast Mktg. Corp.* . . . There are differences, of course. MB Parent was not intended to be, and has not been, liquidated as promptly as the intermediary in *West Coast Mktg. Corp.* Additionally, MB Parent was putatively formed by the acquirer rather than by the party divesting itself of the property. Given the terms of MB Parent's governing documents and the structure of its several classes of stock, however, it has no more function than the intermediary in *West Coast Mktg. Corp.* . . . To disregard the existence of MB Parent is not to ignore any meaningful step in the transfer of Bender from Times Mirror to Reed. . . . MB Parent clearly serves no purpose and performs no function apart from Times Mirror's attempt to secure the desired tax consequences. . . .

The evidence compels the conclusion that Times Mirror intended a sale, assured that it would receive the proceeds of sale for use in its strategic plans, used the proceeds of sale in its strategic plans without limitation attributable to any continuing rights of Reed, and represented to shareholders and to the SEC that it had full rights to the proceeds of sale. None of these actions were inconsistent with the contractual terms. Thus, we need not "substitute respondent's version" for "what actually transpired." We deal only with what actually transpired and give effect to the legal documentation of the Bender transaction, with key points emphasized by the terms of the documents and the statements made by Times Mirror representatives about what was accomplished in the Bender transaction.

In a different but analogous context, the Court of Appeals for the Seventh Circuit has stated:

> The freedom to arrange one's affairs to minimize taxes does not include the right to engage in financial fantasies with the expectation that the Internal Revenue Service and the courts will play along. The Commissioner and the courts are empowered, and in fact duty-bound, to look beyond the contrived forms of transactions to their economic substance and to apply the tax laws accordingly. That is what we have done in this case and that is what taxpayers should expect in the future. . . . [Saviano v. Comm'r, 765 F.2d 643, 654 (7th Cir. 1985), affg. 80 T.C. 955 (1983).]

From any perspective, the "true economic effect" (petitioner's words . . . ) of the Bender transaction was a sale. Because the consideration paid by the buyer, to wit, unfettered control over $1.375 billion in cash, passed to the seller from the buyer, the Bender transaction does not qualify as a reorganization under section 368(a)(1)(B), which requires that the exchange be solely for stock. Because the MB Parent common stock lacked control over any assets, its value was negligible in comparison to the $1.1 billion value that would be required to qualify the Bender transaction as a tax-free reorganization under section 368(a)(1)(A) and (a)(2)(E). . . .

*NOTES*

1. *The tax department "profit center."* In 1998, when news of the Matthew Bender transaction first became public, one commentator wrote that the disposition of Bender represented Times Mirror's "fifth major tax-dodging transaction since 1995. . . . The company's tax department seems to be growing faster than its newspapers are, and is probably more profitable." Allan Sloan, "Did Times-Mirror Deserve That Tax Break? It Depends on Your Definition of 'Sale'," Washington Post, Oct. 13, 1998, p. C-3. The Tribune Company filed Chapter 11 bankruptcy petitions in December 2008.

2. *Settlement.* In 2007, just prior to the oral arguments scheduled before the Seventh Circuit to hear the company's appeal of the Tax Court decision, Tribune announced that it had settled its dispute with the IRS. After the Tax Court decision, the company paid about $1 billion to the government, representing tax and interest, and then sued for a refund pending the appeal. The settlement resulted in a net cash payment back to Tribune of $344 million.

## *5. Summary—Acquisitive Transactions as Reorganizations*

The preceding sections describe the reorganization conditions for five economically similar acquisitive transactions. Each transaction must satisfy COI, COBE, and have a business purpose (unless a more stringent statutory condition applies). Beyond that, the requirements for each transaction diverge. Certain qualifying reorganizations must comply with a "substantially all" test (section 368(a)(1)(C), (2)(D), and (2)(E)), one permits *only* voting stock as consideration (section 368(a)(1)(B)), and others require *mostly* voting stock (section 368(a)(1)(C) and (2)(E)) or impose no (or different) statutory conditions on the permissible consideration (section 368(a)(1)(A) and (2)(D)). There are further differences, such as whether a qualifying stock acquisition must merely result in the acquiring corporation having control of the target (section 368(a)(1)(B)) or must also involve a passage of a controlling interest in the transaction (section 368(a)(2)(E)). Test your understanding of these provisions by determining whether the transaction described in **problem 11-6** qualifies as a reorganization. To understand the IRS's answer to the question, read the excerpt following the problem.

**Problem 11-6:** T corporation is owned by individual A. T has $150x assets and $50x liabilities. P, a corporation unrelated to A and T, has net assets of $410x. P forms corporation X, a wholly-owned subsidiary, for the sole purpose of acquiring all of the stock of T by causing X to merge into T in a statutory merger (the "Acquisition Merger"). In the Acquisition Merger, P acquires all of the stock of T, and A exchanges the T stock for $10x cash and P voting stock worth $90x. Following the Acquisition Merger and as part of an integrated plan that includes the Acquisition Merger, T completely liquidates into P (the "Liquidation"). In the Liquidation, T transfers all of its assets to P and P assumes all of T's liabilities. The Liquidation is not accomplished through a statutory merger. After the Liquidation, P continues to conduct the business previously conducted by T.

## Rev. Rul. 2008-25

2008-1 C.B. 986

. . . If the Acquisition Merger and the Liquidation were treated as separate from each other, the Acquisition Merger would be treated as a stock acquisition that qualifies as a reorganization under § 368(a)(1)(A) by reason of § 368(a)(2)(E), and the Liquidation would qualify under § 332. However, as provided in § 1.368-1(a), in determining whether a transaction qualifies as a reorganization under § 368(a), the transaction must be evaluated under relevant provisions of law, including the step transaction doctrine. In this case, because T was completely liquidated, the § 1.368-2(k) safe harbor exception from the application of the step transaction doctrine does not apply. Accordingly, the Acquisition Merger and the Liquidation may not be considered independently of each other for purposes of determining whether the transaction satisfies the statutory requirements of a reorganization described in § 368(a)(1)(A) by reason of § 368(a)(2)(E). As such, this transaction does not qualify as a reorganization described in § 368(a)(1)(A) by reason of § 368(a)(2)(E) because, after the transaction, T does not hold substantially all of its properties and the properties of the merged corporation.

In determining whether the transaction is a reorganization, the approach . . . is . . . to ignore P's acquisition of the T stock in the Acquisition Merger and to treat the transaction as a direct acquisition by P of T's assets in exchange for 10x dollars in cash, 90x dollars worth of P voting stock, and the assumption of T's liabilities.

However, . . . a direct acquisition by P of T's assets in this case does not qualify as a reorganization under § 368(a). P's acquisition of T's assets is not a reorganization described in § 368(a)(1)(C) because the consideration exchanged is not solely P voting stock and the requirements of § 368(a)(2)(B) are not satisfied. Section 368(a)(2)(B) would treat P as acquiring 40 percent of T's assets for consideration other than P voting stock (liabilities assumed of 50x dollars, plus 10x dollars cash). . . . Additionally, the transaction is not a reorganization under § 368(a)(1)(A) because T did not merge into P. Accordingly, the overall transaction is not a reorganization under § 368(a).

Additionally, P's acquisition of the T stock in the Acquisition Merger is not a transaction to which § 351 applies because A does not control P (within the meaning of § 368(c)) immediately after the exchange.

*NOTE*

*Protecting section 338.* Since integration of the two steps (the Acquisition Merger and the Liquidation) did not produce a reorganization or section 351 transaction, the ruling concludes that the two steps should be given independent significance and treated as a taxable qualified stock purchase of T followed by a liquidation of T into P under section 332. This analysis prevents any change in the basis of T's assets unless a section 338 election is made. See Reg. § 1.338-3(d). See also Rev. Rul. 2001-46, 2001-2 C.B. 321 (collapsing qualified stock purchase with subsequent statutory merger because transaction qualified as a reorganization, no change in basis was claimed, and therefore policy of section 338 was not frustrated by the integration of steps).

### 6. *Other Nondivisive Reorganizations*

This section briefly describes the reorganization conditions for three final nondivisive transactions. These transactions are quite different from the acquisitive transactions previously examined. Two of them — the "E" and "F" reorganization — explicitly concern nondivisive changes to just a single corporation. The remaining transaction, which may qualify as a nondivisive "D" reorganization, involves a transfer of substantially all of the assets of one corporation to another corporation and a distribution of the transferor's remaining properties. The transferor or one or more of its shareholders, however, must control the transferee corporation immediately after the transaction. As we will see, this additional condition distinguishes a nondivisive D reorganization from other acquisitions and generally changes the tax stakes involved.

#### a. Transfer of Assets to Controlled Corporation

Read I.R.C. §§ 368(a)(1)(D), (a)(2)(A) and (H)(i), 354(a)(1) and (b)(1). A transfer by one corporation of all or part of its assets to another corporation may qualify as a "D" reorganization if (1) immediately after the transfer, the transferor or one or more of its shareholders controls the transferee, and (2) stock or securities of the transferee are distributed in a transaction qualifying under section 354, 355, or 356. A transaction qualifying as a "D" reorganization may be either divisive or nondivisive, depending upon the particular provision under which the "distribution" qualifies. As explained in chapter twelve, if the distribution qualifies under section 355, the transaction may be a divisive reorganization. In contrast, if the distribution qualifies under section 354 (or 356), then the transaction must involve a transfer of substantially all of the assets of the transferor corporation and a distribution of its remaining properties, thereby resulting in a nondivisive reorganization. I.R.C. § 354(b)(1). This section only describes nondivisive "D" reorganizations.

As discussed in prior sections, a principal issue in the reorganization area is whether a transaction actually constituting a taxable "sale" is masquerading as a tax-deferred reorganization. Under prior law, however, the opposite strategy of disguising a reorganization as a sale also potentially provided tax advantages, such as a step-up in the basis of corporate assets at the cost of only a single, shareholder-level tax. The "D" reorganization has traditionally been one of the government's principal weapons to attack the latter strategy.

Under prior law, a classic case illustrating this function of the "D" reorganization is Davant v. Comm'r, 366 F.2d 874 (5th Cir. 1966), cert. denied, 386 U.S. 1022 (1967), involving four families who owned in equal proportions each of two corporations, X and Y. The corporations were involved in successful, integrated businesses, and had accumulated sizable amounts of E&P. The taxpayers developed a plan for X to sell all of its operating assets to Y for cash and then to liquidate. Under prior law, if this plan were respected, Y would have obtained a cost basis in the former X assets (section 1012), X would not have recognized any gain or loss (former section 337), and the X shareholders would have recognized long-term capital gain (section 331). Homer Bruce, the attorney for the taxpayers, advised against this plan, however, because of existing precedents that might have permitted the IRS to recharacterize the distribution as a dividend. (Mr. Bruce argued one of the famous early COI cases before the Supreme Court, LeTulle v. Scofield, 308 U.S. 415 (1940).) Instead, the attorney suggested that the shareholders of X first sell all of their stock to an unrelated person before having X and Y carry out the planned steps. At some point, it was decided that the attorney's *son*, Homer Bruce, Jr. (also a practicing attorney), would purchase the stock. The hope, of course, was that a sale to the son would be respected as a separate transaction in which the X shareholders recognized long-term capital gain (or would perhaps cause the transaction to be overlooked on audit). The father arranged all of the remaining details, including obtaining the loan (using the X stock as collateral) to finance the stock purchase and having the loan repaid after the liquidation of X. As the court explained:

> On August 26, 1960 . . . [i]n accordance with a detailed instruction sheet, the respective parties went through the motions of making a loan, selling stock, electing new corporate officials, selling [X]'s assets, liquidating [X], and repaying the loan. Thanks to the careful prearrangement of all the details, the parties were able to act out their respective roles in approximately one hour. [366 F.2d at 878-79.]

The son, who did nothing other than attend the closing, was paid about $16,000 for his involvement, still fairly good compensation even by today's standards.

Not surprisingly, the Fifth Circuit refused to accept the taxpayers' claim. The court disregarded the son's involvement and found that the liquidation provisions were inapplicable due to the continuation of X's business in corporate solution. Instead, the court held that the transaction qualified as a "D" reorganization, with the result that there was no change to the basis of X's assets and that the distribution to the shareholders was potentially taxable as a dividend. The court disregarded the absence of any distribution of stock or securities of Y, as required by section 368(a)(1)(D), because the issuance and distribution of such stock or securities would have been a meaningless gesture under these facts.

With the repeal of *General Utilities* (p. 175) and the currently comparable tax treatment to individuals of dividends and long-term capital gain, the possible advantage of the *Davant* strategy has been largely eliminated and, accordingly, the role of the nondivisive "D" in unmasking disguised reorganizations has been reduced. As the following excerpt explains, another factor diminishing the number of nondivisive "D"-related controversies was the deterrent effect of a 1984 amendment (prior to the repeal of *General Utilities*) that conformed more closely the control requirements under sections 368(a)(1)(D) and 304(a)(1). As discussed in chapter eight, section 304(a)(1) preserves potential dividend treatment in the case of a transfer of stock involving commonly owned corporations, and the nondivisive "D" reorganization serves a similar function in the case of a transfer of assets between such corporations.

## Staff of Joint Committee on Taxation, General Explanation of the Revenue Provisions of the Deficit Reduction Act of 1984 (1984)

pp. 192-94

. . . Under prior law, for purposes of determining whether a transaction qualified as a D reorganization, the term "control" was defined as the ownership of stock possessing at least 80 percent of the total combined voting power of all classes of stock entitled to vote and at least 80 percent of the total number of shares of all other classes of stock of the corporation. No attribution rules were explicitly made applicable. . . .

[U]nder prior law, liquidation-reincorporation transactions (i.e., transactions involving the liquidation of a corporation coupled with a transfer of its operating assets to a new corporation in which the shareholders of the transferor corporation have a substantial stock interest) that were not treated as reorganizations could be used to accomplish a bail-out of earnings and profits at capital gains rates. Further, these transactions could be used by a shareholder (or group of shareholders) to obtain a step-up in the basis of assets that were held in corporate solution largely at the cost of a shareholder-level capital gains tax without a significant change in ownership of those assets.

The D reorganization provisions generally envision the continuation of the transferor corporation's business in a corporation in which the transferor corporation or its shareholders have a substantial interest. In many liquidation-reincorporation transactions, the liquidating corporation's business is being continued by a related corporation. The Congress believed that many of these transactions should be treated as D reorganizations. However, in some instances, the control requirement that applied in the case of a D reorganization prevented the Service from successfully asserting that these transactions constituted D reorganizations.

. . . [T]he D reorganization provisions and section 304 both operate to prevent the bail-out of earnings and profits at capital gains rates. The D reorganization provisions address the bail-out problem in the context of a transfer of assets by 1 corporation to another. Section 304 deals with the problem in the context of a transfer of stock by shareholders to a corporation they control. Nonetheless, the definition of control that applied for purposes of the D reorganization provisions differed from the definition that applies for purposes of section 304. Further, attribution rules applied for purposes of determining stock ownership under section 304, but not for purposes of determining stock ownership under the D reorganization provisions.

The Congress believed that the D reorganization control requirement should more closely conform to the control requirement under section 304. In addition, the Congress believed that the absence of explicit attribution rules to determine ownership of stock for purposes of the D reorganization control requirement may have enabled taxpayers to bail out earnings and profits at capital gains rates by having their corporation transfer assets to a corporation controlled by related persons rather than to a corporation controlled by them. Generally, because attribution rules are applicable for purposes of section 304, such a bail out would not be possible if the transaction were structured as a transfer of stock rather than of assets.

. . . Under the provision, for purposes of determining whether a non-divisive transaction qualifies as a D reorganization, "control" is defined as ownership of stock possessing at least 50 percent of the total combined voting power of all classes of stock entitled to vote, or at least 50 percent of the total value of all shares of all classes of stock. Further, the constructive ownership of stock rules contained in section 318(a), as modified, are applicable for purposes of determining whether the transferor corporation or its shareholders are in control of the acquiring corporation.

It was not intended that recharacterization as a D reorganization under this provision be the exclusive means for the Service to challenge liquidation-reincorporation and similar transactions. Thus, it was not intended that this provision supersede or otherwise replace the various doctrines that have been developed by the Service and the courts to deal with such transactions. . . .

## *NOTES*

1. *Inexact parallel to section 304.* Despite the 1984 amendment and the similar purpose of the two provisions, sections 368(a)(1)(D) and 304(a)(1) do not apply in exactly the same circumstances. The main difference is that for section 304(a)(1) to be operative, the parties who control the transferee must also control the transferor. I.R.C. § 304(a)(1)(A). In contrast, in a "D" reorganization, common control of both corporations is not required; there must simply be control of the transferee on the part of the transferor corporation, one or more of its shareholders, or any

combination thereof. Thus, the threshold requirement for a "D" is less stringent than for section 304(a)(1).

2. *Liberally interpreted conditions.* Consistent with its role of preventing tax abuse, the "D" reorganization provisions have been interpreted quite liberally. *Davant* illustrates the disregard of the distribution condition when satisfying the condition would be a meaningless gesture. The regulations now specifically authorize an all-cash "D" reorganization if the same person or persons own, directly or indirectly, all of the stock of the transferor and transferee corporations in identical proportions. (*De minimis* differences in ownership are disregarded for this purpose.) If the value of the assets transferred is greater than any consideration received by the transferor corporation, the transferee is deemed to issue its stock in an amount that reflects the excess and that stock is treated as distributed by the transferor. If the consideration received is equal to the value of the assets transferred, the transferee is deemed to issue a nominal share of stock that is deemed distributed by the transferor. Reg. § 1.368-2(*l*)(2)(i) and (iii). The "substantially all" requirement in a "D" reorganization has also been interpreted liberally. For example, in Smothers v. U.S., 642 F.2d 894 (5th Cir. 1981), involving a transfer between two identically owned corporations, the court concluded (at the urging of the government) that 15 percent of the net assets (but 100 percent of the operating assets) constituted substantially all of the transferor's assets. Given the anti-abuse context of these decisions, they should not be relied upon as interpretations of the substantially all requirement for purposes of other types of reorganizations.

3. *Affirmative use of the "D" by taxpayers?* The loose threshold requirement for a "D," combined with the liberal interpretation of some of its conditions, raises a question whether taxpayers may increasingly use the provision to qualify a transaction as a reorganization in cases where other reorganization categories cannot be satisfied. For example, suppose A owns 99 percent of corporation T and B (who is unrelated to A) owns the remaining one percent. B also owns 100 percent of the common stock of corporation P. If T transfers all of its assets to P for cash (95%) and nonvoting P preferred stock (5%), the transaction would not qualify as a reorganization (apart from section 368(a)(1)(D)) because there is too much boot. But might it qualify as a nondivisive "D" reorganization? One of T's shareholders (B) controls the transferee (P) immediately after the transfer (assuming that P's common stock represents at least 50 percent of the value of the corporation). In addition, the transaction could include a distribution of the P preferred stock and cash received by T pursuant to the reorganization. Although almost all of the proceeds would be distributed to A, who has little continuing interest in the transferred business, the substantially all requirement may be satisfied.

An obvious possible problem is the absence of COI. But does COI for purposes of a nondivisive "D" reorganization have the same meaning as for other reorganizations? As you recall, COI is generally determined by the mix of stock and non-stock consideration used in the transaction. Yet, both *Davant* and the regulations expressly bless as a "D" reorganization certain transactions in which no stock at all is used. One might argue that the "continuity" requirement in a reorganization is satisfied by the existence of control over the transferee after the transaction, a precondition for a "D" reorganization. The regulations carve out somewhat enigmatically the application of COI in a "D" reorganization (Reg. § 1.368-1(b) (third sentence)) and the IRS continues to study this area. See T.D. 8760, 1998-1 C.B. 803, 805.

4. *Overlap.* Under section 368(a)(2)(A), the "D" reorganization provisions generally apply if a transaction qualifies as both a "C" and "D" reorganization. In Rev. Rul. 2004-83, 2004-2 C.B. 157, P corporation owned all the stock of both S and T corporations, S acquired all of the T stock from P for cash, and T subsequently liquidated into S as part of the plan. The IRS concluded that the transaction should be treated as a "D" reorganization (i.e., an acquisition of T's assets by S) rather than a section 304 transaction followed by a section 332 liquidation of T into S.

5. *Liquidation-reincorporation and the step-transaction safe harbor.* The *Davant* case is an illustration of the venerable "liquidation-reincorporation" doctrine long used by the IRS to recharacterize, in accordance with its substance, a purported liquidation preceded or followed by a reincorporation of some or all of the liquidated corporation's assets. The step-transaction safe harbor in Reg. § 1.368-2(k)(1) may, however, prevent application of the liquidation-reincorporation doctrine in certain cases, with uncertain consequences.

For example, suppose X corporation owns two subsidiaries, Y and Z, and in a single transaction, Y is liquidated into X, which drops down Y's former operating assets into its other subsidiary, Z. Under the liquidation-reincorporation doctrine, this transaction would be recharacterized as a direct transfer by Y of its operating assets to Z followed by a distribution of its remaining assets to X. Yet, because the Y stock held by X prior to the liquidation is not treated as boot under the regulations reversing *Bausch & Lomb* (p. 403) (Reg. § 1.368-2(d)(4)), the liquidation of Y into X qualifies as a "C" reorganization (followed by a dropdown of assets under section 368(a)(2)(C)). In the liquidation, X acquires substantially all of Y's assets solely for a deemed issuance of X voting stock, and Y subsequently liquidates. (The failure to actually issue X stock would be disregarded since X would simply receive this stock back in the liquidation. Cf. Reg. § 1.368-1(e)(1)(i) (third sentence) and (10) (ex. 7).) Regulation § 1.368-2(k)(1), therefore, respects the first step as a reorganization and prevents its recharacterization, notwithstanding the subsequent step. In short, the transaction will be taxed in accordance with its form — a "C" reorganization followed by a section 351 transaction — and not as a direct transfer from Y to Z and a distribution to X. Whether this degree of planning flexibility is appropriate remains to be seen.

6. *Triangular acquisitions and the all-cash "D" regulations.* The all-cash "D" regulations described in note 2 above do not apply in the case of certain triangular acquisitions. Reg. § 1.368-2(*l*)(2)(iv). The reason is explored in **problem 11-7**.

**Problem 11-7:** P corporation owns all of the stock of corporations S and T. In order to combine their assets within one corporate entity, T transfers all of its assets to S in exchange for voting stock of P, and T then liquidates into P. If the all-cash "D" regulations (Reg. § 1.368-2(*l*)) apply to this transaction, how would it be treated for tax purposes? Would it matter if, instead of transferring its assets to S, T simply merges into S? See I.R.C. §§ 354(a)(1) and 368(b).

### b. Mere Change in Identity, Form, or Place of Organization of One Corporation

Read I.R.C. § 368(a)(1)(F). For many years, an "F" reorganization was defined as "a mere change in identity, form, or place of organization, however effected," and was an infrequently used provision with seemingly little significance. As the Tax Court stated in Berghash v. Comm'r, 43 T.C. 743, 752 (1965), aff'd, 361 F.2d 257 (2d Cir. 1966):

> . . . the (F) reorganization . . . is distinguishable from the [other] types of reorganizations [because it] encompass[es] only the simplest and least significant of corporate changes. The (F)-type reorganization presumes that the surviving corporation is the same corporation as the predecessor in every respect, except for minor or technical differences. . . . For instance, the (F) reorganization typically has been understood to comprehend only such insignificant modifications as the reincorporation of the same corporate business with the same assets and the same stockholders surviving under a new charter either in the same or in a different State, the renewal of a corporate charter having a limited life, or the conversion of a U.S.-chartered savings and loan association to a State-chartered institution.

This state of affairs changed dramatically following the Fifth Circuit's decision in *Davant*. In that case, the government raised the possibility before the trial court that the transaction might constitute an "F" reorganization but backed away from that position before the Fifth Circuit. Nevertheless, the Fifth Circuit found that the transaction in question qualified as *both* a "D" *and* an "F" reorganization. This decision was the first to find that a combination of two operating companies could constitute an "F" reorganization. Once that pandora's box was opened, taxpayers attempted to classify a variety of amalgamating transactions as "F" reorganizations.

Why was classification as an "F" reorganization important? Under section 381(b)(3), except in the case of an "F" reorganization, an acquiring corporation may not carry back losses arising in post-acquisition years to offset pre-acquisition income of the target corporation. The IRS argued that this special treatment could only be explained by a Congressional intent to limit an "F" reorganization to changes affecting a single business enterprise and not multiple enterprises. If an "F" reorganization were so limited, then the permissible carryback of losses would be only against income of the same enterprise.

Although the IRS continued to challenge the claims of taxpayers who argued that combinations of two or more operating companies qualified as an "F" reorganization, it kept losing its cases. The zenith of this effort was probably Home

Construction Corp. v. U.S., 439 F.2d 1165 (5th Cir. 1971), involving a consolidation of 123 active, affiliated corporations into their common parent corporation. Relying on *Davant*, the Fifth Circuit held that the mergers all qualified as "F" reorganizations. (The potential breadth of this holding was diminished by the court's insistence that post-merger losses could only be carried back to offset pre-merger income of the same business unit producing the loss, although the practicality of that restriction may be doubtful in certain cases.) Eventually, the IRS capitulated to this judicial onslaught and sought Congressional help. In 1982, Congress inserted "of one corporation" into the definitional provision. Congress made clear that the limitation does not preclude the use of more than one corporate entity to consummate the transaction so long as only one operating company is involved.

The limitation of "one operating company" does not mean that a combination of an active business enterprise with a corporation holding passive investments would qualify as an "F" reorganization. Rather, the non-operating company should hold no property and have no tax attributes. See Prop. Reg. § 1.368-2(m)(1)(i)(D). This interpretation is consistent with Congressional intent to allow a merger of a business corporation into a newly formed *shell* corporation to qualify as an "F" reorganization, if the merger is necessary to accomplish the corporate change. The transaction should ordinarily result in no change to the business, assets, capital structure, and shareholders of the corporation affected. The proposed regulations would allow the transaction to include a redemption of less than all of the corporation's stock in order to permit, for example, the buyout of a shareholder who dissents from the corporate change. Prop. Reg. § 1.368-2(m)(1)(i)(B) and (5) (ex. 2). The proposed regulations would also allow a nominal amount of new capital to be added to the corporation. Id., -2(m)(1)(ii)(B). The finalized portion of the regulations makes clear that this non-amalgamating type of transaction does not require either COI or COBE to qualify as an "F" reorganization. Reg. § 1.368-1(b) (eighth sentence).

The limited nature of an "F" reorganization reduces its potential overlap with other reorganizations. Still, a merger between two commonly owned corporations could easily qualify as an "A," "D," and "F" reorganization. Where there is overlap, the "F" classification prevails (so that, for example, the special exception in section 381(b) would be applicable). Rev. Rul. 57-276, 1957-1 C.B. 126. As the following ruling illustrates, if a transaction qualifying as an "F" is part of a broader transaction, the IRS's position is generally to treat the "F" portion as neither affected by, nor having any effect on, the tax treatment of the remaining part of the transaction. This position is reflected in the proposed regulations. Prop. Reg. § 1.368-2(m)(3)(ii).

## Rev. Rul. 96-29

1996-1 C.B. 50

. . . Do the transactions described below qualify as reorganizations under § 368(a)(1)(F) of the Internal Revenue Code?

. . . *Situation 1.* Q is a manufacturing corporation all of the common stock of which is owned by twelve individuals. One class of nonvoting preferred stock, representing 40 percent of the aggregate value of Q, is held by a variety of corporate and noncorporate shareholders. Q is incorporated in state M. Pursuant to a plan to raise immediate additional capital and to enhance its ability to raise capital in the future by issuing additional stock, Q proposes to make a public offering of newly issued stock and to cause its stock to become publicly traded. Q entered into an underwriting agreement providing for the public offering and a change in its state of incorporation. The change in the state of incorporation was undertaken, in part, to enable the corporation to avail itself of the advantages that the corporate laws of state N afford to public companies and their officers and directors. In the absence of the public offering, Q would not have changed its state of incorporation. Pursuant to the underwriting agreement, Q changed its place of incorporation by merging with and into R, a newly organized corporation incorporated in state N. The shares of Q stock were converted into the right to receive an identical number of shares of R stock. Immediately thereafter, R sold additional shares of its stock to the public and redeemed all of the outstanding shares of nonvoting preferred stock. The number of new shares sold was equal to 60 percent of all the outstanding R stock following the sale and redemption.

*Situation 2.* W, a state M corporation, is a manufacturing corporation all of the stock of which is owned by two individuals. W conducted its business through several wholly owned subsidiaries. The management of W determined that it would be in the best interest of W to acquire the business of Z, an unrelated corporation, and combine it with the business of Y, one of its subsidiaries, and to change the state of incorporation of W. In order to accomplish these objectives, and pursuant to an overall plan, W entered into a plan and agreement of merger with Y and Z. In accordance with the agreement, Z merged with and into Y pursuant to the law of state M, with the former Z shareholders receiving shares of newly issued W preferred stock in exchange for their shares of Z stock. Immediately following the acquisition of Z, W changed its place of organization by merging with and into N, a newly organized corporation incorporated in state R. Upon W's change of place of organization, the holders of W common and preferred stock surrendered their W stock in exchange for identical N common and preferred stock, respectively.

. . . Section 368(a)(1)(F) provides that a reorganization includes a mere change in identity, form, or place of organization of one corporation, however effected. . . . Certain limitations contained in § 381(b), including those precluding the corporation acquiring property in a reorganization from carrying back a net operating loss or a net capital loss for a taxable year ending after the date of transfer to a taxable year of the transferor, do not apply to reorganizations described in § 368(a)(1)(F) "in recognition of the intended scope of such reorganizations as embracing only formal changes in a single operating corporation." . . . Although a change in the place of organization usually must be effected through the merger of one corporation into another, such a transaction qualifies as a reorganization under § 368(a)(1)(F) because it involves only one operating corporation. . . .

A transaction does not qualify as a reorganization under § 368(a)(1)(F) unless there is no change in existing shareholders or in the assets of the corporation. However, a transaction will not fail to qualify as a reorganization under § 368(a)(1)(F) if dissenters owning fewer than 1 percent of the outstanding shares of the corporation fail to participate in the transaction. Rev. Rul. 66-284, 1966-2 C.B. 115.

The rules applicable to corporate reorganizations as well as other provisions recognize the unique characteristics of reorganizations qualifying under § 368(a)(1)(F). In contrast to other types of reorganizations, which can involve two or more operating corporations, a reorganization of a corporation under § 368(a)(1)(F) is treated for most purposes of the Code as if there had been no change in the corporation and, thus, as if the reorganized corporation is the same entity as the corporation that was in existence prior to the reorganization. See § 381(b); § 1.381(b)-1(a)(2); . . .

In Rev. Rul. 69-516, 1969-2 C.B. 56, the Internal Revenue Service treated as two separate transactions a reorganization under § 368(a)(1)(F) and a reorganization under § 368(a)(1)(C) undertaken as part of the same plan. Specifically, a corporation changed its place of organization by merging into a corporation formed under the laws of another state and, immediately thereafter, it transferred substantially all of its assets in exchange for stock of an unrelated corporation. The ruling holds that the change in place of organization qualified as a reorganization under § 368(a)(1)(F).

Accordingly, in *Situation 1*, the reincorporation by Q in state N qualifies as a reorganization under § 368(a)(1)(F) even though it was a step in the transaction in which Q was issuing common stock in a public offering and redeeming stock having a value of 40 percent of the aggregate value of its outstanding stock prior to the offering.

In *Situation 2*, the reincorporation by W in state N qualifies as a reorganization under § 368(a)(1)(F) even though it was a step in the transaction in which W acquired the business of Z. . . .

### c. Recapitalization

Read I.R.C. §§ 368(a)(1)(E) and (b) (first sentence) and 354(a)(1), Reg. § 1.368-2(e), and the following case.

## Bazley v. Commissioner

331 U.S. 737 (1947)

Mr. Justice FRANKFURTER delivered the opinion of the Court.

. . . [T]he Commissioner of Internal Revenue assessed an income tax deficiency against the taxpayer for the year 1939. Its validity depends on the legal significance of the recapitalization in that year of a family corporation in which the taxpayer and his wife owned all but one of the Company's one thousand shares. These had a par value of $100. Under the plan of reorganization the taxpayer, his wife, and the holder of the additional share were to turn in their old shares and receive in exchange for each old share five new shares of no par value, but of a stated value of $60, and new debenture bonds, having a total face value of $400,000, payable in ten years but callable at any time. Accordingly, the taxpayer received 3,990 shares of the new stock for the 798 shares of his old holding and debentures in the amount of $319,200. At the time of these transactions the earned surplus of the corporation was $855,783.82.

The Commissioner charged to the taxpayer as income the full value of the debentures. The Tax Court affirmed the Commissioner's determination, against the taxpayer's contention that as a "recapitalization" the transaction was a tax-free "reorganization" and that the debentures were "securities in a corporation a party to a reorganization," "exchanged solely for stock or securities in such corporation" "in pursuance of a plan of reorganization," and as such no gain is recognized for income tax purposes. [I.R.C. §§ 368(a)(1)(E) and (b), 354(a)(1).] The Tax Court found that the recapitalization had "no legitimate corporate business purpose" and was therefore not a "reorganization" within the statute. The distribution of debentures, it concluded, was a disguised dividend, taxable as earned income. . . . The Circuit Court of Appeals for the Third Circuit, sitting *en banc*, affirmed, two judges dissenting. . . .

Unless a transaction is a reorganization contemplated by [§ 368], any exchange of "stock or securities" in connection with such transaction, cannot be "in pursuance of the plan of reorganization" under [§ 354(a)(1)]. While [§ 368] informs us that "reorganization" means, among other things, "a recapitalization," it does not inform us what "recapitalization" means. "Recapitalization" in connection with the income tax has been part of the revenue laws since 1921. . . . Congress has never defined it and the Treasury Regulations shed only limited light. . . . One thing is certain. Congress did not incorporate some technical concept, whether that of accountants or of other specialists, into [§ 368], assuming that there is agreement among specialists as to the meaning of recapitalization. And so, recapitalization as used in [§ 368] must draw its meaning from its function in that section. It is one of the forms of reorganization which obtains the privileges afforded by [§ 368]. Therefore, "recapitalization" must be construed with reference to the presuppositions and purpose of [§ 368]. It was not the purpose of the reorganization provision to exempt from payment of a tax what as a practical matter is realized gain. Normally, a distribution by a corporation, whatever form it takes, is a definite and rather unambiguous event. It furnishes the proper occasion for the determination and taxation of gain. But there are circumstances where a formal distribution, directly or through exchange of securities, represents merely a new form of the previous participation in an enterprise, involving no change of substance in the rights and relations of the interested parties one to another or to the corporate assets. As to these, Congress has said that they are not to be deemed significant occasions for determining taxable gain.

These considerations underlie [§ 368] and they should dominate the scope to be given to the various sections. . . . In a series of cases this Court has withheld the benefits of the reorganization provision in situations which might have satisfied provisions of the section treated as inert language, because they were not reorganizations of the kind with which [§ 368], in its purpose and particulars, concerns itself. . . .

No doubt there was a recapitalization of the Bazley corporation in the sense that the symbols that represented its capital were changed, so that the fiscal basis of its operations would appear very differently on its books. But the form of a transaction as reflected by correct corporate accounting opens questions as to the proper application of a taxing statute; it does not close them. . . . What is controlling is that a new arrangement intrinsically partake of the elements of reorganization which underlie the Congressional exemption and not merely give the appearance of it to accomplish a distribution of earnings. In the case of a corporation which has undistributed earnings, the creation of new corporate obligations which are transferred to stockholders in relation to their former holdings, so as to produce, for all practical purposes, the same result as a distribution of cash earnings of equivalent value, cannot obtain tax immunity because cast in the form of a recapitalization-reorganization. . . . And so it is hard to escape the conclusion that whether in a particular case a paper recapitalization is no more than an admissible attempt to avoid the consequences of an outright distribution of earnings turns on details of corporate affairs, judgment on which must be left to the Tax Court. . . .

What have we here? No doubt, if the Bazley corporation had issued the debentures to Bazley and his wife without any recapitalization, it would have made a taxable distribution. Instead, these debentures were issued as part of a family arrangement, the only additional ingredient being an unrelated modification of the capital account. The debentures were found to be worth at least their principal amount, and they were virtually cash because they were callable at the will of the corporation which in this case was the will of the taxpayer. One does not have to pursue the motives behind actions, even in the more ascertainable forms of purpose, to find, as did the Tax Court, that the whole arrangement took this form instead of an outright distribution of cash or debentures, because the latter would undoubtedly have been taxable income whereas what was done could, with a show of reason, claim the shelter of the immunity of a recapitalization-reorganization. . . . A "reorganization" which is merely a vehicle, however elaborate or elegant, for conveying earnings from accumulations to the stockholders is not a reorganization under [§ 368]. . . .

Judgments affirmed.

Mr. Justice Douglas and Mr. Justice Burton dissent in both cases for the reasons stated in the joint dissent of . . . the court below. . . .

*NOTES*

1. *The limited significance of an "E" reorganization.* A recapitalization is a change in the capital structure of a corporation and does not ordinarily raise tax issues common to other types of reorganizations. For example, there is generally no issue regarding the recognition of corporate-level gain or loss, change in corporate asset basis, or survival of corporate tax attributes as a result of a recapitalization. Indeed, section 381(a), which generally authorizes the acquiring corporation in a reorganization to succeed to certain tax attributes of the target corporation, does not even reference an "E" reorganization. A recapitalization may cause a corporation to have cancellation of indebtedness income or affect its future use of net operating loss carryovers (if the transaction results in an "ownership change" of the corporation (see chapter thirteen)), but these consequences are independent of whether the transaction is a reorganization.

The principal tax issue of a recapitalization is its effect on the investors of the corporation. *Bazley* evidences a concern that the reorganization provisions not be used to avoid the potential dividend consequences of the transaction. The regulations show the same concern; every example involves an issuance of stock of the corporation to an existing stockholder or bondholder, as opposed to the opposite situation (the issuance of bonds to a stockholder) that the Court in *Bazley* found to be problematic. Reg. § 1.368-2(e).

But even when an investor receives bonds, it may not make much difference whether the transaction qualifies as a reorganization. As we will see in part C, if a shareholder in a recapitalization receives *only* bonds in exchange for stock, the bonds are taxed under the ordinary distribution rules of section 302 or 301 even though the transaction qualifies as a reorganization. I.R.C. § 354(a)(2)(A)(ii); Reg. § 1.354-1(b) and (d) (ex. 3). The one case where reorganization status may be important is if the shareholder receives both bonds *and* stock in exchange for stock (the specific situation in *Bazley*). In that case, if the transaction is a reorganization, the bonds may be taxable as a dividend but only to the extent of the shareholder's gain in the transaction. I.R.C. § 356(a); Reg. § 1.354-1(d) (ex. 2). If the transaction is not a reorganization and the bonds are taxed as an ordinary distribution, there is no similar limitation on dividend treatment. But even in the case of a reorganization, the regulations preserve the possibility that the receipt of the bonds might be treated as separate from the reorganization exchange. Reg. §§ 1.301-1(*l*), 1.356-1(f). In other words, receipt of the debentures in *Bazley* might be taxable as an ordinary distribution under current law even though the stock-for-stock exchange qualifies as an "E" reorganization. As in the case of "F" reorganizations, the regulations make clear that the COI and COBE doctrines do not apply in the case of an "E" reorganization. Reg. § 1.368-1(b) (eighth sentence).

2. *Section 305(c).* The tax consequences of a recapitalization may also be affected by section 305(c) (chapter nine). Under that provision, certain transactions (including a recapitalization) may be treated as a constructive distribution with

respect to any shareholder whose proportionate interest in the E&P or assets of the corporation is increased as a result of the transaction. The regulations apply section 305(c) to a recapitalization if either (1) it is pursuant to a plan to periodically increase the shareholder's proportionate interest in assets or E&P of the recapitalized corporation, or (2) the shareholder surrenders preferred stock with dividend arrearages for other stock, which results in an increase in such proportionate interest. For example, if, in a recapitalization qualifying under section 368(a)(1)(E), a shareholder exchanges preferred stock with dividend arrearages for substantially identical new preferred stock (but without arrearages) plus shares of common stock, the common stock is treated as a distribution taxable under sections 305(b)(4) and 301. Reg. § 1.305-7(c)(1), -5(d) (ex. 1(ii)).

## C. Tax Consequences of a Nondivisive Reorganization

This part summarizes the principal tax consequences of a nondivisive reorganization to the participants of the transaction. The general result of the "operative" reorganization rules is to defer the tax consequences of the corporate- and shareholder-level exchanges in the transaction and to preserve the target's tax attributes in the hands of one of the acquiring parties.

### 1. *Threshold Considerations*

Several of the operative rules refer to "stock or securities" of "a party to a reorganization" received pursuant to a "plan of reorganization." See, e.g., I.R.C. §§ 354(a)(1), 361(a). Read I.R.C. § 368(b), which identifies which corporations are a "party to a reorganization." As you can see, the term includes the corporation involved in a single-corporation reorganization, both the target and acquiring corporations in an acquisitive reorganization, and all three corporations in a triangular reorganization. In addition, the acquiring corporation remains a party to the reorganization even if it transfers the acquired stock or assets to a subsidiary, provided the subsequent transfer satisfies Reg. § 1.368-2(k). I.R.C. § 368(b) (third sentence); Reg. § 1.368-2(f) (sentences 2, 3, 13, 14). Importantly, the transferee who obtains the acquired stock or assets in the subsequent transfer is *not* treated as a party to the reorganization. Therefore, the tax consequences of the subsequent transfer are not controlled by the reorganization provisions but by other rules, such as section 351. This distinction may be important, for example, if the properties transferred are subject to liabilities in excess of basis. Section 357(c), which may require the transferor to recognize gain in that situation, applies to section 351 transactions but not to transfers pursuant to a nondivisive reorganization. I.R.C. § 357(c)(1).

The statute clearly contemplates the existence of a "plan of reorganization" but does not specify what constitutes a plan. The regulations similarly require that a plan exist and be adopted by each party to the reorganization, but provide no formal description. Reg. § 1.368-1(c) (seventh sentence), -3(a) (first sentence). In general, the regulations indicate that a plan should delineate the parameters of the reorganization transaction and describe its business purpose. Reg. § 1.368-1(c) (sentences 8-10), -2(g). Of course, the existence of a plan does not preclude the government from recharacterizing either the parameters or the purpose of the transaction.

Finally, several of the operative provisions distinguish between "stock or securities" of a party to the reorganization and all other property (boot). See, e.g., I.R.C. §§ 354(a), 356(a)(1), 361(a) and (b)(1). As you know, in order to qualify as a reorganization, certain transactions must include "voting" stock as consideration. The operative provisions, however, are generally applicable to all reorganizations and therefore do not distinguish between voting and nonvoting stock. As a result, once the critical determination has been made that a transaction qualifies as a reorganization, its tax consequences are not dependent upon whether the stock received is voting or nonvoting. See Reg. § 1.361-1. Similarly, in certain circumstances, "securities" of a party to the reorganization may be received tax-free even though they do not constitute qualifying consideration for any reorganization. The term "securities" is not defined and generally refers to a debt obligation having a sufficiently long term, such as five or ten years, although other factors may also be important.

The following discussion assumes that P corporation controls S corporation and, in a qualifying reorganization, S acquires the assets or stock of T corporation in exchange for stock of S or P (but not both) and (if permissible) certain additional consideration (boot).

## 2. *Tax Consequences to T*

Read I.R.C. §§ 361, 358(a), (f). If T transfers its assets to S solely for stock or securities of S or P in a qualifying reorganization, T does not recognize gain or loss. I.R.C. § 361(a). The general rule suggests that T might recognize gain if it transfers its assets for boot, but that impression is deceptive. Section 361(b)(1)(A) and (3) make clear that so long as any boot received is distributed by T (or transferred to T's creditors) pursuant to the plan of reorganization, T does not recognize any gain. Since a distribution is required in a "C" and nondivisive "D" reorganization and is deemed to occur in a merger, this provision should generally be satisfied. Therefore, in general, T does not recognize gain or loss upon transferring its assets to S no matter what consideration is provided by S. The required distribution ensures that any boot paid by S will potentially have tax consequences to T's shareholders. T obtains an exchanged basis (reduced by any boot received) in the stock or securities of S or P received, and a fair market value basis in any boot received. I.R.C. § 358(a), (f).

Other than a distribution of "qualified property," which includes stock or securities of S or P, T must recognize gain on the distribution. I.R.C. § 361(c)(2). Since T obtains a fair market value basis in any boot received from S, however, the distribution of the boot should produce little or no tax consequences. Therefore, the principal consequence of section 361(c)(2) is to require T to recognize gain (but not loss) upon distribution of any of its properties not transferred to S in the reorganization. In addition, T must recognize gain or loss if it sells (rather than distributes) the qualified property it receives. A transfer of the qualified property to T's creditors in connection with the reorganization, however, is treated as a distribution of such property to T's shareholders. I.R.C. § 361(c)(3). Thus, T generally recognizes no gain or loss when it transfers property received in the reorganization to creditors.

### 3. *Tax Consequences to S and P*

#### a. Recognition of Gain or Loss

Read I.R.C. § 1032(a) and Reg. § 1.1032-2. S does not recognize gain or loss if it issues its own stock in the transaction. If it exchanges P stock in a triangular reorganization, the "zero basis" problem described in chapter seven potentially arises since S would ordinarily have a zero basis in any P stock contributed to S in the transaction, and section 1032(a) by its terms is limited to a corporation's exchange of its *own* stock. The same transaction, however, could be carried out (without recognition of gain or loss by either S or P) if P acquired T's assets directly (in exchange for P stock) and then transferred such assets to S (referred to as an "over-the-top" acquisition). The regulations therefore treat a triangular reorganization as if the over-the-top acquisition had occurred, as long as the P stock exchanged by S was provided by P pursuant to the reorganization. As a result, there is no recognition of gain or loss by S or P. Reg. § 1.1032-2(b), (d) (ex. 1). If S exchanges P stock not provided by P pursuant to the reorganization, however, S must recognize gain or loss. Reg. § 1.1032-2(c), (d) (ex. 2).

#### b. S's Basis in T Assets or Stock

Read I.R.C. §§ 362(b) and (e), 358(e). In general, S obtains a transferred basis in any T assets acquired in a reorganization. Although the statute permits S to increase its basis by any gain recognized by T in the transfer, T ordinarily does not recognize any gain even when it receives boot. Therefore, S's basis in T's former assets is generally unaffected by any boot paid or liabilities assumed, a somewhat counterintuitive but necessary result to preserve fully the gains or losses not recognized by T in the transaction. In certain circumstances, to prevent the importation of a net built-in loss that could not have been used (such as if T were a foreign corporation not taxed by the U.S.), S's basis in the property acquired is limited to fair market value. I.R.C. § 362(e)(1). In addition, although section 362(e)(2) (the rule prohibiting the duplication of net built-in losses in certain circumstances) is limited to section 351 transactions (see chapter seven), proposed regulations apply this rule to a reorganization that also satisfies section 351. For example, if X corporation owns all of the stock of corporations Y and Z and X transfers its Z stock to Y solely for voting stock of Y, the transaction is a "B" reorganization and also satisfies section 351. Under the proposed regulations, if X's basis in the Z stock transferred is greater than its fair market value, Y's basis in such stock is generally limited to fair market value. Prop. Reg. § 1.362-4(b)(5) and (d) (ex. 2).

Section 362(b) also applies to T *stock* acquired by S in a reorganization. This rule presents practical difficulties in certain cases, such as where T's stock is widely held in street name. In that situation, it may be impossible for S to discover the identity of the beneficial owners of T (and, therefore, obtain their basis in the stock transferred to S). The IRS has issued guidelines to help overcome the administrative problems. See Notice 2009-4, 2009-1 C.B. 251. Aside from the practical issue, there is a theoretical issue concerning the appropriateness of this rule. As described in the next section, any gain or loss realized and not recognized by the T shareholders in the transaction is preserved in the stock they receive in exchange. Furthermore, the stock acquisition has no effect on the amount of corporate-level gains and losses. Thus, it is not entirely clear why S should obtain a transferred (as opposed to fair market value) basis in any T stock acquired.

### c. P's Basis in S Stock

If the acquisition of stock or assets constitutes a triangular reorganization, P's basis in its stock of S is generally increased by the amount of T's former basis (net of liabilities) in its assets (or the T shareholders' former basis in their T stock). This adjustment again conforms the results of the transaction to an "over-the-top" acquisition in which P acquires the T assets (or stock) directly and then transfers them to S. The positive adjustment is reduced (but not below zero) by the value of any consideration provided by S (and not by P) in the reorganization. Reg. § 1.358-6(a), (b), (c)(1) and (3), and (d)(1) and (2). **Example 11-3** illustrates this adjustment:

> **Example 11-3:** T owns a single asset with basis of $100 and subject to a $10 liability. In a qualifying triangular reorganization, S assumes the liability and exchanges P voting stock (worth $200) for T's asset. Assuming that section 362(e) does not apply, S's basis in the asset acquired from T is $100. I.R.C. § 362(b). In addition, P's basis in its stock of S is increased by $90, which is T's basis (net of liabilities) in its asset. Reg. § 1.358-6(c)(1)(i) and (4) (ex. 1(e)). This adjustment produces the same result as if P had acquired the T asset (and assumed the liability) directly (for P stock), and then transferred the asset to

S (which assumed the liability). I.R.C. §§ 362(b), 358(a)(1) and (d)(1). If S acquires the T asset in exchange for $195 of P voting stock (provided by P), $5 cash (provided by S), and S's assumption of the liability, S's basis in the T asset is again $100. In this case, P's basis in its S stock is increased by only $85. Reg. § 1.358-6(d)(1) and (3) (ex. (a) and (b)).

### d. Survival of T's Attributes

Finally, read I.R.C. § 381(a) and (b) and skim I.R.C. § 381(c). In an asset acquisition qualifying as a reorganization, the target's tax attributes, including its loss carryforwards and E&P, generally survive in the hands of one of the acquiring corporations. If one corporation ultimately acquires all of the target's assets, it succeeds to the attributes. If there is no such corporation because the target's assets are split among several corporations, the corporation that directly acquires the assets succeeds to the attributes. Reg. § 1.381(a)-1(b)(2). In a "C" or "D" reorganization, regulations are authorized (but not yet promulgated) to allocate E&P between the target and acquiring corporation. I.R.C. § 312(h)(2). Chapter thirteen describes circumstances in which the successor corporation's use of the target's loss carryforwards may be limited after the reorganization.

## 4. *Tax Consequences to T Shareholders and Security Holders*

### a. Recognition of Gain or Loss

Read I.R.C. §§ 354(a), 356(a), (c)-(e). In general, a taxpayer who exchanges T stock or securities for stock or securities of S or P in a reorganization does not recognize gain or loss. For the reasons expressed in *Bazley*, this rule does not apply if, in general, the taxpayer receives an interest in a corporation that is more senior than the one surrendered. Thus, a taxpayer who surrenders a T security may generally receive tax-free either stock or securities of S or P. If the principal amount of the security received exceeds the principal amount of the security surrendered, however, the fair market value of the excess is treated as boot. I.R.C. §§ 354(a)(2)(A)(i), 356(d). A taxpayer who surrenders T stock (and no securities) may generally receive tax-free only stock of S or P. If the taxpayer also receives a security of S or P, the fair market value of the security is treated as boot unless receipt of the security is properly characterized as separate from the stock-for-stock exchange. I.R.C. §§ 354(a)(2)(A)(ii), 356(d); Reg. §§ 1.356-1(f), 1.301-1(*l*). If the taxpayer *only* receives a security (and no stock) in exchange for stock, then section 356(a)(1) does not apply since the taxpayer has not received any qualifying property, i.e., property permitted to be received, under section 354, without the recognition of gain. The security received is therefore taxed under sections 301 and 302. Reg.

§ 1.354-1(d) (ex. 3). Similarly, if a security holder receives anything other than stock or securities, the transaction is taxed under section 1001.

An exception applies if the S or P stock received constitutes "nonqualified preferred stock" ("NQPS"), as defined in section 351(g)(2) (see chapter seven). For purposes of sections 354 and 356, this stock is generally treated as boot (and not stock) if it is received in exchange for stock other than NQPS. I.R.C. §§ 354(a)(2)(C)(i), 356(e). Since NQPS is defined as stock that has "debt-like" features, this exception is consistent with the general rule that the receipt of an interest more senior than the one surrendered is taxed as boot. For example, a taxpayer who surrenders stock (which is not NQPS) for NQPS is treated as receiving boot, whereas a taxpayer who surrenders a security for NQPS does not recognize gain or loss. Unless the regulations provide otherwise, NQPS is treated as "stock" for other purposes, such as section 368. Thus, for example, voting NQPS of S or P is qualifying consideration in a "B" reorganization even though receipt of such stock may be taxable to the T shareholder.

Because existing judicial precedents classify a right to acquire stock (a "warrant") as not stock, the regulations treat a warrant as a security with a zero principal amount. Reg. §§ 1.354-1(e), 1.356-3(b). The general effect of this rule is to treat a warrant essentially like stock. For example, a taxpayer who exchanges T stock for both stock and a warrant of S or P does not recognize gain or loss; even though the warrant is a security, its value (as boot) is zero. Reg. § 1.356-3(c) (ex. 7). On the other hand, a taxpayer who surrenders a T warrant in exchange for a security of S or P is treated as receiving boot equal to the fair market value of the security. Id. (ex. 9). Warrants are *not* treated as stock for purposes of section 368 and COI.

### b. Amount and Character of Gain or Loss

Read I.R.C. § 356(a). A taxpayer who receives boot in connection with a section 354 exchange must recognize gain but not in excess of the boot received. The taxpayer may have a dividend if the exchange "has the effect of the distribution of a dividend" and the taxable amount does not exceed the taxpayer's ratable share of the target's accumulated E&P. I.R.C. § 356(a)(2).

Comm'r v. Clark, 489 U.S. 726 (1988), involved a forward triangular merger of a target corporation into a subsidiary of a public corporation. The taxpayer owned all of the shares of the target and surrendered them in the merger for stock of the public corporation and boot. In determining whether the boot constituted a dividend, the Court resolved a split in the Circuits regarding the proper interpretation of section 356(a)(2). In Shimberg v. U.S., 577 F.2d 283 (5th Cir. 1978), cert. denied, 439 U.S. 1115 (1979), the Fifth Circuit had held that the boot should be treated as received in a hypothetical redemption of a portion of the taxpayer's target stock immediately prior to the merger. Under this test, the boot qualified as a dividend because the taxpayer owned all of target both before and after the hypothetical redemption.

In contrast, in Wright v. U.S., 482 F.2d 600 (8th Cir. 1973), the Eighth Circuit had held that the transaction should be tested as if the issuing corporation issued only stock to the taxpayer in the merger and then used the boot to redeem a portion of such stock immediately after the merger. Under this test, since the public corporation was widely held and the hypothetical redemption resulted in a disproportionate reduction of the taxpayer's interest in such corporation, the redemption qualified under section 302(b)(2) and therefore the boot was not a dividend. Although neither test really took into account the effect of the reorganization on the taxpayer—the focus presumably of section 356(a)(2)—the Court concluded that the *Wright* test was more consistent with the language and history of the statute.

In general, a taxpayer is less likely to receive a dividend under the *Wright* test than the *Shimberg* test. If the acquiring corporation is widely held and more than 20 percent of the consideration received by the taxpayer is boot, such boot will generally not be a dividend under the section 302 tests. Although neither a "C" nor an "A" reorganization by reason of section 368(a)(2)(E) permits boot consideration in excess of 20 percent of the value of the target corporation, that limitation is applied in the aggregate and not on a shareholder-by-shareholder basis. Thus, a given target shareholder in either of those reorganizations, as well as in an "A" reorganization and one qualifying under section 368(a)(2)(D), may generally receive enough boot to avoid dividend characterization.

Under current law, dividend characterization of the boot often has minimal tax consequences. A corporate shareholder of the target must, in certain circumstances, treat any dividend received as an extraordinary dividend without regard to the period such taxpayer held the target stock. I.R.C. § 1059(e)(1)(B). In addition, individuals generally pay tax at the same rate on their qualified dividend income and long-term capital gain and, even if any boot received is properly characterized as a dividend, the distributee's realized gain limits the amount of dividend recognized. I.R.C. § 356(a)(2). Thus, for individuals, both the taxable amount and the tax rate are generally the same, regardless of the characterization of the boot. The so-called dividend-within-gain rule, which has been a part of the statute since 1924, is inconsistent with the general treatment of dividends, as illustrated by **example 11-4**:

**Example 11-4:** Individual A owns all of the stock of corporations X and Y. A's basis in each corporation's stock is $500. X is worth $2,000, has E&P of $1,500, and excess cash of $600. Y is worth $600 and has minimal E&P and no excess cash. If X distributes its $600 excess cash to A, the full amount is taxable as a dividend under section 301. The same result occurs even if A surrenders some X shares, or transfers her Y shares, to X in exchange for the $600. I.R.C. §§ 302(d), 304(a). If, however, X purchases all of Y's *assets* for $600 cash, which Y distributes to A, the transaction qualifies as a "D" reorganization; a nominal share of X is deemed issued to Y (in addition to the $600 cash) and deemed distributed by Y to A. Reg. § 1.368-2(*l*)(2)(i). Therefore, the amount of the dividend to A is limited to the $100 gain realized by A in the surrender of Y stock.

The "dividend-within-gain" limitation and the prohibition on loss recognition place a premium on the manner in which consideration is allocated to the stock surrendered by the taxpayer. In general, if a taxpayer exchanges target stock acquired at different times with different bases, the taxpayer should allocate as much boot received as possible to the high-basis stock to minimize gain. The regulations permit this flexibility so long as the allocation is economically reasonable. Reg. § 1.356-1(b) and (d) (ex. 4). **Example 11-5** illustrates:

> **Example 11-5:** Taxpayer owns two blocks of T stock, A and B, each worth $500. Taxpayer has a $400 basis in block A and a $100 basis in block B. In a reorganization, taxpayer surrenders both blocks for P stock worth $500 and $500 cash. Without a specific allocation, the consideration is allocated pro rata to each block based on its relative fair market value. Thus, P stock worth $250 plus $250 cash is allocated to each block. Taxpayer recognizes $100 gain on disposition of block A and $250 gain on disposition of block B, all of which may be a dividend. The taxpayer, however, may allocate all of the cash to block A and all of the P stock to block B. Assuming that the allocation is economically reasonable, the taxpayer's gain (including potential dividend) is limited to $100 on disposition of block A.

### c. Basis in Properties Received

Read I.R.C. § 358(a). In a reorganization, a taxpayer receives an exchanged basis in any nonrecognition property received, reduced by the boot (including money) received and increased by the gain (including any amount treated as a dividend) recognized. A taxpayer receives a fair market value basis in any boot received. The regulations generally adopt a tracing method under which the basis of each stock or security received in a reorganization is traced to the basis of the stock or security surrendered for it. For this purpose, the terms of a specific allocation made by the taxpayer are respected if it is economically reasonable. Reg. § 1.358-2(a)(2)(i) and (ii). To illustrate, if there is no specific allocation made by the taxpayer in **example 11-5**, the taxpayer's basis in the P stock acquired in exchange for block A would be $250 ($400 basis in block A plus $100 gain (or dividend) recognized less $250 cash received for block A) and the basis for the P stock acquired for block B would be $100 ($100 basis in block B plus $250 gain (or dividend) recognized less $250 cash received for block B). Under the taxpayer's allocation, the taxpayer would take a basis in the P shares acquired for block B of $100 (basis in block B); none of the P shares is received in the exchange for block A. Reg. § 1.358-2(c) (exs. 4 and 5). In short, the allocation permits the taxpayer to defer paying tax on $250 gain and potentially convert it from dividend income to long-term capital gain.

*NOTES*

1. *Even more flexibility.* Proposed regulations issued in 2009 increase the flexibility provided taxpayers by permitting an economically reasonable allocation of consideration received in a reorganization to result in the recognition of losses by target shareholders, notwithstanding section 356(c). To illustrate, assume in **example 11-5** that taxpayer's basis in the block A target shares was $600 (rather than $400). Without a specific allocation, taxpayer would not recognize a loss upon the disposition of the block A shares (I.R.C. § 356(c)) and would recognize $250 gain upon disposition of the block B shares. If, however, taxpayer allocated all $500 cash to the block A shares and all of the P stock to the block B shares, taxpayer could recognize a $100 loss on the block A shares (while not recognizing any gain on the block B shares). Prop. Reg. § 1.354-1(d) and (e) (ex. 5). Although section 354 would apply to the block B exchange, neither that section nor section 356 would apply to the block A exchange (since no nonrecognition property would be received in that exchange). Thus, assuming the exchange is not equivalent to a dividend, the block A exchange would be controlled by section 302, which permits loss recognition. It remains to be seen whether this type of cherry-picking, generally curbed by the tax law, will be allowed in reorganizations. Cf. I.R.C. §§ 311(a) and (b), 1211; Rev. Rul. 68-55 (p. 257).

2. *Possible legislative change.* Over the years, the "dividend-within-gain" rule in section 356(a)(2) has been frequently criticized, with many proposals for reform. In 2010, the House of Representatives approved a repeal of the limitation. H.R. 4213 (2010) (as passed by the House on May 28, 2010), § 422. Under the House bill, except as provided in regulations, the full amount of boot received in a reorganization may be taxed as a dividend even if the shareholder receiving the boot realizes a lesser amount of gain. The proposal retains the *Clark* test for determining whether the exchange has the effect of a dividend. The House bill also repeals the "ratable share" limitation under section 356(a)(2) on dividend treatment; moreover, both current and accumulated E&P would be taken into account, consistent with the rule in section 316(a). Finally, the bill provides that, except as provided in regulations, the E&P of both corporations in a nondivisive "D" reorganization must be taken into account (in the same manner as under section 304(b)(2)) in determining whether boot constitutes a dividend. Under regulatory authority, the same rule could be extended to other reorganizations when the target and acquiring corporations are under common control.

**Problem 11-8:** T corporation is owned equally by individuals A (100 shares) and B (100 shares). A's basis in the T stock is $10 and B's basis is $50. T owns a single asset worth $100, with a basis of $30, and subject to a $10 liability. Pursuant to a valid business purpose, T transfers the asset to S corporation in exchange for S voting stock ($80), cash ($10), and S's assumption of the liability. As part of the plan, T liquidates and distributes pro rata to A and B (in exchange for their T shares) the S stock and cash received from S.

Assume that the S stock is not nonqualified preferred stock and there is a plan of reorganization.

(a) Determine the tax consequences of this transaction to all parties.
(b) Same as (a), except that the stock exchanged by S is voting stock of P corporation provided by P in the transaction, and P controls S. Thus, in the exchange between T and S, S transfers P voting stock worth $80 (provided by P in the transaction), $10 cash (provided by S), and S assumes the liability.
(c) Same as (b), except that T's asset is subject to a $60 liability. In the transaction, S exchanges P voting stock (worth $40) and assumes the liability, but pays no cash.
(d) Same as (a), except that the T shares owned by A and B are all owned by a single shareholder, C, in two blocks. C has a $50 basis in one block and a $10 basis in the other. To minimize the amount of gain recognized in the transaction, how should C allocate the consideration received in exchange for C's shares in T?

## D. Final Observation

At this point, you may understandably feel overwhelmed by the number of issues and amount of detail provided in this chapter. Moreover, the material covered just begins to scratch the surface of the questions raised by reorganizations. Many transactions involve corporations that are members of consolidated groups (chapter fourteen) or joint-ventures (taxed as partnerships), or are engaged in cross-border activities. These factors multiply the tax issues that must be considered.

A comparison of the material provided in chapter ten and this chapter reveals part of the cost of the reorganization exception. Chapter ten examined the issues involved in taxable corporate acquisitions. As long as the U.S. continues to have a corporate income tax and to treat a corporation as separate from its shareholders for tax purposes, issues like those presented in chapter ten must be resolved when one corporation acquires the stock or assets of another. In that sense, the material in chapter ten represents a structural part of the corporate income tax.

By contrast, the reorganization exception represents, for the most part, a policy choice rather than a structural component of tax law. Once an exception is provided that allows taxpayers in certain circumstances to achieve significant tax savings, it is understandable that taxpayers and their advisors will want to know and push the limits of the exception, and the IRS and courts will have to respond. The result (in abbreviated form) is what you see in this chapter. To a given tax advisor and client, the reorganization exception can be a boon; a famous tax lawyer once quipped that corporate reorganizations had paid for the college education of all of his children. From a societal standpoint, however, policymakers must weigh not only the economic effects of the reorganization exception but also the administrative costs to taxpayers and the government in deciding whether the exception should remain part of the law.

# Chapter 12

# Divisive Reorganizations

This chapter describes the tax consequences of transactions that divide a corporation into two or more parts. If they satisfy a multitude of conditions, such transactions are generally treated as nonrecognition events at both the corporate and shareholder levels and are referred to in this book as "divisive reorganizations" (even though the transaction may not be defined in section 368(a)(1)). The basic pattern of a divisive reorganization involves a transfer of assets by one corporation (the "distributing corporation") to a corporation it controls (the "controlled corporation"), followed by a distribution of the controlled corporation's stock to the shareholders of the distributing corporation. Part A provides background on the nature and origins of the divisive reorganization statute. Part B then describes the tax consequences of divisive reorganizations to the distributee, the traditional focus of tax policy. Finally, part C examines the tax consequences of these transactions to the distributing corporation; this issue has gained importance because divisive reorganizations represent one of the few remaining opportunities for taxpayers potentially to avoid the repeal of *General Utilities*.

## A. Introduction

### Rockefeller v. United States

257 U.S. 176 (1921)

Mr. Justice Pitney delivered the opinion of the court.

... In and prior to the year 1914, the Prairie Oil & Gas Company, a corporation of the State of Kansas, was engaged in producing, purchasing and selling crude petroleum, and transporting it through pipe lines owned by the company in the States of Kansas and Oklahoma, and elsewhere. ... In the month of June, 1914, it was judicially determined by this court ... that with respect to the transportation business [the company was a common carrier] in interstate commerce, subject to the Act to Regulate Commerce ... and as such subject to the supervision of the

Interstate Commerce Commission. By Act of September 26, 1914, the remainder of [the] business became subject to the supervision of the Federal Trade Commission. In order to avoid a probable conflict of federal authority in case the combined business of production and transportation should continue to be carried on as theretofore, it was . . . upon advice of counsel, determined that the pipe line property should be owned and operated by a separate corporation. . . . For [this reason,] the stockholders of the Prairie Oil & Gas Company caused a corporation to be organized under the laws of the State of Kansas, by the name of the Prairie Pipe Line Company, to which all the pipe line property of the Prairie Oil & Gas Company was transferred in consideration of the issue and delivery of the entire capital stock of the new company, to be distributed pro rata to the stockholders of the Prairie Oil & Gas Company.

. . . [T]he oil company had a surplus in excess of the stated value of its pipe lines and of the par value of the total stock of the corresponding pipe line company; so that the transfer of the pipe lines and the distribution of the stock received for them left the capital of the respective oil companies unimpaired and required no reduction in their outstanding issues.

Messrs. Rockefeller and Harkness respectively were holders of large amounts of the stock of . . . the Prairie [Oil & Gas Company] and in the [distribution] each received an amount of stock in . . . the pipe line [company] proportionate to his holdings in the oil companies. This occurred in the year 1915. Neither Mr. Rockefeller nor Mr. Harkness nor the latter's executors sold any of the stock in the pipe line companies.

[The issue is] whether the distribution of the [pipe line stock] . . . among the stockholders of the oil [company] constituted, under the circumstances, dividends. . . .

Under the facts as recited we deem it to be too plain for dispute that . . . the new pipe line company shares were in substance and effect distributed by the oil company to its stockholders. . . . In each case the consideration moved from the oil company in its corporate capacity, the new company's stock issued in exchange for it was distributed among the oil company's stockholders in their individual capacity, and was a substantial fruit of their ownership of stock in the oil company, in effect a dividend out of the accumulated surplus.

The facts are in all essentials indistinguishable from those presented in *U.S. v. Phellis*. . . . [A]s in that [case], . . . there was apparently little but a reorganization and financial readjustment of the affairs of the companies concerned . . . without immediate effect upon the personnel of the stockholders, or much difference in the aggregate corporate activities or properties. As in the *Phellis* Case, the adoption of the new arrangement did not of itself produce any increase of wealth to the stockholders, since whatever was gained by each in the value of his new pipe line stock was at the same moment withdrawn through a corresponding diminution of the value of his stock. Nevertheless the new stock represented assets of the oil [company] standing in the place of the pipe line properties that before had constituted portions of [its] surplus assets, and it was capable of division among stockholders as the pipe line properties were not. The distribution, whatever its effect upon the aggregate interests of the mass of stockholders, constituted in the case of each individual a gain in the form of actual exchangeable assets transferred to him from the oil company for his separate use in partial realization of his former indivisible and contingent interest in the corporate surplus. It was in substance and effect, not merely in form, a dividend of profits by the corporation, and individual income to the stockholder. . . .

Mr. Justice VAN DEVANTER and Mr. Justice MCREYNOLDS dissent.

## *NOTES AND QUESTIONS*

1. Phellis. U.S. v. Phellis, 257 U.S. 156 (1921), decided on the same day as *Rockefeller*, involved a change in the DuPont Corporation's corporate charter from New Jersey to Delaware. The New Jersey corporation transferred virtually all of its assets to a new Delaware subsidiary and the transferor then distributed pro rata to its shareholders all of the stock of the Delaware company. Following the transaction, the Delaware company continued to operate the business formerly conducted by the New Jersey company with the same assets, officers, and shareholders; the New Jersey company continued to exist but did no business. Applying the same reasoning as in *Marr v. U.S.* (p. 370), the Court distinguished *Eisner v. Macomber* and concluded that the receipt of the Delaware stock constituted a taxable dividend to the shareholders.

2. *Arguments for the taxpayer*. Evaluate the strength of the following reasons why the *Rockefeller* transaction should not have resulted in any immediate tax consequences to the taxpayers:

a. The transaction did not enrich the taxpayers.
b. The transaction was undertaken for legitimate business purposes in order to separate a newly regulated business from an unregulated one.
c. The transaction did not change the substance of what the taxpayers owned since, both before and after the transaction, they owned stock in companies engaged in the same business activities.

3. *The Court's reasoning*. In *Rockefeller*, the majority of the Court concluded that the distribution should be taxable to the shareholders because the transaction offered them an opportunity they did not previously have:

> the new [pipe line] stock represented assets of the oil [company] standing in the place of the pipe line properties that before had constituted portions of [the oil company's] surplus assets, and it was capable of division among stockholders as the pipe line properties were not. The distribution . . . constituted in the case of each individual a gain in the form of actual exchangeable assets transferred to him from the oil

> company for his separate use in partial realization of his former indivisible and contingent interest in the corporate surplus. [217 U.S. at 183-84.]

In determining the tax consequences of the distribution, why was the existence of this new opportunity so important?

4. *Distinguishing* Rockefeller *from* Gregory. Review *Gregory v. Helvering* (p. 120), which involved a transaction structured along the same lines as the one carried out in *Rockefeller*. If Congress were to conclude that the distribution in *Rockefeller*, but not in *Gregory*, should be a nonrecognition event, how should it distinguish the two transactions?

5. *Terminology*. Divisive reorganizations are commonly referred to as "spin-offs," "split-offs," or "split-ups," depending upon whether the distribution of the stock of the controlled corporation is an ordinary distribution or pursuant to a redemption or liquidation of the distributing corporation, respectively.

6. *Statutory developments*. In response to *Rockefeller* and *Phellis*, Congress in 1924 provided tax-free treatment to shareholders who receive stock or securities of the controlled corporation in a spin-off transaction. This provision, however, was repealed in 1934 as part of Congress's consideration of a broad anti-tax avoidance proposal to repeal the tax-free treatment of *all* reorganizations. Congress rejected the broad proposal in part because of its revenue loss, since many reorganizations at the time (if made taxable) would have resulted in the recognition of losses. During this same period, however, the *Gregory* transaction was being considered by the lower courts, and Congress was persuaded that repeal of the spin-off provision was necessary to protect the tax on dividend income. The tax-free treatment of divisive reorganizations was reinstated in 1951 and has remained in the law (with many modifications and an increasing number of conditions) ever since.

## B. Tax Consequences to the Distributee

### 1. *Introduction*

Read I.R.C. §§ 355(a)(1) and (2), 368(a)(1)(D), and Reg. § 1.355-1(b) and -2(a). If the various conditions of section 355 are satisfied, no gain or loss is generally recognized by the distributees upon distribution of stock or securities of the controlled corporation (and, as described in part C, no gain or loss is generally recognized by the distributing corporation as well). Qualifying divisive transactions generally follow one of two patterns. One pattern is illustrated by the two steps in *Rockefeller*: a transfer of the pipe line assets by the distributing corporation to a controlled corporation followed by a distribution of the controlled corporation stock to the distributing corporation's shareholders. A transaction consisting of both steps constitutes a divisive "D" reorganization if the distribution satisfies section 355 and the other conditions of section 368(a)(1)(D) are met. Certain corporate divisions, however, only involve the second step because the assets to be separated are already held by a controlled corporation prior to the distribution. In this pattern, the tax consequences of the distribution are determined exclusively by section 355. Cf. I.R.C. § 355(a)(2)(C). Although a division satisfying only section 355 is not technically a "reorganization" within the meaning of section 368(a)(1), it has the same general effect as one and is therefore also referred to here as a "divisive reorganization."

The common feature of all divisive reorganizations is a distribution of stock or securities of the controlled corporation that satisfies section 355. In general, under that provision, the distributing corporation must control the controlled corporation immediately before the distribution and must distribute at least an amount of stock constituting control of the controlled corporation. In addition, the transaction may not be used principally as a device for the distribution of the E&P of the distributing or controlled corporation (or both). Finally, certain "active business" requirements applicable to both the distributing and controlled corporations must be met and certain nonstatutory conditions must also be satisfied. As discussed in part A, the original purpose of these conditions was to prevent avoidance of the tax on dividend income. The following sections describe each of the conditions of this provision.

### 2. *"Control" and "Distribution of Control"*

Read I.R.C. §§ 355(a)(1)(A) and (D), 368(c), and Reg. § 1.355-2(e). Two independent conditions of section 355 require the distributing corporation to control the controlled corporation immediately prior to the distribution and to distribute an amount of stock at least constituting control of such corporation. For these purposes, "control" is defined by section 368(c). In general, together with the rest of section 355, these conditions help to distinguish a major fission of a corporation from a mere separation of surplus assets (including a portfolio stock investment) of the distributing corporation. A possible analogy is to the acquisitive reorganization rules, which generally are limited to major corporate acquisitions and not piecemeal sales of individual assets between corporations. The following case illustrates the "distribution of control" requirement.

#### Commissioner v. Gordon

391 U.S. 83 (1968)

Mr. Justice HARLAN delivered the opinion of the Court.

. . . American Telephone and Telegraph Company (hereafter AT&T) conducts its local communications business through corporate subsidiaries. Prior to July 1, 1961, communications services in California, Oregon, Washington, and Idaho were provided by Pacific Telephone and Telegraph Company (hereafter Pacific). AT&T

held about 90% of the common stock of Pacific at all relevant times. The remainder was widely distributed.

Early in 1961, it was decided to divide Pacific into two separate corporate subsidiaries of AT&T. The plan was to create a new corporation, Pacific Northwest Bell Telephone Company (hereafter Northwest) to conduct telephone business in Oregon, Washington, and Idaho, leaving the conduct of the California business in the hands of Pacific. To this end, Pacific would transfer all its assets and liabilities in the first three States to Northwest, in return for Northwest common stock and debt paper. Then, Pacific would transfer sufficient Northwest stock to Pacific shareholders to pass control of Northwest to the parent company, AT&T.

Pacific had, however, objectives other than fission. It wanted to generate cash to pay off existing liabilities and meet needs for capital, but not to have excess cash left over. It also feared that a simple distribution of the Northwest stock would encounter obstacles under California corporation law.[1] Consequently, the "Plan for Reorganization" submitted to Pacific's shareholders on February 27, 1961, had two special features. It provided that only about 56% of the Northwest common stock would be offered to Pacific shareholders immediately after the creation of Northwest. It also provided that, instead of simply distributing Northwest stock pro rata to shareholders, Pacific would distribute to its shareholders transferable rights entitling their holders to purchase Northwest common from Pacific at an amount to be specified by Pacific's Board of Directors, but expected to be below the fair market value of the Northwest common.

In its February 27 statement to shareholders, Pacific said that it was seeking a ruling from the Internal Revenue Service "with respect to the tax status of the rights to purchase which will be issued in connection with the offerings of capital stock of the New Company to shareholders of the Company." The statement warned, however, that "(t)axable income to the holders of such shares may result with respect to such rights."

The plan was approved by Pacific's shareholders on March 24, 1961. Pacific transferred its assets and liabilities in Oregon, Washington, and Idaho to Northwest, and ceased business in those States on June 30, 1961. On September 29, 1961, Pacific issued to its common stockholders one right for each outstanding share of Pacific stock. These rights were exercisable until October 20, 1961. Six rights plus a payment of $16 were required to purchase one share of Northwest common. The rights issued in 1961 were sufficient to transfer about 57% of the Northwest stock.

By September 29, 1961, the Internal Revenue Service had ruled that shareholders who sold rights would realize ordinary income in the amount of the sales price, and that shareholders who exercised rights would realize ordinary income in

1. The record indicates that Pacific's attorneys had advised that if Pacific distributed the Northwest shares without payment of consideration by Pacific's shareholders, the distribution would have to be charged to earned surplus; the attorneys further advised that Pacific had insufficient earned surplus for this purpose, and that if this difficulty were avoided by creation of a reduction surplus, the reduction surplus would, under California law, have to be used first to redeem Pacific's preferred shares.

the amount of the difference between $16 paid in and the fair market value, measured as of the date of exercise, of the Northwest common received. The prospectus accompanying the distributed rights informed Pacific shareholders of this ruling.

On June 12, 1963, the remaining 43% of the Northwest stock was offered to Pacific shareholders. This second offering was structured much as the first had been, except that eight rights plus $16 were required to purchase one share of Northwest.

The Gordons . . . and the Baans . . . were minority shareholders of Pacific as of September 29, 1961. In the rights distribution that occurred that day the Gordons received 1,540 rights under the plan. They exercised 1,536 of the rights on October 5, 1961, paying $4,096 to obtain 256 shares of Northwest, at a price of $16 plus six rights per share. The average price of Northwest stock on the American Stock Exchange was $26 per share on October 5. On the same day, the Gordons sold the four odd rights for $6.36. The Baans received 600 rights on September 29, 1961. They exercised them all on October 11, 1961, receiving 100 shares of Northwest in return for their 600 rights and $1,600. On October 11, the agreed fair market value of one Northwest share was $26.94.

In their federal income tax returns for 1961, neither the Gordons nor the Baans reported any income upon the receipt of the rights or upon exercising them to obtain Northwest stock at less than its fair market value. The Gordons also did not report any income on the sale of the four rights. The Commissioner asserted deficiencies against both sets of taxpayers. He contended, in a joint proceeding in the Tax Court, that the taxpayers received ordinary income in the amount of the difference between the sum they paid in exercising their rights and the fair market value of the Northwest stock received. He contended further that the Gordons realized ordinary income in the amount of $6.36, the sales price, upon the sale of their four odd rights.

The Tax Court upheld the taxpayers' contention that the 1961 distribution of Northwest stock met the requirements of § 355 of the Code, with the result that no gain or loss should be recognized on the receipt by them or their exercise of the rights. The Tax Court held, however, that the Gordons' sale of the four odd rights resulted in ordinary income to them. The Commissioner appealed the *Baan* case to the Court of Appeals for the Ninth Circuit, and the *Gordon* case to the Court of Appeals for the Second Circuit; in the latter, the Gordons cross-appealed. The Ninth Circuit reversed the Tax Court, holding that the spread between $16 and fair market value was taxable as ordinary income to the Baans. The Second Circuit disagreed, sustaining the Tax Court on this point in the *Gordon* case, Judge Friendly dissenting. The Second Circuit went on to hold that the amount received by the Gordons for the four odd rights was taxable as a capital gain rather than as ordinary income, reversing the Tax Court on this point.

Because of the conflict, we granted certiorari. We affirm the decision of the Court of Appeals for the Ninth Circuit, and reverse the decision of the Court of Appeals for the Second Circuit on both points.

Under §§ 301 and 316 of the Code, subject to specific exceptions and qualifications provided in the Code, any distribution of property by a corporation to its shareholders out of accumulated earnings and profits is a dividend taxable to the shareholders as ordinary income. Every distribution of corporate property, again except as otherwise specifically provided, "is made out of earnings and profits to the extent thereof." It is here agreed that on September 28, 1961, Pacific's accumulated earnings and profits were larger in extent than the total amount the Commissioner here contends was a dividend—the difference between the fair market value of all Northwest stock sold in 1961 and the total amount, at $16 per share, paid in by purchasers.

Whether the actual dividend occurs at the moment when valuable rights are distributed or at the moment when their value is realized through sale or exercise, it is clear that when a corporation sells corporate property to stockholders or their assignees at less than its fair market value, thus diminishing the net worth of the corporation, it is engaging in a "distribution of property" as that term is used in § 316. Such a sale thus results in a dividend to shareholders unless some specific exception or qualification applies. In particular, it is here agreed that the spread was taxable to the present taxpayers unless the distribution of Northwest stock by Pacific met the requirements for nonrecognition stated in § 355. . . .[2]

Section 355 provides that certain distributions of securities of corporations controlled by the distributing corporation do not result in recognized gain or loss to the distributee shareholders. The requirements of the section are detailed and specific, and must be applied with precision. It is no doubt true, as the Second Circuit emphasized, that the general purpose of the section was to distinguish corporate fission from the distribution of earnings and profits. However, although a court may have reference to this purpose when there is a genuine question as to the meaning of one of the requirements Congress has imposed, a court is not free to disregard requirements simply because it considers them redundant or unsuited to achieving the general purpose in a particular case. Congress has abundant power to provide that a corporation wishing to spin off a subsidiary must, however *bona fide* its intentions, conform the details of a distribution to a particular set of rules.

2. It is important to begin from this premise. In our view, the Court of Appeals for the Second Circuit erred in its approach to the § 355 problem because it assumed, at the outset, that the Commissioner essentially sought to tax a transaction that brought no "income" to Pacific shareholders. Whether the shareholders received income, however, cannot in practice be determined in the abstract, before looking at § 355. Any common shareholder in some sense "owns" a fraction of the assets of the corporation in which he holds stock, including those assets that reflect accumulated corporate earnings. Earnings are not taxed to the shareholder when they accrue to the corporation, but instead when they are passed to shareholders individually through dividends. Consequently it does not help to note, as the Second Circuit here did, that the distribution of Northwest stock merely changed the form of ownership that Pacific's shareholders enjoyed and did not increase their wealth. This is only very roughly true at best, but in the rough sense in which it is here true, it is true of any dividend. The question is not whether a shareholder ends up with "more" but whether the change in the form of his ownership represents a transfer to him, by the corporation, of assets reflecting its accumulated earnings and profits. There may be a genuine theoretical difference between a change in form representing a mere corporate fission, separating what the shareholder owns into two smaller but essentially similar parts, and a change in form representing a dividend, separating what a shareholder owns *qua* shareholder from what he owns as an individual. This difference, however, must be defined by objectively workable tests, such as Congress supplied in § 355. Neither the Second Circuit nor the taxpayers have suggested any other way of identifying a true fission.

The Commissioner contends that the 1961 distribution of Northwest stock failed to qualify under § 355 in several respects.[3] We need, however, reach only one. Section 355(a)(1)(D) requires that, in order to qualify for nonrecognition of gain or loss to shareholders, the distribution must be such that

> "as part of the distribution, the distributing corporation distributes —
>
> (i) all of the stock and securities in the controlled corporation held by it immediately before the distribution, or
>
> (ii) an amount of stock in the controlled corporation constituting control within the meaning of section 368(c), and . . ."

Section 368(c) provides in relevant part that

> "the term 'control' means the ownership of stock possessing at least 80 percent of the total combined voting power of all classes of stock entitled to vote and at least 80 percent of the total number of shares of all other classes of stock of the corporation."[4]

On September 28, 1961, the day before the first rights distribution, Pacific owned all of the common stock of Northwest, the only class of securities that company had issued. The 1961 rights offering contemplated transferring, and succeeded in transferring, about 57% of the Northwest common to Pacific shareholders. It therefore could not be clearer that this 1961 distribution did not transfer "all" of the stock of Northwest held by Pacific prior to it, and did not transfer "control" as that term is defined in § 368(c).

Nevertheless, taxpayers contend, and the Second Circuit agreed, that the requirements of subsection [355(a)(1)(D)] were here met because Pacific distributed the remaining 43% of the Northwest stock in 1963. The court said that the purpose of the subsection "in no way requires a single distribution." The court apparently

3. The Commissioner contends, first, that Pacific did not distribute "solely stock or securities" as required by § 355(a)(1)(A), because it distributed rights rather than stock. He contends, second, that Pacific did not distribute the Northwest stock "to a shareholder, with respect to its stock" as required by § 355(a)(1)(A)(i), because it did not distribute the stock to shareholders but sold it to holders of transferable rights, for cash consideration. He contends, third, that Northwest did not meet the quantity requirements of § 355(a)(1)(D) because it parted with only 57% of the stock in 1961. Any one of these arguments, if established, would support the result the Commissioner seeks. The Court of Appeals for the Second Circuit perforce rejected all three. The Court of Appeals for the Ninth Circuit accepted all three. We reach only the last.

4. In the Tax Court, the Commissioner did not argue that Pacific had failed to meet the requirement that it distribute at least 80% of the Northwest stock, but rested upon his other arguments against applying § 355. When the Tax Court rejected these arguments, the Commissioner raised the 80% question, as well as his other arguments in both Courts of Appeals. Both considered the point on the merits, dividing on it as on the others. Since the general issue of the applicability of § 355 has been in the case since its inception, taxpayers do not contend that the 80% question is not properly before this Court. Since the record leaves no disputed issue of fact with respect to this question, we find it proper to decide it here without reference to a trier of fact.

concluded that so long as it appears, at the time the issue arises, that the parent corporation has in fact distributed all of the stock of the subsidiary, the requirements of § [355(a)(1)(D)(i)] have been satisfied.

We are forced to disagree. The Code requires that "the distribution" divest the controlling corporation of all of, or 80% control of, the controlled corporation. Clearly, if an initial transfer of less than a controlling interest in the controlled corporation is to be treated for tax purposes as a mere first step in the divestiture of control, it must at least be identifiable as such at the time it is made. Absent other specific directions from Congress, Code provisions must be interpreted so as to conform to the basic premise of annual tax accounting. It would be wholly inconsistent with this premise to hold that the essential character of a transaction, and its tax impact, should remain not only undeterminable but unfixed for an indefinite and unlimited period in the future, awaiting events that might or might not happen. This requirement that the character of a transaction be determinable does not mean that the entire divestiture must necessarily occur within a single tax year. It does, however, mean that if one transaction is to be characterized as a "first step" there must be a binding commitment to take the later steps.

Here, it was little more than a fortuity that, by the time suit was brought alleging a deficiency in taxpayers' 1961 returns, Pacific had distributed the remainder of the stock. The plan for reorganization submitted to shareholders in 1961 promised that 56% of that stock would be distributed immediately. The plan went on,

> "It is expected that within about three years after acquiring the stock of the New Company, the Company by one or more offerings will offer for sale the balance of such stock, following the procedures described in the preceding paragraph. The proceeds from such sales will be used by the Company to repay advances then outstanding and for general corporate purposes including expenditures for extensions, additions and improvements to its telephone plant.
>
> The prices at which the shares of the New Company will be offered pursuant to the offerings referred to . . . will be determined by the Board of Directors of the Company at the time of each offering."

It was further stated that such subsequent distributions would occur "[a]t a time or times related to its [Pacific's] need for new capital." Although there is other language in the plan that might be interpreted as preventing Pacific management from dealing with the Northwest stock in any way inconsistent with eventual sale to Pacific shareholders, there is obviously no promise to sell any particular amount of stock, at any particular time, at any particular price. If the 1961 distribution played a part in what later proved to be a total divestiture of the Northwest stock, it was not, in 1961, either a total divestiture or a step in a plan of total divestiture.

Accordingly, we hold that the taxpayers, having exercised rights to purchase shares of Northwest from Pacific in 1961, must recognize ordinary income in that year in the amount of the difference between $16 per share and the fair market value of a share of Northwest common at the moment the rights were exercised.

. . . [W]hether the $6.36 received by taxpayers Gordon upon the sale of four rights was taxable as ordinary income, as a capital gain, or not at all, does not require extended discussion in light of our view upon the first question. Since receipt and exercise of the rights would have produced ordinary income, receipt and sale of the rights, constituting merely an alternative route to realization, also produced income taxable at ordinary rates. . . .

The judgment of the Court of Appeals for the Second Circuit is reversed. The judgment of the Court of Appeals for the Ninth Circuit is affirmed. It is so ordered. . . .

## *NOTES AND QUESTIONS*

1. *Step-transaction doctrine.* In *Gordon*, the taxpayer argued that two distributions occurring roughly 21 months apart should be treated as a single transaction in order to qualify both distributions under section 355. Since taxpayers are ordinarily bound to accept the tax consequences of the form of their transactions, including the existence of nominally independent steps, the Court could have dismissed the taxpayer's claim out of hand. Instead, the Court considered the argument but minimized taxpayer opportunism by requiring satisfaction of the "binding commitment" test, the formulation of the step-transaction doctrine that requires the strongest evidence to integrate steps.

Two other common formulations of the step-transaction doctrine are the "end result" and "mutual interdependence" tests. Under the former test, nominally separate transactions with independent legal significance are, nevertheless, integrated with other steps if they were all intended from the outset to be undertaken in order to achieve a particular end result. Under the latter test, individual steps are collapsed if they are so interdependent as to be fruitless without completion of all of the steps. Under either of these two tests, would the distributions in *Gordon* have been stepped together?

2. *Rights to acquire stock.* As stated in footnote 3, the Court did not reach the Commissioner's other arguments that the distribution consisted merely of rights to acquire Northwest stock (as opposed to stock of such corporation) and that the subsequent receipt of Northwest stock by the taxpayers was pursuant to their exercise of those rights (and not with respect to their stock in Pacific). The regulations at the time provided that stock or securities of the controlled corporation did not include rights to acquire stock. In Redding v. Comm'r, 630 F.2d 1169 (7th Cir. 1980), cert. denied, 450 U.S. 913 (1981), the distributing corporation distributed to its shareholders transferable rights to acquire over 80 percent of the stock of the controlled corporation and all such rights were exercised within 15 days. The court refused to collapse the two steps and thus treat the events as a single transaction involving a distribution of over 80 percent of the stock of the controlled corporation. Accordingly, the court held that the receipt of stock rights constituted a taxable dividend to the shareholders. Crucial to the court's conclusion was the issuance of *transferable*

stock rights, which potentially enabled the distributing and controlled corporations to raise capital from new investors. Thus, the intended end result of the two steps was not simply to distribute a controlling interest in the controlled corporation to those shareholders who owned the distributing corporation just prior to the distribution. As the court observed, had that been the sole objective, it could have been easily accomplished by distributing controlled corporation stock (and not stock rights) to those shareholders.

The regulations have since been amended generally to treat (for purposes of section 355) stock rights as securities with no principal amount. Reg. § 1.355-1(c). This resolution avoids having to determine how a distribution of stock rights, if treated as "stock" of the controlled corporation, affects the "distribution of control" requirement of section 355. The regulation, however, leaves open the issue raised by the Commissioner in *Gordon* and decided by the Seventh Circuit in *Redding*. In the absence of a successful recharacterization of the transaction, it appears that a distribution of stock rights that is not accompanied by a distribution of a controlling interest in the controlled corporation does not satisfy section 355. There is a remaining question whether the taxable event in that case is the receipt or exercise of the rights. In *Gordon*, the Court appears to have followed the Commissioner's position and treated the exercise (or sale) of the rights, and not their mere receipt, as the taxable event.

3. *Hot stock cooled off.* Read I.R.C. § 355(a)(3)(B). This provision generally treats certain stock of the controlled corporation (referred to as "hot stock") as taxable boot (and not stock), for purposes of sections 355 and 356 (other than section 355(a)(1)(D)), if it was acquired by the distributing corporation in a transaction that was taxable to the transferor and occurred within five years of the distribution. The purpose of the rule is to prevent the distributing corporation from using its surplus assets to purchase stock of the controlled corporation and then distributing such stock tax-free in a qualifying section 355 transaction. If the distribution were tax-free, the net effect of the transaction might be avoidance of the dividend that would have arisen if the surplus assets had instead been distributed to the shareholder. As noted, this rule does not apply for purposes of section 355(a)(1)(D). Thus, hot stock is treated as stock in order to determine whether, in the transaction, the distributing corporation distributes at least a controlling interest in the controlled corporation.

Temporary regulations have significantly narrowed the scope of the hot stock rule to conform it to an amendment to section 355(b) involving the active trade or business requirement. In general, the hot stock rule does not apply if, following the acquisition of stock (but prior to its distribution), the distributing corporation's stock ownership of the controlled corporation satisfies section 1504(a)(2) (i.e., constitutes at least 80 percent of the voting power and value of the controlled corporation). Temp. Reg. § 1.355-2T(g)(2)(i) and (3). Since section 355(a)(1)(A) requires the distributing corporation to control (within the meaning of section 368(c)) the controlled corporation immediately prior to the distribution (i.e., to own at least 80 percent of the voting power and each class of nonvoting stock of such corporation), the regulation effectively limits the hot stock rule to those few circumstances where the distributing corporation's stock ownership satisfies section 368(c) but not section 1504(a)(2). Temp. Reg. § 1.355-2T(g)(5) (exs. 1 & 2). For example, suppose that just prior to a distribution, the distributing corporation owns all of the voting common stock, but none of the voting preferred stock, of the controlled corporation. This stock would constitute control for purposes of section 368(c) if the common stock has at least 80 percent of the voting power of the corporation. The stock would not, however, satisfy section 1504(a)(2) if the preferred stock represents over 20 percent of the value of the corporation. Thus, if both of these were true, then controlled corporation stock acquired by the distributing corporation in a taxable transaction within the previous five years would generally be treated as taxable boot to the distributee even though the transaction otherwise satisfies section 355.

4. *Retained stock or securities.* The distributing corporation must establish that its failure to distribute in the transaction any stock or securities of the controlled corporation is not for a tax avoidance purpose. I.R.C. § 355(a)(1)(D)(ii). According to the regulations, the business purpose of the transaction ordinarily requires a distribution of *all* of the controlled corporation's stock and securities, and a failure to distribute stock to avoid the effect of the hot stock rule is evidence of a tax avoidance purpose. Reg. § 1.355-2(e)(2). Thus, if a distributing corporation owns hot stock, it is generally preferable to distribute the stock in a qualifying section 355 transaction (with the hot stock being treated as taxable boot) rather than to retain such stock (and potentially cause the entire transaction to be taxable). The IRS has ruled that a distributing corporation's retention of some controlled corporation stock or securities to serve as collateral for a bank loan does not violate section 355(a)(1)(D). According to the IRS, the transaction resulted in a genuine separation, with the retained interest not enabling the distributing corporation to maintain practical control over the controlled corporation. Rev. Rul. 75-321, 1975-2 C.B. 123; Rev. Rul. 75-469, 1975-2 C.B. 126.

5. *Impact of post-distribution acquisition or restructuring of controlled corporation.* In Rev. Rul. 98-27, 1998-1 C.B. 1159, the IRS indicated that it would not apply the *Court Holding Co.* or similar doctrine to recharacterize (solely by reason of a post-distribution acquisition or restructuring of the controlled corporation) whether a transaction satisfies the "control" and "distribution of control" conditions of section 355. Assume that D corporation owns all of C corporation and distributes pro rata all of the C stock to D's shareholders. Subsequently, C is acquired by Y corporation in a tax-free reorganization in exchange for Y stock constituting 25 percent of Y. Assume that these steps are recharacterized under the *Court Holding Co.* or similar doctrine as: (1) an acquisition of D's stock in C by Y in exchange for 25 percent of Y, followed by (2) a pro rata distribution by D to its shareholders of such Y stock. In this event, the distribution would not qualify under section 355 because D would neither control Y prior to the distribution nor distribute at least a controlling interest in Y. In amendments enacted in 1997 and 1998, Congress clarified that such a recharacterization is not appropriate for purposes of determining the tax consequences of any transfer by D to C prior to the distribution and whether D's shareholders control C immediately after the distribution, as required by section 368(a)(1)(D). I.R.C.

§§ 351(c)(2), 368(a)(2)(H)(ii). In Rev. Rul. 98-27, the IRS sensibly reached the same result for purposes of section 355. As described in part C of this chapter, however, an acquisition or restructuring of the controlled corporation following the distribution may affect the tax consequences of the transaction to the distributing corporation.

6. *Footnote 4*. Surprisingly, the Commissioner failed to even raise at trial the issue that eventually proved crucial to the Court. In *General Utilities* (p. 175), a similar failure by the Commissioner to raise an issue at trial may have been key to the Court's decision in favor of the taxpayer.

### 3. *Not a "Device"*

Read I.R.C. § 355(a)(1)(B). The section 355 condition most clearly directed towards the concern expressed by Justice Pitney in *Rockefeller* is the requirement that a qualifying transaction not be used principally as a device for the distribution of the distributing or controlled corporation's E&P. Since a purported divisive reorganization does not generally result in anything being distributed out of corporate solution, the focus of the requirement is on whether the transaction provides a future bailout *opportunity* that would not otherwise have existed. The following ruling illustrates the device test.

## Rev. Rul. 64-102

1964-1 C.B. 136

Advice has been requested as to the Federal income tax consequences of a non pro rata distribution by a corporation of stock of a controlled corporation to certain of its shareholders in exchange for all their stock where such distribution is immediately preceded by a large contribution by the distributing corporation to the capital of the controlled corporation.

A corporation, engaged for more than five years in the active conduct of a business, owned all the capital stock of another corporation, which was also engaged for more than five years in the active conduct of a separate business. All the stock of the subsidiary corporation had been acquired more than five years previously by the parent corporation.

A minority group of shareholders owning one third of the stock of the parent was primarily involved in the management of the subsidiary. In order to resolve managerial policy differences between this group of shareholders and the majority group, it was decided to distribute all the stock of the subsidiary to the minority shareholders in exchange for all their stock in the parent. Prior to the distribution, the parent made a capital contribution of 13x dollars to the subsidiary in order to equalize the value of the subsidiary's stock with the value of the parent's stock owned by the exchanging shareholders. The capital contribution did not cause changes of such character as to constitute the acquisition of a new or different business. After the contribution to capital and prior to the distribution of the stock of the subsidiary, the stock of the parent corporation had a value of 72x dollars and the stock of the subsidiary corporation had a value of 24x dollars. The one-third of the parent's stock owned by the minority shareholders was then surrendered in exchange for all the subsidiary's stock.

Section 355 of the Internal Revenue Code of 1954 provides rules for the separation of two or more existing businesses formerly operated directly or indirectly by a single corporation without recognition of gain or loss to the shareholders and security holders. . . .

Section 355(a)(2) of the Code states that the general rule set forth in section 355(a)(1) of the Code will be applied without regard to whether the distribution is pro rata or whether the shareholders surrender stock in the distributing corporation. However, section 355(a)(1)(B) of the Code provides that the transaction must not be used principally as a device for the distribution of earnings and profits of the distributing corporation or the controlled corporation or both.

Although the parent corporation made a large contribution to the capital of the subsidiary immediately before the distribution of the subsidiary's stock to the minority shareholders, the minority shareholders who received the controlled corporation's stock surrendered in exchange all their stock in the distributing corporation. This distribution, if it were considered taxable, would not result in dividend income to the shareholders receiving the subsidiary's stock because the exchange would be in complete redemption of all their stock interest in the distributing corporation and could be qualified under section 302(b)(3) of the Code. Hence, the test prescribed by section 355(a)(1)(B) of the Code is satisfied. Accordingly, notwithstanding the large contribution to capital, there can be no device to distribute earnings and profits (that is, to convert dividend income into capital gains) because of the non pro rata distribution. Furthermore, the active business requirements of section 355(b) of the Code are met. Consequently, the distribution qualifies for tax-free treatment under section 355 of the Code. . . .

Revenue Ruling 58-68, C.B. 1958-1, 183, is distinguishable from the instant case. There the parent corporation made a large contribution to the capital of its subsidiary immediately before the distribution of the subsidiary's stock to its sole shareholder. The Internal Revenue Service concluded in that ruling that the transaction was used principally as a device for the distribution of the earnings and profits of the parent to its sole shareholder. Here, for the reasons noted above, the non pro rata distribution of the controlled corporation's stock to the minority shareholders in exchange for all their stock in the parent could not be used as a device for the distribution of earnings and profits.

Accordingly, it is held that no gain or loss is recognized to those shareholders who received stock in the subsidiary corporation in exchange for all their stock in the parent corporation under section 355 of the Code. . . .

*NOTES AND QUESTIONS*

1. *Device and nondevice factors.* Read Reg. § 1.355-2(d). The regulations generally determine the existence of a device based on a weighing of various "device" and "nondevice" factors. Factors that indicate the presence of a device include a pro rata distribution, a subsequent sale or exchange of the distributing or controlled corporation's stock, and a division of assets between the distributing and controlled corporations that facilitates a future sale of one corporation and retention of the other. Reg. § 1.355-2(d)(2). "Nondevice" factors include a corporate business purpose for the transaction, a distributing corporation that is publicly traded and widely held, and a distribution to a corporate distributee entitled to the 80 or 100 percent (but not 70 percent) dividends-received deduction. Reg. § 1.355-2(d)(3). In assessing the significance of the claimed corporate business purpose for a transaction, the regulations consider whether there were easy, nontaxable alternatives to the transaction that would have accomplished the same purpose without the same potential avoidance of a dividend. Reg. § 1.355-2(d)(4) (ex. 1). Further, to trump a device factor, a corporate business purpose must relate specifically to the step that provides the evidence of device. Id. (ex. 3).

2. *Quasi-safe harbors.* The regulations also identify certain transactions that are ordinarily not considered a device. These include transactions in which neither the distributing nor the controlled corporation has any E&P, and distributions that would result in exchange treatment to the distributee under section 302(a) or 303(a) if section 355 did not apply. Reg. § 1.355-2(d)(5). Because a taxable distribution under these circumstances would not qualify as a dividend, the distribution is ordinarily not considered a device to avoid a dividend. The "no E&P" quasi-safe harbor is quite limited since a corporation must have no current, accumulated, or "built-in" E&P (in the form of appreciated property (including stock of the controlled corporation) held by the distributing corporation). Reg. § 1.355-2(d)(5)(ii); South Tulsa Pathology Laboratory v. Comm'r, 118 T.C. 84, 94-96 (2002).

3. *Capital contribution.* Rev. Rul. 64-102 suggests that but for the fact that the distribution completely redeemed the interest of the minority shareholders in the distributing corporation, the large capital contribution preceding the distribution may have been evidence of a device. What is the concern with a capital contribution preceding a distribution?

4. *Subsequent reorganization exchange.* Under the regulations, a subsequent disposition of stock that is wholly or substantially tax-free by reason of the reorganization provisions is not treated as evidence of device, but a taxable disposition of the stock received in the reorganization exchange may be such evidence. Reg. § 1.355-2(d)(2)(iii)(E). What is the reason for this exception and qualification?

**Problem 12-1:** Will any of the following transactions ordinarily not be considered a device for the distribution of E&P of the distributing corporation or one or more controlled corporations? Why or why not? Assume that the corporations involved in each transaction all have current and accumulated E&P.

(a) Corporation X, owned by unrelated individuals A, B, and C, has three lines of business: *x*, *y*, and *z*. X transfers business *y* to a new subsidiary, Y corporation, and business *z* to a new subsidiary, Z corporation. Following those transfers, all of the Y and Z stock is distributed pro rata to shareholders B and C in complete redemption of their stock in X. Thus, after the transaction, A owns all of the stock of X corporation (which continues to operate business *x*) and B and C own stock interests in both corporations Y and Z (which operate businesses *y* and *z*, respectively).
(b) Corporation D, wholly owned by individual J, has a wholly-owned subsidiary, C corporation. J sells a portion of her D stock to unrelated individual K. Following the sale, D distributes all of its C stock to K in complete redemption of K's interest in D. Thus, after the transaction, J owns all of D and K owns all of C.
(c) Corporation M is owned by unrelated individuals F, G, H, and I. M has a wholly-owned subsidiary, N corporation. M distributes all of its N stock pro rata to its four shareholders. Following the distribution, F's stock in both M and N is completely redeemed by those two corporations.

### 4. *Active Business Requirement*

Read I.R.C. § 355(a)(1)(C) and (b). In general, in order for a transaction to qualify under section 355, both the distributing and controlled corporation must be engaged immediately after the distribution in a trade or business actively conducted for at least five years prior to the distribution. This condition also seeks to distinguish a qualifying divisive reorganization from a mere separation of surplus assets whose distribution would have resulted in a dividend.

The interpretation of this condition has been modified over the years. In initial regulations, the IRS generally construed the test to require the existence and division of at least two separate active businesses with five-year histories. Thus, the division of a single business generally did not qualify for section 355 treatment. The courts, however, invalidated this portion of the regulations, concluding that either a "vertical" division of a single business (in which each function of the business prior to the division is performed by each of the separate corporations after the division) or a functional or "horizontal" division (in which only certain functions of the business prior to the division are performed by each of the separated corporations) could satisfy the active business requirement. See Coady v. Comm'r, 289 F.2d 490 (6th Cir. 1961); U.S. v. Marett, 325 F.2d 28 (5th Cir. 1963). The current regulations, issued in 1989, adopt this interpretation and focus mainly on whether there is an impermissible separation of assets along "active" and "passive" lines. As a result, although the active business requirement remains an independent condition of section 355, it acts essentially as a backup to the device test.

In 2006 and 2007, Congress further loosened the active business condition; it is now possible to satisfy this condition based on business assets held by any member of an affiliated group headed by the distributing or controlled corporation. See I.R.C. § 355(b)(3). Prior to this change, taxpayers sometimes had to undertake elaborate restructurings to ensure that immediately after the distribution, active businesses were housed in the specific corporate entities required by the active business rule. Proposed regulations issued in 2007 integrate this statutory change with the rest of the active business condition and foreshadow its further liberalization.

As noted, the current regulations no longer require the existence of two or more distinct active businesses prior to a purported divisive reorganization. Nevertheless, as illustrated by the following ruling, taxpayers and the IRS may still sometimes need to determine the number of businesses existing at the time of the distribution. The notes after the ruling describe the current regulations in somewhat more detail and also summarize the new affiliated group rule and proposed regulations.

## Rev. Rul. 2003-38

2003-1 C.B. 811

. . . Whether the creation by a corporation engaged in the retail shoe store business of an Internet web site on which the corporation will sell shoes at retail constitutes an expansion of the corporation's business rather than the acquisition of a new or different business under § 1.355-3(b)(3)(ii). . . .

Corporation D has operated a retail shoe store business, under the name "D," since Year 1 in a manner that meets the requirements of § 355(b) of the Internal Revenue Code. D's sales are made exclusively to customers who frequent its retail stores in shopping malls and other locations. D's business enjoys favorable name recognition, customer loyalty, and other elements of goodwill in the retail shoe market. In Year 8, D creates an Internet web site and begins selling shoes at retail on the web site. To a significant extent, the operation of the web site draws upon D's experience and know-how. The web site is named "D.com" to take advantage of the name recognition, customer loyalty, and other elements of goodwill associated with D and the D name and to enhance the web site's chances for success in its initial stages. In Year 10, D transfers all of the web site's assets and liabilities to corporation C, a newly formed, wholly owned subsidiary of D, and distributes the stock of C pro rata to D's shareholders. Apart from the issue of whether the web site is considered an expansion of D's business and therefore entitled to share the business's five-year history at the time of the distribution in Year 10, the distribution meets all the requirements of § 355. . . .

Section 355(a) provides that a corporation may distribute stock and securities in a controlled corporation to its shareholders and security holders in a transaction that will not cause the distributees to recognize gain or loss, provided that, among other requirements, (i) each of the distributing corporation and controlled corporation is engaged, immediately after the distribution, in the active conduct of a trade or business, (ii) each trade or business has been actively conducted throughout the five-year period ending on the date of the distribution, and (iii) neither trade or business was acquired in a transaction in which gain or loss was recognized, in whole or in part, within the five-year period. Sections 355(b)(1)(A), 355(b)(2)(B), and 355(b)(2)(C).

In determining whether an active trade or business has been conducted by a corporation throughout the five-year period preceding the distribution, the fact that a trade or business underwent change during the five-year period (for example, by the addition of new or the dropping of old products, changes in production capacity, and the like) shall be disregarded, provided that the changes are not of such a character as to constitute the acquisition of a new or different business. Section 1.355-3(b)(3)(ii). In particular, if a corporation engaged in the active conduct of one trade or business during that five-year period purchased, created, or otherwise acquired another trade or business in the same line of business, then the acquisition of that other business is ordinarily treated as an expansion of the original business, all of which is treated as having been actively conducted during that five-year period, unless that purchase, creation, or other acquisition effects a change of such character as to constitute the acquisition of a new or different business. *Id.*

In Example (7) of § 1.355-3(c), corporation X had owned and operated a department store in the downtown area of the City of G for six years before acquiring a parcel of land in a suburban area of G and constructing a new department store. Three years after the construction, X transferred the suburban store and related business assets to new subsidiary Y and distributed the Y stock to X's shareholders. Citing § 1.355-3(b)(3)(i) and (ii), the example concludes that X and Y both satisfy the requirements of § 355(b).

In Example (8) of § 1.355-3(c), corporation X had owned and operated hardware stores in several states for four years before purchasing the assets of a hardware store in State M where X had not previously conducted business. Two years after the purchase, X transferred the State M store and related business assets to new subsidiary Y and distributed the Y stock to X's shareholders. Citing § 1.355-3(b)(3)(i) and (ii), the example concludes that X and Y both satisfy the requirements of § 355(b).

Rev. Rul. 2003-18, 2003-7 I.R.B. 467, concludes that the acquisition by a dealer engaged in the sale and service of brand X automobiles of a franchise (and the assets needed) to sell and service brand Y automobiles is an expansion of the brand X business and does not constitute the acquisition of a new or different business under § 1.355-3(b)(3)(ii) because (i) the product of the brand X automobile dealership is similar to the product of the brand Y automobile dealership, (ii) the business activities associated with the operation of the brand X automobile dealership (*i.e.*, sales and service) are the same as the business activities associated with the operation of the brand Y automobile dealership, and (iii) the operation of the brand Y automobile dealership involves the use of the experience and know-how that the dealer developed in the operation of the brand X automobile dealership.

ANALYSIS

The product of the retail shoe store business and the product of the web site are the same (shoes), and the principal business activities of the retail shoe store business are the same as those of the web site (purchasing shoes at wholesale and reselling them at retail). Selling shoes on a web site requires some know-how not associated with operating a retail store, such as familiarity with different marketing approaches, distribution chains, and technical operations issues. Nevertheless, the web site's operation does draw to a significant extent on D's existing experience and know-how, and the web site's success will depend in large measure on the goodwill associated with D and the D name. Accordingly, the creation by D of the Internet web site does not constitute the acquisition of a new or different business under § 1.355-3(b)(3)(ii). Instead, it is an expansion of D's retail shoe store business. Therefore, each of D and C is engaged in the active conduct of a five-year active trade or business immediately after the distribution. . . .

*NOTES*

1. *Division of a single business.* Examples in the regulations make clear that a division of a single business may satisfy the active business requirement. Reg. § 1.355-3(c) (ex. 4) (vertical division permissible based on *Coady* facts), (exs. 9, 10) (horizontal division permissible). A horizontal division may, however, be evidence of a device if the principal function of one of the separated corporations is to serve (and thereby be secondary to) the business of the other corporation. Reg. § 1.355-2(d)(2)(iv)(C). The concern is the potential accumulation of a disproportionate share of the entire enterprise's profits in the corporation serving the secondary function, since it may have few, if any, market transactions with outsiders. The separation (in two corporations) of the primary business from its profits may enable the profits to be realized by the shareholders without a dividend.

2. *Active versus passive assets.* Read Reg. § 1.355-3(b)(2) and (c) (exs. 1-3, 12, 13). The active business condition reinforces the device test's concern about the possible accumulation in one of the corporations of assets not used in an active trade or business. See Reg. § 1.355-2(d)(2)(iv)(B). In general, immediately after the distribution, each of the separated corporations must be engaged in the active conduct of a trade or business, which requires the performance of active and substantial management and operational functions and does not include the mere passive

holding of investment assets. Leasing activities constitute an active trade or business only if the owner performs significant services with respect to the leased property.

3. *Certain prohibited taxable acquisitions during five-year period.* Read I.R.C. § 355(b)(2)(C) and (D). In general, a qualifying trade or business does not include one that was acquired in a taxable transaction within the five years prior to the distribution, or one conducted by a corporation whose control was acquired by the distributing corporation in such a transaction during such period. This rule addresses a concern similar to that prompting the "hot stock" rule in section 355(a)(3)(B). Since the mere separation of non-trade or business assets does not meet the active business condition, taxpayers cannot satisfy the condition by using such assets to *purchase* a qualifying active business (or a corporation holding such business). For purposes of this rule, a redemption by the controlled corporation resulting in the distributing corporation gaining control over such corporation may constitute a prohibited acquisition of control by the distributing corporation. See McLaulin v. Comm'r, 276 F.3d 1269 (11th Cir. 2001). Section 355(b)(2)(D) also prohibits certain acquisitions by a "distributee corporation"; this part of the rule, discussed in part C, addresses an issue concerning the taxation of the distributing corporation.

4. *Modification or new business?* Read Reg. § 1.355-3(b)(3) and (c) (exs. 5 and 7). Rev. Rul. 2003-38 illustrates the difficult (and largely metaphysical) question of whether a business change constitutes a mere modification (or expansion) of the business, or a new business altogether. As a new business, it must be seasoned for at least five years if its existence is needed to satisfy the active business requirement. In contrast, as a modification or expansion, the change inherits the operating history of the existing business. In addition, a mere modification or expansion of a business by means of a taxable acquisition within the five-year period does not constitute a prohibited section 355(b)(2)(C) acquisition. See Reg. § 1.355-3(b)(3)(ii) and (c) (ex. 8).

5. *Section 355(b)(3) and proposed regulations.* In general, in determining whether a corporation is engaged in an active trade or business, all of the assets held by any member of the corporation's "separate affiliated group" ("SAG") may be taken into account. A corporation's SAG is generally the affiliated group (determined under section 1504(a)) of which the corporation is the common parent. I.R.C. § 355(b)(3)(A) and (B). Under this SAG rule, if different business segments are held by individual members of a corporation's SAG, the corporation is treated as engaged in an active business so long as the segments, taken together, qualify as one. As noted, this rule further liberalizes the active business condition.

Perhaps illustrating how the elaboration of a rule expands as its significance contracts, the IRS in 2007 proposed a lengthy replacement of the existing regulations to take into account the SAG rule. (The preamble to the proposed regulations spans 14 pages of the Federal Register and the text includes 51(!) examples.) The proposed regulations modify the current regulations in three principal ways. First, the SAG rule is applied to all aspects of section 355(b), including throughout the pre-distribution period. Thus, for example, whether the distributing or controlled corporation conducted an active business during the five years prior to a distribution is determined by taking into account the assets and business activity of the members of such corporation's SAG during that period. Prop. Reg. § 1.355-3(b)(1)(ii) (second sentence), -3(d)(2) (ex. 3). Second, SAG members other than the common parent are generally treated as divisions, and not subsidiaries, of the parent. This change has several important implications. It means, for example, that transactions between SAG members are generally disregarded, and that an acquisition of a corporation that becomes a member of the SAG is treated as an acquisition of the corporation's assets. This deemed acquisition of assets may, therefore, be prohibited by section 355(b)(2)(C) (and not section 355(b)(2)(D)) or may qualify as a mere modification or expansion of an existing business. Prop. Reg. § 1.355-3(b)(1)(ii) (third and fourth sentences), -3(b)(3)(ii) (second sentence), -3(b)(4)(i)(A) (third sentence). Finally, the proposed regulations modify the interpretation of section 355(b)(2)(C) and (D) to apply them generally only to acquisitions in which the acquiring corporation uses its assets (as opposed to its stock or the stock of a corporation in control of the acquiring corporation) as consideration. Prop. Reg. § 1.355-3(b)(4)(ii).

### 5. *Nonstatutory Requirements*

The nonstatutory requirements of continuity of interest ("COI"), continuity of business enterprise ("COBE"), and business purpose are all applicable to divisive reorganizations, although these doctrines function somewhat differently here than in the case of an acquisitive reorganization. In connection with section 355, COI requires the distributing corporation's historic shareholders to own a sufficient continuing interest in each of the corporate forms that result from the division. Reg. § 1.355-2(c)(1). COI thus supplements the device test by taking into consideration the consequences of both pre- and post-distribution dispositions of stock. In a divisive transaction, however, COI focuses on the percentage interest of the historic shareholders in the resulting corporations. In contrast, COI in an acquisitive reorganization scrutinizes the percentage of the target corporation acquired for stock of the issuing corporation. The historic target shareholders need not obtain any minimum interest in the issuing corporation as a result of the transaction.

COBE supplements the active business condition by requiring the "continued operation" after a division of the business or businesses existing prior to the division. Reg. § 1.355-2(b) (sixth sentence). COBE, therefore, also places restrictions on both pre- and post-distribution dispositions. Finally, the business purpose condition generally requires the existence of a substantial nontax corporate business purpose (as distinguished from a shareholder purpose) for both the corporate separation and distribution. If the business purpose of the transaction can be achieved by a nontaxable alternative (not involving a distribution) that is neither impractical nor unduly expensive, then the transaction will not be treated as having a valid business purpose. Reg. § 1.355-2(b)(1)-(3). Although a corporate business purpose is a "nondevice" factor, it is an independent requirement of section 355 even if the device test is satisfied.

Read Reg. § 1.355-2(b) and (c) and do the following problem.

**Problem 12-2:**

(a) Review the facts of the *Gregory* (p. 120) and *Rockefeller* (p. 451) cases. Would the transactions in those cases satisfy the business purpose requirement described in the section 355 regulations? Why or why not?

(b) D corporation conducts Businesses 1 and 2. Because certain investors who are attracted to investing in one of the businesses are averse to investing in the other, D's investment banker informs D that if the two businesses were conducted in separate and independent corporations, the aggregate value of the stock of the resulting corporations would likely be greater than the value of D's stock without a separation. Any increase in aggregate stock value would benefit D because it would enhance the value of its equity-based incentive compensation to employees and preserve capital in subsequent corporate acquisitions using D stock as consideration. Accordingly, D transfers Business 2 to newly formed C corporation and distributes pro rata the C stock among D's shareholders. Does this transaction satisfy the business purpose requirement?

(c) Unrelated individuals A and B own all of the stock of X corporation, which has a wholly-owned subsidiary (Y). X distributes all of the stock of Y to B in exchange for all of B's stock in X. Thus, after the transaction, A owns all of X and B owns all of Y. Does this transaction satisfy the COI requirement even though, following the transaction, A has no continuing interest in Y and B has no continuing interest in X?

(d) Assume the same facts as (c), except that X is owned 20 percent by A, 50 percent by B, and 30 percent by C. A and B have owned their shares in X for a number of years, but C acquired his interest fairly recently. As in (c), X distributes all of the stock of Y to B in exchange for all of B's stock in X. Thus, after the transaction, A and C jointly own X and B owns all of Y. Does this transaction satisfy the COI requirement?

(e) Unrelated individuals J and K own exactly one-half each of both corporations Y and Z. J and K transfer their Y and Z shares to new corporation X solely for stock of X. X then distributes all of its Y stock to J in exchange for all of J's stock in X. As a result of the transaction, J owns all of Y and K owns all of X (which owns all of Z). Describe a purpose for this transaction that would satisfy the corporate business purpose requirement of section 355. Assuming that the transaction is carried out for this purpose and also satisfies the active business requirement, does it qualify under section 355? Should it? See Reg. § 1.355-4.

### 6. *Tax Consequences to Distributee in Qualifying Section 355 Transaction*

Read I.R.C. §§ 355(a)(1), (3), and (4)(A), 356(a)-(e). In general, no gain or loss is recognized by a distributee who receives stock or securities of the controlled corporation ("nonrecognition property") in a qualifying section 355 transaction. A security of the controlled corporation qualifies as nonrecognition property only if the recipient surrenders a security in the distributing corporation whose principal amount equals or exceeds that of the security received. I.R.C. § 355(a)(3)(A). Similarly, nonqualified preferred stock (NQPS) (as defined in section 351(g)(2)) of the controlled corporation qualifies as nonrecognition property only if such stock is distributed with respect to NQPS of the distributing corporation. I.R.C. § 355(a)(3)(D). Property received in a section 355 transaction other than nonrecognition property is taxable as boot under section 356. As previously noted, certain other stock of the controlled corporation (termed "hot stock") also constitutes boot, and not nonrecognition property, for this purpose. I.R.C. § 355(a)(3)(B).

Boot is taxed under section 301 if received in a section 355 distribution in which no stock or securities is surrendered. I.R.C. § 356(b). If stock or securities is surrendered, the distributee must recognize gain but not in excess of the boot received. The gain may be a dividend if the exchange "has the effect of the distribution of a dividend" and the amount does not exceed the distributee's ratable share of the distributing corporation's accumulated E&P. I.R.C. § 356(a). According to the IRS, the dividend equivalence test (for purposes of section 355) is determined by assuming that the boot received is in redemption of the distributee's stock in the distributing corporation just prior to the exchange of stock or securities for nonrecognition property. Rev. Rul. 93-62, 1993-2 C.B. 118. For example, suppose in a qualifying section 355 transaction, (1) a taxpayer surrenders her entire 40 percent interest in the distributing corporation for controlled corporation stock (worth $200x) plus $200x cash, (2) all other stock in the distributing corporation is held by unrelated persons, and (3) no other distributions are made. The dividend equivalence of the taxpayer's gain is determined by assuming that half of her stock in the distributing corporation is redeemed for $200x cash prior to the exchange of stock for stock. Since this redemption qualifies under section 302(b)(2) (it reduces the taxpayer's interest in the distributing corporation from 40 to 25 percent, a greater than 20 percent reduction), the boot is taxable under section 302(a) and not section 301. As discussed in chapter eleven, any dividend to the taxpayer is limited by the amount of gain realized by the taxpayer in the exchange.

Read I.R.C. §§ 358(a)-(c), 1223(1). In general, the basis of any nonrecognition property received in a section 355 transaction is determined by the distributee's basis in the stock or securities of the distributing corporation prior to the transaction. The pre-distribution basis is increased by the amount of gain (including dividend) recognized by the distributee in the transaction and decreased by the amount of boot received. I.R.C. § 358(a)(1). The adjusted basis is then generally allocated between the nonrecognition property received and any retained interest in the distributing corporation following the transaction in proportion to their fair market values after the transaction. I.R.C. § 358(b). These rules apply regardless of whether the distributee surrenders any stock or securities in the transaction. I.R.C. § 358(c). The distributee's basis in any boot received is its fair market value. I.R.C. § 358(a)(2). Finally, the distributee's holding period in nonrecognition property received is the same as the taxpayer's holding period in her stock or securities of the distributing corporation if such property is a capital asset or section 1231 asset at the time of the distribution. I.R.C. § 1223(1).

> **Example 12-1:** Taxpayer A owns stock in D corporation with a value and basis of $100x and $30x, respectively. In a qualifying section 355 transaction, A surrenders $40x of D stock for stock in C corporation (worth $30x) and $10x boot. A's pre-distribution basis of $30x in all of her D stock is increased by $10x (gain or dividend recognized) and decreased by $10x (fair market value of boot received), for a total adjusted basis of $30x. This adjusted basis must be allocated between A's D and C stock following the transaction in proportion to their fair market values ($60x and $30x, respectively). Thus, two-thirds of the $30x total basis (or $20x) is allocated to A's remaining D stock and one-third of such total basis (or $10x) is allocated to A's stock in C. If A had not surrendered any D stock in the transaction (and still received $30x C stock plus $10x boot), the result should be the same because A's remaining D stock after the transaction should again be worth approximately $60x. In either case, A obtains a $10x basis in the boot.

## *NOTES*

1. *Tracing and allocation.* As in the case of nondivisive reorganizations, the regulations generally adopt a tracing method under which the basis of nonrecognition property received in a divisive reorganization is traced to, and determined by, the basis of the stock or securities surrendered (or deemed surrendered) in the exchange. Reg. § 1.358-2(a)(2)(i) and (iv). For this purpose, a specific allocation made by the distributee (including an allocation of nonrecognition property and boot received to stock or securities surrendered or deemed surrendered) is respected if consistent with the terms of the distribution and economically reasonable. Reg. § 1.358-2(a)(2)(ii), (v), and (vii) and -2(c) (exs. 12 & 13).

2. *Possible legislative change.* As described in chapter eleven, legislation approved by the House of Representatives in 2010 would repeal the "dividend within gain" rule and determine a dividend based upon the current or accumulated E&P of the distributing corporation. H.R. 4213 (2010) (as passed by the House on May 28, 2010), § 422.

## C. Tax Consequences to the Distributing Corporation

Read I.R.C. § 355(c). In general, the distributing corporation does not recognize gain or loss on the distribution of stock or securities of the controlled corporation in a qualifying section 355 transaction. If the distributing corporation distributes any other property, it must recognize gain (but not loss). The consequences to the distributing corporation are generally the same if the distribution is pursuant to a divisive "D" reorganization. See I.R.C. § 361(c)(1) and (2). This general tax treatment of the distributing corporation is consistent with the principle, examined in chapter eleven, that "reorganization" status confers a nonrecognition result at both the shareholder and corporate levels.

In at least two respects, however, a divisive reorganization presents corporate-level issues not present in an acquisitive reorganization, and important modifications to the general rule of sections 355(c) and 361(c) reflect these differences. First, a divisive reorganization expands the circumstances in which a distributing corporation may avoid recognizing gain on the transfer of corporate assets or stock. Suppose D corporation would like to transfer one of several appreciated businesses to a corporate buyer for cash. The divisive nature of the transaction, as well as the desired cash consideration, probably foreclose the possibility that the transfer of the business by D would qualify for nonrecognition treatment as an acquisitive reorganization. If D transferred the business to a new subsidiary and then sold the stock of the subsidiary, D would ordinarily have to recognize gain or loss on the stock sale. Such gain or loss could be avoided if a section 338(h)(10) election were made, but only at the cost of triggering corporate-level gain or loss of the subsidiary. Finally, D's shareholders could transfer their D stock to the buyer for cash without the recognition of corporate-level gain, but such transaction would result in a disposition of *all* of D's businesses, not just the one to be sold.

If D's businesses could first be separated into different corporations and distributed to D's shareholders without the recognition of gain or loss, however, then it might be possible to avoid corporate-level gain by disposing of the stock or assets of the corporation holding the business to be sold. In short, a tax-free separation and distribution of D's businesses potentially provides a *corporate-level* as well as a shareholder-level tax opportunity that did not exist without the division. If D's owners had had the foresight to incorporate separately each business, they could have avoided the later problem of disentangling them, but separate incorporation entails its own tax and nontax difficulties. For example, it may prevent losses from one business from being used to offset income from some other.

Second, in contrast to the consequences of an acquisitive reorganization, any gain or loss realized but not recognized by the distributing corporation in a divisive reorganization is *not* preserved for later recognition because the transaction is a distribution. Thus, as the following example illustrates, a divisive reorganization potentially allows avoidance of *General Utilities* repeal:

**Example 12-2:** D corporation wishes to transfer one of several of its appreciated businesses to P corporation for $300x. D transfers the desired business to a new wholly-owned subsidiary (C), and P acquires five percent of the stock of D for $300x. D then distributes all of its C stock to P in exchange for all of P's shares in D. If the transaction qualifies as a divisive reorganization, P does not recognize any gain or loss and obtains a $300x basis in the C stock received. I.R.C. § 358(a)(1). If D also does not recognize gain or loss in the transaction, its gain or loss in the subsidiary (and the business transferred to it) is eliminated. Only the former D shareholders who sold their stock to P recognize gain or loss.

To be sure, *C's* corporate-level gain or loss in its assets is fully preserved following the transaction in **example 12-2**. Thus, the gain or loss not preserved—D's gain or loss in its C stock—represents a *second* corporate-level gain or loss. As discussed previously, the second corporate-level gain or loss is eliminated in a parent-subsidiary liquidation under sections 332(a) and 337(a), and in certain sales or distributions of target stock (if a section 338(h)(10) or 336(e) election is made). But a parent-subsidiary liquidation arguably represents a mere change in form and not substance, and sections 338(h)(10) and 336(e) permit one corporate-level gain or loss to be eliminated only on condition that the other corporate-level gain or loss—the target's gain or loss in its assets—is immediately recognized. Without modification, sections 355(c) and 361(c) would allow nonrecognition treatment in circumstances broader than any of those provisions.

For these reasons, section 355(d) and (e) (enacted in 1990 and 1997, respectively) modify sections 355(c) and 361(c) by requiring the distributing corporation in a divisive reorganization to recognize gain (but not loss) upon the distribution of stock or securities of the controlled corporation if, in general, the reorganization is part of an acquisitive transaction. The general goal is to protect *General Utilities* repeal and to limit divisive reorganizations to nonacquisitive transactions in much the same way that acquisitive reorganizations are generally precluded from having divisive elements. Unfortunately, as we will see, section 355(d) and (e) overlap one another as well as certain of the section 355 conditions examined in part B, including the device test, COI, and COBE. Importantly, unlike the section 355 conditions considered thus far, section 355(d) and (e) *only* affect the tax consequences of the transaction to the distributing corporation. Thus, even if the distributing corporation is taxed as a result of section 355(d) or (e), the distributees may still receive nonrecognition treatment.

The first two sections below separately describe section 355(d) and (e). The third section discusses an even more recent section 355 development concerning the taxation of "cash-rich split-off" transactions; as we will see, this development marks a potential change in our understanding of the scope of tax-free corporate divisions. The final section briefly considers some alternatives to qualifying section 355 transactions.

### 1. *Distributions Preceded by Certain Stock Purchases*

Read I.R.C. § 355(d)(1)-(5). In the case of a "disqualified distribution," the distributing corporation in a divisive reorganization must recognize gain upon the distribution of stock or securities of the controlled corporation. In general, a distribution is disqualified if, immediately after the distribution, any person owns at least 50 percent of the stock (by vote or value) of either the distributing or controlled corporation attributable to certain purchases during the five years preceding the distribution. As **example 12-3** illustrates, the 50-percent-or-greater interest in the controlled corporation may result from a combination of purchases of controlled corporation stock within the five-year period or a distribution on stock of the distributing corporation purchased during such period.

> **Example 12-3:** Three years prior to a qualifying divisive reorganization, P corporation acquires by purchase 25 percent of corporation D and 10 percent of corporation C (previously D's wholly-owned subsidiary). In the reorganization, D distributes 40 percent of C to P in exchange for P's 25 percent interest in D. (D's remaining C stock is distributed to other D shareholders.) Under sections 355(c)(2) (or section 361(c)(2)) and 355(d)(1), D must recognize gain on the distribution of C stock (including the distribution to shareholders other than P) because immediately after the distribution, P owns 50 percent of C attributable to D or C stock purchased within five years of the distribution. I.R.C. § 355(d)(2) and (3)(B).

For purposes of this provision, "purchase" generally refers to a transaction (including a section 351 exchange) in which property is acquired with a cost (or equivalent) basis (but not by reason of section 1014(a)). I.R.C. § 355(d)(5)(A) and (B). It also includes certain transferred basis acquisitions in which the basis of the person from whom the property is acquired was determined by purchase. I.R.C. § 355(d)(5)(C). Finally, under the regulations, it also includes certain exchanged basis acquisitions of property if the property surrendered in exchange was acquired by purchase. Reg. § 1.355-6(e)(3).

> **Problem 12-3:** D corporation has a wholly-owned subsidiary, C corporation. For each of the following, assume that all stock acquisitions occur after October 9, 1990 (the effective date of section 355(d)) and that D's distribution of the stock of C satisfies section 355(a)(1). Identify which of the following distributions constitutes a "disqualified distribution" within the meaning of section 355(d)(2).
>
> (a) P corporation acquires 40 percent of D's stock for cash. Three years later, D distributes all of the stock of C to P in exchange for all of P's stock in D.

(b) Same as (a), except that P acquired the D stock in exchange for stock of T corporation in a qualifying "A" reorganization in which T merged into D, with D surviving. Would it matter if P acquired its T stock for cash four or six years prior to the distribution? See Reg. § 1.355-6(e)(3).
(c) Same as (a), except that P acquired 80 percent of D's stock in exchange for P stock in a qualifying "B" reorganization in which P acquired control of D.
(d) Same as (a), except that P acquired the D stock in a section 351 transaction in exchange for cash transferred to D by P.
(e) Same as (a), except that the distribution is in complete liquidation of D, which distributes the C stock pro rata to all of its shareholders (including P).
(f) Same as (a), except that following P's acquisition of 40 percent of D (but before the distribution), D redeems the stock of certain other D shareholders, which increases P's interest in D to 50 percent. D then distributes its C stock pro rata to all of its shareholders.
(g) Same as **example 12-3**, except that P's purchase of 10 percent of C (from other D shareholders) occurs *after* the distribution by D. See Reg. § 1.355-6(b)(4).

*NOTES*

1. *Aggregation, attribution, and suspension.* In determining whether a person owns at least 50 percent of the distributing or controlled corporation immediately after the distribution, interests owned by certain related persons or those acting pursuant to a plan or arrangement are aggregated. I.R.C. § 355(d)(7). In addition, taxpayers who purchase an interest in an entity are treated as having purchased the proportion of stock or securities held by such entity and attributed to the taxpayer by section 318(a)(2) (attribution from entity to owner or beneficiary). I.R.C. § 355(d)(8). For this purpose, the 50 percent threshold test in section 318(a)(2)(C) is reduced to 10 percent. Finally, the running of the five-year period is suspended during certain periods in which the taxpayer's risk of loss with respect to the holding of stock or securities is substantially diminished. I.R.C. § 355(d)(6).

2. *Purpose of section 355(d) and regulatory exceptions.* The purpose of section 355(d) is to prevent taxpayers from using a divisive reorganization to facilitate a disposition of certain corporate interests without a corporate-level tax. Consistent with this objective, the regulations carve out of section 355(d) certain transactions that do not violate this purpose. For example, suppose P corporation purchases 60 percent of the stock of D corporation for cash. Within five years of the purchase, D-1 (D's wholly-owned subsidiary) distributes all of the stock of its wholly-owned subsidiary (C) to D in a qualifying section 355 transaction. Technically, since P is

treated as having purchased 60 percent of both D-1 and C within five years of the distribution (I.R.C. § 355(d)(8)), section 355(d) applies to require D-1 to recognize gain on the distribution of the C stock to D. But the distribution does not facilitate the disposition of any interest without a corporate-level tax because P's cost basis in its D stock has no effect on D's basis in the stock of either D-1 or C following the distribution. Accordingly, the regulations exclude this transaction from section 355(d). Reg. § 1.355-6(b)(3)(i)-(iii) and (vi) (ex. 1). If, however, D immediately thereafter distributes its C stock pro rata to P and D's other shareholders in a divisive reorganization, section 355(d) applies. In this case, P's basis in the C stock received is determined in part by P's cost basis in its D stock (I.R.C. § 358(a)(1), (b), and (c)); thus, if D does not recognize gain in distributing C, such gain may never be recognized since P may be able to dispose of C in the future with little or no corporate-level tax. Reg. § 1.355-6(b)(3)(vi) (ex. 2).

Suppose, in the foregoing example, P purchases 100 percent (and not just 60 percent) of the stock of D for cash. Within five years of the purchase, D is completely liquidated into P (under sections 332 and 337) and D-1 (now wholly-owned by P) distributes all of its C stock to P in a qualifying divisive reorganization. Once again, this transaction is technically covered by section 355(d) since P is treated as having purchased 100 percent of both D-1 and C within five years of the distribution (I.R.C. § 355(d)(8)). The transaction, however, also does not violate the purpose of section 355(d) because P's cost basis in its D stock is eliminated in the section 332 liquidation. Rather, in the liquidation, P succeeds to D's basis in its D-1 stock (and allocates that basis between its D-1 stock and the C stock received in the section 355 transaction). I.R.C. §§ 334(b), 358(a)(1), (b), and (c). Thus, the transaction does not facilitate the disposition of D-1 or C without a corporate-level tax. The regulations exclude this transaction from section 355(d) because P's cost basis in D is eliminated. Reg. § 1.355-6(b)(2)(iii)(A), (B), and (C)(*1*), -6(b)(3)(vi) (ex. 7).

3. *Section 355(b)(2)(D)*. Under this provision, enacted prior to section 355(d), the active business requirement is not satisfied if any "distributee corporation" acquires directly or indirectly in a taxable transaction (during the five years preceding the distribution) control of a corporation conducting the active trade or business. The focus on certain pre-distribution acquisitions by a distributee corporation was designed to prevent the same avoidance of *General Utilities* repeal that is targeted by section 355(d), which has largely subsumed section 355(b)(2)(D). The latter provision is generally narrower than section 355(d) because it is limited to acquisitions of "control" (80 percent test of section 368(c)) by a corporation that is a distributee in the distribution. When it applies, however, section 355(b)(2)(D) is more draconian than section 355(d) since failure to satisfy the active business requirement affects the tax consequences of the entire transaction, not just those applicable to the distributing corporation. The second example described in note 2 (involving P's purchase of 100 percent of D for cash), although exempted from section 355(d) by the regulations, is technically caught by section 355(b)(2)(D) because P (the "distributee corporation") indirectly purchased control of D-1

(and C) when it acquired control of D in a taxable transaction to the former D shareholders. Proposed regulations, however, exempt the transaction from section 355(b)(2)(D) for the same reason section 355(d) does not apply to it. Prop. Reg. § 1.355-3(b)(4)(iii)(C); 72 Fed. Reg. 26012, 26017 (2007).

4. *Overlap*. As is evident, section 355 contains overlapping rules that restrict certain acquisition activity both before and after the distribution. Section 355(d) generally concerns only pre-distribution acquisitions although the regulations permit consideration of post-distribution transactions if engaged in with a principal purpose to avoid that provision. Reg. § 1.355-6(b)(4). Section 355(b)(2)(D), COI, and COBE also limit dispositions preceding the distribution, and COI, COBE, and the device test all restrict post-distribution dispositions. As described in the next section, to complicate matters further, section 355(e) also limits acquisition activity occurring both before and after the distribution.

## 2. *Distributions That Are Part of Certain Planned Acquisitions*

In 1997, Congress expanded the scope of acquisitive transactions that might cause the distributing corporation in a divisive reorganization to recognize gain upon the distribution of stock or securities of the controlled corporation. The specific transaction of concern was described in Comm'r v. Morris Trust, 367 F.2d 794 (4th Cir. 1966), and is illustrated by **example 12-4**:

> **Example 12-4:** D corporation agrees to merge into P corporation, with P surviving. Because P is a national bank not permitted under the banking laws to operate one of D's businesses (an insurance business), D first transfers the insurance business to a new wholly-owned subsidiary (C) and then distributes the C stock to D's shareholders. D then merges into P in a qualifying "A" reorganization.

The Fourth Circuit concluded that the distribution qualified as a divisive "D" reorganization despite the planned merger between D and P subsequent to the distribution.

Part B of this chapter described how a corporate division followed by a *taxable* acquisition of one of the resulting corporate entities may violate the device test or COI and jeopardize the tax-free nature of the division. In contrast, a subsequent *tax-free* acquisition (illustrated in **example 12-4)** does not have the same effect. See Reg. § 1.355-2(d)(2)(iii)(E) (subsequent acquisition of stock pursuant to reorganization is not evidence of device). The traditional explanation for this distinction has been the continuity of interest and business enterprise that is necessarily part of the tax-free acquisition. So long as the transaction as a whole does not result in any significant "cashing in" (or "monetization") of interests, each step of the transaction has been viewed as a mere readjustment of continuing interests in modified corporate form, and therefore not a proper occasion for taxation. The same principle is implicit in the "purchase" requirement contained in section 355(d). See I.R.C. § 355(d)(3) and (5).

The view of a reorganization as not monetizing interests may, however, be illusory. Suppose in **example 12-4**, prior to forming C, D incurs a liability and transfers the proceeds (but not the repayment obligation) to C along with its insurance business. After distributing the C stock to its shareholders, D then merges into P, with P assuming D's obligation. Even if the merger between D and P qualifies as an "A" reorganization, the transaction may have the economic effect of a "sale" of certain of D's businesses (other than its insurance business) for cash. Accordingly, Congress enacted section 355(e) to focus more broadly on whether a divisive reorganization is part of a change of ownership of the original corporate businesses, however effected. According to the Senate Report, section 355 is

> intended to permit the tax-free division of existing business arrangements among existing shareholders. In cases in which it is intended that new shareholders will acquire ownership of a business in connection with a spin off, the transaction more closely resembles a corporate level disposition of the portion of the business that is acquired. [S. REP. NO. 105-33, 105TH CONG., 1ST SESS. 139-40 (1997).]

Read I.R.C. § 355(e)(1)-(3) and (4)(A). In general, a distributing corporation in a divisive reorganization must recognize gain upon distributing stock or securities of the controlled corporation if the distribution is part of a plan pursuant to which one or more persons acquires at least 50 percent of the stock (by vote or value) of either the distributing or controlled corporation. Unlike section 355(d) (which has priority if there is overlap between the two provisions), section 355(e) does not require the stock to be acquired by "purchase" and takes into account acquisitive transactions occurring both before and after the distribution. The triggering event of section 355(e) is the requirement of a "plan" linking the distribution to the acquisition. For purposes of section 355(e), a merger or an acquisition of the assets of a corporation that qualifies as a reorganization (such as the merger in **example 12-4**) is treated as an acquisition of the corporation's stock by the shareholders of the acquiring (or surviving) corporation. I.R.C. § 355(e)(3)(B).

The focus of section 355(e) is on *new* owners obtaining at least 50 percent of the distributing or controlled corporation. Accordingly, acquisitions are generally taken into account only to the extent they reduce the pre-acquisition interest of the direct or indirect owners of those corporations. I.R.C. § 355(e)(3)(A). For example, assume in **example 12-4** that because D was slightly larger than P just prior to the merger, the former D shareholders received 54 percent of the surviving corporation (P) and the P shareholders retained only 46 percent of that corporation (and there was no overlap between those two groups of shareholders). In this case, the merger would not be treated as an acquisition of at least 50 percent of D because it decreases the interest of the former D shareholders in D by only 46 percent. The *Morris Trust* transaction presented exactly these facts; thus, although section 355(e) is commonly referred to as the "anti-*Morris Trust*" provision, it would not have affected the outcome of that case.

The key (and tricky) interpretive question in section 355(e) is the definition of a "plan." A very restrictive definition limited only to certain acquisition activity explicitly tied to the distribution might enable taxpayers to avoid the consequences of section 355(e) too easily by arranging their transactions in informal, indirect ways. On the other hand, a very expansive definition that would include any acquisition activity occurring within reasonable proximity of the distribution, even though not explicitly connected to it, might permit section 355(e) to be used as a form of "shark repellent" to fend off a hostile acquisition. For example, a target corporation subject to such a threat might distribute a valuable subsidiary in a qualifying section 355 transaction prior to the anticipated acquisition. If the potential acquirer knows that the distribution and subsequent acquisition will be treated as part of a prohibited plan triggering the application of section 355(e) and the recognition of a large gain by the distributing corporation, the acquirer might be deterred from completing the acquisition. Section 355(e)(2)(B) establishes a rebuttable presumption that treats as part of a prohibited plan any distribution and acquisitions occurring during the four-year period immediately surrounding the distribution. Regulations issued in 2005 (after four earlier attempts at guidance), however, cut back on that presumption. The following ruling illustrates the highly facts-and-circumstances approach developed in the regulations.

## Rev. Rul. 2005-65

2005-2 C.B. 684

. . . Under the facts described below, is a distribution of a controlled corporation by a distributing corporation part of a plan pursuant to which one or more persons acquire stock in the distributing corporation under § 355(e) of the Internal Revenue Code and § 1.355-7 of the Income Tax Regulations? . . .

Distributing is a publicly traded corporation that conducts a pharmaceuticals business. Controlled, a wholly owned subsidiary of Distributing, conducts a cosmetics business. Distributing does all of the borrowing for both Distributing and Controlled and makes all decisions regarding the allocation of capital spending between the pharmaceuticals and cosmetics businesses. Because Distributing's capital spending in recent years for both the pharmaceuticals and cosmetics businesses has outpaced internally generated cash flow from the businesses, it has had to limit total expenditures to maintain its credit ratings. Although the decisions reached by Distributing's senior management regarding the allocation of capital spending usually favor the pharmaceuticals business due to its higher rate of growth and profit margin, the competition for capital prevents both businesses from consistently pursuing development strategies that the management of each business believes are appropriate.

To eliminate this competition for capital, and in light of the unavailability of nontaxable alternatives, Distributing decides and publicly announces that it intends to distribute all the stock of Controlled pro rata to Distributing's shareholders. It is expected that both businesses will benefit in a real and substantial way from the distribution. This business purpose is a corporate business purpose (within the meaning of § 1.355-2(b)). The distribution is substantially motivated by this business purpose, and not by a business purpose to facilitate an acquisition.

After the announcement but before the distribution, X, a widely held corporation that is engaged in the pharmaceuticals business, and Distributing begin discussions regarding an acquisition. There were no discussions between Distributing or Controlled and X or its shareholders regarding an acquisition or a distribution before the announcement. In addition, Distributing would have been able to continue the successful operation of its pharmaceuticals business without combining with X. During its negotiations with Distributing, X indicates that it favors the distribution. X merges into Distributing before the distribution but nothing in the merger agreement requires the distribution.

As a result of the merger, X's former shareholders receive 55 percent of Distributing's stock. In addition, X's chairman of the board and chief executive officer become the chairman of the board and chief executive officer, respectively, of Distributing. Six months after the merger, Distributing distributes the stock of Controlled pro rata in a distribution to which § 355 applies and to which § 355(d) does not apply. At the time of the distribution, the distribution continues to be substantially motivated by the business purpose of eliminating the competition for capital between the pharmaceuticals and cosmetics businesses. . . .

Section 355(c) generally provides that no gain or loss is recognized to the distributing corporation on a distribution of stock in a controlled corporation to which § 355 (or so much of § 356 as relates to § 355) applies and which is not in pursuance of a plan of reorganization. Section 355(e) generally denies nonrecognition treatment under § 355(c) if the distribution is part of a plan (or series of related transactions) (a plan) pursuant to which one or more persons acquire directly or indirectly stock representing a 50-percent or greater interest in the distributing corporation or any controlled corporation.

Section 1.355-7(b)(1) provides that whether a distribution and an acquisition are part of a plan is determined based on all the facts and circumstances, including those set forth in § 1.355-7(b)(3) (plan factors) and (4) (non-plan factors). The weight to be given each of the facts and circumstances depends on the particular case. The determination does not depend on the relative number of plan factors compared to the number of non-plan factors that are present.

Section 1.355-7(b)(3)(iii) provides that, in the case of an acquisition (other than involving a public offering) before a distribution, if at some time during the two-year period ending on the date of the acquisition there were discussions by Distributing or Controlled with the acquirer regarding a distribution, such discussions tend to show that the distribution and the acquisition are part of a plan. The weight to be accorded this fact depends on the nature, extent, and timing of the discussions. In addition, the fact that the acquirer intends to cause a distribution and, immediately after the acquisition, can meaningfully participate in the decision regarding whether to make a distribution, tends to show that the distribution and the acquisition are part of a plan.

Section 1.355-7(b)(4)(iii) provides that, in the case of an acquisition (other than involving a public offering) before a distribution, the absence of discussions by Distributing or Controlled with the acquirer regarding a distribution during the two-year period ending on the date of the earlier to occur of the acquisition or the first public announcement regarding the distribution tends to show that the distribution and the acquisition are not part of a plan. However, this factor does not apply to an acquisition where the acquirer intends to cause a distribution and, immediately after the acquisition, can meaningfully participate in the decision regarding whether to make a distribution.

Section 1.355-7(b)(4)(v) provides that the fact that the distribution was motivated in whole or substantial part by a corporate business purpose (within the meaning of § 1.355-2(b)) other than a business purpose to facilitate the acquisition or a similar acquisition tends to show that the distribution and the acquisition are not part of a plan.

Section 1.355-7(b)(4)(vi) provides that the fact that the distribution would have occurred at approximately the same time and in similar form regardless of the acquisition or a similar acquisition tends to show that the distribution and the acquisition are not part of a plan. Section 1.355-7(h)(6) provides that discussions with the acquirer generally include discussions with persons with the implicit permission of the acquirer. Section 1.355-7(h)(9) provides that a corporation is treated as having the implicit permission of its shareholders when it engages in discussions.

## ANALYSIS

Whether the X shareholders' acquisition of Distributing stock and Distributing's distribution of Controlled are part of a plan depends on all the facts and circumstances, including those described in § 1.355-7(b). The fact that Distributing discussed the distribution with X during the two-year period ending on the date of the acquisition tends to show that the distribution and the acquisition are part of a plan. See § 1.355-7(b)(3)(iii). In addition, X's shareholders may constitute acquirers who intend to cause a distribution and who, immediately after the acquisition, can meaningfully participate (through X's chairman of the board and chief executive officer who become D's chairman of the board and chief executive officer) in the decision regarding whether to distribute Controlled. See id. However, the fact that Distributing publicly announced the distribution before discussions with X regarding both an acquisition and a distribution began suggests that the plan factor in § 1.355-7(b)(3)(iii) should be accorded less weight than it would have been accorded had there been such discussions before the public announcement.

With respect to those factors that tend to show that the distribution and the acquisition are not part of a plan, the absence of discussions by Distributing or

Controlled with X or its shareholders during the two-year period ending on the date of the public announcement regarding the distribution would tend to show that the distribution and the acquisition are not part of a plan only if X's shareholders are not acquirers who intend to cause a distribution and who, immediately after the acquisition, can meaningfully participate in the decision regarding whether to distribute Controlled. See § 1.355-7(b)(4)(iii). Because X's chairman of the board and chief executive officer become the chairman and chief executive officer, respectively, of Distributing, X's shareholders may have the ability to meaningfully participate in the decision whether to distribute Controlled. Therefore, the absence of discussions by Distributing or Controlled with X or its shareholders during the two-year period ending on the date of the public announcement regarding the distribution may not tend to show that the distribution and the acquisition are not part of a plan.

Nonetheless, the fact that the distribution was substantially motivated by a corporate business purpose (within the meaning of § 1.355-2(b)) other than a business purpose to facilitate the acquisition or a similar acquisition, and the fact that the distribution would have occurred at approximately the same time and in similar form regardless of the acquisition or a similar acquisition, tend to show that the distribution and the acquisition are not part of a plan. See § 1.355-7(b)(4)(v), (vi). The fact that the public announcement of the distribution preceded discussions by Distributing or Controlled with X or its shareholders, and the fact that Distributing's business would have continued to operate successfully even if the merger had not occurred, evidence that the distribution originally was not substantially motivated by a business purpose to facilitate the acquisition or a similar acquisition. Moreover, after the merger, Distributing continued to be substantially motivated by the same corporate business purpose (within the meaning of § 1.355-2(b)) other than a business purpose to facilitate the acquisition or a similar acquisition (§ 1.355-7(b)(4)(v)). In addition, the fact that Distributing decided to distribute Controlled and announced that decision before it began discussions with X regarding the combination suggests that the distribution would have occurred at approximately the same time and in similar form regardless of Distributing's combination with X and the corresponding acquisition of Distributing stock by the X shareholders.

Considering all the facts and circumstances, particularly the fact that the distribution was motivated by a corporate business purpose (within the meaning of § 1.355-2(b)) other than a business purpose to facilitate the acquisition or a similar acquisition, and the fact that the distribution would have occurred at approximately the same time and in similar form regardless of the acquisition or a similar acquisition, the acquisition and distribution are not part of a plan under § 355(e) and § 1.355-7(b). . . .

**Problem 12-4:** For good business reasons, two public corporations, X and Y, decide to combine a business owned separately by each. As part of a plan, X transfers its business to a new wholly-owned subsidiary, X-Sub, and distributes the X-Sub stock to X's shareholders in a qualifying divisive reorganization. Y similarly transfers its business to a new wholly-owned subsidiary, Y-Sub, and distributes the Y-Sub stock to Y's shareholders in a qualifying divisive reorganization. A new corporation (Newco) is then formed, with two wholly-owned subsidiaries, N-1 and N-2. N-1 is merged into X-Sub, and N-2 is merged into Y-Sub, in transactions qualifying as "A" reorganizations by reason of section 368(a)(2)(E). As a result of the mergers, the shareholders of X-Sub and Y-Sub each receive exactly 50 percent of the stock of Newco in exchange for their stock of X-Sub and Y-Sub, and X-Sub and Y-Sub become wholly-owned subsidiaries of Newco (with a possibility of combination in the future). Must X and Y recognize gain on distributing stock of X-Sub and Y-Sub, respectively, to their shareholders? Does your answer depend upon whether any person immediately prior to the distributions owned stock in *both* X and Y?

## *NOTES*

1. *Reg. § 1.355-7.* As mentioned in Rev. Rul. 2005-65, the regulations identify a series of factors that tend to show that a distribution and acquisition are either part of a plan (termed "plan factors") or not part of a plan (termed "non-plan factors"). An example of a plan factor is the existence within two years prior to a distribution of an agreement, understanding, arrangement, or substantial negotiations regarding an acquisition (other than a public offering) that takes place after the distribution. Reg. § 1.355-7(b)(3)(i). An example of a non-plan factor is an unexpected change in market conditions that occurs after a distribution and results in an acquisition. Reg. § 1.355-7(b)(4)(ii). The regulations also provide nine "safe harbors" describing a series of fact patterns that allow a distribution and acquisition not to be treated as part of a plan. Reg. § 1.355-7(d). Finally, the regulations contain the equivalent of a tenth safe harbor providing that a distribution and subsequent acquisition (other than a public offering) are treated as part of a plan only if, within two years prior to the distribution, there is an agreement, understanding, arrangement, or substantial negotiation regarding the acquisition. Reg. § 1.355-7(b)(2). This safe harbor is important because it means there must be some degree of bilateral negotiations for an acquisition following a distribution to be treated as part of a plan. Thus, unilateral strategic planning and other purely internal discussions about an acquisition following a distribution, as well as limited, preliminary bilateral negotiations, will generally not be enough to constitute a plan. As previously noted, the existence of substantial bilateral negotiations during the two years prior to the distribution does not establish conclusively that a plan exists; such evidence is merely a plan factor.

2. *Section 355(f).* Under section 355(f), except as provided in regulations, certain distributions from one member of an affiliated group to another do not qualify under section 355 if such distributions are part of a plan described in section 355(e).

> **Example 12-5:** D corporation owns all of C corporation, which owns all of S corporation. As part of a plan, (1) C distributes all of its S stock to D; (2) D distributes all of the S stock to D's shareholders; and (3) D is merged into P corporation, with P surviving, and the former D shareholders end up with 50 percent or less of P. In this transaction, C's distribution to D does not qualify under section 355 (section 355(f)), and D recognizes gain upon the distribution of S stock to D's shareholders under section 355(c)(2) and (e).

The purpose of section 355(f) is to allow Treasury to determine the basis and other consequences of the transaction for affiliated groups either filing or not filing a consolidated return (chapter fourteen) in order to prevent inappropriate results. See also I.R.C. § 358(g). Thus far, no guidance has been provided. If the intragroup distribution is part of a plan that results in both the distributing and controlled corporations being members of a single affiliated group, then the plan is disregarded for purposes of section 355(e) (and therefore section 355(f) does not apply). I.R.C. § 355(e)(2)(C). For example, if only the first and third steps in **example 12-5** occur (so that C and S are both subsidiaries of P following the merger), then neither section 355(e) nor (f) applies (despite the 50-percent-or-greater change in ownership resulting from the merger).

3. *E&P*. In a divisive reorganization, the distributing corporation must allocate a portion of its E&P to the controlled corporation. In general, if the controlled corporation is newly created, the allocation is in proportion to the fair market value of the assets of the corporations immediately after the transaction. I.R.C. § 312(h); Reg. § 1.312-10.

4. *Policy*. In addition to being quite complex, section 355(d) and (e) can produce questionable policy outcomes. Suppose D corporation is a holding company with two wholly-owned subsidiaries, C-1 and C-2, and would like to transfer C-2's business to P corporation for cash. As we have seen, one way to achieve this objective would be for P to acquire stock in D and then have D distribute to P, in a qualifying section 355 transaction, all of the stock of C-2. However, an alternate way to reach the same outcome (following P's acquisition of D stock) would be for D to distribute all of its stock in *C-1* to the D shareholders *other than P*. Even if section 355(d) or (e) applied to each transaction, their tax consequences would vary, depending upon the amount of D's gain in each subsidiary. Furthermore, following recognition of gain by D, there is no basis adjustment to prevent future recognition of the same corporate-level gain (such as when the assets of the subsidiary are sold), in contrast to the policy of sections 338(h)(10) and 336(e). Both problems could be addressed by *not* requiring D to recognize gain or loss (under the general rule of section 355(c)). Instead, assuming a sufficient change of ownership of a corporation (C-2 in each case), there would be a deemed section 338 election with respect to that corporation. The deemed election would result in the corporation recognizing gain or loss but also obtaining a commensurate change to its asset basis.

Another criticism of section 355 is its linkage of corporate and shareholder tax consequences in certain cases. Although section 355(d) and (e) only affect the tax consequences to the distributing corporation, the conditions of section 355(a)(1) affect the consequences of the entire transaction. As a result, whether the distributing corporation recognizes gain in the transaction oddly may depend on whether the distribution is a spin-off or split-off, since those two forms may determine if the transaction violates the device test.

### 3. *Cash-Rich Split-Offs and the Problem of Disguised Exchanges*

In 2006, Congress added section 355(g) to respond to a monetizing transaction known as a "cash-rich split-off":

> **Example 12-6:** X corporation would like to sell (mostly for cash) its minority interest in Y corporation without incurring a corporate-level tax. Y transfers a five-year active business plus a substantial amount of cash (or other liquid investment assets) to a new subsidiary (S), and then distributes all of the S stock to X in exchange for all of X's stock in Y. Thus, X exchanges its minority interest in Y for 100 percent of S. After the distribution, the cash held by S can easily be distributed tax-free to X, thereby enabling X to monetize most of its investment in Y.

Although the transfer of cash may be evidence of a device (Reg. § 1.355-2(d)(2)(iv)(B)), the device test would ordinarily not be violated because of the non-pro rata split-off (Reg. § 1.355-2(d)(5)(iv)) and (absent section 355(g)) the other section 355 conditions may also be satisfied. Further, the distribution may not implicate either section 355(d) (assuming that there is no purchase of stock within the preceding five years) or section 355(e) (since X's acquisition of S stock is disregarded for purposes of that provision (I.R.C. § 355(e)(3)(A)(ii)). Thus, if section 355(g) does not apply, both X and Y may succeed in exchanging their respective corporate interests without incurring a corporate-level tax. Reportedly, in a cash-rich split-off, Time-Warner exchanged the Atlanta Braves baseball team plus about $1 billion for most of Liberty Media's minority interest in Time-Warner without recognition of gain or loss by either corporation.

Read I.R.C. § 355(g)(1), (2)(A) and (B)(i), and (3). Under section 355(g)(1), section 355 does not apply to a corporate division if, immediately after the transaction, any person holds a 50 percent or greater interest (by vote or value) in a "disqualified investment corporation" and such person did not hold such an interest immediately prior to the transaction. Unlike section 355(d) and (e), which generally apply only if new owners acquire at least 50 percent of the distributing or controlled corporations, the ownership test in section 355(g) allows it to apply to certain non-pro rata transactions that merely change the ownership interests of existing shareholders. For example, if a shareholder owns less than 50 percent of a disqualified investment corporation before a transaction and at least 50 percent thereafter, section 355(g) (but not section 355(d) and (e)) applies.

In general, a "disqualified investment corporation" is the distributing or controlled corporation if at least two-thirds of the value of its assets consists of cash or certain passive investment assets. I.R.C. § 355(g)(2). (The Time-Warner transaction was timed to fit within the one-year post-enactment period when up to three-fourths of a corporation's assets could be cash or investment assets without the corporation being considered a "disqualified investment corporation." I.R.C. § 355(g)(2)(A)(ii).) In **example 12-6**, assuming that S is a disqualified investment corporation and X owned less than 50 percent of Y prior to the transaction (so that there was no attribution to X of Y's stock in S (I.R.C. §§ 355(g)(3)(B), 318(a)(2)(C))), section 355(g)(1) applies to prevent the split-off from qualifying under section 355. Importantly, the distribution is, therefore, taxable to *both* the distributee and the distributing corporation.

The high investment assets threshold for treatment as a "disqualified investment corporation" means that section 355(g) will likely affect few transactions in the future. Nevertheless, enactment of this provision may foreshadow other statutory amendments to prevent possible variations on monetizing transactions. Suppose, for example, D corporation owns a valuable business that it would like to use to pay off certain D security holders. Instead of selling the business and using the cash proceeds to pay off the security holders, D transfers the business to a subsidiary (C) in exchange for stock and securities of C, and D then distributes its C stock to D's shareholders and the C securities to D's security holders. This transaction might qualify under section 355 and not violate section 355(d), (e), or (g). If so, D might be viewed as having satisfied its security holders with the proceeds of its valuable business without incurring a corporate-level tax. Legislation approved by the House of Representatives in 2010 would require D to recognize gain on the transfer of the business to C to the extent the value of any securities (or NQPS) of C distributed to D's creditors exceed D's basis in the assets transferred to C. H.R. 4213 (2010) (as passed by the House on May 28, 2010), § 421.

More broadly, section 355(g) represents a possible rethinking of the permissible scope of section 355 transactions. As we have seen, the focus of section 355(d) and (e) is on whether a section 355 transaction results in a disposition of corporate interests to *new* owners without the recognition of corporate-level gain. In contrast, section 355(g) shows that certain non-pro rata distributions, even among *existing* owners, may constitute disguised exchanges not entitled to nonrecognition treatment. Section 355(g) thus illustrates a *third* possible policy objective for section 355—to prevent disguised exchanges as well as corporate bailouts and avoidance of *General Utilities* repeal. These goals may not be fully compatible with one another. For example, the anti-bailout concern favors non-pro rata over pro rata distributions, while the concern about disguised exchanges has the exact opposite preference. Ultimately, as evidenced by the steady accretion of section 355 conditions (with more on the horizon), it may be that a tax-free corporate division simply cannot be reconciled with all of the other policy objectives for those transactions.

### 4. *Section 355 Alternatives*

The following IRS Notice describes a corporate inversion, a transaction that does not involve or qualify under section 355. The inversion raises, however, some of the same issues as a divisive reorganization, including the impact of the transaction on *General Utilities* repeal. In the transaction described, there is no change in the identity or shares of the owners of the enterprise, the amount of assets held in corporate solution, or the underlying business activities of the corporations involved. Yet the inversion may set the stage for meaningful and possibly inappropriate future tax consequences. How should such transactions be analyzed? The IRS has not yet issued the guidance promised in the notice.

## Notice 94-93

1994-2 C.B. 563

The Internal Revenue Service and Treasury Department are concerned with transactions that invert the positions of related corporations. Such inversion transactions typically involve a transfer of stock of a corporation by one or more of its shareholders to a wholly or partially owned subsidiary of that corporation in exchange for newly issued shares of subsidiary stock. Depending on the facts and circumstances, an inversion transaction may improperly create losses or permit the avoidance of income or gain in circumvention of the repeal of the *General Utilities* doctrine or other applicable rules. . . .

The following is an example of an inversion transaction that is of particular concern to the Internal Revenue Service and Treasury Department. Owner (who may be a single shareholder or a group of shareholders) holds 100 percent of the outstanding stock of P. P holds land worth \$300 and the 10 outstanding shares of stock of its wholly owned subsidiary, S. S holds land worth \$100. P's adjusted basis in the S stock is \$85. Owner transfers all of its stock of P to S in exchange for 90 newly issued shares of S stock. After this exchange, Owner holds 90 percent of the S stock, P holds the remaining 10 percent, and S holds 100 percent of the P stock. Assume that an unrelated third party would have paid \$400 to Owner for the P stock before the inversion transaction and would pay \$400 to Owner for the 90 shares of S stock after the inversion transaction.

As a result of this inversion transaction, P's percentage interest in S has been reduced from 100 percent to 10 percent. An unrelated third party would pay only \$44.44 for P's stock in S after the inversion transaction (disregarding any minority discount or control premium), compared to the $100 that a third party would have paid for the stock before the inversion transaction. This reduced amount reflects the fact that, after the inversion transaction and the sale by P of its S stock to the third party, the third party buyer would have a 10 percent interest in the PS group and the PS group would hold assets with a value of $444.44 ($400 in land plus $44.44 cash from the sale of P's stock in S). The inversion transaction also reduces the amount that a third party would pay for the P stock from $400 ($300 in land plus $100 in S stock) to $344.44 ($300 in land plus $44.44 in S stock).

No such reductions in the amount a third party would pay for P's stock in S or S's stock in P would occur if S issued 40 shares (instead of 90 shares) to Owner. In that case, P's percentage interest in S would decline from 100 percent to 20 percent (instead of 10 percent) and an unrelated third party still would be willing to pay P $100 for its S stock (disregarding any minority discount or control premium). This $100 purchase price reflects the fact that, after the inversion transaction and subsequent sale, the PS group would hold assets with a value of $500 ($400 in land plus $100 cash), the third party would have a 20 percent interest in the PS group worth $100 (disregarding any minority discount or control premium), and Owner would have an 80 percent interest in the PS group worth $400 (disregarding any minority discount or control premium). In addition, the amount an unrelated third party would pay for the P stock would remain unchanged at $400 after the inversion transaction ($300 for the land plus $100 for the S stock).

Owner and the PS group might take the position that they do not recognize income or gain on an inversion transaction. In addition, the PS group might take the position that as a result of the issuance of 90 shares of S stock to Owner, P can avoid the $15 of gain ($100 selling price before the inversion transaction minus $85 adjusted basis) inherent in its S stock before the inversion transaction and even recognize a $40.56 loss ($44.44 selling price after the inversion transaction minus $85 adjusted basis) on the sale of its S stock. The PS group might also take the position that the inversion transaction can generate a loss for S in the P stock transferred to S by Owner because of the decrease in the amount a third party would pay for the P stock from $400 to $344.44 after the inversion transaction.

The Internal Revenue Service and Treasury Department will issue guidance that addresses the tax consequences of inversion transactions. For the purpose of such guidance, an inversion transaction means any transaction that inverts or otherwise reverses (in whole or in part) the positions of related corporations (including predecessor or successor corporations). Such guidance is expected to include regulations that will require, as appropriate: (i) recognition of income or gain at the time of an inversion transaction, or (ii) reductions to the basis (or increases in gain on the sale or other disposition) of the stock of one or more corporations that are involved in inversion transactions. Any such regulations will apply to an inversion transaction occurring on or after September 22, 1994, in which, as a result of an issuance or transfer of stock or stock rights, there would be a reduction in the amount a third party would pay for the stock of one or more corporations involved in an inversion transaction. However, a reduction in the amount a third party would pay for the stock of a corporation involved in an inversion transaction will not be taken into account to the extent it is solely attributable to any minority discount or control premium arising in the inversion transaction.

No inference is intended as to (i) the qualification of an inversion transaction under §§ 351, 368, or any other non-recognition provision of the Internal Revenue Code, or (ii) any other tax treatment of an inversion transaction under current law. Thus, for example, depending on the facts and circumstances, §§ 269, 301, 311, 1248(i), 1.1502-20 of the Income Tax Regulations, or other principles of law such as substance over form, could apply to an inversion transaction, or to the sale or other disposition of stock involved in an inversion transaction, regardless of the date on which the inversion transaction occurred. . . .

## *NOTES*

1. *Section 304.* In the ruling, the Owner's transfer of P stock to S in exchange for S stock is not covered by section 304 since S is considered the "distributing corporation" for purposes of that provision and therefore its stock does not constitute "property." I.R.C. §§ 304(a)(2)(A), 317(a); *Bhada v. Comm'r* (p. 310).

2. *Tracking stock.* "Tracking stock" is stock with dividend or liquidation rights determined directly or indirectly by reference to only a portion of the issuing corporation's assets, such as a division or subsidiary of the issuing corporation. The issuance of tracking stock raises questions similar to the policy issues presented in a section 355 transaction. For example, if tracking stock is tied to the economic performance of a subsidiary of the issuing corporation, should the issuance of such stock be viewed as, in effect, a disposition of the subsidiary to the holders of the stock, resulting in the recognition of gain by the issuing corporation? Should the issuance of such stock be treated as a section 301 property distribution to the holders because (assuming that they continue to hold non-tracking stock of the issuing corporation) the holders have effectively realized a portion of their interest in the issuing corporation? (Recall the concern of Justice Pitney in *Rockefeller* (p. 451).) Despite prior government proposals, no legislation has been enacted dealing specifically with the tax consequences of tracking stock. One reason is that evidence of a very close correlation between the economic performance of tracking stock and that of the tracked property has been inconclusive. In addition, tracking stock can serve important nontax purposes, such as enhancing capital formation and providing incentive compensation for employees involved with the tracked property.

# Chapter 13

# Limitations on Net Operating Loss Carryovers

In certain corporate acquisitions, the target corporation's net operating loss (NOL) deduction — in general, the deduction representing the excess of the target's deductions (other than its NOL deduction) over gross income in a prior taxable year — is not extinguished, but remains available to offset taxable income after the acquisition. Over the years, Congress and the courts have struggled with protecting the policy of the NOL deduction in a corporate acquisition while not encouraging "loss trafficking," i.e., the purchase and sale of corporations principally to acquire their NOL deduction. Part A of this chapter introduces the key issues and summarizes the main pre-1986 efforts to achieve these goals. Part B then reviews the current-law limitations, which are principally found in section 382.

## A. Introduction and Prior-Law Limitations

### *1. Developments Prior to 1954 Code*

The NOL deduction dates back to the Revenue Act of 1918, which permitted a taxpayer sustaining a loss in one taxable year (the "loss year") to deduct it against the taxpayer's net income of the preceding taxable year and to carry forward any remaining loss for deduction in the succeeding taxable year. The purpose of the deduction is to mitigate the arbitrariness of the annual accounting system. The deduction is currently found in section 172, and generally permits an NOL to be carried back two years and forward twenty. In essence, the rule enables taxpayers to determine their taxable income after taking into account their gross income and deductions over a rolling 23-year period. Losses are generally carried back to the earliest possible year with any remaining losses carried forward consecutively to each subsequent permissible year. The NOL deduction comprises both the "carryback" of losses to a year preceding the loss year and the "carryover" or "carryforward" of losses to a succeeding year. Read I.R.C. § 172(a), (b)(1)(A) and (2), (c), and (d)(1).

For corporate taxpayers, the "averaging" purpose of the deduction may be uncontroversial as long as there is no change to the corporation, its owners, or its business. But difficult interpretive questions arise if one or more of those conditions is not satisfied. In New Colonial Ice Co. v. Helvering, 292 U.S. 435 (1934), the Supreme Court held that only the corporation incurring the loss could claim the NOL deduction. Although this strict "entity" approach was soon modified to permit the surviving corporation in a statutory merger to deduct the NOL carryforwards of the corporation that merged into it, the highly formalistic position produced some surprising results.

For example, in Alprosa Watch Corp. v. Comm'r, 11 T.C. 240 (1948), certain individuals made a cash purchase of all of the stock of the Esspi Glove Corporation, which was engaged in the manufacture and sale of women's gloves. Following the purchase, the corporation was renamed the Alprosa Watch Corporation, its principal place of business was altered, its business was changed to that of selling watches, and its old glove business assets were sold back to the former owners of the corporation. The court held that despite the complete change in owners, business, assets, and place of business, the pre-acquisition losses arising from the glove business could be used to offset post-acquisition income generated by the watch business. The key factor unchanged was the corporate entity, the "taxpayer" that had incurred the loss and was, therefore, entitled to the carryforward deduction.

In 1943, Congress first imposed a statutory restriction on the transferability of favorable tax benefits (including the NOL deduction) in certain corporate acquisitions. Under section 129 of the 1939 Code (the predecessor to current section 269), if the principal purpose of the acquisition was to avoid taxes by securing the benefit of a deduction, credit, or other allowance that the taxpayer would not otherwise enjoy, the Secretary was authorized to disallow the benefit. Although this provision was primarily directed at restricting the utilization of unused excess profits tax credits following an acquisition, cases such as *Alprosa Watch* (which involved a taxable year prior to the effect of this provision) soon made evident its potential applicability to the transferability of the NOL deduction.

In the following case arising under the 1939 Code, the Supreme Court set forth yet another standard that conditioned entitlement to the NOL deduction to continuation of the business generating the loss. Hence, prior to enactment of the 1954 Code, the survival of an NOL deduction following a corporate acquisition was subject to at least three different tests: the "entity" approach of *New Colonial Ice*, the statutory "tax avoidance purpose" test, and the "business continuity" requirement of the following case.

## Libson Shops, Inc. v. Koehler

353 U.S. 382 (1957)

Mr. Justice BURTON delivered the opinion of the Court.

The issue before us is whether . . . a corporation resulting from a merger of 17 separate incorporated businesses, which had filed separate income tax returns, may carry over and deduct the pre-merger net operating losses of three of its constituent corporations from the post-merger income attributable to the other businesses. We hold that such a carry-over and deduction is not permissible.

Petitioner, Libson Shops, Inc., was incorporated on January 2, 1946, under the laws of Missouri . . . to provide management services for corporations selling women's apparel at retail. Its articles of incorporation also permitted it to sell apparel. At about the same time, the same interests incorporated 16 separate corporations to sell women's apparel at retail at separate locations. Twelve were incorporated and went into business in Missouri; four in Illinois. Each of these 16 sales corporations was operated separately and filed separate income tax returns. Petitioner's sole activity was to provide management services for them. The outstanding stock of all 17 corporations was owned, directly or indirectly, by the same individuals in the same proportions.

On August 1, 1949, the 16 sales corporations were merged into petitioner under the laws of Missouri and Illinois. New shares of petitioner's stock were issued, pro rata, in exchange for the stock of the sales corporations. By virtue of the merger agreement, petitioner's name was changed, the amount and par value of its stock revised, and its corporate purposes expanded. Following the merger, petitioner conducted the entire business as a single enterprise. Thus, the effect of the merger was to convert 16 retail businesses and one managing agency, reporting their incomes separately, into a single enterprise filing one income tax return.

Prior to the merger, three of the sales corporations showed net operating losses [which totaled $22,432.76]. . . . In the year following the merger, each of the retail units formerly operated by these three corporations continued to sustain a net operating loss.

In its income tax return for the first year after the merger, petitioner claimed a deduction of the above $22,432.76 as a carry-over of its pre-merger losses. . . . The Commissioner of Internal Revenue disallowed it. . . .

We are concerned here with a claim to carry over an operating loss to the immediately succeeding taxable year. The particular provision on which petitioner's case rests is as follows:

> "If for any taxable year beginning after December 31, 1947, and before January 1, 1950, *the taxpayer* has a net operating loss, such net operating loss shall be a net operating loss carry-over for each of the three succeeding taxable years. . . ." (Emphasis supplied.) . . .

The controversy centers on the meaning of "the taxpayer." The contentions of the parties require us to decide whether it can be said that petitioner, a combination of 16 sales businesses, is "the taxpayer" having the pre-merger losses of three of those businesses.

In support of its denial of the carry-over, the Government argues that this statutory privilege is not available unless the corporation claiming it is the same taxable entity as that which sustained the loss. In reliance on New Colonial Ice Co. v. Helvering, 292 U.S. 435, and cases following it, the Government argues that separately chartered corporations are not the same taxable entity. Petitioner, on the other hand, relying on Helvering v. Metropolitan Edison Co., 306 U.S. 522, and cases following it, argues that a corporation resulting from a statutory merger is treated as the same taxable entity as its constituents to whose legal attributes it has succeeded by operation of state law. However, we find it unnecessary to discuss this issue since an alternative argument made by the Government is dispositive of this case. The Government contends that the carry-over privilege is not available unless there is a continuity of business enterprise. It argues that the prior year's loss can be offset against the current year's income only to the extent that this income is derived from the operation of substantially the same business which produced the loss. Only to that extent is the same "taxpayer" involved.

The requirement of a continuity of business enterprise as applied to this case is in accord with the legislative history of the carry-over and carry-back provisions. Those provisions were enacted to ameliorate the unduly drastic consequences of taxing income strictly on an annual basis. They were designed to permit a taxpayer to set off its lean years against its lush years, and to strike something like an average taxable income computed over a period longer than one year. There is, however, no indication in their legislative history that these provisions were designed to permit the averaging of the pre-merger losses of one business with the post-merger income of some other business which had been operated and taxed separately before the merger. What history there is suggests that Congress primarily was concerned with the fluctuating income of a single business.

This distinction is recognized by the very cases on which petitioner relies. In Stanton Brewery, Inc. v. Comm'r, 176 F.2d 573, 577 (2d Cir.) the Court of Appeals stressed the fact that the merging corporations there involved carried on "essentially a *continuing enterprise*, entitled to all . . . benefits (of the carry-over provisions) in ameliorating otherwise harsh tax consequences of fluctuating profits or expanding business." (Emphasis supplied.) And in Newmarket Manufacturing Co. v. U.S., 233 F.2d 493, 497 (1st Cir.), the court expressly distinguished the case before it from the instant case on the ground that there "one single business" was involved in the merger, while in this case there were "several businesses."

. . . In the present case, the 16 sales corporations, prior to the merger, chose to file separate income tax returns rather than to pool their income and losses by filing a consolidated return. Petitioner is attempting to carry over the pre-merger losses of three business units which continued to have losses after the merger. Had there been no merger, these businesses would have had no opportunity to carry over their losses.

If petitioner is permitted to take a carry-over, the 16 sales businesses have acquired by merger an opportunity that they elected to forego when they chose not to file a consolidated return.

We do not imply that a question of tax evasion or avoidance is involved. [The predecessor to section 269] does contain provisions which may vitiate a tax deduction that was made possible by the acquisition of corporate property for the "principal purpose" of tax evasion or avoidance. And that section is inapplicable here since there was no finding that tax evasion or avoidance was the "principal purpose" of the merger. The fact that [section 269] is inapplicable does not mean that petitioner is automatically entitled to a carry-over. The availability of this privilege depends on the proper interpretation to be given to the carry-over provisions. We find nothing in those provisions which suggest that they should be construed to give a "windfall" to a taxpayer who happens to have merged with other corporations. The purpose of these provisions is not to give a merged taxpayer a tax advantage over others who have not merged. We conclude that petitioner is not entitled to a carry-over since the income against which the offset is claimed was not produced by substantially the same businesses which incurred the losses.

The judgment of the Court of Appeals is Affirmed.

Mr. Justice DOUGLAS dissents.

Mr. Justice WHITTAKER took no part in the consideration or decision of this case.

### *NOTE*

Libson Shops *test*. The Supreme Court appears to allow use of the pre-merger losses only against income of the same business producing the loss. This business continuity test is different from the COBE doctrine in reorganizations, which merely requires that at least one of three historic businesses of the target corporation be continued following the acquisition. The *Libson Shops* transaction failed to satisfy the Supreme Court's stricter test but appears to have complied with COBE. Moreover, because taxpayers are generally entitled to offset income and losses generated by different business activities they conduct, the Supreme Court's test arguably restricts the use of losses following an acquisition more stringently than had no acquisition occurred. The test, therefore, may create a disincentive for certain acquisitions. Finally, the test discourages corporations from making business changes following an acquisition.

## *2. Developments Between 1954 and 1986*

In 1954, Congress enacted section 381 to provide that in a section 332 liquidation and an asset acquisition qualifying as a nondivisive reorganization, the acquiring corporation generally succeeds to the tax attributes, including the NOL carryovers, of the transferor corporation. This rule modified the "entity" doctrine and was designed to create symmetry with the results of corporate stock acquisitions where, ordinarily, the tax attributes of the acquired corporation are unaffected by changes in ownership. Perfect symmetry was not achieved, however, since section 381 applied only to certain "tax-free" asset acquisitions, whereas even taxable stock acquisitions preserve tax attributes. Read I.R.C. § 381(a) and (c). Under current law, section 381 is essentially unchanged from its original enactment. If one corporation ultimately acquires all of the target's assets in a nondivisive reorganization, it succeeds to the attributes. If the assets are split among different corporations, the corporation that directly acquires the assets succeeds to the attributes. Reg. § 1.381(a)-1(b)(2)(i).

In 1954, Congress also enacted section 382 to limit the transfer of NOL carryovers in certain ownership changes of loss corporations resulting from a stock purchase or reorganization. In general, if a stock purchase changed the ownership of a loss corporation by at least 50 percentage points over a two-year period *and* the corporation's trade or business was not continued, the corporation's NOL carryovers were extinguished. I.R.C. § 382(a) (1954). In contrast, in certain reorganizations, the amount of a loss corporation's NOL carryover was reduced proportionately, depending upon the degree to which shareholders of the corporation were provided with less than 20 percent of the stock of the acquiring corporation in the reorganization. I.R.C. § 382(b) (1954). These new anti-loss trafficking provisions were "objective" and applied regardless of tax avoidance purpose. Congress retained the tax avoidance test in section 269, and it remains part of current law.

The 1954 rules contained a number of defects. There was no policy justification for applying a different change of ownership threshold to stock purchases and reorganizations, permitting a proportionate reduction of the NOL deduction only in reorganizations, and requiring business continuity only for stock purchases. In addition, the statutory tests were not comprehensive; certain transactions resulting in an ownership change of a loss corporation, such as a section 351 transaction or "B" reorganization, potentially escaped both limitations.

In 1976, Congress approved a revised set of rules that largely corrected the technical deficiencies. As with the 1954 version, however, the 1976 version was criticized for curtailing the *amount* of NOL carryovers surviving a corporate change of ownership rather than the *use* of such carryovers following the acquisition. In its study proposing what became the foundation of current law, the American Law Institute critiqued the 1954 and 1976 versions of the statute:

> [e]xisting law is too harsh when it disallows any part of a loss carryover that is only a minor incident in an acquisition transaction; at the same time it is too lenient, assuming we are to have any limitations at all, when it allows any fraction of a loss carryover in the absence of any other elements of value. [American Law Institute, Federal Income Tax Project: Subchapter C (1982) at 201.]

Because the 1976 amendments were drafted hastily, Congress delayed their effective date until 1978. This proved to be a fatal mistake, as the delayed effective date was subsequently extended several times, and the amendments were ultimately repealed in 1986 without ever having gone into effect.

## *NOTE*

*Loss recoupment and free transferability.* Rules limiting the transferability of losses would be unnecessary if corporations could recoup from the government the "tax value" of their losses as they arise. With loss recoupment, the government would share in both the profits *and* losses of taxpayers in the same manner as a full (though silent) partner, and there would be no losses to transfer in a corporate acquisition. Loss recoupment has been debated primarily by academics and raises many challenging technical and policy questions. Past opposition to refunds of unused corporate minimum tax credits — which, unlike loss recoupment, generally represent mere returns of prepaid corporate taxes — foreshadows the likely political reaction to a loss recoupment proposal.

An alternative to loss recoupment — alluded to in the ALI excerpt noted above — would be to allow corporations to transfer freely their losses without restriction. Free transferability might at first seem to allow purchasers of the losses to obtain windfalls to the extent they capture some of the difference in value of the loss to the buyer and loss corporation seller. But if there were a sufficient number of potential buyers, they could be expected to "bid up" the value of the loss so that most of the benefit would be obtained by the loss corporation. Thus, the effect of free transferability might be similar to loss recoupment without need for government payments to any taxpayers. Free transferability (as well as loss recoupment) would enable the government to use tax incentives to induce business activity even among taxpayers with little or no income tax liability.

Free transferability was tried on a small scale in 1981 when taxpayers were allowed to transfer certain excess deductions and credits to other taxpayers in a practice known as "safe harbor leasing." Public reaction to this program was not positive and safe harbor leasing was repealed in 1982. Moreover, during the program's brief existence, the Joint Committee on Taxation estimated that only about 75 percent of the tax benefit from the transferred deductions and credits was obtained by the transferor; most of the rest resulted in windfalls to buyers, with a small amount attributable to transaction costs. Free transferability might transfer tax benefits even less efficiently than safe harbor leasing if buyers were required to acquire the loss corporation's business along with its losses. In addition, such businesses would potentially be more valuable to loss corporations if sold rather than retained, thereby encouraging acquisitions. Finally, whether justified or not, free transferability would no doubt reintroduce conduct — such as corporate ads soliciting purchasers of available losses — that was found objectionable by earlier legislators.

## B. Current-Law Limitations on NOL Carryovers

### 1. *Section 382 Limitation and Required Business Continuity*

In 1986, Congress adopted an entirely new version of section 382. Like the former version, the 1986 rules apply only upon a significant change in ownership of a loss corporation. But if they apply, the *consequences* of the two sets of rules are dramatically different. Rather than reducing (or eliminating) the amount of the NOL carryover, the 1986 provisions limit the *rate* at which the carryover may be used after the change. The theory behind current law is a principle of "neutrality": use of loss carryovers surviving an ownership change should be limited to the use that would have been available to the loss corporation, had there been no change. Under this principle, the tax law provides neither an incentive nor a disincentive for an ownership change.

Since NOL deductions are "used" to offset taxable income, the neutrality principle is implemented by limiting the annual amount of taxable income after an ownership change that may be shielded by losses arising prior to the change. The statutory limit, known as the "section 382 limitation," is equal to the value of the loss corporation immediately prior to the ownership change multiplied by the "long-term tax-exempt rate"; in general, this rate equals the highest yield in any month (during the three months prior to the ownership change) on outstanding U.S. obligations with terms of over nine years (adjusted to provide a tax-exempt rate). Read I.R.C. §§ 382(a), (b)(1), (d), (e)(1), (f), and (k)(1)-(3), 1274(d)(1). The statutory formula was derived from the estimates of the Joint Committee on Taxation indicating that at the time section 382 was enacted, the rate at which loss corporations used their losses to offset taxable income was only about 4.4 percent of the book value of their assets.

Congress specified a *tax-exempt* (rather than taxable) rate because, in determining the value of the loss corporation, the value of its loss carryovers is not excluded. Hence, a tax-exempt rate is necessary to replicate the rate of taxable income of a loss corporation's assets *exclusive* of its carryovers. For example, assume that a loss corporation's only asset is a $100 bond with a taxable market-rate yield of 12 percent, or $12, per year. Assuming that tax rates are a flat 33.3 percent, the bond's after-tax yield is 8 percent, or $8, per year. However, because the loss corporation has a sufficient amount of NOL carryovers to shield all of its income from taxation, the bond it holds is effectively tax-exempt and yields $12 after taxes. Therefore, disregarding any effect of the bond being held in corporate solution, a purchaser could be expected to pay about $150 for all of the loss corporation's stock, which represents the value of its bond *and* its carryovers ($12 after-tax yield/$150 = $8 after-tax, market-rate yield/$100). Since the section 382 limitation is a function of the value of the loss corporation's stock immediately prior to the ownership change ($150 in this example) (I.R.C. § 382(e)(1)), a tax-exempt rate (8 percent under these assumptions) is necessary to determine the rate of taxable income of the corporation's assets exclusive of its carryovers ($150 value × 8% = $100 × 12% = rate of taxable income of corporation's $100 bond).

Finally, read I.R.C. § 382(c)(1). If the loss corporation's business is not continued for at least two years following the ownership change, the section 382 limitation is zero. This provision was included to ensure that an acquisition resulting in a transfer of losses has some business element apart from the loss transfer. According to the legislative history, this condition is the same as the COBE doctrine for reorganizations, and not the rule in *Libson Shops* (which was explicitly not followed). Thus, continuation of at least one out of three of the loss corporation's historic businesses (or continued use of at least one-third of the corporation's historic business assets) should generally suffice. Reg. § 1.368-1(d)(5) (ex. 1). Moreover, unlike *Libson Shops*, there is no requirement that the business producing the loss be the one continued. The "two-year" requirement in section 382(c)(1) is slightly different from COBE, which ordinarily does not provide any required minimum period of continuity.

## *NOTE*

*Terminology*. Loss corporations are termed "old" or "new," depending upon whether they are entitled to use an NOL carryover before or after an ownership change. The same corporation may be both an old and new loss corporation, such as a loss corporation whose stock acquisition results in an ownership change. I.R.C. § 382(k)(1) - (3). In general, losses arising prior to an ownership change are termed "pre-change losses" and taxable years ending after the date an ownership change occurs are termed "post-change years." I.R.C. § 382(d).

## 2. *Ownership Change*

The section 382 limitation applies only if there is an "ownership change" of the loss corporation. Read I.R.C. § 382(a), (d), (j), and (k)(1)-(3). In general, an ownership change occurs if one or more shareholders owning at least five percent of the stock (a "5-percent shareholder") increase their stock ownership of a loss corporation by over 50 percentage points compared to the lowest percentage they owned at any time during the prior three years (termed the "testing period"). For this purpose, stock held by all shareholders owning less than five percent of the stock of the loss corporation is generally aggregated and treated as held by a single 5-percent shareholder. Read I.R.C. § 382(g)(1) and (4)(A), (i)(1), and (k)(7). In general, percentage ownership changes resulting from gifts, bequests, transfers incident to a divorce, or fluctuations in the relative value of different classes of stock, are disregarded. I.R.C. § 382(*l*)(3)(B) and (C).

An ownership change may arise as a result of either an "owner shift involving a 5-percent shareholder" or an "equity structure shift." The latter term refers to nondivisive reorganizations (other than an "F" reorganization) and, to the extent provided in regulations, other transactions (such as a nonqualifying (taxable) reorganization). In contrast, an "owner shift involving a 5-percent shareholder" is a broad term that generally encompasses any transaction that changes the stock ownership of a 5-percent shareholder (and may, therefore, include an equity structure shift if it affects the percentage of stock owned by a 5-percent shareholder). Read I.R.C. § 382(g)(2) and (3).

Congress developed these two terms to make sure that only *certain* stock changes involving shareholders holding less than five percent of a loss corporation's stock would be disregarded in determining whether an ownership change occurred. For example, changes resulting from the public trading of stock by such shareholders are disregarded as a practical necessity. But changes resulting from a reorganization of a loss corporation are *not* disregarded even if before and after the transaction, all shareholders of the loss corporation own less than five percent of its stock. In the latter case, the transaction is a single, integrated transaction for which an ownership change can be determined, notwithstanding the lack of any 5-percent shareholder. In general, the shareholders of the corporations involved in the reorganization are each treated as separate 5-percent shareholders, with the result that the reorganization may constitute an ownership change. I.R.C. § 382(g)(4)(B)(i).

Read I.R.C. § 382(g), (k)(6), (*l*)(3) and the following excerpt from the Conference Report to the Tax Reform Act of 1986 describing the definition of an ownership change.

## H. Conf. Rep. No. 99-841

99th Cong., 2d Sess. II-170 (1986)

### OWNERSHIP CHANGE

... An ownership change occurs, in general, if the percentage of stock of the new loss corporation owned by any one or more 5-percent shareholders (described below) has increased by more than 50 percentage points relative to the lowest percentage of stock of the old loss corporation owned by those 5-percent shareholders at any time during the testing period (generally a three-year period). The determination of whether an ownership change has occurred is made by aggregating the increases in percentage ownership for each 5-percent shareholder whose percentage ownership has increased during the testing period. For this purpose, all stock owned by persons who own less than five percent of a loss corporation's stock is generally treated as stock owned by a single 5-percent shareholder. The determination of whether an ownership change has occurred is made after any owner shift involving a 5-percent shareholder or any equity structure shift.

Determinations of the percentage of stock in a loss corporation owned by any person are made on the basis of value. Except as provided in regulations to be prescribed by the Secretary, changes in proportionate ownership attributable solely to fluctuations in the relative fair market values of different classes or amounts of stock are not taken into account.

In determining whether an ownership change has occurred, changes in the holdings of certain preferred stock are disregarded. Except as provided in regulations, all "stock" (not including stock described in section 1504(a)(4)) is taken into account. . . . [T]he conferees expect the Treasury Department to publish regulations disregarding, in appropriate cases, certain stock that would otherwise be counted in determining whether an ownership change has occurred, when necessary to prevent avoidance of the special limitations. For example, it may be appropriate to disregard preferred stock (even though voting) or common stock where the likely percentage participation of such stock in future corporate growth is disproportionately small compared to the percentage value of the stock as a proportion of total stock value, at the time of the issuance or transfer. Similarly, the conferees are concerned that the inclusion of voting preferred stock (which is not described in section 1504(a)(4) solely because it carries the right to vote) in the definition of stock presents the potential for avoidance of section 382. . . .

## OWNER SHIFT INVOLVING A 5-PERCENT SHAREHOLDER

An owner shift involving a 5-percent shareholder is defined . . . as any change in the respective ownership of stock of a corporation that affects the percentage of stock held by any person who holds five percent or more of the stock of the corporation (a "5-percent shareholder") before or after the change. For purposes of this rule, all less-than-5-percent shareholders are aggregated and treated as one 5-percent shareholder. Thus, an owner shift involving a 5-percent shareholder includes (but is not limited to) the following transactions:

(1) A taxable purchase of loss corporation stock by a person who holds at least five percent of the stock before the purchase;
(2) A disposition of stock by a person who holds at least five percent of stock of the loss corporation either before or after the disposition;
(3) A taxable purchase of loss corporation stock by a person who becomes a 5-percent shareholder as a result of the purchase;
(4) A section 351 exchange that affects the percentage of stock ownership of a loss corporation by one or more 5-percent shareholders;
(5) A decrease in the outstanding stock of a loss corporation (*e.g.*, by virtue of a redemption) that affects the percentage of stock ownership of the loss corporation by one or more 5-percent shareholders;
(6) A conversion of debt (or pure preferred stock that is excluded from the definition of stock) to stock where the percentage of stock ownership of the loss corporation by one or more 5-percent shareholders is affected; and
(7) An issuance of stock by a loss corporation that affects the percentage of stock ownership by one or more 5-percent shareholders.

*Example 1.*—The stock of L corporation is publicly traded; no shareholder holds five percent or more of L stock. During the three-year period between January 1, 1987 and January 1, 1990, there are numerous trades involving L stock. No ownership change will occur as a result of such purchases, provided that no person (or persons) becomes a 5-percent shareholder, either directly or indirectly, and increases his (or their) ownership of L stock by more than 50 percentage points. . . .

*Example 3.*—On January 1, 1987, individual I owns all 1,000 shares of corporation L. On June 15, 1987, I sells 300 of his L shares to unrelated individual A. On June 15, 1988, L issues 100 shares to each of B, C, and D. After these owner shifts involving I, A, B, C, and D, each of whom are 5-percent shareholders, there is no ownership change, because the percentage of stock owned by A, B, C, and D after the owner shifts (approximately 46 percent—A-23 percent; B, C, and D-7.7 percent each) has not increased by more than 50 percentage points over the lowest percentage of stock owned by those shareholders during the testing period (0 percent prior to June 15, 1987). On December 15, 1988, L redeems 200 of the shares owned by I. Following this owner shift affecting I, a 5-percent shareholder, there is an ownership change, because the percentage of L stock owned by A, B, C, and D (approximately 55 percent—A-27.3 percent; B, C, and D-9.1 percent each) has increased by more than 50 percentage points over the lowest percentage owned by those shareholders during the testing period (0 percent prior to June 15, 1987).

*Example 4.*—L corporation is closely held by four unrelated individuals, A, B, C, and D. On January 1, 1987, there is a public offering of L stock. No person who acquires stock in a public offering acquires five percent or more, and neither A, B, C, nor D acquires any additional stock. As a result of the offering, less-than-5-percent shareholders own stock representing 80 percent of the outstanding L stock. The stock ownership of the less-than-5-percent shareholders are aggregated and treated as owned by a single 5-percent shareholder for purposes of determining whether an ownership change has occurred. The percentage of stock owned by the less-than-5-percent shareholders after the owner shift (80 percent) has increased by more than 50 percentage points over the lowest percentage of stock owned by those shareholders at any time during the testing period (0 percent prior to January 1, 1987). Thus, an ownership change has occurred. . . .

*Example 7.*—On January 1, 1987, L corporation is owned by two unrelated shareholders, A (60 percent) and C (40 percent). LS corporation is a wholly owned subsidiary of L corporation and is therefore deemed to be owned by A and C in the same proportions as their ownership of L (after application of the attribution rules, as discussed below). On January 1, 1988, L distributes all the stock of LS to A in exchange for all of A's L stock in a section 355 transaction. There has been an ownership change of L, because the percentage of L stock owned by C (100 percent) has increased by more than 50 percentage points over the lowest percentage of L stock owned by C at any time during the testing period (40 percent prior to the distribution of LS stock). There has not been an ownership change of LS, because the percentage of LS stock owned by A (100 percent) has not increased by more than 50 percentage points over the lowest percentage of stock owned by A at any time during the testing period (60 percent, after application of the attribution rules, as discussed below), prior to January 1, 1988.

EQUITY STRUCTURE SHIFT

An equity structure shift is defined . . . as any tax-free reorganization within the meaning of section 368, other than a divisive reorganization or an "F" reorganization. In addition, to the extent provided in regulations, the term equity structure shift will include other transactions, such as public offerings not involving a 5-percent shareholder or taxable reorganization-type transactions (*e.g.*, mergers or other reorganization-type transactions that do not qualify for tax-free treatment due to the nature of the consideration or the failure to satisfy any of the other requirements for a tax-free transaction). A purpose of the provision that considers only owner shifts involving a 5-percent shareholder is to relieve widely held companies from the burden of keeping track of trades among such shareholders. For example, a publicly traded company that is 60 percent owned by less-than-5-percent shareholders would not experience an ownership change merely because, within a three-year period, every one of such shareholders sold his stock to a person who was not a 5-percent shareholder. The conferees believe, however, that there are situations involving transfers of stock involving less-than-5-percent shareholders, other than tax-free reorganizations (for example, public offerings), in which it will be feasible to identify changes in ownership involving such shareholders, because, unlike public trading, the changes occur as part of a single, integrated transaction. Where identification is reasonably feasible or a reasonable presumption can be applied, the conferees intend that the Treasury Department will treat such transactions under the rules applicable to equity structure shifts.

. . . [F]or purposes of determining whether an ownership change has occurred following an equity structure shift, the less-than-5-percent shareholders of each corporation that was a party to the reorganization will be segregated and treated as a single, separate 5-percent shareholder. Moreover, the conference agreement provides regulatory authority to apply similar segregation rules in cases, such as a public offering or recapitalization, that involve only a single corporation.

*Example 8.* — On January 1, 1988, L corporation (a loss corporation) is merged (in a transaction described in section 368(a)(1)(A)) into P corporation (not a loss corporation), with P surviving. Both L and P are publicly traded corporations with no shareholder owning five percent or more of either corporation or the surviving corporation. In the merger, L shareholders receive 30 percent of the stock of P. There has been an ownership change of L, because the percentage of P stock owned by the former P shareholders (all of whom are less-than-5-percent shareholders who are treated as a separate, single 5-percent shareholder) after the equity structure shift (70 percent) has increased by more than 50 percentage points over the lowest percentage of L stock owned by such shareholders at any time during the testing period (0 percent prior to the merger). If, however, the former shareholders of L had received at least 50 percent of the stock of P in the merger, there would not have been an ownership change of L.

It is anticipated that the same results would apply in a taxable merger in which the loss corporation survives, under facts as described above, pursuant to regulations treating taxable reorganization-type transactions as equity structure shifts.

*Example 9.*—On January 1, 1987, L corporation is owned by two unrelated shareholders, A (60 percent) and C (40 percent). On January 1, 1988, L redeems all of A's L stock in exchange for non-voting preferred stock described in section 1504(a)(4). Following this recapitalization (which is both an equity structure shift and an owner shift involving a 5-percent shareholder), there has been an ownership change of L, because the percentage of L stock (which does not include preferred stock within the meaning of section 1504(a)(4)) owned by C following the equity structure shift (100 percent) has increased by more than 50 percentage points over the lowest percentage of L stock owned by C at any time during the testing period (40 percent prior to the recapitalization).

Assume, however, that on January 1, 1987, the stock of L corporation was widely held, with no shareholder owning as much as five percent, and that 60 percent of the stock was redeemed in exchange for non-voting preferred stock in a transaction that is otherwise identical to the transaction described above (which would be an equity structure shift, but not an owner shift involving a 5-percent shareholder because of the existence of only a single 5-percent shareholder, the aggregated less-than-5-percent shareholders, who owns 100 percent of L both before and after the exchange). In such a case, the Secretary will prescribe regulations segregating the less-than-5-percent shareholders of the single corporation, so that the group of shareholders who retain common stock in the recapitalization will be treated as a separate, single 5-percent shareholder. Accordingly, such a transaction would constitute an ownership change, because the percentage of L stock owned by the continuing common shareholders (100 percent) has increased by more than 50 percentage points over the lowest percent of stock owned by such shareholders at any time during the testing period (40 percent prior to the recapitalization).

*Example 10.*—L corporation stock is widely held; no shareholder owns as much as five percent of L stock. On January 1, 1988, L corporation, which has a value of $1 million, directly issues stock with a value of $2 million to the public; no one person acquired as much as five percent in the public offering. Under the statutory definitions contained in the conference agreement, no ownership change has occurred, because a public offering in which no person acquires as much as five percent of the corporation's stock, however large, by a corporation that has no five-percent shareholder before the offering would not affect the percentage of stock owned by a 5-percent shareholder. In other words, the percentage of stock owned by less-than-5-percent shareholders of L immediately after the public offering (100 percent) has not increased by more than 50 percentage points over the lowest percentage of stock owned by the less-than-5-percent shareholders of L at any time during the testing period (100 percent).

Under the conference agreement, however, to the extent provided in regulations that will apply prospectively from the date the regulations are issued, a public offering can be treated as an equity structure shift. Rules also would be provided to segregate the group of less-than-5-percent shareholders prior to the offering and the new group of less than-5-percent shareholders that acquire stock pursuant to the offering. Under such regulations, therefore, the public offering could be treated as an equity structure shift, and the less-than-5-percent shareholders who receive stock in the public offering could be segregated and treated as a separate 5-percent shareholder. Thus, an ownership change may result from the public offering described above, because the percentage of stock owned by the group of less-than-5-percent shareholders who acquire stock in the public offering, who are treated as a separate 5-percent shareholder (66.67 percent), has increased by more than 50 percentage points over the lowest percentage of L stock owned by such shareholders at any time during the testing period (0 percent prior to the public offering). The conference agreement anticipates that the regulations treating public offerings as equity structure shifts also may provide rules to allow the corporation to establish the extent, if any, to which existing shareholders acquire stock in the public offering. . . .

## ATTRIBUTION AND AGGREGATION OF STOCK OWNERSHIP

*Attribution from entities.*—In determining whether an ownership change has occurred, the constructive ownership rules of section 318, with several exceptions, are applied. The rules for attributing ownership from corporations to their shareholders are applied without regard to the extent of the shareholders' ownership in the corporation. Thus, any stock owned by a corporation is treated as being owned proportionately by its shareholders. Moreover, except as provided in regulations, any such stock attributed to a corporation's shareholders is not treated as being held by such corporation. Stock attributed from a partnership, estate or trust similarly shall not be treated as being held by such entity. The effect of the attribution rules is to prevent application of the special limitations after an acquisition that does not result in a more than 50 percent change in the ultimate beneficial ownership of a loss corporation. Conversely, the attribution rules result in an ownership change where more than 50 percent of a loss corporation's stock is acquired indirectly through an acquisition of stock in the corporation's parent corporation.

*Example 15.*—L corporation is publicly traded; no shareholder owns as much as five percent. P corporation is publicly traded; no shareholder owns as much as five percent. On January 1, 1988, P corporation purchases 100 percent of L corporation stock on the open market. The L stock owned by P is attributed to the shareholders of P, all of whom are less-than-5-percent shareholders who are treated as a single, separate 5-percent shareholder. Accordingly, there has been an ownership change of L, because the percentage of stock owned by the P shareholders after the purchase (100 percent) has increased by more than 50 percentage points over the lowest percentage of L stock owned by that group at any time during the testing period (0 percent prior to January 1, 1988). . . .

*Utilization of holding company structures.*—The mere formation of a holding company unaccompanied by a change in the beneficial ownership of the loss corporation will not result in an ownership change. The attribution rules of section 318, as modified for purposes of applying these special limitations, achieve this result by generally disregarding any corporate owner of stock as the owner of any loss corporation stock. Instead, the attribution rules are designed to provide a mechanism for tracking the changes in ownership by the ultimate beneficial owners of the loss corporation. The creation of a holding company structure is significant to the determination of whether an ownership change has occurred only if it is accompanied by a change in the ultimate beneficial ownership of the loss corporation.

*Example 20.*—The stock of L corporation is owned equally by unrelated individuals, A, B, C, and D. On January 1, 1988, A, B, C, and D contribute their L corporation stock to a newly formed holding company ("HC") in exchange for equal interests in stock and securities of HC in a transaction that qualifies under section 351.

The formation of HC does not result in an ownership change with respect to L. Under the attribution rules, A, B, C, and D following the incorporation of L corporation are considered to own 25 percent of the stock of L corporation and, unless provided otherwise in regulations, HC is treated as not holding any stock in L corporation. Accordingly, the respective holdings in L corporation were not altered to any extent and there is thus no owner shift involving a 5-percent shareholder. The result would be the same if L corporation were owned by less-than-5-percent shareholders prior to the formation of the holding company.

## *NOTES*

1. *"Testing date," "change date," and allocations during "change year."* Unless disregarded, every change in stock ownership of a loss corporation must be tested to determine whether an "ownership change" has occurred (after taking into account other stock changes during the preceding three-year testing period). The date of the test is the "testing date" (Reg. § 1.382-2(a)(4)(i)) and, if an ownership change has occurred, the date is the "change date." I.R.C. § 382(j). If an ownership change results from an equity structure shift, the change date is the date of the reorganization. Id. In general, only losses arising prior to the change date are affected by section 382, and only taxable income arising after the change date is subject to the section 382 limitation. I.R.C. § 382(a) and (d).

In determining the applicability of section 382, loss corporations must generally allocate ratably (by number of days) their income or loss, as well as the amount of the section 382 limitation, in the taxable year in which a change date occurs (termed the "change year" (Reg. § 1.382-6(g)(1)). For example, assume that a change date occurs halfway through a loss corporation's taxable year and the section 382 limitation is $80,000 per year. If the corporation has $100,000 of income (before any NOL deduction) in the change year, then one-half of that income, or $50,000, is unaffected by section 382 since it is treated as arising prior to the change date. I.R.C. § 382(b)(3)(A). Of the $50,000 income treated as arising after the change date, only $40,000 (one-half of the section 382 limitation) may be offset by pre-change losses. I.R.C. § 382(b)(3)(B). As a result, the loss corporation can shelter $90,000 of its change year income with losses arising prior to that year. If, on the other hand, the loss corporation has a $100,000 net operating loss in the change year, only one-half of the loss, or $50,000, is treated as arising prior to the change date and is therefore a pre-change loss subject to limitation. I.R.C. § 382(d)(1)(B). In addition, since the loss corporation has no taxable income in the year, no part of the allocable section 382 limitation ($40,000) may be used in that year. The unused limitation is carried forward and the corporation may offset in the subsequent year as much as $120,000 of its taxable income ($80,000 section 382 limitation plus $40,000 carryforward amount) with pre-change losses. I.R.C. § 382(b)(2). Reg. § 1.382-6 allows a loss corporation to make a closing-of-the-books election (in lieu of the allocation based on number of days) in order to determine the amount of its change year income or loss affected by section 382.

2. *Regulations*. Regulations have clarified certain of the issues left unresolved by the Conference Report. For example, the regulations specify the ownership interests treated or not treated as "stock" for purposes of section 382. Reg. § 1.382-2(a)(3); Temp. Reg. § 1.382-2T(f)(18). The "segregation rules" referred to in the Conference Report's example 9 (where L corporation has no actual 5-percent shareholder) generally treat the shareholders redeemed in that example as separate from those who continue to own L common stock after the redemption (each group is treated as a separate 5-percent shareholder). Thus, the redemption is an ownership change of L. Temp. Reg. § 1.382-2T(j)(2)(i) and (iii)(C)(*1*) and (*2*) (ex. 2). Regarding the public offering in the Conference Report's example 10 (where there is no actual 5-percent shareholder before or after the offering), the regulations also segregate (and treat as separate 5-percent shareholders) the shareholders owning stock before the offering from those acquiring stock in it. Temp. Reg. § 1.382-2T(j)(2)(i) and (iii)(B)(*1*)(*ii*) and (*2*) (ex. 3). The regulations generally assume, however, that if the offering is solely for cash, the pre-offering shareholders acquire a portion of the stock issued equal to one-half of their pre-offering interest in the corporation. Thus, the transaction described in example 10 does not result in an ownership change; after the offering, only $1 million of the $3 million of L stock (33.3 percent) is deemed owned by the new shareholder group. Reg. § 1.382-3(j)(1), (3)(i) and (13) (ex. 3). Finally, Temp. Reg. § 1.382-2T(g) specifies the conditions under which indirect ownership of stock qualifies a shareholder as a 5-percent shareholder. No regulations have yet been issued that would treat a taxable reorganization-type transaction as an equity structure shift pursuant to section 382(g)(3)(B). Temp. Reg. § 1.382-2T(e)(2)(ii).

3. *Policy*. Notice 2010-49, 2010-2 C.B. 10, previews a possible change in the interpretation of an ownership change. Under one policy rationale for section 382 expressed in the 1986 legislative history, the shareholders of the loss corporation who bore the economic burden of the losses should be the ones to obtain any tax benefit from the losses. See H.R. Rep. No. 99-426, 99th Cong., 1st Sess. 256 (1985); S. Rep. No. 99-313, 99th Cong., 2d Sess. 232 (1986). Under this view, the goal of section 382 is to prevent new owners of a loss corporation following an ownership change from gaining any windfall benefit from the losses. The rules attempt to achieve this objective by making the tax benefit to the new owners (the section 382 limitation) a

function of the amount paid for the stock of the loss corporation (including the value of its losses). Under this "anti-windfall" view of section 382, the exception for ownership changes resulting from public trading of a loss corporation's stock is needed for practical (and not theoretical) reasons, due to the difficulty of determining the existence of an ownership change in that circumstance.

In Notice 2010-49, the IRS emphasized a slightly different policy rationale for section 382, one that is also included in the legislative history. As explained in the Notice, the purpose of section 382 is to limit the use of losses in those cases where an ownership change may be followed by contributions of income-producing assets (or diversion of income-producing opportunities) to the loss corporation. See H.R. Rep. No. 99-426, 99th Cong., 1st Sess. 256 (1985); S. Rep. No. 99-313, 99th Cong., 2d Sess. 232 (1986). Under this "anti-abuse" view of section 382, the public trading exception is theoretically sound and not merely a practical imperative: following such trades, the new shareholders (all of whom own less than five percent of the stock) would ordinarily have little ability (and no incentive) to shift income to the loss corporation.

These two approaches differ on whether an owner shift of a single corporation should be treated as an ownership change if, following the shift, there is no actual 5-percent shareholder of the loss corporation. Examples 9 and 10 of the Conference Report, involving a redemption and public offering by a public corporation, are illustrations. The "anti-windfall" approach would treat both transactions as ownership changes so long as there is insufficient overlap between the pre- and post-transaction groups of shareholders. The "anti-abuse" approach would exempt each transaction from section 382 for the same reason as the public trading exception. Notice 2010-49 invited public comment on possible modifications to the ownership change regulations.

4. *SRLY limitation.* A separate restriction exists if the loss corporation is part of an affiliated group filing a consolidated income tax return following the acquisition. In that case, if there is no section 382 ownership change, the "separate return limitation year" ("SRLY") rule generally permits pre-acquisition losses of the loss corporation to offset post-acquisition income of the consolidated group only to the extent the loss corporation contributes to the income of the group. See Reg. § 1.1502-21(c)(1)(i). In other words, the rule imposes a *Libson Shops*-type restriction except that the limitation is along *corporate* lines rather than *business* lines. In general, if the section 382 and SRLY restrictions both apply, the former has exclusive jurisdiction. See Reg. § 1.1502-21(g)(1).

5. *Ownership changes among family members.* Section 382(*l*)(3)(A)(i) treats an individual and all members of his family (as defined in section 318(a)(1)) as one person for purposes of section 382. As a result, stock transfers among such family members are disregarded in determining whether an "ownership change" has occurred. In Garber Industries, Inc. v. Comm'r, 435 F.3d 555 (5th Cir. 2006), a shareholder of a loss corporation transferred stock to his brother, thereby increasing the latter's interest in the corporation by over 50 percentage points compared to his lowest share during the preceding three years. The taxpayer argued that because the

two brothers had common parents (and grandparents), they should be treated as members of the same family under section 382(*l*)(3)(A)(i) and the transfer should therefore be disregarded. The court rejected this view and concluded that the transfer constituted an ownership change. The court found that the "individual" whose family is identified in section 382(*l*)(3)(A)(i) must be a shareholder of the loss corporation. Since the parents (and grandparents) of the brothers were all deceased, the only family to be tested was one headed by each brother, and under section 318(a)(1), each brother was not treated as a member of the family headed by the other.

6. *More shark repellent.* Because section 382 is activated by a change of ownership, some loss corporations have adopted "poison pill" provisions to try to prevent unintended changes that might jeopardize the tax value of the corporation's losses. For example, a loss corporation might distribute stock rights to existing shareholders that become effective upon some shareholder approaching five percent ownership of the corporation's stock. Exercise of the stock rights would be designed to dilute the interest of the shareholder potentially owning five percent to prevent the threshold from being reached. Reportedly, Citicorp, GM, and AIG all adopted such plans in 2009 to protect their sizable losses. In Versata Enterprises v. Selectica, 5 A.3d 586 (2010), the Delaware Supreme Court upheld the validity of one such plan.

**Problem 13-1:**

(a) A owns all of the stock of X corporation (a calendar year taxpayer) and B (unrelated to A) owns all of the stock of Y corporation (also a calendar year taxpayer). At the very end of year 3, X is merged into Y, with Y surviving, in a transaction qualifying under section 368(a)(1)(A). In the merger, A exchanges her X stock for Y stock representing 10 percent (by value) of the surviving corporation. At the time of the merger, X and Y have NOL carryovers of $500,000 and $200,000, respectively, each as a result of losses arising in year 1. In addition, at the time of the merger, X is worth $2 million, Y is worth $18 million, and the long-term tax-exempt rate is 10 percent. If the surviving corporation has taxable income (before reduction for any NOL deduction) of $250,000 during year 4, how much of the pre-year 4 losses of X and Y may be used to offset this taxable income? See Temp. Reg. § 1.382-2T(e)(2)(iv) (ex. 1 and 2); I.R.C. § 382(*l*)(2)(B). Would your answer change if Y had merged into X, with X surviving, and B received 90 percent of the stock of X (by value) in exchange for her Y stock? See Temp. Reg. § 1.382-2T(e)(2)(iv) (ex. 3). Would it matter if neither X nor Y had a 5-percent shareholder both before and after the merger? See Temp. Reg. § 1.382-2T(j)(2)(i) and (iii)(B)(*1*).

(b) L corporation (a calendar year taxpayer) has two business divisions and a $2 million NOL carryover arising from a year 1 loss. At the very end of year 2, L redeems all of the stock of a 60 percent shareholder (by value) in exchange for $6 million of assets (comprising one of its operating divisions). Immediately prior to the redemption, the value of L's stock was $10 million. Assume that at the time of the redemption, the long-term tax-exempt rate is 10 percent and that following the redemption, L continues to operate its other division. If L has taxable income (before reduction for any NOL deduction) of $500,000 in year 3, how much of that income may be offset by the NOL carryover arising from year 1? See Temp. Reg. § 1.382-2T(e)(1)(i)(C), (j)(2)(iii)(C)(*1*) and (*2*) (ex. 1); I.R.C. § 382(e)(2). Do you think your answer is consistent with the "neutrality" principle underlying section 382?

**Problem 13-2:** Determine which corporation has an ownership change in the following transactions and specify the change date. Assume that in each question, all shareholders are unrelated and all stock ownership interests are based on value.

(a) A, B, and C own all of the stock of X corporation (100 shares each). On January 1 of year 1, C transfers 70 X shares to B. On January 1 of year 2, A transfers 100 X shares to C. On January 1 of year 3, C transfers 130 X shares to D. See I.R.C. § 382(g)(1) and (i)(2); Temp. Reg. § 1.382-2T(c).

(b) E owns 100 percent of Z corporation. On January 1 of year 1, E transfers 12 percent of Z to F. On January 1 of year 2, Y corporation (owned equally by G and H) merges into Z, with Z surviving, and G and H receive 20 percent each of Z in exchange for their Y stock. The merger qualifies under section 368(a)(1)(A). On January 1 of year 3, H transfers 10 percent of Z to J. See I.R.C. § 382(g)(4)(B)(ii).

(c) R corporation's 6,000 shares are owned by a group of shareholders (termed "public group I"), no one of whom owns five percent of R. On January 1 of year 1, A acquires 2,000 R shares from public group I. On January 1 of year 2, public group I transfers 3,000 R shares to a group of shareholders (termed "public group II"), no one of whom owns five percent of R. On January 1 of year 3, R issues 1,000 new shares each to B and C. See Temp. Reg. § 1.382-2T(e)(1)(ii) and (iii) (ex. 3).

(d) J owns 100 percent of S corporation and K owns 100 percent of T corporation. On January 1 of year 1, in a qualifying "B" reorganization, T acquires all of the stock of S from J solely for T voting stock representing 60 percent of T. On January 1 of year 2, K transfers one-half of her T stock to L. See I.R.C. § 382(*l*)(3)(A)(ii); Temp. Reg. § 1.382-2T(e)(2)(iv) (ex. 4).

### 3. *Built-In Gains and Losses*

Read I.R.C. § 382(h), (c)(2), and (k)(1) (second sentence). Section 382 takes into account both unrealized gains and losses (including certain economically accrued income and deduction items) at the time of an ownership change if they exceed a threshold amount. In general, built-in gains recognized within five years of the change date can be offset by losses without limitation because such gains economically represent pre-change taxable income. The statute carries out this objective by generally increasing the section 382 limitation by the amount of such gains in the year recognized. I.R.C. § 382(h)(1)(A)(i). For the same reason, built-in losses recognized within five years of the change date are generally treated the same as pre-change losses and therefore subject to the section 382 limitation. I.R.C. § 382(h)(1)(B)(i). The statute places the burden on the taxpayer to establish that a recognized gain was unrealized, and a recognized loss was *not* unrealized, at the time of the change. I.R.C. § 382(h)(2).

### *NOTES*

1. *Notice 2003-65.* Other than providing that certain prepaid income is not a recognized built-in gain (Reg. § 1.382-7(a)), the IRS has not issued regulations interpreting section 382(h). In Notice 2003-65, 2003-2 C.B. 747, the IRS indicated that taxpayers may identify their built-in items for purposes of section 382(h) using the rules of either section 1374 (the built-in gains tax on S corporations) or 338.

2. *Notice 2008-83.* In September 2008, the IRS issued Notice 2008-83, 2008-2 C.B. 905, indicating that effective immediately, any deduction with respect to losses on loans or bad debts of a bank properly allowable after an ownership change would not be treated as a built-in loss or deduction for purposes of section 382(h). Upon issuance of the Notice, Wells Fargo immediately announced a proposed acquisition of Wachovia Bank for $15 billion (which was subsequently consummated); just two days earlier, Wells Fargo had indicated that it would not compete with Citigroup's $2 billion offer for Wachovia, the only bid then outstanding. At the time of its acquisition, Wachovia reportedly held approximately $74 billion in bad mortgage debts, potentially producing an immediate tax benefit of $25.9 billion ($74 billion × 35%) if losses from such debts were not limited by section 382. In contrast, had Wachovia been acquired for $2 billion and all of these debts treated as pre-change losses, the tax benefit from the losses would have been limited to about $32.6 *million* per year ($2 billion × 4.65% (long-term tax-exempt rate for ownership changes occurring in October 2008) × 35%).

In response to a Congressional inquiry, the Treasury Department indicated that the Notice represented a continuation of its ongoing effort to provide guidance on section 382(h) (Notice 2003-65), and was necessary in light of the dysfunctional nature of the market for certain financial assets that made valuation of those assets impossible to determine. According to the Treasury, the Notice enabled bank transactions to be undertaken with greater certainty in the unusual market environment, and was not issued with an eye towards any particular transaction or taxpayer. In section 1261 of P.L. 111-5 (the economic stimulus legislation enacted in February 2009), Congress nullified Notice 2008-83 but only on a prospective basis, thus not affecting the Wells Fargo acquisition of Wachovia and certain other transactions. Among other things, Congress found that the delegation of authority under section 382(m) "does not authorize the Secretary to provide exemptions or special rules that are restricted to particular industries or classes of taxpayers." As a footnote, the acquisition of Wachovia by Wells Fargo, although consummated solely for Wells Fargo stock, was apparently structured not to qualify as a reorganization in order to enable Wachovia shareholders to recognize losses in the transaction.

**Problem 13-3:** On December 31 of year 1, L corporation (a calendar year taxpayer) owns only three assets: asset A (FMV = $100,000, basis = $200,000), asset B (FMV = $100,000, basis = $100,000), and asset C (FMV = $100,000, basis = $80,000). On that day, all of L's stock is sold in a transaction constituting an ownership change with respect to L. Assume that none of L's assets is a cash item, marketable security, or nonbusiness asset described in section 382(h)(3)(B)(ii) and (*l*)(4)(C).

(a) During year 3, when L's basis in asset B is still $100,000, L sells it for $50,000. Is the resulting loss subject to limitation under section 382?
(b) During year 4, when L's basis in asset C is still $80,000, L sells it for $110,000. Does the resulting gain increase the section 382 limitation?
(c) During year 5, when L's basis in asset A is still $200,000, L sells it for $100,000. Is the resulting loss subject to limitation under section 382?
(d) Instead of selling asset A, assume that L uses it in its business in years 2 and 3 and is entitled (under applicable cost recovery rules) to claim a $100,000 depreciation deduction in each of those years. If L has no NOL carryovers at the time of its ownership change and the section 382 limitation with respect to the change is $30,000 per year, how much may L deduct in years 2-5 as a result of depreciating asset A?
(e) Would any of your answers to (a)-(d) change if on December 31 of year 1, L's basis in asset C had been $40,000 instead of $80,000? Would it make any difference if asset C had been transferred to L by Mr. K, a shareholder of L, in a capital contribution on December 31 of year 0? See I.R.C. § 382(*l*)(1).

### 4. *Anti-Avoidance Rules*

Finally, section 382 contains certain rules to prevent circumvention of limitations intended by the provision. For example, to preclude taxpayers from artificially increasing the value of a loss corporation (and resulting section 382 limitation) prior to an ownership change, section 382(*l*)(1) provides authority to disregard certain capital contributions prior to the change date (an "anti-stuffing" rule). Read I.R.C. § 382(c)(1), (e)(2), and (*l*)(1) and (4), and the following case, which discusses certain other anti-avoidance rules.

## Berry Petroleum Co. v. Commissioner

104 T.C. 584 (1995), aff'd (unpubl. op.), 98-1 U.S.T.C. ¶50,398 (9th Cir. 1998)

BEGHE, Judge.

[This case involves five corporations engaged in the oil and gas business: petitioner (Berry Petroleum Co.) and its wholly-owned subsidiary, Bush Oil Co. (Bush); Tosco Corp. (Tosco) and its wholly-owned subsidiary, Tosco Enhanced Oil Recovery Corp. (Teorco); and Tenneco Oil Co. (Tenneco). Teorco's principal assets consisted of leasehold interests in four California oil properties, Placerita, McKittrick, Edison Grove, and Jasmin. Only Placerita had generated significant gross receipts. Tosco viewed the other properties as liabilities because of possible environmental responsibilities.

Prior to November 1987, Tenneco offered to purchase Placerita from Teorco for $7.5 million. Tosco rejected this offer because it wished neither to sell Teorco's properties separately nor to retain responsibility for its contingent liabilities. Tosco offered to sell Teorco stock to Tenneco, but Tenneco declined.

Tosco then solicited interest in Teorco stock from 20 companies, including petitioner. After receiving the solicitation, petitioner engaged in discussions with Tenneco leading to an agreement for Tenneco to purchase Placerita from Teorco for $7.75 million if petitioner was successful in acquiring Teorco from Tosco.

In May 1988, petitioner, through its subsidiary Bush, acquired all of the stock of Teorco from Tosco for $6.5 million. Immediately thereafter, Bush caused Teorco to change its name to C.J. Co., and to sell Placerita to Tenneco for $7.75 million. Immediately prior to the acquisition of Teorco, the gross value of its assets were as follows:

| | |
|---|---:|
| Placerita | $7,750,000 |
| McKittrick (50-percent interest) | 2,000,000 |
| Jasmin | 250,000 |
| Jasmin Equipment | 385,000 |
| Edison Grove (35-percent interest) | 200,000 |
| Jasmin note receivable | 1,588,155 |
| Accounts receivable | 289,278 |
| Inventory | 165,787 |
| Prepaid expenses | 12,274 |
| Total gross asset value | $12,640,494 |

Known liabilities totaled $535,569, and after the transfer of stock, C.J. Co. reserved an additional $200,000 for unknown contingencies.

Petitioner's due diligence did not disclose any liabilities of which its management was not aware. Petitioner believed that Tenneco was excessively concerned about possible environmental liabilities associated with McKittrick, Edison Grove, and Jasmin.

Immediately after the purchase, C.J. Co. had NOL carryovers of $8,109,272 arising from pre-acquisition years. In calculating the amount of taxable income that could be offset by the carryovers, petitioner used $6.5 million as the value of the loss corporation.

Between December 1988, and March 1989, C.J. Co. advanced Bush a total of $3,625,946, evidenced by interest-bearing demand notes. After paying interest through May, 1989, Bush caused C.J. Co. to distribute a $3,625,946 dividend to Bush by canceling the repayment obligation. In September 1989, C.J. Co. sold its interests in Jasmin and Edison Grove to unrelated parties. It also attempted to sell its half-interest interest in McKittrick, but eventually acquired the remaining half-interest and developed the property.]

... Section 382(a) ... provides that, after certain significant changes in corporate ownership, the amount of income of a "new loss corporation" that may be offset by loss carryovers arising prior to the ownership change shall not exceed the "section 382 limitation." The section 382 limitation is equal to the "value of the old loss corporation" multiplied by the long-term tax-exempt rate. ... Sec. 382(b).

The section 382 limitation does not directly limit the amount of the loss carryovers of an old loss corporation. It limits only their continuing usefulness. ... The section 382 limitation is intended to approximate the annual income that the business capital of the old loss corporation would have generated, and thereby prevent the new loss corporation from using the loss carryovers faster than the old loss corporation could have used them in the absence of a change in ownership. ...

Although the basic mechanical approach as described above arguably embodies the "neutrality" principle, Congress was concerned that the mechanical rules of section 382(b) would provide opportunities to structure transactions that would literally satisfy those rules but be inconsistent with their spirit and intent. ... To address those concerns, section 382 includes a series of somewhat overlapping responses, which impose obstacles to a new loss corporation's use of the old loss corporation's net operating loss carryovers in various situations. See, e.g., sec. 382(c), (e), (*l*)(1), (4). The operations of three of those statutory responses are at issue in this case. ...

The parties agree that Bush's acquisition of Teorco was an ownership change under section 382(g) and that the applicable long- term tax-exempt rate under section 382(f) is 7.47 percent. The parties disagree whether C.J. Co. continued the business enterprise of Teorco during the 2 years after the ownership change. If we should find that C.J. Co. did not continue Teorco's business enterprise, the section 382 limitation would be zero under section 382(c). If we find that C.J. Co. did continue Teorco's business enterprise, we must decide what was the value of

Teorco immediately prior to the ownership change and whether that value should be reduced under section 382(e)(2) by reason of the canceled advances from C.J. Co. to Bush and under section 382(*l*)(4) on the ground that C.J. Co. had enough non-business assets to invoke that provision.

We hold that C.J. Co. continued Teorco's business enterprise at all times during the 2 years after the ownership change, that the fair market value of Teorco was $6.5 million immediately prior to the ownership change, and that value should be reduced by $3,625,946 (the canceled advances to Bush) under section 382(e)(2) and $1,520,866 (the Jasmin receivable less its share of Teorco's indebtedness) under section 382(*l*)(4).

## CONTINUITY OF BUSINESS ENTERPRISE—SECTION 382(c)(1)

Section 382(c)(1) provides that if a new loss corporation does not continue the business enterprise of the old loss corporation at all times during the 2 years following an ownership change, the section 382 limitation is equal to zero. . . . This is similar to the continuity-of-business requirement that a transaction must satisfy in order to qualify as a tax-free reorganization under section 368. . . .

The fact that an acquired corporation and the acquiring corporation are in the same line of business tends to establish continuity, but is not determinative. Reg. § 1.368-1(d)(3). The new loss corporation must retain a link to the business enterprise of the old loss corporation, either by continuing the old loss corporation's historic business or by using a significant portion of the old loss corporation's historic business assets in a business. Reg. § 1.368-1(d)(2). This continuity-of-business requirement is broader, more objective, and more lenient than the corresponding requirement under section 382(a)(1)(C) of the 1954 Code, which required the acquired corporation "to continue to conduct a trade or business 'substantially the same' as its historic business." . . . Thus, a new loss corporation may discontinue more than a minor portion of the old loss corporation's historic business, or dispose of more than a minor portion of the old loss corporation's historic assets, and still satisfy the continuity-of-business requirement. . . .

At all relevant times, petitioner was engaged in the exploration, development, production, and sale of domestic heavy oil. Teorco had acquired and operated heavy-oil properties while it was owned by Tosco. Throughout the 2-year period after the ownership change, C.J. Co. continued to acquire and hold heavy-oil properties. Although C.J. Co. sold Placerita, the most valuable property owned by Teorco, C.J. Co. continued to hold, and tried to develop, McKittrick, its second most valuable property, and it acquired its coowner's interest in Edison Grove, which it developed and operated and then sold.

Respondent contends we should conclude that petitioner intended to dispose of all the assets of Teorco, particularly in view of C.J. Co.'s contingent offer to sell its interest in McKittrick. . . . However, neither the statute, the regulations, nor the legislative history provides persuasive support for respondent's contention; we consider only what actually happened during the 2 years following the ownership change, not what might have happened. . . .

Although the sale of Placerita substantially reduced what had been Teorco's historic business enterprise, C.J. Co. continued that business enterprise at all times during the 2-year period after the ownership change. Therefore, section 382(c)(1) does not reduce the section 382 limitation to zero, and the section 382 limitation must be calculated under section 382(a). . . .

## REDEMPTION OR OTHER CORPORATE CONTRACTION—SECTION 382(e)(2)

To limit bootstrap acquisitions of loss corporations' net operating loss carryovers, section 382(e)(2) provides that the value of the old loss corporation (and therefore the amount of the section 382 limitation) is determined after taking into account any "redemption or other corporate contraction [that] occurs in connection with an ownership change." . . . A redemption or corporate contraction can occur in connection with an ownership change regardless of whether it occurs before or after the ownership change. . . .

Respondent contends that the advances from C.J. Co. to Bush, which were subsequently distributed as a formal dividend to Bush by cancellation, were a "corporate contraction" because Bush never intended to repay them and that the advances therefore had no economic substance. Respondent contends further that the advances were made "in connection with the ownership change" because Bush would not have needed to borrow substantial funds if it had not paid for Teorco with cash.

Petitioner contends that "corporate contraction" does not include loans or distributions between members of an affiliated group that files a consolidated return because such loans and distributions do not transfer equity value out of the affiliated group. Petitioner also contends that, if the canceled advances amounted to a corporate contraction, it did not occur in connection with the ownership change.

If we were to accept petitioner's contention that "corporate contraction" does not include distributions between members of an affiliated group, a corporation could acquire a loss corporation (without suffering a reduction in its value for the purposes of section 382) by causing the loss corporation to redeem some of its stock or pay a substantial dividend immediately after the ownership change and then use the proceeds of the distribution to pay the old shareholders. An acquisition so structured is the kind of bootstrap acquisition that section 382(e)(2) is intended to inhibit. Structuring the payment to the acquiror as a loan that is intended to be forgiven would reduce the loss corporation's assets in the same way as a redemption or formal dividend.

When a controlling shareholder withdraws funds from its controlled corporation, the relationship invites special scrutiny to determine whether the withdrawal is a bona fide loan, or a dividend at its inception or some later time. . . . This is a factual question, which depends in the first instance upon the shareholder's intent to repay at the time of the withdrawal, and the intention of the corporation to enforce collection. . . . The parties' intent must be inferred from all the facts and circumstances. . . .

When Bush received the advances from C.J. Co., Bush executed unsecured demand notes providing a market rate of interest. Although interest was paid monthly, no principal payment was ever demanded or made, and the advances were discharged by cancellation less than 6 months after the first payment and less than 3 months after the second payment. The cancellation so soon after the advances were made is strong evidence that, when C.J. Co. made the advances to Bush, neither Bush nor C.J. Co. intended them to be repaid. Bush's financial position . . . also indicate[s] that Bush had no intention or ability to repay the advances from its own resources at the times they were received from C.J. Co.

Even if the advances standing alone did not amount to corporate contractions, C.J. Co.'s formal payment of a dividend by canceling the notes from Bush was a corporate contraction. C.J. Co.'s cancellation of the notes completed the process that the advances initiated, reimbursing Bush for a substantial portion of its investment in C.J. Co.

Because we find that Bush did not intend to repay the advances, and that these advances and their cancellation reduced the equity capital and value of C.J. Co., these events amounted to a corporate contraction. We must therefore determine whether the contraction occurred in connection with the ownership change.

. . . The ownership change caused Bush to need a cash infusion, a need that was foreseeable in April 1988 and that would not have continued through March 1989 but for the acquisition of Teorco. Bush's needs for cash were satisfied by the advances from C.J. Co., making the advances a direct and foreseeable result of Bush's acquisition of Teorco. . . . We think that . . . the advances were canceled in connection with the ownership change. Although the advances and the formal dividend in this case were not as closely connected to the ownership change as they would have been if a portion of the proceeds of the Placerita sale had been paid directly to Tosco, Bush would not have received or needed the funds represented by the advances if it had not acquired Teorco. . . .

The question in the case at hand is . . . whether one transaction — the contraction of C.J. Co. — occurred in connection with a prior transaction — the ownership change of Teorco. In this case, Bush's need for cash and its ability to borrow from C.J. Co. had their origins in, and were connected causally with, Bush's acquisition of Teorco and C.J. Co.'s sale of Placerita. We conclude that the canceled advances occurred in connection with the ownership change for the purpose of section 382(e).

The value of Teorco is to be determined after taking into account the corporate contraction caused by the advances and their cancellation in the amount of $3,625,946.

### SUBSTANTIAL NONBUSINESS ASSETS — SECTION 382(*l*)(4)

To discourage "stuffing" a loss corporation with liquid assets or liquidating its active business assets before an ownership change, the value of the *old* loss corporation is reduced by the value of its nonbusiness assets (adjusted for their share of indebtedness), but only if the *new* loss corporation has substantial nonbusiness assets immediately after the ownership change. Sec. 382(*l*)(4)(A). . . . Although a loss corporation may be both the old loss corporation and the new loss corporation, it cannot be both at the same time. Sec. 382(k)(1), (2), and (3). Upon the ownership change, the old loss corporation becomes the new loss corporation. . . .

Petitioner asserts that "both the plain language of the statute and the legislative history indicate that the Section 382(*l*)(4) nonbusiness asset limitation only applies if the old loss corporation has nonbusiness assets *prior to* the ownership change," and that "Section 382(*l*)(4) was enacted solely to prevent the *seller* of a loss corporation from liquidating the loss corporation's assets and then selling a shell corporation." Petitioner concludes that section 382(*l*)(4)(A) focuses solely on the assets of the old loss corporation, and that for section 382(*l*)(4) to apply, we must reorder the sequence of the purchase of the Teorco stock and the sale of Placerita. We disagree.

We do not find the language of section 382(*l*)(4) to be "plain"; it seems to us that the paragraph includes what might be taken to be conflicting references to "the new loss corporation" and "the old loss corporation." The reduction in the value of the old loss corporation is triggered by the substantial nonbusiness assets of the *new* loss corporation, but the amount of the reduction is measured by the value of the nonbusiness assets of the *old* loss corporation. Sec. 382(*l*)(4)(A). In addition, "substantial nonbusiness assets" of the *new* loss corporation is defined by reference to the nonbusiness assets of the *old* loss corporation. Sec. 382(*l*)(4)(B)(i).

Although section 382(*l*)(4) is not a model of clarity, its focus does not appear to us to be solely on the assets of the old loss corporation, as petitioner contends. Section 382(*l*)(4)(A) uses the terms "old" and "new," focusing on the assets of both the old loss corporation and the new loss corporation. [The Conference Report] supports this interpretation. . . . Although in most cases neither the value nor the character of the loss corporation's assets will change when the loss corporation is the subject of an ownership change, in this case Placerita was changed from a business asset to a nonbusiness asset when Bush purchased the Teorco stock, and, pursuant to prearrangement, caused C.J. Co. to sell Placerita to Tenneco.

Nonbusiness assets are defined as "assets held for investment." Sec. 382(*l*)(4)(C). [The Conference Report] states that assets held for investment include cash and marketable securities that are not held as an integral part of the conduct of a trade or business. . . . The definition of nonbusiness assets that was finally enacted is considerably less specific than the definition included in the House bill, which included:

(i) cash,
(ii) marketable stocks or securities, and
(iii) any other asset which is—

(I) not held for active use in a trade or business, or
(II) disposed of (other than in the ordinary course of the old loss corporation's trade or business) pursuant to a plan or arrangement in existence before . . . [the ownership change]. [House bill, sec. 321(a).]

The amendments . . . in the Senate . . . completely disallowed net operating loss carryovers if, immediately prior to the ownership change, at least two-thirds of the old loss company's assets were held for investment . . . [but] did not otherwise specify what types of assets were to be considered as held for investment.

Respondent cites the House report . . . for the proposition that "assets held for investment" includes assets disposed of pursuant to a plan. Petitioner, on the other hand, notes that the language of that report reflects the intent of the House, not the Senate. Neither party seems to recognize that the language of the House bill was not included in the law as enacted.

We think Congress recognized that it could not foresee all the ways that transactions could be structured, and that, to prevent avoidance of the mechanical rules of section 382(b), Congress provided a flexible, general definition of nonbusiness assets. We interpret the definition of nonbusiness assets so as to implement the antiavoidance purpose of section 382(*l*)(4). . . .

Neither petitioner, Bush, nor C.J. Co. was ever interested in acquiring or retaining Placerita and the benefits associated with its operation, nor was any of them ever at risk with respect thereto. C.J. Co. did not earn any income or incur any expenses with respect to the operation of Placerita. C.J. Co. never had an operating interest in Placerita because it was immediately bound, through Bush's commitment, to sell Placerita to Tenneco upon Tosco's sale of Teorco to Bush. We see no practical difference between a corporation's acquiring a corporation that has converted its business assets to investment assets before being sold, and an acquiring corporation's obligating itself, before it contracts to purchase the acquired corporation, to convert those business assets to investment assets immediately after it acquires control of them.

As petitioner contends, "it can hardly be said that Petitioner converted Teorco's operating assets to nonbusiness assets . . . *and then* sold the stock of Teorco as a corporate shell." What can be said, however, is that petitioner bound itself to convert Teorco's most important business asset to a nonbusiness asset, purchased the stock of Teorco, and then effected the conversion pursuant to the preexisting, binding obligation.

We look to the definition of "immediately after" as that phrase is used in the regulations under section 351 as "a situation where the rights of the parties have been previously defined and the execution of the agreement proceeds with an expedition consistent with orderly procedure." Reg. § 1.351-1(a)(1). Momentary ownership of what might otherwise be a business asset is insufficient where the owner's rights and obligations with respect to that asset have been previously defined, and must be subsequently carried out, pursuant to a prearrangement, in this case, an agreement whose enforceability was triggered by the ownership change. . . .

We stress that the Teorco and Placerita transactions made good business sense, regardless of the net operating loss carryovers. As respondent has conceded, petitioner did not arrange those transactions with the principal purpose of evading or avoiding Federal income tax. See sec. 269(a). However, immediately after the ownership change, C.J. Co. held Placerita as the functional equivalent of the cash proceeds from its impending sale. . . .

The Jasmin receivable was also a nonbusiness asset. The primary purpose of section 382(*l*)(4) is to discourage the conversion of a loss corporation's active business assets into passive assets prior to a change in ownership of the corporation. . . . The Jasmin receivable was created as part of just such a transaction, and resulted, prior to the ownership change, in the conversion of one of Teorco's business assets into a passive investment asset.

Placerita and the Jasmin receivable were nonbusiness assets immediately after the ownership change, and therefore C.J. Co. had substantial nonbusiness assets immediately after the ownership change.[1] Because C.J. Co. had substantial nonbusiness assets immediately after the ownership change, the value of Teorco immediately prior to the ownership change must be reduced by the value of the nonbusiness assets owned by Teorco immediately prior to the ownership change.

Although immediately after the ownership change C.J. Co. held Placerita as a nonbusiness asset, immediately prior to the ownership change, Teorco held Placerita as a business asset. Teorco, unlike C.J. Co., had earned income and incurred expenses with respect to Placerita. We do not impute Bush's or C.J. Co.'s intent or contractual obligation to sell Placerita to Tosco or Teorco because neither Tosco nor Teorco was a party to the Placerita agreement or any other agreement for the sale of Placerita. Tosco and Teorco were not interested in selling Placerita. Neither Tosco nor Teorco was obligated to convert Placerita to cash, and the sale of Teorco to Bush was not dependent on Bush's being able to sell Placerita. Because Placerita was not a nonbusiness asset of Teorco immediately prior to the ownership change, the value of Teorco immediately prior to the ownership change is not reduced by the value of Placerita.

Because Placerita was a nonbusiness asset immediately after the ownership change, it triggers section 382(*l*)(4). However, because Placerita was not a nonbusiness asset immediately before the ownership change, it does not reduce the value of Teorco immediately before the ownership change for the purposes of section 382. The only nonbusiness asset that Teorco held immediately before the ownership change was the Jasmin note receivable, which had a value of $1,588,155. Therefore, for the purposes of section 382, the value of Teorco immediately before the ownership change, $6,500,000, must be reduced by $1,520,866 ($1,588,155 – (($1,588,155 / $12,640,494) × $ 535,569)), the amount by which value of the Jasmin note receivable exceeds its proportionate share of the $535,569 of debt for which Teorco was liable. Sec. 382(*l*)(4)(A)(i) and (ii).

The amount of petitioner's section 382 limitation with respect to C.J. Co. will be calculated using a "value of the old loss corporation" of $1,353,188 ($6,500,000 – $3,625,946 – $1,520,866) and a "long-term tax-exempt rate" of 7.47 percent. . . .

---

1. Although sec. 382(*l*)(4)(A) tests the nonbusiness assets of the *new* loss corporation, sec. 382(*l*)(4)(B)(i) provides that "The *old* loss corporation shall be treated as having substantial nonbusiness assets if at least 1/3 of the value of the total assets of such corporation consists of nonbusiness assets." (Emphasis added.) Over 70 percent (($7,750,000 + $1,588,155) divided by $12,640,494) of the value of C.J. Co.'s assets consisted of nonbusiness assets, and we find that percentage to be substantial without recourse to sec. 382(*l*)(4)(B)(i).

*NOTES*

1. *The enigmatic section 382(l)(4).* In *Berry Petroleum*, the court struggles with what appears to be a drafting error in this provision. Read literally, the provision reduces the value of the old loss corporation (and the resulting section 382 limitation) if the *new* loss corporation has substantial nonbusiness assets. Under this interpretation (and the court's holding), an ownership change resulting from a merger of a loss corporation is potentially affected by section 382(*l*)(4) if the surviving corporation (but not the loss corporation) has too many nonbusiness assets. Since the purpose of this provision was presumably to reduce the section 382 limitation in transactions that too closely resemble the trafficking of losses, the *new* loss corporation's holding of nonbusiness assets after the transaction would not seem to be a relevant consideration. As the court notes in footnote 1, the literal language of section 382(*l*)(4)(A) also contradicts the test provided in section 382(*l*)(4)(B).

2. *Guidance and legislation in response to economic crisis of 2008-09.* In addition to Notice 2008-83, 2008-2 C.B. 905 (relating to the treatment of built-in losses of banks), the IRS issued a series of notices, and the Congress passed legislation, to address the application of section 382 to government efforts in 2008 and 2009 to stabilize the economy. Among other things, the notices and legislation explain that the government's acquisition and disposition of ownership interests in Fannie Mae, Freddie Mac, and certain other corporations do not constitute ownership changes for purposes of section 382. See, e.g., Notice 2010-2, 2010-1 C.B. 251 and Notice 2008-76, 2008-2 C.B. 768; I.R.C. § 382(n). In addition, in guidance of general application, Notice 2008-78, 2008-2 C.B. 851, vitiates the presumption in section 382(*l*)(1)(B) that a capital contribution made within two years of a change date shall not be taken into account for purposes of section 382. The Notice replaces the presumption with a facts-and-circumstances test and describes four safe harbors in which a contribution will be taken into account even though made during such two-year period.

3. *Bankruptcy.* An NOL deduction may be a bankrupt firm's most important asset whose value would be significantly reduced if the section 382 limitation applied following an ownership change. Under section 382(*l*)(5)(A), the section 382 limitation generally does not apply to an ownership change of a loss corporation involved in a title 11 or similar case (i.e., a bankruptcy proceeding) if the shareholders and certain long-term creditors of the corporation own (solely as a result of being shareholders and creditors of the corporation) stock representing at least 50 percent of the voting power and value of the new loss corporation. This exception recognizes the "equity-like" interest of certain creditors of the loss corporation prior to the ownership change. Consistent with that view, the loss corporation is not entitled, during generally the three years prior to the ownership change, to deduct interest on debt that is converted into stock in the title 11 or similar case. I.R.C. § 382(*l*)(5)(B). Loss corporations may elect out of the exception (and therefore be subject to the section 382 limitation) in order to preserve their interest deduction. I.R.C. § 382(*l*)(5)(H).

4. *Section 383.* This provision extends the principles of section 382 to certain other tax benefits of a target corporation, including net capital loss and excess credit carryovers surviving an ownership change.

5. *Section 384.* This provision is essentially the opposite of section 382 and prevents a loss corporation from using its losses to offset income from built-in gains of another corporation. The provision applies following certain asset acquisitions qualifying as reorganizations or an acquisition of 80 percent or more (by vote and value) of the stock of one corporation by another. I.R.C. § 384(a), (c)(4) and (5). For this purpose, the built-in gain affected is generally the same as that described in section 382 (with the same threshold limitation generally being applicable), with one important exception. Since, in contrast to section 382, the presence of built-in gain is generally unfavorable to taxpayers for purposes of section 384, the taxpayer has the burden of establishing that any gain recognized was *not* a built-in gain at the time of the acquisition. I.R.C. § 384(c)(1) and (8); compare I.R.C. § 382(h)(2)(A). If the provision applies, income attributable to recognition of the built-in gain (if realized within five years of the acquisition) may not be offset by pre-acquisition NOLs (including built-in loss and deduction items) of the other corporation. I.R.C. § 384(a), (c)(3). An exception applies if the two corporations were members of the same controlled group at all times during the five-year period prior to the acquisition. I.R.C. § 384(b). The rules also apply to pre-acquisition net capital losses and excess credits. I.R.C. § 384(d).

The original version of section 384 was enacted in 1987 and applied only to certain acquisitions *by* loss corporations of another corporation with built-in gains. This transaction is ordinarily not affected by section 382 as long as there is no ownership change of the loss corporation. Section 384 was expanded, however, in 1988 to apply generally to such combinations, regardless of which corporation is the acquirer. If the gain corporation acquires the loss corporation, there is potential overlap between sections 382 and 384. Under the former provision, pre-acquisition losses may be used to offset post-acquisition income (including income from the recognition of the gain corporation's built-in gain) only to a limited extent. In contrast, under section 384, no offset at all is allowed.

# Chapter 14

# Consolidated Returns

## A. Introduction

Some business enterprises operate through divisions of a single corporate entity but others are organized as separate corporations having common ownership. To tax the income of these enterprises as similarly as possible, the law permits the separate members of a commonly owned group of corporations, termed an "affiliated group" of corporations, to join together to file a single income tax return, known as a "consolidated return." Affiliated groups that file a consolidated return are referred to as "consolidated groups." This final chapter introduces some special tax rules for consolidated groups.

To conform to the income taxation of a single corporation with divisions, the consolidated return rules disregard for certain tax purposes the separate existence of members of a consolidated group and include all of their tax items on a single consolidated return, which might be viewed as a return of the parent corporation covering the activities of the entire group. This system resembles passthrough treatment under subchapters S and K. As we have seen, in different ways and to a different extent, both subchapters S and K disregard the existence of a business entity (corporation, partnership, or other unincorporated business organization) for certain tax purposes in order to achieve parity in the income taxation of such entities and sole proprietorships. As we conclude this course, it may be reassuring to discover that the taxation of complex corporate groups poses many of the same issues examined initially concerning the taxation of S corporations and partnerships.

Although some of the issues presented in this chapter are therefore familiar, their resolution is generally more complicated than in subchapters S and K. A consolidated group may consist of numerous members, all of which must be disregarded (for certain purposes) simultaneously. In contrast, subchapters S and K generally only "look through" a single entity at a time for tax purposes, even when passthroughs hold ownership interests in one another. Among other things, this difference requires special consolidated return rules relating to transactions between members of the same consolidated group and investments and disinvestments by one member of the group in the stock of another.

As with subchapters S and K, the threshold question in the consolidated return area is whether to treat the members of a consolidated group as a "single" entity for tax purposes or a collection of "separate" entities. For example, should the taxable income of the group be computed by ignoring all corporate identities and treating each member as if it were a division of a single corporation? Or should such corporate identities be preserved for this purpose, with each member first computing its taxable income as a separate corporation and then having the group report the aggregate amount on a joint tax return?

Although a single entity approach might seem more consistent with the underlying purpose of the provisions, it presents some difficulties. For example, suppose a member of a consolidated group (P) acquires all of the stock of another corporation (S), which previously existed outside the group. Under a pure single entity approach, this transaction might be viewed as an acquisition by P's group of S's assets rather than its stock. But what basis should the group take in those assets? Should the group's basis be the same as S's former basis in those assets or should the group's basis be conformed (in some manner) to P's basis in the S stock? Further, how should the tax consequences of subsequent transactions involving S's stock be determined? These issues generally would not arise if P had actually acquired S's assets rather than its stock.

Another issue raised by a single entity approach is the taxation of members that have special tax status. Suppose one of the corporations in a consolidated group is a bank that is taxed under rules different from those for regular business corporations. If the law disregards the separate corporate identities of the members of such a group, how should the income tax liability of the group be determined?

On the other hand, the separate identities of each member of a group presumably cannot be respected in all instances. For example, treating a sale of property between two members of a consolidated group as a taxable event would certainly seem inconsistent with the goal of taxing the group like a corporation with multiple divisions. A transfer between divisions of a single corporation ordinarily does not produce any income tax consequences.

Thus, like subchapters S and K, the consolidated return rules involve a blend of the single and separate entity approaches, and much of the difficulty in the law arises from efforts to resolve this conflict. Over the years, the taxation of a consolidated group has oscillated between these two extremes, with the latest approach reflecting a move toward the single entity approach.

Finally, because a consolidated return is elective for taxpayers, it is useful to consider its principal advantages and disadvantages. The principal advantage is to allow losses of one member of a consolidated group to offset income of another. Thus, rules that liberalize the transfer of deductions and losses between unrelated corporations tend to reduce the advantage of a consolidated return (potentially transforming the corporate sector into one giant consolidated group). The consolidated return rules also generally attach no immediate tax consequences to transactions between group members and try to avoid imposing more than one level of corporate tax on the group's income.

The principal disadvantage of filing a consolidated return is the cost of complying with the consolidated return rules. It is generally easier for each member of a consolidated group to determine its income tax liability as a separate taxpayer. In addition, each member surrenders some flexibility when it joins in a consolidated return. For example, each member must adopt the same annual accounting period for tax purposes (but may adopt different methods of accounting).

The law affecting consolidated groups is complicated, spanning over 50 regulation sections. This chapter merely introduces the basic issues so that the law will not seem quite so mysterious when encountered in the future. Part B begins by describing the eligibility requirements for filing a consolidated return. Part C discusses the computation of a consolidated group's taxable income, including the special treatment of intercompany transactions. Part D introduces the "investment adjustment" rules affecting intercompany ownership. Finally, part E briefly discusses limitations on the recognition of losses upon disposition of a member's stock.

## B. Eligibility

Read I.R.C. § 1501. To be able to join in a consolidated return, a group of corporations must qualify as an "affiliated group" and all members must consent to the law governing such returns. A group filing such a return is deemed to have consented.

Read I.R.C. § 1504(a) and (b). An "affiliated group" is defined as two or more "includible corporations" that have certain stock ownership relationships with one another. Prior to 1984, the ownership condition required possession of at least 80 percent of the voting power of a corporation's stock and at least 80 percent of each class of the corporation's nonvoting stock (the same test as under current section 368(c)). Upon learning of the transaction described in the following case, Congress changed the rule to require at least 80 percent of the voting power and at least 80 percent of the *value* of a corporation's stock.

### Alumax Inc. v. Commissioner

165 F.3d 822 (11th Cir. 1999)

Cox, Circuit Judge:

Alumax Inc. appeals a tax court decision concluding that Alumax owes about $129,000,000 in taxes for the years 1981-86. The tax court's decision rested on its ruling that for the years 1984-86 Alumax could not join the consolidated return of one of its shareholders, Amax Inc., under Internal Revenue Code §§ 1501 and 1504(a). We affirm.

. . . Alumax is a Delaware corporation and Atlanta-based manufacturer of aluminum products. Since 1974, Alumax's voting stock has belonged to Amax and to a changing group of Japanese interests that has included at various times Mitsui & Co., Ltd., and Nippon Steel Corporation. From 1974 until 1984, Amax and the Japanese interests shared power equally: in shareholder matters, board election, and board voting, each controlled 50% of the votes. Amax and the Japanese interests also shared dividends equally.

At the beginning of 1984, however, Alumax underwent a significant restructuring. First, shareholder votes were redistributed. While Amax and the Japanese interests continued to hold equal numbers of common shares, Amax held stock of a class that had four votes per share while the Japanese-interest stock belonged to a class with only one vote per share. Amax thus had a four-to-one advantage over the Japanese interests in most shareholder matters. But Amax's voting power had its limits. A majority of each class of stock had to approve any action touching any of the following six matters:

—any merger;
—purchase or sale of any asset worth at least 5% of Alumax's net worth (about $36 million between 1984 and 1986);
—partial or complete liquidation or dissolution of Alumax;
—capital appropriation or asset disposition worth more than $30 million (about 1.8% of Alumax's total assets);
—election or dismissal of Alumax's chief executive officer; and
—loans to affiliated corporations not in the ordinary course of business.

Amax's voting advantage did, however, extend to the election of Alumax's board of directors: the Amax shares were entitled to elect four of the board's six voting members, while the Japanese interests could select only two. The Amax-elected directors each held two votes, moreover, while the Japanese-interest directors had only one each. While this arrangement gave the Amax-elected directors 80% voting power over most matters, the Amax-elected directors suffered the same limitations on their powers as Amax did as a shareholder: in the same six matters listed above, any action had to be approved by a majority of the Amax-elected directors *and* a majority of the Japanese-interest directors.

There was yet another restriction on the Amax directors' authority. If any Japanese-interest director objected to a board action, and that objection was ratified within fourteen days by the Japanese corporation, then the Alumax board vote would become ineffective. Amax had an out: upon notice within five days, Amax could challenge the "veto," and the vote would become effective if Amax persuaded a panel of arbitrators (who had fourteen days to rule) that the vote would not have a material and adverse effect on the Japanese interests' investment. On the other hand, if Amax challenged the "veto," but lost before the panel of arbitrators, the vote would remain ineffective. . . .

Besides these limitations on the voting authority of the Amax-elected directors, Alumax's board itself suffered a significant limitation on its traditional authority.

Absent contrary provision in corporate documents, under Delaware law the board of directors determines when and in what amount distributions will be made, subject to priorities awarded to certain classes of stock. . . . Alumax's certificate of incorporation, however, *required* Alumax to pay dividends amounting to 35% of its net income. Those dividends were not divided equally: the Japanese interests received 80%, Amax only 20%.

During the tax years 1984 through 1986, Alumax was included on Amax's consolidated tax return. This consolidation yielded a tax benefit to Alumax, which was able to offset its profits with losses from other Amax subsidiaries. . . . The Internal Revenue Service determined that consolidation was not allowed for the years 1984-86 under I.R.C. §§ 1501 and 1504(a) because Amax did not have 80% of the voting power in Alumax. . . .

. . . [C]orporations belonging to an "affiliated group" may file a consolidated return. In 1984 (the relevant year for our purposes), I.R.C. § 1504(a)(2) defined "affiliated group" to mean a member of a chain of corporations in which a parent "owns directly stock possessing at least 80 percent of the voting power of all classes of stock." Congress amended § 1504(a) in 1984 to create a two-pronged test for "affiliated group": loosely stated, a subsidiary may now join the return of a parent that holds both 80% of the voting power in the subsidiary and 80% of the subsidiary's stock, measured by value. . . . This amendment contained a grandfather clause, however, that extended the pre-1984 test through 1988 for all corporations that met the old test on June 22, 1984. . . . Alumax completed its 1984 restructuring before that date. Hence, if the restructured Alumax was entitled to join the consolidated return under the pre-1984 standard, it was entitled to do so through 1986. Because Alumax's right to consolidation thus turns simply on whether Amax held 80% of the voting power in Alumax, the central question is what 80% voting power means.

According to Alumax, 80% voting power is a bright line: it means nothing but the power to elect directors who hold 80% of the total board votes. Alumax accordingly argues that the power of the Amax-elected directors, or of the board itself, to manage corporate affairs is irrelevant. The IRS, on the other hand, rejects this mechanical test and argues that 80% voting power must mean not only the power to elect a certain percentage of the board votes, but also the actual power to run the corporation that would normally accompany control of such a supermajority of the board.

This is a question of statutory construction. The statute's language would control, of course, if it were plain. . . . But it is not: the naked phrase "80 percent of the voting power" does not answer the question "Power to do what?" We do not, moreover, have the benefit of on-point Treasury regulations that, if reasonable, would control. . . . The analysis must therefore rely on extrinsic sources of congressional intent. . . . Congress's acquiescence has imbued [the] judicial and agency interpretation with the significance of congressional intent. . . .

[The] historical judicial and IRS interpretation is that "voting power" means the power to control the corporation's business through the election of the board of directors.... This interpretation is rooted in the reason behind the privilege of consolidation: § 1501 was "based upon the principle of levying the tax according to the true net income and invested capital of a single business enterprise, even though the business is operated through more than one corporation." ... A single enterprise exists by virtue of common control of business affairs.... Thus, the relevant voting power is the power to run the corporation's business—through the board of directors....

There are two implicit assumptions ... from §§ 1501 and 1504's first principles (common control = common enterprise) to the election-of-directors rule. Those assumptions—which are completely sound as a matter of default state corporate law—are: (1) that the directors manage a corporation's business; and (2) that a supermajority of directors controls the board.... These assumptions make it natural in most cases to equate the power to elect 80% of the board with the power to operate the subsidiary as part of a common enterprise.

But when these assumptions are belied—as here—there is no longer any reason for equating the power to elect directors with control, and hence to assume that the parent and subsidiary operate as a single enterprise. Consider, for example, a two-shareholder corporation whose board may act only by unanimous vote; the power to elect 80% of that board is equivalent to the power to elect 50% of a "normal" board. Or consider the corporation that gives its board only the power to recommend courses of action to the officers; power to elect 80% of that board is not per se the power to manage the corporation's business. Thus, it is unjustified in such circumstances to make the step from the purpose of § 1501 (to permit single enterprises to file one return) to a rule defining 80% voting power to mean exclusively the power to elect 80% of the directors. Rather, the principle ... implicitly espoused by Congress, requires taking into account not only the power to elect 80% of the votes on the board of directors, but also the extent to which those directors, and the board itself, have the authority to manage the corporation's business.

Here, the tax court properly concluded that the voting authority of the Amax-elected Alumax directors was too diluted, and the power of Alumax's board itself too restricted, for Amax to reach the 80% voting power threshold. It is obvious from the Delaware statute cited above that mandatory dividends robbed the Alumax board of some customary discretion. But more significantly, the measures eliminating the Amax-elected directors' supermajority voting power in certain situations reduced Amax's control over Alumax even further. The Japanese interests retained the unusual and impressive power to delay the effectiveness of any board action by at least 28 days and to force Alumax to persuade a panel of arbitrators that the action did not have a material and adverse effect on the Japanese interests' stock. Because of the cumbersomeness of the procedure prescribed for overcoming the Japanese interests' objection, the Japanese interests in essence held a right to veto that reached to important matters.

On the six matters in which the directors voted by class, moreover, the Amax-elected directors' voting power effectively declined to 50%. Many of these matters lie at the core of the board's authority to run a corporation's business. Selection of a chief executive officer, for instance, is one of the board's "basic management functions." . . . Purchases and dispositions of assets (unless they involve "substantially all" of the corporation's assets . . . ) also fall within the board's oversight and have obvious importance to the operation of a manufacturing business.

All in all, these restrictions on both the power of Alumax's board and that of the Amax-elected directors prevented Amax from operating Alumax as part of Amax's single enterprise, notwithstanding Amax's facial power to control 80% of the board votes. In §§ 1501 and 1504, Congress extended the consolidation privilege to single enterprises, identified by a shorthand test. Applying the test mechanically here would thwart Congress's intent to give the privilege only to single enterprises. We hold, therefore, that Amax did not have 80% of the voting power in Alumax under § 1504(a), and that Alumax was not entitled to join Amax's consolidated return. . . .

## *NOTES*

1. *Stock ownership test.* As the court explains, the grandfather provision meant that the 1984 stock ownership amendment aimed at the Alumax transaction ended up largely missing its target. Moreover, the court's decision raises a question whether the legislation should have been enacted in the first instance. Although addition of a "value" requirement in section 1504(a) precludes the type of planning carried out by Amax and Alumax, the test potentially introduces uncertainty for other taxpayers—particularly corporations with more than one class of stock—not attempting to "game" the eligibility rules. Section 1504(a)(5)(C) and (D) authorize regulations to provide relief from the value requirement, and the IRS has issued interim guidance in Notice 2004-37, 2004-1 C.B. 947.

2. *De- and reconsolidating.* Once a group files a consolidated return, its ability to deconsolidate is limited. In general, a group must continue to file a consolidated return unless it can convince the Commissioner that there is good cause for some or all of its members to cease doing so. Reg. § 1.1502-75(a)(2), (c)(1)(i). Permission is ordinarily granted if, because of a change in the law, continued filing of a consolidated return has a substantial adverse effect on the tax liability of the group. Reg. § 1.1502-75(c)(1)(ii). In the last 30 years, however, the Commissioner has granted such permission only once. In general, if a corporation ceases to be part of a consolidated group, it must wait at least five years before being eligible to rejoin the group. I.R.C. § 1504(a)(3). The waiting period is generally waived if the change in filing status does not produce any incremental tax benefit. Rev. Proc. 2002-32, 2002-1 C.B. 959, § 5.14.

Corporations may try to change their filing status by disaffiliating from the group filing the consolidated return (e.g., by issuing high-vote but low-value stock to nonmembers). Section 1504(a)(5)(E) and (F) authorize regulations to disregard certain transactions that may be designed to achieve only a technical disaffiliation.

3. *Reverse acquisitions*. In general, a group is deemed to remain in existence from one year to the next as long as the common parent continues as the common parent and at least one corporation affiliated with the parent at the end of the prior taxable year remains affiliated at the start of the current taxable year. Reg. § 1.1502-75(d)(1). Thus, another way for a group to deconsolidate is to change the common parent of the group. A "reverse acquisition" rule ensures, however, that any change in the common parent is bona fide. For example, suppose corporation X acquires all of the stock of corporation Y in a "B" reorganization in which the former Y shareholders end up owning over 50 percent of the value of the X stock. In that case, any group headed by Y is deemed to continue (with X replacing Y as the common parent of the group). Any group headed by X is deemed to terminate as a result of the acquisition. Reg. § 1.1502-75(d)(3)(i). The reverse acquisition rule is ordinarily helpful to taxpayers seeking to avoid an unintended deconsolidation that would produce adverse tax consequences.

4. *Application of section 1504(a)*. In addition to determining which groups are eligible to file a consolidated return, the "affiliated group" definition in section 1504(a) also controls for purposes of other sections, including sections 243, 332, 337, and 338. The reorganization provisions and section 351, however, generally rely upon the definition of "control" contained in section 368(c).

**Problem 14-1:** In each of the following alternatives, unless otherwise specified, assume that all corporations are domestic and unrelated, pay the section 11 tax, and are engaged in general business activities. Determine which corporations in each situation would be eligible to join together in a consolidated income tax return.

(a) Each of corporations X1 through X4 owns 100 percent of the next lower numbered corporation, that is, X1 owns 100 percent of X2, which owns 100 percent of X3, and so forth. The same ownership pattern is true for corporations Y1 through Y4. Both X1 and Y1 are wholly owned by individual A.
(b) Same as (a), except that P corporation owns all of the stock of X1 and Y1.
(c) Same as (b), except that X2 is a foreign corporation.
(d) Same as (b), except that X2 is a bank as defined in section 581.
(e) Same as (b), except that X4 and Y4 own 50 percent each of the voting power and value of Z corporation.
(f) Same as (e), except that P's stock in Y1, consisting of 100 percent of its voting common stock, represents only 50 percent of its value. The balance of Y1 stock consists of nonvoting common stock owned by Q corporation.
(g) Same as (f), except that the Y1 stock owned by Q (representing 50 percent of the value of Y1) consists exclusively of nonvoting preferred stock meeting the definition of section 1504(a)(4).

## C. Computation of Consolidated Taxable Income and the Special Treatment of "Intercompany Transactions"

Read I.R.C. §§ 1502, 1503(a). As you can see, thanks to an extraordinary delegation of authority by Congress, virtually all of the substantive tax rules for consolidated groups are contained in a lengthy set of Treasury Regulations. In general, the income tax liability of a consolidated group is equal to the group's consolidated taxable income multiplied by the regular corporate income tax rate. Reg. § 1.1502-2(a). The starting point for the computation of "consolidated taxable income" is the separate taxable income of each member of the group. Each member, however, must adjust that amount to take into account certain tax items that must be determined on a consolidated basis. Reg. §§ 1.1502-11(a), -12. For example, as is the case for corporations generally, the group's charitable contribution deduction may not exceed ten percent of the group's consolidated taxable income, as adjusted for certain items. I.R.C. § 170(b)(2)(A). Thus, each member must disregard its charitable contributions in calculating its separate taxable income. Instead, all such contributions must be aggregated, with the total compared to the group's consolidated taxable income to determine the permissible charitable deduction for the year.

Another item that must be calculated on a consolidated basis is the group's net operating loss ("NOL") deduction. Recall that the principal advantage of a consolidated return is the ability to offset the losses of one member against the income of another member. Thus, the income and deductions of each member of the group are separately computed but then netted for the year, and any excess of aggregate deductions over the group's gross income represents the group's consolidated NOL ("CNOL"). This CNOL may be carried back and forward as a deduction against past or future income of the group. In certain cases, a portion of the group's CNOL must be allocated back to individual members in order to allow that portion of the CNOL to be carried back or forth to a year in which the member filed a separate return or a return with a different consolidated group. See Reg. § 1.1502-21(b)(1) and (2).

If a member has an NOL that arose in a year in which the member was not part of the group, the use of that loss by the group may be subject to the "separate return limitation year" (or "SRLY") rules. (These are commonly referred to as the "surly" rules, making the acronym particularly apt.) In general, such losses may only be used to offset the portion of the consolidated group's income that is attributable to the member incurring the loss. Reg. § 1.1502-21(c)(1)(i). For example, suppose T corporation (owned entirely by individual A) incurs an NOL in year 1. At the beginning of year 2, X corporation (also owned entirely by individual A) acquires all of the stock of T and the two corporations file a consolidated return in that year. T's year 1 loss is a SRLY loss that may offset only that portion of the group's year 2 income that is attributable to T. Thus, if T continues to incur losses in year 2, no part of its year 1 loss may be deducted in year 2, even though the group has net income in year 2.

The SRLY limitation resembles the section 382 limitation because its general effect is to limit the use of losses to the amount that would have been usable by the loss corporation itself absent consolidation with other corporations. Moreover, the purpose of each limitation is the same—to discourage acquisitions of loss corporations solely for tax purposes. The SRLY rules are supplanted by the section 382 rules if both limitations are applicable. Reg. § 1.1502-21(g)(1). In the above example, because A owned both X and T, there is no "ownership change" of T (within the meaning of section 382(g)). Hence, the SRLY rules (and not section 382) would apply to the X group's use of T's pre-acquisition NOLs. Section 382 also only limits the use of NOL *carryovers* following an ownership change. Thus, if a corporation ceases to be a member of a consolidated group and subsequently incurs a loss, only the SRLY rules limit the *carryback* of that loss potentially to offset the income of the consolidated group.

Finally, in calculating the separate taxable income of each member, special rules apply for transactions (known as "intercompany transactions") between members of the same consolidated group. See Reg. §§ 1.1502-12(a), -13. These rules generally attempt to treat intercompany transactions as if they were carried out by divisions of a single corporation, with the result that any income or loss from the transaction is deferred until an event with a nonmember occurs.

Beck Builders v. Comm'r, 41 T.C. 616 (1964), illustrates the need for these rules. In that case, a parent corporation filed a consolidated tax return with its wholly-owned subsidiary, and had a zero basis in the subsidiary's stock. The parent constructed a building for about $1 million and sold it to the subsidiary for about $1.3 million. Almost the entire purchase price was financed by a borrowing incurred by the subsidiary from outside of the group, and the subsidiary had almost no assets other than the borrowed proceeds.

The regulations at the time provided that a sale between two members of a group filing a consolidated return was not a taxable event. If, for example, the two members had simply been separate divisions of a single corporation, the transfer of property from one division to the other would not ordinarily have resulted in any income tax consequences. To preserve the parent's $300,000 gain from sale of the building, the regulations provided the subsidiary with a $1 million transferred basis in the building (equal to its basis in the hands of the selling member). This transferred basis treatment ensured that upon a subsequent disposition by the subsidiary of the building outside of the group, the gain not recognized by the parent would be taken into account.

Prior to a disposition of the building by the subsidiary, however, the parent sold its *stock* of the subsidiary for nominal consideration to a buyer outside of the group. (Because the value of the building held by the subsidiary was largely offset by its indebtedness, the stock had nominal value.) The stock sale resulted in gain of about $25,000. The government contended that upon sale of the stock of the subsidiary, the parent should recognize the $300,000 gain previously realized (but ignored) when the building was sold to the subsidiary. Nothing in the regulations required that result, however, and the court denied the government's claim.

*Beck Builders* illustrates the potential conflict between the "single" and "separate" entity approaches in determining the tax consequences of intercompany transactions. The rules at the time essentially followed a single entity approach: they disregarded the separate corporate existence of the parent and subsidiary and treated them like divisions, thus ignoring the sale of assets between them for tax purposes. When the parent sold the stock of the subsidiary (which retained the low transferred basis asset) — a transaction with no easy analogue in the divisional model — the rules failed to provide an appropriate tax adjustment to take into account the deferred gain on the original asset sale.

In response to *Beck Builders*, the Treasury promulgated regulations in 1966 to deal more comprehensively with the tax consequences of intercompany transactions. Those regulations tilted the law more towards the "separate entity" approach. The current regulations, effective since 1995, partially reversed course, tilting the law back towards the "single entity" approach. Although differing in emphasis, both sets of regulations effectively implement a hybrid approach.

Under the current regulations, "intercompany transactions" are defined as transactions between corporations that are members of the same consolidated group immediately after the transaction. They include sales, distributions, the performance of services, and the licensing, leasing, or loaning of property by one member (generally referred to as "S" in the regulations for "selling member") to or for another member (generally referred to as "B" in the regulations for "buying member"). Reg. § 1.1502-13(b)(1)(i). In general, the *amount* of the tax items belonging to S and B as a result of an intercompany transaction is determined by treating them as separate entities. However, the timing, character, and other attributes of the items are determined as if S and B were divisions of a single corporation. Reg. § 1.1502-13(a)(2).

The current rules implement two principles. Under the "matching" principle, the parties to an intercompany transaction are generally treated like divisions of a single corporation for purposes of taking into account the tax items from the transaction. Under the "acceleration" principle, the tax items are recognized sooner than under the matching rule if an event occurs that makes treatment of the parties as divisions no longer possible. Reg. § 1.1502-13(a)(6)(i). The following example illustrates the basic operation of these principles in the context of a sale of property by one member to another:

> **Example 14-1:** P owns all of the stock of X and Y and the three corporations file a consolidated income tax return. On July 1 of year 1, X purchases some nondepreciable investment property for $1,000. On January 1 of year 2, X sells the property for $1,500 to Y, which also holds it as an investment. On March 31 of year 3, Y sells the property to Q, an unrelated corporation, for $1,800.

Under the regulations, X is treated as having an "intercompany item" of $500 gain from the sale in year 2, and Y is treated as obtaining a $1,500 basis in the property (both results corresponding to separate entity treatment). X's gain is taken into account, however, at such time (and in such amount) as the difference (if any) between Y's "corresponding item" and "recomputed corresponding item" with respect to the property. Reg. § 1.1502-13(b)(2)(i), (c)(2)(ii). Y's corresponding item is $300 gain ($1,800 amount realized less $1,500 basis), which must be recognized in year 3. Reg. § 1.1502-13(b)(3)(i), (c)(2)(i). Y's recomputed corresponding item is $800 gain (the amount of Y's gain if the transfer of property from X to Y had been between divisions) ($1,800 amount realized less $1,000 basis); this amount is not recognized but would have arisen in year 3. Reg. § 1.1502-13(b)(4). Thus, in addition to Y's $300 gain, X must recognize $500 gain in year 3 (the excess of Y's $800 recomputed corresponding item less its $300 corresponding item in that year). The character and other attributes of X's and Y's items are determined as if the transfer between X and Y had been between divisions, and their holding periods are aggregated. Reg. § 1.1502-13(c)(1). Therefore, even though X held the property for only six months before selling it to Y in year 2, X's $500 gain is long-term capital gain. Finally, the recognition of intercompany items is accelerated if there is an event (such as P's sale of Y stock outside the group prior to Y's sale of the property (as in *Beck Builders*)) that makes it impossible to treat X and Y as divisions. Reg. § 1.1502-13(d).

Test your understanding of these rules by doing the following problem. Read Reg. § 1.1502-13(a)(1), (2), and (6) (providing an overview of the rules); -13(b)(1)(i), (2)(i), (3), (4), and (6) (providing definitions); -13(c)(1)-(4) (describing matching rule); and -13(d)(1) and (2) (describing acceleration rule). Helpful examples include Reg. § 1.1502-13(c)(7)(ii) (ex. 1, 2 and 4) and -13(d)(3) (ex. 1 and 2).

**Problem 14-2:** In each of the following alternatives, assume the same facts as in **example 14-1** except as modified. What are the federal income tax consequences of these transactions and when do they occur?

(a) Y sells the property to Q in year 3 for, alternatively, $1,200 or $900.
(b) The property is inventory property to Y (but nondepreciable investment property to X).
(c) Y transfers the property to Q in exchange for like-kind property qualifying under section 1031.
(d) X acquires the property (which is depreciable property) for $1,000 on January 1 of year 1 and depreciates it on a straight-line basis over ten years. Assume that X therefore claims a $100 depreciation deduction in year 1, and that Y continues to depreciate the ten-year property on a straight-line basis after acquiring it from X for $1,500 on January 1 of year 2. Finally, assume that Y sells the property to Q for $1,500 on January 1 of year 3. Disregard application of the half-year convention. See I.R.C. § 168(i)(7); Reg. § 1.1502-13(c)(7)(ii) (ex. 4).
(e) On March 31 of year 3, Y continues to own the property but P sells all of the stock of X to R, an unrelated corporation. Disregard the specific tax consequences to P of its sale of the X stock.

*NOTE*

*Intercompany ordinary distributions — consequences to distributing corporation.* In general, an ordinary distribution between members of a consolidated group is an intercompany transaction that is taxed in accordance with the matching and acceleration principles. Any gain realized by the distributing corporation is treated as an intercompany item that is recognized under those principles. Any *loss* realized by the distributing corporation is also treated as an intercompany item, notwithstanding the general prohibition against loss recognition by a distributing corporation in an ordinary distribution. I.R.C. § 311(a) and (b)(1); Reg. § 1.1502-13(f)(2)(iii). This preserves the item for later recognition if the distributee disposes of the property outside the group in a transaction not subject to section 311(a). If, however, the distributee's later disposition *is* subject to section 311(a), then the distributing corporation's intercompany item may be redetermined. Reg. § 1.1502-13(c)(6), (f)(2)(iii) (last sentence); cf. Reg. § 1.1502-13(c)(7)(ii) (ex. 1(g)). (The tax consequences to the distributee are described immediately after **problem 14-3**, below.)

To illustrate, assume that P owns all of S and the two corporations file a consolidated return. If S acquires property for $100 and distributes it to P when it is worth $90, S's intercompany item is treated as a $10 loss, notwithstanding section 311(a), and P's basis in the property is $90 (I.R.C. § 301(d)). S would recognize this loss under the matching rule upon certain dispositions of the property by P to a nonmember. If, for example, P were to sell or distribute the property when it is worth $130, the $30 net gain recognized by P and S ($10 loss recognized by S and $40 gain recognized by P) would equal the amount of gain that would be recognized if P and S had been divisions of the same corporation. If, however, P subsequently distributes the property to a nonmember when it is worth $90 (or less), S's intercompany item (the $10 loss) would be eliminated. Once again, this result would be the same as if P and S were divisions of the same corporation.

## D. Investment Adjustment Rules

The investment adjustment rules in the consolidated return area are designed to achieve the same general objective as the basis adjustment rules in subchapters S and K. They try to prevent income or loss recognized by a member of a consolidated group from being recognized again in a transaction involving the member's stock. Although the principle is fairly straightforward, the following case illustrates the difficulty of implementing the policy correctly. Subsequent to *Woods Investment*, Congress and then the Treasury intervened to remedy the defect identified by the court.

## Woods Investment Co. v. Commissioner

85 T.C. 274 (1985), acq. 1986-2 C.B. 1

[The petitioner sold all of the stock of four wholly-owned subsidiaries and reported a capital gain of about $1.5 million. The government asserted a deficiency based on its contention that the petitioner's basis in the stock of the subsidiaries was less than the amount claimed by the petitioner. The petitioner and the subsidiaries had filed a consolidated return in the years prior to the sale, and the subsidiaries had depreciated their business property using permissible accelerated methods during those years.]

FAY, Judge.

. . . The consolidated return regulations . . . provide a detailed and comprehensive set of rules for adjusting the basis of a subsidiary's stock held by a parent corporation. . . . [E]ither a positive or a negative basis adjustment must be made annually to the basis of such stock in an amount equal to the difference between the required "positive adjustment" and the required "negative adjustment." The primary positive adjustment is "An allocable part of the undistributed earnings and profits of the subsidiary for the taxable year." Conversely, the primary negative adjustment is "An allocable part of the deficit in earnings and profits of the subsidiary for the taxable year."

Pursuant to section 1.1502-32, petitioner first computed the earnings and profits of the subsidiaries and then used those figures to adjust its basis in the subsidiaries' stock. In computing the earnings and profits of the subsidiaries, petitioner followed section 312(k), which provides that, for purposes of computing the earnings and profits of a corporation for any taxable year beginning after June 30, 1972, the allowance for depreciation . . . shall be deemed to be the amount which would be allowable for such year if the straight-line method of depreciation had been used. Thus, pursuant to section 312(k), petitioner reduced its subsidiaries' earnings and profits only by the amount of straight-line depreciation available rather than the amount of accelerated depreciation actually taken on its consolidated returns.

Petitioner argues that its basis adjustments to the subsidiaries' stock are in accordance with [the regulations], that it correctly followed section 312(k) in calculating the subsidiaries' earnings and profits, and that no further adjustments are required by the consolidated regulations which exclusively govern basis adjustments. Respondent concedes that petitioner properly adjusted its basis in the subsidiaries' stock to reflect the subsidiaries' increase or decrease in earnings and profits. Respondent argues, however, that petitioner must further reduce its basis in the subsidiaries' stock for the excess amount of accelerated over straight-line depreciation in order to prevent petitioner from obtaining what respondent perceives to be a "double deduction."[1] . . .

1. Respondent contends that petitioner has received a double deduction because petitioner and its subsidiaries received a tax deduction for the excess of accelerated over straight-line depreciation, and, on the disposition of its subsidiaries' stock, since petitioner's basis was not reduced by such excess

Pursuant to his delegated power, respondent has promulgated detailed regulations [including] section 1.1502-32, which specifically requires each member of a consolidated group owning stock of a subsidiary to "adjust the basis of such stock" in the manner prescribed therein. That regulation specifies that the relevant basis adjustments are to be made by reference to a subsidiary's earnings and profits.

The rule . . . that basis adjustments are to be made in accordance with earnings and profits, rather than taxable income or loss, was first promulgated in 1966. The history of the regulations reveals that respondent's decision to use earnings and profits was a conscious and deliberate one. Prior to 1966, the regulations did not provide for any positive adjustments to a subsidiary's stock, but required a reduction in the basis of a subsidiary's stock measured by the excess of (a) the net operating losses incurred by the subsidiary over (b) the taxable income of the subsidiary against which the net operating losses could have been applied. Thus, the negative basis adjustment was measured by a subsidiary's taxable losses. . . . [In 1966, the Treasury] replaced net operating losses with deficits in earnings and profits as the principal negative adjustment and for the first time provided for a positive adjustment equal to the subsidiary's undistributed earnings and profits for the taxable year. . . .

Respondent chose earnings and profits as the measuring rod for adjusting basis . . . even though he was well aware that various items and transactions are treated one way in computing taxable income and another way in computing earnings and profits. . . . [R]espondent . . . made no special provisions for any differences that did not reduce earnings and profits by the entire amount deducted from taxable income.

Although section 312(k) was not enacted in 1966, respondent was aware of the interplay between that provision and section 1.1502-32 prior to issuing the notice of deficiency in this case. Respondent had previously issued several technical advice memoranda concerning the identical issue with which we are faced, and, in fact, respondent initially concluded that no further basis adjustment in a subsidiary's stock for the excess of accelerated over straight-line depreciation was required, thus agreeing with petitioner's position herein. In 1982, although respondent changed his position to the one he advances herein, he failed to amend his regulations to reflect his new position.

Based upon the foregoing, we conclude that petitioner reached the result mandated by respondent's consolidated return regulations and section 312(k) in computing its basis in the subsidiaries' stock. . . . If respondent believes that his regulations and section 312(k) together cause petitioner to receive a "double deduction," then respondent should use his broad power to amend his regulations. . . .

---

amount, petitioner realized a second tax advantage in the form of a higher basis which resulted in a lower gain on the sale.

*NOTE*

*Revised regulations.* Subsequent to the decision in *Woods Investment*, Congress amended the statute to negate its effect. The rather inelegant solution fashioned by Congress was to redefine the E&P of a member of a consolidated group solely for purposes of determining the group's stock basis adjustments. (The redefinition brought the calculation of E&P closer to the amount of the member's taxable income.) See I.R.C. § 1503(e). The Treasury Department subsequently made this amendment obsolete by breaking the link between basis adjustments and E&P altogether. Instead, basis adjustments are now determined by the amount of a member's taxable income or loss, tax-exempt income, noncapital and nondeductible expenses, and distributions. Reg. § 1.1502-32(b)(2). You will recognize these adjustments as virtually identical to the ones authorized in subchapters S and K. See I.R.C. §§ 1367(a), 705(a). One reason the intercompany transaction rules (described in part C) generally determine the *amount* of a member's tax items based on separate entity principles is to ensure that there is a proper basis adjustment to the stock of such member. Basis adjustments are made at the end of each consolidated return year and also when necessary to determine the tax liability of any person. Reg. § 1.1502-32(b)(1)(i).

One aspect of the consolidated return basis adjustments not found in subchapters S and K is the "tiering up" of any adjustment in the stock basis of lower-tier members to that of higher-tier members. For example, assume that P owns all of S, which owns all of T, and the three corporations file a consolidated return. If T's contribution to consolidated taxable income is $100 and S's contribution (determined independently from T) is $150, S must increase its basis in T stock by $100 and that adjustment is tiered up and also taken into account by P in its stock of S. Thus, P must increase its basis in S stock by $250 to reflect the income of both S and T. Reg. § 1.1502-32(a)(3)(iii), (5)(ii) (ex. 7).

Read Reg. § 1.1502-32(a), (b)(1)(i), (2), (3)(i), (ii)(A) and (B), and (iii)(A), and do the following problem. Question (e) introduces the concept of negative basis, referred to as an "excess loss account" ("ELA"); read also Reg. § 1.1502-19(a), (b)(1)(i) and (iii), and (c)(1)(i) and (ii) to answer it. In general, the ELA represents the amount of a subsidiary's losses that exceed the consolidated group's economic investment in the subsidiary. The ELA is generally triggered (resulting in income to the group) at such time as it becomes evident that the excess losses will not be offset by additional earnings of the subsidiary or investment by the group.

**Problem 14-3:** At the beginning of year 1, X organizes two wholly-owned subsidiaries, Y and Z. The three corporations join in a consolidated income tax return in each of the following years.

(a) During year 1, Y invests $1,000 in depreciable property. Assume that for income tax purposes, Y is entitled to a $100 depreciation deduction in year 1 but for E&P purposes, Y may reduce E&P by only $50. Y has no other tax items in year 1 and its deduction is used to reduce taxable income of other members of the group in that year. What adjustment, if any, must X make to its basis in Y stock at the end of the year? If X is wholly owned by M Corp., which is also part of the consolidated group in year 1, what adjustment, if any, must M make to its basis in X stock at year's end?

(b) During year 2, Y swaps with a nonmember a parcel of land (Blackacre) for another parcel (Whiteacre) in a like-kind exchange under section 1031. Immediately prior to the swap, Y's basis in Blackacre (which is worth $500) is $300. Whiteacre is also worth $500. What adjustment, if any, must X make to its basis in Y stock as a result of this exchange by Y?

(c) During year 3, Y acquires some portfolio stock in nonmember corporations and receives $200 in dividends. Y is entitled to the 70 percent dividends-received deduction with respect to these dividends. What adjustment, if any, must X make to its basis in Y stock as a result of the dividends and dividends-received deduction?

(d) During year 4, Y sells nondepreciable property to Z for $1,000. Y's basis in the property just prior to the sale was $400. If X sells all of its Y stock to a nonmember while Z continues to hold the property, what adjustment, if any, must X make to its basis in Y stock immediately prior to such sale? See Reg. §§ 1.1502-13(c)(2)(ii) and (d)(1)(i), -32(b)(5)(ii) (ex. 1(c)).

(e) At the beginning of year 5, X's basis in its Z stock is $1,000. During year 5, Z earns $600 of tax-exempt interest and has a $5,000 tax loss that is used to offset other income of the group in that year. What are the tax consequences if, at the end of year 5, X sells its Z stock to a nonmember for $3,000?

## *NOTE*

*Intercompany ordinary distributions — consequences to distributee.* In general, an intercompany ordinary distribution is excluded from the distributee's income if (and to the extent) there is a negative adjustment to the distributee's basis in the stock of the distributing corporation (including any increase in the distributee's ELA). Reg. §§ 1.1502-13(f)(2)(ii), -32(b)(2) and (3)(v). For example, assume X owns all of Y, the two corporations file a consolidated return, and in a given year, Y has $100 of taxable income and distributes $20 to X. The distribution is excluded from X's income and X's basis in its Y stock is increased by a net amount of $80. If X is wholly owned by M Corp. during the year (and M joins in the consolidated return), then M's basis in its X stock increases by $100 as a result of Y's income and distribution. The $80 net increase to X's basis in Y is tiered up to M's basis in X; in addition, M's basis in its X stock is increased by $20 to reflect the $20 tax-exempt distribution (from Y to X). M's total basis increase in its X stock ($100) reflects the combined inside basis increase of X and Y ($100); Y's inside basis is increased by $80 ($100 income less $20 distribution) and X's inside basis is increased by $20. See Reg. § 1.1502-32(c)(5)(ii) (ex. 5(a) and (b)).

## E. Loss Limitations on Dispositions of Member Stock

The consolidated return rules impose special limitations if a member of a group would recognize a loss upon disposing of stock of another member. One reason for the limitations is to prevent taxpayers from using consolidated groups to avoid the repeal of *General Utilities.*

**Example 14-2:** Individual A owns all of the stock of S corporation, which holds a single asset with value and basis of $100 and $10, respectively. The value and basis of A's S stock is similarly $100 and $10. If A were to sell her S shares to individual B for $100, she would recognize $90 gain. If S (while owned by B) were to sell its asset for $100, it would also recognize $90 gain. The potential double taxation of a single economic gain is, of course, standard fare for investments through C corporations.

Suppose, instead of selling her shares directly to B, A sells her shares to P corporation for $100 and P and S thereafter file a consolidated return. While consolidated, S sells its asset for $100 and recognizes $90 gain, which increases P's basis in its S stock to $190 under the investment adjustment rules, even though S holds only $100 of sale proceeds. If no loss limitation applied, P would recognize a $90 loss upon its subsequent sale of S stock to B for $100. The $90 loss would in effect offset S's $90 gain from sale of its asset. Thus, by using P as an intermediary and having P and S file a consolidated return, A and B would effectively avoid recognizing the $90 of corporate-level gain, contrary to the policy of *General Utilities* repeal.

In this example, P's initial $100 basis upon acquiring the S stock already reflects the built-in gain in S's asset. Thus, P should not receive a positive investment adjustment to its basis in S when S recognizes that gain; otherwise, a $90 tax loss would arise (when P sells the S stock) that is not matched by any economic loss (P purchased and sold the stock for $100). The possible use of a passthrough entity to circumvent *General Utilities* repeal is not unique to consolidated groups; as discussed in chapter ten, but for the "built-in gains" tax in section 1374, S corporations could be used to accomplish the same end. Section 1374 prevents the avoidance of *General Utilities* repeal through a "tracing" approach that requires corporations for a limited period of time to distinguish built-in gains from items accruing subsequent to the acquisition.

Another reason for the loss limitation rules is to prevent the possible recognition of two tax losses for a single economic loss suffered by a consolidated group. The investment adjustment rules described in part D only mandate certain "outside" tax consequences (stock basis adjustments) in the case of certain "inside" events affecting a group member (such as the recognition of gain or loss by the member and change in inside asset basis). As under subchapter S, there is no general requirement of an "inside" tax consequence (such as an inside basis adjustment) if there is an "outside" event (sale of member stock). Compare the section 754 inside basis adjustments that may be elected (or required) under subchapter K. Absent the loss limitation rules, the failure to require matching of inside and outside basis would potentially allow the duplication of losses for tax purposes.

> **Example 14-3:** P contributes $1,000 to S and the two corporations file a consolidated return. S invests the $1,000 in property that declines in value to $600. If S sells the property for $600, it recognizes a $400 loss and P's basis in S stock is reduced to $600 under the investment adjustment rules. The basis reduction therefore prevents P from recognizing a second loss if it should subsequently sell its S stock for $600. If, however, P sells its S stock first and recognizes a $400 loss without restriction (including any required reduction to S's basis in its asset), a subsequent sale of the asset by S would trigger a second $400 tax loss, despite the single $400 economic loss.

The possible duplication of tax losses, however, is not unique to consolidated groups, since the same result may arise if P and S file separate returns.

To prevent the recognition of both noneconomic losses (**example 14-2**) and duplicated losses (**example 14-3**), the Treasury in 1991 adopted a "loss disallowance rule" that generally disallowed recognition of loss by a consolidated group member upon a disposition of the stock of another member. The Treasury recognized that both problems addressed by the loss disallowance rule might in certain circumstances produce tax consequences *un*favorable to taxpayers. For example, the failure to allow inside basis adjustments might result in a single economic gain of a consolidated group being recognized twice for tax purposes. Treasury believed, however, that taxpayers had adequate self-help mechanisms to avoid such adverse results. Thus, the loss disallowance rule focused on preventing opportunistic use of the consolidated return rules.

Some analysts criticized the breadth of the loss disallowance rule. For example, disallowance of P's $400 tax loss upon its disposition of S stock in **example 14-3** arguably denies P's group any tax loss for the $400 economic loss suffered. The "duplicate" tax loss embedded in S's assets would arise only after S's departure from the group.

In Rite Aid Corp. v. U.S., 255 F.3d 1357 (Fed. Cir. 2001), the court upheld the taxpayer's recognition of a loss upon sale of a subsidiary in the "duplicated loss" scenario. The court found that the Treasury's authority under section 1502 to promulgate rules that change the application of Code provisions was limited to addressing problems created by the filing of a consolidated return. Since the duplicated loss problem was not unique to taxpayers filing a consolidated return, the court invalidated the loss disallowance rule in that circumstance.

Congress responded to *Rite Aid* by adding the second sentence to section 1502, which authorizes the promulgation of tax rules for consolidated groups different from those applicable to corporations filing separate returns. This amendment was, in a sense, a mere placeholder to enable Congress to reiterate (in the legislative history) the authority granted to the Treasury by the *first* sentence of section 1502 (which was left unchanged by the legislation). S. REP. NO. 108-192, 108TH CONG. 1ST SESS. 117 (2003). Specifically, Congress restated Treasury's authority to change the application of Code provisions to consolidated groups if necessary to clearly reflect the income tax liability of the members of the group both during and after the period of affiliation. Congress, thus, rejected the Federal Circuit's narrow interpretation of the Treasury's authority as addressing only problems created by the filing of a consolidated return. Yet, Congress also stated its intention to preserve the specific result of the *Rite Aid* decision, perhaps reflecting its view that denial of the taxpayer's loss distorted, rather than clearly reflected, the taxpayer's income. H.R. REP. NO. 108-548 (PART 1), 108TH CONG., 2D SESS. 311 (2004); S. REP. NO. 108-192, 108TH CONG. 1ST SESS. 117 (2003).

Subsequent to *Rite Aid*, the Treasury suspended application of the loss disallowance rule and issued additional guidance addressing the recognition of losses upon a disposition of the stock of a consolidated group member. The current law provision—the "unified loss rule"—was finalized in 2008 in Reg. § 1.1502-36. In very brief summary, current law consists of three different sub-rules, applied successively, if (but for the application of one of the sub-rules) a member ("P") would recognize a loss upon the disposition of stock of another member ("S"). In general, the sub-rules either disallow the loss or provide certain additional tax consequences if the loss is recognized. Current law attempts to achieve greater precision than the former loss disallowance rule while not imposing administratively infeasible requirements on taxpayers, such as tracing. Unfortunately, achieving this "middle-ground" objective introduces considerable complexity.

In general, the first sub-rule (termed "basis redetermination") applies only if P (or other members of P's group) continues to own S stock following P's disposition of S stock at a loss, and the per-share bases of S stock held by P or other members are not identical. In that case, immediately prior to P's disposition of S stock, P must reduce (not below the stock's value) its basis in the S stock by the amount of prior positive investment adjustments with respect to such stock, and the amount of the reduction must be reallocated to other S stock to reduce the per-share disparity in basis. Reg. § 1.1502-36(b)(1)(i), (2)(i)(A). Thus, the sub-rule generally affects only the "noneconomic loss" scenario (**example 14-2**) and permits the deferral, rather than the disallowance, of that loss.

**Example 14-4:** P and M form S in exchange for all 100 shares of S, and all three corporations are members of the same consolidated group. P transfers asset 1, with value and basis of $80, to S in exchange for 80 shares, and M transfers asset 2, with value and basis of $20 and $0, respectively, to S in exchange for 20 shares. S sells asset 2 for $20, and S's $20 gain increases P's basis in S stock by $16 (to $96) and M's basis in S stock by $4 (to $4) under the investment adjustment rules; thus, P and M each increase their basis in the S stock by their proportionate share (80% and 20%, respectively) of S's gain on the asset sale. Reg. § 1.1502-32(c)(1)(iii) and (2)(i). If P sells its S stock to a nonmember for $80, P would recognize a $16 loss but for the unified loss rule. Under the basis redetermination sub-rule, just prior to the disposition, P must reduce its basis in S stock by $16 (the prior positive investment adjustment with respect to such shares), which amount is reallocated to M's shares in S (to reduce the per-share disparity between P's and M's basis in S). Thus, P recognizes no loss on the disposition of S shares and M's basis in S is increased to $20.

The basis redetermination sub-rule generally does not apply if, following P's disposition of its S shares at a loss, there are no remaining S shares held by members of the group. Reg. § 1.1502-36(b)(1)(ii)(B). In that case, a second sub-rule (termed "basis reduction") potentially applies generally to reduce (and not merely reallocate) P's basis in S stock (but not below value) by the amount of prior positive investment adjustments (net of prior negative investment adjustments (other than adjustments for distributions)) with respect to such stock. The amount of the reduction is generally limited, however, by the excess of P's basis in the S stock over such stock's share of S's net inside attributes (including money, asset basis, and losses). Reg. § 1.1502-36(c)(1)-(5).

**Example 14-5:** Assume the same facts as **example 14-2** involving P's acquisition of S for $100 when S holds a single asset with value and basis of $100 and $10, respectively. Upon S's sale of the asset for $100, S's $90 gain increases P's basis in S to $190 under the investment adjustment rules. If P sells its S stock to a nonmember for $100, P would recognize a $90 loss but for the unified loss rule. The basis redetermination sub-rule does not apply because no member of the P group owns stock in S after the disposition. Under the basis reduction sub-rule, just prior to the disposition, P must reduce its basis in S stock by $90 (the prior net positive investment adjustments with respect to such shares). The reduction is limited, however, by the excess of P's basis in the S stock ($190) over such stock's share of S's net inside attributes ($100 (the cash proceeds from S's sale)), or $90. Thus, P reduces its basis in S stock to $100 just prior to the disposition and P recognizes neither gain nor loss upon selling the S stock to the nonmember.

As is evident, the first and second sub-rules generally operate to defer or disallow all or part of a noneconomic loss resulting from application of the investment adjustment rules. Neither sub-rule, however, affects the potential recognition of a duplicate loss. For example, if in **example 14-3**, P sells its S stock to a nonmember for $600 prior to S's disposition of its asset, P would recognize a $400 loss but for the unified loss rule. Neither the basis redetermination nor basis reduction sub-rules apply, however, since there were no prior positive investment adjustments made to P's stock in S. In that case, a third sub-rule (termed "attribute reduction") potentially applies generally to reduce S's net inside attributes (such as inside asset basis or loss carryovers) by the lesser of the aggregate built-in loss in S's stock or S's assets (determined immediately prior to the transaction). Reg. § 1.1502-36(d)(1)-(3). Thus, in **example 14-3**, P recognizes a $400 loss on sale of its S stock, but S must reduce its asset basis by $400 (the lesser of the aggregate built-in loss in S's stock and assets, which are both $400) to $600, thereby eliminating the potential duplicate loss in the future.

In summary, the unified loss rule ultimately borrows from another feature of passthrough taxation — the inside basis adjustments permitted (and in some cases required) under subchapter K. See I.R.C. §§ 734, 743. The attribute reduction sub-rule is only triggered, however, when certain losses are recognized on the disposition of member stock. Purchasers of corporations from consolidated groups will need to perform due diligence to determine whether the attribute reduction sub-rule applies (and the transaction therefore results in a reduction in the net inside attributes of the acquired corporation).

# Table of Authorities

*Italics indicate reprints of authorities.*

**Cases**

## Legislative Materials



## Notices and Announcements

**Revenue Procedures**



**Revenue Rulings**



**Other Administrative Guidance**



**Other Reference Materials**

# Index